THE MIDDLE EAST IN TRANSITION

Contributors

SIR HAMILTON A. R. GIBB
HANS TÜTSCH
CHARLES ISSAWI
SA'ID B. HIMADEH
MORROE BERGER
A. F. MILLS
GABRIEL BAER
ELIE KEDOURIE
G. F. HUDSON
W. KHALIDI
JEAN VIGNEAU
NISSIM REJWAN
P. M. HOLT
ANDREW J. A. MANGO
F. KAZEMZADEH
SIR ISAIAH BERLIN
STEWART PEROWNE
MIZRA KHAN
HAL LEHRMAN
SYLVIA G. HAIM
BERNARD LEWIS
WALTER Z. LAQUEUR
GEBRAN MAJDALANI
DR. NABIH AMIN FARIS
A. BENNIGSEN
LT.-COL. G. E. WHEELER
IVAR SPECTOR
H. CARRÈRE D'ENCAUSSE
PAUL B. HENZE
A. V. SHERMAN
DR. MUHAMMAD KAMEL AYYAD
GEORGES KETMAN
L. N. VATOLINA
V. B. LUTSKII

THE
MIDDLE EAST
IN TRANSITION

*Studies in
Contemporary History*

Edited by
WALTER Z. LAQUEUR

FREDERICK A. PRAEGER · NEW YORK

*Published in the United States of America in 1958
by Frederick A. Praeger, Inc.
Library of Congress Catalog Card Number: 58-8181
Printed in Great Britain*
© *1958 Walter Z. Laqueur*

By the same author
COMMUNISM AND NATIONALISM
IN THE MIDDLE EAST

CONTENTS

Part Two: COMMUNISM, THE SOVIET UNION, AND THE MIDDLE EAST

CONTENTS

LIST OF CONTRIBUTORS

AYYAD, MUHAMMAD KAMEL, teaches philosophy in the Higher Teachers' College, Damascus. Author of studies on contemporary political and cultural problems in the Arab world.

BAER, GABRIEL, PH.D., Department of Oriental Studies, Hebrew University, Jerusalem. Editor of *Hamizrakh Hehadash* (*New East*), the periodical of the Israel Oriental Society.

BENNIGSEN, ALEXANDRE, Head of Section 'U.S.S.R. and Middle East', Direction de la Documentation de la Présidence du Conseil (Paris). Author of studies on Islam in the Soviet Union in *Revue des Études Islamiques, Islamic Review, Encyclopédie de l'Islam*, etc.

BERGER, MORROE, Associate Professor of Sociology at Princeton University, where he teaches courses on the contemporary social institutions of the Middle East. Author of *Bureaucracy and Society in Modern Egypt*, etc.

BERLIN, SIR ISAIAH, C.B.E., Chichele Professor of Social and Political Theory in the University of Oxford; Fellow of the British Academy.

CARRÈRE D'ENCAUSSE, HELENE, Chargé de Conférences au Centre des Hautes Études d'Administration Musulmane. Author of studies on the Soviet Union and the Middle East in *Revue des Études Islamiques, Esprit, Revue de Défense Nationale*, etc.

FARIS, NABIH AMIN, Curator of Arabic Manuscripts, Princeton University (1936–42); Head of Arabic Desk, Office of War Information, New York (1942–45); Professor of Arab History, American University, Beirut, 1947.

GIBB, SIR HAMILTON A. R., Professor of Arabic, London University, 1930; Laudian Professor of Arabic, Oxford

University, 1937; University Professor, Harvard University, 1955; Member of Academy of Arabic Language, Cairo, from 1934.

HAIM, SYLVIA G., PH.D., engaged in research on the history of ideas in the Arab world. Author of studies published in Orientalist journals.

HENZE, PAUL B., Graduate of Harvard University Regional Program on Soviet Union (1950). Author of studies on Caucasian and Central Asian Affairs published in the *Royal Central Asian Journal*, etc.

HIMADEH, SA'ID B., Professor of Applied Economics, American University, Beirut; Vice-President Economic Development Board of Lebanon. Editor of *Al-Abhath*.

HOLT, P. M., Lecturer in the History of the Near and Middle East, School of Oriental and Asian Studies, University of London; formerly in the Sudan Ministry of Education, and subsequently government archivist. Author of *The Mahdist State in the Sudan*.

HUDSON, G. F., Director of Far Eastern Studies, St. Anthony's College, Oxford; Formerly Fellow of All Souls College, Oxford. Worked during the war in the Research Department of the Foreign Office.

ISSAWI, CHARLES, Associate Professor of Near and Middle Eastern Economics, Columbia University. Author of *An Arab Philosophy of History*, *Egypt at Mid-Century*, etc.

KAZEMZADEH, FIRUZ, Department of History, Yale University. Author of *The Struggle for Transcaucasia (1917–1921)*, and other studies.

KEDOURIE, ELIE, Lecturer in Politics and Public Administration at London School of Economics. Author of *England and the Middle East: The Destruction of the Ottoman Empire, 1914–21*.

KETMAN, GEORGES, pen-name of a French writer, born in Cairo in 1929 of Syrian, Afghan, and German origin. Author of *Un Personnage sans Couronne*, etc.

KHALIDI, WALED, formerly Lecturer in Arabic, Oxford University. Author of studies on the contemporary history of the Middle East.

LAQUEUR, WALTER Z., Editor of *Survey* (London). Author of *Communism and Nationalism in the Middle East*, etc. At present Visiting Associate Professor, University of Chicago.

LEHRMAN, HAL, former Foreign Editor of *Newsweek*; Chief, Office of War Information, in Turkey, during the Second World War; Special Correspondent of *New York Times* for Middle East and North Africa. Author of *Russia's Europe, Israel: The Beginning and Tomorrow*, etc.

LEWIS, BERNARD, F.R.Hist.S., Professor of History of the Near and Middle East, University of London, since 1949. Author of *Handbook of Diplomatic and Political Arabic*, etc.

LUTSKII, PROFESSOR V. B., a leading Soviet student of the modern history of the Middle East. Author of several books.

MAJDALANY, GEBRAN. Author of essays on the contemporary history of the Middle East. Leading member of Ba'ath Party.

MANGO, ANDREW J. A., PH.D., Specialist in Turkish and Middle Eastern Affairs. Born Istanbul, 1926. Specialized in medieval Persian literature. Worked in the British Embassy in Turkey during the war.

MILLS, ARTUR F., formerly Assistant Professor in the Department of Business Administration, American University of Beirut; has taught and worked for the last seventeen years in various Middle Eastern countries.

MIZRA KHAN, pen-name of a student of Middle Eastern affairs.

PEROWNE, STEWART, O.B.E., served for many years in the Colonial Administration Service and as a diplomat in the Middle East; Oriental Counsellor, Baghdad, 1944. Author of *The One Remains, Herod the Great*, etc.

REJWAN, NISSIM, born in Baghdad, now lives in Jerusalem, Israel. Student of contemporary Arab affairs; specializes in the analysis of cultural trends in the Arab world.

SHERMAN, A. V., Economist and Sociologist. Wrote for the London *Observer* and broadcast for the B.B.C. from the Balkans and North Africa; formerly Economic Advisory Bureau, Ministry of Finance, Jerusalem, Israel.

SPECTOR, IVAR, Associate Professor, University of Washington, Seattle. Author of *The Soviet Union and the Muslim World, 1917–1956*, etc.

TÜTSCH, HANS E., since 1946 Foreign Editor and Foreign Correspondent of *Neue Zuercher Zeitung*. 1954–55, Visiting Professor, Wayne University. Has extensively travelled in the Middle East in recent years. Author of *Die Arabischen Voelker am Kreuzwege*, etc.

VATOLINA, L. N., leading Soviet student of Middle Eastern affairs. Has published a book on Egypt and many articles in Soviet periodicals on Egypt, Palestine, Syria, etc.

VIGNEAU, JEAN, Directeur-général du Centre de Documentation et de Synthèse, Paris.

WHEELER, LT.-COLONEL GEOFFREY E., C.I.E., C.B.E., director of Central Asian Research Centre since 1953; Military Attaché, Meshed, 1926; Intelligence Duties, Iraq, 1928–31; Director, Publications Division, Government of India, 1941–46; Counsellor, British Embassy, Teheran, 1946–50.

ACKNOWLEDGEMENTS

The articles mentioned in this list were originally published in the periodicals named below and have been reprinted (some with revisions subsequently made by the authors) by permission of the publishers.

P. M. HOLT: 'Sudanese Nationalism and Self-determination'— *The Middle East Journal.*

SIR HAMILTON A. R. GIBB: 'Social Reform: Factor X'—*The Atlantic Monthly.*

LT.-COL. G. E. WHEELER: 'Recent Soviet Attitudes towards Islam'; and IVAR SPECTOR: 'Soviet Cultural Propaganda in the Middle East'—*Soviet Survey.*

SIR ISAIAH BERLIN: 'The Origins of Israel'—The Anglo-Israeli Association.

GEORGES KETMAN: 'The Egyptian Intelligentsia'—*Preuves.*

DR. NABIH AMIN FARIS: 'The Islamic Community and Communism'—*The Islamic Review.*

CHARLES ISSAWI: 'Economic and Social Foundations of Democracy in the Middle East'; and BERNARD LEWIS: 'Communism and Islam'—*International Affairs.*

MIZRA KHAN: 'The Arab Refugees'—*Midstream.*

A. F. MILLS: 'Middle Eastern Development—Another Missing Link'—*Middle East Forum.*

ANDREW J. A. MANGO: 'Turkey and the Middle East'; and ELIE KEDOURIE: 'Pan-Arabism and British Policy'—*The Political Quarterly.*

WALED KHALIDI: 'Political Trends in the Fertile Crescent'— *The World To-day.*

SA'ID B. HIMADEH: 'Social Awakening and Economic Development in the Middle East'—*International Social Science Bulletin*.

'Development in Iraq,' Part I—HAL LEHRMAN—*The New York Times Magazine*; Part II—*The Economist*.

SYLVIA G. HAIM: 'Islam and the Theory of Arab Nationalism' —*Die Welt des Islams*.

STEWART PEROWNE: 'Levant Dusk: The Refugee Situation'— *Journal of the Royal Central Asian Society*.

GEBRAN MAJDALANY: 'The Arab Socialist Movement'— *Cahiers Internationaux*.

H. CARRÈRE D'ENCAUSSE: 'The Background of Soviet Policy in the Middle East'—*Les Cahiers de la République*.

A. BENNIGSEN: 'Sultan Galiev: the U.S.S.R. and the Colonial Revolution'—*Esprit*.

A. BENNIGSEN: 'The "National Front" in Communist Strategy in the Middle East'—*Politique Étrangère*.

G. F. HUDSON: 'The Great Catastrophe'—*The Twentieth Century*.

L. N. VATOLINA and V. B. LUTSKII: 'Two Soviet Views on the Middle East'—*Sovetskoe Vostokovedenie*.

W. Z. LAQUEUR: 'Syria: Nationalism and Communism'— *Commentary*.

INTRODUCTION

THIS COLLECTION of essays is a contribution to the analysis of recent political and social trends in the Middle East. Most of the topics it covers have not as yet been adequately discussed, although, as recent developments in the area have shown, they are of the greatest importance. For the same reason of urgency, the essays selected are those that reveal most of the ideology and activities of the local political and social forces, and a relatively large space has been allotted to the analysis of Soviet attitudes towards the Middle East, Islam, and the Arab national movement. Certain aspects, such as those of the Arab-Israeli conflict and the exploitation of the oil resources of the area, have been excluded from anything more than incidental allusion, because they have been amply publicized elsewhere. These limitations may be regretted, but they are really unavoidable, for an encyclopedia would now be needed to cover *all* the problems of the Middle East.

Some of the essays have been specially written for inclusion in the present volume, others have been previously published in English, French, Russian, and Arabic periodicals, and most of the latter have been revised and brought up to date by their authors. They represent a wide range of political opinion; no reader is expected to agree with all the views they express. But the editor, who emphatically disagrees with some of them, is persuaded that they all represent currents of thought that are significant and have to be taken into account.

The essays in the first section deal with social developments in the Arab world, and some aspects of its recent political history, as well as with the relations between the Arabs and the West. The main theme of the second section is the effect that Russia and Communism have had upon the Middle East, and this includes some essays whose relevance may not be obvious at first sight. What connection is there, it may be asked, between contemporary Middle Eastern politics and the discussions going on in the Soviet Union about the merits of the Imam Shamil, an obscure Caucasian tribal leader of the nineteenth century? Or of what topical interest is it to review the ideas of Sultan Galiev, a Tatar Communist leader of the nineteen-twenties?

Yet closer scrutiny will show that the wavering judgments pronounced upon Shamil in the Soviet Union reveal, more clearly than
any of its foreign political documents, the predicament of that
government in its contacts with Islam; and that Sultan Galiev's
ideas, long forgotten and never considered to be of much importance, are in more than one respect prophetic of the policies pursued
by President Nasser and the Syrian colonels. The two Soviet contributions may not strike a Western reader as particularly illuminating;
nevertheless, they are worthy of study as fairly typical of Soviet
writing on Middle Eastern questions.

While a knowledge of the history of the Middle East is of great
value towards the understanding of current tendencies in that area,
it is not the only, nor always the most important, prerequisite.
When all is said and done, the problems of the Middle East today
are much more similar to those of, for instance, Indonesia, Indo-
China, or of some of the Latin-American countries than to those
of eighteenth-century Syria or Egypt. A knowledge of the Leninist
theory of imperialism, of populism, or of certain German right-wing
political philosophers of the early twentieth century, may be as
helpful towards the understanding of Arab nationalism as a knowledge of Tahtawi and Kawakibi.

Several contributors to this volume discuss the comparatively
recent emergence of radical movements in the Arab world—Nasserism, the Ba'ath, and Communism—some in a sympathetic and others
in a highly critical spirit. These show the need for a re-appraisal of
new and unfamiliar factors in the situation; they may help to do
away with certain misconceptions by which Western thinking about
the Middle East, and therefore Western policy towards it, has been
badly misled for a considerable time past.

Besides these misconceptions of the situation there are also mistaken attitudes towards it. To a certain school of thought, which
assumes that there is nothing new under the sun, whatever happens
in the Middle East has happened once or often before; so that a
correct study of its past history will always explain present developments. But this is to overlook the fact that there is always something
new and unique in a new situation; and in the present concatenation
of circumstances there is much that is completely unprecedented.
Another school of thought tends to view the Middle East through
Western spectacles, thereby receiving distorted impressions and
drawing fallacious conclusions. For instance, seeing a highly critical
situation in the Middle East, it assumes that, as would undoubtedly
be the case in the West, this cannot possibly endure for long without
revolution, civil war, or some equally drastic action or reaction.
This Western feeling for order and stability is natural, but it is quite

misleading if projected upon the Middle East, a part of the world where standards of stability and order are different, where people react differently to crises and disturbances; and where things do not produce the same consequences as they would in the West. In other words, it is by no means certain that any significant new element will emerge out of the present turmoil in the Middle East.

A third school in the West has for some considerable time argued that there is a natural community of interests and ideals between Arab nationalism and the West; that, but for the regrettable nineteenth-century record of certain imperialist powers, the clash between France and Algeria, British involvements in the Arabian Peninsula, and, above all, the existence of the State of Israel, agreement between the West and Arab nationalism would not be too difficult to bring about. This is a serious argument which deserves due consideration. But the idea that there is a natural community of interest between the Western and Asian nations is, at best, a hopeful generalization. The Western nations themselves are not held together by their nationalism, but by common beliefs in supra-national values such as freedom, democracy, and their common European heritage. Even so, it has often been difficult enough in the West to find a common denominator between national interests; and between the Western and some Asian nations in their present stage of development it may be impossible. Or there may prove to be common ground with some countries in Asia and the Middle East but not with others. Some of these, such as India, Burma, Ceylon, and the Lebanon, have directed their energies mainly towards peaceful reconstruction and domestic problems ever since they won their independence. But others have been much more influenced by considerations of military strength and glory; by desire for territorial gains, or even, perhaps, by dreams of new empires. With such countries it is difficult to see how a clash could have been prevented even if the West had moved out of all its remaining possessions and spheres of influence. Generalizations about 'Asian nationalism' are even less trustworthy than those about European nationalism.

Israel is, of course, an important issue: there can be no doubt that the Israeli-Arab conflict has exacerbated or, to be more precise, did much to precipitate the struggle between Arab nationalism and the West. Even here, however, the different effects upon different countries should not be forgotten. For Jordan, and perhaps for Syria, Israel is a major factor: but the course of events within Egypt has seldom been palpably altered by the existence of Israel. To ask whether developments in the Middle East would have been fundamentally different if this new state had not been founded is a hypothetical question to which there is no sure answer. But other developments in Asia—in, e.g., Indonesia, in Kerala and in Persia (under Dr. Mossadeq)—where Israel was in no way involved, make it seem unlikely that Middle Eastern events would have taken a very different course in the absence of Israel. To ascribe all that has gone wrong between the Arab world and the West to the Arab-Israeli conflict is to mistake the symptom of a malady for its cause.

Another thing that is often overrated in the West is the importance of the economic factor. Well-meaning observers have from time to time suggested that if only all the countries concerned would get together and co-operate in a scheme for the economic development of the whole area, all the outstanding problems would be solved, or at least become tractable. Advocates of this solution tend to forget that economic development, desirable though it is, is no cure for problems that arise on the political and social planes, where alone they can be successfully dealt with. Of all the Asian countries, Syria has shown the most economic progress during the last ten years, yet Syria's political development, internal and external, can hardly be said to have taken a direction expected or desired in the West.

There has been much searching of hearts and consciences in the capitals of the West, to discover mistakes that were made in the past and that may even now, perhaps, be remedied. It has been suggested that a lack of humility on the side of the West, or of friendliness or willingness to understand, has been the root of all the troubles. All these qualities are invaluable; they will always be as much appreciated in the Middle East as elsewhere, whenever they are displayed. In the conduct of international affairs, however, the manifestation of them will not always bring the response that is desired: humility, for instance, may be misunderstood as weakness, which has never been highly esteemed in Arab capitals—or in many other quarters, for that matter. Often, what is most needed is tact, firmness, and friendliness—towards friends.

The lack of co-operation between the Western Powers, especially between France and Britain on the one hand and America on the other, has also been blamed for most of the Western failures. This negative factor has been, and is, indeed, highly regrettable; but here again one may over-estimate the amount of difference that closer collaboration could have made. For there are some irremovable limitations to the scope of Western action in the Arab countries. The shaping of their future depends almost wholly upon their own political *élites*. Any Western interference, however well-intentioned, will be greatly resented and probably self-defeating; for there is nothing these countries want more than to work out their destinies by themselves. Towards Syria and Egypt, for example, the only possible policy is one of inactivity: military intervention is excluded by the international situation, and minor acts or gestures of hostility are ineffective, for they only irritate the people they are meant to impress, and preclude any improvement in their policy towards the West. Even friendliness, however sincere, is unlikely to ripen any political harvest for the West, because it is a psychological necessity for the political organizers of these countries to proclaim a state of danger, to point to an enemy Power—and Israel by itself is too small to fulfil this role. What these countries need, even more than economic development, is a gain in self-esteem; and how can they better prove to themselves their independence, and their new-won political power, than by displaying ability to defy the West?

Not that this state of affairs need go on for ever. Passions may calm down in course of time: the radical movements in the Arab lands may grow in positive content until hatred and resentment, their present *raisons d'être*, will be gradually abandoned as unnecessary. But there is nothing that the West can do at present, or presumably for years to come, that is likely to expedite this process—apart from a policy of studied non-interference and demonstrative disinterest. The risks that this involves are admittedly formidable. Some of the countries involved may gradually and almost imperceptibly be drawn into the Soviet sphere of power. This possibility, which in one or two cases is a probability, has to be accepted as outside our preventive powers. Everything now depends upon whether the political *élites* of the Middle East will prove that their professed ability to maintain their national independence was more than an idle boast. Real independence, that is, not the forensic façade of a virtually satellite status—however voluntarily that may at first be entered into. It seems unlikely that all will succeed in this; but it is not inevitable that all will fail.

WALTER Z. LAQUEUR

London,
  January, 1958

Note: There is no universally accepted system of transliteration for Arabic names. The editor has therefore preferred not to take liberties with the transcriptions used by the various contributors—some of whom are 'purists' and others very liberal in this respect. Only in cases of major divergence, or where confusion might be occasioned, have a few minor adjustments been made.

I should like to record my obligation to Nissim Rejwan, Philip Mairet, and Mrs. Jane Degras for their translations from Arabic, French, and Russian. Over and above this assistance, the advice of the two latter has been of great value in editing the present volume.

Part One

SOCIAL AND
POLITICAL CHANGE

SOCIAL REFORM : FACTOR X

The Search for an Islamic Democracy

by SIR HAMILTON A. R. GIBB

I

THE 'EASTERN QUESTION' of today differs profoundly from the 'Eastern Question' of the nineteenth century. Then, the Concert of Europe, jealous competitors, stood around the death-bed of the irremediably disintegrating Ottoman Empire, disputing its ultimate inheritance. Today the Western Powers seek to promote the stability and cohesion of ten resurgent sovereign states, with a fringe of colonial or semi-colonial fragments, and to find a basis for their integration. Yet repeated eruptions and revolutions show that 'The Question' remains, and even grows in perplexity.

Since these manifestations are usually linked with foreign policy, political issues might seem to be the dominant factors. Political factors are real enough, especially the issues of foreign controls and the State of Israel; yet there is a growing perception that they alone cannot explain the region's volcanic instability. The other factors, in prevailing Western opinion, are economic, and the most urgent question is seen as helping these 'under-developed' countries to build new and efficient economic structures. Certainly the economic factors are crucial—and in Egypt, at least, frighteningly complex. But the internal causes of unrest can no more be cured by economic gadgets—even of such size as the High Dam on the Nile or a Jordan Valley Authority—than by a few clever political adjustments. Economic development may help if integrated with social development; but if it cuts across deep-seated social forces it may even intensify the inner instability.

For the third element is the social factor. It is, not surprisingly, often overlooked. Political factors, if confusing, at least lie close to the surface; economic potentialities can be evaluated with fair accuracy. But the social factor has been the least studied, not only by outside observers but by those most concerned within the region. Many of the weaknesses of the Middle Eastern states are arguably the result of their failure to recognize and meet adequately the problems of a prolonged social crisis.

A social organism is the resultant of a great variety of continually changing spiritual and material forces, producing strains which require adjustment to maintain a relatively stable equilibrium. If any maladjustment becomes too widespread and prolonged, the situation is felt to be intolerable and a violent demand arises for 'reform'. The effectiveness of this demand depends on: (1) the kinds of organ for expressing social needs, the leadership for canalizing them, and the instruments available for promoting reforms; (2) the ability of the governing elements to diagnose the true causes of the maladjustment and so cure them that the society's vital inner forces and external activities are again brought into harmony.

Every living society includes 'devices' or organs whereby relative tensions can find adjustment; and the speed and ease with which they operate is a measure of its viability. In general, the older a society, the more its social institutions become fixed, and the means of adjustment restricted to minor reforms within a standardized framework. Yet these are usually adequate, precisely because the need for reforms in so experienced and equilibrated a society is correspondingly less. But when the need of a major adjustment shows the traditional instruments to be inadequate, new methods and organs must be created. The real vitality of a society can be measured by its success in providing them without excessively violent reactions or dislocation.

The organ evolved by Islamic society was the religious brotherhood. Considerations of space make it impossible to trace in detail here the origins and history of these brotherhoods. Suffice it to say that in face of the challenge of the Turko-Mongol invasions starting in the eleventh century, two existing currents—the spiritually reformist 'methodism' of the cities, and the militant 'frontier warfare' organizations—gradually coalesced and forced the invaders to respect established religious and economic institutions and co-operate with the settled agricultural and industrial communities. Ultimately the brotherhoods encompassed all social classes and reinforced the functional groupings by trade-guild and corporation.

After the establishment of the Ottoman Empire, they took on predominantly the role of mediators in a situation of recurrent military violence or usurpation or administrative tyranny. In Islamic thought, the state should be only the public exponent of Islamic ideology, ensuring the security and well-being of the Muslim peoples, and enforcing the Law of Islam but itself subject to that Law; and its authority derives wholly from the degree to which it is considered to do so. The religious leaders, though they created a Muslim community, had failed to control the centres of political power. This was the main socio-political tension within Islam. The political organizations, tainted by usurpation, violence, and corruption, were only passively accepted. The state always exists, but dynasties and governments are transient. Violation of a government's man-made laws carried no moral reprobation or violation of conscience— rather, indeed, the contrary. Civil penalties inflicted by government officers carried no stigma. The citizen owed his loyalty primarily to Islam itself, and after Islam to his own social group or guild and its ethic.

Finally, a reasonable *modus vivendi* was reached, with the religious brotherhoods mitigating inner tensions or conflicts of loyalties. Yet the limitation of their civic function to the removal of grievances and restoration of the *status quo ante*, reinforced the tendency, natural to every religious institution, to oppose 'innovations' and resist all change.

The religious leadership was thus wholly unprepared and ill-equipped, and indeed contributed not a little to its own impotence, when in the nineteenth century this precarious balance was entirely destroyed. It was destroyed less by the direct intrusion of the West than by immensely complicated internal developments, which have been so insufficiently studied that it might almost be said that we know more about the internal history of the Muslim world in the ninth than in the nineteenth century. Only three things are reasonably certain: (1) the old corporative functional groups decayed or dissolved; (2) the old brotherhood organizations also decayed— these two results involving the loss of the personal link between the individual and the community and of social and religious integration; (3) the power of the state was disproportionately enlarged, by both the increased efficiency of its own instruments and the decay of the counterbalancing ones.

II

Whether the dissolution of the old community structure will ultimately prove beneficial depends on the principles and forms of social cohesion that will take its place. Rural co-operatives and industrial trade unions are still in their infancy, and fail to satisfy the deeper emotional and spiritual needs. The average individual belongs to his family and to Islam, but Islam no longer has any concrete social organization. This social void is intensely real and creates a spiritual dissatisfaction which craves a uniquely Muslim form of expression. Meanwhile, social maladjustments and disequilibrium have grown so severe that the cry for relief and reform has become articulate and insistent.

Simultaneously with this disintegration there were growing up in all the Arab countries (save Arabia) new administrative and professional classes: lawyers, civil servants, doctors, journalists, teachers, entrepreneurs, and professional army officers. It would seem that, ignorant or careless of the old social structure, and fascinated by Western political theories, these elements overlooked the social issues altogether and concentrated on counteracting their countries' inorganic political structures. They aimed at reorganizing political life on Western models, introducing Western legal codes and courts, and co-operated with the orthodox religious leaders to discredit the old Sufi brotherhoods as superstitious, while dreaming of reforming Islam itself in terms of Western thought.

Clearly this Westernized intelligentsia never thought in terms of a 'Muslim State', but unconsciously applied the Western division between church and state to the traditional Muslim separation of political and social functions. They would create organized constitutional governments and leave the religious institution as guarantor of social relationships in the new and enlightened society produced by the spread of education.

But the religious institution was no longer capable of carrying out this function. Only through the brotherhoods had orthodox Islam acquired a social integration. The religious leaders imagined that the 'purification' of religion by the elimination of 'superstition' would lead to an Islamic revival; but (leaving aside the question whether any religion can be truly effective in human society without an outer ring or protective covering of 'superstition') Islam's abstract doctrines and personal duties, not backed by a social organization, lacked the force to guide social development. And the intelligentsia's growing secularization and hostility to the 'medievalism' of the *ulema* (religious teachers) nullified any purely religious sanctions.

The rift between political and social policy was strangely widened by the resounding campaign of the late-nineteenth-century reformer Jamal el-Din el-Afghani for a pan-Islamic programme of spiritual unification of all Muslims under the Ottoman caliphate to oppose European political, economic, and cultural penetration. Jamal el-Din did align the Muslim masses behind movements to oppose the West; but they paradoxically emerged, in the Middle East at least, under the leadership, not of the caliphate, but of local nationalists already becoming hostile to the Ottoman government. And it was by this mass support that the nationalist movements finally succeeded in setting up their parliamentary governments.

III

Though the nationalist leaders were primarily concerned with political emancipation, they had to let it be assumed, to hold the support of the masses, that it would be followed by positive measures to meet social discontents. They were thus committed to internal 'reforms'. The vague identification of political and social ends was rendered easier by the obvious fact that the most extensive maladjustments were connected with the importation of Western systems, processes, and ideas. But underneath this superficial identification lay a real divergence of aims: between independence as an end in itself and independence as the means to the end of reknitting the threads of social cohesion supposedly severed by Western penetration and controls.

Even after political independence, the nationalist leaders failed to recognize this divergence. Maladjustments continued and even became more severe. For the main causes were not (as the masses naïvely thought) due to the presence of foreign governors and entrepreneurs, but to the pervasive effects of Western intellectual, legal, and economic systems, to new patterns of land tenure, to population growth and pressure on means of subsistence, and to the expansion of urban proletariats. While claiming to 'choose out' the useful elements from Western civilization and reject those conflicting with national traditions, the nationalist leaders have made social discontents more acute by themselves continuing and expanding under nationalist auspices just those imported administrative and legal systems which had been responsible for dissolving the traditional community institutions.

Granted that the intricate nexus of material and psychological factors was difficult of comprehension, yet the nationalist leaders faced their problems like politicians everywhere. Either they remained immobile, putting up a stiff front of opposition to 'disturbances', or they attempted to placate by promises; and only recently, as the idea of the 'welfare state' has percolated to the Middle East, have they started on social-welfare legislation, modelled on the West and not very specifically related to the actual social situations, economic possibilities, or psychological dispositions. Or they have pinned their hopes on industrialization or other economic panaceas, again without much consideration of the social problems involved.

If this were all, the politicians could not be blamed overmuch. In a democratic system political leaders are expected to respond to popular will as expressed in institutions from parish councils and town meetings right up to the most comprehensive organizations. But it is precisely the great weakness of Arab countries that, since the breakdown of the old corporations, no social institutions have been evolved through which the public will can be canalized, interpreted, defined, and mobilized. Elective institutions at the lower levels practically do not exist. No functional associations link representatives from different areas. There is, in short, no functioning organ of social democracy at all.

The political leaders have demonstrated no awareness of this inorganic state of social institutions, have not aided them to develop, and indeed have shown jealousy of any potential institution which might rival and eventually oppose the political parties. But their still greater disservice to the welfare of their peoples has lain in their party rivalries, open pursuit of private interests, scandals pinned upon one another in their wrangling, subservience to the wealthy and powerful, and toleration of bitter inequalities. By this behaviour the parliamentary leaders have discredited themselves and the system, and disillusioned the masses. To these the new kind of state differed little from its predecessors. So-called 'democracy' in practice was scarcely distinguishable from the old sultanates: corruption was as rife as ever in the administration, and violence was not less violence because clothed in incomprehensible legal forms. Like the old sultanates, the new governments were passively accepted in virtue of their power, but they had no real moral authority: in the people's eyes they were merely associations of self-interested persons using power for their own advantage during their transient ministries.

Inevitably, as the nationalist leaders felt mass support slipping away, they made ever more violent efforts to regain it by persistent harping on the continued presence of European forces or enterprises or controls, or on the hidden hand of Western diplomacy and on Western support of Zionism. When accused of neglecting social issues, they insisted that those were secondary and controversial, and must not disrupt the nation's united determination to achieve its national aims. However genuinely the politicians desired national independence, they did not know what to do with it. Concentrating on its negative aspect as freedom from foreign interference, and without positive programme, they could only try to fill the void of policy by propaganda.

IV

It must, of course, be frankly admitted that the policies adopted by Great Britain and France on the disintegration of the Ottoman Empire gave bitter offence to nationalist sentiment. And since the Second World War, the positive actions of these Powers plus the United States have given further offence, especially through their support of Israel, while their open and concealed rivalries have intensified Arab suspicions and hostility towards the West. The grievances are real and deep-seated. But it is a fallacy to suppose that the Western countries could have escaped becoming the butt of nationalist propaganda. The weakness of the political leadership forced it to distract public resentment into anti-Western channels, and the Western Powers, whatever their policies had been, were cast for the role of scapegoats.

The consequences of this emphasis on propaganda have been disastrous in at least two respects. First, propaganda is the most vicious of the habit-forming drugs. It engenders group delusions which so root themselves in the minds of the propagandists themselves that they finally inhibit rational judgment of real issues. Drifting helplessly on waves of mass emotion, they become an easy mark for exploitation even by their enemies, provided these enemies subtly minister to the delusions which the propagandists have implanted. And when the political leaders find it necessary or opportune to change course, their own propaganda recoils on them and they find themselves branded as turncoats and traitors.

Second, because its content was merely political, propaganda has inhibited positive thought on real internal problems. No stable state can arise or endure without a basic social philosophy, accepted by the mass of its citizens, more or less consciously pursued in public life and private associations, and guaranteed by its laws, whether it be the *Respublica Christiana*, or the ideology of the Islamic Community, or *Liberté, Égalité, Fraternité*, or 'Life, Liberty, and the Pursuit of Happiness'. Nationalism by itself is not such a philosophy; the 'nation' is merely a political concept. In most Arab countries, indeed, it is not even a universally accepted concept, and has as yet acquired no inherent authority.

Thus the internal instability of the Arab world has been increased by the clash of different definitions of the content of the national concept. The Westernized professional classes define it in terms of Western political and social institutions, plus naïve faith in universal education, or at least primary literacy. The professional armies define it in terms of military strength. The small Socialist and Communist Parties define it in terms of their own doctrinaire ideologies. All of them may and do profess their desire to relieve social pressures, and many are sincere therein. But their programmes are designed to serve their special interests, and in power give way to those interests in the competition for shares of the limited national revenue.

One factor, however, is common to all of them. All regard the masses as so much plastic material to be moulded, without will or vision of their own. But the masses do have their vision, in terms of their Arab heritage through thirteen centuries of Islam. Politically, their aspirations are not narrowly national, but pan-Arab. Socially, their disillusion with the failure of national governments to meet their social needs is slowly beginning to find expression in new forms corresponding to the old religious associations, such as the Muslim Brotherhood (el-Ikhwan el-Muslimin), which demand a programme of social order based on the principles of Islam and which through local lodges restore the lost sense of 'belonging'.

How such a programme could be applied in the modern world is an open question. But these are only the first inchoate gropings towards a restatement of Muslim values in face of the invasion of Western values, and as such show an inherent vitality in Muslim society. Understandably the Westernized politicians and professionals view them with suspicion and disfavour, especially when they break into open political action. Yet, since nationalism has hitherto manifestly failed to meet the social needs and aspirations of the Arab peoples, and even the new government in Egypt—though more positively affirming its good intentions—has not yet proved that it grasps the material or psychological dimensions of the social problem, these vital forces, even if repressed, will probably continue to find stronger and more coherent expressions and create new organs and institutions of their own.

To sum up, then. The Arab world is in the profound crisis of a dialectical process (outwardly concealed by a common hostility to the Western Powers) which drags it in two different directions. On the one hand is the movement towards authoritarian régimes, whose principal aim is to build up the political and military power of the state and restore Arab unity by political alliances. On the other are tentative movements to rebuild the social organism on Islamic principles, and so recreate a moral reunion of the Arab peoples.

Although complementary in appearance, these movements stand on conflicting principles. The first gears social and economic development to Western-type administration, military organization, and expansion of technical skills. Because these imported systems are artificial structures, imposed by the few, and not rooted in the national psychology, this programme requires sustained propaganda and the use of state power to remould the life and thought of the nation to conform with the ideas and objectives of the ruling groups. The second stresses organic internal development, relating economic to social needs, not rejecting Western experience where consistent with these, but subordinating it to the directives derived from the Islamic traditions of the masses. But because there is no vitality left in the lingering remains of the old Islamic social organizations, its leaders must forge the appropriate new organizations and institutions to canalize their ideals—a task calling for a long period of germination, probably often in conflict with the state, and continuing adaptation to changing social needs and situations.

Both movements are thus partial and provisional experiments towards adjusting Arab political, economic, and social life to the play of world-wide forces. Probably neither can by itself fill the inner void, but through their opposition and interplay there may in time emerge the solution by which the restless social problems of the Arab world can be satisfied in a social order which meets their psychological needs within the framework of expanding international relationships. Only then will the Middle Eastern countries gain the stability which is to their own greatest interest and to the interest of the world at large.

ARAB UNITY AND ARAB DISSENSIONS

by HANS E. TÜTSCH

THE 'COLD WAR', which since the second world-wide conflagration in this century keeps real peace away from humanity, has shifted its storm-centre several times in the past twelve years. First, Soviet expansion far into the heart of Central Europe, which reached its zenith with the *coup d'état* in Prague, was checked by the air-lift into blockaded Western Berlin; a sort of trench warfare has developed since then in which neither party has won any notable gains—the West not even when the workers in Eastern Germany, Poland, and Hungary rose against their Communist oppressors. The emphasis of the 'cold war' then shifted to the Far East, where in Korea and Vietnam the bloody battles ended in a stalemate that found its diplomatic recognition and confirmation in the first Geneva Conference of 1954. Since then the vortex of political strife has moved to the Middle East, especially to the Arab states. Not all the problems there are direct outgrowths of the 'cold war'—as the Cyprus conflict shows best—but their role in the international struggle confers on them a potentially pernicious character. The Arab countries are fighting for national independence against the former colonial Powers and sometimes also against their brother states. The form, or forms, in which the Arab peoples will achieve their final being as a nation or as several nations, are still in a provisional stage. Trouble brews where the transition is taking place from the personal dominion of tribal chieftains to the modern territorial state encompassing a particular national entity. It is extremely difficult to arrive at the root of the real problems in a region where legend becomes history and history becomes legend before the sun has set on an eventful day.

The saying that the Middle East is a world in transition is too much of a cliché not to be true. Only the border-zones of this area—Istanbul, Beirut, and Cairo—were drawn before World War I into the modern world, while the Arab countries between the Suez Canal and the Zagros Mountains, between the Indian Ocean and the Mediterranean, remained in a sort of medieval existence. When the Arabs marched forth under the banner of the Prophet and created an empire from central France to Samarkand, they also acquired great cultural accomplishments. Nevertheless, as in every empire, after a few centuries of flourishing civilization, disintegration and decay set in. While other empires disappeared completely, the Arab world in this phase of decadence was overrun and kept for centuries in a sort of anaesthesia by the Turks, who have the same religion but in mentality and behaviour are a world apart from the Arabs. The Turkish military and administrative system was imposed upon the Arabs, whose language and customs, however, remained practically unaffected by this foreign domination. The Arab way of life continued in a state of hibernation during the four centuries of Turkish rule. Total night fell upon the Arab world about the same time as the lights of the Renaissance began to glow in Europe, and only after World War I were the Arabs violently shaken out of their centuries-old lethargy. Their cultural and economic achievements during the long period of stagnation were extremely small compared with those of former times.

After the fall of the Ottoman Empire the entire Islamic world came, for a short while, under the rule of European Powers. Immediately after World War I not a single Moslem country was in possession of all the attributes of sovereignty. Today, less than forty years later, most of the Islamic countries have acquired full independence. In an extremely short span of time the Arabs—largely under Western influence—have again become conscious of their identity and realized their desire for independence. A whole series of new states has arisen: Iraq, Syria, Lebanon, Jordan, Egypt, Sudan, Libya, Tunisia, and Morocco; *but their boundaries have been drawn by European Powers*. The dividing-lines, in some cases, are artificial and do not correspond to natural factors. In other cases Arab populations have been draped in the mantle of a great past that does not fit them. No clear national consciousness has as yet developed in the Arab countries; nowhere do the peoples identify themselves completely with the territory within whose boundaries they live. Local and regional nationalisms compete with the pan-Arab ideal. The mosaic of tribes and ethnical and religious groups has not yet been consolidated into an integrated whole, or into clear and distinct parts. The entire process of development into nations and states is still under way. Of the three constituent elements of a modern state—territory, nation, and constitution—the territory has been circumscribed by an alien will, and the laws—with the exception of the law of persons—have been taken over almost completely from European countries, while the people struggle to achieve the future form of a nation. In the economic field, however, almost unimaginable progress has been made, especially since World War II, although the social structure of the Arab countries is still deeply entangled in the bonds of the Middle Ages.

THE PREDOMINANCE OF WESTERN TECHNOLOGY

Modern technology has taken hold of the Arab world. From Cadillacs to hydro-electric power plants, from radio and—in Iraq—television to oil refineries, technology as developed in Europe and the United States determines the daily life of the Arabs. Their total dependence on Western production, from the aeroplane down to the last rivet, is evident to every eye. Even if one rejects the idea of technological determinism, one must acknowledge its validity in the Arab world. But it is not the technology of the people of this area which dominates their life to an almost unlimited degree; it is the *technology of alien nations* on far-away continents. In the past six centuries no important invention has originated in the Middle East. Not only has the inventive genius disappeared, but there is practically *no mechanical production* to be found in the whole area which is not totally dependent on the great production centres of the modern world: Western Europe, North America, the Soviet Union and its satellites, and Japan. Mass products of Western industries fill the stalls in the bazaars of Arab cities, while the artisans of old have all but disappeared. The decadence of the local handicrafts is all too obvious, as inquiries in the bazaar of Damascus will show: the once-famous Damascene steel blades have not been produced since Hulagu Khan's Mongols overran the city in 1258; the renowned Damascene glass has been made since the eighteenth century in Bohemia; damask is not to be found, and brocade, once a speciality of the Omayyad capital, is still woven for tourists on fewer than a dozen looms, while the merchants cover local consumption with imports from Japan. Even the little cups in which the Bedouin tribesmen serve coffee—bitter with the taste of cardamom—come from Germany or Japan. Boxes and furniture, inlaid with silver and ivory, are still made for the tourist trade; but what a disappointing sight these unimaginative products, which have not undergone the slightest artistic development since the Middle Ages, present in a Western *salon*. Imported goods dominate the market wherever one looks.

Even more striking is the total lack of any non-agricultural production in the small towns and the villages of the fellahin. While in Turkey even the smallest village has a smith and a carpenter, in the Arab countries local handicraft is all but non-existent. The Arabs, however, claim a living standard and a supply of consumer goods which are not proportionate to the development in their countries, but which correspond to the highest level reached in the Western world.

What is the cause of this gulf between the Middle East and the West? Islam is founded on a static *Weltanschauung*; the Western thirst for knowledge and the theories of cognition are alien to it. It already has the answers to all the questions of a simple life. The truth was revealed long ago through the Prophet. The thirst for knowledge, which has led the Western world since the Renaissance and the Reformation to revolutionary discoveries, is missing in Arab countries. In vain do we look for 'do-it-yourself' fans, for men who experiment and others who ponder the mysteries of their visible and invisible surroundings; there are no laboratories and no philosophical schools which are not hedged in by the barriers of dogma. The large majority of young Arabs who study at Western universities turn to science, and succeed in mastering it. Only a few, however, receive an education in the humanities. They do not study the intellectual, moral and spiritual foundations that made possible the development of Western science and its application in modern technology; the Greek-Jewish-Christian foundations of the civilization which dominates the twentieth-century world—and it must not be forgotten that Soviet civilization also rests on the same basis—remain a closed book to most Arab students. The technology is accepted without question, but the foundations on which it rests remain unexplored. One cannot help feeling concerned about the materialistic solutions that many Arabs now seek—without success—to problems of a spiritual nature. If they do not succeed in their quest, they easily succumb to the feeling that they are thrown into a world of which they really understand and accept only the most superficial manifestations. The *feeling of insecurity*, from which the intellectuals in particular suffer, is often strangely paired with a *feeling of superiority* bestowed upon the Arabs by their religion. Therefore they oscillate constantly between complexes of inferiority and superiority. While the rootless intellectual is deplored as an exception in the West, one gets the impression that in the Arab world he is the rule.

Countless Arab writers attempt to explain the one-sided development of their countries by the oppressive policies of the European 'colonialists':

'Why don't we have industrial production?—The colonial Powers prevent us from developing it!'

'Why have we become familiar only with the technology of the West and not with its culture as well?—The colonial Powers keep us in ignorance and prevent the development of education!'

These are two of the stereotyped questions and answers with which the visiting observer is presented all the time. Yet even where education has been on a high level for decades, where money abounds and where no colonial Power stands in the way of progress, hardly any industrial production can be found; nowhere is any machinery produced through local initiative, but only some textiles. Why is all the money invested in real estate or trade? A story from *A Thousand and One Nights* significantly begins:

"There once lived in Baghdad a wealthy man, who lost all his fortune and became so destitute that he could earn his living only by hard labour." The hedonistic consumer's mentality of the Arabs could hardly be better summarized. This mentality also has its roots in Islam, and is expressed in the social order prevailing in the Middle East since medieval times. The German saying, 'Working with one's hands brings no dishonour', has no validity in the Arab world; manual labour, dirtying one's fingers, is considered degrading—not only in the Arab countries but in most of the Mediterranean lands.

METAMORPHOSIS OF THE BEDOUINS

Life in the Arab countries is determined by two poles: the ideal picture of the free-roaming Bedouins, on the one hand; the cities on the other. Hardly any cultural or political impulses emanate from the fellahin. Since pre-Islamic times the Arab bards have praised the life of the Bedouin who tends his herds, races on his fiery stallion or his camel across the endless deserts, pounces in sheer exuberance on peaceful peasants, and bows to no authority. Every Arab will try to derive his ancestry from a Bedouin chieftain or, at the worst, from a city family; never will he claim to be of peasant stock. Like the European snob who claims descent from Charlemagne, the modern Arab seeks his ancestors among the proud tribes of the desert. The Bedouin, however, is disappearing from the modern world. Fixed boundaries check his migrations, roads traverse his pastures—and the ride in an air-conditioned car, after all, is more comfortable and faster than the ride on a camel, horse, or donkey. The peasant's plough makes ever deeper inroads upon the steppe where the Bedouins' herds used to graze. Forays are no longer profitable where the police move in with machine-guns, and aeroplanes easily control the country's remotest corners. The authority of the modern state makes itself felt everywhere.

The Bedouins, however, profit most from the new order of things. Where new land becomes available through irrigation, it is assigned to the Bedouins. They receive seed, fertilizer, livestock, agricultural machines, water, and houses from the state, which wants to induce them to settle down for good. The Bedouin gets land which is not given to the fellahin, He becomes a *beneficiary of the land reforms* and of modern technology, while the peasant remains caught in the old economic and social fetters. The Bedouin readily finds work in the oil-fields and on building sites, thanks to his mobility. The jump into the twentieth century is easier for him than for the settled peasant, because he has not first to rid himself of a complicated social and economic order. He steps down from his mount into a car and moves unhampered into the 'world on wheels' which modern technology has created. He is not burdened with the débris of ancient history. Where he is torn directly from an archaic way of life into the domain of modern technology, he profits from the transition. But where the tribal chiefs—by way of misused land reforms— managed to reduce the Bedouins to the status of fellahin, there is trouble brewing. In the early land reforms of the second half of the nineteenth and in the early twentieth century the land was registered for the sake of convenience in the name of the tribal chiefs, whose position changed from that of charismatic or chosen leaders to landowners whose wealth and leadership became hereditary. Their tribesmen, on the other hand, were reduced to the status of share-croppers on the chief's property, of fellahin, who do not own the land they till.

DISREGARD OF AGRICULTURE

Ploughing the land under any condition is considered by the Arabs of the Middle East the worst of hardships—with the notable exception of the Egyptian fellahin, whose different outlook is obviously due to their non-Arab descent. Whoever can possibly do so moves from the countryside into a city to live there from the rent of his land, from the work of others, or from trade. No 'Georgics' exists in Arab literature, no praise of agriculture, no Arab Cincinnatus is known in the Middle East. While the Bedouin's life is overrated, not only by the Arabs themselves but also by some romantic Europeans—especially from the British Isles—the toiling fellahin are disregarded. And, indeed, no political influence eman- ates directly from the peasantry, who live in abject misery and dependence upon the landlords, and who never won any preferential position through military or administrative services, as did their feudal counterparts in Europe.

The present distribution of *property* is extraordinarily complicated, because the system goes back to the Arab conquest of the seventh century. Originally full landed property (*mulk*) was admitted only in towns and cities, while the open land fell to the conquerors. The theoretical proprietor of all the conquered lands remained, till the end of the Turkish suzerainty, the caliph or sultan, who disposed of the land in the name of the community of the believers. In practice one part of these lands remained the full property of the sultan as state domain (*recaba*), while another part (*amirieh*) was handed over to individuals or villages with such far-reaching rights of use (*tessaruf*) that it developed into a sort of *de facto* property. This land could be freely sold or transmitted by inheritance, and the right of disposal was limited only by the prohibition—which in fact was not enforced—against handing it over to a pious foundation (*waqf*), and the right of the sultan to take the land back if it lay fallow for three to five years. There was full individual property in city land (*mulk*); there were the state domains (*recaba*), and there was land which in theory remained the property of the ruler, but upon which individuals or communities had established *de facto* property rights. The rights of the pious foundations were different. Only private property was supposed to be given to the *waqf*—a limitation which was not kept—because the land remained the property of the foundation for 'eternity'. The founder, however, could retain the right of usufruct for himself and his heirs; he thus protected it from the greedy hand of the tax collector or a powerful chieftain while suffering no notable loss of income. The *waqf* lands developed into latifundia.

The proprietor does not cultivate the land himself, if he can avoid the dishonour of dirtying his hands. He leases it to a tenant or employs day-labourers. The leases are as complicated as the ones which are customary in southern Europe, and different contracts for sharecropping prevail. A whole cascade of proprietors, *de facto* proprietors, usufructuaries, tenants, day-labourers make their living from the same piece of land. And where absentee-landownership prevails, the soil is exhausted, owing to the lack of personal interest in keeping it fertile. In Syria we find a particular sort of collective village property, the *moushaa*, resembling the ancient land co-operatives in German and Slavic countries.

The peasant who does not own the soil he tills lives in dependence upon the proprietor. His village is not much better than a dormitory. and he leaves his adobe hut as easily as the Bedouin his tent. A deeply rooted peasantry, as in Europe, does not exist in the Asian-Arab lands.

POLITICS ARE MADE IN THE CITIES

The Bedouin ideal lives on even in the cities of today. The dream of wide-open spaces, in which the Nomads freely roam, does not take into account the gradual disappearance of the Bedouin. This dream inspires the ideal picture of a gigantic Arab empire extending from the Indian to the Atlantic Ocean. With the extension of living space (*Lebensraum*), all problems, be they of economic, political, or spiritual nature, are expected to be automatically solved; this at least is the main credo of the pan-Arab nationalists who revel in the glories of the early Arab conquests.

In his *Philosophy of the Revolution*, Colonel Nasser, having described his dream of Arab unity, writes: 'I do not hesitate for one moment to say that our united struggle could achieve for us and our peoples everything we wish and aspire to.'

The counterpart to the idealized Bedouin life is formed by the city. Trade and crafts are traditionally concentrated there. To the city retires the man who has drawn enough wealth fron his lands so that he no longer needs to work, i.e. the beneficiary of the ground-rent, the landowner. The city offers entertainment; it also contains the mosques, churches, and schools. It is the administrative centre and disposes of the public services. A surprisingly high percentage of the population lives in the cities; even in Jordan and Syria it is as much as one-third of the total population. The social order shows an even more subtle stratification and ramification than that developed in Europe in the Middle Ages. This stratification corresponds to an equally differentiated *division of labour* which is not only characterized by a specialization based on different operations, but also on ethnical and religious differences; personal services are often reserved for Christians—therefore the personnel in hotels and restaurants, and the taxi drivers with whom the foreign visitor makes his first contacts, are very often members of a Christian church, while the Iraqi tribe that specializes in archaeological excavations has now become famous. The complicated vertical division of labour in the Arab countries could be compared to the horizontal division of labour of the modern assembly line. A characteristic feature, however, is the multiplicity of personal services as compared to the number of people engaged in productive work. Every worker performs only one narrowly circumscribed function, which after him is performed by his children and grandchildren and becomes a hereditary family privilege, lowly as it may appear to Western eyes. To each function corresponds a guild-like organization. In fact the guild systems of the Arab cities are based on such a highly developed division of labour that the guild organizations of the medieval

Central European cities appear very crude instruments by comparison.

But the social order based on this extremely subtle division of labour is everywhere broken up by Western technology. It loses its meaning where finished products can be imported cheaper and in better quality from abroad. Thus the crafts disappear more and more, and personal services are supplied by an ever-shrinking group. Nowhere is this development more evident than in the arts and crafts which the travellers of old used to praise so highly. Where they persist, stereotyped, unimaginative products dominate the scene. Western mass production has led most of the artisans to abandon their crafts and to dedicate themselves to trade, more lucrative and respect-commanding. In this way urban society is overwhelmed by Western technology. The old complex structure has begun to disintegrate. No new production facilities have absorbed the former craftsmen, who, having lost the professional and social stability guaranteed by the guild organizations and ancient privileges, have now for the greater part joined the rootless masses.

It is in the cities, moreover, that the rootless intellectuals collect. High schools and universities in the Arab countries were originally founded with the primary purpose of training administrators in the countries formerly administered by the Turkish overlords. But many of the graduates now find no adequate occupation, while others have to accept poorly paid work with little social standing. The city thus becomes the stage for the formation of *masses* in the sociological sense. The phenomena of mass psychology are nowhere more evident than in the Arab cities. And it is there that all the politics originate. The special interests of the economically powerful—the tribal chiefs, the big landowners, and the rich merchants—clash and merge in the narrow space of the city. Below them moves the amorphous mass of the people who have lost their orientation in the disintegrating social order. More and more the 'street' and the 'bazaar' influence politics. This mass can be manipulated, as experience has all too often shown, but in many cases there exists no determined leadership; the masses move by their own momentum and are wide open to the influence of agitators who come from outside the particular city or country.

Economics, education, and technology all lead in a Western direction. It is in the cities also that a counter-movement is beginning to assert itself. One of its main organizational expressions is the *Moslem Brotherhood*, which demands a return to the old laws of Islam—regardless of whether this is practicable or not. Similar tendencies dominate the *Arab Liberation Party* in Syria and Jordan. In the light of the main stream of development these are reactionary movements which want to turn away from modern civilization. They find support, however, among the petty bourgeoisie of the cities, the class which still imposes the veil on women. Hardly any reform movement aiming at a full assimilation of Western achievements—as in Turkey—has yet developed in the Arab countries. Technology, economic reforms, and the legal order of the West are accepted; the social order is in a state of disintegration; the spiritual balance, in the face of the irresistible invasion of new values and new methods, has still to be looked for by the Arabs.

ELEMENTS OF ARAB UNITY

One way out of the conflict-laden situation into which the Arabs have drifted is sought by many in the ideal of pan-Arab unity. What the Arabs have in common is their language, and many Arabs think that on this foundation—which is endangered by the growth of different dialects—an economic, political, and spiritual edifice should be built—a proposal which recalls the remark of an objective and observant Arab, Edward Atiyah (*The Arabs*, p. 96): 'It is a characteristic of the Arab mind to be swayed more by words than by ideas, and more by ideas than by facts.' Philip K. Hitti supports this statement in his *Précis d'Histoire des Arabes*: 'No nation in the world feels such an enthusiastic admiration for the literary expression, no one is moved to such a degree by word and writing as the Arabs. No other language seems to influence the spirit of those who speak it in such an irresistible way. Even in our time one can find audiences in Baghdad, Cairo, and Damascus who are moved to delirium by the recitation of ancient poems and speeches in literary Arabic, which in fact only a few of them really understand. The rhythm, the rhyme, the music produce an effect upon the listeners which they themselves describe as "pleasant magic".' Pleasant magic to the ears of many Arabs are the alluring sounds of the propagandists of Arab unity who never fail to refer to the long-past glories of early Islam. The allegedly limitless freedom of the Bedouin is projected upon the modern ideal of pan-Arab unity, ignoring all the weaknesses of the social and economic structure, and the resulting political instability in Arab lands. Between the urge to expand in space and the extreme individualism of the people runs an unbridgeable abyss. The greatest Arab historian, Ibn Khaldun, was of the opinion that 'generally speaking, the Arabs are incapable of founding an empire, except on a religious basis such as the Revelation of a Prophet or a Saint . . . because their fierce character, pride, roughness, and jealousy of one another, especially in political matters, make them the most difficult of peoples to lead'.

PAN-ARAB NATIONALISM

It seems to be in the nature of Islam that only a single personality can take over the leadership of the people. The whole history of the Arabs is characterized by authoritarian rule. Even in the countries where democratic rule of a Western type has been introduced, it is only one man, be it king or president, who has decisive influence in politics. Islam does not recognize class differences between men, but social equality should not be mistaken for political democracy. The personalities who determine Arab politics often oppose the movement of pan-Arab unity. But will one man be able to accomplish the difficult task of unifying all Arabs? In the light of Ibn Khaldun's theory it is significant that the men aspiring to the leadership of all Arabs are trying to use religious forces for their own aims—for a while they even succeeded in mobilizing the conservative religious groups against the 'heretics and infidels' of the Baghdad pact. Yet these same religious forces, i.e. the Moslem Brotherhood, are being steadily pushed out from modern Arab society into the wastes of a social and economic stone age.

At the present time large groups are emotionally committed to the pan-Arab ideal. Their concentration on a distant goal creates secondary effects of far-reaching importance: the solution of urgent local problems, social, economic, and political, is postponed or neglected; the integration of the Arab peoples within narrower confines is hampered. The development of a healthy social and political structure remains an unfulfilled postulate, as long as some of the best intellectual forces are absorbed by the remote dream of Arab unity. But propaganda for this goal has progressed so far that even the ones who oppose it have to express themselves in terms of pan-Arab nationalism to make themselves heard. In the field of foreign politics the pan-Arab nationalists have succeeded in forcing all politicians to pay at least lip-service to their ideal. Anti-Zionist, anti-colonialist, and anti-Western declamations are obligatory as the credentials of fidelity to the pan-Arab ideal: a negative solidarity has thus developed. Even the West must look on while its plans, proposals, and assistance are reduced throughout to the simplified formulas of pan-Arabism.

Pan-Arabism has combined lately with a highly aggressive nationalism of anti-Western orientation, and Cairo has become the propaganda centre of this movement. The rejection of Israel as a sovereign state has a pronounced anti-Western character, and the French colonists in the Maghreb are placed on exactly the same level as the Jewish settlers in Israel. Pan-Arab propaganda has made the strongest inroads in the cities where the formation of the masses is farthest advanced. The masses call for strong leadership, and in so doing invoke the entire political past of the Islamic area in which, almost without exception, individual leaders have prevailed, while the forms of democracy were imported from a foreign world.

NATIONALISM COMBINED WITH SOCIALISM

Recently this over-heated nationalism has initiated attempts to solve, by Socialist methods, the problems posed by the break-through of twentieth-century technology. Socialism in this part of the world is merely a label covering all sorts of government inter-vention. There is hardly any serious study of Socialist doctrines, and even among the followers of Moscow there is hardly anyone, except Khaled Bakdash, the chief of the Communists in Syria and Lebanon, who has thoroughly studied the writings of the high priests of Marxism and Leninism. On the desk of a pan-Arab nationalist in Damascus, who expects salvation from the Kremlin, we found the works of Friedrich Engels, and to our question whether these consti-tuted material for advanced studies, he answered that they only had to be checked to see if they contained anything subversive. This superficial approach to the problems of Socialism and Communism is typical. But where this vague Socialism is combined with extreme nationalism it produces phenomena all too familiar from recent European experience. In practice it is Colonel Nasser in Cairo, and the Socialist Party of the Arab Renaissance (Ba'ath) in Damascus, who most fervently promote the fateful alliance of nationalist and Socialist elements today. While many Western observers' attention is absorbed by the manoeuvres of the Communists, the immediate danger of the rise of a *pan-Arab national-Socialism* seems to escape them. One has to see the distorted, hate-filled faces of those who gather around the radio sets listening to the inflammatory 'Voice of the Arabs' to understand what is going on in this region.

THE COMMUNISTS ENTER THE SCENE

The Communists have cleverly exploited the pan-Arab agitation and they have sought, whenever possible, an alliance with the nationalists. Communism alone cannot hope, at the present time, to grasp power in the Arab countries—not even in Syria. But it uses the wave of nationalist excitement to steer the masses towards its special goal. The Communists have shed the shabby overcoat of the agitator in the Arab countries and changed it for the emperor's purple; instead of sneaking in through the back door, they march in full daylight through the main portal accompanied by a host of nationalist train-bearers. They cleverly use the fascination of power, which radiates from their 'strong leadership', they boost the Arabs' self-confidence by courting their favour and, since the West is pre-occupied with the growing Communist influence, confer on them a greater possibility to manoeuvre in the field of foreign politics.

The interest of Soviet imperialism in the Arab states is not recent. Moscow was the first to recognize Ibn Saud as king of the Hedjaz and Nejd in 1926. In Yemen a Soviet mission was already active for years before World War II. The demand for a United Nations Mandate over Libya, and the attempt to establish Soviet republics in Iranian Azerbaidjan and Kurdistan, were made only a few years ago. The supply of arms to some Arab states—like diplomatic sup-port for Abdul Nasser, and other moves—is designed to secure a foothold for the Soviet Union in the Middle East, the landbridge between Africa, Asia, and Europe, and also to capture eventually a share of the oil wealth of the area. If successful, Communist infiltra-tion in the Middle East would constitute a *turning of the Western positions* in the Near and Middle East. If the oil and communications by land, air, and sea in this region were dominated by weak govern-ments open to Soviet influence and pressure, Moscow would gain a dangerous stranglehold over the Western world.

GROWING SELF-CONFIDENCE OF THE NATIONALISTS

Two other events have strengthened the pan-Arab nationalists: the Bandung Conference and the taking over of the Suez Canal by Egypt. The effect of the Bandung Conference of Asian and African states has obviously been under-estimated by most Western obser-vers, who concentrated their attention on the anti-Soviet speeches by the Turkish, Pakistani, Filipino, and Ceylonese delegates. True, no decisions of immediate consequence were taken. The fact, however, that the countries formerly under Western domination came to-gether at a conference, at which neither European nor American representatives were present, has strengthened the self-confidence of the Arabs—and other nations—tremendously, the more so as the Conference adopted the Arab point of view on the Palestine ques-tion, and approved a solution on the basis of the United Nations' resolutions, which do not correspond to the conditions created after the 1948 war of the Arabs against the newly emerged State of Israel.

The evacuation of the Suez base after the agreement of 1954 by the British acted like the bursting of a dike, and this was, perhaps, due less to the evacuation itself than to the circumstances in which it took place. That an Arab state was able to force the mighty

British to withdraw from one of their strongest positions made a deep impression on the Arabs. That the two strongest Powers of the West, Great Britain and the United States, did not collaborate, but were at odds in this conflict—this, at least, is how the Arabs understood American mediation, which seemed to favour Egypt—opened new horizons to Arab policy. When Abdul Nasser reached out on July 26, 1956, to nationalize the Suez Canal Company, and when the United Nations, backed strongly by the United States and by the Soviet threat of military intervention, forced the British and French expeditionary corps and later the Israeli troops to withdraw from Egypt, Abdul Nasser's influence seemed to have reached its apex— but only from the outside. In fact he had opened the eyes of many who slowly turned their back on Nasser's brand of pan-Arab nationalism. His initial successes had concealed the fact that other nationalisms were at work in the Arab world.

PARTICULARISM OPPOSED TO PAN-ARAB NATIONALISM

European history, and even recent African history, should have taught that pieces carved out of an empire tend to develop a strong will to live, and very often consolidate into durable states. In a similar way in the Arab countries, national consciousness and local nationalisms are emerging which are opposed to pan-Arab nationalism. The force of this local nationalism or patriotism should not be under-estimated. The boundaries of the Arab states have, as was mentioned before, been artificially drawn by Western Powers. But this does not exclude the formation of a local patriotism. Many observers dispose lightly of the manifestations of local patriotism, because they accept the dreams of a large group of Arab intellectuals as reality. They disregard the fact that the Arab Empire of the eighth and ninth centuries had already fallen into many parts at feud against each other when the Turks reunified the Arab lands under Ottoman rule. They disregard the differentiation which has formed the various spoken dialects out of a single classic language. Local patriotism in the different countries is more than a manifestation of special material interests, and it draws its strength not only from foreign influence. Since World War II, its centrifugal forces have, in most critical periods, prevailed over the pan-Arab idea. The development of the Arab League, a sort of Council of Europe, as its secretary-general aptly calls it, is only one example of the vital power of local nationalism against the centripetal force of pan-Arab unity.

Why is it, then, that local nationalism inside the borders of the existing Arab states has so rarely been regarded as a vital force by

Arab intellectuals and foreign observers? The answer lies in the Arab states' internal structure. *Personalism* in politics is still the rule. The heads of families, clientèles, and tribes are regularly elected to the various parliaments, and there they represent the interests of their special groups, and not always—as the theories of the French Revolution proclaim—the single and indivisible nation. But this is also the case in several European 'nations', especially in the Mediterranean area, where—as in the Arab countries—the process of forming a nation has not yet come to an end.

CENTRIFUGAL FORCES: PERSONALISM AND THE MILLET SYSTEM

The different social, ethnic, and religious groups which form the electoral basis of the candidates for parliament in the Arab countries have a long history. The Turkish *Millet system*—the *millah* of the Arabs—has preserved the ancient differentiations, often corresponding with a division of labour. Under the Millet system, legal and even political functions were conferred on the religious groups. 'The laws', writes Albert H. Hourani in *Syria and Lebanon*, 'by which the life of the individual and of society was regulated sprang not from positive enactments of the ruler, but from the religious doctrines and ancestral customs to which individual and society adhered. It is true that since the ruling power was Moslem by faith, the Moslem religious law and the courts had a special relation to the government. But a Moslem would no more have thought of compelling Christians and Jews to conform to Moslem law in matters of personal life and relationships than of abandoning his own religious codes. Law was personal. Not simply was there no concept of equality before the law, there was no idea of sameness.' The Jews and the different Christian denominations, as well as the heterodox Moslem communities, were preserved as separate entities, and their spiritual leaders were responsible to the ruler for administration, the collection of taxes, the personal relations, and the good behaviour of the members of their groups. The law of the religious communities, not that of the secular authorities, prevailed in all these matters, and it followed the person not the territory.

The Millet system preserved the particularities of the different groups; it also separated them from each other. The modern state tries to abolish these historical barriers, but it has not yet succeeded. In most of the Arab states special representation is conceded to religious or ethnic communities. The most striking example is to be found in Lebanon, where the safeguarding of minorities has become a sort of *'raison d'être'*. There the religious groups each have their own representation in parliament. The minorities also send representatives to the legislative assemblies of Syria, Iraq, and Jordan. Since separate laws rule the different communities, and since the ethnic or religious or social group is accepted as the basis for representation, it is only natural that personalism and not party rule or ideology dominates politics in the Arab states. More than egotistical material interests are at stake: historical differences have been carried over by the tolerance of Moslem law into the age of the modern nation-state.

Where personalism is the rule, democracy does not correspond to twentieth-century conceptions. The leaders of different groups dominate politics, as did the oligarchy in England before 1832. There are no parties with nation-wide organizations held together by a common programme or ideology. Personalities rather than ideas determine the line of the government. Decisions are not made in open debate in parliament, but rather in secret talks in back rooms over endless cups of coffee. *The differences between democracy and an authoritarian régime tend to disappear.* No Arab parliament has ever dared to pass a vote of no-confidence in any government. Crises develop through pressures on the local 'strong man', king or president, and when he withdraws his protecting hand from the Prime Minister, the cabinet falls. Political parties in the modern sense with permanent organizations and programmes are only now beginning to emerge in the border-zones of democracy. Totalitarian groups first use modern methods to bind together the rootless masses of the cities who have cast off the fetters of the social, ethnic, or religious communities to which they originally belonged.

LOCAL PATRIOTISM ON THE MARCH

The existence of a variety of different groups does not preclude their collaboration for the sake of preserving the state's integrity and sovereignty. The national 'pact of unity' of 1943 concluded by the Lebanese 'parties' may serve as an example. In Iraq, national consciousness or national pride opposes the pan-Arab ideas emanating from Cairo, and the old conflict between the Two-Stream Land and the Nile Valley, familiar since earliest times, continues in new forms. Even Syria, the Poland of the Middle East, which lacks natural frontiers, has so far resisted all attempts to incorporate its territory into a larger state. In Egypt, the hope of creating a 'new-pharaonic' state had taken shape before Abdul Nasser's pan-Arabism got the upper hand.

Out of the autonomy enjoyed by Lebanon under Turkish suzerainty since 1860, and the relative liberty of the Christian and heterodox Moslem mountain tribes, 'new-Phoenician' dreams spread down to the centre of the present administration. The events of May, 1957, when pan-Arab nationalists forced a show-down with the government—which stood for liberty for all groups and individuals, for neutrality between the warring factions in the Arab world, and for the preservation of the country's sovereignty and independence—showed clearly the strength of local patriotism against the forces stirred up by Colonel Nasser and his followers. Similarly King Hussain of Jordan, who at first had given free rein to the Suleiman Nabulsi government, took up the gauntlet thrown to him by the introduction of a Communist into the cabinet and the opening of diplomatic relations with the Soviet Union, and defeated, for the time being, the pan-Arab nationalists. Many observers were astonished by the extent to which this daring fight for his throne and, in the final analysis, for the existence of his country as a sovereign state, received support from large segments of the population—whether the majority or not, is still an open question. Nuri es Said's régime in Baghdad, the near demise of which has been predicted by various interested parties practically since its beginning, has remained in power for several years, and may even survive the final abdication of the old authoritarian chief of government. More than special material interests and foreign influences are at work to preserve the various states into which the Arab world split after the crumbling of the Turkish Empire.

REGIONAL GROUPINGS: THE FERTILE CRESCENT

The fight for unity or local independence will probably go on for decades. Regional units may be formed, as distinct from pan-Arab unity or local sovereignty. The tendency to federate or unite several Arab states, without reaching as far as the pan-Arab ideal, cannot be overlooked. The 'Fertile Crescent' idea still has many adherents in Baghdad and in the other countries of the Asian Middle East. One of its earliest advocates, Antoun Saadeh, wanted it to comprise the territory between the Suez Canal and the Persian Gulf which now belongs to Egypt (the Sinai Peninsula), Israel, Jordan, Lebanon, Syria, Turkey (the Sanjak of Alexandretta), Iraq, and even Cyprus, 'the star before the Fertile Crescent'. Since Saadeh fell, in 1950, before the bullets of a Lebanese execution squad, and since his party has been banned and prosecuted in Syria and Lebanon, his followers have lost much of their influence and have reduced their aspirations to a Greater Syria. Plans to create a Greater Syria have been put forward by King Abdullah of Jordan and by at least four different groups that are still at work in Syria, Jordan, Iraq, and Lebanon;

but none so far has been able to muster many partisans. The 'unity of the Nile Valley' which fascinates most Egyptians and not a few Sudanese—though obviously not the ruling ones—would form another regional grouping, and this has some possibility of being realized eventually. In the Maghreb the strong tendency to build a North African Arab Federation cannot materialize so long as France holds on to the Algerian departments and to her desert empire in the Sahara.

The main problems which the Arabs have to solve consist in overcoming their consumer position with respect to modern technology, and adopting twentieth-century production methods by which the labour potential could be put to better use; in shedding the fetters of the medieval social system, and, thirdly, integrating the people into one or several nations in the social and political sense of the word. While the West could help the Arabs in the difficult task of assimilating modern technology, and might, to a certain degree, be instrumental, by advice and example—given, for instance, by foreign enterprises and international organizations—in changing social conditions, the underlying spiritual problems must be solved by the Arabs themselves. Political integration, the formation of one or several nations, can be accomplished only by the Middle Eastern peoples themselves—any foreign interference would automatically discredit the proposed solution. This will certainly take a long time, judging by other examples. For, notwithstanding the innumerable declamations of unity already achieved or of unity aspired to, the Arabs of today are as much divided as ever in their history.

ARAB INTEGRATION AND THE PALESTINE CONFLICT

The Arabs have achieved a certain identity of purpose only with respect to Israel—and it is a strictly negative purpose. The Palestine conflict cannot be considered as an isolated struggle between Israelis and Arabs; it forms part of the deep-rooted political crisis which keeps the Near and Middle East and Northern Africa in a permanent state of turmoil. The foundation of the Jewish state has acted as a catalyst around which Arab nationalism coagulates and inflames itself; but it has not created Arab nationalism and its problems. That Jewish nationalism, which found its expression in Zionism and realized its main goal with the creation of Israel, grew simultaneously with the Arabs' striving for nationhood, must be considered one of the tragic coincidences of history; both movements gained irresistible momentum after World War II. The Palestine conflict acquired an important function in the painful birth of Arab nations. The Arabs understand the struggle against Israel in this sense, and they put the Jewish settlers in Israel on the same level as the French colonists in the Maghreb and the British soldiers and administrators in the sheikdoms along the Persian Gulf.

The Palestine conflict, therefore, is only one part of a far-reaching commotion where the issues at stake emerge with special virulence. The number of the parties to this conflict has grown continuously since it first started, and practically embraced the world with the intervention of the Soviets in the Middle East area. The protagonists are, to be sure, Israel and the Arab states; but in the background all the big Powers are involved in the drama. From the end of the nineteenth century, but especially after World War I, Britain and France had been driving the Turks from the Arab countries they had conquered four hundred years earlier. At the same time the Western European Powers kept the Russians out of this region. World War II brought the elimination of the French Mandates, a process in which Britain played a part that the French have not yet forgotten. Under the double pressure of awakening Arab nationalism and the traditional anti-colonial attitude of its most powerful ally, the United States, Britain was forced in the post-war period to evacuate important positions in Egypt, on the Suez Canal, in Iraq, and in Jordan. The pressure on the remaining British positions in Cyprus, Aden, and the Persian Gulf is still mounting.

THE UNITED STATES AGAINST SOVIET IMPERIALISM

The assumption that the newly-created states in the Middle East would be quite capable of standing on their own feet has proved a fallacy. Not a single state in the Near and Middle East, not even Greece and Turkey, can do so without foreign support. The Arab countries are dependent on outside aid in the field of technology, Israel financially. An overwhelming proportion of their material requirements is produced in those parts of the world which, on the foundation of Hellenic-Jewish-Christian civilization, have brought technology to its present high stage of development. The liquidation of the antiquated forms of Western European influence, and the refusal of the United States to replace it—a refusal modified only recently, to a certain degree, by the proclamation of the Eisenhower doctrine—have created a vacuum in the Middle East which the Soviets would be only too happy to fill.

The American maxim that the spreading of Communism must at all costs be stopped enables the Arabs to play the United States and the Soviet Union against each other—and the pan-Arab nationalists have used it to further their special aims. It seems ironical that the very Powers which make such a point of forswearing colonialism—

the one out of genuine tradition, the other at best for propaganda purposes—now stand in the forefront of the struggle for hegemony in the Middle East. The discussions about the appeal of Communist doctrine to the peoples of the Middle East very often miss the principal point: for what the Arabs are interested in at present is not the ideology of Communism but the economic, technical, and military aid of Moscow. The number of Communists who have studied Marxism and Leninism is still minute, because the vast majority is obsessed by nationalist and national-Socialist dreams. Communism may be a danger in some states because there are no checks and balances to prevent a small determined group—which may gain the support of some influential leaders, as happened in Syria—from grabbing what little power the Arab administrations provide. The most important problem in the Middle East is not Communist subversion but the alliance of nationalist forces with Soviet imperialism. The Arab world today is in the phase of a Molotov-Ribbentrop pact, with Colonel Nasser as one of the two participants.

The pan-Arab nationalists are bent on eliminating all the elements they resent as alien, as foreign bodies in the Arab and Islamic spheres. These elements include the European outposts, the Jews in Israel, and the Christians wherever they are not satisfied with a subordinate function. The pan-Arab nationalists, whose principal spokesman Colonel Nasser has become by self-appointment, exploit every weakness of their opponents to eliminate the centres of foreign influence. A rich prize would await them if they were successful: the oil resources of the Middle East upon which Western Europe is dependent, since it imports from there as much liquid fuel as all the Communist states produce together, and furthermore the domination of the air, sea, and land communications between the continents. Nothing would please the Soviet rulers more than to see Western Europe become economically dependent on the favours of weak Arab states which could be manipulated from Moscow.

PEACE IN THE MIDDLE EAST: THE WESTERN POWERS' TASK

The conflict with Israel serves the pan-Arab nationalists as a means to heighten Arab emotions and to canalize them as required by Colonel Nasser and his advisers. Even if the Palestine conflict were settled, no peaceful development in the Arab countries would result, because what troubles the Arab world lies much deeper. The problems of the Middle East cannot be solved in Palestine alone. A Solomon's judgment in twentieth-century style, which—as in

Korea, Vietnam, Kashmir, Trieste, and Germany—would divide the cause of dispute, could not eliminate the conflict. Even if the provisions of the United Nations' resolutions about the division of Palestine, and the return of the Arab refugees to what has since become the State of Israel, were to be enforced, as the Arabs now wish, no Arab leader would dare to recognize the sovereignty of Israel, or be prepared to lift the boycott or blockade against the Jewish state. The recognition of Israel by all the Great Powers, and its admission to the United Nations, should be sufficient reason to exclude any solution affecting the very existence of the Jewish state.

The stabilization of the Middle East must be sought, not at the cost of Israel, but by comprehensive action of the Western Powers in the whole area, by strengthening the forces in the Arab countries which are prepared to fight for liberty and democracy, and social and economic evolution. These forces have often felt let down, and they are still on the defensive today: they often feel deserted by the Western Powers who appear unable to pull themselves together and take concerted action. The insufficient support given to the Baghdad Pact, which should have become a bastion against Soviet imperialism, is but one example of the weakness of the West. For more than two years Colonel Nasser's 'Voice of the Arabs' and Moscow's propaganda dominated the air waves, till Iraq was given a radio station powerful enough to counteract the anti-Western tirades. The Eisenhower doctrine constitutes a first attempt by the United States to take on the anti-Western forces. But co-ordination of Western strength is of the utmost importance: no single Power can go its way alone. The influence of France and Britain has declined, but —as Syria's stand against the Baghdad Pact brought clearly into evidence—it is still enough to condemn any move by another Western country to abject failure, if Paris or London so decide. Only collaboration of the Western Powers at all levels—not only at the summit, but down to the intelligence services and economic enterprises—could guarantee peaceful development in the Middle East and prevent it from becoming the Balkans of the second half of the twentieth century.

ECONOMIC AND SOCIAL FOUNDA-TIONS OF DEMOCRACY IN THE MIDDLE EAST

by CHARLES ISSAWI

IT HAS BECOME commonplace that the parliamentary-democratic[1] form of government has not functioned satisfactorily in the Middle East. During the last few years, a series of *coups d'état* have proclaimed, in no uncertain terms, the dissatisfaction of several countries with their parliamentary governments, and in more than one country the army has taken over power.

The failure of democracy in the Middle East has been attributed to widely divergent, though not necessarily incompatible, causes. One explanation, which is current in the West, is that democracy is a plant of slow growth, which gradually developed, over several centuries, in the congenial climate of Europe and North America and which could not possibly be expected to thrive when suddenly transplanted to an alien Eastern soil which, since the dawn of recorded history, had bred nothing but the thorns and thistles of despotism. The absence of democratic traditions, and of the historical customs, habits, and attitudes required to make democracy work, was one of

---

[1] In this article 'democracy' denotes exclusively a system of parliamentary government, based on free, popular elections, contested by two or more parties. The term usually covers a much wider range of meaning, and in this broader sense several aspects of Middle Eastern life may be said to be 'democratic'; in particular, there is a genuine and widespread social democracy in most Middle Eastern countries. It is moreover true that political democracy can express itself in other forms than parliamentary government, and does so in several Middle Eastern countries. However, a study of these broader aspects of democracy would carry the discussion too far afield and the present article is therefore exclusively concerned with the narrow meaning given above.

M.T.—3

the first aspects of the East to strike nineteenth-century Europeans, and no one has expressed this better than Lord Cromer, who wrote: 'Do not let us for one moment imagine that the fatally simple idea of despotic rule will readily give way to the far more complex conception of ordered liberty.'[2]

In the Middle East itself, a more popular explanation is that external political factors have been mainly responsible for the inability of democracy to thrive and prosper. The title of Morgan Shuster's book, *The Strangling of Persia*,[3] is indicative of this attitude. It has been cogently argued that no real democracy could develop in Egypt, Iraq, Jordan, Lebanon, and Syria as long as British or French armies of occupation were the determining factor in all political matters and as long as the population continued to be preoccupied, not to say obsessed, with the problem of its relations with the foreign Power. Nor was the situation of unoccupied countries, such as Iran and Turkey, very much better, for both have lived under the shadow of two powerful neighbours, one or other of whom periodically made attempts, often successful, to dominate them.

A third explanation, prevalent in both the West and the Middle East, is that, with the exception of the Turks, Middle Easterners are incapacitated, by their extreme individualism, from achieving the degree of co-operation required for the successful functioning of democracy. It is recognized that Middle Easterners develop intense loyalty to certain small units, such as the family, the clan, the tribe, or the religious sect, but they do not seem to be able to transcend those groups and feel towards any larger body, for example the city or the nation, enough devotion and responsibility to subordinate their individual selfish propensities to some common goal. In other words, the notion of the general will aiming at the general good seems to be absent, and with it any hope of making democracy function. Perhaps the best expression of this view is that of Ibn Khaldun, the most penetrating social scientist who has ever studied the region: '. . . every Arab regards himself as worthy to rule, and it is rare to find one of them submitting willingly to another, be it his father or his brother or the head of his clan, but only grudgingly and for fear of public opinion.'[4]

Each of the three views mentioned undoubtedly contains a large measure of truth. Taken together, they may well constitute a sufficient explanation of the shortcomings of Middle Eastern democracy.

[2] See 'The Government of Subject Races', *Edinburgh Review* (January, 1908).
[3] New York, The Century Co., 1912.
[4] *An Arab Philosophy of History: Selections from the Prolegomena of Ibn Khaldun of Tunis, 1332–1406*, translated by Charles Issawi (London, John Murray, 1950), p. 57.

Nevertheless, it seems relevant to draw attention to another group of factors which have also had a deep effect, the sociological factors. Briefly put, it is the contention of the writer that democracy does not thrive in the present-day Middle East[5] because the economic and social basis which it requires is as yet non-existent. That basis presents the following aspects: size of territory and population, level of economic development, distribution of wealth, industrialization, homogeneity of language and religion, degree of education, and habit of co-operative association. In this paper the common economic and social characteristics of those countries which at present successfully practise democracy[6] will be adopted as yard-sticks against which the development of the Middle Eastern countries can be measured.

It is necessary to make explicit one basic assumption which underlies the following argument. For democratic institutions to develop, and for the democratic spirit to flourish, two conditions seem necessary: the community must be bound by a strong social solidarity; and at the same time it must contain enough diversity to produce tension between its constituent parts. In the absence of solidarity, the community is constantly threatened with disintegration, democratic government is too weak to hold it together, and there is a powerful tendency to resort to a strong, absolutist government. On the other hand, unless there is diversity and tension, resulting in the clash of ideas and interests represented by different groups, no effective check on the power of the government is likely to be established.

In western Europe during the last three or four hundred years, and in the overseas societies which sprang from it, the cementing force has been nationalism which, although only recently articulate and still more recently virulent, has been present since the close of the Middle Ages. The tensions were provided first by the religious differences following the Reformation, and then by economic and social conflicts, as first commercial and then industrial development brought into being new classes which could challenge the old landed aristocracy.

[5] The Middle East is here defined as the territory bounded by and including Libya in the west, the Sudan in the south, Turkey in the north, and Pakistan in the east, a territory with an aggregate population of not much below 200 millions. With the qualifications noted below, much the same economic and social pattern prevails in the whole region, except in Israel, which is consequently not included in this article.

[6] The countries covered by the term 'democratic' are: the United States, Canada, the United Kingdom, France, Iceland, Ireland, Switzerland, Luxemburg, Belgium, the Netherlands, Denmark, Norway, Sweden, Finland, Australia, New Zealand, and Uruguay. Germany and Italy have joined the democratic ranks only recently, while Czechoslovakia has been snatched away from them; the inclusion of these three countries would not, however, in any way affect the conclusions drawn.

Size of Population and Territory. Whatever errors of application he
may have committed, Aristotle was essentially right when he stated
that 'States, like all other things, have a definite measure of size. Any
object will lose its power of performing its function if it is either
excessively small or of an excessive size', and further that 'experience
shows that it is difficult, if not indeed impossible, for a very populous
state to secure a general habit of obedience to law'.[7] With the exception of the United States, Canada, and Australia, which will be discussed later, none of the democratic countries is very extensive. Of
the rest, France, the largest, has an area of 200,000 square miles and
most of the others are distinctly smaller. Again, with the exception
of the United States and the United Kingdom, none of these countries has a population of over 50 millions, and the majority fall below
the 10-million mark.

It is germane to inquire how the Middle Eastern states compare
with the democracies in respect of population and territory. Only
Pakistan, with its 75 million inhabitants, ranks among the world's
giants. The other countries do not go beyond the 25-million mark,
and several of them have fewer than 5 million inhabitants. It cannot
therefore be maintained that the size of the population of Middle
Eastern countries is, in principle, such as to place great obstacles in
the path of the democratic process. Indeed, from the economic point
of view, several of them are too small to constitute a market in which
division of labour can be carried far enough to secure a high national
income and standard of living, a fact which, as will be shown later,
has a bearing on their political life. It is worth while noting, however,
that in the more populous democracies, for instance, the United
Kingdom and France, constitutional government developed at a
time when the population was only a fraction of its present size, and
that even when the democratic form of government was well established the number of inhabitants was much smaller than at present.
Regarded from the point of view of size, the Middle East is not so
favourably situated. Iraq is almost as large as present-day France;
Afghanistan and Turkey are distinctly larger; and Pakistan, Iran,
and Saudi Arabia are twice,[8] three and a half times, and nearly four
times as large, respectively.

Experience seems to support the assumption that great size is a
handicap in the quest for democracy. In the first place it tends to

[7] *The Politics of Aristotle*, translated with notes by Ernest Barker (Oxford,
Clarendon Press, 1948), p. 341.

[8] Egypt has not been included in this list. Her area is nearly twice as large as
that of France, but the population is concentrated in only 5 per cent of the whole
territory, making it, in spite of its elongated shape (Napoleon once said that Italy
was too long: and Egypt is longer), one of the most compact countries in the
world.

promote regionalism; French and German political divisions have run on regional lines to a greater extent than have British, while in the United States regional divergences produced a great and disastrous Civil War and have continued to confuse national politics. In a country as large and varied as Iran, regional divergences would have constituted an important political factor even if the population had been perfectly homogeneous, which of course it is not, and the same is true of Pakistan, Turkey, Afghanistan, and Iraq.

The second effect is more fundamental. At any given stage of technical knowledge, there are definite limits beyond which the control exercised by a government ceases to be effective. As Ibn Khaldun put it: 'Each state has its apportioned share of territories which it cannot exceed . . . the state is stronger at the centre than at the periphery, weakening at the borders and becoming inoperative outside them, like rays and beams radiating from a centre, or like circles spreading out on the surface of the water from the point at which it has been impinged upon.'[9] For responsible democratic government an additional condition is necessary, formulated by Aristotle as follows: 'The citizens of a state must know one another's characters.'[10] It is safe to state that, given the very inadequate means of communication, several of the Middle Eastern states are far too large for effective, let alone democratic, government. The table on p. 38 shows two criteria, the density of railways, defined as a length of line per unit of area and population, and the number of radios per head; other means of communication, such as roads, telegraphs, and telephones, are no better developed.

It may be objected that the United States, Canada, and Australia have succeeded in running a very satisfactory form of democratic government over areas far wider than those of the largest Middle Eastern countries. This is true, but easily accounted for by their very different historical background. For in all three, constitutional government was introduced at a very early stage, in colonies which were small in size and had a tiny population, and responsible government was first practised on the state or provincial level, by such entities as Massachusetts, Lower Canada, or New South Wales. It was only after democratic government had become firmly established that those states or provinces ventured to federate in a bigger union. And it is very doubtful whether that union would have held together (as in the United States at the time of the Civil War) or even come about (as in Canada and Australia) but for the rapid development of railways and telegraphs.

In the Middle East, however, democracy was introduced at the national level into large areas inadequately provided with means of

[9] *An Arab Philosophy of History*, p. 127.　　[10] *The Politics of Aristotle*, p. 341.

MEANS OF COMMUNICATION IN PRINCIPAL MIDDLE EASTERN
COUNTRIES AND SELECTED WESTERN DEMOCRACIES, 1948

Railway route kilometres

	Per 100 square kilometres of total area	Per 10,000 inhabitants	Registered radio sets per 1,000 inhabitants
Afghanistan	0	0	1
Egypt	0·61	3·2	11
Iran	0·19	1·9	11
Iraq	0·34	3·2	6
Jordan	0·37	8·3	2
Lebanon	4·50	3·5	33
Pakistan	1·23	1·5	1
Syria	0·67	2·5	11
Turkey	1·00	4·0	15
Australia	0·59	55·6	258
Canada	0·75	65·2	189
Belgium	29·03	10·6	164
France	7·55	10·4	172
Sweden	3·38	21·7	307
United Kingdom	23·33	12·0	245
United States	5·13	26·7	600
Uruguay	1·61	13·1	125

communication. A glance at the not so distant past, forty years ago,
when the bulk of the non-colonial parts of the Middle East belonged
to two large states, the Ottoman Empire and Iran, and when the
railway and road systems embraced only a few thousands of miles,
shows why, until recently, effective government, let alone democratic
government, was impossible.

Economic Structure. The influence of economic structure on politics may be studied from three angles: level of national income,
distribution of wealth and income, and occupational structure. It
has been stated that democracy is the child of prosperity, and it is
certain, first, that the development of democracy has been intimately
connected with the expansion of capitalism and, secondly, that a
very close correlation can be established between high *per capita*
income and the successful working of democracy. A perusal of *per
capita* incomes computed by the United Nations[11] shows that the

[11] Statistical Office of the United Nations, *National and Per Capita Incomes,
Seventy Countries, 1949* (New York, October, 1950).

fifteen countries with the highest incomes are, in order: the United States, Canada, New Zealand, Switzerland, Sweden, the United Kingdom, Denmark, Australia, Norway, Belgium, Luxemburg, the Netherlands, France, Iceland, and Ireland—in other words, fifteen of the seventeen democracies listed on p. 35. The *per capita* annual income of the poorest of them, Ireland, was computed as $420, and twelve of the fifteen had incomes of over $500 per annum.[12] At the same date, none of the Middle Eastern countries except Lebanon and Turkey had a *per capita* income of over $100. Even making all the reservations which are necessary in any international comparison, it is evident that there is a vast difference in the levels of real income in the Middle East and in the Western democracies.[13]

It is hardly necessary to repeat what has so often been said, namely, that it is only when their basic needs have been satisfied that citizens can find the leisure and energy for active and intelligent participation in politics. Unless real incomes in the Middle East are doubled or trebled, the masses, obsessed by their daily needs, will continue to be the prey of every demagogue who promises relief.

The absolute level of the national income is not, however, the only criterion; no less important is its distribution. Wealth is power, and the concentration of wealth in a few hands means that a small group wields excessive political power while the mass of the population, having no economic independence, is in no position to exercise its political rights. This has been clearly realized since the time of Plato, who, in the *Laws*, laid it down that in the ideal commonwealth the richest should not be more than four times as wealthy as the poorest. It has often been remarked that, since the emergence of parliaments in the Middle Ages, and even in ancient Greece, democratic government has rested mainly on the shoulders of the middle class, and it is no coincidence that the most perfect democracies, Switzerland, New Zealand, and the Scandinavian countries, have the most equal distribution of wealth.

Few data are available on the distribution of wealth and incomes in the Middle Eastern countries, but the main outlines stand out only too starkly. A study of pre-war Egypt concluded that 'the gap between the two extremes is . . . enormously greater than anything

[12] The figure for the United States was $1,453; the second highest, Canada, stood at $870. The figures for the two other democracies listed on p. 35 were Finland $348, Uruguay $331.

[13] Other criteria of economic and social development, such as consumption of energy and steel, foreign trade, literacy, newspaper circulation, etc., tend to fall in line with *per capita* incomes. See Charles Issawi, 'The Conditions of Economic Progress in the Middle East', *Economic Development and Cultural Change* (Chicago, December, 1952).

met with in Europe',[14] and since that time war-time inflation has, if anything, accentuated inequality still further. In Lebanon, Pakistan, and Turkey the situation is distinctly better, but in the other Middle Eastern countries the same pattern of inequality prevails. Hence the often repeated statement that these countries do not have a middle class, a judgment which in this extreme form is certainly untrue, but which does bring out one of the basic weaknesses of the region. Hence, too, until recently, the complete domination of political life by the large landowners.[15]

The third economic factor to be considered here is the occupational structure. Democracy seems to flourish only when an appreciable proportion of the population is engaged in industry and trade; it appears to be unable to strike roots in an overwhelmingly agricultural country.[16] This generalization seems to be as true of ancient city states, such as Athens, and medieval republics, such as Florence, as of modern nation states such as England or Denmark. Perhaps the best index of industrial and commercial development available for international comparison is the percentage of the working population engaged in agriculture. A table compiled by the Food and Agriculture Organization[17] gives the following percentages for the period 1939–49: United Kingdom 4 per cent, United States 13 per cent, Australia 15 per cent, New Zealand 20 per cent, Switzerland 20 per cent, Sweden 21 per cent, Canada 24 per cent, Denmark 27 per cent, France 36 per cent, and Finland 50 per cent. Pre-war figures are also available for another group of countries, for which more recent data are lacking; in the period 1926–39, when the level of employment in agriculture was everywhere distinctly higher than in 1939–49, the percentage of the occupied population

---

[14] Charles Issawi, *Egypt: An Economic and Social Analysis* (London, Oxford University Press, for the *Royal Institute of International Affairs*, 1947), p. 54.

[15] See *ibid.*, pp. 173–4, for a discussion of the part played by landlords in Egyptian politics.

[16] The United States in the eighteenth century, and perhaps Canada, Australia, and New Zealand in the nineteenth, may be quoted as contrary examples of agrarian democracy. Moreover, it may be recalled that, according to Jefferson, democracy can flourish only in an agrarian environment. These facts, however, only apparently contradict the statement made above. For in all the above-mentioned countries, an immigrant population, from a country with highly developed free political institutions, settled in an empty continent. This meant that, in their new homes, the colonists were not burdened with feudal institutions hampering their economic, social, and political progress; it also meant that agriculture could yield them an exceptionally high income. Neither of these factors could possibly exist in an old, settled society until an economic, social, and political revolution, generated by the expansion of commerce or industry, had broken down their feudal or quasi-feudal system.

[17] *Yearbook of Food and Agricultural Statistics*, Vol. 4, Pt. 1, 1950, Table 5A.

working in agriculture was Belgium 17 per cent, Netherlands 20 per cent, Norway 26 per cent, and Ireland 49 per cent.

The only comparable Middle Eastern figures refer to the two most industrialized countries, Egypt and Turkey, where the percentage of working population engaged in agriculture in the period 1926–39 was 70 per cent and 82 per cent respectively. Since that time, industry has developed considerably in both countries, but in neither has it succeeded in drawing away any of the surplus rural population. As for the other Middle Eastern countries it is only in the Lebanon that the proportion is lower than in Egypt, owing to the leading parts played in the economy by trade, tourism, and other services; in all the others, a still higher percentage of the working population is engaged in agriculture.

Industrialization and the development of commerce and other services affect political life in several ways. First, they contribute greatly to the raising of the national income. In almost all countries for which figures are obtainable, *per capita* incomes in industry are higher than in agriculture, while in commerce and other services they are higher than in industry.[18] Available data for Egypt, Lebanon, and Turkey show that *per capita* incomes in industry are twice as high as in agriculture,[19] and that the gap between agriculture and other services is, if anything, greater than in more advanced countries.[20] It is only in such sparsely populated countries as Australia, Argentina, New Zealand, and Canada that a predominantly agricultural economy succeeded in providing a high standard of living and even there, as has been seen, the bulk of the population is no longer engaged in agriculture.

Industrialization and commercialization also promote democracy in a more direct way. By drawing the peasant away from the land, they at once weaken the power of the landowners and bring into being two new classes, the middle class and the industrial working class. A society consisting predominantly of two classes, landlords and peasants, cannot possibly hope to develop democratic institutions. The emergence of other groups, however, gives it a certain articulation; new interests come into being and with them new points of view. The struggle of the middle class for participation in government is the historical origin of most modern—and even ancient and medieval—democracies. And since the middle class is usually unable to achieve its ends without the help of the urban working class, the

---

[18] See, among others, Colin Clark, *The Conditions of Economic Progress*, new ed. (London, Macmillan, 1951).

[19] United Nations, *Review of Economic Conditions in the Middle East, 1951-2*, pp. 37–42.

[20] *Egypt: An Economic and Social Analysis*, p. 163.

latter acquires some share of the benefits.[21] Finally, it often happens that both the landed interest and the bourgeoisie compete for the support of the peasantry, which is then drawn into political life.

A special aspect of this process is urbanization. By concentrating large numbers in towns, and thus multiplying their social contacts, industrialization stimulates the intelligence and sharpens political awareness. It is not by chance that democracy has always flourished in an urban environment, in Athens, Florence, Geneva, London, Paris, and Boston. At the same time, it should be noted that in the past, European cities were in closer touch with their rural surroundings than were Middle Eastern cities and that democratic ideas were thus more easily diffused.

National, Linguistic, and Religious Homogeneity. It is generally agreed that the absence of national and linguistic[22] homogeneity constitutes a serious obstacle to the working of democratic government. The Scottish and Welsh national movements represent only minor and picturesque anachronisms, and the same may be said of Breton and Provençal nationalism. In Belgium, however, the struggle between Flemings and Walloons has often perilously rocked the ship of state, and in Czechoslovakia even the statesmanship of Masaryk and Beneš could not prevent the quarrel between Czechs, Slovaks, Germans, and Ruthenians from splitting it wide open. Canada's politics are dominated by the tug-of-war between the French and British elements, and United States politics have often been distorted by the centrifugal pull of ethnic groups. The shining success of the Swiss Confederation in fusing its three national ingredients is the more conspicuous because it is the only state of its kind.

In this respect, conditions vary widely in the Middle East.[23] Egypt, Jordan, the Arabian Peninsula, Lebanon, and Syria are entirely homogeneous or contain only insignificant national minorities; the only sizeable non-Arab groups in these countries are the Kurds (some 120,000) in Syria and the Armenians (some 150,000)

---

[21] It cannot, however, be denied that at present there is a danger that the working class of under-developed countries may choose the path of Communism rather than democracy. It may be found possible to counteract this tendency by raising the economic, social, and cultural level of the working class.

[22] In this paper, linguistic and national divisions are assumed to be identical. This may not have been true in the past, but since the national awakenings of the nineteenth century it may be taken that every large group speaking a language differing from those of its neighbours will, sooner or later, experience a feeling of cultural distinctness which will generally translate itself into national consciousness.

[23] The best study on this subject is A. H. Hourani's *Minorities in the Arab World* (London, Oxford University Press, for the Royal Institute of International Affairs, 1947).

in Syria and Lebanon, and neither of these presents any real problems. In Iraq, however, the Kurds constitute nearly one-fifth of the total population, and there are also small groups of Persians, Turcomans, and Assyrians. Turkey has been largely 'homogenized' by the elimination of its Armenian and Greek minorities, but it still contains a fairly large Kurdish population, estimated at from 1·5[24] millions to 2 millions.[25] Iran contains many linguistic minorities including the Turks of Azerbaidjan (about 1·5 millions), Turcomans, Kurds (some 800,000), Arabs (300,000) and Armenians.[26] In Afghanistan there are important differences between Pushtu-speaking Afghans, Persian-speaking Tajiks, and Turkish-speaking Uzbeks, and the task of national integration is complicated by this factor. The situation in Pakistan is difficult to assess, but strains have begun to make themselves felt between the Urdu-speaking West and the Bengali-speaking East, which are separated by over a thousand miles of Indian territory.[27]

It is unnecessary to dwell at length on the effects of the existence of these minority groups, since all students of Middle Eastern affairs agree that they constitute a great handicap to the development of sound government. It may, of course, be said that the minorities are a problem only because the governments have not evolved suitable policies for integrating them into a multi-national whole. This is partly true, but it does not dispose of the fact that their presence adds one more to the many obstacles to democratic government confronting the Middle East. In Iraq, the Kurdish problem has created friction which has occasionally flared up in armed revolt. In Turkey, the friction has been still greater, repression has been more severe, and for a long period the eastern, i.e. predominantly Kurdish, provinces have been under military rule. Afghanistan is in the very earliest stages of nation building.[28] As for Iran, it is periodically threatened with disintegration, as was vividly illustrated by the Azerbaidjani and Kurdish separatist movements of 1945 as well as by the Arab separatist movement in Khuzistan after the First World War. What has preserved the country's unity has

[24] A. M. Burton, 'The Kurds', *Royal Central Asian Journal* (London, January, 1944).

[25] Lewis V. Thomas and Richard N. Frye, *The United States and Turkey and Iran* (London, Cambridge University Press, 1951), p. 78. A figure of 4 millions is given by the Kurdish leader, Emir Kamuran Bedir Khan, 'Kurdistan', *Cahiers de l'Est*, Beirut, No. 1, 1945.

[26] *The United States and Turkey and Iran*, pp. 188–90. Somewhat different estimates are given by Haas, Groseclose, and Wilber in their books on Iran.

[27] European minorities which, when protected by the Capitulations, presented a major obstacle in many countries, now no longer constitute a serious problem.

[28] Vladimir Cervin, 'The Problems in the Integration of the Afghan Nation', *Middle East Journal*, Autumn, 1952.

generally been the Shī'īsm of the great majority of its inhabitants, which has both drawn Iranians together and marked them off sharply from their Sunnī neighbours.

Middle Eastern minority problems are intensified by the fact that several national minorities still have a predominantly tribal structure. This is true of the Kurds in Iran, Iraq, and Turkey, and of the Turcomans and Turkish-speaking Qashqais in Iran, of the Pathans in Pakistan, and of all the main groups in Afghanistan. The existence of large bodies of tribesmen presents a truly formidable obstacle to any central government attempting to establish a framework of order covering the whole country and to enact uniform legislation for all its parts. This question, too, is not dwelt upon at length here because it has been fully recognized and often discussed by Middle Eastern experts.

While practically all students recognize that the co-existence of more than one national group imposes a great strain on a State, they are not so categorical about religious groups. Indeed, it is often maintained that modern liberty and democracy owe their existence to religious diversity. To quote only one of many thinkers who have given this matter their attention, 'Political liberty, as a fact in the modern world, is the result of the struggle of religious organisms to live'.[29] But while it may be true that without the Reformation and the ensuing religious strife the medieval, all-embracing, Catholic church would not have given way to the modern, secular, limited state, it is equally true that, once that state has been firmly established, the presence within its borders of large religious minorities does nothing to promote, and may often retard, political democracy. The conflict between Catholics and Protestants nearly wrecked the Swiss Confederation and has put a great strain on both Germany and the Netherlands, while the struggle between Catholics and anti-clericals has bedevilled the politics of half of Europe. One of the major reasons for the smooth working of the democratic system in the Scandinavian countries is their religious, as well as their national, homogeneity. Now, except for the Arabian Peninsula and present-day Turkey, the Middle East is a veritable mosaic of religions. The fact that the Kurds, Arabs, and Turcomans are Sunnī Muslims further differentiates them from the Shī'ī Muslim Persians. Pakistan contains a 15 per cent Hindu and Sikh minority and it is also divided into Shī'īs and Sunnīs. In Iraq, the Shī'īs are almost as numerous as the Sunnīs; in the other Arab countries there are substantial Christian minorities, constituting 7 per cent of the population in Egypt, about 8 per cent in Jordan, and 12 per cent in Syria;

[29] J. N. Figgis, *Studies of Political Thought from Gerson to Grotius*, 2nd ed. (London, Cambridge University Press, 1916), pp. 6–7.

in the last-mentioned country, heterodox Muslim sects constitute a further 15 per cent of the total population. As for Lebanon, it may be said to consist of nothing but minorities: of the seven leading sects, the largest, the Maronite, constitutes 30 per cent of the total population, and the smallest, the Armenian Orthodox, under 6 per cent.

But it is not merely a question of statistics; much more important is the difference in attitude towards religion prevailing in the West and in the Middle East. In the West, the centrifugal effects of religious divergences have been effectively checked by the centripetal force of nationalism. As Hilaire Belloc somewhat unkindly put it, the predominant philosophy has been: 'Worship the nation and you may hold what lesser opinions you please.'[30]

In the Middle East, on the other hand, religion is still the strongest social force and the one which arouses the fiercest passions. In the past, after the convulsions of the first few centuries, Sunnī Islam was the cement which held together the greater part of the Middle East; in Iran, after the sixteenth century, Shī'ī Islam performed the same function. Christian and other minorities had a definite, if subordinate, place in society and did not give any trouble.

With the decay of the Ottoman Empire, however, religion, sometimes in alliance with nationalism and sometimes working against it, has proved to be a most disruptive force, and one which has greatly slowed down the formation of stable states. The part played by religious minorities in the different Middle Eastern countries has been fully described in a vast body of literature and need not be discussed here.[31] No unbiased student can deny that their presence, and particularly the pretext they offered for foreign intervention, has greatly complicated the task of government in the region.

Education. This question, too, needs little elaboration, for the main facts are well known. In the West, democracy came into being largely because of the combination of a highly educated ruling class and a literate electorate. The eighteenth- and nineteenth-century British aristocracy, the Virginia dynasty, and the French middle class during the Restoration and the July Monarchy provide examples of highly educated ruling classes which prepared their

[30] Hilaire Belloc, *Survivals and New Arrivals* (London, Sheed & Ward, 1939), p. 42.

[31] Two points, however, deserve to be made. First, that intermarriage between members of different religious communities was, until very recently, unthinkable and even today is numerically negligible. Secondly, that each religious or national group has generally tended to specialize in one or two occupations, practising what Professor C. S. Coon has called 'an ethnic division of labour'. It may also be mentioned that, until recently, each group had its own distinct form of dress.

countries for democracy. In all European countries, the expansion of education more or less kept step with the broadening of the electorate. This was dramatically signalled in England by the passing of the Education Act in 1870, following the Reform Bill of 1867, which enfranchised the urban artisan class.

In the Middle East, both conditions have been absent. The Middle Eastern states adopted parliamentary-democratic institutions without having either an educated ruling class or a literate mass, although in both respects the situation is improving greatly, thanks to the admirable efforts made after the achievement of independence. Thus, to take only two examples, in Turkey the number of pupils in all schools rose from 360,000 in 1923 to nearly 1,800,000 in 1950, and in Syria, between 1943 and 1950, the school population rose from 147,000 to 301,000. In Egypt, Turkey, and Lebanon competent specialists have begun to appear in the natural and social sciences. But the limited progress achieved serves only to mark the distance from the goal ahead. In only one Middle Eastern country, Lebanon, is more than half the population literate; in Syria the proportion is about one-third, in Turkey one-quarter, in Egypt one-fifth, and in the other countries considerably less. Similarly, while Lebanon provides education for nearly four-fifths of her children of school age, Turkey, Syria, and Egypt can accommodate about half, and the other countries one-quarter or less. Another indication is the newspaper circulation per thousand inhabitants, which stands at 81 in Lebanon, 28 in Jordan, 21 in Syria, 18 in Egypt, 15 in Turkey, 6 in Iraq, 5 in Iran, 2 in Pakistan, and one in Afghanistan. Corresponding figures for some Western democracies are 599 for the United Kingdom, 455 for Australia, 441 for Luxemburg, 415 for the three Scandinavian countries, 357 for the United States, 281 for the Netherlands, and 187 for Uruguay.

It is true that the level of political consciousness of the Middle Eastern masses is much higher than these figures would seem to indicate. Owing to the habit of listening, in groups, to the radio or to a newspaper reader, Middle Easterners have an acquaintance with international and local politics which always astonishes foreigners. But such alternative methods, welcome as they may be, are not a satisfactory substitute for literacy, and the level of public opinion remains, of course, very much lower than in the developed countries of Europe and America.

Co-operative Associations. One of the aspects of the Middle East which impresses, and depresses, Western observers most is the inability of its peoples to associate for co-operative action or to act on the level of local government. Whenever a social need is felt, be it for a village road, an electric station, a school, a football field, or a marketing co-operative, the first impulse is to turn to the central government for help. Recent Middle Eastern history teems with instances of government-sponsored schemes. The great majority of schools and hospitals are government-owned and run, and so are the railways and most of the airlines. In Turkey a great part, and in Iran a substantial portion, of industry and mining belongs to the state. In the few countries where it has made headway, i.e. Egypt, Turkey, and Arab Palestine, the agricultural co-operative movement has been sponsored and directed by the government. And it should be noted that in all these cases it is the central government, rather than the provincial or municipal authorities, which is in charge.

It would be foolish in the extreme to condemn such government action outright in the name of abstract principles of individualism and free enterprise. If individual initiative is not forthcoming to build a railway or school, it is surely better that the state should do so rather than that it should be left undone. But at the same time it should be clearly realized that a society which lacks numerous and strong associations, and in which local governments play a negligible part, is not one in which democracy can flourish.

It would be equally rash to conclude that Middle Easterners are congenitally incapable of co-operative association, still less that they lack initiative. There is some evidence that, in its heyday, Islamic civilization was the scene of intense activity conducted by partnerships and joint enterprises. International commercial ventures were on a scale well beyond the financial capacities of any individual, and were carried out by partnerships involving large numbers. Similarly the network of banking, which made it possible to cash in Morocco, Ceylon, or Zanzibar a cheque drawn on Basra, indicates widespread contacts and habits of trust and co-operation. The collapse of Islamic civilization, following the Crusades and Mongol invasions, seems, however, to have eliminated both individual initiative and co-operation, both of which became equally impossible under the arbitrary and extortionate governments which oppressed the poverty-stricken region.

In the last fifty or hundred years, conditions having become more propitious, there has been a re-birth of individual initiative which is best exemplified by the activities of Persians in India, South Arabians in Indonesia, and, above all, the exploits of the Lebanese in West Africa, the United States, and South America. Action by associations responded much more slowly to the improvement in the environment, being often hampered by the very qualities which account for the increase in individual enterprise, but during the last thirty years there have been such welcome steps as the Banque Misr enterprises

and the Committee for Translation and Publication in Egypt, and
the foundation of hundreds of societies for educational or philan-
thropic purposes, such as the Red Crescent, in all the more advanced
Middle Eastern countries. Trade unions have also begun to assume
some importance. But such associations still play only a minor part
in national life. As for local governments, with very few exceptions,
such as the municipality of Alexandria—which owes its importance
and activity to the large number of foreigners who still serve on it—
their functions continue to be negligible and there are few signs of
an increase in their scope and power. It is significant that Cairo, the
largest city in the region, was not allowed to have a municipality
until after the Second World War.[32]

The Case of Lebanon. The validity of the observations made in
this article may be tested by applying them to the Middle Eastern
country which is furthest advanced on the road to full and genuine
democracy, Lebanon. However great the imperfections of her
governments it remains true that Lebanon has enjoyed a freedom of
thought, expression, and association far greater than that prevailing
in the Middle East—and in many more advanced countries as well.
And the bloodless overthrow of the seemingly all powerful President,
in September, 1952, was an encouraging sign of the power of public
opinion and its ability to translate itself into action.[33]

An examination of the criteria enumerated shows Lebanon to be
much more favourably situated than any other Middle Eastern
country studied here. The very small size of Lebanon's territory and
population, which is distinctly hindering her economic growth, has
favoured her political development. Her means of communication
are adequate, an excellent system of roads compensating for the
deficiency in railways. Her *per capita* income, recently estimated at
over $250, is well above that of any other Middle Eastern country.
Owing to the prevalence of small-scale landholdings in many parts
of the country, and to the relatively large number engaged in services, the distribution of wealth and income is less unequal than in
other parts of the region. Her population is highly urbanized; only
half the population is rural, and of this a substantial fraction earns
its livelihood in non-agricultural occupations; the income from

[32] It may be noted that Islamic civilization never witnessed the kind of corporate municipal activity which flourished in ancient Greece and Rome or
medieval and renaissance Europe. Only in Spain, where Islam impinged on a
European society, did such cities as Toledo, Cordoba, and Seville play an
independent part.

[33] For an interesting and sympathetic account see: 'Peaceful Change in the
Lebanon', *The World Today* (Royal Institute of International Affairs, April,
1953), p. 162.

industry and building combined is greater than the agricultural income; and commerce plays a most important part in the economy. Education is much more developed than elsewhere; over two-thirds of the population are literate, and nearly four-fifths of children of school age attend school. Newspaper circulation is comparable to that of the less advanced European countries, and the number of radios is relatively high. Nationally and linguistically, Lebanon is homogeneous, the very small Armenian minority presenting no problem whatsoever. The one great handicap of Lebanon is the multiplicity of religious sects, and all observers agree that this, more than anything, has stood in the way of efficient government.

It may therefore be taken that the case of Lebanon confirms the choice of the criteria adopted. A further confirmation is provided by Turkey. The remarkable economic and social advance of the last decade (reflected by such indices as *per capita* income, literacy, school attendance, and book publishing) following the basic social reforms of Atatürk, paved the way for the emergence of political democracy in that country. These considerations lend support to the hope that economic and social development will bring about, in the other countries, conditions more propitious for the growth of political democracy.

Conclusion. One negative conclusion stands out sharply from the preceding analysis: in the Middle East the economic and social soil is still not deep enough to enable political democracy to strike root and flourish. What is needed is not merely constitutional or administrative reforms, not just a change in government machinery or in personnel. It is not even the adjustment of an obsolete political structure to bring it in line with a new balance of forces reflecting changing relations between various social classes, as was achieved by the Reform Bills in nineteenth-century England. What is required is a great economic and social transformation which will strengthen society and make it capable of bearing the weight of the modern state. Such a development is a necessary, if not a sufficient, condition for the establishment of genuine democracy in the region. For, in politics as in religion, a Reformation must be preceded by a Renaissance.

What should be done in the meantime? Clearly, while it is futile to lament the absence of democracy in a region still unprepared for it, it is absolutely necessary to set in motion the forces which will transform Middle Eastern society in the desired manner. Great efforts must be made to improve means of communication, multiply schools, and, so far as possible, bring about a cultural and spiritual unity which will bridge the chasms separating linguistic groups and religious sects. Great efforts must also be made to develop the economy of the different countries in order to raise the general level and to create opportunities which will allow the individual to emancipate himself from the grip of the family, tribe, and village.

So much would be admitted by all, but the question still remains: who is to carry out all these changes? Most Middle Easterners look to the government for the necessary guidance and initiative, and many of them seek a short cut by way of a military dictatorship. Both these tendencies deserve more understanding and consideration than they usually receive from Anglo-Saxon observers. In under-developed countries attempting to transform themselves within a twentieth-century economic, social, and political context, the government must inevitably play a large, perhaps a leading, part. This is especially true where it happens to own the main sources of funds which can be used for development, as is the case in the oil-producing countries in the Middle East. Nor need the desire for a military dictatorship spring from ignoble, ultra-nationalistic, or reactionary motives. In Asian countries the officer corps tends to be recruited from the middle class and is therefore—unlike the upper-class European officer corps—more often a spearhead of change than a bulwark of conservatism. Finally, the need for strong governments is an essential prerequisite of progress, and perhaps even of eventual democracy. Most existing democracies have passed through a pro-longed stage of despotic or dictatorial government in which the country was forcibly welded into a coherent whole. One has only to recall the Tudors, the Stuarts, and Cromwell in England and Richelieu, Louis XIV, and Napoleon in France. What Atatürk and Riza Shah attempted to do, with a greater or less measure of success, was to transform a congeries of villages, tribes, and sects into a nation state. The methods were often ill chosen, but it is impossible to deny that without a greater degree of national unity than pre-vailed when they took power, orderly and efficient government, let alone democratic government, would have been utterly impossible.

All this is true, but it does not represent the final answer to the problem. Ultimately, Middle Eastern society must save itself through the individual and co-operative efforts of thousands of men and women in all walks of life, who will educate and regenerate the people and develop and exploit the human and natural resources of the region. Most Middle Easterners will answer that such efforts are useless under existing conditions, because a malevolent government can thwart the best intentioned and most devoted individuals. This is true, but only up to a point. Sooner or later these efforts will bear fruit, however great the opposing forces may be. And then, the present vicious circle, in which bad governments prevent society from bettering itself and them may be replaced by a 'virtuous circle', in which private and public bodies co-operate for the common good. Another objection may also be briefly discussed. Individual, and still more co-operative, action tends to work through, and therefore to reinforce and perpetuate, the existing social framework. This applies particularly to sectarianism. Thus the remarkable expansion of education in Lebanon, which was mainly carried out by church groups, has greatly helped the general development of the country but has undoubtedly strengthened its chronic sectarianism. In recent years, however, there has been an encouraging tendency to transcend sectarian, ethnic, and other group barriers by non-denominational associations working for common political, economic, or social ends. A conspicuous example is that of the *Ruwwad* in Egypt, a group of social workers founded some twenty years ago, several of whose members have served in recent cabinets. Another example is that of the Village Welfare Service in the American University of Beirut.[34] Finally, political parties are tending more and more to cut across sectarian and ethnic lines.

One final remark may be made. The task outlined above is one for the Middle Easterners themselves. Foreign aid can be of great use, but it must be indirect and limited, taking the form of deeper and more sympathetic understanding as well as the provision of technical and financial assistance. The bulk of the work, and all the major policy decisions, must be left to the nationals of the country concerned. The most disastrous mistake would be the belief that because the Middle Eastern countries are unprepared for democracy they are unfit for independence. For one thing, the vast majority of independent states, throughout history and in all parts of the world, have not been democracies. For another, nothing is better calculated to distract Middle Easterners from their real problem than foreign interference. A long and arduous road lies ahead of the Middle East and it is essential that it be not pushed or stampeded into blind alleys but on the contrary encouraged and aided to find the right path.

October 1955

[34] In this connection it may be noted that Anglo-Saxon schools in the Middle East have done much to break down sectarian barriers and that a great degree of inter-denominational harmony has been achieved by their students and graduates.

SOCIAL AWAKENING AND ECONOMIC DEVELOPMENT IN THE MIDDLE EAST

by SA'ID B. HIMADEH

PRIOR TO World War I the economic and social structure of Middle East society was basically medieval. Agriculture and animal husbandry were the chief occupations of the people, and industry was of secondary importance. A very large proportion of agricultural production went to satisfy the producers and their families and a relatively small proportion went to market, so that trade was of relatively minor importance.

Rural communities lived largely under a feudalistic system, with land concentrated in the hands of a small absentee landowning class and cultivated by peasants under a system of share tenancy, which could be terminated at the will of the landlord. Like European feudalism, Middle East feudalism made the cultivator a serf dependent in every way upon his landlord; but one of the main characteristics of European feudalism was absent, namely, the personal relationship between the landlord and the cultivator. The effect of Middle East feudalism was to reduce appreciably the productivity of the land and to demoralize and impoverish a considerable proportion of the rural population.

Industry consisted mainly of shop and home handicrafts, with only a small proportion of enterprises using power-driven machines and hired labour. Most of the industries were of an agricultural character; and almost all industrial production was undertaken for local consumption. A number of factors hindered industrial as well as agricultural development: lack of security, poor means of transport and communication, lack of capital, scarcity of mechanical engineers and skilled labour, the ignorance and traditionalism of the masses, lack of a legal system designed to ensure the fruits of labour, and the capitulations, which prevented countries under Turkish rule from adopting a tariff policy favourable to the development of industry and agriculture. These handicaps were scarcely given attention by Middle East governments. The administration of the Ottoman régime was almost completely indifferent to national economy. In countries under foreign influence, industrial development was considered prejudicial to the interests of the mother country.

With an under-developed economy and a poor public administration, and with a backward fiscal system based very largely on indirect taxation—the chief direct taxes being those on land, buildings, and animals—the means and the will to provide educational, health, and other social services were very deficient. The poverty of the masses was accompanied by widespread illiteracy and disease.

These conditions were regarded by religious leaders as inevitable, and by most intellectuals as capable of evolutionary change through the action of spontaneous forces. The Moslem 'sheikhhood' (priesthood) viewed certain laws and regulations, which Islam laid down to deal with temporary conditions, as true for all times, and were therefore against social change that was in opposition to these laws and regulations. The majority of the intellectuals failed to see that economic and social development could hardly take place under conditions of extreme inequality of opportunity and fatalism; and the few intellectuals with more penetrating minds did not dare to express their ideas openly, as they were afraid to antagonize the government and the religious leaders. The stage preceding the First World War may, therefore, be regarded as essentially a stationary one, with technological modernization limited to projects undertaken by Europeans in their own interests, such as concessionary public utility undertakings, railways, and other enterprises of a monopolistic character.

During the First World War, the importation of manufactured wares and certain foodstuffs not produced in the region, or produced there only in small quantities, was almost completely checked, and the people suffered considerable deprivation. The resulting hardship, coupled with the post-war struggle for political liberation, created a strong desire for industrialization and economic nationalism in all Middle East states. In Turkey and Iran the initiative came from the dictatorship governments themselves, with strong backing from the intellectual elements in those countries. In Egypt and the Mandated territories of Syria and Lebanon, Palestine, Transjordan, and Iraq, the governments were compelled, under pressure of political parties, economic associations, and owners of capital seeking investment, to respond to a number of demands for the encouragement and protection of industry, chiefly protective tariff and duty exemptions on industrial machinery and raw materials for use in local industries. As a result, many domestic industries previously using primitive methods and tools were converted into factory industries equipped with modern machinery and applying modern methods, such as the cotton-spinning and weaving industries; and a variety of new industries was established, such as cement, tiles, and matches.

Change in the taste of the people as regards dress, food, furniture, etc., in consequence of contacts with the West, shifted the demand from articles manufactured by traditional local industries to manufactured goods of foreign patterns. The old textile, tanning and shoe-making, food and drink industries were those most affected.

Perhaps the greatest single factor contributing to economic development in Mandated territories was the improvement in public administration, though it fell short of what was required. This included improvement in public security, means of transportation and communication, the taxation system, education, and health. In agriculture, the chief reform was the establishment of a system of land registration based upon technical survey and settlement of land rights. The Mandatory Powers neglected, however, to deal with the problems of large estates and the insecurity of tenants. In part, they strengthened the power of the landlords by legal recognition of their doubtful claims to their lands. They also failed to provide plans for agricultural development. Irrigation, on which progress in agriculture very largely depends, was given but little consideration. Poor agricultural technique, under-employment, and usury were also given little or no attention, except in Palestine. In Egypt and the Mandated territories, the stage between the two world wars may, therefore, be regarded as ameliorative. The countries of the Arabian Peninsula remained stationary throughout the period between the two wars.

Drastic measures took place only in Turkey and Iran. The chief aim of Mustafa Kemal during his absolute rule in Turkey between 1923 and 1938 was to maintain and strengthen political independence and to develop the productive power of the nation. To this end, his immediate concern was to free the Turkish populace from traditionalism and superstition, and to develop a progressive mentality among the masses. The measures used, however, were for the most part superficial and had little effect, especially in the rural areas. The most effective measures were the separation of church from state and the development of education, including adult training.

Economic development was also handicapped by lack of private initiative and by the fact that industry and trade were mainly in the hands of foreigners, who, in many cases, were nationals of countries with which Turkey was technically still at war. Accordingly, economic development had to depend largely on government initiative and finance. Two developmental plans were made, one for industry and the other for agriculture. The first was a five-year plan put into effect in 1934, which included the establishment or development of: cotton textiles, hemp products, rayon, coke, iron foundries, copper refining, chemicals, paper, porcelain, and electric power plants. The second was a four-year plan instituted in 1937, which comprised a number of agricultural developmental works, chiefly irrigation. The war interfered with the execution of the plan, although two irrigation projects were substantially advanced.

Riza Shah Pahlawi had as his first aim the strengthening of Persia's power, so as to enable her to resist foreign interference. But he was aware that such power could not be achieved without economic development. Improvements were made in industry, transport and communication, education, health, and public administration. But little or no attention was given to land reform, probably in order not to antagonize the influential landlords. The chief single accomplishment was the building of the Trans-Iranian Railway.

Plans for development continued in Turkey and Iran during the post World War II period. In both countries they were directed towards the improvement of living standards. In Turkey they included: limitation of landownership and distribution of expropriated excess and state land among landless tenants and agricultural workers; better transport and communication facilities, erection of grain-storage warehouses, and development of industries more directly related to the needs of the masses. A comprehensive five-year investment programme involving an investment of about $730 million over a period of five years—originally 1948–53—is the most spectacular and far-reaching developmental endeavour that has yet been planned in Turkey. It includes expenditures of about 100·6 million dollars on agriculture, 105·9 million on mining, 416 million on transportation, 41·9 million on power production, 60·6 million on industry, and 4·8 million on studies and control.[1] About half the total expenditure was to be defrayed from internal sources. To help Turkey to draw away from *étatisme* in industry, a Turkish Industrial Development Bank, sponsored by the International Bank for Reconstruction and Development, was established in April, 1950, to provide financial facilities for private entrepreneurs.

[1] H. V. Cooke, *Challenge and Response in the Middle East* (New York, 1952), p. 276.

In Iran a comprehensive seven-year plan was prepared in 1948 after a survey of Iranian economy by an American engineering firm, and was enacted into law by the parliament. Upon recommendation of the I.B.R.D., a fuller survey of Iran's economy was made by a group representing eleven American firms. Later the group recommended allocations of the funds (amounting to $650 million) for the plan as follows: 46·6 million dollars to public health, 31 million to education, 101·7 million to agriculture, 57·4 million to water resources, 85·3 million to town improvement and housing, 155·3 million to transportation, 15·8 million to communications, 68·3 million to industry and mining, 31·4 million to electric power, 23·4 million to petroleum, 1·1 million to meteorology, 3·8 million to statistical organization, 0·4 million to distribution, and 18·5 million unallocated.[2] The plan was to be financed largely from internal sources, mainly oil royalties. Several factors interfered with its execution, notably the fear of corruption in the execution of the programme, the fear that it would be used to provide more profits and power for the wealthy classes, the opposition of Iranian landlords to the insistence of the Shah that the programme should include land reform, and the crisis between the Iranian government and the Anglo-Iranian Oil Company. To set a good example, the Shah recently embarked on the distribution of some of his land to tenants and agricultural labourers at nominal prices to be paid in instalments over a period of years. The seven-year plan for economic development was formulated in response to the struggle of the intellectuals for substantial reform and as a measure to check the growth of Communism. This struggle for reform, however, has subsided as a result of strained relations with the Anglo-Iranian Company and the resulting diversion of attention to nationalism.

In the Arab countries of the Middle East, the war in Palestine and its aftermath, and continued foreign influence or interference, have prevented concentration of public opinion on economic and social problems. For a time, their governments were able to find excuses for delaying attention to these matters and continuing palliative measures; and when important projects such as irrigation works were undertaken they were mainly for the benefit of the big landlords. The fact that the Arab states gained varying degrees of independence did not help to improve the sense of public responsibility, the political system in most cases having been inherited from the Mandatory régimes and not having had time to develop. The governments were essentially oligarchies, the dominating elements being the landlords and influential rich. Their voice and that of the capitalists was most heard by government, although concerted action

[2] Cooke, *op. cit.*, pp. 247–8.

on the part of factory labourers, supported by enlightened public opinion, succeeded in bringing about legislation permitting organization of labour unions and protecting factory labour and commercial employees. Industrialists received more protection in the form of higher tariffs and wider customs exemptions on imported machinery and raw materials for industry.

This increased protection, together with the great impetus given to industry during and immediately after the last war by the decline in imports and the high profits realized, brought about a relatively considerable industrial development. Many existing industries expanded, particularly cotton-spinning and weaving, rayon-weaving, knitting, and electric power. Others which also developed were oil-pressing, soap-making, and the various food and drink industries. Besides, new industries were created for which modern factories were erected, such as: the glass, sugar, and dye factories in Syria; the oil-refining, the dye and print, and the vegetaline factories in Lebanon; woollen and chemical factories and the steel mill (smelting domestically available scrap) in Egypt; and the vegetable-oil extraction plants in Iraq and other Arab countries. With the exception of the large electric power plants, practically all these are financed by local capital. Mention should also be made of the great expansion of petroleum-oil extraction and refining in the Middle East, though this has not been influenced by the foregoing promoting factors.

While conditions in urban areas of the Arab countries were improving as a result of the large windfall profits accumulated by merchants and industrialists during and immediately after the war, and on account of post-war industrial development, conditions in the rural areas were deteriorating, with little or no heed given to them by the oligarchical governments dominated by the landlords and the influential rich. In the meantime, traditionalism and fatalism were beginning to decline in the rural areas as a result of recent increases in rural education and the penetration of new ideas through the newspaper and radio. The peasants began to question old opinions and customs, and to realize that their difficulties were not predetermined and inescapable, Their dissatisfaction and desire to be free from poverty and serfdom led many of them to join Communist Parties as a vague protest against their misery, and even, in some quarters, to rise in arms against their landlords. But the Arab governments continued until recently to think that by outlawing Communism and suppressing it they could escape the consequences of their negligence.

Meanwhile, several studies dealing with the causes of rural poverty and the centuries-old lethargy and submissiveness of the peasant masses have appeared; warnings to governments from national intellectuals have been given in books, articles, addresses, and parliamentary speeches regarding the dangers of their indifference; Socialist Parties have been formed, and the United Nations Economic and Social Council has organized social-welfare seminars to discuss economic and social problems in the Arab Middle East. Among the best-known works dealing with conditions in rural areas and causes of poverty is that of Doreen Warriner,[3] which has had considerable influence on enlightened public opinion, university students, and statesmen. Among the best works that have discussed the causes of traditionalism and fatalism of the Arab masses are those of two Moslem scholars, Abdullah Ali al-Qasim[4] and Khaled Muhammad Khaled.[5] Al-Qasim presents a reasoned statement of the merits of Western civilization, condemns the traditionalism which has kept Arab and Moslem society in chains, and makes a plea for the adoption of the spirit of Western civilization. He points out that the essence of modern man's greatness is his intellectual daring, which has harnessed nature and conquered such enemies as poverty, disease, and ignorance; that, through an erroneous concept of religion, religious leaders have indoctrinated the people with a defeatist attitude to life, with unquestioning acceptance of authority and resignation to their miserable lot in this world. He asserts that the mission of Islam is to redeem man from the enslavement of mind and will, from submission to the tyranny of leaders and government systems which inflict poverty, distress, and misery upon men, and from the grip of fixed doctrines and beliefs which hinder men from liberation and stunt the development of their creative faculties. He criticizes man's tyranny over woman and ascribes her degraded status to false interpretation of religion.

Khaled Muhammad Khaled stresses the need for social change, and proposes a just Socialism as the only solution of the problems of Egypt. He urges a sound understanding of the spirit of religion and denounces the prevailing 'sheikhcraft' (priestcraft) for having misinterpreted religion and its mission, held the people in chains of superstition, and defended poverty and ignorance. He asserts that religion is essentially democratic and humane, contrary to the teachings of the sheikhcraft, which deny freedom of mind and oppose democracy. He pleads for the emancipation of women and for granting them full civil and political rights. He also utters a warning that the toiling masses, long forgotten, are beginning to wake up.

Space does not allow a discussion of all contributions to post-war

[3] *Land and Poverty in the Middle East* (London, 1948). This book was translated into Arabic and has had a wide circulation in the Middle East.

[4] *These Are the Chains* (in Arabic) (Cairo, 1946).

[5] *From Here We Begin* (in Arabic) (Cairo, 1949).

social awakening, and only a brief sketch can be given of its manifestations. It is now recognized that poverty is the fundamental problem of Arab society, and that its cause does not lie so much in the meagreness of resources as in their inadequate development, the glaring inequality in wealth and income, and the age-long submissiveness of the masses. Xenophobia is declining, and the Arab countries' economic under-development and political dependence is now recognized as due more to internal weakness than to foreign imperialism. There is a fuller appreciation of the modern conception of the state, especially as regards its economic and social functions, which include a fuller development of the natural resources for the general good, the provision of adequate educational and social services, and a reduction of inequalities of wealth and income and of inequality of opportunity. There is a greater sense of public responsibility, though in most Arab countries this is not yet sufficiently strong to introduce radical reforms. The recent change of government in Egypt may be largely attributed to the failure of the king and his governments to heed the demand for social reconstruction.

The result of all this has been a determination on the part of the Arab governments, varying in strength between one country and another, to embark on the task of economic and social development. This includes: expanding the cultivated areas, or intensifying cultivation, by harnessing more of the river and underground waters; increasing agricultural productivity; generating hydro-electric power; reducing the extreme inequality in landownership (in Egypt, Iraq, and Syria); encouraging industrial development; improving means of transport and communication; creating financial facilities for agriculture and industry (in Egypt, Iraq, Syria, and Jordan); establishing central banks (in Egypt, Iraq, and Syria); improving the taxation system with a view to providing a more adequate public income and a more just distribution of the tax burden, and the use of customs duties and other taxes as instruments of economic policy; expanding elementary education and health services in rural areas; and other economic and social works. In Egypt, Iraq, Lebanon, and Jordan, economic development boards have been established with a view to making comprehensive studies of resources and planning comprehensive economic development; while in Syria such a board is contemplated.

In most Arab countries, developmental programmes are handicapped by the absence of adequate finance. The only countries which have no such difficulty are Iraq and the countries of the Arabian Peninsula. Oil royalties in these countries are financing considerable economic and social development. The budget of the Economic

Development Board of Iraq for 1951 involved an expenditure of about 9½ million dinars, of which were assigned: 3 million for irrigation projects, 2 million for roads, about 2½ million for buildings, and the remainder for other projects.

Space does not allow discussion of economic achievements in the various Arab countries, but since the extreme inequality in land-ownership is the chief immediate cause of mass poverty, it may be worth sketching how it is being dealt with by the countries that have embarked on its solution. In Egypt, the solution found by the military régime involves expropriating—with compensation—ownerships exceeding 200 feddans (a feddan is roughly one acre). The land expropriated in any village will be distributed to small farmers, so that each will have a plot of not less than 2 feddans and not more than 5 feddans, according to the quality of the soil. In Syria a recent law provides for the distribution of public land to landless tenants and small landowning farmers within the limits of 125 acres of unirrigable land and 12·5 acres of irrigable land. In Iraq, newly irrigated public land is being distributed, and some of the political parties are demanding limitation of ownership. No other Arab country has yet attempted to solve this problem. In Lebanon, limitation of ownership is on the programme of the Progressive Socialist Party.

The Middle East countries may, therefore, be regarded as passing into a constructive stage of economic and social development. The degree and rapidity of progress will depend, as in the past, upon social awakening, which in turn is dependent upon freedom of thought and intellectual development. Judging from recent experience, a more complete reconstruction is bound to come—either peacefully or by revolution.

1953.

THE MIDDLE CLASS IN THE ARAB WORLD

by MORROE BERGER

INDUSTRIALIZATION of Western societies in the eighteenth and nineteenth centuries was intimately bound up with the rise of the middle classes and with their prosperity. Inevitably, we ask whether the Middle East (and other technologically under-developed areas) can give birth to the same kind of dynamic middle class, the catalyst that stirs up a placid economy.

When we speak of a middle class in terms of its economic role, we are referring to two related but distinct elements within it: an entrepreneurial class that accumulates, organizes, and allocates capital, and a technical-administrative bureaucracy that manages industrial enterprises. In an earlier era of Western industrial society, these two tasks were more likely to be fulfilled by the same persons than they are now. Especially in the last fifty years or so, the West has experienced two well-documented processes: first, the separation between entrepreneurship and management, and second, the relative decline of the individual entrepreneur and the concentration of the entrepreneurial function in management boards (in private or state enterprises).

If individual entrepreneurship in the West is becoming a rare commodity, can the Middle East develop it in abundance? It will be our thesis that the Arab world is not likely to become highly industrialized (if at all) through the efforts of a local entrepreneurial class of individuals acting in their private capacities, but that the society is likely to be more successful in nurturing a 'salariat' to manage industries set up by whatever combination of local or foreign and public or private capital proves to be feasible. In the course of establishing the basis for this conclusion we shall have to (1) clarify the meaning of the term 'middle class' in the Arab world today in relation to the historical meaning of that term in the West, (2) examine the position of the middle class in the Middle East today, and (3) consider its cultural and political role.

THE MEANING OF 'MIDDLE CLASS'

The idea of a socio-economic class can be a very simple one. Aristotle remarked that, 'In every city the people are divided into three sorts: the very rich, the very poor, and those who are between them'. This classification illustrates the elusive quality of the middle class: a residue after easily identifying the rich and the poor. With the development of trade and manufacture, the criterion of function was systematically added to that of wealth, so that middle class came to mean not only middling income, but those who gained it in economy's exchange and manufacture. To these criteria, those of status or prestige and socio-economic power were added, giving us four bases for the ascription of class position of any kind.

The triumph of the industrial system in Western society brought with it vast social changes and the loosening of class positions. During the rise of capitalist enterprise, urban merchants and manufacturers—formerly occupying a middle-class position in terms of income, status, function and power—moved into the upper class when their incomes became large enough to enable them to adopt at least the outward aspects of upper-class life. Such movement was made possible by (and further stimulated) the eradication of feudal and other privilege embodied in law, by changes in standards of behaviour, and by the advent of new social values. The upshot was to raise the middle-class capitalist to the level of the upper classes. Yet we still speak, often, of the large-scale entrepreneurs as middle class or 'bourgeois'. This is, in most parts of Western society, merely an anachronism of linguistic usage, for since the latter part of the nineteenth century the entrepreneurs, managers, and merchants in large-scale enterprises can hardly be called middle class from any modern point of view.

But the situation in the Arab world is somewhat different. There the changes we have just summarized are only beginning to appear, so that, in most cases, the merchant and the manufacturer (perhaps we ought to say, the artisan) still occupy a middling position in terms of status, function, power, and income. I put income last, because it is in this respect that changes are occurring. As in the case of Western society in the eighteenth and nineteenth centuries, the first break in middle-class position in the Middle East is in income.

Many merchants and industrialists have the income commensurate with upper-class position, but not the power or prestige.

SIZE OF THE MIDDLE CLASS

We take the middle class to encompass two groups between the rich and the poor: (1) those merchants and small manufacturers, self-employed, whose income and influence are not great enough to place them among the really powerful men in political or economic life; (2) a more mixed group, including independent professionals such as doctors and lawyers; employed managers, technicians, and administrative workers such as clerks and bureau chiefs; and the civil service.

If we ask so simple a question as, What is the size of the middle class in the Arab world? we run into problems posed by the lack of data. Only Egypt among the Arab states conducts a regular census, and even that one has serious limitations, as we shall see. The table on page 64 shows the composition and size of the urban middle class in Egypt in 1947, the year of the most recent census.

As we define it, the Egyptian middle class in 1947 numbered only about half a million persons, or about 6 per cent of the total gainfully employed population. Even if all possible miscalculations owing to errors in the original census data or to faulty interpretation are in the direction of an under-estimation (which is not likely), the middle class in Egypt in 1947 could not have constituted more than 10 per cent of the gainfully occupied population. This proportion, moreover, is undoubtedly larger than is the case in the other Arab countries (with the exception of Lebanon), for industry and commerce are less developed there than in Egypt. Let us compare this proportion to the comparable one for the United States, where about two-fifths of the labour force is in urban middle-class occupations.[1] I am not implying, of course, that Egypt and the United States are at all comparable in this respect; rather my purpose is only to show the far greater numerical strength of the middle class in an industrial, urban society. Now even in the United States, there are observers who say the middle class is weak, unorganized, and with little economic power. Even if we are not so pessimistic about the middle class in the United States or other Western societies, certainly the middle class in the Arab world shows little economic influence in view of its numerical weakness and the large proportion in it of 'merchants', mainly owners of small shops, and clerks in private and government offices.

[1] U.S. Bureau of the Census, *Statistical Abstract of the United States: 1956* (Washington, D.C., U.S. Government Printing Office, 1956), Table 252, p. 208.

Urban Middle Class* in Egypt, 1947

Occupation	Number	% of all middle class	% of total population gainfully occupied†
Merchants . . .	254,388	51	3·00
Chief clerks and clerks .	127,876	26	1·51
Professionals‡ . . .	94,339	19	1·11
Business men and agents .	22,561	4	·27
Totals .	499,164	100	5·89

(*) We omit the agricultural middle class, however defined, as not sufficiently relevant as yet to our present interest in the middle-class rôle in industrialization. If we define this rural middle class as the owners of holdings between 5 and 30 feddans (a feddan is slightly larger than an acre), then there were only 134,562 in this class in 1947, constituting 5 per cent of the 2,662,800 owners of holdings of all sizes (see Republique d'Égypte, Département de la Statistique et du Recensement, *Annuaire Statistique 1949–1950 et 1950–1951* (Cairo, Imprimerie Nationale, 1953), Chapter X, Table II, pp. 352–3). In 1952, on the eve of the land reform, there were 139,200 such holders, again constituting 5 per cent of all 2,802,000 landowners (see Republic of Egypt, Ministry of Finance and Economy, Statistical Department, *Statistical Pocket Year-book, 1953* (Cairo, Government Press, 1954), Table 24, p. 33). In neither case would the addition of this agricultural group to the urban middle class in the table significantly alter the low proportion of the middle class to the total population gainfully employed. Nor does the agrarian reform since 1952 affect our point much either, since the holders who benefit from it are precluded, after the redistribution, from owning more than 5 feddans (National Bank of Egypt, *Economic Bulletin*, 1957, Vol. X, No. 1, p. 48).

(†) The figure used to calculate this percentage is 8,479,503 as the total number of persons gainfully occupied. The census data, however, give as this total 14,155,168 (see source indicated below, Table 11, p. 23). We prefer not to use this larger figure because it is based in part on what is apparently a mere re-definition of two occupational categories for women, rather than upon actual changes in the Egyptian economy between the two census years 1937 and 1947. Our use of the lower figure yields a higher proportion in the middle class, but it is nevertheless a more accurate indication of its relative size.

(‡) Includes actors, doctors, chemists and pharmacists, school administrators, professors, teachers, authors and editors, lawyers, engineers.

Source: Egyptian Government, Ministry of Finance and Economy, Statistical Department, *Statistical Pocket Year-Book, 1952* (Cairo, Government Press, 1953), Table 12, pp. 24–9.

In a political sense the middle class is stronger. In the West its strength, at least on election day, is proportionate to its numbers. In the Arab world the political influence of the middle class takes another form. There the middle class is numerically the largest articulate and literate one in the society; the leaders who emerge from this class, however, do not act especially in *its* interests but usually in those of a combination of the wealthiest urban and rural groups, or an aristocracy (where one exists) in league with other upper-class groups, or a military class that exercises control. It is true that leftist politicians, whose influence has grown considerably in recent years, tend to come from the educated middle classes, but their power derives not from this fact but from their appeal to the depressed masses and their association with the wealth, prestige, and power of the Soviet Union.

Level of education itself has been a useful guide to class position in the Middle East. A secondary school graduate, for example, who was likely to become a clerk in the civil service or a private firm, could until recently be considered middle class despite his low income. With the rapid expansion of compulsory primary education in the last decade,[2] it is possible that middle-class status is no longer automatically assumed by secondary-school graduates but that it takes a university degree now to confer that position. Emphasis on formal education as a means of social mobility has set up a strong expectation in Middle Eastern society that a certificate or diploma entitles one to prestige and a certain kind of employment. In a largely rural-agricultural economy, however, outlets for such a class have been too few. In response to this and other pressures, governments have been willing to swell the ranks of the civil service, fearing to increase the already large number of unemployed, educated, articulate young men.

Middle-class weakness in the Arab world is not merely a matter of small numbers. Weakness also stems from its economic position. The foregoing table shows that about half of the urban middle class in Egypt, for example, are merchants, that is, small retailers who employ few people outside the members of their own families. Another quarter are clerical workers. The middle class in the Arab world is thus largely a self-employed or an employed class and is less an *employing* class than its Western counterpart is today or was in an earlier era. Indeed, there is a serious difficulty of classification regarding an Arab middle class that must now be faced. It has just been mentioned that a modicum of formal education by Western standards virtually guarantees middle-class status there. In much the same way, an employer in commerce or manufacturing who, in the West, would be placed and would feel himself to be in the middle class would, in the Arab world, be considered in or very near the upper class. This is the limitation of applying to the Middle East the

[2] See *Compulsory Education in the Arab States* (Paris, U.N.E.S.C.O., 1956), p. 29.

concepts and techniques evolved in the study of Western society; but it is only a limitation of this approach and does not invalidate it.

As a non-employing group, the middle class in the Arab world has little economic power and has been, as a class, rather distant from the fount of all power in that area, the government. The other major component of the middle class, the civil servants, are of course closer to the seat of power, but are a rather pliant instrument in the hands of the real holders of political and economic power.[3]

MIDDLE CLASS AND INDUSTRIALIZATION

In order to industrialize, an economy needs to develop the two kinds of talent mentioned at the beginning: entrepreneurial (based on either public or private capital), and administrative-technological. Traditionally the middle class in the West supplied these abilities. Thus far it has failed to do so in the Middle East, chiefly because it has not engaged in that kind of activity. In its turn, this failure is undoubtedly the result in part of an unfavourable economic environment, for there is certainly plenty of entrepreneurial talent there in a commercial sense, and administrative talent as well. Religious and educational traditions, however, have combined with economic weakness and the lack of certain natural resources to discourage the acquirements most needed for industrial development—those of entrepreneurial and technological skills associated with the machine process. In the past, but to a declining degree today, foreigners, non-Muslims, and non-Arabs performed these functions. More and more the Arab world will need, if it is going to industrialize, a new middle class of technicians and managers, engineers, skilled workers, and foremen—an industrial and not merely an administrative bureaucracy.

What will be the source of such a new middle class in the Middle East? Will the engineers and managers, the technicians and foremen, emerge from the middle-class groups from which the *administrative* bureaucracy in government and trade has been drawn? If so, there will have to be a change in the social estimation of occupations, for the prejudice against technology and engineering is still intense, and the attraction of clerical work, administration, and law very strong. It is entirely possible that the source for such a technological-managerial 'salariat' may be not the present middle class but the sons of the socio-economic layer just below it—the upper reaches of the peasantry and the urban industrial workers. For them, the chance to rise to middle-class status through technical education and

[3] See this writer's *Bureaucracy and Society in Modern Egypt* (Princeton, Princeton University Press, 1957), Chapter 7.

modern industrial employment would be welcomed as an unequivocal advance. For the sons of the middle class as now constituted, however, such an opportunity would not be so eagerly seized.

The new régimes in the Arab countries may well find it in their interest to create other sources of support by encouraging the growth of a new social group. To draw these lower socio-economic elements into a different kind of middle class will require an even greater expansion of primary and secondary education and a greater emphasis on technical education. Public schools, beyond the primary grades especially, are still luxuries which a majority of the people in the Middle East cannot afford for their children. Yet, as has been mentioned, compulsory elementary education is reaching an increasing proportion of the children of school age. A study in 1952 of the manual labourers of a foreign-owned firm in Cairo revealed, for example, that nine out of ten of their school-age sons were actually attending school; equally impressive is the finding that half of their school-age daughters were in school too.[4] But the number receiving a technical education in the preparatory and secondary schools in Egypt actually declined in the early 1950's, although at the university level it increased slightly.[5]

The opportunities which would be created for such a new element of the middle class by industrialization and the execution of industrialization plans by such a group would be a stabilizing influence in the Middle East. It would probably reduce the tendency of the educated élite to concentrate on politics, provide employment for many of them who cannot find useful work of a kind they have come to expect by virtue of their education, and in general open wider the door to social and personal advancement.

Can the Middle East breed the second middle-class component necessary for industrialization?—the accumulators, organizers, and allocators of capital for industrial enterprises. Historically, Western entrepreneurs in private ventures emerged from the urban merchant class and the artisans, rather than from the employed administrative bureaucracy or the independent professions. But the day seems to be past when a small merchant in the Arab world (such as constitute about half of the Egyptian middle class, for example) can accumulate enough capital or technical knowledge to go into industry on a scale that would make a real difference in the nature of the economy. For the same reasons that a firm starting out to manufacture a product today does not have to go through the stages of technological development that older firms did, an entrepreneur today, even in a

---

[4] Unpublished study, Socony-Vacuum Co., Cairo, Industrial Relations Dept., *Survey of Laborers' Living Conditions*, 1953.

[5] National Bank of Egypt, *Economic Bulletin*, 1957, Vol. X, No. 1, p. 46.

non-industrial country, cannot establish an industrial enterprise
with only the small amount of capital needed in an earlier era of
modern capitalism. Estimates of the capital requirements for a
modest rate of industrialization of essentially agricultural economies
are so high that it is unlikely that a large proportion of either this
capital or the talent needed to apply it will be obtained from private
domestic sources. Capital and talent both are likely to be provided,
if industrialization is to proceed substantially, from foreign sources
(private, governmental, or inter-governmental) and domestically by
the state itself.

To be sure, various inducements, such as easy tax arrangements
and compensated expropriations of large agricultural holdings, may
divert domestic capital into industry, but this process will create
investors rather than entrepreneurs. There is indeed a growing
respect in the Arab world for the possibilities of personal and
national benefits to be realized from modern industry, but there is
also suspicion of certain features and effects of it.

The expansion of the oil industry in several Arab countries and
the profit to others from shipments of oil to the Mediterranean area
have led to the growth of some small ancillary private enterprise in
the oil-producing countries and a desire in those and in others for
employment in the private, foreign firms (which produce and ship
the oil), in which the conditions of work are so much more attractive
than in government or domestic private firms. The high prestige
traditionally associated with a government post has not yet declined
much, but there are signs, at least in Egypt, that it is beginning to
lose its status in the eyes of the younger men and that it seems a
less attractive career than formerly.[6] The careers which are gaining
in prestige, however, are not private trade or manufacture but the
independent professions and employment on the professional level
in the large, well-established companies already engaged in manufacturing.

Private entrepreneurship is thus not growing much more attractive
in the Arab world. Aside from the purely economic or traditional
factors discouraging it, there is a political or ideological element
worth mentioning. A socio-economic class or a type of economy
needs a rationale or an ideology to justify it. Western capitalism
developed or found (depending on one's philosophy of history) its
rationale in a certain kind of religious orientation, a secularization
of social relationships, and in political liberalism. Its advocates and
defenders (and even some of its most fervent enemies, such as Marx
and Engels) could point not only to its productive power but also to

[6] See this writer's *Bureaucracy and Society in Modern Egypt*, cited above,
Chapters 4 and 5.

its loosening of tradition, its role in scientific and technological progress, its relationship to political democracy and even to the arts. Now what sort of rationale can the Arab world develop for private entrepreneurship today? I do not mean a rationale for industrialization itself—such a rationale comes easily because modern industry is associated with a higher standard of living and with national power. I mean a rationale for industrialization through domestic private capital and entrepreneurial talent.

The Middle East has in this respect become a victim of its own ideology. For many years its leaders and its Press have attacked the West as imperialist. In recent years, however, they have identified imperialism with capitalism. Rightly or wrongly, and irrespective of the quasi-colonial background which impels them in this direction, they have identified private enterprise as the evil demon behind Western imperialism and expansion. And the foreign-owned oil companies are considered, in the Arab world, as conclusive evidence of such claims. Thus the spokesmen for the articulate classes, who are themselves opposed to Socialism at home, fully accept the Leninist and Soviet Russian view of Western expansion. As Russian influence in the area has grown, this view has been further spread. With such a notion daily pounded into their minds, can the Arabs now, across the threshold of political independence at last, build up a rationale for private enterprise?

Our conclusion must be that if the Arab countries are to industrialize at all in the near future, it will be substantially through means other than private capital and private entrepreneurial talents. They will probably be able to produce the technological skills needed, and it is through this process that the middle class is likely to play an important part in industrialization. Managerial and even entrepreneurial skills put to work by the state or through governmental stimulation in some other form is more likely to be the pattern of economic growth in the Arab world than the creation of a swarm of busy individual entrepreneurs acting for themselves in the image of the older Western pattern.

MIDDLE CLASS AND MODERNIZATION

Despite its small size, lack of power, and the limited role it will probably play in industrialization, the middle class has had enormous influence as a vehicle of modernization and the introduction of Western elements into the Arab world. Since this is too vast a subject to discuss in detail, I want to mention only one very important aspect of this middle-class role: the education and emancipation of women. We might first, however, bear in mind that as a vehicle of modernization in family roles, relations between the sexes, and patterns of consumption, the middle class has exerted an extraordinary influence simply in showing the Arab world that change itself is possible, that there are other traditions and ways of doing things, and that even the Middle East itself has varied styles of life and attitudes.

In regard to the education and emancipation of women (itself, incidentally, a process not irrelevant to industrialization and urbanization), the middle class has been quicker than the others to send their daughters into the public schools, the shops, and even into the secondary schools and universities, especially in Egypt. The upper classes have sheltered their daughters or Westernized them abroad. The lower classes have not yet been drawn into this process. It is thus the middle class that has felt the impact of changing family roles and of new employment opportunities which have changed the status and behaviour of women.

Interesting evidence on this point emerges in a study made a few years ago by an Egyptian social scientist at the Institute of Sociology and Social Science in Alexandria University.[7] He interviewed five hundred girls in the secondary schools of that city, of whom three-quarters were between 16 and 18 years of age, and their mothers, three-quarters of whom were 39 to 48. He found, of course, that the daughters enjoy more freedom in their personal lives and have more schooling than their mothers. They are freer to leave the house alone and to stay out later, and to choose their own clothing; their amusements are less sedentary and secluded than were those of the older generation, and no longer include such pastimes as playing cards and breeding birds. Now the most interesting thing about the findings in this study is that for the daughters the degree of emancipation increases as the income and education of their fathers increase, whereas for the mothers their degree of emancipation *declined* as their fathers' income and education increased. This means, if these findings are representative, that today the higher a family's socio-economic status, the more emancipated the daughters are likely to be, whereas a generation ago the higher the status of the family, the less emancipated the daughters were. In other words, a generation ago the daughters of middle-class families were more emancipated than those of the upper-class families, which were apparently rela-

[7] Muhammad A. S. Mito, 'The Social Change of Daughters' Position in Egyptian Middle Class Families in Alexandria', unpublished thesis at the Institute of Sociology and Social Science, Alexandria University, 1953, p. 118 of typed manuscript. This study was made under the supervision of the director of the Institute, the late Dr. Zdenek K. Ullrich, who kindly made it available to me.

tively conservative. Thus emancipation and education of women seem to have spread upward and downward from the middle class. In this critically important realm of social relations it was the middle class that made the first tentative but unmistakable moves towards change.

SOCIAL STABILITY

Technological change is stirring Arab society and shifting socio-economic classes. Once accepted, as it is coming to be in the Middle East, it places different values on certain skills and brings with it new social relationships and ideological commitments. The most powerful and articulate elements in the Arab world want technological change, especially industrialization. In such change the middle class has played an important part by introducing the idea of change itself, by supplying leaders and an articulate following in nationalist causes, and by beginning to transform itself from a largely clerical-administrative bureaucracy into a managerial-technological one. The specific impulse and drive towards actual industrialization, however, will probably come, if it comes at all, from other sources in the society.

Economic growth, if it takes place steadily and to a substantial degree, or even if it is sought seriously, may lead to an important change in orientation in the Arab world: from the highly political concerns of the era in which it sought complete independence, to economic and technological projects, as means of raising living standards and of enhancing national power. Military régimes and the decline of parliaments and political parties may reduce the immediate attractiveness of politics and administration as careers. If economic growth can open up new ones, and if new social groups can acquire a stake in continued economic advance and in the sharing of political power, the Middle East may well enter a period of greater social and political stability. The middle class can play a limited but important part in such changes, especially by its example; through its flexibility and its familiarity with the new patterns, and its close relationship with those elements of the population that want to cling to the old. If the various types of *élite* groups in the middle class can develop a spirit of independence and of responsibility to the entire society rather than only to their own narrow and immediate interests, they may be able to provide a good measure of the leadership that may take some parts of the Arab world into a new era of spiritual and political development as well as of economic growth.

MIDDLE EASTERN DEVELOPMENT
—ANOTHER MISSING LINK

by A. F. MILLS

MOST OF US have gone through phases of hope and gloom as we have contemplated Arab economic development during the years since the war. Some of the achievements, in Iraq, Egypt, Lebanon, or Syria, in both public and private enterprise, have given deep satisfaction to those of us who wish to see the Middle East bloom again with the wealth and culture which were its glory in past ages. The new dams, irrigation and drainage schemes, the new ports, the lofty new edifices all remind us that the Arab world is alive to what is modern, efficient, and large-scale in conception in this dynamic twentieth century. But these moments of hope are overtaken all too rapidly by reminders elsewhere of the obstacles to progress. The conflicting undercurrents in the political field, the gulf between rich and poor which, through the insidious pressure of inflation, has been widening in many communities in the Middle East, the voices of men who are suspicious of Western values as also of Western science: these are only the worst of the obstacles.

One of the most stimulating comments on Middle Eastern development that have appeared in recent years referred to a missing link in the economic process, namely *entrepreneurship*. It appeared in the 1954 issue of the *Middle East Economic Papers*, published by the Economic Research Institute of the American University of Beirut, in an article by Professor A. J. Meyer. We realized that by a stroke of insight Professor Meyer had focused our minds on one of the deeper secrets of thwarted progress. You cannot develop an economy unless there are the persons with vision to discover where change can occur, and who have the initiative, the

venturesomeness, and the resources to see it through. It is that kind
of initiative and risk-taking blended with imaginative skill which has
created the dams, the power stations, the factories, and the airlines,
which kindle our hopes.

There has been long discussion as a result of this intellectual squib.
Though there is some disagreement as to the part private initiators
are able to play in this immature social and economic environment
where the industrialist or farmer is often at a distinct disadvantage,
most of us are agreed on the need for an innovating leadership,
whether in the private or in the public sectors of the economy.

It is not my main purpose in this article to argue one way or the
other on whether 'entrepreneurship' is a 'missing link'. In some
regions there is no doubt that it is. In many others—in Egypt, in
Lebanon, Syria, and even Iraq—it may be less the top leadership
that is missing than conditions favourable to its exercise. You cannot
expect a man to found a factory if the risks of its collapsing after a
year or two are greater than its chances of success. Risk is very great
where so much of the economic, social, and political outlook is
uncertain; and such insecurity is hardly inviting for the man with
ideas and money to venture them in a long-term undertaking which
a single arbitrary event, such as an armed conflict, monetary inflation, a capricious change in trade or tariff policy, or a revised
taxation scheme, can wreck. Above all, it is tempting to avoid such
adventures when safer channels exist for the money and skills.
Nevertheless, in spite of the clouds, many an Arab entrepreneur has
believed in the sun behind them. In Egypt, Syria, Lebanon, and, to
a lesser extent, in Iraq, there have been men prepared to risk savings
in new lines of production, from pig iron to clothing and hosiery,
paper products, beverages, macaroni, biscuits, chocolates, tennis
shoes, and a growing variety of cast-iron, brass, and other metal
articles. Others have experimented with new farming methods, invested large sums in equipment, and specialized in fruits and vege-
tables as in Lebanon, or in cotton and sugar-beet as in Syria. There
are signs indeed that 'entrepreneurship' is perhaps less a missing link
than was at first thought. Certain types of 'top leader' are no doubt
in acutely short supply, including administrators, directors of research, planners, statesmen, quite besides the risk-takers, innovators,
and organizers whom the economist usually has specifically in mind
when he refers to 'entrepreneurs'. We have certainly here a *weak*
link. But what is perhaps far more a *missing* link is the *middle leadership* on which top leaders have to rely to execute their policies and
plans. If we look closely enough at the Arab social and economic
order, we see a profound lop-sidedness: a mass of unskilled labour
at the bottom, a small group of trained or partially trained leaders

and risk-takers and organizers at the top, and an almost completely denuded series of middle ranks. It is like an inverted mushroom.

Let us look at the way institutions function in this setting. Where the top leadership does exist and where men have had the courage and vision to set up an enterprise, even so progress is often arduous and slow. There are factories, banks, wholesale and retail houses, and entire departments in the public administration of every country in the Middle East where, beyond a certain point, little progress has been made. Something calls a halt. Enthusiasm evaporates as the initial spurt peters out. How often after that first brilliant expansion, the rot 'creeping in' sets off a real decline, and the whole enterprise, once so fresh and promising, folds up and dies. This type of experience is known over the wide world in every century, but in the Middle East, as in every other of the less developed regions in the world, the frequency and scale of such abortive schemes are far greater than in the developed countries. It is not a chance phenomenon. Its roots go deep. There must be a cause, and it would be of inestimable value to discover it.

Most people I have met have ideas on this topic, and these ideas put together embrace almost the entire field of management. To catalogue them would give the impression that the Arabs are the worst managers in the world. But quite obviously the same procedure would have given the same result in Britain in 1820 or in the U.S.A. in 1860. Each person's ideas are based on his own personal observation, and, of necessity, this is usually limited. A shortcoming that might be common to one group of institutions in a given locality might not be universal in the area as a whole, even in the same type of institution. The shortcoming that might prove fatal in one set of circumstances might not be of particular importance in a different set. So we must not be quick to generalize on the basis of personal observation. Scientific research methods alone can throw definite light on the problem, and give guidance on the way to tackle it.

THE NEED FOR PLANNING

My own observations in administrative institutions and commercial enterprises in the Middle East, during and since the war, have evoked a few tentative suggestions. In industrial firms, for instance, where policies made today may not bear fruit till several years have passed, it would appear that the most elementary procedure necessary to safeguard investment is planning ahead. Most firms in developed economies plan for at least a year ahead, a large proportion for five years, and a steadily growing number for as much as ten. In official circles the need to plan even further ahead has been recognized. Britain, in its problem of power supply, has plans for the generation and commercial utilization of nuclear energy that cover more than twenty years. In this way firms and whole communities avoid being caught off their guard by unforeseen events. The plan sets a path, and that path gives confidence in dealing with the uncertain changes over the years before us. But there is no rational planning in the vast majority of Middle East firms; and in those few cases where plans are worked out, they cover usually not more than three months ahead. If this is so, it might account for many of the failures; many a firm which had not planned for its working capital, raw materials, spare parts, or for new markets, has now disappeared.

What perhaps is even more serious is that the great bulk of factory owners do not understand what a business man in Europe or America means by internal control. He does not mean merely ensuring that accounts are kept so that one employee cannot put the firm's money into his pocket without being found out. He means knowing exactly what is being done day by day and comparing it with what he had planned for, discovering at once where the strong and weak spots are, and taking immediate corrective action. To do that needs appropriate accounts and statistics, and regular reports from every section of the business, presented so that unusual conditions stand out clearly for action, and indicate the persons responsible for taking the action. If this control procedure is not even understood, it is not strange that owners and managers should be unaware of the weak points in their enterprises, should not seem anxious about what to the economist appears to be irritatingly low productivity, and should blame third parties for their difficulties. How many owner-managers have demanded protection—high protection—as their right? And how many have received it and so remained blind to their real weakness? Only perhaps in Lebanon have tariffs been pitched sufficiently low for many industrial enterprises to feel the chill blast of foreign competition; yet even here I have found hardly an instance of systematic control. I do not wish to imply that protection is not justified for infant industries in the Middle East, but that protection is not conducive to competent leadership in the economic field. In official institutions the main causes of poor performance may be less a lack of planning and control; there is reason to believe that ill-advised methods of recruiting and selection, the blocking of the flow of information through the departments, and the fear of assuming responsibilities which might bring down on one's head the wrath of superiors and even lead to dismissal, may be more important factors in this sphere than in business. Only research on a wide scale can tell us.

THE NEED FOR 'MIDDLE LEADERSHIP'

But whether imperfect performance be through lack of planning and control or whether through poor selection, blocked communication channels, fear of responsibility, and over-centralized power, there is one factor missing which makes it impossible to remove any of these deficiencies even when top leadership is alert and competent. That factor we may call 'middle leadership'. It comprises all the levels between the top level of owner-manager, director, permanent secretary (whatever the title), and the lowest of operative or clerk. It comprises the gang-boss, foreman, supervisor, superintendent, head of section, factory manager, administrative officer, chief clerk, personnel officer, and the numerous other posts responsible for executing the policies and instructions of the top level of authority, communicating information and orders down to the operative in the workshop or the clerk in the office, bank, shop, or warehouse, and then reporting back information on action taken and its results.

Every firm I have visited in the Middle East has complained of the difficulty of finding supervisors; it is a problem worse even than that of finding competent technicians, engineers, scientists, statisticians, and cost accountants. It is just as important. Only in the smallest family firm can the top level personally supervise the operative level and thus ensure that orders are carried out as desired and the best use is made of men and machines. In most industries now, in Egypt, Lebanon, Syria, the firms making headway are larger than this and so need the intermediate levels; they have usually between 20 and 50 employees, and a small proportion (responsible for a growingly significant part of total production in their industry) has over 200. There are examples of over 1000. In official organizations and public utilities, of course, the typical number goes into many hundreds. The same is true in the military services, hospitals, port authorities, nationalized industries, and the larger commercial institutions.

This lack of middle leadership constitutes a severe bottle-neck. It is easy to see what happens to letters and instructions when those who have to take the action they involve are untrained, unqualified, apprehensive of their superiors, and distrustful of their subordinates. It is the almost universal situation in the larger organizations that clerks have not learned how to file documents, type accurately, use office machines, route files to those concerned, and keep track of them; accountants have not learned how to present their facts for control purposes; and factory machine-operators for the most part cannot fill in a job-ticket or read instructions. How can the foremen or chief clerks or supervisors secure even moderately efficient performance, when they are themselves untrained, underpaid, and over-worked (in the textile mills foremen often supervise up to eighty operatives)?

This is, in my view, the most serious 'missing link' in Middle Eastern development. Many are aware of it, some acutely so. The answer is a simple one, of course—training: technical training, supervisory training, and clerical training. There have been good beginnings in some countries. In the Sudan, after the war, a centre was set up to train government clerks and bookkeepers, and in 1951 the Khartoum Technical Institute began to train technicians, build-ers, carpenters, engineers, accountants, and commercial teachers. In Egypt a similar centre for clerical training was set up in 1955 as part of the United Nations Institute of Public Administration, and there have been efforts to improve technical training facilities, and bring up-to-date commercial teaching syllabuses in the schools, which are still based on pre-1914 ideas. There have been attempts to fill the gap elsewhere. But still it yawns.

TECHNICAL TRAINING

If we take Lebanon, the most literate of the Arab countries, we find the training problem is just as acute as elsewhere, even though a considerable proportion of the educational facilities are provided by private, often foreign, institutions and paid for privately, so that the burden on the official budget is relatively less heavy than in other Arab countries. Indeed, the official failure to provide technical and supervisory training for the growing industries, commercial under-takings, and administrative departments within the government itself appears incredible to the observer. There was in 1957 (as in 1943) only one governmental vocational school, the 'Arts et Métiers', in Beirut, with three minor branches in Tripoli, Sidon, and Zahle. It began offering diplomas in vocational subjects in 1927, and from then till the end of the academic year 1955–56 the number of gradu-ates amounted to less than 1700. Not only has this supply of trained men been ludicrously small in relation to the needs of the country, but no plan has ever been made to ensure that each of them should be given the opportunity of systematically imparting his skills to other workers in industry. The 'Arts et Métiers' is supplemented by vocational curricula in not more than 30 schools out of the 2135 schools in the country; this small fraction had in 1954 enrolments of less than 2000 students out of a total enrolment of 248,000 (less than four-fifths of one per cent). Of the 30 schools, only 9 with enrolments of 300 pupils had programmes for teaching technical-mechanical skills; the rest had a variety of courses in nursing, dressmaking, bookkeeping, wireless and radio operation or repair, hotel service, and music. This official lethargy in the provision of technical training stands in contrast to the enthusiastic provision of primary educational facilities. In 1943 the total number of government schools was 248; in 1956 it was 1107, an increase of 342 per cent. Of these, 1047 (92 per cent) are primary schools for pupils of ages 6 to 11. In 1957 there were only 8 government secondary schools. Among private schools, 88 per cent, or 911 of a total of 1028, were primary.

Literacy has been given priority over technical proficiency and leadership training. As in all educational systems in Arab countries, the underlying philosophy seems still to be that education, to be truly so, must be intellectual. The boy who is not fit for the academic programme is forced to undergo it, for there is no technical stream in the schools for him. A new curriculum has been planned with streams for the commercial and industrial alongside the existing academic *brevet* and *baccalaureat* courses. But the change has yet to be implemented.

The Department of Commerce of the American University of Beirut offers a well-balanced training in business administration which not only acquaints students with the principles, problems, and techniques of marketing, finance, accounting, and statistics, but also gives some insight into the tasks of supervisors and junior managers in business institutions. Between 35 and 45 students now graduate annually. The same Department offers a Brief Business Course for the training of clerks in typing, stenography, bookkeeping, filing, and business methods.

The U.S. Operations Mission in Lebanon (Point IV) has done valuable work assisting the Ministry of Education to improve technical training and the training of teachers for schools. It contracted for U.S. experts from the Delgado Central Trade School, New Orleans, Louisiana, to spend three years in Lebanon preparing job analyses and courses of study in motor-car mechanics, radio electronics, electricity, carpentry, and drafting. Together with government officials the team drew up plans for a professional trade school and technical institute, and ordered equipment for them. This work is already having some effect. In the Arts et Métiers the number of first-year students at present (1956–57) is 240, compared with 180 second-year and only 97 third-year. This rate of expansion is highly desirable, if standards can be maintained. The demand for trained teachers, as a result of the expansion of schools since 1946, has been largely unsatisfied. U.S.O.M. has assisted in the construction of a new home for the Teachers' Training Institute at Bir Hassan, but the intake of trainees needs to be stepped up appreciably. Measures need to be taken also to train teachers for the commercial and technical streams in the secondary schools which will develop as the new syllabuses are introduced.

The Engineering School of the American University, likewise aware of the gap in training of foremen and supervisors in industry, has devised a new course of study leading to a Degree of Technology. Half of the time of students will be devoted to engineering subjects, and the balance to management, to give them the knowledge, skills, and insight required to perform the tasks of supervisors and middle managers in industry. But this plan, too, awaits implementation.

Meanwhile, industrial firms have to train their men as best they can. There is an apprenticeship system in certain trades. But training is costly for the small firm, especially when labour turnover proves to be high. This is related, of course, to the remuneration offered to semi-skilled, skilled workers, and foremen. The small firm burdened with training costs pays relatively low wages, which fail to attract the best-qualified persons. The semi-skilled worker and foreman in most small factories earn usually between £L 150 and £L 300 monthly, which compares with clerical salaries in commercial enterprises of from about £L 175 to £L 450 monthly. This, too, reflects the low social status of manual and industrial work, which is a legacy of the feudal past.

A radical reform of this situation awaits an equally radical change of attitude in top leaders. In all Arab countries, teachers still have to be trained to use modern teaching methods to replace the bookishness which characterizes so much of classroom activity today. There must be a marked expansion in teacher-training facilities. New syllabuses need to be introduced, and schools provided with the equipment required to train students for the more practical tasks they will have to perform in industry and agriculture. The governments, on behalf of the communities, must assume full responsibility for planning the training facilities, organizing, financing them, and finding the teachers. It is a difficult and expensive task, but there are many hands already extended to aid in completing it.

Will top leaders refuse to see where their true interest lies: in creating trained middle leaders, without whom their own failure is inevitable?

EGYPTIAN ATTITUDES TOWARDS
LAND REFORM, 1922-1955

by GABRIEL BAER

I. VIEWS ON AGRARIAN REFORM PRIOR TO THE MILITARY REVOLUTION

A. *The Social and Political Background*

FEW PEOPLE would deny that the distribution-structure of landed property in Egypt prior to the Military Revolution seriously impeded Egyptian economic development. This fact alone, however, or even the realization of its significance on the part of Egypt's leaders or sections of Egyptian public opinion, was not sufficient to give rise to a popular demand for agrarian reform, let alone its implementation. The question of the distribution of private landed property engaged Egyptian public opinion only to a slight degree before the 1940's. Apart from the proposal advanced by the insignificant Communist Party in the early 1920's,[1] no demand was made to limit the size of the great estates or to confiscate them, and there was no public discussion of the question.

This phenomenon requires some explanation, since it might appear strange in the light of two other facts: (*a*) the inimical effect on the economy of the prevailing distribution of land was marked before the 1940's, and two attempts to stabilize smallholdings—the Five Feddāns Law and the sale of state domain—had already ended in failure; and (*b*) during the 'twenties, agrarian reforms were carried out in many countries of Eastern Europe, and there was the

[1] *Cf.* J. Castagné, *Les Indes et l'Égypte vues de Russie.* Extrait de la *Revue du Monde Musulman* (Paris, Leroux, 1925), p. 112.

possibility that the movement might prompt, if not the Egyptian government and its leaders, at least certain circles of Egyptian public opinion, to demand similar action in Egypt, which so desperately needed it.

If, nevertheless, the question of land reform was ignored by Egyptian public opinion, we must look further into the socio-political structure of Egypt for an explanation. Great landowners were in positions of control in all the representative bodies which had been established in Egypt up to the First World War; afterwards, the 1923 Constitution granted wide legislative and executive powers to the King—the biggest landowner in the country—and provided for the rule of the great landlords in the Senate. In addition, the landowners acquired the most influential positions in Parliament and in all the political parties. On the other hand, prior to the Customs Reform Act of 1930, industrial activity was insignificant and there existed no organized urban *bourgeoisie* capable of disputing the supremacy of the landowners. Moreover, the struggle for political and national sovereignty generally overshadowed the internal social and economic problems. Thus, for example, Sa'ad Zaghlūl, in a speech to the Legislative Assembly in 1914, condemned the Five Feddāns Law, claiming that it discriminated against Egyptian money-lenders in favour of foreign banking institutions, since the former lent to the fallāhīn while the latter dealt with the large landowners.[2] Finally, the fact that the fallāhīn, the class most directly interested in agrarian reform, were entirely inarticulate, was one of the chief reasons for the problem's being neglected. The Egyptian peasant had been oppressed for hundreds of years; his standard of living was so low, his ignorance so abysmal, and his strength so enervated by disease, that he was apathetic rather than rebellious.

This situation was decisively altered in the 1940's. In its 'agrarian programme' of 1935, the *Wafd* Party was still able to ignore completely the question of the distribution of landed property,[3] and as late as 1938 a political writer like Dr. Hāfiz 'Afīfī could publish a full-length book dealing with the economic, social, and political problems of Egypt without even once mentioning the subject.[4] Even the authoress Ibnat ash-Shāti' did not touch the problem in her book, *qadīyat al-fallāh* (*The Problem of the Fallāh*), published shortly afterwards.

However, during the Wafd administration of 1942–44, the question of the distribution of landed property came to be one of the most

---

[2] 'Abbās Mahmūd al-'Aqqād, *Sa'ad Zaghlūl* (Cairo, 1936), p. 160.

[3] See the report on the Wafd Conference in the Wafdist paper *al-Balāgh*, January 8, 1935.

[4] Hāfiz 'Afīfī, *'alā hāmish as-siyāsa* (Cairo, 1938).

controversial subjects of public discussion, and was frequently
dealt with by cabinet members in their public pronouncements.[5]
The Prime Minister, Mustafā Nahhās, in a speech on the malaria
epidemic raging at the time in Upper Egypt, laid the blame for the
poverty of the residents of the Aswān and Qenā districts on the
exaggerated concentration of property in the hands of the great
landowners of the area.[6] At the end of the same year (1944)
Muhammad Khattāb submitted to the Senate a bill whose purpose
was to limit the size of landholdings. In 1945 at least three books
appeared demanding agrarian reforms: one by the Communist
author Sādiq Saʿad, called *mushkilat al-fallāh*; the second edition of
The Economic Development of Egypt in Modern Times, by Rāshid
al-Barrāwī and Muhammad Hamza ʿUlaish, who demanded the
limitation of large landholdings in an additional chapter entitled
'Several Problems of the Future' (which did not appear in the first
edition, published a year earlier); and finally Mirrīt Ghālī's book
The Agrarian Reform, containing a detailed blue-print for land
reform (Ghālī opposed such a reform in his *Policy of Tomorrow*,
which first appeared in 1938).[7]

What was it that made Egyptian leaders and thinkers devote such
serious consideration during the 1940's to the problem of land
reform? First of all, following the 1936 Treaty with Great Britain,
and the abolition of the Capitulations in 1937, politicians and
publicists were free to turn their attention to Egypt's internal
problems. At least four books published in 1938 and dealing with
social problems emphasized the necessity of stabilizing, reorganizing,
and reforming Egyptian society now that Egypt had achieved her
independence.[8] Secondly, during those same years inflation automatically solved the problem of mortgage debts—which had engaged Egyptian political attention during the 'thirties to the exclusion
of almost all other internal problems—and it became possible to
consider other aspects of the agrarian régime in Egypt. The chief
reason, however, for the sudden interest in land distribution arose
out of the social problems generated by the war: the widespread
inflation, entailing much suffering for broad sections of the population and widening the gulf between rich and poor; the dislocation
of the food supply, particularly in 1942; and finally the malaria
epidemic in Upper Egypt, that carried off tens of thousands of
victims.

Publications of this period reveal how directly the proposals for

[5] Cf. *al-Misrī*, March 15, 1943; February 16, 1944; April 18, 1945, etc.
[6] *al-Ahrām*, February 29, 1944.
[7] Mirrīt Ghālī, *Siyāsatal-ghad*, 2nd ed. (Cairo, 1944), pp. 71, 74–5.
[8] ʿAfīfī, *op. cit.*, pp. 3–4; Ibnat ash-Shāti', *op. cit.*, p. 14; Ghālī, *op. cit.*, p. 7;
Tāhā Husain, *mustaqbal ath-thaqāfa fī misr* (Cairo, 1938), introduction and
pp. 4–5.

agrarian reform were linked with these events. Thus, for example, Muhammad Khattāb writes: '. . . The rich accumulated wealth while the poor were plunged yet deeper into poverty. . . . As a result, the disparity between the classes grew and the social structure was undermined to such a degree that does not bode well for the future of the country.'[9] Mirrīt Ghālī speaks in his book of the 'increased profits of the landowner, while the income of the small tenant and of workers has fallen to a level which makes the maintenance of a stable economic and social order an impossibility'. He points out that this phenomenon also heightened general interest in the question of the redistribution of landed property: 'The present war, even if it has not altered the basic premises of our situation, is fraught with danger for it. It implanted in the masses a realization of their rights in society and brought in its wake shortages and disastrous epidemics that emphasize the awful conditions in which the rural citizen lives. It is a problem which can no longer be ignored.'[10] Sādiq Sa'ad puts the same interpretation on the situation in these words: 'The present war may be seen as an important turning-point in our lives in general and in our attitude towards reform in particular. Our economy is rapidly developing, industry has taken gigantic strides forward, and the number of workers has grown enormously. The problems of food supply, the rise in prices, and the other domestic hardships brought about by the war have made people aware of the faults in our social structure and made them give some consideration to their remedy—not superficial or stop-gap measures, but thorough-going reform.'[11] Finally, the ideas of social justice and freedom from want which were sweeping the world and which had been expressed in the Beveridge Report and the Atlantic Charter unquestionably left their mark on the Egyptian intelligentsia, arousing in them the desire that Egypt should not lag behind 'the spirit of the times'.[12]

Despite all this, the results were disappointingly poor. The subject of land distribution and the agrarian question in general were aired by politicians and cabinet ministers and debated in Parliament, but the actual demand to carry out an agrarian reform was limited to a small circle of intellectuals. Although several extremist organizations, such as the Communists and the Moslem Brotherhood,

[9] Muhammad Khattāb, 'āfaq gadīda fi-s-siyāsat-il-misrīya', al-Ahrām, March 5, 1943.

[10] Mirrīt Ghālī, al-islāh azzirā'ī (Cairo, 1945), pp. 11, 12.

[11] Sādiq Sa'ad, mushkilatal-fallāh (Cairo, n.d.—published about the middle of 1945), pp. 7–8.

[12] See, e.g., Khattāb, loc. cit.; Fu'ād Sirāg ad-Dīn, 'al-islāh al-igtimā'ī fī misr', al-Misrī, June 7, 1944; Dr. Ahmad Husain in al-Misrī, April 18, 1945, etc.

issued calls for agrarian reform, this was only a side issue raised on rare occasions; their principal interests lay elsewhere. All the parties represented in the various Egyptian Parliaments were at one in consistent opposition to agrarian reform.

This opposition to a fairer distribution of farmland—the disinclination to enter the lists against the economic and social supremacy of the great landowners—was engendered not only by the fact that the great proprietors were represented in the leadership of those parties (and that their strength in the leadership of the Wafd Party even increased after 1936).[13] It was also partly a result of the character of the new urban middle class, which had grown in the wake of the industrial, commercial, and financial expansion encouraged by the Second World War. Although this *bourgeoisie*, in virtue of its interests and its economic and social standing, was logically the most likely heir to the rule of the landowners, several factors militated against its taking up the challenge.

First, members of minority communities and foreigners still made up the backbone of the middle class, thus lessening its ability to play an independent role in the Egyptian political arena. Secondly, its interests were bound up with those of the landowners, for example by the steadily increasing participation of landowners in urban enterprises and the acquisition of landed property by urban capitalists. Thirdly, the period of the development of this class was one of social tension in the cities themselves, with famine riots in 1942, and waves of labour disputes, strikes, and demonstrations punctuating the later 'forties. Consequently, the middle class felt the need for co-operation with the ruling classes; it was apprehensive of any demand for social reform and refrained from any action that might awaken it for fear that, once started, it could not be contained within predetermined bounds.[14]

To these positive restraints a negative one must be added. Whereas in the cities, during the 'forties, social movements often took the shape of organized activity on the part of the workers, who banded together in trade unions to press their specific social and economic demands (and even began to form political organizations) among the fallāhīn there was no organized movement for improving conditions. Social tension in the villages found its outlet in scores of isolated murders—of landlords, their agents, overseers, watchmen,

---

[13] See 'Abd ar-Rahmān ar-Rāfi'ī, *fī ā'qāb ath-thawra al-misrīya*, III (Cairo, 1951), p. 51; and Rāshid al-Barrāwī, *haqīqatal-inqilāb al-akhīr fī misr* (Cairo, 1952), pp. 148-9.

[14] For an excellent analysis of this dilemma of the Egyptian middle class see Charles Issawi, *Egypt at Mid-Century* (Oxford University Press, 1954), pp. 258-9; *cf.* also Ghālī, *al-islāh az-zirā'ī*, p. 14.

and village '*omdas*[15]—but the fallāhīn never succeeded in voicing a corporate demand or creating a functioning organization for themselves. Thus from no direction was pressure exerted on the Egyptian governments of the day to make any fundamental adjustments. Towards the end of the decade, it became apparent that in spite of the urgency of agrarian reform, and in spite of the detailed plans for such reform worked out by several Egyptians, there was little likelihood of a redistribution of land 'so long as the existing political régime remained in power'.[16]

B. Discussion of the Land Distribution Question

1. The Position of the Parties Represented in Parliament

None of the parties represented in the Egyptian Parliament ever had a clearly defined social or economic programme. Before 1940 the distinctions between them were expressed chiefly in their respective attitudes towards the monarchy or towards Great Britain, and even in this there were occasional reversals of policy. To arrive at their position on agrarian affairs, we must examine empirically what party leaders had to say in this respect and what they accomplished during their terms of office.

The most striking feature in the parties' approach to the agrarian question was their common opposition to any reform in the existing distribution of land in Egypt, a position which they maintained even after the 1952 Revolution. All the parties believed that it was possible to evade drastic reform through the sale of state domain to small farmers, although none of them ever in fact carried out that programme. One may, however, discern differences of emphasis between the proclamations issued by spokesmen of different parties and differences between the alternative proposals suggested and implemented (or not) during the parties' periods in power.

Opposition to any state intervention whatsoever in the distribution of private property beyond the sale of state domain to small farmers was first expressed in public by political and party leaders during the 1940's, when the question began to occupy public attention. In 1939, 'Alī Shamsī Pasha, for many years President of the Egyptian National Bank, urged the sale of state domain only to small farmers, for whom credit should be made easier and the tax burden lighter 'in order to prevent the confiscation of big estates, such as occurred in Rumania after the First World War and which is now going on in

[15] See, e.g., 'Azīz Khānqī, 'hawādith al-ightiyāl fī-l-aryāf', *al-Ahrām*, October 23, 1944.

[16] *Cf.* Charles Issawi, *Egypt, an Economic and Social Analysis* (Oxford University Press, 1947), p. 198; Doreen Warriner, *Land and Poverty in the Middle East* (Royal Institute of International Affairs, 1948), p. 50.

Sicily, where the Italian government is dealing with a situation similar to that of Egypt'.[17]

The policy of the *Liberal Constitutionalist* Party was outlined in detail by Muhammad 'Alī 'Allūba Pasha in his book *mabādi' fi-s-siyāsati-l-misrīya*, which appeared in 1942. 'Allūba was one of the founding members of the party and, although in later years he was not one of its recognized spokesmen, his statements still express the prevailing opinions within the party. In his book, 'Allūba attacks 'the belief generally held by a number of people' that there are rich men in Egypt who have acquired vast estates, the same belief that leads 'several of them to demand in journals, books, and in public addresses the limitation of the size of land holdings. . . . In my opinion, this plan is not the way to extricate Egypt from its distressing situation; our country is a democracy, and it would be far better for us to safeguard the freedom of the individual and his initiative. . . . Moreover, because of the large numbers who need land and the relatively small amount available, the breaking up of private estates and their redistribution would not produce the benefits expected of it.'[18] The contention that an equal distribution of Egypt's land among all its citizens would leave each one with only a tiny plot was, of course, one of the principal arguments against agrarian reform, and was frequently advanced.[19] The Liberal Constitutionalist Party consistently maintained its opposition to agrarian reform, and even in the programme published in August, 1952, at the request of the Revolutionary régime, it agreed only 'to the transfer of state farmlands to the people in order to increase the number of smallholdings, in accordance with existing legislation'. Explaining this programme, the President of the party, Husain Haikal, declared: 'The limitation of private property is a delicate matter that would be likely to provoke class war. I do not believe that the government will put its very existence in jeopardy by urging legislation which the country as a whole rejects.'[20] The Secretary of the party, Ibrāhīm Disūqī Abāza, suggested that the traditional Moslem charity tax (*zakāt*) should be imposed as a substitute for the proposed land reform.[21]

[17] Quoted from Jean Anhoury, 'Les Grandes Lignes de l'Économie Agricole de l'Égypte', in *L'Égypte Contemporaine*, 1941, pp. 552–3.

[18] 'Allūba, *op. cit.*, pp. 51–2, 67.

[19] E.g. in an article by Murād Wahba, *al-Ahrām*, April 8, 1945, and by many others. This was also Ghālī's main argument against land reform in his first book (*Siyāsatal-ghad*, pp. 71, 74–75); he refutes his own argument in *al-islāh az-zirā'ī*, p. 11.

[20] 'mabādi' hizb al-ahrār ad-dusturiyīn fi-l-'ahd al-gadīd', art. 16, *al-Ahrām*, August 7, 1952.

[21] *al-Misrī*, August 22, 1952.

Leaders of the *Sa'adist* Party, until asked to do so by the new régime in 1952, had virtually refrained from making their views on land distribution known. During one of their periods in office (the Nuqrāshī Government, February, 1945–February, 1946), the Senate voted down Muhammad Khattāb's proposal to limit the size of agricultural holdings to 50 feddāns.[22] Like the Liberal Constitutionalist Party (with which it shared the responsibility of office in 1945–46), the Sa'adist Party, as late as August, 1952, opposed any alteration in the distribution of private landed property other than the 'distribution of State Domain, after its amelioration, among small landholders'.[23]

The *al-Kutla al-Wafdīya* Party, founded by the former Wafd leader Makram 'Ubaid, avoided all reference to the agrarian question in the programme which it had to publish after the Revolution.[24] But one of its spokesmen, Tāhā as-Sibā'ī, went on record against agrarian reform, which at the time was still only a proposal.[25] Against the suggestion to limit the area which a landowner might possess and to redistribute the rest, as-Sibā'ī marshalled the following arguments: (*a*) such a distribution would discriminate in favour of the owners of fertile lands, since all land is obviously not of the same quality; (*b*) the plan involved enormous expenditures and would lead to inflation; (*c*) it would not produce a corresponding increase in agricultural output, but on the contrary, a drop; (*d*) monetary compensation paid to landowners would not necessarily find its way into industrial investment, as this required foreign currency; (*e*) in the event of a fall in prices for agricultural produce, particularly cotton, the fallāhīn would be unable to meet the annual payments for the land they had received; (*f*) the area which could be distributed to the fallāhīn was very small. In place of agrarian reform, as-Sibā'ī urged the distribution of cultivable state and *Waqf* lands among the fallāhīn and a progressive tax on the large landowners.

This last proposal was seized upon by other circles as well as a loophole through which they hoped to escape the necessity of legally limiting the size of estates. Moreover, while the leader of the *Kutla* arrived at this conclusion only after it had become clear that the Revolutionary régime was intent on confiscating the land belonging to estates above a certain size, the group led by 'Alī Māhir had already adopted this line in 1946. This group (*Gibhat*

[22] ar-Rāfi'ī, *op. cit.*, II (Cairo, 1949), pp. 357–8. See below.

[23] "barnāmig al-hai'a as-sa'adīya fi-l-'ahd al-gadīd', art. B. 3, *al-Ahrām*, August 8, 1952.

[24] See *al-Misrī*, August 1, 1952.

[25] *Le Progrès Égyptien*, August 19, 1952.

Misr) published in the same year a political programme demanding
the imposition of a progressive tax on all estates exceeding a certain
minimum in size. This, the group believed, would discourage capitalists from investing in land. In the same programme 'Alī Māhir also
suggested establishing a minimum size for smallholdings in order to
prevent their being further broken up into plots too small for
efficient cultivation.[26] But when 'Alī Māhir became Prime Minister
under the Revolutionary régime, he announced that although he
supported 'those who agree to the establishment of a limit to the
size of large landholdings, I do not wish to subject the country to a
violent economic upheaval, especially at this time'.[27] His opposition
to the land reform was one of the chief reasons for his being deposed
from the office of Premier by the military junta in September, 1952.[28]

The two demands noted above—to impose a progressive tax on
large landowners and to prevent the further breakdown of small
landholdings—were the most extreme views ever expressed by the
Wafd Party, and even then only by one particular wing of the party.
This wing, which recognized the need to emphasize the importance
of social reforms, found its spokesmen in Mustafā Nusrat, Minister
of Agriculture in the Wafd government of 1943–44, and Dr. Ahmad
Husain, Director of the 'Fallāh Division' in the Ministry for Social
Affairs and later Minister of Social Affairs in the Wafd administration of 1950–51. In one of his speeches, Nusrat expressed his view as
follows: 'With regard to large landholdings, their further growth
may be impeded by the levying of progressive taxes on agricultural
land to the point where investment in land beyond a certain limit
will prove impractical'.[29] The same reasoning is followed in the
programme presented by Dr. Ahmad Husain in a research paper on
the problems of the fallāh: 'The imposition of a progressive tax on
large estates will mean that purchases beyond a certain limit—100
feddāns, for example—will not prove worth while.'[30] In the above-
mentioned speech, Nusrat also suggested putting a minimum
limit to the size of smallholdings, while Dr. Husain, who made a
similar proposal in an address before the Congress of Graduate
Egyptian Agronomists, added that it was also advisable to reintegrate
smallholdings which had been divided up in the past.[31]

These views, however, were held by only a small circle within the
Wafd, while the leadership of the party never took any steps to

[26] Gibhat Misr, *mashrū' barnāmig lirasm siyāsa qawmīya* (Cairo, 1946), p. 13.
[27] *al-Misrī*, August 8, 1952.
[28] *Cf.* a speech by Gamāl 'Abd an-Nāsir, *al-Ahrām*, April 14, 1954.
[29] *al-Misrī*, February 16, 1945.
[30] *ibid.*, April 18, 1945.
[31] *al-Ahrām*, April 24, 1945.

arrest the disintegration of smallholdings. With respect to the progressive tax on large estates, the Wafd administration did ask Parliament to agree to additional levies on the rich estates in the Aswān and Qenā provinces at the time of the malaria epidemic in the early 1940's. But this was only an emergency measure confined to a certain area, and not a planned attempt to inhibit the growth of large estates or to divert investment capital into other branches of the economy; its goal was the temporary readjustment of the fiscal burden in two areas in which the fallāhīn were sorely stricken. Nevertheless, even this limited proposal was rejected by a Parliament with a Wafdist majority.[32] The Wafd programme published in August, 1952, at the request of the junta, was printed in the party organ al-Misrī under a banner headline, 'The Levying of Progressive Taxes on Large Estates', but the text of the programme mentioned only progressive income and inheritance taxes generally,[33] and its purpose was definitely not to prevent the accumulation of large estates.

Indeed, the predominant trend in the Wafd was opposed to any encroachment upon the large landed properties. This opposition was expressed not only by leaders who were themselves large land-owners, like Fu'ād Sirāg ad-Dīn, who proclaimed, in a speech on agrarian reforms in Europe, that 'we do not wish to follow their lead; we will be content with the just distribution of state domain without molesting other property'.[34] Even 'Abd-al-Hamīd 'Abd al-Haqq, the Minister of Social Affairs in the Wafd government of 1942, announced his objections to Senator Khattāb's proposals in these words: 'I do not believe that we need consider the present unfair distribution of land—Egypt still has millions of feddāns which can be reclaimed for cultivation. . . .'[35] Moreover, the Ministry of National Economy in the Wafd government of 1950 advised the 'Congresses Committee' of the Egyptian government not to participate in the Islamic Conference called in Teheran 'because several proposals for the redistribution of land, the limiting of large agricultural property, and a number of other subjects which have been adopted from Communist doctrine and are opposed to the Constitution and laws of Egypt, are included on the agenda'.[36] The Egyptian delegate to the Second Social Welfare Seminar for Arab States in the Middle East, held under U.N. auspices in Cairo in

[32] ibid., February 29, 1944; Ghālī, al-islāh az-zirāʻī, p. 15.
[33] al-Misrī, August 1, 1952.
[34] ibid., March 15, 1943.
[35] at-Talīʻa (monthly journal of the Graduates' Association of the Egyptian University), No. 1, September 15, 1945.
[36] According to al-Ahrām, September 18, 1950.

November–December, 1952, also opposed a sub-committee recommendation that a limit be set to the size of landholdings.[37]

2. *The Views of the Protagonists of Land Reform*

The protagonists of agrarian reform in Egypt, while dealing chiefly with the limitation of the size of the large estates, also gave some attention to the question of the disintegration of smallholdings. Thus, for example, Barrāwī and 'Ulaish suggested a minimum limit of five feddāns to the holding of a family. This property would fall to the eldest son, who would be obliged to pay compensation to the other heirs for their share of the estate, the payments to be effected following the sale of each harvest. To enable him to do this, Barrāwī and 'Ulaish recommended the establishment of banks to furnish, in such cases, special loans at low interest.[38]

A minutely detailed plan on these lines was worked out by Mirrīt Ghālī in his writings on agrarian reform.[39] According to Ghālī, the minimum area should be set at three feddāns. Heirs who did not share in the land would be paid compensation by the competent authorities, who would in turn collect the money in the course of time from the heir to the land. Ghālī adds that it would not be worth while to apply the law to farms of less than one feddān, since in any case plots of this size do not support their cultivators. He further urged exemption for the heir to the land from interest on his debt, and priority in the purchase of state domain for those who did not inherit land. Ghālī also tried to find a remedy for the existing fragmentation of small landholdings. In his opinion, the owners of tiny and uneconomic plots should be encouraged to dispose of their property either through sale or through exchange. The families would later be settled by the state on its reclaimed lands (part of the cost of the alternative lands would be covered by the sale of the previous plots). The state would then consolidate these tiny holdings into larger units, which could be resold to fallāhīn as well. However, Ghālī himself pointed out that the process would of necessity be a difficult and prolonged one. Moreover, from the examples he gives of the proposed inheritance procedure, it is clear that the debt to the other heirs which the heir to a patrimony of three feddāns would have to pay amounted to approximately the entire income from such an area over six years, whereas three feddāns of good land produces barely enough to meet the minimum requirements of a single family.

[37] *al-Ahrām*, December 7, 1950.
[38] Barrāwī-'Ulaish, *op. cit.*, pp. 291, 292. Also al-Barrāwī in *al-Kutla*, April 16, 1945.
[39] Ghālī, *al-islāh az-zirā'ī*, pp. 47–8, 52–3. Mirrīt Ghālī Bey, 'Un Programme de Réforme Agraire pour l'Égypte', in *L'Égypte Contemporaine* (1947), pp. 31–6.

However, the principal change advocated in most of the plans, and the one that aroused the greatest opposition, was the proposal to limit the size of large estates. Its advocates (prior to the Military Revolution) fall into two distinct categories. The first was a group of intellectuals; they were moderate reformers whose proposals were to be carried out within the existing social and political framework through the existing parliamentary institutions. Aware of the decisive influence of the large proprietors over these institutions and over the Egyptian public as a whole, they hoped to persuade the landowners and their political supporters to agree to limiting any further expansion of large estates above a certain maximum. They pointed out that if the proprietors did not make such a concession, a day would come when the demand for forcible confiscation of their property would be raised. 'Limitation of existing property . . . is a cruel measure which governments as a rule do not agree to carry out except under the threat of social revolution. We hope that the implementation of the agrarian reform proposed by us . . . will relieve us of the necessity of confiscating landed property.' 'Every year of delay makes the problem of the large estates more critical and strengthens the arguments of those who demand more extreme measures.'[40] The adherents of this group emphasized again and again that their programme did not affect existing landed property.[41]

The opinions of this moderate group on the subject of agrarian reform were voiced chiefly by Muhammad Khattāb, Dr. Ibrāhīm Bayūmī Madkūr, and Mirrīt Ghālī. Khattāb's draft law, which was tabled in the Senate in 1944, stated in the first article that it would be illegal for any person possessing 50 feddāns of land or more to acquire additional acreage. The second article made an exception of lands transmitted through inheritance.[42] The Social Affairs Committee of the Senate approved the bill, but raised the limit to 100 feddāns. However, when the debate was resumed on the Senate floor on June 25, 1945, the government opposed the bill, and a majority of the Senators voted to return it to committee. The latter had, in the meantime, changed its mind and decided to oppose the draft. On June 16, 1947, it was finally rejected by the Senate.[43] A similar proposal was presented to the Senate by Dr. Ibrāhīm Bayūmī Madkūr during the Wafd administration of 1950–51 and was discussed by the Social Affairs Committee.[44]

[40] Ghālī, *al-islāh az-zirā'ī*, p. 65; *Un Programme de Réforme Agraire*, p. 15.
[41] E.g., Ghali, *Un Programme de Réforme Agraire*, p. 14. See also Rāfi'ī, *op. cit.*, II, p. 357.
[42] According to Ghālī, *al-islāh az-zirā'ī*, p. 62, note.
[43] Rāfi'ī, *op. cit.*, II, pp. 357–8.
[44] *al-Ahrām*, January 30, 1951.

Mirrīt Ghālī's agrarian reform programme was published in booklet form by the '*Gamā'at an-Nahda al-Qawmīya*' in 1945, and two years later in French in the quarterly *L'Égypte Contemporaine*. Ghālī at the very outset fixed the limit beyond which a landowner would be prohibited from acquiring more land at 100 feddāns. His objection to the 50-feddān limit was supported by the argument that it would 'restrict the initiative of the rural middle class, those rural notables who, in our opinion, have the vital task of infusing life into rural society'. These 'medium-sized' landowners must be protected, Ghālī went on, so that they could play a responsible role in the district councils and other local institutions. In his essay published in 1947, Ghālī added one more argument: the limit of 100 feddāns had a better chance of being accepted by a parliament in which the large landowners controlled a majority.[45] Ghālī, too, exempted from the proposed law lands transmitted by inheritance, but he thought that by enacting his law the large estates would be broken up after two or three generations through inheritance, and that there was, therefore, no necessity to reduce existing estates. The following additional reasons against such a measure are given: (*a*) compensation payments would lay too great a burden on the state at a time when it would be better to use government funds for the amelioration of new lands; (*b*) it would raise extremely difficult administrative problems; (*c*) it would be impossible to carry out the confiscation of large estates within the framework of the Constitution and the measure would lead to serious disturbances. Only those landowners whose property encompassed entire villages should be made to relinquish part of their holdings—through either forced sale or confiscation.[46]

The second group of agrarian reformers insisted on more extreme measures, including the confiscation of large estates and their redistribution among the fallāhīn. As it was impossible to reconcile such a step with the character of the existing régime in Egypt, this second group also sought a change in the political régime. The cause of a more just distribution of the land was taken up in the last years before the Revolution by the two extreme nationalist factions which had grown up outside the pale of Egyptian parliamentary life during the 'thirties and 'forties, the *Moslem Brotherhood* and *Misr al-Fatāt*. In his book on Egyptian religious movements.[47] J. Heyworth-Dunne

---

[45] Ghālī, *al-islāh az-zirā'ī*, p. 60, note; *Un Programme de Réforme Agraire*, p. 12.

[46] Ghālī, *al-islāh az-zirā'ī*, pp. 61–5; *Un Programme de Réforme Agraire* pp. 13–18.

[47] J. Heyworth-Dunne, *Religious and Political Trends in Modern Egypt* (Washington, 1950), p. 51.

mentions that in 1948 the Moslem Brotherhood issued a leaflet calling upon the government to distribute farmland in accordance with the precepts of the Prophet, viz. to forbid the leasing of land and to deny any person the right to possess more land than he himself could cultivate, the remainder to be distributed gratis to landless peasants. Although the Misr al-Fatāt group did not touch on the question of distribution of landed property in its political programme published in 1940 (which included various demands concerning the fallāhīn and agriculture),[48] in 1950–51 it began to advocate redistribution of village lands.[49]

However, these two groups never regarded this aspect of their respective programmes as of great importance, and did not work out a detailed practicable plan for the implementation of the agrarian reforms they advocated. Only after the Military Revolution, when the Moslem Brotherhood was requested, together with all other parties, to publish its programme, and after the junta's own plan for agrarian reform had already become known, did the Brotherhood elaborate their demands in greater detail and include among them a maximum size to large estates. They relinquished their championship of free distribution to the fallāhīn of all lands above the maximum and agreed instead that 'they should be sold to landless peasants at a reasonable price and on easy terms'. They also waived their slogan that lands should not be leased.[50] Ahmad Hussain, a former leader of the Misr al-Fatāt, now urged before a meeting sponsored by the Liberation Movement of the Revolutionary officers that the implementation of the Agrarian Reform Law of 1952 be speeded up and steps be taken for the confiscation of estates exceeding 50 feddāns in area.[51]

As against these nationalist extremist groups, whose programmes for a more just distribution of landed property were rather vague and general, several leftist authors were turning out a more explicit plan for agrarian reform. Thus, Dr. Rāshid al-Barrāwī advocated fixing the maximum size of all landed property in Egypt at 50 or 100 feddāns. The remaining area would be bought by the government or, if means were lacking, would be confiscated for distribution among smallholders.[52] A pamphlet on *The Problem of the Fallāh*, with a

---

[48] See *Oriente Moderno*, April, 1940, p. 186. At that time the group was called 'al-hizb al-watanī al-islāmī,'

[49] See Barrāwī, *haqiqat-ul-inqilāb*, p. 189. By then the group's name had been changed into 'al-hizb al-ishtirākī'.

[50] *al-Misrī*, August 2, 1952.

[51] *al-Ahrām*, September 4, 1953.

[52] See his article in *al-Kutla*, April 16, 1945. In this article Barrāwī expressed more radical views than those to be found in the book of which he was co-author with 'Ulaish (see above).

complete programme for agrarian reform, was published in 1945 by the Communist writer Sādiq Sa'ad. Sa'ad called for legislation to 'prohibit individuals and companies from increasing in future their landed property above an area of 50 feddāns of farm land. In this way, large areas would become available which should be apportioned equally among landless fallāhīn and agricultural workers, that is to say, among nearly 2 million impoverished peasants'. Land in excess of 50 feddāns per owner was to be confiscated without compensation, 'since the poor smallholders have a much greater right than anyone else to the land which they cultivate with their own hands'. However, as larger farms are technically and economically superior to smaller ones, the redistribution of the land must go hand-in-hand with a campaign to encourage producers' co-operatives among the fallāhīn, i.e. collective farms. Sa'ad assumed from the start that he would be accused 'of spreading ideas dangerous to the existing social order', and to these accusations he replied that 'official economists in Great Britain suggested even more revolutionary changes in the social order when they urged the abolition of all farm property'.[53] (He meant, of course, the abolition of private ownership of agricultural land, i.e. nationalization; other leftist publicists also stressed that they did not advocate nationalization of the land.[54])

Although several leftist and Communist writers pieced together a kind of 'agrarian programme' that included the elimination of the large estates, these demands, and the agrarian question as a whole, did not occupy an important place in their political and social struggle. Even during the 1940's, when Communist activity was legal, their principal periodical at that time—*al-Fagr al-Gadīd*—hardly touched on the agrarian question at all. In contrast with most of the other parties, the Communists had no roots in the Egyptian villages.

II. SOCIO-POLITICAL BACKGROUND OF LAND REFORM UNDER THE MILITARY RÉGIME

On July 23, 1952, a group of army officers seized power in Egypt. Only two months after the *coup d'état*, an Agrarian Reform Law was enacted and about a year later all lands of the reigning Muhammad 'Alī family were confiscated. The early date of these reforms indicates that they have been an integral part of the Military Revolution. To explain this, one must look into the factors which led to this Revolution.

[53] Sa'ad, *op. cit.*, pp. 61–9.
[54] See, e.g., Barrāwī's article in *al-Kutla* quoted above.

A detailed analysis of the political factors leading to the Military Revolution would be out of place in this article. They can be summarized as follows: the old parliamentary system had been undermined to such a degree that in 1952 it was no longer capable of forming a stable administration; during the first six months of that year Egypt had five different governments. Egypt's foreign relations had been brought to an impasse by the unilateral abrogation of the Anglo-Egyptian Treaty and by anti-British guerrilla warfare, hopeless as it was under the political conditions of that time. On the other hand, the army had been strengthened as a result of the conflict with Israel, and at the same time its indignation against the civil administration and the Court had been aggravated by their conduct during the Arab-Israel war (which was regarded by the army officers as one of the principal causes of the defeat). The impotence of the old régime on the one hand, and on the other the self-confidence of the army officers, who realized that they were the only factor with real power, found a drastic expression in the events of 'Black Saturday' on January 26, 1952, when the King and his government were shown to be no longer capable of ruling Cairo's ravaging mob without calling upon the army for help.

Even if these political conditions had been the only factor inducing the army officers to attempt the complete annihilation of the old system of parliamentary monarchy, it would be enough to explain the eagerness and speed with which a land-reform law was introduced and carried out. Since large landowners had been the controlling power of Egypt's legislative and executive institutions and political organizations, the attempt to prevent an eventual restoration of the old régime was bound to involve an attack on the basis of their social and political power, i.e. on large landed property. Like agrarian reforms in most countries where they have been implemented, the Egyptian land reform, too, derived powerful impetus from such political considerations: 'The decision to carry out a land reform crystallizes the determination to break with the past in an irrevocable way.'[55] In speeches delivered by the leading Revolutionary officers, phrases like the following were not uncommon: 'We have wiped out agrarian feudalism (*iqtā'*) in order to eliminate political feudalism.'[56]

In many countries this political aspect of agrarian reform had a nationalist flavour: either because the old agrarian régime had been introduced by foreign rule and was abolished in the wake of a successful struggle for independence—as happened in some Asian

[55] Doreen Warriner, *Land Reform and Economic Development* (National Bank of Egypt, Cairo, 1955), p. 9.
[56] Bikbāshī (Lt.-Col.) Husain ash-Shāfi'ī, *al-Ahrām*, April 29, 1953. See also Ahmad Kāmil Qutb in *al-Ahrām*, April 9, 1954.

countries;[57] or because 'the struggle against minorities of foreign origin who owned the largest area of land (gave) considerable impulse to the (agrarian) reform movement'—which was the case in many of the eastern European countries after the First World War.[58] As far as this factor was of any importance in Egypt, it took the eastern European form rather than the Asian one. In contrast to many of the Asian countries, land reform was carried out in Egypt in the wake of internal changes, and not as a corollary of liberation from foreign rule. Yet the relation between land reform and 'the struggle against minorities of foreign origin' had been weakened in Egypt by the fact that the area of land owned by foreigners had been decreasing rapidly in the years preceding the Revolution,[59] and that a part of these lands was owned by companies to whom the land reform did not apply. Nevertheless, some such relation existed, the 'foreigners' in this case being the remnants of the 'Turco-Egyptian' elements, headed by the Muhammad 'Alī family, which ruled Egypt in the nineteenth century, rather than the non-Egyptians owning the lands which are shown in the statistics as 'owned by foreigners'. Although the Turco-Egyptians, except the Muhammad 'Alī family, had ceased to be an important group of large landowners, the fact that the income from many large *waqfs* established by them had been dedicated to Turkish institutions was given great publicity.[60] Moreover, the non-Egyptian origin of the Muhammad 'Alī family (and some of its members' ignorance of the Arabic language) was frequently mentioned in connection with the land reform, and stress was laid on the argument that the lands it held had been taken forcibly from the Egyptian people.[61] The nationalist agitation in connection with the land reform reached its climax with the announcement that the Turkish Ambassador to Egypt, Fu'ād Khulūsī Togāi, had intervened in the expropriation of the estate of his wife, Princess Amina

---

[57] *Cf.* United Nations, Department of Economic Affairs, *Progress in Land Reform* (New York, 1954), p. 52. See also Konrad Bekker, 'Land Reform Legislation in India', in *The Middle East Journal*, Summer, 1951, p. 320.

[58] League of Nations, *European Conference on Rural Life*, 1939, No. 2, p. 44. *Cf.* H. T. Montague Bell, *The Near East Year Book, 1931–32* (London, 1931), pp. 597–608, 933–8; Doreen Warriner, *Economics of Peasant Farming* (Oxford University Press, 1939), p. 16.

[59] From 408,683 feddāns in 1940 to 215,783 feddāns in 1950 (or from 7·0 per cent to 3·6 per cent of all privately owned lands).

[60] See, e.g., *al-Ahrām*, November 30, 1953, and December 4, 1953. The *waqf* problem, including Egyptian views on this question, has not been mentioned in this paper since we dealt with some of its aspects in a separate paper.

[61] *Cf. hādhā-l-fallāh wa-usrat Muhammad 'Alī* (Cairo, Matba'at garīdatas-Sabāh, n.d.). See also *al-Ahrām*, November 13, 1953, and 'Abd an-Nāsir's speech to beneficiaries of the land reform at Nag' Hamādī, *al-Ahrām*, July 4, 1955.

Mukhtār of the Muhammad 'Alī family, claiming that she was not an Egyptian citizen and that therefore her property was not liable to expropriation.[62]

Political factors, however, had not been the only cause of the Military Revolution; Egyptian society, too, had undergone important changes which found their expression in the early 'fifties. Up to 1950 social tensions following the Second World War found their release in the villages in outbursts of individual violence; in 1951, for the first time in modern Egyptian history, there occurred some rebellions of fallāhīn making common cause against their landlords. This unrest may have been in part due to the rise in rents following the tremendous rise in cotton prices. One of the fiercest incidents occurred in June at Buhūt, a village on the estates of the Badrāwī-'Āshūr family in Gharbīya Province. The main outlines, emerging out of conflicting stories, are as follows[63]: an argument between the *nāzir* (manager) of the Buhūt estate and some of the tenants concerning the rent to be paid by them led to the use of violence. Other fallāhīn from Buhūt village gathered and moved in a hostile manner towards the mansion of the Badrāwī family. They were shot at from the mansion and more fallāhīn joined them. Then security forces were summoned by the landlord and a battle broke out in which there were several fatal casualties. Similar events occurred, in the same year, on the Kufūr Nigm estates (Sharqīya Province) of Prince Muhammad 'Alī Tawfīq (then Crown Prince).[64] In October, 1951, the tenants of state domain at as-Sirū (Daqahlīya Province) squatted on lands formerly rented by them, demanding that the government should sell these lands to them, as promised, and not implement its new decision to put them up for sale by auction.[65]

This unrest in the Egyptian village revealed that the equilibrium of Egyptian society had been unsettled. Yet the old régime reacted only by announcing its intention to introduce some minor reforms (which were never carried out); the landlords, and the social system in general, were not affected. Moreover, there was no organized civilian group or power willing and able to fight for more radical reforms and to implement them. There were only the army officers, whose social origin was in the lower middle classes (except some of the highest ranks); as soon as their loyalty to the old régime had been undermined they were the only force interested in overthrowing

---

[62] *Cf.* the Egyptian Press of November–December, 1953, especially *al-Ahrām*, November 21, 1953, and December 5, 1953.

[63] According to *al-Ahrām*, June 24, 1951; December 30, 1953; January 18, 1954.

[64] Barrāwī, *haqīqat al-inqilāb*, pp. 92, 189; *al-Ahrām*, June 18, 1954.

[65] *al-Misrī*, October 25, 1951.

M.T.—7

it and carrying out the necessary reforms, and at the same time capable of doing so.

Thus the Military Revolution was the result not only of political difficulties but also of social ferment; and the agrarian reform was conceived not only as a means to prevent the restoration of the old political system but also as a response to social unrest. In order to re-establish social equilibrium in the Egyptian countryside and to forestall Communist revolution, landed property would have to be redistributed and the relation between landlord and peasant regulated. This purpose of the Egyptian land reform has been formulated most clearly by Sayyid Mar'ī, the leading administrator of the Reform, in the following words: 'We all remember the days preceding the revolution of July, 1952; we remember how the Egyptian village became restless as a result of dangerous agitation; we remember the events which led to bloodshed and destruction of property—for the first time in the history of the Egyptian village. Would the large landowners have preferred to be left exposed to the wind blowing through this unrest, exploiting want and poverty, until it became a tempest uprooting everything . . . and endangering, perhaps, the peace of our entire fatherland? Do they not fare better under stable conditions, the income from the land being given to its tillers and its price to its former owners to be invested by them in the development of Egyptian industry and commerce? . . .'[66]

The last words quoted from Sayyid Mar'ī reveal that the land reform as conceived by the Egyptian army officers had yet another purpose. They were conscious of Egypt's deficient industrial development, in which they saw the source of its backwardness and military weakness. It was the third purpose of land reform to divert capital from the acquisition of landed property to investment in industry.[67] To what extent land reform in Egypt has succeeded in its political, social, and economic purposes as conceived by its initiators is a question which needs a more detailed analysis than the scope of this article allows.

Summing up, we may discern three stages in the development of Egyptian attitudes towards land reform since Egypt became an independent country: (1) complete unconcern until the Second World War; (2) public discussion in the 'forties between the parliamentary parties, the moderate reformers, and the protagonists of

[66] al-Ahrām, September 4, 1954.

[67] Cf. also the official explanation of the Agrarian Reform Law, Journal de Commerce et de la Marine (Alexandria). September 12, 1952. Mar'ī himself has frequently elaborated this subject, e.g., in al-Ahrām, April 13, 1954, and Sayed Marii, 'The Agrarian Reform in Egypt' in International Labour Review, February, 1954, p. 150.

radical reform; and (3) the 'fifties, in which land reform was carried out by the military régime. The change from the first to the second stage was caused by the social upheaval resulting from World War II, as well as by the emergence of a group of intellectuals giving thought to Egypt's social problems and of extremist leftist and rightist parties outside the framework of Parliament. The change from the second to the third stage was caused by the spreading of social ferment into the countryside, as well as by the emergence of a power both interested in overthrowing the old régime and capable of doing so.

PAN-ARABISM AND BRITISH POLICY

by ÉLIE KEDOURIE

PAN-ARABISM AND EGYPT

IN THE YEARS following the First World War, pan-Arabism was the only political doctrine to make headway and to exert a powerful appeal in the Arab-speaking lands. The nature of the war settlement itself and the political power which some of its leading votaries acquired in consequence of this settlement contributed alike to such a result. The situation developed suddenly, with revolutionary abruptness. Men who, before the destruction of the Ottoman Empire, were quite obscure, emerged all at once after 1919, not only to preach a doctrine which got the Arab East into its grip, but actually to exercise political power in one of the former provinces of the Empire. In 1914 such a state of affairs was impossible to imagine. It is true that there were then murmurings in Beirut, and that Syrian *émigrés* in Cairo were demanding a decrease in meddling from Constantinople and the enlargement of local initiative. But these grievances were local and specific; they related to the quality of government services, or to the financial relations between the centre and the provinces, or to the proper scope of local administration; and those who sought redress for such grievances were mostly men well known in their communities, able perhaps to conduct a sober constitutional opposition, but not to entertain grandiose, limitless ambitions. How they would have fared under imperial rule, where their opposition would have taken them, how the Arab provinces would have developed under their leadership, it is now impossible to say. The war made England and the Ottoman Empire enemies; England fomented a revolt in the Hijaz against the Turks, and to this revolt gravitated a number of disaffected Ottoman officers who, when the war ended with the triumph of their patron, claimed the leadership of the Arab movement and were eventually enabled, by devious and complicated means, to obtain political control of Mesopotamia, where they set up government as the Kingdom of Iraq.

The new leaders thrown up by the war were pan-Arab by nature. They came to politics not through consideration of concrete difficulties or the grind of pressing affairs or daily responsibility, but by way of a doctrine. Their doctrine was compounded of certain European principles which made language and nationality synonymous, of a faith in sedition and violence, and of contempt for moderation. They believed that the Arabs, because they spoke Arabic, a language different from Turkish, were *ipso facto* entitled to secede from the Ottoman Empire and to form a state where everybody who spoke Arabic would be included. They were not ambitious for the community they knew, or the locality where they were born and reared. The European doctrine of linguistic nationalism with which they were imbued, the oecumenical claims of the Arabian Caliphate the glories of which they aspired to revive, the impetuosity of their youth, and the insignificance of their origins and their prospects alike combined to help them nurse ambitions to which only their dreams could set a bound. As one sympathizer with Arab nationalism, Professor Sir Hamilton Gibb, put it: 'The Arab nation . . . like all other nations, is not an entity delimited by ethnographical data, nor the fortuitous result of geographical or historical association, but the function of an act of will.'[1]

The will of these young officers willed an Arab nation, and ethnography, geography, or history were of consequence only as they offered sustenance to their imagination. When, therefore, the miraculous circumstances gave them suddenly a country to govern, it was not gratitude to fate and their patrons that they felt, but rather that they were cheated of their dream. They had desired an Arab nation and an Arab state, and they got Iraq, a specific country with specific frontiers. They denounced the imperialist dismemberment of the Arab nation, and called the boundaries drawn up at the peace settlement arbitrary and artificial. This was indeed true, for what otherwise can boundaries be when they spring up where none had existed before? These officers, of course, did not think to blame themselves for having, by their disaffection, helped the Powers they were now denouncing to defeat the Ottoman Empire, and thus to erect these hated boundaries. With the establishment of these men in the government of Iraq, therefore, pan-Arabism itself was endowed with a political base from which to prepare future incursions.

[1] *The Near East: Problems and Prospects*, P. W. Ireland, editor (Chicago, 1942), p. 70.

The settlement of 1921, which created the Kingdom of Iraq, contained the seeds of its own destruction; for it gave power to men who were intent precisely on overthrowing such a settlement.

The ambitions of these men were, to start with, confined to the Fertile Crescent—Iraq, Syria, Palestine, and the Lebanon—the stage on which, during their youth under the Ottoman Empire, their dreams were accustomed to play. Between the wars, and after the outbreak of the Second World War, their efforts were bent on securing a dislodgement of the French from Syria and the Lebanon, and a curtailment or, if possible, a suppression of Zionist activities in Palestine; thereafter, on putting together a unitary or a federal Arab state embracing the Fertile Crescent. This was the burden of Nuri al-Sa'id's proposal to Mr. Casey, Minister of State in the Middle East, in December, 1942. This was the original pan-Arab programme, on the realization of which the original pan-Arabs had always set their hearts. But this was not yet to be. Instead, after negotiations lasting from 1943 to 1945, a quite different scheme of Arab unity was set afoot. In this scheme, there was no amalgamation or federation of states; it provided, rather, for an alliance of sovereign states in which, unexpectedly, Egypt figured as the leader.

Egypt had never before manifested any interest in Pan-Arabism, and though we do not yet know all the negotiations which led to the formation of the Arab League, we do have a few details which throw light on Egyptian policy, and which explain in some measure this new and sudden development. A pan-Arab policy for Egypt seems to have been throughout the handiwork of King Farouk and some of his entourage. The evidence for this is cumulative and convincing.

Farouk's father, King Fouad, is said to have nursed the ambition of becoming the Muslim Caliph in succession to the dethroned Ottomans, and Farouk to have desired to follow his father's policy. In 1939, on the occasion of a meeting in Cairo of Arab magnates to discuss Palestine, while the King, his entourage, and his foreign guests were present at a mosque for the Friday prayers, the palace officials prevented the Imam of the mosque from officiating as usual, and the King himself led the congregation in prayer—a traditional prerogative and attribute of the Caliph—and on emerging from the mosque was proclaimed a true Caliph and a pious ruler. In 1946, again, when Ismail Sidqi was Prime Minister, the King, on his own initiative, assembled a meeting of Arab kings and presidents on his estate at Inshass to which neither the Prime Minister nor the Foreign Minister were invited, and at which decisions on pan-Arab policy and on Palestine were taken. 'People then understood', writes Muhammad Husain Haikal, the eminent Egyptian statesman who recounts the incident in his *Memoirs*, 'that King Farouk's personal policy had for its aim the establishment of his personal leadership over the Arab states. However, the Ministry raised no protest, and did not wish to make an issue of what happened.'[2] In May, 1948, also, when the Egyptian troops went into Palestine to oppose the establishment of the State of Israel, they did so at the King's instance and on his orders. Hostilities began on May 15, and until May 11, writes Haikal who was at the time President of the Senate, al-Nuqrashi, the Prime Minister, was quite unwilling to intervene in Palestine; 'he used to say that he would not commit the Egyptian army to a position such that the British troops stationed on the Canal would be able to take them in the rear, . . . but from one day to the next this opinion changed. On May 12 al-Nuqrashi asked me to summon Parliament to a secret session to ask authority for Egyptian troops to enter Palestine. People learnt a little while later that the Minister of Defence, General Muhammad Haidar Pasha, the King's man and his private aide-de-camp, received an order direct from the King, and he then ordered battalions of the Egyptian army to cross the frontiers into Palestine, without the knowledge of the Prime Minister, and without waiting for the decision of Parliament and the decision of the Cabinet.'[3]

The same story, with minor variations, emerged from Muhammad Haidar's examination at the trial in October, 1953, by the Revolutionary Court in Cairo, of Ibrahim Abd el-Hadi who was, in 1948, chief of the Royal cabinet.

Farouk, of course, did not carry out his pan-Arab policies single-handed. He had coadjutors and instruments, and of these the most prominent were Ali Mahir and Abd al-Rahman Azzam. Ali Mahir became chief of the Royal cabinet soon after Farouk came to the throne, and acquired great influence as the King's political adviser. It was during his tenure of office that an active pan-Arab policy was initiated. In 1939 the British government convened a Round-Table Conference on Palestine to which the Arab states and Egypt were invited. The Egyptian Prime Minister, then Muhammad Mahmud Pasha, decided to lead, himself, the Egyptian delegation to the Conference. It was then suddenly announced that Ali Mahir would go instead, and would take with him Abd al-Rahman Azzam—later to become Secretary-General of the Arab League. 'I do not know', writes Haikal, who was a member of Muhammad Mahmud's Ministry, 'that the Cabinet ever delegated this matter to Ali Mahir Pasha, for the question never came before the Cabinet.'[4] Haikal

---

[2] Muhammad Husain Haikal, *Memoirs* (Arabic text), Vol. II (Cairo, 1953), p. 319.

[3] *ibid.*, p. 330. [4] *ibid.*, p. 155.

then goes on to say how, when Ali Mahir was away in London, certain notions relating to the restoration of Islamic principles of government, to the efficacy of quick dictatorial reforms, and such-like, began to get increasing publicity, and he adds: 'It is true that these notions were current before the chief of the Royal cabinet's visit to England; but those who advanced them had done so somewhat shamefacedly. After his departure, however, this propaganda became more active, and the Palace was not averse to such notions being attributed to it.'[5]

In August, 1939, the King dismissed Muhammad Mahmud's cabinet, and appointed Ali Mahir Prime Minister, who included in his cabinet Azzam, as Minister first of Religious Foundations, and then of Social Affairs. As soon as this government was formed, it set up a so-called 'Territorial Army', which seems to have been Azzam's invention and of which he was put in charge. This territorial army seems to have been devised to indoctrinate youth and to prepare armed bands which could be used by the government for political purposes. In this, Ali Mahir and Azzam were merely following a fashion made popular by the Nazis and the Fascists, a fashion already adopted in Iraq, and in Egypt itself, where Blueshirts and Greenshirts organized by the Wafd and by the Young Egypt Party made the streets of Cairo hideous with riots and molestations.

The territorial army attempted, as the eminent Orientalist Ettore Rossi observed at the time, to take up again 'with new regulations and new aims'[6] the traditions of these organizations which had been dissolved by Muhammad Mahmud Pasha when he took office in 1938. A writer knowledgeable in Muslim Brotherhood affairs, Dr. Heyworth-Dunne, thinks that Azzam took the idea of a territorial army from Hasan al-Banna, the Leader of the Brotherhood,[7] and it is worthy of note that the Brotherhood had its own private army organized in battalions and regiments, members of which had to swear to defend the faith and to obey orders unquestioningly.[8] Among other members of Ali Mahir's Cabinet were Salih Harb and Mustafa al-Shurbatchi, known for anti-British agitations and for their connections with the Muslim Brotherhood and similar bodies; as was the Chief of Staff appointed by Ali Mahir, Aziz Ali al-Misri, who 'never', says Haikal, 'at any time hid his admiration for Germany'.

Ali Mahir's Ministry lasted from August, 1939, until June, 1940. Britain was at war with Germany, which took the offensive in the

[5] *ibid.*, p. 156.

[6] *Oriente Moderno* (Rome, 1939), p. 512.

[7] J. Heyworth-Dunne, *Religious and Political Trends in Modern Egypt* (Washington, 1950), p. 36.

[8] Ishaq Musa al-Husaini, *The Muslim Brotherhood* (Arabic text) (Beirut, 1955), pp. 108–9.

spring of 1940 and soon scored a brilliant and resounding victory. Egypt was bound to Britain by an alliance, but under Ali Mahir's administration and especially in its last days, Egypt was lukewarm towards her ally, and perhaps worse. The British, comments Haikal, 'were seeing with their own eyes what was taking place in Egypt, and hearing that Abd al-Rahman Azzam Bey, the Minister of Social Affairs, and Saleh Harb Pasha, the Minister of War, were talking at every social gathering of German victories and British defeats. . . .'[9] The British Ambassador demanded the resignation of Ali Mahir; the King dismissed him, and Ali Mahir delivered a bitter speech in Parliament denouncing the British for meddling in the internal affairs of Egypt.

It was these men and their party who, inspiring the King or inspired by him, invented and propagated pan-Arabism as a policy for Egypt. It is true that Egypt negotiated the formation of the Arab League when they were under a cloud, the Wafd in power, and Mustafa al-Nahhas Prime Minister. We do not yet know what convinced al-Nahhas that pan-Arabism was a paying policy, but no doubt the desire to please the King, to dish his opponents by adopting their policy, the dislike of Iraq's aggrandizement should Nuri al-Sa'id's scheme be realized, the approval of the British, and visions of future grandeur had their part to play. But it is clear that the policy originated neither with the Wafd nor with al-Nahhas. It originated with the King or with men who, out of either personal ambition or doctrinaire conviction, conceived the dream of an authoritarian Muslim state in Egypt embracing gradually all the Arabs, and perhaps in the fullness of time all the Muslims. Their inspiration was not strictly the same as that of the original pan-Arabs; but this is not to say that they contradicted each other. The ideal of the pan-Arabs was authoritarian also. They desired to transform the heterogeneous, fissiparous, sceptical populations of the Fertile Crescent to the likeness of their dream, with all differences suddenly annihilated, and external unity the emblem of a deeper, still more fundamental internal unity: one state, one nation, one creed.

It is said that pan-Islamism and pan-Arabism are contradictory. Owing to an historical accident the pan-Arabs had acquired the reputation of being opposed to pan-Islamism. Pan-Islamism was used by the Ottomans to provide a support for their Empire; when the pan-Arabs rose, they necessarily had to emphasize the opposition between pan-Arabism and pan-Islamism. In Egypt, of course, there was no place and no need for such opposition: the enemy was Britain, not the Ottoman Empire. Islamic sentiment and Islamic solidarity gave body and passion to the struggle against the foreigner. A remark-

[9] Haikal, *op. cit.*, II, pp. 180–1.

able illustration of this appeared in a prayer written by Hassan al-Banna, the Leader of the Muslim Brothers, for the use of his followers:

'O God, Lord of the Creation who giveth assurance to the insecure, who humbleth the vainglorious, and who layeth low the tyrants, accept our prayer and answer our call. Enable us to obtain our right, and give back to us our freedom and independence. O God, those British usurpers have occupied our land and made free with our rights; they have oppressed the country and spread evil in it. O God, turn their intrigues away from us, weaken their strength and disperse their hosts; annihilate them and those who have helped them to victory, or have aided them, or have made peace with them, or have befriended them, in a manner worthy of an all-powerful and majestic One. O God, let their actions rebound on them, let calamities descend on them, humiliate their kingdom, release Your land from their power, and let them have no sway over any of the Believers. Amen.'[10]

Here we see well exemplified the general character of Islam as at once a political and a religious creed. The pan-Arabs desired the unification of the Arab lands; they desired to expel the foreigner. These aims are acceptable to, and indeed mandatory on, Muslims, for the Arab world is the cradle of Islam and to expel the foreigner from it is a meritorious action. Such is the agreement in principle between pan-Islamism and pan-Arabism. It explains how the original pan-Arabs in the Fertile Crescent, though different in outlook and assumptions from Farouk and his advisers, could effect some kind of junction with them, and sign after long and no doubt difficult negotiations the Pact of the Arab League.

At this further stage in the progress of pan-Arabism, the revisionism implicit in the settlement of 1921 became explicit. To the Pact of the League two annexes were attached, one dealing with Palestine, and the other with 'Arab countries which are not members of the Council of the League'. In both cases the League served notice of its right to meddle in the affairs of countries outside the jurisdiction of its members, and of its claim to advise and direct Powers ruling over or having interests in countries inhabited by Arabs, until such Powers should agree to liquidate their authority and their interests in favour of pan-Arabism. The Zionists did object to the annex on Palestine, and pointed out to the Mandatory Power that it was a derogation of its authority.[11] The Mandatory Power remained

[10] Al-Husaini, *op. cit.*, p. 119.

[11] At a meeting between Jewish Agency officials and Foreign Office officials on March 21, 1945, and in a letter from Dr. Weizmann to the Secretary of State for Foreign Affairs, of March 27. I am indebted for this information to the Weizmann Archives, Rehovoth, Israel.

serene and unmoved, not thinking that a day would come when claims such as these would affect more than mere Zionists.

BRITAIN AND THE ARAB LEAGUE

Such were the men and such the policies which the British government encouraged with its support and blessing. On two public occasions during the Second World War, once in a speech at the Mansion House in 1941—to which great importance seems to have been attached, for it was published as a White Paper—and once in answer to a question in the House of Commons in February, 1943, the Foreign Secretary declared that it was 'natural and right' that cultural, economic, and political ties among the Arab countries should be strengthened: 'many Arab thinkers' desired, it seemed, a greater degree of unity than was then enjoyed by the Arab peoples; 'no such appeal from our friends should go unanswered'; and the British government would give 'full support to any scheme that commands general approval'.

It is well known that in the 1930's, Germany and Italy—by skilful propaganda, by judicious disbursements, by the powerful appeal of their efficiency and success—established themselves as the champions of, and could set the pace for, Arab nationalism. And yet when one comes to examine what—with their freedom from local and imperial responsibilities, and their lack of scruple—they were in the end prepared to concede, one is struck with their discretion and circumspection, compared with the generous and insouciant abandon of British policy. In the summer of 1940, when Rashid Ali al-Kailani was engaged in the preliminaries of his conspiracy to take power in Iraq and range it alongside the Axis, he sent an emissary to Turkey who presented to von Papen, the German Ambassador, a list of demands which included the confirmation by the Axis of the independence of all Arab countries, the abolition of the Jewish National Home, and the recognition of Arab unity.[12] But neither Germany nor Italy would be drawn so far and, after months of consideration, they made a declaration in October stating that they desired to see the Arab countries prosper and occupy among the peoples of the world a position commensurate with their natural and historical importance, that they had always followed with interest the Arab struggle for independence, that in this struggle the Arabs could count on the full sympathy of the Axis.

Again, in April, 1941, when Rashid Ali was in power, and before he declared war on Britain, he concluded, as the official history of the Indian army records, a secret Treaty whereby in return for

[12] The list is reproduced in *al-Irfan* (Sidon, August, 1951).

recognizing a union—whenever effected—between Iraq and Syria the Axis would receive oil and pipeline concessions, the lease of three ports on the Syrian coast, and the right to construct naval and military bases thereon.[13] And even when Rashid Ali's movement against the British was under way in May, 1941, and Hitler was persuaded to give some help, he was not ready to go beyond careful and qualified generalities. In his directive of May 23, 1941, he laid down the policy on which propaganda was to be based: 'Victory by the Axis Powers will liberate the lands of the Middle East from the British yoke and give them the right of self-determination [handwritten note: except Syria]. Let those who love liberty join the anti-British front.'[14]

Exactly the same demands as were made to the Germans were made—albeit by different persons—to the British government. And the sympathy of the British government was full indeed, and active. They elbowed the French out of the Levant, to the Zionists they turned a deaf ear, and the scheme of Arab unity, realized by a fortuitous agreement between Farouk and the original pan-Arabs, they supported and blessed. What, then, was anticipated from such a policy?

The policy rested on a theory and a hope of which there are many expressions, official and unofficial. The Arab League, as Lord Altrincham (who was Minister of State in the Middle East from the assassination of Lord Moyne until 1945) said in an address at the Sorbonne in May, 1947, was encouraged by Britain; but he claimed that it was an autonomous Power created by the Arabs themselves and represented their unanimous resolve to act independently in world affairs. Theirs was an ancient civilization now being reborn, and it was possible to capture their friendship and goodwill by helping them in this enterprise. Lord Altrincham buttressed his hopes by a curious argument. If the Palestine White Paper of 1939, he explained, had not been issued, the whole Arab world would have been against the Allies in the most dangerous years of the war, from 1940 to 1942; hence the way to safeguard Western interests in general and British interests in particular was to act with the Arabs, assembled in their new League.[15] This was to confuse the wishes and anticipations of those who invented the White Paper of 1939 with what, in fact, happened. For it was precisely in these years between 1940 and 1942 that the Arab world manifested great hostility to Britain.

[13] Compton Mackenzie, *Eastern Epic*, Vol. I, 1951, p. 93.
[14] *History of the Second World War: the Mediterranean and Middle East,* Vol. II, 1956, p. 334.
[15] The address is printed in *Politique Étrangère* (Paris, July, 1947).

What saved the British position in the Middle East was not the White Paper, but military power, Mr. Churchill's daring, and Hitler's obsession with the conquest of Russia. Such arguments deserve mention to show the foundations on which such grandiose hopes were built. Lord Altrincham's views are worthy of notice because they provide evidence of the terms in which someone who had held high office connected with the Middle East was prepared to think of policy.

But to appreciate the full scope and ramifications of this theory, we must go to unofficial sources, to the writings of some British academics on Middle Eastern affairs, among which those of Professor Sir Hamilton Gibb are noteworthy. The theory, we find, is concerned, in the first place, with a presumed Muslim ethic, and, in the second, with a presumed difference within the ranks of Arab nationalists. As to the first, Gibb explains that though Muslim society has suffered from violence and lawlessness, and from corruptions introduced by non-Arabs,[16] its true principles, which had been so particularly safeguarded by Arab Muslim orthodoxy, could still be applied in the Arab Muslim East. 'Islam', for instance, "still maintained the balance between the exaggerated opposites of *bourgeois* capitalism and communism,' and 'while hostile to banking capital and unrestricted exchange it sanctioned private property and commercial capital'; Islam 'had not succumbed to the obsession with the economic side of life which was characteristic of almost all our Western societies'. Gibb asserted that 'it is by these and similar ideas that the thought of the Arab nationalists is being more and more strongly influenced'.[17] After the Arab League was formed, Gibb explained that the 'duty laid upon the Arab leaders is, in its essence, closely parallel to that laid upon the leaders of the United Nations'.[18]

As to the Arab nationalists, Gibb said that there were 'two kinds of Arab nationalists: those whom I call by that name, and those whom I call pan-Arabs'. The pan-Arabs were intolerant bigots, while the nationalists, though certainly respectful of Islam, desired also to adopt Western ideas in order to combat feudalism and internecine rivalries, and to collaborate with the non-Muslim minorities. 'Such there are in all the regions of the Arab East—Egypt, Palestine, Syria, Iraq, even', he asserted, 'Arabia—and it is upon them that the hopes of a revived, progressive, respected and self-respecting Arab nationhood depend.' Let, therefore, said Gibb, advocating some such plan

[16] The question is discussed at greater length in my article, 'Islam and the Orientalists,' *British Journal of Sociology*, September, 1956.

[17] *The Near East: Problems and Prospects*, P. W. Ireland, editor (Chicago, 1942), p. 62.

[18] 'Toward Arab Unity,' *Foreign Affairs* (New York, October, 1945), p. 129.

as that being then pushed by Nuri al-Sa'id in British official quarters, let a federation of the Arab lands in Asia be constructed, and the sound Arab nationalists would be able to get on with the work which centuries of Sassanid corruption and Ottoman malpractice had left undone: 'it is a rational, reasonable, eminently practical objective'.[19]

Such were the doctrinal foundations on which a policy was based to encourage Farouk, Azzam, and the triumphant doctrinaires of the Fertile Crescent to come together and emulate the ideals of the United Nations. Many people must have felt misgivings as to how such an adventure would end, but it is safe to say that nobody of position or standing, whether British or Arab, was ready to question in public the assumptions and execution of this policy as Haikal coolly and soberly questioned it. He is reported to have declared at the time of the first formal conference on Arab unity in 1944: 'It is doubtful whether the union will be a political union; it is doubtful whether, in case one of the Arab states is attacked, the others will hurry to its aid. It is also doubtful if an effective cultural union, or a union of some other kind, could take place, because the history, the legal codes, agriculture, and industry are necessarily different in the different Arab states.'[20]

The 'rational, reasonable, eminently practical objective' has failed of its attainment, and the policy which sought to promote it is now dust and ashes. It disintegrated on the battle-fields of Palestine in 1948, three years after the foundation of the League. It was a swift reckoning. Policies are meant to succeed; if they fail, then they are bad policies; unless, that is, new and powerful circumstances which could not have been foreseen impinge to falsify calculations and up-set expectations. But between 1945, or indeed 1943, or 1939, and 1948 no new elements, no alien factors were introduced into the Middle Eastern situation. The Zionists were there, the pan-Arabs were there, Farouk and his men were there, and their antecedents, capacities, and ambitions were for all to see. To argue that the policy failed because the Zionists were not docile enough, the Arabs united enough, or wise enough, is to argue either from ignorance or from fancifulness or from sentimentality. It may indeed be said that the formation of the Arab League made quite inevitable a violent out-come to the quarrel opposing the Arabs of Palestine to the Zionists, and the consequent injury to public morality, settled society, and British interests in the Middle East. Any kind of compromise solu-tion enforced or facilitated by the Mandatory became quite impos-sible, because the doctrine in terms of which the Arab League claimed to operate spurned and abhorred the idea of compromise, and be-cause each of the principal states constituting the League looked on

[19] Ireland, *op. cit.*, pp. 95, 98.   [20] *Oriente Moderno*, 1944. p. 2.

a military victory in Palestine as a quick and easy means of securing the leadership of the Arab world.

It may be said that whether they knew it or not, the makers of the Baghdad Pact have thereby abandoned at last the policy which led to the encouragement of the Arab League. If so, it is a return to common sense and prudent calculation. Friends made friendly by the persuasion of tangible interests, by a reckoning of risk and advantage, by a provident quest for military and economic security: such is a conceivable objective of foreign policy. But will it be easy to extricate oneself from the quicksands of a doctrinaire adventure?

Years of official pan-Arabism mean that inevitably the Middle Eastern political debate is securely confined within the pan-Arab groove. When the Baghdad Pact was made, its Arab enemies denounced it as a betrayal of the pan-Arab cause. To reply to them when they became most vociferous at the time of the Suez operation, Nuri al-Sa'id made a long broadcast in December, 1956. The burden of his argument was that Communism, Zionism, and France were allies against whom Iraq has always fought and will always fight. Iraq, he said, was the only true servant of pan-Arabism. How can those, he asked, who maintain the frontiers created by imperialism (here alluding to Syria, and the well-known pan-Arab argument that all frontiers in the Fertile Crescent were artificial and arbitrary) be called patriots and nationalists? It may be that the Iraqi Minister was trying to pay back his enemies in their own coin, but it is as probable that he is sincere in what he says: 'The call to Arab nationalism', he declared at the end of his broadcast, 'is not something new and accidental with me. It is my very being, of which I am proud, which I seek to protect and to tend, whether I am in power or not. If such has been my way in my youth and in my middle age, it is not strange that I should remain the same in my old age.' This is quite true, and to the extent that it is true and represents the terms in which, whether from habit, inclination, or necessity, the rulers of Iraq talk of politics, disengagement from the quicksand is difficult. Britain may perhaps find itself facing obligations and being involved in quarrels and complications not envisaged within the text of the Baghdad Pact.

In the circumstances, one further remark remains to be made. Pan-Arabs are quite fond of citing German unity in the nineteenth century by way of precedent and analogy to prove that Arab unity in the twentieth century is inevitable. They forget, however, that German unity was made not only at the expense of the French, but also at that of a fellow German, the Habsburg Emperor. The pan-Arabs have fought their Sedan—and lost it—in Palestine in 1948. Sadowa still remains to be fought. Who shall be its Bismarck, and who its victim, only the future will tell.

THE GREAT CATASTROPHE

by G. F. HUDSON

AN ALLIANCE between two states for a specific common purpose can remain stable only as long as disagreements which may arise on other matters are of an order of importance so greatly inferior that the factors of disruption are always outweighed by the community of will. If there is serious conflict on an issue which appears to one or other of the parties as vital as that for which the partnership was formed, their solidarity cannot long be maintained. For two nations to be allies in one part of the world and enemies in another part is possible only if the latter region is regarded by both as relatively unimportant.

The N.A.T.O. coalition, built round an Anglo-American alliance that was a revival of the original war-time partnership against Hitler, was brought into being to defend Western Europe against domination by the Soviet Union. But for Britain, and to a lesser extent for France, the affairs of Europe could not be entirely separated from those of the Middle and Far East, traditional fields of their maritime commercial and colonial expansion where the Soviet Union, as heir to the continental empire of the Tsars, was also present and politically active, It was necessary in these regions, too, to achieve a close co-ordination of policies with the United States, not only in order to contain the advance of Soviet power in Asia as well as in Europe, but also because discord over Asian affairs could gravely impair the good understanding they had reached on European problems. The last six years, however, have been marked by a series of quarrels between the British and American governments, first over Far Eastern, and then over Middle Eastern, policy, which have imposed severe strains on their alliance. The crisis over the Anglo-French action against Egypt merely brought to a climax a long process of mutual irritation and misunderstanding.

After the failure of the Russian blockade of Berlin a position of stalemate was reached between the opposing forces in Europe and the storm-centre of international politics shifted to the Far East, where an entirely new situation was created by the final triumph of the Communists over the Kuomintang on the mainland of China and the conclusion of a treaty of military alliance between the Soviet Union and the Chinese People's Republic. The response of the British government to these developments was to transfer diplomatic recognition from the Kuomintang to the Communists, without waiting to reach any agreement on the matter with the United States; the American government did not follow suit, but withheld recognition from the Chinese Communists and has continued to do so to this day. It is not here relevant to discuss either the causes for this divergence of policies or the pros and cons of the arguments on each side; it is sufficient to point out that failure to agree—or even seriously to seek agreement—on an issue of such importance condemned Britain and America to endless frustration in their efforts to co-operate in dealing with the problems raised by the subsequent course of events in the Far East. Britain joined with America in armed intervention in Korea after the United Nations Security Council had endorsed the initial American action there, but did not approve the parallel American policy of neutralizing Formosa. When Communist China in turn intervened in the Korean War, Britain at first opposed any move to get the new antagonist declared an aggressor by the United Nations and for several days adopted a defeatist attitude which called forth some violent anti-British outbursts in Congress. Later there were sharp disputes between London and Washington over moves to seat Chinese Communist delegates in the United Nations, over possible extensions of the Korean War operations to Chinese territory, over the stand to be taken in the negotiations for a truce in Korea, over the question of inviting India to a Korean peace conference, over the timing of presentation of the South-East Asia Defence Pact, over measures proposed in Washington for the relief of Dien Bien Phu, and over the implications of American commitments to aid Chiang Kai-shek in the event of Communist attacks on the islands of Matsu and Quemoy. In every case Britain stood for a milder and weaker policy towards Communist China than that which the American government wished to pursue, and the British were constantly reproached for 'appeasement' by the more extreme advocates of the American anti-Communist policy in the Far East. Britain, on the other hand, kept in close touch with India throughout these controversies and laid great emphasis on the importance of conciliating 'Asian opinion', which was sympathetic to the new China and only alienated by the toughness of American policy. But the arguments used by each side had little effect on the other, and the basic British and American attitudes towards Far Eastern affairs remained far apart. These attitudes, moreover, were to a remarkable extent 'bi-partisan' in both countries; since the outbreak of the Korean War there has been little difference in America between Democrats and Republicans with regard to China, and in Britain the Conservatives in office have continued in essentials the Far Eastern policy pursued by the Attlee cabinet. Both nations have been fairly solid in their disagreement with each other.

That the disputes over Far Eastern affairs never led to an open head-on collision with America was due mainly to the fact that in the end Britain always shied away from a situation in which she would have had to line up with the Soviet Union in direct antagonism to American policy. Once or twice it seemed that the combined efforts of Britain and the Soviet bloc were about to muster enough support in the United Nations to seat Communist China there, and thus put America into the dock as an aggressor for support of the nationalists in Formosa. But that point was never actually reached, and as a result America has always been able to keep on the right side of the United Nations Charter in her Far Eastern policy; as long as China is represented in the world organization by nationalist delegates, there can be no legal objection even to the use of American bombers for the defence of Matsu and Quemoy. However unwise and provocative British opinion may think American actions—or proposed actions—in the Far East to have been, they have never taken the form of an armed attack on a fellow member of the United Nations.

Behind the Anglo-American disputes over policy towards China there was the fundamental fact that America was strategically deeply involved in the Far East, while British power was in process of withdrawal from the area. As a result of the Pacific War the United States held a system of strategic bases covering Japan and the Philippines and pivoted on Okinawa; the defensive alliances with South Korea and nationalist China were bound up with this system, and any challenge to it from Russia or Communist China was regarded as affecting vital American interests. Britain, on the other hand, was writing off her former position in the Far East as part of the necessary contraction of British power after the Second World War; it had already been virtually made over to America as a strategic sphere during the struggle against Japan. Hong Kong had become a hostage rather than a stronghold, and the only way to save anything from the wreck of British economic interests in China seemed to be by conciliation carried to the point of self-abasement, as in the policy of keeping a British mission in Peking for month after month supplicating for the favour of diplomatic relations which the Chinese declined to grant.

In the Middle East it was just the other way round; it was the British, with their continuing strategic involvement, who were inclined to strong and positive policies, while the Americans, with only economic interests in the area, tended towards appeasement and political *laissez faire*. Britain had had forces of occupation in Egypt for more than sixty years, and the defence of the country had been a crucial part of British strategy in two world wars; how crucial it had been held to be had been shown by the decision in 1940 to send reinforcements to Egypt at a time when Britain herself was threatened with invasion. The base in Egypt was maintained not only for the security of communications through the Canal, but also for support of a system of protection for the British oil interests in Iraq and eastern Arabia; Jordan—with its R.A.F. bases and British-officered Arab Legion—being the link between Egypt and the more easterly region of the Persian Gulf, otherwise virtually inaccessible to British power. The strategic scheme originally devised to meet the threat of Italo-German penetration of the Middle East had to be revised after 1945 to provide against the possibility of a Russian advance from the north, but it remained as before pivoted on Egypt, and without Egypt it was meaningless, since after the British withdrawal from Palestine contact with Jordan through Aqaba depended on security of passage between the Mediterranean and the Red Sea. It was therefore extremely embarrassing for Britain that Egypt was unwilling to prolong the Treaty authorizing British troops to remain in the Canal Zone, and eventually began to follow up demands for their removal with an officially sponsored guerrilla warfare.

The Americans had never, before 1945, been involved in the political affairs of the Middle East and did not feel any need to underwrite, or associate themselves with, the British security system in the area. Their approach to the problems of the area was through the economic interests created by the investments of American oil companies, particularly in Saudi Arabia. The Saudi connection came to dominate American diplomacy in the Middle East. As Saudia was the enemy of Iraq and the ally of Egypt, American policy favoured Cairo rather than Baghdad in the rivalry for leadership of the Arab world; as Saudia was hostile to the British protectorates in southern and eastern Arabia, American policy was to avoid any entanglement with Britain which might cause offence in Riyadh. This line was naturally in harmony with the anti-colonialism which the Americans had had to forget in Okinawa, and the role of champion of the Arabs against an outmoded European domination was one which came easily to certain American Foreign Service officials in the Middle East.

Middle Eastern affairs, however, were complicated not only by oil, but by Israel, and with regard to this question the British and American governments, from 1952, when Truman vacated the Presidency of the United States, were able to achieve a happy agreement on a policy which led ineluctably to disaster. Both of them regarded Israel as an intolerable nuisance getting in the way of good relations with the Arab states; since hostility towards Israel was the most universal sentiment held in common by the Arabs, there could be little difference in this respect between pro-Iraqi Britain and pro-Saudi America. The aim of both the Foreign Office and the State Department was to avoid offending the Arab states by any action on behalf of Israel; Britain and America therefore took no steps to press the Arab states to end the state of war against Israel or to give effect to the Security Council resolution of 1951 on the closing of the Suez Canal to Israeli shipping or to prevent Egypt from extending the blockade to the Gulf of Aqaba. A blind eye was turned on the Egyptian *fedayeen* raids on Israel, although there was plenty of evidence that these guerrilla units were a part of the Egyptian army and their exploits were celebrated as national enterprises by Cairo radio; only when reprisals were carried out by Israeli regular forces did London and Washington find cause for indignation at the breaches of the peace. On the other hand, neither Britain nor America was prepared to facilitate the complete destruction of the Israeli nation as desired by the pan-Arab extremists, and they sought to prevent an all-out Arab attack on Israel by maintaining a balance of armaments in the Middle East such that the Arab states would not be able to attain the decisive military superiority it would require. This policy was thwarted when Russia entered the field with supplies of arms for Egypt. It was then open to Britain and America either to announce that Russian deliveries of arms to the Arabs would be matched by increased supplies to Israel or to guarantee the existing frontiers of Israel, so that Arab leaders would know for certain that they could not launch a full-scale attack on Israel without going to war with the major Western Powers. But Britain and America did neither of these things. Instead, they declared that they would not take part in an 'arms race' and that they would only guarantee 'agreed' frontiers for Israel—which, since there was no possibility of any voluntary agreement on Israel's frontiers as long as there was a prospect of changing them by force, meant no guarantee at all. But this evasion, though it may have avoided the outburst of Arab wrath which a clear warning would have provoked, did nothing either to check the drift towards an

Arab-Israeli war or to curb the new ascendancy of Soviet influence involved in the Russian moral and material support for the extreme anti-Zionist programme. Only two alternatives now lay ahead: either Israel's Arab neighbours, combined under Egyptian leadership, would attack in overwhelming force when their preparations were complete, or else Israel would attack first, before they were ready.

Meanwhile, a year before Russia had begun to exacerbate the conflicts of the Middle East by supplying arms to Egypt, the British government had agreed to remove its troops from the Canal Zone on the basis of a Treaty which permitted it to 'reactivate' the base in certain circumstances. The critics of the agreement, who came to be known as the 'Suez Group', did not fail to point out that the abandonment of the Suez base undermined the whole British strategic position in the Middle East, that Cyprus could not be a substitute, and that the assurances given by Nasser were worthless in view of the rabid anti-British nationalism characteristic of the new revolutionary régime in Egypt. The nationalization of the Anglo-Iranian Oil Company's assets by Persia was fresh in the memory of everyone, yet the British government fatuously assumed that the Suez Canal Company was safe for the rest of its lease and made no attempt to obtain new international guarantees for the future operation of the Canal while its troops were still in military control of it. The evacuation of Suez should logically have meant a writing-off of all British strategic commitments in the Middle East, since it had become almost impossible to sustain them. But, instead of this, Britain recklessly embarked on entirely new commitments of a most dangerous kind by the conclusion of the Baghdad Pact, directly impinging on the frontiers of the Soviet Union. The United States declined to join in the Pact, for to have done so would have been to incur the disapproval of Saudi Arabia. How Britain by herself was to give any effective military support to the Pact after giving up the Suez base it passed the wit of man to discover; those who clung to the belief that there must somehow be sense in this madness did their best to discern an intelligent motive behind the contradictions of British policy, but could find nothing but a vast, formless, uncomprehending muddle.

The withdrawal from Suez was a gamble on the improvement of relations with Egypt which was expected to follow from it. When, therefore, it was in fact followed not by reconciliation but by an intensification of anti-British propaganda, covering the whole Arab world with a radio barrage of lies and insults of unprecedented malevolence, by the incitements and intrigues which led by stages to the complete destruction of British influence in Jordan, and finally by the nationalization of the Suez Canal, Sir Anthony Eden, as the chief architect of the policy, was left defenceless before the Suez Group, who had correctly predicted that these would be its consequences. The only way for him to forestall their reproaches was for him to join them and make himself their leader, to become the man of iron who would recover the security he had previously given away. But it was no longer possible, having once quitted Suez, merely to walk in again and resume possession. Egypt could now no longer be coerced except by military invasion from outside—which would be incidentally a violation of the Charter of the United Nations.

The nationalization of the Canal by an openly hostile Egyptian dictator was a very serious matter for Britain, in both its economic and its political implications. If it had been decided at the outset that force must not be used against Egypt, the right course would have been to accept nationalization as an act within Egypt's jurisdiction, but at the same time to launch an emergency programme of building fast tankers (or buying them from America) in order to reduce the stranglehold of the Suez traffic monopoly and to start urgent consultations with Australia on the best means to provide for common strategic interests in the Indian Ocean on the assumption that communications through Suez must be written off in any critical situation. But the course taken was to begin highly publicized military and naval preparations and to adopt in the most insistent manner the position that Britain could never allow the Canal to fall under the control of 'one government or one man'. This meant that force must be used unless Nasser could be induced to climb down by pressure and threats, for if he did not submit, Britain would be faced with a disastrous diplomatic defeat which could only further reduce what remained of her prestige in the Middle East.

In taking the line they did in the early days after the nationalization, the British Prime Minister and his Foreign Secretary undoubtedly counted on a degree of American support much greater than they ultimately received, for the earlier American benevolence towards the Nasser régime had been considerably modified, and Dulles seemed at last to be steering on an anti-Nasser course. His withdrawal of the offer to finance the Aswan Dam had precipitated Nasser's seizure of the Canal, and he had told American journalists in an off-the-record conference that Egypt had 'passed the point of no return' in her commitments to Russia. It was therefore to be expected that, even if he was not prepared to approve the use of force against Egypt, he would at any rate be in favour of the maximum diplomatic and economic pressure to bring about a tolerable settlement of the Suez issue. At first the course of events seemed to confirm this hope; the United States joined Britain and France in advocating a scheme for international administration of the Canal at the London Conference. But from the beginning there were strange vacillations and reservations in the attitude of the American Secretary of State, as if he were being jerked away by some invisible force from co-operation with his European colleagues. During these weeks the disapproval of King Saud cast an increasingly dark and oily shadow over the endeavours to present Egypt with a joint policy of the Western Powers. Dulles appeared to have forgotten what he had said about Nasser having passed the point of no return and began to deprecate any talk of exerting even economic pressure on Egypt. Finally, he refused to agree to the withholding of dues from Egypt by the Canal Users' Association, which the British and American governments had understood was to be a means of bargaining for the attainment of the purposes laid down at the London Conference. The Dulles *volte-face* led to a complete breakdown of confidence between Washington and London. The British and French leaders now fell back on their original intention to use force and they repaid what they regarded as American bad faith by concealing their preparations from the American government. But two wrongs do not make a right, and mutual deceptions do not add up to relations of trust. The Anglo-French ultimatum brought the quarrel immediately into the open and the partners of N.A.T.O. were split wide apart over the invasion of Egypt.

Earnest endeavours are now being made on both sides to mend the broken alliance. But even if new relations of mutual confidence and co-operation can be established—and it will take time—it is evident that a disaster of great magnitude has taken place. The situation in the Middle East has gone from bad to worse at a time when a new dangerous instability has been created in Europe as a result of the revolutions in Poland and Hungary. The American government was, indeed, in spite of its opposition to the British and French policies, quick to counter to the best of its ability any threat of Soviet intervention in the Middle East; it denounced the proposal to send Soviet 'volunteers' to Egypt and subsequently warned Russia against attacking any Asian member of the Baghdad Pact—the nearest it has ever got to endorsing that combination. But it has not been able to prevent a great increase of Soviet influence throughout the Middle East. Although America took a leading part in the condemnation of the Anglo-French action by the United Nations, and was even more effective in halting the action by the threat of economic sanctions, it was Russia alone which threatened—and that in the most dramatic manner—to wage war on behalf of Egypt, and to Russia therefore goes in Arab eyes the credit for having compelled the invaders to call off their war. The victory lies with the extremists of pan-Arabism, who can claim that the West is divided and impotent, that Soviet protection has shown its power, and that the way ahead is open for new campaigns with Soviet aid against the French in North Africa, against the British in Arabia, and, above all, against Israel. Iraq remains the main obstacle to the Nasser-led unity of the Arab world, and against Iraq therefore must the main effort of the Moscow-Cairo axis be directed—with help perhaps from India, because for India the enemy is Pakistan, and therefore also Iraq as the ally of Pakistan. Great forces of revolutionary violence have been unleashed in the Middle East, and it would not take much in present circumstances for all the oilfields, containing the world's largest petroleum reserves, to be transferred into the hands of the bitter enemies of the Atlantic Alliance. In the period now beginning the limitation of the catastrophe which has already occurred will depend on the speed and resolution with which the United States is prepared to act in any crisis which may now arise in the affairs of the Middle East; otherwise the whole area may soon fall under Soviet domination.

In the Middle East, as in Europe, the only wisdom is to decide once and for all where to stand and to make the stand definite. Keeping them guessing, waiting for the dust to settle, can lead only to fresh disaster. But it is now for America to play the hand. With the withdrawal from Port Said Britain ceases to be a Great Power in the Middle East, but by the same event America has become heir to all the troubles of the world between Bab el Mandeb and Kirkuk. Every *djinn* of the Thousand and One Nights has now gone to make its home in Washington. The British have been defeated and they must bear the consequences of their failure. The Americans have been victorious and they must bear the consequences of that, too.

January, 1957

POLITICAL TRENDS IN THE FERTILE CRESCENT

by W. KHALIDI

IN ALL THE Arab countries of the Fertile Crescent political power is at the moment (if only nominally) in the hands of a group which may be called traditional Arab nationalists. Many of these fought against the Turks in the First World War. They also led the nationalist struggle against the Mandatory régimes. They belong to a vague nineteenth-century school of liberalism, are secular in outlook, and basically pro-Western. On the question of Arab unity they favour the *status quo* policy of the Arab League, for which indeed they were responsible. On the question of Palestine, they do not lead but are led by public opinion. They are representative of the old aristocratic families of the towns and the feudal and tribal chiefs of the countryside. They are also in alliance with powerful local industrial and commercial interests. They are the Middle Eastern group upon which Western policy is based.

Everywhere they are on the defensive, and in some countries in thinly camouflaged rout. In Lebanon, the requirements of denominational equilibrium and a clever policy of replenishment from younger members of the same group have kept them more firmly in power than anywhere else, but they are not by any means unchallenged there. In Syria, a series of *coups d'état* has considerably weakened their hold over the country, and the recent return of President Kuwatly gives them only a momentary and precarious respite. In Jordan, the discrediting of the old Palestinian oligarchy of Jerusalem families, the murder of Abdullah, and the removal of Glubb have all but destroyed their power. In Iraq they seem to be supreme, but the very measures to which Nuri Pasha has to resort show that, to say the least, their supremacy is not effortless.

These traditional Arab nationalists were their own worst enemies. Under the Mandates, their object was to show that it was too costly and impracticable for the foreign Powers to continue the direct occupation of their countries. This could be achieved by a purely negative policy, by civil agitation, and by administrative sabotage. In this they succeeded, but they could never afterwards shed their negativeness. Moreover, with independence achieved, the *raison d'être* of their cohesion—the presence of the foreigner—was removed and with his removal the solid front with which they had faced him collapsed. They now fell to fighting with one another for the fruits of office. The countless parties with pompous titles into which they divided were entirely meaningless except in terms of clashes of will and personality. Because of the aristocratic and feudal background of most of them, office became synonymous to them with the protection and expansion of the particular land or commercial interest which they represented. Their triumph over the foreigner was erroneously taken by them as proof of their own importance and placed them in a false moral position *vis-à-vis* their public. They felt that they had satisfactorily fulfilled their duties to the people and that they could now start attending to themselves.

None of this was lost upon the rapidly growing educated classes and the people in general. These now began to look upon the traditional nationalists not as leaders but as targets. Two great post-war international developments made a deep impression upon the educated classes in particular: the rise of British Socialism, and the emergence of the U.S.S.R. as the greatest Power in Europe and Asia. Both these developments focused the attention of the intelligentsia upon such mundane matters as the necessary conditions of a welfare state.

The gap between the ruling classes and the rest of the people was further widened by the Arab, or rather non-Arab, policies of the rulers. Before independence the traditional nationalists were pan-Arabists. After independence they became jealous particularists. To satisfy the popular feeling of pan-Arabism the Arab League was formed as a half-hearted attempt in that direction. But the Palestine War of 1948 exposed the bankruptcy not only of the Arab League but also of its authors.

One aspect of the Palestine War is of special importance. It is seldom realized that this was launched by the Arab politician, not the Arab soldier. The soldier had no illusions about Zionist strength, but the politicians were under tremendous pressure from public opinion at home and had to make some gesture, however feeble. It is of course arguable that if the Arab armies had not entered the Arab part of Palestine in 1948 the whole of the western bank of the

Jordan would have been lost, but that is beside the point. The unpreparedness of the armies and the humiliating terms imposed upon them by the armistice agreements inevitably caused them to turn against their governments. The Arab officer became the spearhead of all the pent-up feelings of the educated people and the masses against the traditional ruling classes. First Kuwatly went and then Farouk. Glubb is only the latest victim of one and the same trend.

The year 1948 is probably the most important single landmark in the modern history of the Arab world. As far as one can see, the future of each Arab country of the Fertile Crescent will depend to a large extent on the political outlook of its particular officer class, on the trend to which this officer class gives whole-hearted support, and on the degree of co-operation between the officer classes in the various Arab countries.

This is not difficult to understand. The tension along the borders of Israel, and the overwhelming superiority of Israel, particularly in comparison with Lebanon, Syria, and Jordan, emphasize the importance of the military. People feel the same confidence in them that the Americans felt in Eisenhower at the height of the cold war. Moreover, the Arabs are keenly aware that they lag far behind in modern developments and look to the military to supply them with the short-cuts to a more egalitarian society, however paradoxical that may sound. Finally, there is the inescapable fact that the Arab officer class has become the repository of self-conscious political power at a time when the traditional ruling class is bankrupt, the other growing forces and trends have not sufficiently crystallized, and the general masses positively look to this class as a saviour. Iraq is no exception to this; for the army there is neutralized only by drastic periodic purges, a process which cannot be carried on indefinitely. After all, the first Arab military *coup d'état* took place in Iraq. Moreover, the will to survive of the traditional Iraqi ruling class, strong as it is, derives to a large extent from the powerful personality of one man, Nuri Said, and Nuri has had his moments of triumph and failure.

What are the forces and trends which are trying to supersede traditional Arab nationalism and to convert the Arab officer class?

Traditional Arab nationalism occupies the centre. On the extreme right is the Islamic trend. This is represented organizationally in the Moslem Brotherhood. It must be remembered that although the Brotherhood has been greatly weakened in Egypt, it has not been altogether smashed, and its branches in the other Arab countries are still intact. It is strongest in Syria and Jordan, and has important nuclei in both Lebanon and Iraq. It has a wide emotional appeal, not only to the lower-middle urban classes and peasants, but also to the students and intellectuals. It is also very active among the Palestinian refugees.

The version of the Brotherhood in the Fertile Crescent is milder than that in Egypt. This is due to consideration for Christian sentiment in Lebanon, Syria, and Jordan and for Shi'ite feelings in Iraq. On the question of world orientation it is neutralist but non-doctrinaire. It has co-operated with Communists but is basically and explicitly anti-Communist. It is anti-'Western policy' but not anti-West, and there are conditions in which it would co-operate with the West. It is very sensitive to Western military occupation and control and sees Israel in this light. It is not against Arab unity, but sees it as an indispensable preliminary step towards Islamic unity. Tactically, it is regrouping its forces and carefully watching the course of events in Egypt.

Facing the Brotherhood, on the extreme left of the traditional nationalists, are the Communists. They have old-established nuclei in select trade unions in all Arab countries, and are possibly strongest in Iraq although they are outlawed there. Their power is growing everywhere, especially among students, workers, and Palestinian refugees. On the question of world orientation they at the moment preach doctrinaire neutralism. They are not enthusiastic about Arab union or Arab rights in Palestine, but are careful to keep up appearances. Their general policy is not only to replace Western influence, political, military, and economic, with Soviet influence: it also aims at preventing any other local trend—Arab, Islamic, or otherwise—from stabilizing the situation. It is interesting that while the Communists are hostile to the concept of the Baghdad Pact, they are delighted with its consequence, which is the isolation of Iraq, potentially the richest Arab country, from the rest of the Fertile Crescent. Tactically, they outwardly conform to the dominant trend.

To the right of the Communists, but at no great distance from them, are the Marxist Socialists represented in the Ba'ath or Renaissance Party. This party has greatly grown in power, particularly after the Palestine War and the deflation of traditional Arab nationalism. It is strongest in Syria and Jordan, and has an important nucleus in both Iraq and Lebanon. It has succeeded in winning over considerable sections of the middle and lower officer ranks of the Syrian army, and was behind some of the Syrian *coups d'état*. It is very popular among schoolteachers, students, and Palestinian refugees, and in certain rural areas. It has not succeeded as much as one would have expected among workers. On the question of orientation it believes in and preaches doctrinaire neutralism. It is anti-Zionist, but its main emphasis is on the ideological contradictions within Zionism, and it sees Israel mainly as a Near Eastern bastion of Western imperialism. It supports Arab unity, but the stress is not on Arab sentiment but on class solidarity against the traditional ruling circles. It is, of course, secularist and will have little to do with either Islam or Christianity. Tactically, its followers adopt a fastidious and carping tone and set themselves up as arbiters of true nationalism. They refuse to take part in any national or coalition government, partly to escape responsibility for failures and partly to allow the traditional ruling classes more rope with which to hang themselves.

To the right of these Marxist Socialists, though still well to the left of traditional Arab nationalism, is the dominant trend of the moment—'Nasserism'. This has swept everything before it. Traditional nationalists, Communists, Marxist Socialists, and even Moslem Brothers bend the knee to it. The one exception is Nuri Pasha and his circle. But while all these trends pay lip-service to Nasserism, they are deeply frightened and suspicious of it because it threatens to undermine their whole position. Most annoying of all, it does not fit anywhere into their ideological manuals. For Nasserism is not an ideology but an attitude of mind. It is eclectic, empirical, radical, and yet conservative. It starts with the fact of an Islamic Arab Egypt and the desirability of perpetuating this fact with its constituent elements. The interests of this Islamic Arab Egypt are its overriding concern, and in pursuing these interests it is untroubled by historical determinism, a divine scripture, or dialectical materialism. This gives it greater scope for manoeuvre and increases rather than decreases the possibility of agreement with it. On the question of orientation it is neutralist, but its neutralism is tactical, not doctrinaire. This neutralism is based upon a realistic appraisal of the popular Arab mood, a mood which has deep roots in the Arab-Western tension of the last fifty years. It is therefore at least as practical as Nuri's approach, if indeed it is not more practical. It is anti-Communist and basically pro-Western. Its system of bilateral treaties has greatly strengthened, and largely displaced, the looser Arab League arrangements. Its purchase of Czech arms has been universally welcome in view of the aggressiveness of Israel's frontier policy.

The appeal of Nasserism lies in the fact that it has transferred, if only partially, to the Arab world itself the centre of decisions concerning the future of that world, from the western European capitals where those decisions have been taken for more than a century. It has also restored to the Arabs a feeling of confidence in themselves, and thus has largely counterbalanced the psychological shock of the loss of Palestine upon which the Communists, Marxists, and Moslem Brothers have been cashing in since 1948. Its policy of radical domestic reform has shown that such reform can be effected without resort to the bloody class struggle of the Communists and Marxists.

The success of Nasserism has revealed three important facts: the vast majority of Arabs are still uncommitted to the extreme Right or Left; the ideological bases of Nasserism, such as they are, are acceptable to this vast majority; and these bases have a counter-dynamism capable of wresting the initiative from the hands of the extreme Right or Left. But an important reservation must be made. Nasserism, with Egyptian nationalism as an indispensable component, cannot in all its details strike permanent roots in the Fertile Crescent countries. What it can do, and is already doing, is to inspire the growth of a parallel local movement, a neo-Arab nationalism. Such a movement would truly reflect the needs of the time, and the mood and aspirations of the majority. It would move in the general direction of the other important trends. It could eventually rally round it most of the groups lying to the right of the Communists. Its regard for Islamic culture and values could serve as a link with the moderate Moslem Brotherhood of the Fertile Crescent. Its genuine pan-Arabism and reformist platform would attract many pseudo-Marxists and fellow-travellers who have turned away in disgust from the more traditional Arab nationalism. The centre parties would also see it as a lesser evil than that of the extreme Right or Left parties. Moreover, since the criterion of this group would be enlightened self-interest, it would be possible for it to come to a business-like agreement with the West, on a more broadly popular basis, than has so far been feasible.

The natural backbone of this movement is Iraq. Only Iraq, with her potential wealth, economic, technical, and military, can give it reality and permanence. But the policy of Iraq at the moment, particularly in relation to the Baghdad Pact, prevents her from taking any lead in Arab affairs in the other countries of the Fertile Crescent. The Baghdad Pact may or may not be a worth-while objective, but, even if it were, it should have been conceived, not as the starting-point, but as the goal to be approached through a number of intermediate stages. While it is true that the Pact was in no sense imposed on the government of Iraq, since Nuri Pasha was perhaps at least as enthusiastic about it as Britain, yet the alacrity with which Britain joined it would seem to reflect particular British interests rather than those of the West as a whole.

The danger of the Baghdad Pact lies in the possibility not only that it may not succeed, with all the consequences that failure would entail for the West, but that it may succeed only too well. For an Iraq truly orientated towards Turkey and Iran and truly integrated within an all-embracing Western organization would, to all intents and purposes, be a de-Arabized Iraq, and a de-Arabized Iraq would, in the long run, be a loss not only to the Arabs but also to the West. Iraq can be regarded in two ways: by herself and *in vacuo*, or as part of the Arab world. From the former standpoint, which seems implied in the Baghdad Pact policy, the most important potential stabilizing factor in the Middle East as a whole seems likely to be wasted; for an Iraq that was not cut off behind the curtain of an untimely or an unnecessary Western Pact could even now be exerting a beneficial influence in Jordan and Syria.

It may be argued that the object of the Pact is first and foremost to build up Iraq into a modern state and to enable her at some future date to exercise her influence for good on the other Arab countries of the Fertile Crescent. But this argument overlooks the following facts: Iraq, having gone her own way for so long, might not wish to do this; an Iraq with such Western credentials, however strong and developed, would be unacceptable to the majority of people in the other Arab countries; and Egypt would almost certainly consider such an Iraq hostile to herself and might physically oppose such a move. Lastly, in the process of thus building up Iraq into a modern state which should in the future be able to exercise its influence on other Arab states, the internal battle to win the vast uncommitted majority on a neo-Arab nationalist basis might be lost for ever.

But assuming the Baghdad Pact were dropped tomorrow and Iraq began to spread her influence westwards, would Egypt stand by and allow this to happen? Such a change in Iraqi policy, if it were to come about, would in itself be a cause of deep satisfaction to Egypt. Moreover, it would entail a change in Iraqi leadership and the coming to power in Iraq of a group that has more in common with the Egyptian leaders from the point of view of age, temperament, background, and outlook. It should also not be forgotten that if Jordan and Syria turn to Egypt today it is because, from their point of view, Iraq has not till now allowed them to turn to her, so that if Egypt is stepping in she is doing so because there is in fact a vacuum into which to step.

On a long-term basis, Egypt has everything to gain from a strong and united Fertile Crescent so long as it is friendly to herself. Such a Fertile Crescent would protect her eastern flank. It would take off her shoulders the immediate military burden of Israel. It could lend her much-needed capital for her development projects and so save her from the necessity of begging for Western or Eastern capital. It would help her to improve the acute situation of the three hundred thousand Palestinian refugees in the Gaza strip. It could even accept some of her surplus population in its under-populated territories.

There is, moreover, the fact that while Egypt, like every other country, enjoys possessing prestige, she does not make a cult of prestige and certainly does not pursue prestige at the expense of her own real interests. There is every indication that the Egyptian leaders are well aware that not only the future of their country but their own personal survival depends on finding solutions for the great economc and domestic problems confronting them. They believe that the present Anglo-Egyptian tension is a transitory phase and that the atmosphere not only in Egypt but throughout East Africa may relax considerably once the High Dam scheme is under way. They also believe that then would come the opportune time for Britain to try to bring Iraq and Egypt together, in her own interest and in the interest of the Arabs and of world peace.

1956.

THE IDEOLOGY OF THE
EGYPTIAN REVOLUTION

Its Evolution with the Course of Events

by JEAN VIGNEAU

'I can assure you that our movement is attached to no political party, either directly or indirectly. It is completely independent and its sole object is to secure the institution of a sound government for the good of the country. . . . This movement in the army has nothing to do with either Communism or Fascism. Its primary aim is to purge the army itself of its corrupt elements, and then to see that the government purges itself. We want to put an end to tyranny and corruption and to strengthen the basis of the Constitution. Political questions, as well as everything to do with the machinery of government, are in the hands of the government, which regulates them under the aegis of the Constitution—that Constitution for whose re-establishment we have striven, with a view to the country's interests.'
—MUHAMMED NAGUIB, July–August, 1952.

I. THE EGYPTIAN AND THE SYRIAN COUPS D'ÉTAT

THE WORDS we have quoted above summarize the character and objectives of the Egyptian *coup d'état* of July, 1952, as defined by the man who was then regarded as its prime mover, General Naguib, and as confirmed, in different words, by the members of the military junta.

Thus presented, the act of the army which, during the night of July 22–23, brought about the fall of the Egyptian monarchy, looked more like an '*Inkilab*' (literally: an upsetting) than a *revolution* inspired by a clear clash of ideologies. Moreover, this *Inkilab*, to judge by the declarations of the men who took over the tasks of government, might have been thought to belong to the series of crises that shook the Arab world in consequence of the war in Palestine, which aroused spectacular commotions in the surrounding countries. Seen from that angle, the Syrian *Inkilab* of March, 1949, cannot but be related to the Egyptian event of three years later which it fore-shadowed. Both were directly caused by the Arab defeat in Palestine and the discredit into which it plunged the existing Arab govern-ments which were held responsible for it.

In the autumn of 1948 there had been a grave crisis in Syria. Mass demonstrations of popular resentment occurred throughout the country. In reality those risings were no more than explosions of popular anger against the leader of the Syrian government, Jamil Mardam, and his previous Minister of Defence, Ahmed Sharabati, who was accused of treason in the Palestine War.

The question of armament, to which the Arab defeat in that same Palestine War was attributed, was also one of the chief and immediate causes of the political crisis which, in Egypt, was marked by the sanguinary revolts of June 26, 1952, the departure of Nahhas, and the unsuccessful attempts upon the lives of Hilali and Serri.

The aims of the Syrian *coup d'état*, as defined by General Husni Zaïm, had been the same as those to be proclaimed three years later by the Egyptian military leaders. Zaïm declared that: 'The *Inkilab* of the 30th March, 1949, was the natural consequence of the existence in the country of corrupt leaders who had managed the affairs of the fatherland according to their own passions and ambitions; of a leadership which had constantly violated the authority of the consti-tution to the detriment of the people's happiness and their interests. It is therefore the intention of the *Inkilab*, after putting an end to this corruption, to ensure the return to a constitutional government which will guarantee the well-being and happiness of the people.'

To put a stop to the corruption and oppression of the people by the feudal potentates; to ensure a return to sound democratic and constitutional government—these were the essential aims which the Egyptian military chiefs, following the example of the Syrian army leaders, professed as their articles of faith. For Zaïm in 1949, as for Shishakli in 1951, and for Naguib in 1952, the people (*al Chaab*) is the spiritual motive of the *Inkilab*. The army is, so to speak, only its secular arm.

'The age of charlatans, politicians, and climbers is finished. Such is the will of the army because it is the will of the people. That is your will, O people, and it is in the name of your will that the army is determined to do its duty by pursuing the interests of the nation above all things.'[1]

---

[1] Shishakli, December 5, 1951.

'It is the people and the nation as a whole who are the architects of our movement. The army is only one fraction of the nation.'[2]

'The army is of the people and for the people.'[3]

Hence the repeated affirmations, on all sides, that the army has no political power or ambitions.

'Our movement was founded from the beginning upon "renunciation". Neither my colleagues nor I have any personal ambitions. We have no intention whatever of filling our own pockets. In that, probably, lies the secret of our success.'[4]

'Our motto has been, and it remains, that of renunciation.'[5]

'We have fixed a date six months ahead for returning to our barracks, after having restored to our country the right to dispose of itself as it will.'[6]

Like the Syrian military leaders before them, the Egyptian army chiefs take pains to protest their disinterestedness and to renounce all political designs by affirming their loyalty to democratic and constitutional government, even to the freedom of political parties.

'The kind of government best suited to modern Egypt is one that is based upon true democratic principles. This government should be directed solely to the public good, and not to private ambitions and interests. Why should we want to have a single-party constitution and establish a dictatorial power now, when the countries which have tried such a system are having to revert to democratic rule and a multiplicity of parties? Why should we not leave a free field for every doctrine which is put forward by a group with goodwill, whose aim is to serve the public good? The present period should therefore be regarded as one of transition only, while we prepare the way for a return to normal, democratic life.'[7]

This period of transition, originally estimated by the Egyptian military chiefs at six months, has since been extended by them to three years. We shall see presently how the Egyptian government has now come to envisage the return to 'normal democratic life' which it promised after seizing power in July, 1952.

In order to give proof of their adherence to democratic principles and to satisfy the public opinion which had greeted their movement with favour if not with acclamation, both the Syrian and the Egyptian military leaders endeavoured from the beginning to 'legitimize' their seizure of power and to buttress it with regular democratic supports. It is to that end that the 'Liberation Movement' (*Al-*

[2] Naguib, September 14, 1952.   [3] Nasser, December 31, 1952.
[4] Naguib, December 14 and 31, 1952.   [5] Nasser, March 27, 1953.
[6] Various declarations made by members of the military junta in the first months after their seizure of power in July, 1952.
[7] Nasser, June 17, 1953.

Tahrir) has been organized in Damascus and in Cairo. And both in Syria and in Egypt this is regarded not as a political party but as a great popular assembly, centring in itself the aspirations to the new régime, and representing all the political forces, at different levels of the population, which can promote and support a national and democratic policy.

'The Liberation Movement is not a political party set up for the benefit of its promoters, nor is it at the service of any ambition for power whatsoever. It is an instrument for the organization of the energies of the people, in new ways based upon *the individual*; for no renaissance can take place unless the individual believes in himself, in his powers, and in his fatherland.'[8]

But while the *Tahrir* in Syria, whose founder and President is Shishakli himself, pretty soon became a political party in competition with the other parties in Syria, the Egyptian *Tahrir* is becoming the Single Party at the behest—political, ideological, and administrative—of the military dictatorship. In this respect the Syrian *Inkilab* is marking time for the Egyptian *Inkilab*. The latter, in its initial phase and as it was conceived by some of its promoters, notably by Naguib, was certainly inspired by the Syrian example and tried to work to the same ends. Nor did General Naguib fear to say so very clearly on December 11, 1952, during General Shishakli's visit to Cairo: 'I thank you for having been the first to pay us a visit, and that you were also the first to bring about an *Inkilab* similar to ours in its circumstances and its aims. The two revolts have been directed to the same ends and aims—to put an end to corruption, and to reform our two countries.'

But the different paths of development subsequently taken by the two *Inkilab* show clearly enough that the Egyptian *coup d'état* of July, 1952, is more than an *Inkilab*. It is a *revolution*; it has an ideological side that is absent in the Syrian military revolts. Moreover, the members of the Egyptian military junta themselves never called their rising of July 22 anything but a revolution, never an *Inkilab*, as the Syrians called theirs. And, from the beginning, the most active and influential members of the junta set up a Revolutionary Council which took practically all power into its hands; whereas, in Syria, the military power tried, until the end, to come to terms with the political parties and the civil authorities.

Is this to say that the Egyptian military chiefs were animated from the first by a definitely revolutionary ideal with precise aims; or did they find themselves obliged, by the force of circumstances and the pressure of events, to become conscious of their position as revolutionary leaders? No positive information is available that would

[8] Nasser, April 9 and June 17, 1953.

justify a plain and certain answer to that question. It can be reasonably maintained that Naguib and a few other officers in the conspiracy saw no more in the deed of July 22 than just another *Inkilab* on the Syrian pattern, meant to bring their country back into a normal and sound democratic way of life; and that they could not, therefore, foresee the subsequent course of the 'Revolution'. But there was one man of the junta who certainly could see farther, and who was nursing revolutionary ambitions in expectation of later developments—Gamal 'Abdul Nasser.

II. NASSER'S IDEOLOGY OF REVOLUTION

Nasser is unquestionably the theorist and ideologist of the July Revolution; what is more, he is a revolutionary by nature and destiny, or at least sees himself as such.

In his booklet entitled *The Philosophy of the Revolution*, Nasser makes much of his long revolutionary past. Before becoming the most active member of the Committee of Free Officers, he took part in students' political organizations and, in 1936, in the 'National Front'. About that time, Nasser tells us, he belonged to a youth organization which proposed to assassinate any person in politics suspected of any action damaging to the sovereignty and independence of Egypt. But after their first attempt upon the life of one of these political personalities, Nasser tells us how he was overcome by a crisis of conscience. He emerged from this experience with the definitive idea for the Revolution of July 22.

'Lying on my bed, a prey to intense emotions, and enveloped in a haze of cigarette smoke, I kept on saying to myself:

'—And then?

'—And then what? asked a voice within me.

'—Then, I said to myself, the system must be changed. . . . *That* deed was not a positive action. . . .

'At once I was filled with a gentle serenity; though it was soon dispelled by the echoes of crying and weeping that would not cease to haunt my memory.

'—If only he wouldn't die, I murmured.

'The strangest thing is that when the dawn broke I had begun to hope that the man I had wanted to see dead might be alive.

'Feverishly scanning the morning paper, with what joy did I learn that the man had not succumbed!

'But the fundamental problem was quite different: it was to discover the way leading to that positive action.

'And straightway we thought of something of the highest importance.

'WE TRACED THE FIRST LINES OF THE PLAN WHICH WAS CARRIED
OUT ON JULY 23 . . . A REVOLUTION SPRINGING FROM THE HEARTS OF
THE PEOPLE, BEARING OUT THEIR HOPES AND SWEEPING ONWARD INTO
THE FUTURE.'[9]

Whilst Naguib and the other members of the junta were insisting,
in their first speeches, upon the immediate and rather ordinary
objectives of the *coup d'état*, Nasser strove from the beginning to
go far beyond the modest frame of an *Inkilab*, in which they wanted
to confine their action. He depicted their revolt in the perspective of
history; he hailed it as the decisive turning-point in the life, not only
of Egypt but of all the Arab peoples. It was not, he declared, the
war in Palestine nor the scandals of the reign of Farouk which had
provoked this movement. 'I dare to say that the Revolution of
July 22 was not the consequence of the war in Palestine, nor was it
caused by that defective armament which cost the lives of so many
soldiers and officers, nor by the electoral crisis in the Officers' Club.
Those are but the factors that hastened its maturity.'[10]

Here, Nasser is seeking to explain the deeper reasons for the
Revolution which the others seem not to have grasped. The com-
mencement of it, which they date from the events of July, is traced
by Nasser to a much more distant past. 'Some people want to regard
July 23, 1952, as the starting-point of our Revolution; but the truth
is quite otherwise. July 23 was only the last phase of the Revolution.
Its beginnings were to be seen on July 11, 1882. On that day the
peaceful city of Alexandria was subjected to bombardment by the
British aggressors. The hateful occupation followed. Egypt re-
volted. The peasant soldier Ahmad Arabi sallied out at the head of
a group of free officers and soldiers to repel the aggressors. But the
Revolution did not then attain its objectives. It was then new-
born, and being only an infant, it had to bide its time, to grow up
and attain its maturity before it could decide to take action. Thus
the first aim of the Revolution, from the first day of its life, has been
TO LIBERATE EGYPT.'[11]

According to Nasser, then, the original cause of the Revolution
was 'the enslavement of the people by the imperialists and their
lackeys the Egyptian feudal lords and politicians'. The essential aim
of the Revolution is, therefore, 'to liberate the slaves, namely the
people, and put them, in place of their masters, in the government of
the country'. The Egyptian revolutionaries, like all those of the past,
dream of establishing the reign of the people. 'The Revolution of
July 23 is the realization of a dream cherished by the people since
the beginning of the last century; to govern themselves and become

---

[9] *The Philosophy of the Revolution*, pp. 33–4.   [10] *op. cit.*, pp. 10 and 17.
[11] Speech of December 31, 1952.

the masters of their own destiny'.[12] But in the mind of Nasser, the way to this realization lies through a 'struggle between the classes', since the power must pass out of the hands 'of the masters into those of the slaves'. There is no mistaking the familiar phrases of the Marxian doctrine, adopted either consciously or unconsciously by the leader of the Egyptian Revolution.

Yet according to this same leader, the representative of the people is the army, because the army is 'of the people and for the people'. It is to the army that the destiny of the nation must be entrusted. True, in several of his declarations, from which we have quoted, Nasser affirms his attachment to a free, democratic constitution and promises a rapid return to it. On June 17, 1953, he can still say: 'I believe in true democracy, because I believe that the people has a right to its own choice in whatever concerns its existence and its future; hence I consider that the people should be left free to choose the system most suitable for its government.' This free democracy is not, however, of the kind that Naguib foresaw in his declarations. For Nasser, although the Revolution is to bring about 'government of the people by the people', it is the army which chooses this government for it, which, indeed, governs on its behalf. The army is, so to speak, its tutor and, what is more, the sole interpreter of its feeling and its will. One may well ask whether such an ideology is not indebted to both Communism and Fascism. Democracy in the mind of Nasser has, anyhow, a meaning quite different from what it has in Western countries. According to him it is something that surges up from below, as in Communism; but is in practice a power exercised by a military dictatorship, as it is in Fascism.

Nevertheless, it seems that Nasser at first looked upon the part to be played by the army as only temporary; it was only to give the signal for the populace to rise:

'I believed that the whole nation was waiting and watching, before July 23, to see the first sparks fly, before launching itself in serried ranks towards the great objective. . . . I believed, no less firmly, that our own part, which was to command, would be played out in a few hours, after which the majestic masses would join in the hallowed march towards the same great end. Sometimes indeed, in my vivid imagination, I could hear the thundering tumult of the masses pressing onward in close array. But it turned out quite otherwise. The events that followed July 23 were disappointing. The spark had been struck, the vanguard had taken the fortress by storm; we were waiting only for that hallowed march of the masses . . . and long did we wait. . . . Crowds without end were flocking around. But how different was the reality from our illusions! The masses were divided

[12] *The Philosophy of the Revolution*, p. 9.

and disordered. There was no hallowed march. . . . My heart was
torn with pain and bitterness, as I realized that the mission of the
vanguard was not finished, but had only begun. We needed order,
and what followed our action was disorder. We needed unity, and
discord had arisen in our wake. We needed zeal and ardour, but in
these masses we found sloth and inertia. It is against these things
that the Revolution set up its slogan of "Union, Discipline, and
Work". For everywhere the cheapest egotism was rampant. The
word "I" was in every mouth, as though it were the solution to all
problems, the remedy for every evil.'[13]

Was it this disillusion and disappointment following upon the
seizure of power which caused Nasser to look beyond the Revolution
to other aims and wider horizons? Or was it the set-back that the
Revolution suffered in its internal policy which led this political
dreamer and mystic to attribute to himself a 'hallowed mission'
transcending the Egyptian and even the Arab frontiers? The fact is
that Nasser, who at first was hesitant, whose declarations had been
vague, obscure, and even contradictory, took a new line after his
travels abroad to Mecca and Bandung. With a new consciousness
of himself as a man with a mission to the whole Arab and Muslim
world, he now threw himself into a new political action directed to
foreign affairs. The course of the Revolution, he said, now depended
upon the factor of 'place' or 'space', the other factor, that of 'time',
being concerned more particularly with the internal history of
Egypt.[14]

Starting from the statement that 'the age of isolation is past',
Nasser announces that the mission of Egypt is to be fulfilled in three
directions: that is, in the Arab zone, the African continent, and the
world of Islam:

'Can we ignore the presence of an Arab zone surrounding us,
constituting with us a compact whole whose interests are intimately
linked with ours?

'Can we ignore the presence of an African continent in the midst
of which we are placed by destiny—the same destiny which has
decreed a fearful struggle for the future of that continent, a struggle
in which we shall be involved willynilly?

'Can we ignore the presence of the Muslim world with which we
are united not only by the bonds of religion but also by history?
Destiny, I repeat, is inexorable.'[15]

It is above all in relation to the 'Arab zone' that Nasser regards
himself in the light of an heroic leader. 'I know not why, but it is clear
to me that in this region, where we live, *an important drama is to be
played which awaits its hero.* I know not why, but it seems to me

[13] *op. cit.*, pp. 18–20.   [14] *op. cit.*, p. 45.   [15] *op. cit.*, pp. 47–8.

that this role cries continually throughout the vast region around us, to be filled by a valiant soul. . . . We have responded to that appeal.'[16] The part to be played is, first of all, that of a 'liberator'—'Be it known, therefore, whether willingly or perforce, that every Arab-speaking country is our country, and our country absolutely must be liberated.' The role in question is a political action throughout the Arab countries, to 'liberate' them; that is, to deliver them from the yoke of Western imperialism and ensure their full independence under the shield of the great Arab brother-country, Egypt. But this role is, equally, that of *the unity and superiority of the Arab race*. In his succinct and simplified review of history, the Egyptian leader proclaims that 'the Arabs are a single nation. . . . We are a part of the great Arab fatherland stretching from the Atlantic shores to the mountains of Mosul. Here as there we are brothers, children of the same father and mother. Widely separated in space, we are united by community of sentiments, as also by our common origins, by the bond of religion and language. . . . The Arab standard has floated over the Arabian fatherland from the Indian Ocean to the Mediterranean, from the mountains of Atlas to the mountains of Mosul. Never has it ceased to wave between its four frontiers from thirteen centuries and more ago until today and tomorrow—and until that day when God will raise up the dead of all nations, Chosroes and Caesar, Roderic and Charles Martel, to bear witness of what they have known.'[17]

And besides their own union, a nobler mission awaits the Arab peoples: that of serving, guiding, and spiritualizing the countries of the whole world.

'In their position midway between east and west, north and south, our countries stand in a relation to all the others of the world, like the relation of a capital city to its state. Why, then, should we not rejoice to play the part of a capital in orientating all the nations of mankind?

'We possess in our earth, in our skies and in our seas, immense resources which are the envy of many a nation to the east and to the west. Why should we not seek to exploit our resources, to take our place and steer our course in the world, so that we can restore the balance of world-forces to the benefit of all humanity?

'We have been endowed with a strength of spirit and a faith in God, as well as a sense of brotherhood, which should render us worthy of opening up a new chapter in the history of man, like that which our ancestors began thirteen hundred years ago. Why do we

[16] *op. cit.*, p. 49.
[17] Preface by Nasser to a work sponsored by the Liberation Movement, entitled *North Africa, Past, Present, and Future* (Cairo, 1954), pp. 5–6.

not again bring to the world a message of peace, compassion, fraternity, and equality, that would dispel the gloom that now darkens so many hearts and minds who no longer believe in anything but the material?

'Once we received a revelation from heaven, so that we might guide humanity towards its destiny. Thence arose the civilization of Islam, which delivered the world from darkness and error, from ignorance and discord. Today a new revelation is springing in our hearts, in order that we should again lead mankind to its destiny. Again our message is worthy to touch hearts and minds that are on the way to perdition; and to save them once more from darkness and error, ignorance and discord.'[18]

Reading such declarations, which are very like confessions of faith, we may well wonder whether this ideology of Nasser is inspired by some religious mysticism, or simply arises from fanatical nationalism; or whether it is borrowed from the racial doctrine of Hitler transposed into terms suitable for the Arab and Muslim masses. It must be noted that Nasser tries to forestall the accusation of 'racialism' which his preaching must incur, and denies that he means any such thing.

'In this we are not giving expression to any fanaticism, religious, racial, or territorial. Our religion is the religion of humanity as a whole, not the religion of one human race. For our race is the first to have proclaimed peace, brotherhood, and humanity over all the earth, and will not listen to any appeals to racialism. For our land is the land of prophecy, out of which it is impossible to send out an appeal to evil.'[19]

Here we see the same contradiction again, both in terms and in ideas. Are we, then, confronting a fanatic, crazed with his own personal ideas about history and ethnography, who thinks he has a 'sacred mission' to which he is dedicated by both the divine and the popular will? Or is he a political leader with admirable insight into the reactions of the populace, able to use them to inflame his eloquence and propel him to power? It is hard to tell: but from this standpoint Nasser's conduct presents striking analogies with that of two dictators notorious in recent history.

On the whole, Nasser's ideology of revolution appears confused and contradictory. It arises from religious mystagogy and emotional thinking more than from any social doctrine or theory, and seems not to be attached to anything systematic. Borrowed from a variety of ideologies, ancient and modern, it presents a mixture of Fascism,

[18] Preface by Nasser to a work entitled *Oil and Arab Policy* (Cairo, 1954), pp. 6–7.
[19] *ibid.*

Communism, racialism, and Kemalism, 'topped off' with some ideas from the Qur'ān. In the sphere of Arab nationalism it only repeats and amplifies, by giving them an expression apt to flatter and excite the crowd, themes that were announced at the beginning of this century by an *élite* of Arab patriots in revolt against the yoke of the Ottoman Empire. Considered as an ideology of revolution, Nasser's contributes no new element and contains very little that is original.

In any case, these ideas diverge considerably from the original intentions of the *Inkilab* as Nasser and his colleagues then defined them. In the light of their earlier principles and professions of faith, it will be instructive at this point to trace the actual course of the Revolution of 1954 at the later stages of its development.

III. FROM THE PRINCIPLES TO THE FACTS

The first government, presided over by Ali Mahir, gave earnest of a sincere desire, on the part of the men who made the Revolution, to pave the way for a return to parliamentary and constitutional rule. But, first, it was under urgent pressure to carry out the reforms for which the revolutionaries had seized power. In August, 1952, Ali Mahir demanded that the political parties should purge their own ranks. A plan of agrarian legal reform was drawn up, calculated to put an end to the vices and misdeeds of feudalism. This was drafted with care not to arouse too great discontent among the landed proprietors, but they opposed it nevertheless, and trouble broke out in several districts. While this was happening the military demanded that Mahir should dissolve the political parties altogether; and he, unwilling to engage himself further in a kind of politics not at all congenial to a man of his political temperament, gave in his resignation on September 7, 1952.

Naguib then assumed leadership of the government: he dissolved the political parties, declared the Constitution abolished, dismissed the monarchy, and proclaimed a Republic of which he became the first President. In reality, these dictatorial actions, which appeared to contradict all Naguib's first declarations and promises, were dictated by certain resolute members of a military junta which was now emerging into prominence. While conferring the supreme magistracy upon Naguib and maintaining him at the head of the government, this 'Council of the Revolution' nominated three of its most eminent members to the key Ministries of the Army, of the Police, and of the 'National Orientation'. But despite these audacious measures the revolutionaries continued, in their public speeches, to promise an early return to parliamentary rule and a free Constitution.

Seeing that Naguib inclined more and more towards moderation and favoured a return to more normal political life, the young leaders in the junta saw to it that their cleverest and most dynamic member should become Naguib's closest associate. This was Colonel Gamal 'Abdul Nasser, who was made Vice-President and thereby practically controlled the exercise of the powers of the head of the government. Sensing this menace to his own position, Naguib looked round for support among the old political leaders and managers of the parties that had been dissolved. This moment of his indecision happened to coincide with certain difficulties which held up the Anglo-Egyptian negotiations over the evacuation of the area of the Suez Canal. Exasperated, the Council of the Revolution deprived Naguib of his functions and put Nasser at the head of the government, an action which provoked great discontent among the public and in part of the army. This obliged the Council of the Revolution to reinstate Naguib, who took advantage of the moment to announce the return to parliamentary rule and fixed a date for the elections; he also promised to liberate persons under political arrest, and an amnesty for those who had been sentenced. Naguib's promises were received with much enthusiasm by the parties, the political associations, and most sections of the Press. Even the Council of the Revolution, at one moment, appeared to approve of Naguib because he abolished the censorship of the Press and seemed determined to accept a free parliamentary system. But there was an immediate outbreak of public demonstrations in acclamation of Naguib. And the Press organs of the old political parties launched violent attacks against the members of the military junta, demanding the return of the army to barracks.

Such was the situation in March, 1954. But on the 19th of that month, to the general astonishment, a decree of the Council of the Revolution reimposed the Press censorship, postponed the date of the elections *sine die*, and instituted proceedings against those who had made attacks upon the military government. At the same time the directors of the junta, reckoning that they had no longer an ally in Neguib but almost an enemy, again deprived him of his functions, maintaining him only in that of President of the Republic.

All power thus became centred in Nasser, who at once sought a new understanding with the English. An Anglo-Egyptian Agreement was signed on July 27, 1954. But the association called the Muslim Brotherhood publicly denounced this Agreement in a violent attack upon the Council of the Revolution. The Council retorted by accusing Hasan al-Hudaybi, supreme head of the Brotherhood, of having collaborated with the English against Egypt. There had been enmity for some time between the military junta and this powerful religious organization, and their opposition now developed into an acute crisis. The Revolutionary Council tried to persuade the committee of the Association to depose Hudaybi; but the Brotherhood's reply to that was to elect him, by an overwhelming majority, to be their supreme leader for life. Thenceforth the leaders of the junta waited only for an opportunity to destroy the Muslim Brotherhood, and one was provided for them on October 26. A member of the Brotherhood, Mahmoud Abd al Latif, fired three shots at Nasser when the latter was addressing a public demonstration. On the 28th of that month the Muslim Brotherhood was dissolved; and on the 30th its supreme head and the other leaders were impeached for high treason and terrorism. In the course of the trial that ensued some of the accused made references to General Naguib himself, who had given some support to the Brotherhood. On November 16 the Council of the Revolution therefore deposed Naguib from the Presidency and put him under house arrest; it was then a moot question whether he would have to stand his trial, but the Sudanese leaders intervened to prevent any further action against him. On December 3 the revolutionary tribunal passed sentence of death upon Hudaybi and six other leaders of the Brotherhood; and, although Hudaybi's sentence was commuted to forced labour for life, the six others were executed on December 7, 1954.

The military junta had now got rid of the most serious menace to the régime installed by the Revolution, and Nasser was the undisputed master of the new Egypt. Thereafter the internal situation seemed to have been stabilized in his favour; and from then onward he devoted all his energies to foreign affairs and to the building-up of his prestige with the Arab masses. Preaching the union of all the Arabs with fire and conviction, he nevertheless continued, on his own account, the policy of rivalry towards the Hashemite dynasty which had been one of those most steadily pursued under King Farouk. It was to strengthen his arm in this competition for prestige that he declared diplomatic war on the Pact of Baghdad and its signatories. He fostered all the nationalist movements that opposed Iraq and the Western Powers, concluded bilateral agreements with Saudi Arabia, Syria, and Jordan. In opposition to Israel he organized suicide commandos, thereby heightening his popularity with the nationalist masses, always highly sensitive about the question of Palestine. It was by raising hope of the liberation of Palestine that he was able to arouse so much popular enthusiasm by the announcement of his agreement with Czechoslovakia for the importation of arms. Finally, the xenophobic element in Arab nationalism found its supreme gratification in the conflict over Suez, which began with the nationalization of the Canal on July 26, 1956.

In home affairs, however, Nasser's successes have been less

spectacular. Since the dissolution of the Muslim Brotherhood, Egyptian national life has been free from crises. It has been marked by three events of importance—Nasser's election to the Presidency of the Republic, by referendum; the proclamation of the new Constitution; and the announcement of the date of the elections to the National Assembly in July 1957.

The New Constitution

The first project for a new Constitution was produced by a commission of fifty members, chosen from among the most eminent Egyptian jurists, but was at last rejected by the government and the Council of the Revolution. The outstanding features of this first design were a parliamentary system, free elections to the legislature and, therefore, the supersession of the military régime. It gave women the right to vote if they were sufficiently educated, and, if they held university diplomas, the right to sit in parliament.

In January, 1956, another plan for the Constitution, drawn up by the Council of the Revolution, was adopted as definitive and proclaimed officially after its acceptance by a referendum.

In the new Constitution important concessions are made to Arab and Islamic nationalism. Egypt is described as a part of the Arab nation (art. 2) and Islam as the religion of the state (art. 3). It may be recalled that the Constitution framed by Shishakli had also adopted these two principles, but with a difference: owing to the opposition of the Christian minorities, it did not say that Islam was the religion of the state, but only that it was the religion of the President and of the Republic.

On the social and economic plane also the new Egyptian Constitution is similar, in a number of points, to Shishakli's creation of 1953. The system it defines is on the whole socialistic, but it leaves wide scope for private capital (arts. 8, 9, 10, 11).

The system of government is *presidential*; that is the outstanding feature of the new Egyptian Constitution. According to the rules it lays down for the exercise of the President's powers and prerogatives, that functionary can dissolve the parliament (art. 111); propose laws and promulgate them (art. 132); and promulgate decrees between sessions of parliament. Further to reinforce this almost absolute power of the President and of the government over Parliament, the Constitution disqualifies the latter from making any modification in the Budget without the government's consent (art. 11).

The powers allowed to Parliament within the frame of this Constitution seem very meagre. They consist principally in the ability to make proposals and suggestions about public affairs to the government (art. 92). Parliament is equally entitled, upon the demand of ten of its members, to open discussions upon government policy but only in order to offer its advice (art. 91). The one real power that Parliament can exercise over the government is that of allowing the Prime Minister to withdraw confidence from a Minister, after interpellation and advice tendered to that Minister by ten members of Parliament. The Minister must then resign (art. 113).

Parliament, then, in its form as the National Assembly and as it was to be elected in July, is to play a chiefly consultative part. The discretionary powers remain in the hands of the President of the Republic and of the government.

The new Constitution having consecrated the presidential régime in a form faintly resembling that of the United States, it might reasonably have envisaged the recognition of free political parties in the form of two large parties, those of the government and the opposition. This would, moreover, have been a fulfilment of what had been promised, more or less, by all the revolutionary leaders. But there is no longer any question of that.

THE NATIONAL UNION AND THE PARLIAMENTARY ELECTIONS

On May 28, 1957, a decree of the President created an additional institution. This is—

'*Art.* 1. The NATIONAL UNION, the purpose of which will be to keep watch over the realization of the aims of the Revolution, and over the reconstruction of a national life that will be sound from the political, social, and economic points of view.

'*Art.* 2. The President of the Republic is charged with the presidency of the National Union.

'*Art* 3. By the President's decree, an executive committee will be appointed, to which will be entrusted the duty of presenting the candidates for election to the National Assembly, in accordance with the regulations of the Constitution and the law No. 146 of the year 1956.

'*Art.* 4. The decisions of the executive committee will be subject to a delay of twenty-four hours for ratification.'

So at first it was the Council of the Revolution, then the Liberation Movement, and later still the National Union which had to take the place of the old political parties.

That is what has become of the Revolution of July, 1952. Tracing the path it has followed, we can now measure the distance between the principles once so loudly professed and what has actually happened to Egyptian and Arab political life. For all that, we can hardly lay all the blame upon men who are suffering the common fate of all revolutionaries when they confront the actual necessities of the exercise of power. It may well seem, indeed, that in the present state of affairs and of ideas in the Middle East, the army remains the only instrument of popular aspiration that is capable of bringing about a social democracy. For the efforts of eminent civilians to promote political democracy have almost everywhere, and particularly in Egypt, been scattered in a defeat which is also, in some measure, that of the liberal West.

June, 1957

Postscript. This paper was not intended for publication. It took shape as a working memorandum, prepared, with the help of our colleagues of the Centre for Documentation and Synthesis, for use at a seminary held at St. Anthony's College, Oxford. It was written in view of the participation, in that interesting meeting, of the Study Centre for Foreign Politics.

That is the reason for the somewhat elliptical character of the exposition, which was meant to raise questions and serve as a basis for discussion, rather than to formulate any judgments of value.

ARAB NATIONALISM

In Search of an Ideology

by NISSIM REJWAN

I

WRITING IN 1942, Professor H. A. R. Gibb lamented the fact that he had not yet seen a single book written by an Arab of any country, in any Western language, that made it possible for a Western student to understand the roots of Arab culture. More than that, he said he had 'not seen any book written in Arabic for Arabs themselves which has clearly analysed what Arab culture means to the Arabs'. In 1956, another prominent Arabist, Professor G. E. von Grunebaum, of Chicago University, deplored the fact that the Arab-speaking world of today had not been able to develop 'an adequate self-image—adequate in the sense that it could reconcile emotional purposiveness with a reasonable respect for facts'.

There is no doubt that these statements still remain largely true, though not altogether so. It is true that no Arab has yet analysed the meaning of Arab culture to Arabs themselves, and that a balance between Arab emotional purposiveness and a sufficient respect for the facts is yet far to seek. Yet the student of Arab culture today cannot help being impressed by a new phenomenon. For to the contemporary Arab intellectual, Arab culture has become epitomized in one comprehensive concept—that of Arab nationalism. And within the limits of that notion there are fairly sincere attempts to pay attention to facts. No Arab today gives a thought to defining the meaning or analysing the content of Arab culture because he sees no reason for doing so. The unity of Arab culture, its content and principles, are taken for granted. The controversies which raged, only a decade ago, about what constitutes Arab culture, whether the Arabs have a uniform and comprehensive cultural heritage, or what constitutes an Arab nation, have suddenly dropped out of fashion and seem even irrelevant. No Arab intellectual now finds it necessary to talk about the Arabs' common historical background, their consciousness of race, their common environment, language, folk-lore, traditions, or their common interests. All that is taken as read. Even such a difficult question as the compatibility of Arab nationalism with Islam and their mutual relations is left aside. Arab nationalism has become a living force, not to be justified theoretically by marshalling historical or sociological facts, but to be embodied in an all-embracing creed. This creed does not consist of any analytic findings about Arab nationality; it is presented as a philosophy of life as well as an ideal of government, a credo as well as a manifesto. It sets out, in fact, to be a complete ideology to match the rival world-ideologies of Communism and Democratic Capitalism. Arab though it is, in the sense that it is formulated by Arabs for their own nation, this new ideology professes to be open to all, and to offer a way of life for humanity as a whole, when the two world giants shall have finished their fight and cancelled each other out.

The purpose of this survey is to present a brief summary of the endeavours of the Arab intelligentsia to formulate this ideology. A word should first be said about the sources of material for such a study. For both ideas and circumstances in the Arab world are changing with such rapidity that most of the discussion of them is to be found not in books but in articles, and the controversies that they provoke, in periodical journals. Dialogue of this kind—which was greatly stimulated after the events in Suez and Sinai in 1956—could hardly be conducted through the medium of books; its topicality and urgency almost limit it to journalism. Typical of the recent change in the mental climate is the fact that, in the late 'thirties and early 'forties, the whole controversy over Arab nationalism, and whether there could be a theory of it at all, was contained in three fairly slim volumes published between 1938 and 1941; and this discussion, ably summarized in a book by Hazem Zaki Nuseibeh, now seems quite out-of-date.

The monthly review *Al-Adaab*, in which most of the discussions we are about to review were published, is itself a witness to the rising force of Arab nationalism. It first appeared in 1953 in Beirut, and has become the foremost monthly published in Arabic. *Al-Adaab*, which is distinguished by the high standard of its contents, is literally as well as politically a pan-Arab organ. Published in the Lebanon, its contributors are almost equally Syrian, Egyptian, Lebanese, Iraqi, Jordanian, and Kuweiti—although the last are probably non-Kuweiti Arab teachers and other white-collar workers in the oil-rich protectorate. In the pages of *Al-Adaab*, Arab intellectuals from any part of the world can join in discussion of the same questions.

It was in *Al-Adaab*, so far as can be ascertained, that the demand for an 'Arab ideology' was first raised, by Abdullah Abdul Da'im, in September, 1955. This was followed by a series of efforts to formulate such an ideology and a controversy about it which is still proceeding, and in which a few of the writers questioned the validity of the idea, or opposed any attempt to elaborate it at the present time.

II

The first and most systematic effort at a formulation was made by Sa'adun Hammadi, of Wisconsin University, in two lengthy essays, the first of which was entitled 'The Question of Arab Nationalism: its Problem, Solution, and Method'. Hammadi's point of departure is that, despite all that has been said and written on the subject in the last fifty years, 'Arab nationalism is still in need of a comprehensive theory of life'. It is true, he admits, that the spirit of Arab nationalism has opened up new vistas of life and thought and aroused 'a tangible aspiration to a better life', but this has not expressed itself in an inclusive and well-knit theory that could illuminate the road to a national renaissance. Direct positive action alone, it is true, can overcome present evils and lead the way to a healthy and progressive future. But this also demands 'an effort of thought, to discover the principles and the involved logic of the present Arab way of life, if blind aspiration is to become organized action under conscious guidance'. The 'rotten present' of the Arabs has a logic of its own, determined not only by the material bases of their social existence. As a problem, therefore, it is definable and has a definite solution.

A society, whether healthy or sick, is of a certain structure or system, has a unique nature to which any reform of it must be appropriate. The function of thought is to find the solution suitable to its problem; otherwise the national spirit will remain in a blind alley from which no devotion or sacrifice can extricate it. Hammadi's essay is 'an initial attempt to discuss some of the theoretical premises of nationalist action'. The differences of opinion between active nationalists about the means and even the ends of their action, point to the need for a new understanding of their problem. First, then, Hammadi summarizes a common misunderstanding, as he sees it, on the part of those Arabs who see their own nationalist future too simply in terms borrowed from Western democracy, or from German and Italian totalitarianism and Marxism. After this he proceeds to his own diagnosis of what is wrong with Arab society; namely, a deeply retarded development, which dates from the disintegration of Arab culture in the later stages of the Abbasid dynasty. For him, this disintegration followed the Arab conquests and expansion; the extension of the Arab domain over so many different peoples, which led to the loss of its own harmony, its cohesion, and, ultimately, of its independence. Foreign intellectual trends infiltrated and diluted the Arab spirit inspired and led by Islam. The Abbasid period was thus one of weakness and decay underneath all the flowering of Arab civilization for which it is famous. A downward process began which, since the original cause was external, affected society rather than its members, and great individuals still emerged, but the deterioration finally overtook the individual life also.

The disintegration is now ubiquitous and deep: it is not confined to one aspect of Arab life, nor limited to its systems and laws. It is a disease whose symptoms can be traced to weaknesses in the soul of the individual Arab. And of these the first and worst, says Hammadi, are egotism and rapacity—a self-seeking wholly undeterred by ethical considerations or public spirit. This selfishness has pervaded every walk of life, however small and unimportant. Hammadi sees it in the very language of official pronouncements, in 'what is called etiquette', in the lack of dissent or criticism: it appears everywhere— in the home, in the office, at school, in the clubs, and in the professions. The danger of such a state of mind is all the more conspicuous because their national salvation calls for a generation of Arabs willing to sacrifice personal interests for the public good; national revival needs men willing to give to it, not expecting to receive from it.

The second weakness of the Arab individual today is his lack of practical initiative, his inability to try to realize his aspirations by his own efforts. As a substitute he sometimes projects a purely imaginary world of pretences unsubstantiated by any positive action—so much so that talking has become very largely the art of evading realities and deluding himself. That is why most Arab political parties present programmes so nearly identical in their professions of independence, equality and justice—though, in fact, they differ widely in the amount of sincerity, consistency, and industry with which they work for them.

This personal weakness appears also in the Arab's submission to what is accepted and traditional in many walks of life, even when it is harmful. School is the only place where the individual is to be found in revolt against the *status quo*; after leaving school he accepts the existing order and fits himself into it instead of breaking with it and joining a nucleus of the new order. Imitative, averse to change, and with a distaste for adventure, he prefers security in a bad and poor livelihood to a good and plentiful life which entails any risk. Another weakness is the inclination to superstition and dislike of anything that is scientific. Together, these enable him to escape from productive exertions into an unreal world, where grandiose hopes are supposed to be realizable by boasting and believing in supernatural signs and portents. Thus we find in the average Arab individual a confused and undecided personality at a moment when the supreme need is for decision and resolution. Hence the instability of his opinions throughout the last half-century; the successive waves of conflicting doctrine that have swept the Arab lands one after another, in whichever direction the international situation seemed to point at the time. Especially was this the case, for instance, in and around the period of the Second World War.

From this diagnosis of the individual Arab's problem, Hammadi proceeds to its social implications. First, he says, 'the problem of Arab society is a nationalist one, because it arises from this society's own experience. "The world" consists of nations, not individuals, and the Arab nation has its own unique experience; its present condition is the product of the peculiar circumstances of its entire history up to the present moment. What might benefit another nation does not necessarily apply to it; nor can the present division of the nations into two rival camps point out the true path to Arab nationalism. There are differences between the nations in the capitalist camp, and also between those in the Eastern camp. The school of thought which regards the Arab problem as simply that of backwardness in comparison with some foreign cultural development is mistaken. The path of progress for Arabs is national, not international.'

Secondly, the nationalist problem lies in the will of the people, not in laws or systems. Some nationalist groups concentrate all their attention upon the systems that obtain in Arab society and regard their defects as the root of the trouble. Some, for instance, think that the division of the Arab world into small, weak nations is the first evil to be remedied, others that foreign influence must first be eradicated; while others again locate the root of all evil in the political system, the Constitution, the electoral laws, the Press laws, or the party regulations. A fourth group traces every evil to the economic systems. But Hammadi says they are all putting the effects before the causes. A system is only the apparatus for the organization of society; the nature and efficiency of a system are determined by the character and condition of the people it governs. Systems do not create the backward or the advanced state of a society so much as reflect it.

Not that he thinks systems unimportant: he does not ignore the parts played by feudalism and imperialism in complicating the Arab problem, nor deny the need for combating these. The present system maintains the present deplorable state of affairs; but the cause of both lies in a deeper social malady. What must be done, then, to start this society on the road to health and progress?

It is the first precept of medicine that the nature of the disease determines the treatment. If the disease of Arab society be so deep-seated and extensive as to have caused a blurring and enfeeblement of the Arab soul, the remedy must be a revolution which begins *there*—in the soul that has been blurred and enfeebled. There must be a spiritual revolution that will awaken the mind, inspire it with the virtue and the strength of will of the whole nation, before that mind can repudiate present conditions and start upon a new life. This must be an intellectual revolution that will clear up obscurities and dissolve complications. It must pervade the Arab soul until the selfishness and greed of the individual are replaced by good citizenship, and he is transformed from a man who lived only for himself into a patriot living for society—at least for the period of transition. The fear which imprisons him in the existing order of things must be dispelled by courage and love of adventure. There are worn-out traditions, both religious and social, still practised by the populace, which need someone to come out openly against them—someone who will sow scepticism and doubts of their usefulness in the minds of the people, and give a lead to those who have courage to defy such traditions but are waiting to be shown how. At the same time the individual needs to be freed from his liability to negativism and extremism; the revolution must take care of this. What the Arab needs today is the restoration of his self-confidence, his belief in his own strength and virtue, through the sense of belonging to a nation which now has a world mission, and is no longer leading a trivial and merely marginal existence.

In addition to drawing up a comprehensive theory of Arab nationalism, Mr. Hammadi outlines a programme of action. Granting that revolution is the only way to a solution of the Arab problem, how, he asks, should it be planned? Could it be achieved by an external factor such as the intervention of a foreign power and the progress of world thought? Could it be brought about by changing the existing political and social systems, liberating them from foreign influence and liquidating feudalism? His answer is that the national character of the problem, as well as its depth, impose the necessity of an internal movement towards revolution. It can be effected only by a patriotic, nationalist struggle, not by foreign political factors. Nor can the required change in the individual Arab soul be brought about by external factors like advice, guidance, the change of systems or of rulers: it can be achieved only through personal commitment to the

Arab cause, through conflict and suffering. Moreover, struggle alone creates the conditions in which the individual identifies himself with the action and appreciates its results. Experience has shown that reforms bestowed from above, or obtained through certain international circumstances, have not endured; while those won after struggle and suffering have been maintained, because those who won them knew their value.

The basic character of this struggle for Arab nationalism is that it is voluntary: its motive-power is that of the free will, not that of an external force, nor of a natural law. Whereas Marxism explains progress by the movement of matter, and Capitalism explains it by the laws of human nature, the Arab nationalist holds that man's free will is the central force in society. Man is the master: he created society out of his own free will, and the story of human civilization is but the record of Man's increasing control over nature and over the forces of evil. The second characteristic of the struggle is its comprehensive aim. It is directed against everything that is rotten in the present, not against selected evils: its aim is to create a new life for the Arabs and not to introduce a partial reform. It cannot be confined to, for instance, the political sphere, because literature and the arts also play a vital part in any national renaissance. Thirdly, the struggle must be not only voluntary and comprehensive, but practical. A movement to transform Arab society, in which ignorance, poverty, and disease reign supreme, cannot indoctrinate the masses with its principles by theorizing; nor can it succeed wholly by sacrifice and effort on the part of the just and the good. It must also take the form of popular campaigns in support of direct, material demands that exemplify the spirit and purpose of the revolution. For this kind of practical work it is not necessary that the whole populace should agree with those demands or be ready for them; nor is it necessary that all, or even a majority, of the people should understand the problem philosophically.

The fourth and final question to which Mr. Hammadi offers an answer is—What is the final aim of Arab nationalism? Is it the liberation of the Arab lands from occupation by foreign imperialism? Or is it the raising of the standard of living? Neither by itself, he says, nor even both together, constitute the complete objective of Arab nationalism, although both are indubitably just and must be attained. These are incidental goals that will fade away when they have been realized; they are relative aims imposed by transient conditions.

The final aim of Arab nationalism is Right (*al-haq*). There is in man an inborn, original tendency towards Right, which manifests itself in the civilizing work done by nations in the service of humanity. This tension towards Right has been eminently manifest in the civilizations that the Arab nation has given to the world, and the mission of Arabs today is the creation of a new Arab civilization whose highest principle shall be Right. The practice of this principle is respect for man; and the new Arab civilization, if it is true to its aim, will reverence man as the most precious being in the universe, for whose sake all else is sacrificed and to whose service all nature is enslaved. Man's happiness should be the criterion of the laws; his welfare the source of all legislation.

The organization of society upon this basis would imply three things: First, that the people is the source of all power. It follows that the political apparatus must be democratic, designed solely to reflect, in an organized manner, the will of the people. Secondly, in order to maintain the dignity of the individual and realize all his potentialities, the economic system must be one that is healthy, that excludes the exploitation of man and frees him from want; it must ensure the good life to everyone, for no other reason but that he is a man. The third implication is toleration. National and religious toleration is deeply embedded in the Arab tradition under Islam; and Arab society, inheriting that principle of toleration, is capable of raising Arab nationalism to a sublimity unknown to the intolerant nationalities of the West.

In foreign relations, this principle of ethics leads to respect for other nations, to co-operation with them to eliminate imperialism and exploitation, and to the establishment of peace. 'Thus', Hammadi concludes, 'the objection that democratic socialist nationalism is only a mixture of alien and independent doctrines is baseless. For socialism and freedom themselves are but the overflow from the well of a nationalism infused with this ethical principle—that is, one whose final aim is Right.'

III

Mr. Hammadi's second essay, 'Realism and Contemporary Arab Thought' (*Al-Adaab*, March, 1957), is an attempt to 'establish in outline one aspect of Arab nationalism—its Realism'. As an historical movement, Arab nationalism has passed the stage of 'knowledge through feeling', which is that of the awakening of consciousness and the resurgence of soul. It has now to enter upon the phase of Reason. The Right, a craving for which is the driving force of the movement, is but a part of the abstract and absolute Right which moves the whole universe. In the march of history the dominant tendency is towards Right: the divided nations struggle to become united, subject nations to free themselves, societies to enlarge and consolidate civil liberties, and economic systems, also, develop in the direction of justice.

When we say that Arab nationalism is humanist (*insaniyya*), we mean, implicitly, that it is a manifestation of abstract, absolute Right in one of its forms. And the framework in which this form of absolute Right is transmuted into social principles and aims, such as justice, equality, and liberty, is fixed and formulated by the intellect. The intellect works upon material from three sources—the national-historical experience, which may be called the national heritage; existing conditions and requirements; and lastly, the experiences of other nations. The soundness of the aims formulated by the intellect depends upon its ability to make a correct evaluation of all these factors.

The discussion of Realism is, therefore, focused upon this intellectual task. The term 'realism', as it is generally used in politics, means working within the possibilities and limitations of reality. That conception of 'realism' is, however, inadequate for an understanding of the revolutionary problem. Such realism sees nothing beyond the present, it is based only upon what now exists. Its aims are limited to what can be achieved within the frame of things as they are. In short, this school of realism tries to derive what should be from what is. But the present is constituted by positive forces which work against the urge to a new creation. In itself the present is too poor to be a basis for any important progress. One can build nothing upon it except superficial and insignificant reforms which soon relapse into the putrescence of the present. Such realism, by trying to reduce the national movement merely to scientific study of the present, leads logically to escapism, simply because it takes its standards from the present.

To illustrate his view of 'the practical side of Realism', Hammadi turns to present Arab policy, notably to the emergence of the 'liberated Arab Front' of Egypt, Syria, Saudi Arabia, and Jordan.[1] During the previous twelve months there have been signs of a new tendency, including a serious endeavour to effect radical change in the conduct of foreign affairs. While the ideas of positive neutralism, Arab union, and social reform became predominant, Arab governments concluded arms deals with the Soviet Union, recognized Communist China, nationalized the Suez Canal, proclaimed agrarian reform in Egypt, and made a number of advances in public health, education, and industrialization. The strengthening of the armed forces in Syria was followed by the unification of that country's army command with Egypt's, a similar pact between Egypt, Saudi Arabia, and Yemen. Passports between Syria and Jordan were

[1] The author was writing before the defection of Jordan.

abolished; federal union was planned between Syria and Jordan, and, finally, an Arab Solidarity Pact in aid of Jordan was signed in Cairo by Egypt, Saudi Arabia, Syria, and Jordan in February, 1957.

These developments have been made possible by three factors in Arab thought which have been constant ever since the beginning of the present century. One of these is the longing for Arab unity which, in spite of physical obstacles and mental confusions caused by conflicting international, provincial, religious, and autocratic interests, has remained persistent, and has grown in force and clarity with the passage of time. Another constant factor is the aspiration to liberty, closely linked in the Arab mind with the aspiration to national unity. Demands for freedom have characterized the Arab national movements since before they overthrew the Ottoman rule. In this connection, there is a notable difference between what has happened here and what took place in the West. Whereas, in the West the nation-state came into being with the rise of absolute monarchies which subjected all the feudal and clerical rulers to one central government, the present trend towards Arab union is combined with a movement towards democratic republican rule. The third of these factors is the steadily growing demand for economic prosperity and a just distribution of its benefits. In Syria, in the Lebanon, and in Tunisia there are considerable labour movements growing in size and in organizing ability. In Egypt a kind of agrarian reform has put an end to land ownership [sic!]; and in the Arab countries as a whole there is a growing belief that the business of the state is to secure the welfare of the people in every respect.

That the Arab nationalist movement is proceeding along these three lines is evidence of the realism with which the Arab mind has conceived its aims. It means that the movement has a sound sociological basis; it is no coincidence that men of sincerity and integrity have come to power, nor is it a fortuitous agreement between their beliefs and their own desires, but a link in the chain of the Arabs' historical evolution.

Since this evolution is natural and inherent and the present effort is both the beginning and a part of a great Arab resurgence, the conscious élite must hail it with confidence and optimism. Their part is to explain it to the people, to exploit everything in it that has evolutionary potency, and protect it from the surrounding drift towards decay. They must refuse to regard the internal struggle as a breach in continuity or a sign of division. Conflict is unavoidable in a creative movement. Real unity is not to be found in continuity between the old and the new, nor in accommodation between right and wrong; unity is achieved by the victory of the new and the triumph of Right, which is the only source of real harmony.

IV

Hammadi's two essays, published at an interval of fifteen months which were decisive in the history of Arab nationalism, represent the most comprehensive and systematic attempt that has been made to formulate the creed of that movement—to define it as an ideology, a faith, as a way of life and thought. His formulation was disputed by critics who objected not so much to its content as to the idea that Arab nationalism was in need of any comprehensive theory.

But whilst this was being debated, another, equally fierce, controversy raged about the problem of priorities. Given Arab nationalism —and in these writings it is invariably 'given'—against what or whom should the struggle first be concentrated? Against imperialism, or foreign influence, or Israel, or against deviationists and traitors in the Arabs' own ranks? Or alternatively, should war be waged upon everything that is opposed to the movement, including all the above-mentioned foes *and* all the social evils which enfeeble Arab society, all at the same time? Two schools of thought emerged. One, commonly known as the 'ideological', calls for a combined action to sweep away every antagonist and inpediment; the other, which includes most of those who deprecate any formulated ideology, proclaims that so long as foreigners remain in any part of the Arab homelands, so long as Israel is there, and while Arab rulers are not uniformly arrayed against imperialism, no elaborate programmes of social and economic reform are of any use. To this latter group belong the anonymous writers of *With Arab Nationalism*, a book published in Cairo in 1957 by the Federation of Kuweiti (Student) Missions. This book sets out to prove three leading theses: That nationalism is as old as human association and is not a product of the eighteenth and nineteenth centuries—it is the socio-historic being produced by the deep, inner workings-out of relations between the members of one same society. That nationalism is not, therefore, an emotional propaganda put out by the *bourgeois* classes in order to maintain their own misrule and exploitation of the people, as historical materialists assume. Finally, that in its authentic form nationalism is *humanist*, and neither racialist nor isolationist. A nonhumanist nationalism treats other nations inhumanly. Such was the nationalism of the West, European but not humanist either internally or externally, because the exploiting classes were able to use it for their own ends of domination, at and after the Industrial Revolution.

The remaining seven chapters of the book deal with various aspects of Arab nationalism. 'Thousands of years ago, successive waves of Arabs moved from the Peninsula to the Fertile Crescent and the Nile Valley.' They were succeeded by the Islamic Arab wave, which was to give the Arab nation its present territorial domain extending from the Persian Gulf to the Atlantic. Arab nationality is not identical with the Islamic religion, though in no way opposed to it. Nationalism differs from religion because nationality is a being, while religion is a mission directed to the reform of certain aspects of that being. 'There is no contradiction between nationalism and religion, but there would be if and when religion ceased to devote itself wholly to the virtues by which man realizes union with the ideal, and became a political movement that denied the socio-historic being of nationality.' Since nationalism is a being, it is above philosophies and doctrines. 'We can say that we are Socialists or non-Socialists, democrats or non-democrats, but we cannot say we are non-nationalists', because the nation is a being to which we belong by nature. As against the Marxist interpretation of history, which is a partial view based upon only one aspect of it, the 'nationalist interpretation of history' is comprehensive, combining all the aspects of human life. It takes account of all the factors which inform human existence and influence it: Arab nationalism, therefore, is not a matter of feeling, or ideas or doctrine, nor is it a philosophy, it is the total expression of a being.

From this theoretical preamble the authors proceed to practical issues, arguing that the Arab nation is suffering from a 'crisis of being', is faced with the need for the renewal of its being. The starting-point for this re-creation of being can be nowhere but in the heart of the Arab reality, from which alone the new being can develop and come to birth, and can be no other thing than the Arab nation's consciousness of itself, as a being extending from the Persian Gulf to the shores of the Atlantic. From that consciousness follows the vision of the re-creation of the Arab nation as a society freed from imperialism and its agents. With its plundered lands restored, with its fear, poverty, ignorance, and disease abolished, the Arab nation will at last be liberated to fulfil its mission in the community of all nations for the good and enrichment of mankind as a whole.

These authors propose a programme of action divided into two phases. The first of these will 'put an end to division by unity, to imperialism by liberation, to Israel by vengeance'. The second phase will be that of the 'building of a Socialist democratic system for the Arab nation'.

On the question of 'priorities' the authors of *With Arab Nationalism* maintain that although 'our political, social, and economic problems are inseparable from each other, yet the political problem is the gravest, the most urgent, and the most acute; it is the problem that first stands in our way and prevents us from dealing with those of economics and social order' (p. 162). And although 'in order to rid ourselves of poverty, of economic and social injustices in general, we have to eliminate exploitation and make our way to Socialism . . . yet imperialism on the one hand, Israel on the other, and the present ruling, deviating, and self-seeking groups among us are certain to put up an obstinate and violent resistance. We must therefore get rid of these before we can turn to the economic and social struggle' (p 165).

The authors seem to fear that the struggle in the economic field may distract attention from the main enemy. 'It is not permissible, at this juncture, to turn the movement into an economic struggle within the nation; it must not be compelled to fight on two fronts. Yet this does not mean, of course, that it must abstain completely from economic reform; what it means is that the Arab struggle as a whole should not take on the general character of an economic revolt, as though its main enemy were the employers, when the primary problem is imperialism. The aims of Arab nationalism are therefore to be attained in two stages. The first is the phase of political struggle aiming at the liberation of the nation within a sound framework of union; the second phase is that of building up . . . the democratic Socialist structure of the nationally-unified Arab society' (p. 167).

V

Like everything written today upon the subject, *With Arab Nationalism* has provoked heated reactions. It did not appease the prevalent craving for an 'Arab ideology' that could challenge those which now divide the world; the book was accordingly attacked for its lack of a clear theory of Arab nationalism and for various other omissions. Farid Abu Atiyya, of Kuwait, writing in the July, 1957, number of *Al-Adaab*, deplored the authors' division of the struggle into two separate phases. He would allow of 'only one liberation, internal and external, both at the same time'. Atiyya agrees with most of what the authors say in definition of the problem and formulation of aims, but he refuses, sharply and significantly, to have the struggle divided into distinct phases. This crisis of the national being, he says, is also a distortion of the personality of the Arab individual. Authentic personality can be restored to this individual only by a reconstruction extending into every sphere of his life. 'To ignore his own struggle in the economic and social spheres would be to fall into sheer contradiction. Where is the type of Arab personality that is capable of doing battle for political liberation? Is it the distorted, sterile personality we now encounter in every corner of the homeland? Can such a struggle be waged by meaningless numbers of individuals without an economic or social existence—as it was, so disastrously, in Palestine? The contradiction is obvious. If we seek political liberation without having the fighting forces to bring it about, we shall never get out of the vicious circle in which we have been turning round and about for the last century or more.'

The truth of the matter, according to Atiyya, is that the Arab individual, on whom success depends, cannot be expected to defeat his enemies—imperialism, Israel, and the selfish ruling cliques within the Arab ranks—until he is provided with the essentials of economic and social existence. The authors of *With Arab Nationalism* seek the end without preparing the means to attain it. They claim that other societies have first emancipated themselves from external oppression and then built up social systems of their own. It is true that the peoples of Russia, China, India, Yugoslavia, Egypt, and Algiers [*sic!*] have gained in control over their internal affairs since they emancipated themselves from foreign domination. Nevertheless, it remains true that there is only one struggle, political and economic, being waged at one and the same time.

To take some concrete examples, says Mr. Atiyya—the Liberation Army and the Algerian people are fighting the imperialists and the traitors at the same time as they are laying the foundations for a future Arab society. And in Egypt, the great political achievements, such as the abolition of monarchy and the expulsion of the British, would have been null and void had they not been followed up by agrarian reform, and by the nationalization of the Suez Canal and of other alien enterprises. Atiyya can see no point in trying, as some people do, to see one kind of reform as a means and another as an end. He thinks it is the sign of a mechanical mentality trying to study Arab individuals as one studies chemicals in a physics laboratory. The free Arab man is the end in himself: to regard him as if he were merely a tool for the construction of some social edifice in the future is to adopt the philosophy of those who—as could be seen all too clearly at the Twentieth Congress of the Soviet Communist Party— are ready to sacrifice one or more generations of men for the sake of a future system which may be no more than a dream. The struggle for unity, liberty, and Socialism must include the renewal of every aspect of Arab life in the present—of habits, traditions, culture, and ways of thinking and reasoning.

VI

Neither the authors of *With Arab Nationalism* nor their critic Farid Abu Atiyya seem to insist on what one Arab intellectual has

called the 'philosophizing of the Arab experience'. The present controversy has become something quite different from that which raged
during the late 'thirties, an outline of which is given in *The Ideas of
Arab Nationalism* by Dr. Hazem Zaki Nuseibeh (published in 1956).
Then, the question was whether 'the life and thought of a nation can
or should be embodied in what is known as a national philosophy'.
Nuseibeh's own comment is that 'National philosophy is, in a sense,
a contradiction in terms . . . for the term "philosophy" denotes a
search for universal truths, and a philosophy which deserts the
universal for the particular, except in so far as the universal pulsates
in the particular, is anything but genuine. In this limited sense . . .
we might venture to speak of national philosophies—of British
empiricism, American pragmatism, French nationalism, German
idealism, Soviet materialism, Indian quietism, and so on' (pp. 57–8).
The old controversy was renewed by Dr. Costi Zureik with his
National Consciousness, in which he argued that a systematic, force-
ful, and clear-cut national philosophy was a necessity for a real
national revival. 'Indeed, there is no hope for an Arab national
renaissance unless it is inspired by a national philosophy which
reflects its spirit, de-limits its orientation, portrays its objectives, and
prescribes its methods.' Another advocate of an Arab national
philosophy, Abdullah al-Alavili, though he deplores the lack of any
systematic Arab ideology, draws a sharp distinction between nationalism as ideology and as a programme of action. A national ideology, he says, should satisfy three conditions: 'It should have its
cornerstone in the heart rather than in the mind, for faith is a
securer bond of union than is the intellect; it should be flexible
enough to accommodate the continual growth of knowledge and to
prevent any hardening of its emotional basis around certain assumed
truths; and it should have profundity as a system of thought, in
order to attract and satisfy the intellectual aspirations of its nationalist adherents.'[2]

It is a far cry from this to the kind of ideology that the younger
generation of Arab intellectuals are trying to formulate. Abdullah
Abdul Da'im, who, as far as can be ascertained, is the originator of
the new controversy, formulates his demand for an ideology in the
following terms: 'Arab nationalism has to draw up its programme
and define its characteristics in a clear-cut manner; it is called upon
to formulate itself in an ideology which will hold its own against
the other ideologies of the modern age.'[3] He bases this on the
assumption that 'Arab nationalism has long ago passed beyond the

[2] *The Constitution of Arab Nationalism* (Beirut), 1941, quoted by Nuseibeh,
pp. 58–9.
[3] 'Humanism, not Internationalism', *Al-Adaab*, September, 1955.

phase of emotion, when it was mere resentment against an Ottoman or a Western imperialism'. This remark provoked many reactions and rejoinders, whose echoes still reverberate in the pages of the Lebanese monthly.

Broadly speaking, these reactions were of two kinds. One came chiefly from the doctrinaire Marxists, who denied the existence of the problem and said that Arab thought was not called upon to frame a distinct ideology 'because the final end of humanity is one'. Some even denied that there was such a thing as an Arab nation, and said that talk of this kind savoured of Nazism and Fascism. We need not consider these objections in detail, however, since our present concern is only to find out what Arab nationalists themselves think about their doctrine and how they propose to present it. Of the other nationalists who opposed the call to an independent ideology, the most persistent—who have also something to say—are Abdul Latif Sharara and Ali Baddour, both literary critics and men of letters. (The latter is also a lawyer and a short-story writer from Aleppo.) Sharara's reaction to Abdul Da'im's call was prompt and final. It is not logical, he protested, to demand from the Arab nation of today an ideology comparable to, say, Communism or Existentialism. The production of an ideology must by its nature and necessity be left to the genius of the nation freely unified on its own conditions. It is unreasonable to ask anyone for what they do not have and therefore cannot give. 'The only thing the Arab nation can be asked for today is to fight for the independence of its lands, to give what it can for the sake of uniting its sons and resisting its enemies both at home and abroad. When it has achieved freedom and union, it will spontaneously, without being asked, create a new literature, a new philosophy, and an ideology—all of which will be expressions of the Arab mind and the Arab genius.'[4]

History has shown, Sharara went on to say, that there are two kinds of nationalism. One is sheer intolerance, a narrow emotionalism, the desire for domination, superiority, and exploitation; in this category we find all European nationalisms ever since the European nations were formed and until this day. The other is 'humanist nationalism', which respects the concepts of right and of justice, which believes in man and in the good, and is charged with a mission to other nations. History records, for instance, no aggressions by the Indian nation against other nations, nor do we find in its philosophies any cruelty, intolerance, praise of evil, or distortion of facts: it has never tried to prevent other nations from leading their own lives.

And so it is with the Arab nation, formed by clearly humanist

4 *Al-Adaab*, October, 1955.

ideals. The rise of Christianity and Islam within it shows that it is humanist in tendency. Zionism, however, is nothing but a reversion to heathenism and the worship of idols: in its moral and political aspects it is an experiment in the methods of primitive barbarism—which is why it has found favour with Europeans, who support it and endorse its aggressions.

VII

An essay, 'Realism and Contemporary Arab Thought', by Sa'adun Hammadi (*Al-Adaab*, March, 1957), provoked another sharp reply from Sharara. In this, he says that the existence, in the Arab world, of foreign influence, feudalism, and illiteracy prohibits the 'philosophizing of the revolutionary experience of the Arab nation'. He goes so far as to accuse the advocates of a cut-and-dried Arab ideology of playing into the hands of the West. The Westerners want to see the Arabs formulate an ideology, because they think it would show the way to an ultimate compromise between the Arabs and the West. 'Arab thought is compelled, by existing political realities, to concentrate upon political independence, even if this retards its progress in other departments of study . . . a drawback which is a direct result of the pressure that Westerners still put upon us.' Sharara concludes that, since the Arab and Moslem nations agree with both the rival world camps about the best things they have, and disagree with them about the worst, it follows that the 'distinct Arab ideology' demanded by some nationalists 'could not, on the one hand, be politically hostile to Communism nor, on the other hand, be hostile to Western democracy'.

VIII

In two separate and lengthy essays, published in June and in September, 1957, Ali Baddour (the lawyer and short-story writer) sets out to refute the advocates of an Arab ideology. They ignore, he says, the special circumstances of the Arab nation living under the special conditions of the modern world. Contemporary ideologies arose, not from the formulation of clear-cut philosophies, but out of the evolution and development of material conditions.

Citing the examples of Italy and Germany, Baddour maintains that the Arabs can find guidance in them. Those two nations possessed all the characteristics required of unified states; the distinctive method by which each achieved its unity was not inspired by a philosophical doctrine that it adopted. The justification for unifying a nation does not reside in its creation or adoption of a doctrine, nor does the absence of one nullify its claim to unification. Now, an ideology exclusively appropriate to the Arabs in their present situation would be impossible to formulate. The attempt to formulate it and at the same time to maintain contact with reality, will bring it within the framework of one of the two leading world ideologies. It will not produce a third, purely Arab, ideology to compete with the other two. That, indeed, would be a highly difficult task.

The truth of the matter, he goes on, is that the Arab world as a whole is suffering from three different diseases—first, from the inordinate number of groups competing for leadership, their differences and rivalries; secondly, from the widely different levels of social progress attained in the various Arab countries and the discrepancy between their political systems; and thirdly, from the continued existence, in some Arab lands, of strongholds retained by certain imperialist Powers. Those Powers would unite for mutual defence if once the flame of Arab nationalism grew hot enough to endanger their interests. And naturally, they are all in favour of Israel, and want to strengthen its foothold in Palestine.

The Egyptian Revolution (of 1952) presents an excellent illustration both of the effects of these diseases and of their cure. That Revolution could not produce a planned economy until it had first cured the 'leadership disease'—by abolishing the political parties. It could not join battle with the imperialists until it had managed to cut the 'supply lines', which they had established through the parties' splits and differences and with the active help of some of them. And as for the country's backwardness in social and economic development, the Egyptian Revolution did not permit elections to be held until it had, to some extent, freed the workers, peasants, salaried employees, and small traders from the tyranny of employers, landowners, and bosses. . . . A revolution does not abolish political parties because it is impatient of opposition—that is a superficial opinion, as far as the Egyptian Revolution is concerned; it abolishes them because they are part of the 'leadership disease', part of the 'sovereignty disease', and because they stand in the way of extending the Revolution beyond its borders—and this is a revolution directed to Arab union and Arab nationalism. Why, then, asks Baddour, are some of the advocates of liberation, unity, and Socialism so frightened of what he calls 'planned dictatorship'? True, there are members of political parties in some Arab countries with ugly memories of life under dictatorships—of prison and exile, torture and the violation of human dignity. 'Yet this does not affect our respect for such a "planned dictatorship" as will lead to unity in home affairs, non-alignment in the world conflict, to Arab nationalism, Arab unity, and a wide front against any aggressor.' It is because this has come to pass in Egypt that all Arabs can now hold up their heads: it is this which has given them the hope of unity, and confidence in their own thought and aspiration.

Democracy is the enemy of continuity. Our battle for unity will be long, it cannot be won without continuity and stability, and a sincere dictatorship is the system which lasts longest. 'Our belief in the value of dictatorship is not theoretical . . . it springs from our need for unity . . . for a system which can under no circumstances be a fluid, democratic one. . . . Liberty is not necessarily identical with democracy. . . . Liberty is synonymous with sufficiency of food, clothes, housing, hygiene; of cultural consciousness and emotional participation in the nation's problems. I do not know whether the Egyptian citizen of today is not getting a greater measure of freedom than he had in the days of monarchy, political parties, of the Constitution, and the freedom of the Press;—when everything was permitted, but everything had its price!'

As for those who want to formulate an Arab Socialist ideology, they may try; but they will fail, because the attempt is premature. We cannot feel like a unified nation before we attain unity. All that we can do towards such an ideology is to list a few preliminary theses. Indispensable, for instance, are the following:

(1) The Arab nation will not achieve unity unless it remains neutral between the two world camps. The world may divide itself into as many camps as it likes; but the Arab nation remains the Arab camp.

(2) This Arab neutrality is not negative; it is positive, in the sense that the Arab nation will co-operate with either of the two world camps, within such limits that this co-operation will not appear, in the eyes of the other camp, to betoken hostility against it. Those limits will be set by the Arab nation itself, not by either or both of the two camps.

(3) Since human civilization is the sum-total of Man's endeavours towards a better and higher life, the Arab nation should emulate the progress of science in both camps; for when the two dominant Powers have finished their bitter struggle in total war, the Arab nation will be the secure refuge of what remains indestructible in the human achievement.

(4) Faithfulness to the Arab nationalist idea is the duty of every Arab country which does not want to fall into the orbit of one of the two world systems. Since any deviation from such fidelity affects the personality of the Arab nation as a whole, the other Arab countries should consider it their duty to bring the deviating country back into the fold, even if it involved the use of force.

(5) The wealth of the Arab homeland is the property of the whole nation, to be applied to the improvement of the lot of all the Arab peoples. Those Arab states which can afford it must aid the needier ones until the time when all will be pooled in one great Arab economy.

(6) Western democracy, based on the plurality of political parties and divided responsibility between parliament and government, paralyses the forces of the nation—forces of growth for which ways and means must be found.

(7) For the federation of the liberated Arab states which are not tied to either of the world camps, action is needed without delay.

(8) Egypt is today the most active and energetic of the Arab states, and is therefore the best suited to the leadership of the Arab nation. This must be acknowledged by all the Arab states, including Egypt herself. Furthermore, Israel, and the imperialism which supports it, is the cancer which retards unification, in both the wider and the narrower senses, of the Arab states. There can be no union so long as Israel exists; and Israel will not disappear so long as Egypt's leading role in the union of all Arabs is not acknowledged.

(9) The ironing-out of contrasts in the social life, and the strengthening of the armed forces, are both incumbent upon every Arab country striving towards union.

IX

These, then, are some of the opinions current today among Arab nationalists. Whether concrete conclusions can be drawn from them, to the general climate of thought in the Arab world—or what such conclusions would be—are questions not easy to answer. In the first place, these views represent the thought of the 'chosen few', and not anything like a consensus of mass opinion. Secondly, neither these theories nor their exponents are necessarily representative even of the Arab *élite*, omitting, as they do—and perhaps under-estimating—the potential force of Communism in the Middle East and the possible repercussions of Russia's progressive penetration of that area.

It can be argued, on the other hand, that it is the *élites* which are the decisive factor in technically under-developed countries such as these. The masses have never counted for much in similar nationalist movements, even in Europe, and still less in the other countries of Asia. Moreover, for the time being, nationalism appears to be a much stronger and more persistent force in the Arab lands than is any European creed, including Communism. Arab rulers and the Arab intelligentsia protest that the present strengthening of relations between certain Arab governments and the forces of world Communism represents no more than a passing phase, and that it is nationalism, not Communism, which is the driving force behind the Arab revival. Nor can that view be lightly dismissed.

The picture that emerges from the studies summarized above is that of a society developing politically towards a kind of benevolent dictatorship which is not Communist in character, neither has it much in common with the capitalist democracy of the West. An illuminating comment has been made upon this by an Arab intellectual whose Western culture and training put him in a good position to survey the Arab scene with a certain measure of detachment. Albert Hourani, a British citizen of Lebanese descent, has observed that the régimes in Egypt and Syria seem to be reverting to patterns which existed in Mamluk and Ottoman days, before the incursions of the modern West. Such democratic régimes as Arab governments have copied from those of the Western nations have indeed shown little capability for efficient or responsible government. And now, in Egypt and Syria, political life appears to be going back to the old pattern of Mamluk and Ottoman times. This consisted of: (1) a military oligarchy, in whose hands lay the final authority, with a rapidly changing personnel but also with a certain continuity owing to its military structure; (2) the permanent officials who carried on the daily business of government undisturbed by political changes going on above them; and (3) the learned class, who provided the principles of social morality by which government was guided.[5]

It is to this 'learned class' that Messrs. Baddour, Hammadi, Atiyya, Abdul Da'im, and the anonymous Kuweiti students belong. And it is not without interest to see Mr. Baddour writing of the undesirability of government 'based on the multiplicity of parties', dividing responsibility and 'rendering the head of the state without responsibility'. . . . Neither is it a coincidence that he writes in such exalted terms about President Abdul Nasser as the leader of Egypt and of Egypt as leader of the Arab nation. Maybe it is really a return to the type of government that existed in Mamluk and Ottoman times. Or maybe not: the controversy is still proceeding.

[5] See 'The Decline of the West in the Middle East' in *International Affairs*, April, 1953 (quoted by Nuseibeh, p. 101).

SUDANESE NATIONALISM AND SELF-DETERMINATION

by P. M. HOLT

THE MOVEMENT towards self-determination in the Sudan is a very recent development. Less than thirteen years ago there was no Sudanese representative body in existence. It was only a little over ten years ago that the British government formally envisaged Sudanese self-determination—a possibility that the Egyptian government did not accept until after the revolution of 1952. The final stages in the accomplishment of national independence have all taken place in the period between the signing of the Anglo-Egyptian Agreement on February 12, 1953, and the termination of the Condominium on January 1, 1956. The developments which have occurred have resulted from the interaction of two factors: the appearance of a Sudanese nationalist movement and the tension existing between the two nominal partners, Great Britain and Egypt, in the Condominium.

THE MAHDIYYAH, THE SAYYIDS, AND THE SUDANESE NATIONALIST MOVEMENT

Many factors, geographical, historical, and social, have militated against the development of a national consciousness in the Sudan. In a sense the state within its present boundaries is an artificial creation, the product of nineteenth-century conquests and Great Power diplomacy. Within its frontiers are the territories of two former indigenous sultanates: the Funj Kingdom of Sennar, which fell to the forces of Muhammad 'Ali Pasha in 1821, and Darfur, which was finally absorbed only in 1916. Suakin in the east had been an Ottoman possession since the sixteenth century. The remnant of the Mamluks, fleeing from Egypt after the massacre of 1811, retained for a few years their independence in Dongola. The Shayqiyyah, farther south, dominated the great bend of the Nile. The autonomy of these and other petty states was brought to an end by the expansion of Egyptian power. Under the Khedive Isma'il (1863–79), Egyptian rule was extended over vast areas in the south and west which had previously known no social and political organization higher than the tribe. The negroid and Nilotic peoples of the upper Nile and the Bahr al-Ghazal, pagan in religion and speaking a great variety of languages, were thus incorporated under one administration with the more advanced northern Sudanese, Muslims by religion and for the most part Arabic-speaking. The Condominium perpetuated this assembling of peoples of diverse ethnic origins and historical experiences, under a common and alien administration. The competition of the Great Powers for the control of Africa led to the delimitation of precise frontiers in place of the often vague and elastic boundaries that had been possible as late as the reign of the Khedive Isma'il. But a frontier, however artificial, becomes sacrosanct once it is drawn, and the suspicion that Britain wished to detach the southern from the northern Sudan has profoundly influenced the attitude of the Sudanese.

Sudanese nationalism was in its origins, and still very largely is today, a development of the northern, Muslim, and Arabic-speaking areas. Even within these limits there were serious obstacles to be overcome. Distances were immense, and communications difficult. The way of life of the townsman differed from that of the cultivator on the river-bank or in the rainlands, and this again from the nomad camel- or cattle-owning tribes. There were wide variations in the degree of literacy and sophistication. Loyalties tended to be limited and local—to the family, the tribe, the *tariqah* or religious order.

Nevertheless, it was in this setting that Sudanese nationalism originated and became an overwhelming force. Its first glimmerings were probably in the Mahdiyyah. The Mahdiyyah began in 1881 as a puritanical movement for religious reform, very similar in its ideals to Wahhabism. It soon acquired a political significance and became involved in war with the Egyptian administration in the Sudan. The Egyptian régime was defeated and overthrown and a Mahdist state was set up which controlled virtually the whole of the northern Sudan and some riverain areas of the south. Although the puritan ideals of the movement were not maintained, especially after the triumph and death of the Mahdi in 1885, and although there was much internal opposition to the rule of his successor, the Khalifah 'Abdallahi, the state did not disintegrate and was extinguished in 1898 only by the superior armament and technical ability of the Anglo-Egyptian forces under Kitchener.

The Mahdiyyah contributed to Sudanese nationalism the tradition of a miraculously successful revolt against alien rule and the memory of an independent and militant Sudanese state. The campaigns and the tribal migrations of the Mahdiyyah shook both nomads and sedentaries out of their customary environments and widened their horizons, both physically and spiritually. The Sudanese, before the Mahdiyyah, had been a member of three communities: his tribe, his *tariqah*, and the Egyptian Sudan. The Mahdiyyah smashed the Egyptian administration, suppressed the *tariqahs*, and seriously weakened the traditional tribal authorities. In 1898 the alien administration returned, the *tariqahs* revived spontaneously, and tribal organization was gradually reconstructed. But the events of the previous thirteen years had shown that social, religious, and political groupings, which were deeply rooted in tradition or had an apparently firm basis of material power, were nevertheless impermanent.

The memory of the Mahdiyyah was not, however, wholly beneficial to the development of Sudanese nationalism. The Mahdi's claims had never received unqualified acceptance from his countrymen. The Sudanese '*ulama*', some of whom had been trained at Al Azhar, were for the most part convinced of the Mahdi's mission rather by his military successes than by his theological arguments and prophetic visions. The leaders of the *tariqahs* were divided in their views, but tended to see in the Mahdi a threat to their own influence. From the first the Mahdi was opposed by the Mirghani family, who controlled the Khatmiyyah *tariqah*. This order was widespread and influential, especially in the eastern Sudan, and enjoyed the favour of the Egyptian administration. After the death of the Mahdi, the Khalifah estranged many of his more pious followers by his failure to maintain the religious standards set when the movement began. This, coupled with the fact that he withdrew the chief military and administrative commands from the riverain Sudanese and gave them to his own western kinsmen and clients, lost him the loyalty of the most sophisticated and experienced of his subjects.

The Mahdiyyah thus polarized the northern Sudanese into two groups. When the Condominium was set up, Mahdism was proscribed, the reading of the Mahdi's *Ratib* (prayer-book) was an offence, and the Mahdist organization apparently ceased to exist. The old *tariqahs* revived, notably the Khatmiyyah. The head of this order is now Sayyid 'Ali al-Mirghani, the son of the leader who had most strenuously combated the growth of Mahdist power in the eastern Sudan. As the heads of the opposition to Mahdism, the Mirghanis were treated with considerable deference by the Condominium and British governments. Sayyid 'Ali was created a K.C.M.G. and K.C.V.O. When a delegation of Sudanese notables visited London in 1919 to congratulate King George V on the Allied victory, Sayyid 'Ali was its leader.

Among the members of this delegation was a younger man, whose position at this time was one of apparent insignificance. This was Sayyid 'Abd al-Rahman al-Mahdi, the posthumous son of the Mahdi by a woman of Darfur. His early life had been one of considerable difficulty. He had been a child during the reign of the Khalifah, when 'Abdallahi was jealously excluding the family of the Mahdi from all positions of influence in the administration. He grew up to young manhood under the early Condominium, dependent on the favours of a government which was keenly on the alert for any revival of Mahdist enthusiasm. He lived on sufferance until the outbreak of the First World War gave him an unexpected opportunity to improve his position with the Sudan government. When Britain went to war with Turkey, Sayyid 'Abd al-Rahman was asked by the Governor-General to use his influence against pro-Turkish sympathies. It was a curious echo of the call to the *jihad* against the Turks, made by the father whom Sayyid 'Abd al-Rahman had never known.

During the next twenty years, Sayyid 'Abd al-Rahman gained open recognition for himself and his *tariqah* from the Condominium government. He himself became a wealthy landowner, and acquired great influence on the White Nile (where his holdings lay) and in the western Sudan. When the first generation of Sudanese nationalists appeared in the 'twenties and 'thirties, several of their leaders were in close contact with him. Thus Sayyid 'Abd al-Rahman came to occupy a dual position. To the members of his *tariqah* he held a mystical position as the son of the Expected Mahdi. To the political nationalists his father was a religious reformer and nationalist leader and he himself was significant as the rival of Sayyid 'Ali al-Mirghani, who displayed no political ambitions and was too much in the favour of the government.

During the 'thirties and 'forties there was a change in the standing of the two Sayyids in regard to the nationalist movement. The rise in Sayyid 'Abd al-Rahman's status brought its own nemesis. He, too, received his knighthood—in 1926, ten years after Sayyid 'Ali. His ambition and undoubted ability began to alarm many Sudanese, who feared the restoration of a Mahdist monarchy in his person. His growing wealth may also have been a cause of offence in a country where great capitalists are few and there is a pronounced feeling of social equality. In contrast, Sayyid 'Ali remained withdrawn from politics but uneasily aware of the rapid rise of his rival to parity with himself in the esteem of the government. He began to strengthen his ties with Egypt—at a time when Egyptian political influence was at its nadir in the Sudan and the government viewed with apprehension any possibility of its revival. Thus the situation of the 'twenties was being reversed. Sayyid 'Ali rather than Sayyid 'Abd al-Rahman now represented opposition to the Condominium government, and political nationalism became associated with him and his *tariqah*.

This change in the position of the two Sayyids explains the apparent paradox in the result of the Sudanese general election of 1953, when to all appearances a strongly nationalist public opinion swept into power a party ostensibly devoted to unity with Egypt. Sayyid 'Abd al-Rahman's party, advocating total independence, was heavily defeated. The key to the situation lay, not in the slogans, but in the relationships of the parties to the two Sayyids and of these to the Condominium government. As Sayyid 'Abd al-Rahman had grown in governmental favour, he had lost in national prestige.

DEVELOPMENT OF POLITICAL PARTIES

Although the two Sayyids played, directly or indirectly, a considerable part in the rise of Sudanese nationalism, the nationalist movement from the later 'thirties developed its own institutions and threw up its own leaders. The institutions were the Graduates' General Congress and the political parties, notably the Ashiqqa' and Ummah Parties. The leaders, of whom the most notable was Sayyid Isma'il al-Azhari, first Prime Minister of the Sudanese Republic, were members of the new middle class which had grown up under the Condominium. Educated along English lines in the Gordon Memorial College at Khartoum, they were the first generation of Sudanese to grow to maturity under the impact and the challenge of Western influences. Their experience was not confined to the Sudan. Some of them, including Sayyid al-Azhari himself, had studied at the American University of Beirut. They were frequent visitors to Egypt, and occasionally reached England. But the direct influence of travel to England was to be felt more by the younger Sudanese, who came over in increasing numbers for training after the Second World War. Men of this stamp regarded nationalism from a secular point of view; the Islamic nationalism of the Mahdiyyah was instinctively felt to be an anachronism and failed to inspire them. Their problem was to communicate their political aims to the mass of their countrymen, to whom the phrases of Western political thought were lacking in emotional and intellectual content. Hence they were driven to ally themselves with one or the other of the Sayyids, whose popular prestige was enormous and who had a firm command over Sudanese emotions.

The relationship between the nationalists and the Sayyids was thus in origin a marriage of convenience. It gave ground for two criticisms which were frequently made in the later years of the Condominium—that the Sudanese nationalists were not representative of the country as a whole, and that the Sudanese political parties were an unreal façade covering the old rivalry between the Mahdist and Mirghanist *tariqahs*. Both these criticisms had a considerable element of truth in them at the outset, but they did not take into account the possibility of development and they have become progressively less true as the Sudan has moved towards independence. The political education of the mass of the Sudanese has as yet been both brief and superficial, but the ancient loyalties to the Sayyids and the *tariqahs* have played their part in mediating to the less sophisticated elements of the population something of the ideas of the political nationalists. By a paradox not unknown in countries passing through this phase of development, the nationalist leaders have become more representative because they have succeeded in communicating their aims to their countrymen. The fact that Sayyid al-Azhari has now become a national figure in his own right, and that political groupings are developing an independence of the *tariqahs*, was shown in December, 1954, when al-Azhari dismissed from his Cabinet an able minister, Sayyid Mirghani Hamzah, who was particularly favoured by the Khatmiyyah leadership.

Political organization began, in a veiled form, after the Anglo-Egyptian Treaty of 1936. Sudanese resentment that their future should be decided by negotiations between two foreign Powers found an outlet in the foundation of a body called the Graduates' General Congress. Its constitution was made known on March 12, 1938. Membership was confined to 'graduates', i.e. persons who had completed at least the intermediate stage of education. Its object was 'to promote the general welfare of the country and its graduates'. The Sudan government from the first refused to regard the Congress as a political body, and would not accept its views as representative of Sudanese opinion.

Controversy over these points arose in 1942. The war was in a highly critical phase. The Atlantic Charter had been published. The Civil Secretary, who controlled the administration, was Sir Douglas Newbold, a man of liberal views and possessed of much goodwill for the educated Sudanese. On April 3 the Committee of the Congress presented to the Civil Secretary a memorandum stating twelve demands. All of these had political implications, and the first went to the heart of the matter. It asked for: 'The issue, on the first possible opportunity, by the British and Egyptian governments, of a joint declaration granting the Sudan, in its geographical boundaries, the right of self-determination, directly after this war; this right to be safeguarded by guarantees assuring full liberty of expression in connection therewith; as well as guarantees assuring the Sudanese the right of determining their natural rights with Egypt in a special agreement between the Egyptian and Sudanese nations.'

The Civil Secretary's reply was crushing. The government was not prepared to discuss the revision of the Condominium Agreement with 'any body of persons'. The Congress had forfeited the confidence of the government by submitting the memorandum, since it had thereby committed the errors of 'claiming to represent all the Sudanese' and 'attempting to turn itself into a political national body'. Finally, the Congress was informed that the government was 'constantly studying and carrying out plans for the closer association of the Sudanese with the direction of their affairs and for the general welfare and orderly development of this country and its people'. This, however, was 'the duty and business of the Sudan Government alone'. Further correspondence took place and the exchange was concluded by Newbold in September.

Although the Congress had stuck to its guns in these exchanges, a rift had appeared between the moderate group, including the president, Sayyid Ibrahim Ahmad (later Minister of Finance), who were prepared to trust the government further, and those who felt that the Civil Secretary's rebuff was aimed at the educated Sudanese as a class and indicated a preference for traditional, if not reactionary, men and methods of government. The leading figure in this second group was Isma'il al-Azhari, who was a teacher of mathematics in the Gordon Memorial College, then a secondary school. From this point al-Azhari's influence steadily increased, both in the Congress and among the students. The capture of the Congress by the Azhari group was, however, accompanied by a decline in the prestige of this body, since the educational qualification for membership was lowered and canvassing was carried on indiscriminately. The attempt to gain political recognition for the Congress had failed. Al-Azhari's attempt to turn it into a political party by swamping the original membership had succeeded but proved unprofitable. The rift between the moderates and extremists in 1942 was the basis of party grouping during the next thirteen years.

The result of the emergence of al-Azhari as a leading political figure was the formation of a party around him known as the Ashiqqa' (Blood-brothers). The aim of this group was unity with Egypt. It worked in alliance with the Khatmiyyah *tariqah*, although Sayyid 'Ali himself remained cautious over entering into any political commitments. From the other Congress groups, which had been prepared to view the acts of the Condominium government with more patience, developed the Ummah Party, under the patronage of Sayyid 'Abd al-Rahman al-Mahdi, whose son, Sayyid Siddiq, became its titular head. Its aim was the complete independence of the Sudan. In the circumstances, the alliance of the moderates with the Mahdist *tariqah* was understandable, but it seriously prejudiced their position in the eyes of many Sudanese, particularly the rising generation of students. The ambition of Sayyid 'Abd al-Rahman, the favour with which he had come to be regarded by the Condominium government, and unhappy memories of the Mahdiyyah obscured the individual merits of members of the Ummah Party, some of whom were among the most able and experienced Sudanese. Even the name of the party had to some ears a slightly ominous sound. Although *ummah* is now the current Arabic word for nation, its older significance of 'the Islamic community' persists. And in Mahdist usage, 'the Islamic community' was restricted to those who accepted the mission of the Mahdi, all other Muslims being regarded as infidels.

There were many Sudanese who deplored the division in the nationalist ranks. At the end of the war it seemed that the Sudanese case might go by default for lack of agreement among the leaders of public opinion. So when the revision of the Anglo-Egyptian Treaty of 1936 was agreed upon between the British and Egyptian governments in 1945, a number of independent members of the Congress worked out a formula which was accepted by both sides. The key demand was for the setting up of a free democratic government in union with Egypt and in alliance with Britain. This government was to decide upon both the form of union and the type of alliance. An all-party delegation then went to Cairo in March, 1946, but talks with Egyptian politicians soon showed that only the Ashiqqa' programme of unity under the Egyptian crown was acceptable there. The supporters of independence thereupon returned to Khartoum with the division of Sudanese nationalism more marked than ever.

The next crisis of Sudanese nationalism occurred in 1948. The Sudan government wished to set up a Legislative Assembly and an Executive Council as a means of associating Sudanese effectively with the hitherto British-controlled administration. The Egyptian government refused to endorse this modification of the Sudanese Constitution, and ultimately the required legislation was promulgated with the unilateral authorization of the British government. The Ashiqqa' responded by boycotting the elections, held in November, and by staging demonstrations. Denunciations of the Legislative Assembly as a stooge of the British found a ready hearing among the students. Throughout the next five years the schools and colleges witnessed recurrent strikes and demonstrations, which menaced the quality and quantity of their output at a time when the need for educated men and women was rapidly increasing. At a demonstration in Omdurman, al-Azhari himself was arrested and underwent a period of imprisonment.

Under the circumstances the Ummah Party naturally won the election and controlled the Legislative Assembly. Meanwhile a new grouping of its opponents was preparing. Al-Azhari's popularity began to suffer from the closeness of his association with Egypt, much as Sayyid 'Abd al-Rahman's had suffered from his relations with the Sudan government. Moreover, some of the Sudanese were becoming less enthusiastic for a close association with Egypt, the political condition of Egypt at that time being in certain respects unhealthy. A new political organization was therefore formed in August, 1949, known as *Al-Jabhah al-Wataniyyah*, the National Front, aiming at nothing closer than 'dominion status' under the Egyptian crown. The backing of Sayyid 'Ali al-Mirghani and the numerical support of the Khatmiyyah *tariqah* were now transferred to this more moderate group. For a time al-Azhari seemed in eclipse. In 1951 the party split between its founder and a rival leader, Sayyid Muhammad Nur al-Din. An Egyptian attempt to compose their differences was later successful.

At the end of 1951 it seemed likely that Sudanese political life might degenerate into a dreary round of boycotts, demonstrations, and party schisms. The picture was dramatically changed by the Egyptian military revolution of July, 1952, which removed King Farouk from the scene and placed at the head of the Egyptian state General Muhammad Naguib, a man half-Sudanese by origin, whose sympathy for the Sudanese was rewarded by the overwhelming devotion which his name inspired in them. The new Egyptian régime acquired an immense fund of goodwill in the Sudan and reversed the inflexible attitude of its predecessor in regard to Sudanese self-determination. In contrast the British proposals now seemed cautious and hesitating. On January 10, 1953, representatives of the chief Sudanese parties signed a pact supporting the proposals of the Egyptian government. Once again the Ummah and their opponents had sunk their differences for common action. The place of the old Ashiqqa' and National Front had now been taken by a National Unionist Party (*Al-Hizb al-Watani al-Ittihadi*), and a new group, the Socialist Republican Party (*Al-Hizb al-Jumhuri al-Ishtiraki*), had come into being. This last, which had published its manifesto in December, 1951, was backed by a number of tribal leaders. It was opposed to union with Egypt and equally opposed to the inception of a Mahdist monarchy. Its appeal was overrated by non-Sudanese observers and its influence upon the course of events was nil.

From what has been said above, it will be clear that relations between Britain and Egypt and the political history of the latter country have had a profound effect and at times a determining influence both upon the development of the Sudanese national movement and upon the steps by which self-government and self-determination were realized. I shall now deal with this aspect of Sudanese political development and, in conclusion, outline the stages by which independence was attained.

EGYPT AND THE CONDOMINIUM

The constitutional and political development of the Sudan has, since 1898, been deeply affected by both the course of internal events in Egypt and relations between that country and Britain. A number of complications arose out of the ambiguous status of the Sudan under the Anglo-Egyptian Condominium. The Condominium itself was devised by Lord Cromer as an instrument of British control over the newly reconquered territory of the Sudan. The formulae of the Condominium Agreement preserved nominal Egyptian authority over the Sudan, but conferred supreme military and civil power on a Governor-General appointed on the initiative of the British government. In effect, from 1899 to 1924 the Sudan had an autonomous administration under the control of senior British officials. Throughout this period the Sudan was never technically a British colony, and at no time did it come under the Colonial Office.

The inconsistencies of the Condominium Agreement were of no great practical importance so long as the British dominated Egypt; however, the position was changed when, in 1922, Britain declared Egypt to be an independent sovereign state. From that point on, Egyptian politicians became more vociferous in their demands that full Egyptian authority over the Sudan be recognized. The British, however, deferred the entire question by insisting upon maintenance of the *status quo* until an Anglo-Egyptian Agreement was reached.

Matters came to a head when, in 1924, the Governor-General and Sirdar, Sir Lee Stack, was assassinated by an Egyptian in Cairo. Allenby, the British High Commissioner, immediately delivered an ultimatum in which he demanded the withdrawal of Egyptian military forces from the Sudan. The Egyptian government complied, and Egyptian civil servants, in addition to troops, were withdrawn. This made possible the creation of the British-officered Sudan Defence Force, and the posting of Sudanese to appointments previously held by Egyptians in the civil service. In all but name the Condominium had ceased to exist, but for a long time to come self-government appeared an infinitely remote contingency.

From 1924 to 1953 the Sudan remained one of the principal obstacles to Anglo-Egyptian co-operation. The Treaty of 1936 again postponed the question of sovereignty but relaxed the policy of excluding the Egyptians. The question remained in abeyance during the Second World War, but from 1945 to 1952 another period of futile negotiations and growing tensions followed.

While successive post-war governments in Cairo, echoed in the Sudan by the Ashiqqa', became more insistent that the two countries be united under the Egyptian Crown, the British in Khartoum displayed increasing sympathy for Sudanese autonomy, from both Britain and Egypt. In London, Egyptian claims to the Sudan were countered with the assertion that the Sudanese must, in due course, be free to decide their own future.

Matters might have remained indefinitely at a deadlock between Britain and Egypt, with the Sudan slowly moving towards self-government under British auspices in spite of Egypt's ineffective fulminations, had it not been for two events. In October, 1951, the Egyptian government denounced the 1936 Treaty and the Condominium Agreement. The Governor-General, supported by Britain, declared this unilateral abrogation to be invalid. To the Sudanese, however, this dissolution of partnership indicated that the question of sovereignty could no longer be deferred. The way to an agreed solution was still blocked by Egyptian insistence on sovereignty over the Sudan, but in July, 1952, the Army Revolution took place. The new régime accepted the proposition of Sudanese self-determination. This dramatic reversal of traditional policy had momentous effects both on the speed and on the quality of constitutional developments in the Sudan.

SUDANESE ASSOCIATION WITH THE ADMINISTRATION

Until the end of the Second World War, British control over the Sudan Government was undiminished. The administration was a model of paternalistic rule devoted to maintaining the security and increasing the prosperity of the country and conscientiously furthering the best interests of the Sudanese as the British political officers saw them. With the less Westernized, unsophisticated Sudanese, the relations of the Sudan Political Service (as the administrative service was called) were generally happy. Between the educated Sudanese and the British administrators there was less sympathy. The administration had a high reputation with British colonial officials and other experts who came into contact with it, but the service neither sought nor received much publicity. In the circumstances the Sudan government was able to proceed on its way with remarkably little external interference.

The association of the Sudanese with the government could take place in either of two ways: by the appointment of Sudanese to administrative posts, or by the establishment of institutions through which Sudanese opinion might exert influence on policy. The first of these ways had been followed from the early days of the Condominium. But incorporation of Sudanese in the official cadres did not for many years include the holding of posts of great responsibility. In tribal and local administration the position was rather different. A series of ordinances between 1922 and 1931 regularized and extended the judicial powers of the notables, and certain administrative functions were also devolved on men of this class. By the educated Sudanese these measures were regarded with mistrust. The tribal system and the authority of the old sheikhly families had been shattered by the Mahdiyyah. The younger generation of educated men saw in the fostering of native administration (in this restricted sense) an attempt to create a client class of subservient local authorities. The experiment was outspokenly criticized by the late Sir James Currie (formerly the first Director of Education in the Sudan), who wrote in 1935 of 'young administrators diligently searching for lost tribes and vanished chiefs, and trying to resurrect a social system that had passed away for ever'.

The second form of association of the Sudanese with the government, namely through institutions influencing policy, was much later in appearing. This new departure was undertaken when Sudanese nationalism and Egyptian activities were gaining in strength and ruffling the superficial calm which had prevailed since 1924. The changing situation was realized by the late Sir Douglas Newbold who, as Civil Secretary from 1939–45, was the effective head of the administration. Under his auspices in 1944 provincial councils were set up, as was an Advisory Council for the northern Sudan. This consisted of the three British Civil, Legal, and Financial Secretaries, and twenty-eight Sudanese members; eighteen represented the provincial councils, two the chamber of commerce, and eight were nominated to represent the educated classes. The Council met twice yearly under the presidency of the Governor-General.

Although this seemed at the time a great concession to Sudanese political consciousness, it was far from satisfying even the moderate nationalists. To begin with, the functions of the Council were purely advisory; the formulation of policy still remained in the hands of the Governor-General's Council, a purely official and British body. Secondly, the limitation of both the membership and the sphere of debate to the northern Arab provinces nourished the old fear that the ultimate purpose of the British was to partition the country and annex the southern Sudan to Uganda. As nationalist opinion became more powerful during the next ten years, any hint of a special status for the South immediately provoked a dynamic reaction in the northern Sudan. Thirdly, the high proportion of tribal notables among the provincial members aroused the suspicion of the educated Sudanese that the government was attempting to preserve a permanent majority of men with an uncritical and conservative outlook.

Since the Council was purely advisory, the argument could be put forward that its establishment did not alter the Constitution of the Sudan and so did not require the approval of the Co-domini. But matters could not remain like this. Under the irresistible pressure of Sudanese nationalism and the need to outbid Egypt, a further step had soon to be taken. In 1946 an Administrative Conference was set up to study the closer association of the Sudanese with the central and local governments, and at the same time, a committee was formed to make recommendations for the Sudanization of the civil service. Both bodies had British and Sudanese members. It is interesting in retrospect to note that the Sudanization Committee suggested that 62·2 per cent of the posts held by expatriates were to be Sudanized by 1962. The recruitment of expatriates on pensionable service was suspended in 1947, but the effect of this was masked by the increase of appointments on contract. The crux of Sudanization lay in the Political Service. After 1947, British officials continued to be recruited to this branch on long-term contracts and there was no rapid increase in the appointment of Sudanese. This lag was defended on the grounds of maintaining standards, but created a serious problem when Sudanization was sharply accelerated in 1954.

The Administrative Conference, which was boycotted by the Ashiqqa', resulted in the passage of an ordinance to establish a Legislative Assembly and an Executive Council in place of the Governor-General's Council. The Executive Council represented a distinct advance in the application of the principle of Sudanese association. It consisted of twelve to eighteen members, of whom at least half were Sudanese. The Executive Council approximated in functions to a cabinet. The Legislative Assembly also embodied a concession to Sudanese political feeling in that it represented the South as well as the North and had genuine legislative powers. But its membership was so constructed as to render it sensitive to administrative control. In the first place, all members of the Executive Council were *ipso facto* members of the Assembly. Secondly, of the remaining seventy-five seats, only ten were filled by direct election. These were held by representatives of seven large towns. Forty-two seats were filled by indirect election in the North. Thirteen were held by Southern members elected by their provincial councils; ten were filled by nominees of the Governor-General.

Thus, although the Assembly was representative, the representation was so filtered as to give the preponderance to the more docile elements. The tribal notables were again present in force. Unfortunately, the inception of the Assembly and Executive Council coincided with (and to some extent caused) a period of intense exacerbation of Anglo-Egyptian relations. Hence the constitutional changes of 1948 were authorized unilaterally by the British government, against Egyptian protests. A precedent was thereby set for the unilateral Egyptian denunciation of the Condominium Agreement three years later. The Ashiqqa' and cognate parties boycotted the elections, and so the majority in the Assembly was composed of Ummah Party members. Although the Sudanese members were capable of wise and statesmanlike action, the Assembly was inevitably regarded by the nationalists outside it as a party instrument rather than a national institution, a British device to conceal control rather than a genuine step towards self-government.

Under the Legislative Assembly from 1948 to 1952, the pattern of events from 1944 to 1948 repeated itself, but the British position in the Sudan weakened. The Ashiqqa', backed by Egypt, were openly hostile to the *status quo* and had much support from the educated Sudanese and students. The Ummah were in power, but in circumstances that made it necessary to outbid their rivals for popular support. The British were committed to Sudanese self-determination and, although they might think it desirable to slow the pace of advance, they could not oppose movement in that direction. In 1951, following a vote in the Assembly, a Constitution Amendment Commission was set up. The Ashiqqa' again refused co-operation. The Commission broke up some months later in a controversy over sovereignty resulting from the Egyptian abrogation of the Condominium Agreement, but a substantial part of its work was enacted as a Self-Government Statute in April, 1952. This Statute provided for an entirely Sudanese Council of Ministers (in which two Ministers were to be from the South) and a bicameral Parliament. The Senate was to consist of fifty members, twenty being nominated by the Governor-General and thirty chosen by provincial electoral colleges. The House of Representatives was to have ninety-five members, of whom thirty-five would be elected directly and fifty-seven indirectly. A gesture was made towards the educated Sudanese by creating a three-member Graduates' Constituency. The Governor-General's position approximated that of a constitutional monarch, but he had certain special responsibilities, notably for the South.

THE ANGLO-EGYPTIAN AGREEMENT OF 1953 AND ITS CONSEQUENCES

Had the Farouk régime continued, this statute would probably have been implemented as it stood and the deadlock of Sudanese parties would have recurred. The revolutionary change in Egyptian policy after the events of 1952 removed the danger of another period of frustration. By accepting the principle of Sudanese self-determination, the new Egyptian government made possible joint action with both wings of the Sudanese national movement—a new grouping of forces which worked to the disadvantage of the British position. Anglo-Egyptian negotiations finally issued in the Agreement of February 12, 1953. This provided for a transitional period lasting not more than three years. During this period the Condominium Administration was to be liquidated and, upon its conclusion, self-determination was to take place.

The governmental institutions of the transitional period were to be basically those of the Self-Government Statute of 1952, but with certain important changes. Most of the Governor-General's residuary powers were to be exercised with reference to a five-member commission, composed of two Sudanese, one British, one Egyptian and one Pakistani member. The special responsibility of the Governor-General for the South disappeared; instead, a colourless phrase spoke of his responsibility 'to ensure fair and equitable treatment to all the inhabitants of the Sudan', while the Agreement emphasized as a fundamental principle 'to maintain the unity of the Sudan as a single territory'. The elections for the Parliament were to be controlled by an Electoral Commission consisting of three Sudanese and one member each from the U.S.A., Britain, and Egypt, under an Indian chairman. This body drew up the electoral rules, reduced the number of indirect-vote constituencies from fifty-seven to twenty-four, and increased the graduates' representation to five members. The election took place during November and December of 1953.

The administration appears to have under-estimated the strength of the popular appeal exercised by al-Azhari and the newly formed National Unionist Party, and correspondingly to have over-estimated the chances of the Ummah and the so-called Socialist Republicans. The radicalism of the title of this last group was belied by its membership, largely composed of the tribal and local notables who had been built up by native administration and had been strongly represented in the Advisory Council and the Legislative Assembly. In the event, success in the elections went neither to the Ummah Party, with its policy of co-operation with the administration, nor to the conservative notables. The National Unionist Party (N.U.P.) won a block of

51 out of 97 seats in the House of Representatives. The opposition was divided; the largest single party was the Ummah with 22 seats. The Socialist Republicans won only 3 seats. In the Senate the N.U.P. won 22 of the 30 elected seats, the Ummah 3, the Socialist Republicans none. A Socialist Republican was subsequently introduced by nomination. During the election there were frequent and vociferous Egyptian complaints that the British administrators were influencing the voters. This accusation was answered by the final results. British counterclaims were less numerous but better founded. Nevertheless, in spite of the propagandist and material assistance given unsparingly by the Egyptians, the victory of the N.U.P. seems to have been spontaneously desired by the majority of those among whom there was any real political consciousness. Paradoxically, the party using the slogan of unity with Egypt seemed to offer the best prospect of genuine independence.

THE PERIOD OF TRANSITION: 1954–55

The victory of the N.U.P. created a situation of great delicacy and some tension. The new Sudanese Parliament had the function of choosing the Prime Minister. On January 6, 1954, it elected Isma'il al-Azhari to this office, and three days later al-Azhari formed his Council of Ministers entirely from N.U.P members. The Ummah Party was excluded from political control. But in spite of its defeat it remained a very powerful organization through its leadership and its links with the Mahdist sect. Ummah hostility to Egypt was unabated. The British administrative officials who carried on the daily routine of government now found themselves under the direction of Sudanese, belonging to a party for which they felt little sympathy and which showed, in its hour of triumph, symptoms of bitter anti-British sentiments. It is to the credit both of the Sudanese ministers and of the British officials that the potential hostility between them never developed. Xenophobic utterances did not prevent friendly personal relations, while the British Political Service publicly accepted with dignity and goodwill its changed status and impending dissolution.

With the establishment of a Sudanese Council of Ministers began the 'transitional period' in which the Condominium Administration was to be liquidated. This process was carried out by a Sudanization Committee, established under the Anglo-Egyptian Agreement. It consisted of three Sudanese members selected by the Governor-General from a list submitted by the Prime Minister, together with a British and an Egyptian member. The object of this body was, as stated in the Agreement, 'to provide the free and neutral atmosphere requisite for Self-Determination'. Its functions were more particularly defined in an Annex:

'The duties of the Sudanization Committee shall be to complete the Sudanization of the Administration, the Police, the Sudan Defence Force, and any other government post that may affect the freedom of the Sudanese at the time of Self-Determination. The Committee shall review the various government posts with a view to cancelling any unnecessary or redundant post held by Egyptian or British officials.'

Since the Sudanese majority on this Committee was nominated by the N.U.P. ministry, these functions were very rigorously exercised. All British administrative officials (the total was 140 on the eve of self-government) and the handful of police and military officers (amounting to 8 and approximately 30 respectively) were dismissed during the course of 1954. In the technical departments—education, agriculture, medicine, and others—the process of replacing British by Sudanese in the chief posts was sharply accelerated. In consequence many expatriate officials in technical posts found the possibilities of promotion limited or totally withdrawn, while others felt their continuation in their existing posts endangered. The possibility that such officials might prefer to leave the service voluntarily had been foreseen, and the Sudanese Parliament enacted in July, 1954, an ordinance which not only provided compensation for officials whose employment was terminated by the rulings of the Sudanization Committee, but also for other expatriate officials giving or receiving due notice. Thus 1955 saw an exodus of British officials from the technical departments. The parting was accomplished without bitterness on either side. A number of British have remained in the service and have maintained a happy relationship with the Sudanese. In various departments, notably that of education, British officials are still being recruited for service in the Sudan.

Relations between the N.U.P. government and its Sudanese opponents developed less auspiciously. Matters came to a head on March 1, 1954. On that day it was intended to have a state opening of the second session of Parliament, attended by representatives of Britain, Egypt, and other Powers. The opponents of unity with Egypt planned a great demonstration against the Egyptian delegation at Khartoum airport. On arrival, the Egyptian party were quietly conveyed to the Palace by an unexpected route. The disappointed demonstrators, their numbers augmented by hundreds of Mahdist tribesmen imported for the occasion, swarmed into the centre of the town. A clash occurred with the police and a number of persons, including a British and a Sudanese officer, were killed. The opening of Parliament was postponed, a state of emergency declared by the

Governor-General, and the distinguished foreign visitors hurried home.

The bloodshed of March 1 came as a shock to Sudanese public opinion. A blow was struck at the prestige of the Ummah Party, a leading member of which was sentenced to death (subsequently commuted to fourteen years' imprisonment) for instigating the riots. On the other hand, the events showed the N.U.P. government that the policy of unity with Egypt could be achieved only at great cost, perhaps civil war. Other considerations were reducing the fervour with which the unity of the Nile Valley was now preached by Sayyid al-Azhari and his associates. With aid from Egypt they had broken the hold of Britain over the Sudan; now, having tasted power, they were less inclined to a union with Egypt which would inevitably imply subordination. Moreover, developments in Egypt were shaking Sudanese confidence in that country, Muhammad Naguib was a hero to many Sudanese. Their leaders had personal memories of him in his youth, and the success of the Army Revolution under what seemed to be his leadership was flattering to Sudanese national pride. The rift between Naguib and Nasser in the early months of 1954 had been watched with anxiety. When, on November 14, 1954, Naguib was finally ousted by Nasser, it was felt by many Sudanese as a personal tragedy. Disillusionment with Egypt spread. 'The blessed movement of the Army' was revealed as a military dictatorship, and stood in unpleasing contrast to Sudanese parliamentary democracy. Nor were extremists any more favourable. Communists remembered the imprisonment of Sudanese Communist students in Egypt. The persecution of the Muslim Brotherhood antagonized pious opinion in general, apart from adherents of the order.

Al-Azhari moved steadily but cautiously in response to the growing popular demand for complete independence. His position was complicated by the fact that the N.U.P. was a composite party and expressed several shades of opinion. A step towards greater homogeneity was taken in December, 1954, when he dismissed three Ministers belonging to the wing most in favour of independence. But during the following months antagonism with Egypt grew. Negotiations over the Nile waters broke down in April, 1955. Al-Azhari now openly championed Sudanese independence and in June, 1955, dismissed two further Ministers—on this occasion members of the wing which still favoured unity with Egypt. One of the dismissed Ministers, Sayyid Muhammad Nur al-Din, was the same man who had split the Ashiqqa' Party in 1951. He and other malcontents now charged the Prime Minister with 'dictatorial methods', but they had lost the ear of the public. The revolution in al-Azhari's policy was complete when he began conversations with leaders of the Ummah Party on the work of the forthcoming parliamentary session.

Meanwhile a storm was brewing in the southern Sudan. Here the electoral procedure which had brought the N.U.P. into power had contrasted incongruously with the character and outlook of the people—for the most part unsophisticated tribesmen, ignorant of and uninterested in the political issues of the North. The British district commissioners and governors had gone and their places were taken by Northerners. These men were doubly at a disadvantage. Not only, like the Sudanese administrators generally, were they new to positions of such responsibility, but also they were working among tribes whose languages, customs, and religious outlook differed profoundly from their own. During most of the Condominium period little intercourse had been permitted between North and South.

With the unforeseen acceleration of self-government this policy of segregation, so recently abandoned, left a tragic legacy of mutual incomprehension and misunderstanding. From the point of view of the Southerners, they also had cause for dissatisfaction. They had lost the administrators to whom they were accustomed. Sudanization had not brought the glittering rewards which the Northerners enjoyed. They had no appeal against the situation in which they found themselves; the Governor-General's 'special responsibilities' were obviously unenforceable in practice. Some of their leaders began to flirt with Egypt. On August 2, 1955, eight of them announced from Cairo that they were working for an independent South, having only a general federal link with the North. The situation was curiously reminiscent of the palmy days of the Ashiqqa'-Egyptian *entente*!

But just over a fortnight later events took a sudden alarming turn. Mutiny broke out in the Equatoria Corps of the Sudan Defence Force. Its motives were partly anti-Northern feeling, partly fear of an impending transfer to the unknown North. Widespread disorders broke out, in which many Northerners lost their lives and many Southerners fled across the borders for refuge. Although the mutineers surrendered unconditionally on August 27, the re-establishment of law and order throughout the South is only gradually being accomplished. It is to the credit of the northern Sudanese that panic-stricken measures of revenge seem to have been exceptional and that attempts are being made to restore the normal life of the southern provinces. The rebellion and its tragic consequences have, like the earlier crisis of March 1, 1954, impressed on the government the seriousness of the issues at stake and the heavy responsibilities of the administration.

SELF-DETERMINATION

While these events were proceeding in the southern Sudan, Khartoum, London, and Cairo were occupied with the final stages leading to Sudanese self-determination. The Anglo-Egyptian Agreement of 1953 had laid down an elaborate procedure. At any time within the three-year transitional period, the parliament might pass 'a resolution expressing their desire that arrangements for Self-Determination should be put in motion'. The Governor-General was to notify the two Co-domini of this fact. The Parliament was then to pass a law for the election of a Constituent Assembly. 'Detailed preparations for the process of Self-Determination, including safeguards assuring the impartiality of the elections and any other arrangements designed to secure a free and neutral atmosphere [were to] be subject to international supervision.' Meanwhile Britain and Egypt were to withdraw their military forces from the Sudan. When the Constituent Assembly met, it was to decide the future of the Sudan, either 'choosing to link the Sudan with Egypt in any form, or . . . choosing complete independence'.

By June, 1955, it was clear that the transitional period was drawing to a close, and representatives of Egypt and Britain met in Cairo to discuss the composition of the international commission which was to supervise self-determination. With Naguib gone, the familiar tensions returned, and in August the British government accepted an Egyptian proposal that this matter, on which they could not reach agreement, should be referred to the Sudanese Parliament. The Parliament selected the commission, composed of representatives of seven neutral states, on August 22. Already on August 16 it had passed a resolution for the evacuation of British and Egyptian forces, and the Prime Minister had expressed his hope that elections would be held early in December. But the Sudanese were rapidly losing interest in the cumbersome procedure laid down by the Agreement. On August 13, Sayyid 'Ali al-Mirghani had suggested the holding of a plebiscite to decide the future of the country. Sayyid 'Abd al-Rahman al-Mahdi agreed in principle, but regarded the unanimous desire of the Sudanese for complete independence as rendering a plebiscite unnecessary. On August 29 the Parliament resolved to ask the Co-domini to allow the holding of a plebiscite. The proposal was accepted by Egypt on October 30 and by Britain on November 7. On the following day the Sudanese government requested the Co-domini to allow the simultaneous holding of the plebiscite and elections for a constituent assembly. This was agreed to on December 3, with the proviso that the international commission should supervise the process.

Thus the initiative in the advance towards self-determination had clearly passed to the Sudanese. The British and Egyptian governments could do little more than formally register the decisions of the Sudanese Parliament and administration. The last outward signs of the Condominium were passing away. Sir Robert Howe, the British Governor-General who had presided over a period of rapid constitutional change since his appointment in 1947, left in March, 1955. His successor, Sir Alexander Knox Helm, was the last of the line that had begun with Kitchener at the Reconquest. The withdrawal of British and Egyptian troops was completed by the middle of November.

At this point, however, a series of governmental crises intervened. The effect of al-Azhari's ministerial changes over the past months had been to confine office to members of his original Ashiqqa' group in the N.U.P. A demand arose, which was voiced by the opposition, that a non-party government should be formed to direct events in this critical phase of the national life. On November 10 the N.U.P. government lost a vote of confidence in Parliament but was re-established five days later, when al-Azhari was re-elected Prime Minister by a narrow majority. Pressure for the widening of the party basis of the government continued, and on December 6 al-Azhari agreed to the formation of a coalition government, but on condition that the suggested plebiscite be dropped and that the existing Parliament should both exercise the function of self-determination and act as a constituent assembly. These conditions seemed to guarantee the continuation of the N.U.P. in office as the nucleus of a national government. The last traces of the self-determination procedure laid down in the Anglo-Egyptian Agreement were swept away on December 19, when the Sudanese Parliament passed a resolution declaring the Sudan's independence, which Britain and Egypt were asked to recognize. The constitutional powers of the Governor-General were assumed by a Supreme Commission of five Sudanese, one of whom was a Southerner. The final scene took place on New Year's Day, 1956, when, in the presence of the Prime Minister and a great gathering at the Palace, the Union Jack and the Egyptian flag were run down for the last time and the standard of the Republic of the Sudan was hoisted over Khartoum.

1956.

TURKEY AND THE MIDDLE EAST

by ANDREW J. A. MANGO

THE INCLUSION of an article on Turkey in a symposium devoted to the Middle East needs to be justified. If a European country is one that tries to live up to European standards, just as a man who acknowledges and seeks to live by Christian standards is commonly presumed to be a Christian, then Turkey is a European country. The proclamation of the Turkish Republic, prepared by a long process of assimilation of European influences and symbolic of the success of that process, has torn Turkey from the Middle East and has propelled her finally into the North Atlantic region. Strategic convenience may produce fanciful geography, but the fancy is based on fact. The fact is that Turkey has gone much farther along the road to the West than her Middle Eastern neighbours, and the inequality of their attainments separates them. They are also separated by an undesirable first product of Westernization, the adoption of the ideology of nationalism.

WESTERNIZATION OF TURKEY

The Westernization of Turkey started long before Atatürk. A century ago a reformed and constitutional Turkey was admitted to the Concert of Europe: the Turkish delegates at Strasbourg follow a long line of Europeans. By the First World War the entire Ottoman ruling class was Westernized: it had been educated abroad or in foreign schools in Turkey, or again on translations of foreign textbooks. The success of the revolution of Atatürk was therefore no accident. What it did was to proclaim the private practices of the rulers as the faith of the state. The Middle East is behind the back of republican Turkey. It is also, to use the unlovely language of Soviet experts, an internal émigré. But let us take the rejection first. It was made easier by the fact that politically there was nothing left to reject: the Arabs had come under the care of a Western head master, and both teachers and pupils looked hopeful. Nevertheless, ram's horns were produced and anathemas pronounced:

'We came near to extinction as we tried to free ourselves from this race [the Arabs] which has lost all nobility and vitality. I personally would much rather see as neighbours on our southern frontiers Paris smarties than Syrian *hajjis* [Moslems who have been on a pilgrimage to Mecca]. At least the Parisians are generous enemies and intelligent and honest friends. For five centuries we gave our blood and our possessions for the Arabs and still could not please them. Let us see how the noble race fares under the French.'

The extract comes from a novel by the mediocre but popular Turkish writer Burhan Cahit. The failure of the Holy War proclaimed against the Allies by the Ottoman Sultan was particularly instructive. Burhan Cahit's hero concluded from it: 'The Arabs are always the same: sweet as lambs when faced with armed might. They care little whether they are governed by Moslem Turks, Roman Catholic Frenchmen, Protestant Englishmen, or Buddhist Japanese. They are always ready to flatter the mighty.' And, of course, intrigue with the mighty. T. E. Lawrence and all that was a symbol of Arab treachery, of treachery compounded in spite of five centuries of common life, of common religion, of the Hijaz Railway built with Turkish money, the aqueducts paid for by pious Turkish Moslems, and all the rest.

Arab nationalists in the meantime were forging a defensive myth, that they had kept faith with the Ottomans until the godless Young Turks arrived and Turanians became more important than good Moslems. But these rival myths were elaborated in different compartments and did not impede each other's growth. When England and France fell out with the Arabs, the usual Turkish reaction was: 'What else could you expect from this ungrateful race? We are well rid of them, but what made you take them on?' This is not all sour grapes. There was and there still is a genuine disinclination among educated Turks to get drawn into the bog of Middle Eastern politics.

The repudiated Middle East had, however, its counterpart in Turkey. Just as the entire population of the Roman Empire did not become Christian with the conversion of Constantine, every Turk did not become a Westerner when the Republic was founded. *Hajjis* were not confined to Syria: the species existed also in Turkey. A former Turkish diplomat, Yakup Kadri Karaosmanoglu, author of

Panorama, an ambitious novel which has the present state of Turkey as its main theme, has drawn the picture of a typical internal émigré, Hajji Emin Efendi. Hajji Emin Efendi believes that the Kaiser Wilhelm was a secret Moslem, that the Ottoman Empire was defeated because Turkish officers in Enver Pasha's suite had entered the sacred enclosure in Mecca while in a state of ritual impurity. 'When the Arabs saw that, they understood that the Turks were done for. The only way out for them was to drive us out of the Sacred Places. Had they not done so, their position would have been as bad as ours now: the last traces of religion would have disappeared from their lands too!' Hajji Emin Efendi believes also that 'it is a sin to speak against the Arabs. It is equivalent to disbelief in the Prophet, who said "I am an Arab."' Having delivered himself of these sentiments, Hajji Emin Efendi goes off to hoard some gold. He is clearly a bad citizen.

Hajji Emin Efendi is also a typical Oriental. *Sarklilik* (the quality of being Oriental) is a term rich in associations; it stands for superstition, inefficiency, lethargy, and dubious morals. These associations derive from experience of Oriental society in decay and have some truth in them. That society is essentially incoherent: the medieval Islamic ideals which once inspired it become and are seen as irrelevant: the new Western ideals are unevenly adopted and applied. Old forms of group and guild solidarity and loyalty disappear and are not immediately replaced by new ideals of citizenship. Religion becomes ignorant superstition. Such incoherent societies lie to the east and south of the Turkish Republic; they make uneasy and rather unattractive neighbours.

In Turkey the battle against 'backwardness and superstition' has been won in principle, although the end of the mopping-up operations is not yet in sight. These local campaigns are absorbing much of the energy of the new generation of Turkish intellectuals. Their main weapon is 'education in the spirit of positive science', which they see as the essential condition of economic and social progress. Their advice to their Middle Eastern neighbours is to adopt the 'Atatürk solution': Westernization, secularization, collaboration with the West. Educated Turks believe that they can save the Middle East by their example. There was a time between the two wars when it was a matter of academic and rather superior interest to the Turkish ruling class whether the Arabs and Persians followed their example or not. But this is no longer so. A distasteful necessity has again forced Turkey to attend to her Oriental neighbours. The need arose some time before the last war, when the influence of Western democracies began to recede. The remedy fashionable at the time was to conclude a feeble *entente*: by concluding the Pact of Saadabad with Iraq, Persia, and Afghanistan, Turkey applied the fashionable remedy. The Pact of Saadabad proved to be a document of no great worth. The present Turkish government hopes that the Baghdad Pact will be different.

TURKEY AND THE BAGHDAD PACT

It is said that the interest shown by the Turkish government in the Baghdad Pact means that Turkey is again facing east. This is a misleading and not very meaningful metaphor. The rulers of Turkey, who are trying to turn their own Orientals into Europeans, are not becoming Orientals themselves to please less-developed neighbours. The Baghdad Pact was born out of strategic necessity, but its success depends largely on the social evolution of its Middle Eastern members, on the growth in numbers and importance of Westernized social groups, to supply a cohesive principle. (Seen from the other side of the Curtain, the growth of these groups in the Middle East is as distasteful to the Soviet Union as was the movement for constitutional reform in Persia to Czarist Russia. There is a Europe of the spirit and a backwoods of the spirit. The rulers of the Soviet Union belong to the latter and seek their allies in similar thickets: 'Mental proletarians of the world unite!') The accession of the United States to the Baghdad Pact, which is the prime aim of Turkish foreign policy at the present moment, would promote both causes, the strategic security of the Middle East and, through American economic and cultural aid, the social evolution of its inhabitants. American aid has been from its inception a civilizing force in the Middle East: American university missions, Fulbright scholarships, the known preference of the Americans for decent social and political practices have helped to raise the tone of civil life in the countries of that region. But in the meantime the attempt of the Turkish government to collaborate with less developed Middle Eastern countries has raised some difficulties. There is the noisy quarrel which Arab nationalists are waging with the West; there are the Arab objections to the existence of Israel. So far the views of the Turkish government on both matters have generally coincided with those of the United States government. But by withdrawing her Minister in Tel Aviv in order to appease Arab nationalists in Iraq, Turkey has, however slightly, fallen out of step with the other members of the Western club to which she is proud to belong. The group of young Ankara intellectuals who produce the fortnightly review *Forum*, a review which resembles the *New Statesman* not only in format, disagreed with this gesture of appeasement. 'In regard to our relations with Israel,' *Forum* said, 'we should know that the existence of that state in the Middle East is in Turkey's interests. If a war were to break out in the Middle East tomorrow, the Israeli army would be the only serious force capable of fighting on our side; its value is greater than the combined value of the Iraqi, Jordanian, and other Arab armies.'[1] *Forum* believes, on the other hand, that Turkey should support the Arabs where their claims are justified, over the North African problem, for example, or over the nationalization of the Suez Canal. 'Turkey,' *Forum* concluded, 'has grown out of the stage of romantic nationalism through which the Arabs are now passing; ours has long been a rational nationalism. In our actions we should not try to play up to the Arabs, but to serve as an example to them. Otherwise the Baghdad Pact will never succeed in solving the problems of the Middle East.'

The trouble is that epithets applied to nationalism tend to be subjective. Would Syrian nationalists agree that their claim to the Turkish province of Hatay was romantic? The essentially ungenerous nature of nationalism is in itself an obstacle to better relations between Turkey and her Middle Eastern neighbours. Geographically contiguous nationalisms are usually antagonistic; national friendships, as extolled in nationalist literature, operate, like the knight in chess, at one remove: the smaller the contact the greater the friendship. The Turkish government is therefore probably right in asking for United States participation in the Baghdad Pact and in seeking the extension of the Pact: American restraining and civilizing influence would help to keep apart rival nationalisms. The peaceful development of the Middle East and Turkish-Arab co-operation within it, require, not the absence but, on the contrary, a multiplicity of conditions to American aid.

TURKEY AND ISLAM

It may be objected that I have neglected the factors which Turkey and the states of the Middle East are believed to have in common: the Islamic religion, Islamic culture, past co-existence in a multinational state. But, as I have already contended, the concept of Islamic solidarity was proved to be politically inoperative in the First World War. Medieval Islamic culture (and there is no other Islamic culture) is dead: fewer traces remain in Turkey than in the Arab lands, and they are growing fainter everywhere. In Turkey, as a result of thirty years of secular nationalist education, the legacy of that culture is fully available only to university-trained Orientalists. Just as Western positivism, or 'positive science' to give it the

[1] 'Clarity in our Middle Eastern Policy' (editorial), *Forum*, December 1, 1956, p. 4.

honorific title by which it is known in Turkey, had dissolved the structure of Islamic society, Western nationalism has torn the links that united the former subjects of the Ottoman Empire. Arab proper names appearing in Turkish newspapers in strange Western trans-literations instead of their traditional Turkish forms are a symbol of Turkish-Arab estrangement; places in the Middle East where Turks fought or which they governed and which were part of their personal experience are now names in dispatches by Western corre-spondents. Today, Turks and Arabs can establish fruitful contacts only as they become citizens of the West. A young Turkish lecturer who recently visited the Arab lands to study cultural co-operation found English and French to be the most useful common languages. The future rulers of Turkey and of the Arab countries will, I hope, for the sake of civilized progress in those lands, first meet as Fulbright scholars or as students at the London School of Economics. They will certainly not meet at the al-Azhar University in Cairo. The most nationalistic Arab parents would choose a proper univer-sity in the West for their children if they were given the choice. Their preference is logical: the West, meaning the North Atlantic region, is the home of the only civilization that is alive today. Clichés about a meeting or a synthesis between East and West, between Eastern spiritual values and Western technology, are mean-ingless and are seen as meaningless by the people who matter in the Middle East today. Islamic civilization can be studied; it can no longer be lived—and even the study is carried on in the West is or directed from it. There is nothing paradoxical or supercilious about such a judgment: it was natural for scholars to go to Alexandria in Hellenistic times, to Baghdad or Cordoba in the Middle Ages. Today the most favourable ecologic conditions for the growth of culture happen to be in the West.

INTEGRATION WITH EUROPE

Seen in this light, the efforts of the Turkish intellectuals to achieve full integration with the West are not funny (*pace* Miss Rose Macaulay), even although they will reduce the incidence of the picturesque. The level of economic and political development is not an index of Westernization: some Western communities are poor, others are or have been governed by dictatorships. They do not become Asiatic for all that. Incidents such as the anti-Greek riots in Istanbul in September, 1955, are adduced as proof that Turkey is not a Western country. It would, indeed, be convenient if nationalist riots did not form part of the Western heritage: like proletarian revolutions, they are unfortunately an excess from which the West has not been immune. We are, of course, all in favour of remedying defects and avoiding excesses, but so are our opposite numbers in Turkey. Political thought, literature, or popular taste in Turkey cannot be studied in isolation from trends in the West. Socialists and Keynesians argue in the columns of *Forum*; Turkish *literati* favour Silone's type of humanism, Faulkner's folksy realism, and the real people of Steinbeck or of Italian film directors; *Waiting for Godot* was produced in Istanbul before it came to London; the Turkish Students' Association is earnestly debating the dangers of rock-'n'-roll. There is, it is true, one basic difference. As long as they remain at home, Turkish intellectuals are disseminators rather than creators of Western culture. But this is true of all intellectuals east of Rome. Today Turkey is badly served by Western writers. Ignorance of the Turkish language is understandable but not inevitable: it should be recognized as a handicap by writers who seek to interpret Turkish public opinion and Turkish literature. No civilized man can object to writers who take an interest in Byzantine or classical Greek remains in Turkey, provided that books on archaeology are not served up as books on modern Turkey. Seekers after the picturesque should go farther afield.

The political scene in Turkey should not be judged too harshly. Radicals have always looked with disfavour on Turkey. They are apt to divide nations into reactionary and progressive, and the Turks are usually consigned to the former category, irrespective of any changes that may have been introduced into the civil government of Turkey. Turkey falls short of West European standards of social and political democracy, although administration in Turkey is much more democratic than in the Socialist sixth of the world. Practical obstacles must be recognized before radical remedies are recommended. The standards of the Turkish Civil Service (which remains, nevertheless, the best in the Middle East) limit the useful range of state administration and intervention; general cultural standards make for high differentials in rewards (for if the habits and standards of life of different sections of the population are profoundly unequal, rewards have, at least to some extent, to be unequal too); powerful incentives are needed if economic development is to proceed quickly. There are arguments for restricting in practice democratic rights to the Westernized part of the population: the extension of these rights since the war beyond the confines of the *élite* has created difficulties. Members of the religious opposition in Turkey, for example, do not behave like Western defenders of spiritual values. They go in for breaking statues and hounding women out of public life. The obstacles to the creation of a social-democratic welfare state in Turkey are formidable, assuming, as many Turkish intellectuals do assume, that this is a worthy object of endeavour. Western aid and sympathy are needed if they are to be overcome: there is no lack of Turkish progressives with whom Western progressives could sympathize.

Similar considerations apply probably to many Middle Eastern countries. What distinguishes Turkey is the extent of Westernization and, consequently, of the growth of Westernized classes, the self-identification of most articulate Turks with the West, and the sense of purpose which they and their rulers seem to have. These phenomena have their social counterparts: the Turkish middle class, for example, is more numerous and more powerful than is the case in any Middle Eastern country. The growth of the middle class was one of the factors in the victory of the Democratic Party in 1950, and was in turn further stimulated by that victory. Indeed, one of the dangers to which the Turkish body politic has been exposed during the last few years was due to the circumstance that rapid economic progress had added, to the socially and politically important classes, elements which had not been fully Westernized. It is they, for example, who produced the appearance of a religious revival, although that phenomenon can perhaps be more accurately described as the open manifestation of existing religious attachments which had been less obvious because they had been harboured by less important people. The middle class is, moreover, not confined to a few cities, as is usually the case in the Middle East. A Turkish actor told me recently that he had witnessed the best theatrical manners in the town of Adana where a large and wealthy audience assembled to watch a performance of *The Rainmaker*. When a branch of the Turkish State Theatre was opened a few months ago in the central Anatolian town of Konya, all available tickets for a season's performances were sold out in a few days. The numbers of the intelligentsia can also be gauged from the fact that an uncompromisingly serious review like *Forum* has a circulation of approximately ten thousand copies. Turkish newspaper circulations generally have doubled or trebled since the war, although here technical improvements are more conspicuous than any new excellence of content. The total circulation of literary periodicals has, however, also increased very considerably. Serious works of foreign literature, particularly American, French, and English, are translated in large numbers and within a remarkably short time of their first publication abroad. Here again it is the extent and the diffusion of cultural and educational activity which differentiates Turkey from the countries of the Middle East.

Turkey is today a member of the North Atlantic Treaty Organization and of the Council of Europe. Many people in the West consider this as a formal strategic or political arrangement; some may even think of it as slightly incongruous. But to the Turks, their country's membership of these organizations is a recognition of their status as Europeans and as Westerners, the formal abandonment of what they call 'the Crusaders' mentality', the hostility of Christian Europeans for Moslem Turks. The recognition has not come suddenly, it has not been unearned. It is in the interest of the democratic countries of the West to give effect to this recognition by helping in the integration of Turkey in the Western community. This in turn would encourage the countries of the Middle East, or rather the people who matter in those countries, to take the road to the West.

IDEOLOGICAL CRISIS IN IRAN

by F. KAZEMZADEH

THE IMPACT of the West upon Iran has had a shattering effect upon the spiritual life of her people. Modes of thought and feeling which had developed over the centuries underwent a radical transformation within two or three generations. The rapid dissolution of traditional cultural patterns precipitated an ideological crisis which is growing more severe every day and promises to continue for a long time.[1]

Iran's contacts with the West did not originate in the twentieth century. However, during the sixteenth, seventeenth, and eighteenth centuries her relations with Europe were sporadic and confined to government officials whose duty it was to receive foreign ambassadors and negotiate with them. Some merchants had dealings with European traders, while occasionally a Jesuit or an adventurer from the West would turn up at Esfahān or Shirāz. The presence of a few Russians, Englishmen, or Venetians had not the slightest effect upon Iranian society.

Those Iranians who came to have some knowledge of the West had little admiration for the 'Franks'. True, the Franks were masters at casting cannon, an art the Iranians hastened to learn; they were good at making pistols, watches, and pocket-knives and sailing the seas. However, this did not make them superior in the eyes of the Iranians, who knew that the Franks could contain the Turks in Central Europe only through coalitions, while Iran withstood them alone. The Franks were Christian, and no Iranian would agree that Christianity was superior to Islam. Thus the West failed to make an

[1] It must be noted that the Iranian masses, predominantly rural, are largely inert politically and ideologically. Even in the cities many are unconscious of any crisis. This article, therefore, discusses the ideas and attitudes of a minority which includes the intellectuals, as well as a portion of the upper and the middle classes.

impression upon a society which until the second quarter of the eighteenth century was relatively prosperous, reasonably well ordered, and united by a devotion to Shiism and by that peculiar cultural cohesion which is the distinguishing mark of Iranian civilization.

Religion occupied the central place in an Iranian's outlook. It permeated his views on politics, philosophy, poetry, and art. He regarded the Shāh as the vicegerent of the hidden Imām,[2] he read of the unity of God in the poetry of Hātef, and saw the faith glorified in the tiled mosques of Esfahān and Mashhad. In school he was taught by a *mollā*, and his first text was the Qur'ān. His whole life passed to the accompaniment of religious festivals, fasts, prayers, and processions. The feeling was especially deep, because it was only in 1500 that Shāh Esmāil Safavi, the new King, made Shiism Iran's official religion. The vigour of the Shiite sentiment and the national revival of the sixteenth and seventeenth centuries gave the Iranians enough self-assurance not to seek to imitate the 'Franks' occasionally appearing in their midst.

The period of anarchy which followed the downfall of the Safavi dynasty ended with the enthronement of Āqā Mohammad Khān Qājār. Under his successor, Fath-Ali, Iran fought with Russia two disastrous wars which resulted in the Treaties of Golestān and Torkamanchāy. Deeply shocked and humiliated, the Iranian ruling class was disunited in its reaction to defeat. A few, such as the heir to the throne, Abbās Mirzā, and his closest adviser, the wise and talented Qāemmaqām, realized that Iran was technically backward. They determined to learn from the West the secret of its military superiority, hoping, perhaps, that under the protection of a Westernized army Iran could remain essentially unchanged.

Abbās Mirzā's attempts at reform failed. Under Mohammad Shah and his Qājār successors Iran continued to regress. Yet it was precisely at this time that it began to be increasingly exposed to Western influence. The construction of telegraph lines, the opening of British and Russian banks, the appearance of various foreign companies, the formation of the Persian Cossack Brigade, brought to Tehran a relatively large number of Westerners who operated in close daily contact with Iranians. An even larger number of Iranians went to Europe as students, diplomats, and merchants.

In the twentieth century the influx of Western ideas into Iran reached the proportions of a flood. The birth of the daily Press contributed to their spreading among a sizeable portion of the population in Tehran, Tabriz, and two or three other major cities.

[2] The *Imām* Mahdi who, according to tradition, disappeared in A.H. 260 and whose triumphal return is expected by the Shiites.

Persian papers published in England and India gained influence. When in 1906–7 a strange coalition of nobles, *mollās*, and *bāzār* merchants fought against Mozaffar ed-Din Shah and his despotic successor, Mohammad Ali Shah, they did it under the banner of Western constitutionalism.

The reign of Rezā Shah Pahlavi was a period of wholesale Westernization. The compulsory unveiling of women and the prohibition of the traditional hat were only external symbols of a deep change which took place with great rapidity between 1925 and 1940. Legal, administrative, educational, and military reforms, together with physical modernization, transformed Iran almost beyond recognition.

The rapid *tempo* of external change was reflected in the spiritual and mental life of the nation. The growing group of Western-educated men and 'emancipated' women could not look at the world through the spectacles of tradition. Moreover, a fair number of people arrived at the thought that Western technological superiority was a product of the totality of European culture, and particularly of Western political systems.

Rezā Shah expressed the new feeling in the official ideology which was established during his reign and was propagated through government-controlled or owned newspapers, radio, and schools. This official ideology taught love of King and country. It proclaimed that the nation was paramount, and the service of the nation a citizen's highest obligation and honour. The nation was conceived of as organic, a living body manifesting its individual spirit through its culture. One could borrow from abroad technical innovations, or even political institutions such as a parliament. These belonged to the material sphere, but one must not pollute the national spirit by an excessive admiration for foreign ways, or by the use of Latin letters in algebra and geometry. A campaign was waged to remove from Persian as many Arabic words as possible. The Arabic alphabet was not denounced, perhaps because Iran had never developed one of its own.

Religion, which had always dominated national life, was subordinated to the interests of the state. The Moslem clergy lost all influence on government, and much of its influence on urban society. Though Islam remained the state religion, it was often openly disparaged. The Moslem conquest of Iran was presented in schools as a national calamity, while the Arabs were shown as the destroyers of Iranian culture, incendiaries and plunderers. Zoroastrianism, formerly the faith of a despised minority, acquired unexpected respectability as a relic of ancient Iran.

The weakening of Islam was a result partly of Rezā Shah's policy and partly of the influx of Western ideas. The belated acquaintance of educated Iranians with European writers had its effect. After all, an anti-clerical remark by Voltaire could be easily applied to a *mollā*. That the knowledge, either of religion or of science and philosophy, possessed by the new converts to agnosticism, positivism, or materialism was pitifully small, did not deter them from stating their views with much heat and conviction.

The official ideology of the Rezā Shah period, though artificial and shallow, served a purpose. The younger generation, severed from traditions of the past, found some satisfaction in the glorification of Iran's history and in the faith in Iran's future. Progress, education, industrialization, prosperity are relative matters. It seemed to educated Iranians that their country had awakened after centuries of lethargy and was about to resume her destined place among the great nations of the world. Some even went so far as to dream of a rebirth of the Sasanian Empire.

In August, 1941, Russian and British troops marched into Iran. The army, which had been lauded for years, could not defend the nation. The imposing façade of Rezā Shah's régime collapsed in three days, revealing the jerry-built structure behind. The Shah himself was exiled first to an island in the Indian Ocean, then to South Africa, where he soon died. The dream of independence and power was destroyed, and Iranians were rudely reminded that their continued existence as a nation depended not so much on themselves as upon the old conflict between Russian and British interests in the Middle East. Rezā Shah's official ideology could not survive the fiasco of August, 1941. Its downfall was accompanied by cynical shrugs and loud cries of indignation, but many shouts were uttered only to disguise disappointment and pain.

The war years left Iranian society ideologically disoriented and morally sick. While the peasantry remained passive, politically conscious strata of the population broke into a large number of ideological groups. Some of these coincided with political parties and were organized. Most are called groups here only as a means for the identification of individuals holding similar views, though such persons may not be organized in any form whatever.

The most active groups are the extremists of the Right and the Left. The Communists formed the Tudeh Party, which was the largest, most disciplined, and most important political party in Iran. Moreover, the Tudeh was the only party to have a coherent ideology. This was Marxism of the Leninist-Stalinist type. Practically all Tudeh literature was translated from Russian. Every statement made by a Tudeh leader faithfully reproduced the current party line as given out by the Communist Party of the Soviet Union. One could find no specifically Persian elements in Tudeh's ideology, except, perhaps, a greater emphasis on nationalism than would be permitted to the Communists of Hungary or Rumania. The Tudeh knew that, in Iran, nationalism was a powerful weapon which could be used against the West, against the monarchy and the ruling class, but also against Communism and Russia. Therefore the Communists set out to appropriate nationalism to themselves, to appear in the eyes of the masses as anti-colonialist, anti-Western, nationalists. Occasionally the Tudeh would be embarrassed by those who reminded the Communists that at the end of the Second World War Russia had made demands for oil concessions in Iran; but Marxist dialectical skill could always be replied upon to provide some sort of an explanation.

Communism has many attractions for Iranians. It appeals to the misery of the poor and the idealism of the rich, the bitterness of those who fail and the guilt-feelings of those who succeed, the ignorance of the mass and the learning of the intellectuals. The crowds which the Communists were able to gather in the streets of Tehran followed them for reasons which were far removed from ideology. Slum dwellers are concerned about bread and shelter first, and the Tudeh generously promised everyone a life of plenty. Hoodlums willing to join any crowd, Communist as well as anti-Communist, were also ready to march under red banners. Some minor officials of the vast bureaucracy, some underpaid teachers, were willing to listen to Communist agitators because their standard of living and social position failed to meet their modest expectations.

To university students, the intelligentsia, and certain members of the upper class, Communism appealed as an ideology. It gave fairly simple answers to all questions, it provided a coherent world outlook, it seemed to unify all experience and to relate the individual to society. Those who had lost faith in Islam and were not satisfied with Western philosophical and political pragmatism found in Marxism a substitute for religion. The very violence of Communism, its disregard of the individual, its reliance on force, attracted those who believed themselves superior, worthy of being the rulers, yet were deprived of power.

At the opposite pole from the Communists stand the extreme nationalists. To call them parties of the extreme Right would be misleading, since they are not necessarily devoted to free enterprise and do not represent the interests of the rich. Unlike the Communists, they do not have a body of recognized scriptures, nor have they a systematic philosophy comparable to Marxism. However, they share certain views which identify them as a group.

The extreme nationalists are totalitarian in outlook. Individual liberty, the rights of man, constitutions and charters mean little or nothing to them. They are not, or pretend not to be, concerned with class struggle, believing that common nationality must transcend all other interests and serve as a bond between all Iranians. In unguarded moments extreme nationalists may talk about the future restoration of the ancient Iranian Empire. They will argue at all times the superiority of Iranian race and culture. All the ills of modern Iran, which the Communists attribute to both Western imperialism and the class structure of Iranian society, the extreme nationalists attribute to imperialism alone. In blaming imperialists for Iran's backwardness, the extreme nationalists strike at both Britain and Russia, though during the famous oil dispute of 1951–53 they naturally concentrated on the former.

The extreme nationalists have fallen heir to some of the ideas which had been part of the official ideology of the Rezā Shah period. They favour a strong, if not absolute monarchy, or a dictatorship; they view Islam as basically an alien faith; they are Westernizers at least to the extent of wanting to absorb Western science and technology, without which Iran could never be great.

Moslem fanatics of the Fadāyāne Eslām type are often classed with extreme nationalists. There is some justification for such a view. Both the extreme nationalists and the Moslem fanatics are anti-foreign. However, the resemblance ends there. Whereas the nationalists have abandoned the old and look to a secular leadership to make Iran strong, the Fadāyān are pure archaists. Their following is recruited from among the most conservative sections of the population, primarily in the *bāzār*. Unlike the nationalists, the Fadāyān and their sympathizers totally reject the West. They have but one remedy for all ills—a return to Islam. Thus they represent the last resisting elements of the old order, a desperate remnant fighting a battle which cannot be won.

The programme of the Fadāyān is entirely negative. They hate the foreigners, despise the Jews and the Armenians, dislike the Zoroastrians, call for the extermination of the Baha'is, oppose the emancipation of women, and decry modern education. They believe in violence and engage in individual terror, which they practised on many occasions until the government smashed their organizations and executed Navvāb Safavi together with several other Fadāyān leaders. It should be noted that the influence of the Fadāyān was never great enough to constitute a real threat, partly because they failed to attract the intellectuals, the bureaucracy, and the army.

The majority of educated Iranians could be classified as political moderates. It is impossible to speak of their ideology, since as a group they have none. As individuals they hold a variety of views,

but in most instances these views are not systematized. The moderates do have certain common characteristics. They are usually
secularist in outlook. The only time they visit a mosque is for a
funeral. They do not observe Moslem dietary laws, look down upon
the clergy, and speak with admiration of the writings of Kasravi, a
brilliant, though superficial, eccentric who attacked religion, preached nationalism, created much controversy, and fell victim to the
terrorism of the Fadāyān. Their mode of life, amusements, interests,
and aspirations have been deeply influenced by Europe and America,
where many of them studied at colleges and universities. They have
lost, or are in the process of losing, much of their cultural heritage,
since the schools through which they go in Iran teach less and less
of the Persian classics, while devoting more and more time to science
and foreign languages. To this group belong many of those who
have lost all sense of direction, who are bitterly cynical or stoically
self-contained.

Within this group one also finds the pragmatically minded young
men who wish to do good, who, amidst general corruption and disillusionment, display some idealism, though it seldom lasts or brings
tangible results. They do not express their sentiments in terms of
philosophical systems, in which most of them do not believe. Their
lot in the midst of a turbulent, unstable, and spiritually impoverished
society is hard.

Apart from all others stand the Baha'is, who constitute Iran's
largest minority. Though born in Iran, their faith is universal in
outlook, transcending the boundaries of race and nation. It proclaims the essential unity of all religions, advocates the abandonment of national and racial prejudices, calls for universal peace,
world government, an international auxiliary language, and incul-
cates in its followers such devotion to their cause that they have been
able to withstand repeated persecution and oppression.

Iran has always been rich in ideas. Fertilized by currents from
Babylon and India, Greece and Rome, exposed to the influences of
Christianity and Islam, its culture has been varied and rich, producing perhaps as many systems, philosophies, and theologies as any
other people on earth. Mithraism and Manicheism, various forms
of Shiism, the Sufism of Sheikh Attār and Jalāl ed-Din Rumi, the
philosophies of Avicenna and Ghazzāli, these constitute a heritage
of great value, demonstrating Iran's ability to originate, absorb, and
integrate. The process of adjustment to new conditions is painful and
full of dangers, yet Iran, unlike Assyria or Egypt, has preserved its
cultural identity through more than two thousand five hundred
years.

The West is a challenge to Iran, but even before the full impact of the West had been felt, Iran's internal development had posed some crucial problems. The ideological crisis of today is not a simple result of Western imperialist pressure. Were this the case, solutions would be relatively easy to find. The crisis is undoubtedly aggravated by the challenge of the West, but its causes are deep in history. In many of its aspects this crisis is not confined to Iran, nor is it shared only with the other nations of the Near and Middle East. At its roots it is a crisis of mankind, all of whom are equally involved. The same constructive and disruptive forces which operate in all changing societies in the twentieth century are at work in Iran. There, as elsewhere, they assume local forms, are expressed in the idiom of a particular culture, sometimes creating the impression of being peculiarly Iranian, yet at bottom they are the same forces.

Today Iranian society is suffering from inner strains and external pressures. The *tempo* of change creates economic, political, social, and psychological problems. The feelings and thoughts of the people reflect the breakdown of an old order. They do not yet reflect the building of the new, for it will be some time before Iran finds the spiritual resources to overcome its present ideological crisis.

THE ORIGINS OF ISRAEL*

by SIR ISAIAH BERLIN

I SHOULD LIKE to begin with the strange fact that the State of Israel exists. It was once said by the celebrated Russian revolutionary, Herzen, writing in the mid-nineteenth century, that the Slavs had no history, only geography. The position of the Jews is the reverse of this. They have enjoyed rather too much history and too little geography. And the foundation of the State of Israel must be regarded as a piece of historical redress for this anomalous situation. The Jews have certainly had more than their share of history, or, as some might say, martyrology. Certainly no community has ever been so conscious of itself, its past fate, its future, and the apparently insoluble character of the problems which beset it. Where were the Jews going? What would happen to them, or should be done about them? Almost every Jew, early or late in his life, has encountered something called the Jewish problem. Englishmen, Frenchmen, Belgians, Chinese, Portuguese are not beset at the beginning of their conscious lives by something called the Belgian, Chinese, or Portuguese problem. This consciousness of themselves as being peculiarly problematical, rendered the creation of the State of Israel a miracle; for if it had been made dependent on the solution of the Jewish problem by the specialists on the subject, if the Jews had been what either some of their friends or some among their enemies have declared them to be, there might well have been no State of Israel at all.

Perpetual discussions went on, particularly during the nineteenth century—the most historically conscious of all ages—about whether the Jews were a race, or solely a religion; a people, a community, or merely an economic category. Books, pamphlets, debates increased in volume if not in quality. But there was one persistent fact about this problem, which was in some respects more clearly perceived by gentiles than by the Jews themselves: namely, that if they were only a religion, this would not have needed quite so much argument and insistence; while if they were nothing but a race, this would not have been denied quite as vehemently as it has been by persons who nevertheless professed to denote a unique group of human beings by the term 'Jew'.

It gradually became clear, both to Jews and to those who took an interest in their affairs, that in fact they constituted an anomaly, which could not be defined in terms of the ordinary definition of nations, as applied at any rate to European nations; and that any attempt to classify them in such terms would lead to unnatural, artificial and Procrustean consequences.

One does not need to be old to remember a time when Jews in the West used to grow indignant when other Jews, mainly from eastern Europe, declared themselves to be members of a nation, and demanded a land in which to lead a national life. And some western Jews did feel sufficiently assimilated to the natives of the country in which they lived to receive this kind of proposition with much amazement and, indeed, honest indignation. It is said that the late Edwin Montagu described the original draft of the Balfour Declaration as bordering on an act of anti-Semitism. No doubt he was sincere, but the fact that he was both sincere and honest was, in this case, only an illuminating sign of his own and his friends' state of mind. Sincerity and honesty are not always guarantees of knowledge of objective truth. Despite passionate denials of this proposition from many sides, it became increasingly clear to almost everyone who approached the problem from outside that the Jews were a unique combination of religion, race, and people; that they could not be classified in normal terms, but demanded an extraordinary description, and their problem an extraordinary solution. The person who saw the problem in the simplest possible terms and provided the most radical solution was Theodor Herzl.

The distinguishing characteristic of Dr. Herzl was that, despite his origin and *milieu*, he came to the problem, as it were, from the outside; and possessed a somewhat romantic conception of the Jews, scarcely recognizable to those who themselves grew up in the thick of a closely-knit traditional Jewish community. There is something about great radical solutions of political questions which seems to make it necessary for them to be born in the minds of those who in some sense stand on the rim, and look in from outside, and have an over-simple ideal, an over-simple purpose, a lucid, usually violent vision, based on an indispensable ignorance of detail. Those who know too much—know too many detailed facts too closely—cannot, as a rule, produce radical solutions. The Jews who grew up in truly traditional Jewish communities, such as those of eastern and central Europe, were usually much too conscious of the difficulties and complications, and lived cooped up in too small a world, ever to conceive anything so bold, so simple, so radical, and, in a sense, so fantastic, as Herzl's original idea.

I shall not, before this learned audience, traverse the familiar ground of how, as a result of the Dreyfus case, Herzl became aware of the total anomaly of the Jewish situation. It presently became obsessively clear to him that the moral and social situation of the Jews was intolerable: that it was painfully and tragically abnormal; that the palliatives had all failed; that the only alternative to apathy or humiliation was a drastic cure. As my friend, the Ambassador of Israel, once told me, Herzl's original solution was to cause all the Jews to be baptized. That was at any rate simple, general, and final; it would surely put an end for ever to all the embarrassment of ambiguous status of the Jews, their three-quarter citizenships, the peculiarity of their relationships in the various *enclaves* which they formed within the various communities to which they half believed, and half did not believe, themselves to belong.

It soon became quite clear to him that this was a genuinely Utopian solution, and he abandoned it. The notion of creating a territorial state for his people was in its own way an idea just as audacious and ruthless and direct. It was regarded as absurd by most of those who heard of it, if only because it sprang from a terrible, Napoleonic simplicity of vision. There is perhaps a quality which statesmen of this type have in common, something possessed by Alexander, Napoleon, perhaps by Mr. de Valera, possibly by Disraeli, and I fear Hitler and Stalin too, which comes of standing apart, at a certain distance, from the people with whose destinies they are engaged, and tending to see things in simple patterns, in contrast to the vision of those who see from within, and, as often as not, simply perceive a patternless heap of minute, unending complications, and see every possible path as blocked by a vast number of obstacles which cannot be overcome in their time. Outsiders romanticize and over-simplify more easily: familiarity breeds if not contempt, then at any rate scepticism and corrosive defeatism.

From this attribute Herzl who, though he came from Budapest, was not an eastern European Jew, was free, perhaps too free. His ideas were nationalist, secular, romantic, liberal, and bore more affinity to the enlightenment of Vienna and Paris than to anything specifically Jewish. And this, *mutatis mutandis*, was true of his followers. Each reflected the leading tendencies of his environment, each conceived the Zionist ideal in terms which, to some degree, derived from the national attitudes of his non-Jewish neighbours. The British Jews came with British ideas, the French Jews with French ideas, the German Jews with German, the Russian Jews with Russian, and the American Jews with American ideas. What happened as a result of this confusion of the tongues? The ideas came into collision with one another. In spite of all that we hear about inexorable laws of history (a metaphysical refrain which nowadays comes with almost equally monotonous frequency from the Soviet Union and Chatham House), one thing seems clear: large revolutions, attempts to upheave existing society and alter the course of events, do, at times, produce a break and change things deeply, but seldom in the direction which their initiators anticipated or desired. Why this is so, I do not propose to discuss—this must not become a lecture on the philosophy of history. It is enough to note that the State of Israel emerged with attributes quite different from those which anyone had previously intended. The intentions and purposes and motives had been many: and differed at times from individual to individual. Nevertheless, certain common national and cultural 'patterns' are discernible among them; and the influence of each is still identifiable in Israel today. Thus the small group of English Jews who accepted Herzl's ideas were to some degree affected by the liberal imperialism of their surroundings. What some among them wanted was a spiritual centre, a source of spiritual light, in a rather nebulous, idealistic sense. Others were more political. What they wanted was a Jewish community which would constitute a Western outpost in the East, a body of missionaries of Western culture, with peculiar duties and responsibilities towards the undeveloped communities of the East, both Jews and Arabs. This was, however unconsciously, a kind of Jewish version of something very British—of the most idealistic liberal conception of the White Man's Burden. The English Jews of whom I speak conceived of the Jewish establishment in Palestine as essentially a civilizing mission carried on by dedicated personalities who would bring the maturest fruit of the most peace-loving and most humane culture of the West to these inchoate, rather wild, rather barbarous Eastern peoples.

The French Jews were on the whole less interested in Palestine; but there were exceptions; and the most notable among them, the great Baron Edmond de Rothschild. His villages—the colonies which he founded—represent a French ideal with pretty French vines and olive trees, elegant, charming, and self-contained, an expression of a peaceful, rural, slightly nostalgic nineteenth-century view of the life of tenant farmers and their labourers; of Jewish farmers on the hill and Arab labourers below, and of the great landlord who owned the land, remote, mysterious, and benevolent, far away beyond the sea.

The German Jews wanted an orderly, modern, spick and span world, with a sufficiency of applied economic and technological knowledge, and a certain degree of democracy, but on the whole a well-disciplined, tidy, competent, late-nineteenth-century—I won't say Prussian, but at any rate, a properly regulated and firmly founded —political and economic organization.

The American Jews wanted something perhaps a little more streamlined and yet sentimentally affecting. They wanted something embodying a great deal of passionate and romantic popular enthusiasm, and, with it, the newest, most up-to-date, most labour-saving, mechanically fertile, twentieth-century gadgets and improvements imaginable anywhere. They wanted Palestine to lead in the van of all spiritual, artistic, material progress, tangibly, palpably, for all to see and admire. And they wanted it at the same time to be the idealized home country, at once biblical and sweetly familiar, by which they could themselves be identified in America among the great groups of immigrants of which that country is composed.

But by far the most important community to be considered is the community most closely concerned with the early foundations of Israel: that is to say, the Jews of Russia and Poland. Both numerically and in influence they outweighed the western Jews. It seems almost self-evident that if there had existed only the Jews of the Western world, or, perhaps, the Jews of the West and the Jews of the Eastern, Moslem, countries, there would have been no Israel. Whatever the genuine problems besetting the Jews of the West, however true and sharp and refreshing Dr. Herzl's extremely ruthless analysis of their diseases might have been, there were in the beginning of our century no sufficiently compelling causes which could uproot the relatively comfortable and well-set-up Jews of the West, materially provided for, and morally and politically unpersecuted, and send them on a general trek in that particular direction. But for the character and needs of the eastern European Jews there would have been no Israel. They were, in that sense, absolutely *sine quibus non*; to grasp their role is indispensable to the understanding of what happened later.

For this reason I should like to say a few words about their establishment. The eastern European Jews, as a result of historical circumstances, possessed a kind of independent establishment of their own. They had, unlike their western brothers, grown to be a kind of state within a state, with their own political, social, religious, and human ideals. I should not like to generalize about the oriental countries, for about them I fear that I know nothing. The Jews of

Russia and Poland, as a result of political and social persecution, had found themselves cooped up in a kind of single extended ghetto, called the Pale of Settlement, and although, or perhaps because, they were not well treated by the Russian government and bureaucracy, particularly towards the end of the nineteenth and the beginning of the twentieth century, they remained within their medieval shell and developed a kind of internal structure of their own. They developed a very powerful inner life and, in a certain sense, remained less touched by modern developments than almost any community of Jews in Europe. If one finds difficulty in conceiving what life was like in the Middle Ages in Europe, I think that the life of a truly religious Jewish small-town in Western Russia, even as late as 1890 or 1900, probably bears a closer analogy to it than any other modern community anywhere. Its inhabitants were affected by, but on the whole comparatively preserved from, the intrusion of outside forces. They lived their own rich, and despite economic misery and social ostracism, often gay, imaginative, and morally satisfying lives. They were surrounded by Russian peasants, against whom they felt no hatred, but whom they regarded as a species of lower beings with whom their contacts were confined. They lived inside the walls of their own community, leading a closely knit traditional, tight-woven form of existence, and they developed their own inner institutions. There was a great deal of persecution and pressure by the Russian government outside; but if you were inside this establishment, you felt morally and spiritually secure; it was a home, and built on solid foundations.

These were the people who to some extent transferred their own institutional basis to the new country. That is what gave Jewish Palestine its profound continuity with the immediate Jewish past. You might well ask, how can a state be constructed artificially? Is it really feasible to put up a pre-fabricated society? Even if one does not fully accept the traditionalist views of Burke and his brand of conservatives, one is liable to be told that states cannot be made, they must grow; that there is such a process as the insensible growth of a civilization by small, scarcely measurable steps; there are imponderables, there is the crucial influence of a multiplicity of untraceable small causes, leading to vast, but individually invisible, unanalysable effects. One cannot, one is informed, create a state in the way in which one makes a machine, or the way one creates any artificial object. There must be roots, growth, soil. There must be an imperceptible traditional accumulation, a sort of precipitate of tradition throughout the ages. And yet the impossible has apparently occurred; we are witnessing the rise of a state which in a few years' existence has been created by, to all appearances, pre-fabricated means: bits of Italy, bits of England, of Germany, bits and pieces from everywhere, quickly screwed together. And yet, like Aaron's rod, this apparently dead entity, this artificial wooden object, hammered together in a haphazard manner under critical conditions and in terrible haste, has burst into green leaf.

This is a very astonishing fact. It is less astonishing only if one realizes that the Jewish community lived by a set of portable values, a tradition on wheels, which, like the Ark of the Covenant, travelled from Jerusalem back into the wilderness of exile across central Europe to Russia and Russian Poland. There it halted, a kind of temporary establishment; a tradition with no roots in specifically Russian or Polish soil, for its roots were not territorial or geographical. It was a very genuine institutional unity, a real pattern of life, a way of living unrelated to almost any other. The Jews of England, Holland, Germany, America, could not claim and would not wish, perhaps, to possess anything like it; their histories in modern times have been different: before Hitler, happier, and, it may be, less interesting.

What kind of institutions were these? They were compounded of at least two elements. On the one hand there was the Jewish religion and the traditional religious Jewish way of living, which, in conditions of common depression, common misery, and common suffering, developed a deep sense of equality, so that all, whether rich or poor, men who were relatively influential and men who were not, felt themselves bound together by the particular ties of solidarity and fraternity which common slavery commonly induces. For this reason it was a more tightly woven community, with more intimate relationships within it, than the freer and looser communities outside. On the other hand, the Jews of every country tend to assimilate to some degree to the movements round them. In Russia and Poland they assimilated the humanist-liberal, radical, and social-democratic traditions of intellectual revolt which the best elements in those countries developed in response to the harsh and unbelievably stupid form of despotism maintained by the Tsarist régime.

It is not easy for those who have not met it to conceive this queer combination of ancient, pious, medieval religion with its immense preservative centripetal power on the one hand, and nineteenth-century liberal-democratic ideals on the other. The emancipated ex-inhabitants of the Pale of Settlement preserved traditional tastes but acquired new beliefs, the creed of the liberal intelligentsia. They believed in human virtue, in knowledge, in science, in reason; they believed in everything in which the Western revolutionaries of 1848 had believed. And if you go to Israel today, a far better key to understanding the minds of the rulers of that country and the methods they employ would be found in the study of the ideals of the nineteenth century than of those of the twentieth. In a certain sense, Israel is an anachronism: a very valuable, interesting, and inspiring anachronism; but still, in the twentieth century, odd and unique. The ideals which the Jews imported, and the culture they were able to build in the relative vacuum of Palestine—with a minimum of counter-influence on account of the evident feebleness of the Moslem culture in this corner of the Arab world—were founded upon typically nineteenth-century principles: belief in freedom from government dictation; in civil liberties, in equality, in human rights, in a form of democracy which in the twentieth century has, alas, proved not very reliable against the furious new forces which have been unleashed against it.

Israel is an *enclave*, a curious corner of the liberal past in which these things were—and are—believed with passionate and single-minded sincerity; and this is what gives it a curiously unfamiliar air. Anyone who wishes to understand the political structure of Israel had best study the nineteenth-century history of liberal ideas in Europe, and then the story of these ideas as reflected in the minds of Russian liberals and socialists. The Russian Jews who set their stamp so deeply on the social and political structure of Jewish Palestine under the Mandate—and Israel is faithful enough to that inheritance— were brothers and heirs to the idealistic Russian intellectuals, and to the poor artisans, struggling land labourers, factory workers, whose cause they fought. Any student of political institutions who wishes to understand the State of Israel must remember that its political parties derive from Russian Westernism, Russian liberal enlightenment, the ideas and aspirations which united the entire opposition to Tsarist oppression, and were, after their short-lived triumphs, so easily and cynically thrown overboard by the Bolsheviks. Nineteenth-century Russian liberals, without the scars of the disenchantments and failures, the crippling frustrations which democrats and liberals had suffered in Europe, remained hopeful; and their Jewish disciples still possess a great deal of hope, optimism, enthusiasm, and a certain inner strength. If you examine, for example, the Mapai and Mapam Parties—the Labour Party, and the Left Radical Party which has mysterious sympathies with the Soviet Union—you will find that they both resemble the idealistic members of Russian Menshevik or Social-Revolutionary Parties, the latter with its agrarian mystique, the former with its peculiar belief in a possible combination of socialization of the basic industries with the preservation of an almost maximum degree of cultural liberty on the part of individuals.

There is a direct link between Russian Social-Revolutionaries and the early Jewish colonists in Palestine, with their Rousseau-like belief in the healing power of contact with the soil, and their affinities to the Russian students who wished to 'go among the people' in the 'seventies and 'eighties of the last century, and were brought up on the purest principles of agrarian liberalism. Both believed in life on the land, contact with the peasants, a healthy existence away from the contaminating sophistication of the great cities, in escape from factors morally destructive for people deformed and maimed by the particular development of modern society, in which they—in one case intellectuals, in the other Jews—found themselves; namely, an abnormal situation of isolation from, and liability to persecution by, the barbarous majority. Not everything came from Russia, of course. The Irgun, a quasi-Fascist Party, is not an imitation of anything Russian, but far more like its Polish origins, having something in common with Pilsudski's colonels of the nineteen-twenties with their belief in honour. It is thence that it derives its terrorism, its heroism, its brutality, and a certain kind of romantic, Byronic inhumanity. And if you look to the opposite end of the scale, at the left-wing terrorists of the 'Stern gang', they are the direct heirs of those small groups of the terrorist section of the Russian left-wing Socialist Revolutionary Party, which believed in individual assassination as a politically necessary method. Misguided—deeply so—they may have been; but the roots from which they sprang are in these same humanitarian, idealistic, these now no longer existent, obsolete circles of the liberal intelligentsia of Russo-Polish society of the nineteenth century. To fail to see this is to misinterpret the facts.

The ideals which inspired the early Russian and Polish Zionists who emigrated to Palestine—ideals which are still dominant—came from Russian liberals. They filled the people who arrived earliest, the people who went without compulsion. There is a very great difference between the moral force exercised by those who went with no obvious economic need and no obvious political pressure, and those who went because they were expelled from the countries of their origin by violence. Obviously the moral influence of people who go of their own volition, and as an act of deliberate moral choice, is likely to be greater than that of people who, dazed and thrown about by the waves of misfortune which they have neither brought about nor understand, find themselves, in a large number of cases, cast up on this shore of refuge, to which they gradually grow assimilated, but which begins by being perhaps as bewildering to them as any other remote and unfamiliar country might have been. The people who went voluntarily, the early generations, certainly imported a flavour of liberal enthusiasm and a kind of mild half-socialist faith—(I do not think one can go much further than that)—

not very Marxist for all its Marxist phraseology, modified by boundless scepticism, individualism, empiricism—a particular brand of outlook which the Jews, particularly in Russia and Poland, derived partly from their own miseries and sufferings, partly from the soft, porous, chaotic, not very well-organized political system in which they were themselves brought up.

In giving this very definite primacy to the Russian settlers and their ideas I may seem guilty of exaggeration. What, it may be asked, of the German element? Where would Israel have been in its most critical hour, at war with the Arab states, and given up by its Western friends, without German skills and capital and talent for organization alike in peace and war? Where indeed? Lost perhaps; defeated and destroyed. And yet, for all the crucial contribution which the German settlers have made—to the arts and sciences, the army and the civilian administration, the judiciary and the manufacture and commerce—to every walk of life and every profession and technique, in spite of all this, the heart of the national life is almost untouched by the values dearest to the German Jews. It is they who are expected to adjust themselves to an outlook often alien to theirs.

Very little in Israel today can be derived from the views or practices of civilized immigrants from Berlin or Vienna or Frankfurt: much by going farther east. Israel is today a kind of welfare state—the kind of state which, by the end of the war, many people wished to see everywhere—a country which is neither Communist, nor moving in a Communist direction—nor yet one in which rampant individualism breeds a great deal of violent social injustice. How has Israel come to embody this ideal? Partly, no doubt, as a result of the pressure of the facts themselves. The country was poor, and its original immigrants came from among the poor; it was founded in an irregular fashion; Socialism preceded Capitalism; trade unions acquired power before industrialists could possibly have done so—Jews, it might be remarked, do everything in the reverse order. But—and this needs some emphasis—partly it is due to the beliefs which these early pioneers brought with them. These are scarcely intelligible unless one knows the peculiarly idealistic political climate, which included an almost mystical worship of British liberalism and British parliamentary institutions, in which the founding fathers (some of whom must surely still be among those whom a celebrated British officer is reported as having this year described as criminals from the ghettoes of Europe) obtained their education in the countries of their origin.

One of the remarkable facts which have helped to form the new society is the recreation of the Hebrew language. Much has been alleged against it. It was maintained that the *réchauffage* of a classical tongue, used largely for ceremonial purposes, would lead to great artificiality; that the language was outlandish, and would isolate those who used it from the community of civilized peoples; that it was violence done to the 'true' language of the Jews, the popular Yiddish language, which was rooted in the life of the people. These arguments have been blown to pieces by events. Hebrew has achieved a remarkable triumph, partly because it was the only common medium which was equally sacred to all the immigrants, partly because it was the ancient vehicle of a noble literature, the associations of which have affected the roots of all European thought and imagination. Because of this it has acted as an educational instrument of unique power. Words, thoughts, and behaviour are not easily divorceable elements. All the warmth, the humour, and the raciness, the splendid expressiveness of Yiddish, all the gaiety and tears of the many centuries of exile embodied in it, cannot compensate for the fact that it is an *argot*; that, like all things created under degraded conditions of life, it is formless, insufficiently disciplined and strict, over-elastic, whereas Hebrew (like much else in Israel, but perhaps more than any of the other factors) became an instrument for the increase of human dignity, a means of recreating a minimum degree of discipline of both emotion and reason. It is an adaptation of a genuine tradition, of long desired, long craved-for forms imposed upon the chaos of bohemian homelessness and blurred outlines, the cosy makeshifts of vagrant exiles—the obliteration, by means of something firm and yet deeply familiar and traditional, of the memories of past wounds and past servitudes. Of all the factors at work in creating a democratic and liberal nation in Israel today, not even excluding the army, it is the most penetrating, the most influential, and the most successful; and not, as is often maintained, a mere means of increasing chauvinism and isolationism.

Another of the factors which welded the diverse elements together and overcame those differences, which might otherwise have been too pronounced, was the fact of war, the war with the Arab states. It is a sad and melancholy fact, and highly discreditable to human nature, that wars produce a cohesion, solidarity, common enthusiasm, which few other phenomena create. I remember being told by a celebrated Israeli statesman that he had been brought up as a Social-Democrat in strict hatred of war, that he regretted the Arab War, had done nothing to bring it about and much to prevent it, and thought it a sad and calamitous thing; but that he could not deny that as a result of this war a tradition had grown up, a basis for the state had come into being. The blood of the martyrs had undoubtedly quickened those seeds of the national spirit which otherwise might have taken much longer to develop. There is no doubt

that, as during the Blitz of 1940–41 in England, a bringing together
and a violent fusion of very different ideals occurred, which, although
the end of the war to some extent (as in Britain) dissolved it, nevertheless still continues to be the essential moral basis of the common endeavours of the people of Israel.

Unless one understands that in some sense these citizens of a new
state feel that they live in a kind of bivouac; if not in an actual armed
camp, at any rate at the cross-roads of hostile armies; unless one
realizes that they feel themselves in constant danger, if not of
extermination, at any rate of attack, and that this, together with
intensifying the vices of chauvinism and puritanism brings out certain
virtues in human beings, certain forms of altruism, a genuine opportunity for generosity and even toleration which they otherwise seldom
show, the whole of their progress becomes unintelligible. Certainly,
in terms of the laws of economics and sociology and many other
respected social sciences, they should have collapsed a long time ago.

The result of the impact of so many abnormal forces was the
emergence of a new species of human beings. If you ask what the
founders of the Zionist movement wanted—they wanted to create
Jews each in his own image. The English Jews doubtless wanted to
see the best kind of English Jew flourish in Israel. The Russian Jews
wanted the best kind of idealistic liberal Russian Jews to predomin-
ate; the Australian Jews hoped for the best-liked Australians, the
Iraqi Jews might desire the most admired Iraqi character. None of
this was to be, because, although man proposes, the forces of
history dispose very differently. There has come into being the
embryo of an Israeli nationality, the like of which has not existed for
two thousand years. What, you may well ask, are these new human
beings like? They are not easy to describe. Their most striking
characteristic seems to me to be their dissimilarity from the concept
of the Jews which is lodged in the minds of almost all non-Jews. This
may be a matter of pride or regret, pleasure or pain, depending on
what one's tastes may be.

There are in Israel very few eminent bankers, very few eminent
lawyers, not many scientists of genius, there are very few persons
principally occupied with the accumulation of wealth. Again, there
are few professional critics (I say nothing of the amateurs); there
are few sophisticated, chess-playing, café intellectuals—late-night
figures, dispensers of a peculiar compound of Freud, Marx, Sartre,
or whatever else is at once shocking and fashionable; seekers after
strong sensations, partly genuine, partly fraudulent, sometimes
interesting, at other times deliberately sordid and obscene, amusing,
destructive, superficial, and liable to exhibitionism and vulgarity;
with a tendency to flourish within declining or insecure cultures—in

the Weimar Republic of Germany, or in certain sections of the United States today. Of such there are very few to be seen in Israel, and such forms of activity are not held at a premium there. Tourists who visit Tel Aviv with the expectation of Jewish activities of this particular kind, and look for these sharp flavours—the fruits of decadence and self-critical desperation—are much disappointed by the relative placidity, relative coarseness; a kind of stubborn normality and a complacent soundness, wholesomeness, dullness—which the Jews have surely richly deserved. For certainly there has been no absence in their lives hitherto of condiment, no absence of salt or acid and exotic spices of all types. They have had these elements, if anything, in rather too high proportions, so high that they tended to poison both themselves and their neighbours. In Israel these elements are at a discount. What you find are natives of a country, not unlike the natives of some other Mediterranean state, and not the artificial products of a liberal European intelligentsia in decay.

That may be a cause for regret, or it may not. Certainly I have known some people who went to Israel and were bitterly disappointed by the fact that the arts do not sufficiently flourish there. There are no great Israeli novelists; there are some good short-story writers, but they are older men who perfected their genius before they went to Palestine. There are on the whole no great thinkers, poets, painters, sculptors, composers; Israeli music is respectable, painting is far from deplorable, writing is moderately good, architecture is improving; and so on. All these activities are reputably carried on. They do not, certainly, lag behind the civilizations of the Middle East, nor, perhaps, even some among the less advanced countries in the west. But the expectation of a sudden efflorescence of genius, this curious hope that the light will come from the east immediately and without delay; that a nucleus of men of superlative gifts would spring forth in this new soil, and at once burst upon the world with a new moral and intellectual message, so that men would wonder how so much astonishing genius could be so marvellously gathered together—that, fortunately, has not happened. Israel, consequently, has a chance of continuing to grow, under conditions which may be described as almost normal. This is surely what Herzl wanted to see, although whether all his followers were equally won to the idea of something normal and ordinary is not clear. Certainly among the early Zionist pioneers there were those who spoke as if what they wished to create was a cultural enclave, a super-university, a shrine, a temple at once sacred and secular whose task would be spiritual and educational, and not a community occupied with the daily tasks of ordinary life. Yet I cannot think that it is the duty of any man to produce works of genius and irradiate the world with wisdom. If he does, so much the better for him and for the world. The principal obligation of human beings seems to me to consist in living their life according to their lights, and in developing whatever faculties they possess without hurting their neighbours, in realizing themselves in as many directions as freely, variously, and richly as they can, without worrying overmuch whether they are measuring up to the peaks in their own past history, without casting anxious looks to see whether their achievements reach the highest points reached by the genius of their neighbours, nor yet looking at other nations, or wondering whether they are developing precisely as they expect them to develop.

I spoke earlier of the peculiar self-consciousness—the heightened, sometimes over-acute awareness of themselves and their condition which is itself a large element in the 'Jewish problem'. To this there was bound to be a reaction. And so in Israel one comes across individuals who say: 'We are not greatly interested in the outside world. We are the natives of this land. No doubt we did come from outside. And the Americans came from Europe, and so did the Australians and Canadians. But it is a mistake to regard the Australians and Canadians as a species of Englishman, and it is a mistake to regard the Americans as a species of Germans, Italians, Dutchmen, Czechs, etc.; they have a mentality of their own. This is more obvious if you go to America, Australia, and Canada than if you simply study history and look at them from a distance as a kind of extension of a mother country. No doubt we too come from outside, and we are composed of very varying elements from different countries; but the 'pressure cooker' is working well. We are gradually assimilating to a common type; and we cannot be tied in our history to perpetual dependence upon, and concern with, the fate of those Jews who have not followed us, and whose fate is determined by their local position in their local communities, in which they have either chosen to stay, or were forced to stay by circumstances.'

This is a very extreme position, and I do not for a moment pretend that it is morally tenable or at all widely held. But in a milder and humaner form it will surely spread. There is nothing unnatural in the fact that there exist people who do not wish to spend their lives in mourning for the six million Jewish dead. They cannot forget them; but neither do they wish to start their lives as the gloomy heirs of a black tragedy; they want to start their lives afresh. Some of them are young, healthy, ordinary men and women who are looking forward to a future of normal activity. They wish to be simple, uncomplicated, and shed the neuroses of their ancestors, without perpetual reminders of their past misfortunes. They cannot develop independently so long as they remain a colony with infinite strands binding it to the entire Diaspora, feeling in its body every tremor of what happens to the end of these strands in other countries. They are today economically dependent on the Jews in the rest of the world; they are, in general, excessively dependent on the rest of the world, because they are not economically viable, their imports exceed the exports, and so forth. Nor is autarky a desirable ideal for any country. But in the end, if they survive at all (as they surely will), this excessive dependence will cease, and a new type of man and citizen will develop. He may produce no very sophisticated art, may produce nothing culturally startling or arresting, but he and his fellows will exist, and be happy, and be a people, and that is surely sufficient.

If a new nation is born which differs from the Jews of the outside world, if a gap occurs—if the Israeli nation gradually becomes almost (never wholly) as different from the Jews of the outside world as other nations are, we should have no ground of complaint. There are those, even among Jews, who say that the entire experiment is a kind of 'exile from exile'. The Jews have been in exile in the Diaspora; and now, in order to escape from its difficulties and burdens, they have voluntarily exiled themselves into a kind of vast ghetto of their own, which still possesses all the properties of those from which they emerged, plus the discomforts of the Middle East. But this, in my view, is quite false. No country gives less impression of a self-enclosed, timid, cowering body of persons, huddling together for mutual protection, which is the idea that a ghetto conjures up.

It is true that Israel's problems are many. Apart from terrifying economic problems which I am incompetent to appraise, it is afflicted, at the fringes of the great liberal, semi-middle-class body of its population, with political unwisdom both of right- and of left-wing kinds: not more so than other countries: but, alas, not less. There is the problem of her relations with her neighbours, and perhaps the greater problem of her relations with the outside world. Israelis are of course a predominantly Western people, they read Western books, they think Western thoughts, they go to Western films. Their outlook is a Western outlook. The symbols, the words in which they think have largely been derived from the traditions of England, of France, of Germany, of America, of all the countries of Western civilization. They are today faced with the problem of assimilating with—or to—their new immigrants from Oriental countries; the army training which the newcomer undergoes is a great leveller. Will the result be Westernization or 'Levantinization'? It is too early to tell.

There is no doubt, moreover, that there is a vast gap between them —even their Oriental portion—and their Arab neighbours, and the

Arabs are certainly consumed with hostile sentiment towards them; indeed, with the desire to exterminate them. Not as great, perhaps, as Arab leaders find it necessary to proclaim; but violent enough. Neither they, nor their Western friends in or out of government offices in London and Washington and New York, are reconciled to the notion that Israel has come to stay. The relations of Israel with the outside world are difficult. Israel is aware that it has relatively little of material value to offer. It realizes that in some sense it is the plaything of the Great Powers: Babylon, Assyria, and Egypt in ancient days; America and the Soviet Union and Britain today. They are still at the cross-roads between the Great Powers, which may support them one day, and desert them the next. The clash of ideologies between the major Powers comes into violent play on the soil of Israel, which is a more impressionable medium than almost any other place in the world. In the circumstances Israelis realize that they are a kind of political and intellectual microcosm, in which almost any tendency of the modern world is more clearly visible, more acutely felt, and more traceable than anywhere else. They realize this, but there is nothing that they can do to escape it. Their daily cares are greater than the anxieties induced by long-distance prospects. They feel—I think perhaps rightly—that if they behave themselves in an intelligent and constructive manner, they will survive. Late or soon a settlement with their neighbours will take place. The geographical and ethnic factors are inescapable. On the whole, I should say, they are too wise to brood too gloomily about them: day-to-day anxieties sufficiently absorb their energies.

If one were a serious sociologist, it is to Israel that one would surely go today. There is no place in the world where a greater degree of variety of humanity is observable. Social scientists complain of the absence of 'laboratory conditions' in which experiments can be conducted in their disciplines. But these almost obtain in Israel. Nowhere else can one witness so extraordinary a collision and 'cross-fertilization' of types—of representatives of some ancient pre-classical culture coming into contact with the most sophisticated modern products of the United States; of the most theoretical, intellectually coherent form of, let us say, Marxist ideology, coming into collision with some dim, mystical, almost inexpressible Oriental attitude to life. There is no country where so many ideas, so many ways of living, so many attitudes, so many methods of going about everyday things, have suddenly been thrown into a more violent clash. It is one of the most fascinating spectacles in the world. Yet the sociologists in the world have paid relatively little attention to Israel, and prefer to study routine phenomena in, let us say, the U.S. Midwest. This is virtuous, there is nothing to be said against it.

Nevertheless it seems curious to me that sociologists, with the opportunity of studying a phenomenon unique in their field, obstinately avert their gaze and go on burrowing into the dullest and most uniform forms of life that they can find. It is as if there were an eclipse only once in the history of the world, from which some kind of crucial data—refuting and confirming essential hypotheses—could be deduced, and as if the world's astronomers were found firmly pointing their telescopes in some other direction.

From the point of view of Israel itself, as a result of this violent clash and collision of various cultures a common denominator is emerging, something identifiable and fascinating, namely a politically liberal, egalitarian, human being, with a mentality not unlike that of the Italian Risorgimento: on the whole, left of centre, of a kind rightly admired by English liberals and radicals in the nineteenth century. This is the kind of outlook which has set its stamp upon the whole economic and social development of Palestine. None of this could have been deduced solely from economic needs or the social necessities of the Israeli community.

This seems to me interesting, because it shows the power of ideas, and not merely of economic and social pressures. It upsets materialist theories of history according to which environment, or economic factors, or the collision of classes is mainly responsible for what happens. It upsets the various doctrines in accordance with which Israel could not have arisen at all; the doctrines which the German Marxists and Russian Bundists used to adduce in order to prove the impossibility of a Jewish state, and all the various doctrines about the inevitable assimilation of the Jews, advanced by both Jews and gentiles, from some set of cut-and-dried premises, or historical theory, or sociological law or system. Nor did the empiricists in the foreign offices of the Great Powers do much better. Very few of the chancelleries of Europe or America seriously believed in the possibility of the rise of even a short-lived independent State of Israel. Very few believed that it would ever have the fighting strength, the unity of spirit which would enable it to triumph over so many obstacles. A great many of the prophets were in the grip of various obsolete theories of how nations rise and fall, or simply of powerful prejudice and emotion; and on the whole they tended to discount too much the sheer power of human idealism and human will-power.

Israel is not a large-scale experiment. It occupies a very small portion of the earth's surface; the number of persons comprising its population is relatively small. But its career confutes a number of deterministic theories of human behaviour, both materialist, and the fashionable brands of anti-materialism. And that, I will not deny, is a source of great satisfaction to those who have always believed such theories to be false in principle, but have never before, perhaps, found evidence quite so vivid and quite so convincing of the hollowness of such views. Israel remains a living witness to the triumph of human idealism and will-power over the allegedly inexorable laws of historical evolution. And this seems to me to be to the eternal credit of the entire human race.

*Lecture given at the Royal Society of Arts to Members of the Anglo-Israel Association, London, April, 1953.

LEVANT DUSK: THE REFUGEE* SITUATION

by STEWART PEROWNE

DURING THE past four years I have been working in Jerusalem with the Anglican Bishop, as one of his assistants on schemes for the welfare of the Arab refugees. I want to tell you today, as best I can, something of the present condition of these unhappy people. Then perhaps some of you may be interested to hear of a small experiment which the Bishop has made, not in providing a future for these people, but in trying to ensure that whatever their future may be, they may face it with confidence, self-respect, and peace of mind. I should like to tell you of other enterprises, particularly those undertaken by Arabs for Arabs, such as those of Musa Alami, Mrs. Antonius, Miss Hussaini, and Miss Nasir. If I speak of the Bishop's work, it is because I have been closest to it.

The refugee problem was created in 1948 when, during the war with the Zionists, nearly one million Arabs fled from their homes. The massacre of Deir Yassin, the latest link in a chain of terror, had struck fear into the hearts of those civilians whose homes lay in the path of the Zionist forces. Just as, in 1940, Frenchmen in their thousands fled before the advancing Nazis, so, in 1948, before the Zionists, thousands of Arabs did the same, and for the same reason. As General Spears has put it in a letter published in the *Daily Telegraph* of November 16, 1955: 'That an honest person should be expected to believe that anything but force or fear for their lives would drive peasants from their age-long holdings is an affront to common sense.' I have talked to many refugees during the past four years. They all support General Spears's view. And I think they should know.

So there were these hundreds of thousands of peasants, with their wives and children, suddenly uprooted from the homes and lands which had been theirs for generations, and the quiet and peaceable possession of which Great Britain had repeatedly guaranteed to them. Overnight they became outcasts, and outcasts they have remained ever since. America recognized the new Zionist state almost before it had uttered its first cry. England, playing a role sadly reminiscent of that of Aaron in the creation of the Golden Calf, of which we read in the 32nd chapter of Exodus, followed America. Nothing was done by either to obtain redress for the Arabs, whom they were, I repeat, solemnly bound to protect from wrong. To this day the Arab refugees have neither been permitted to return to their homes, nor have they received one penny in compensation for what has been taken from them by alien force.

> *In the corrupted currents of this world,*
> *Offence's gilded hand may shove by justice;*
> *And oft 'tis seen, the wicked prize itself*
> *Buys out the law.*

So there they are, this million of victims, 'Strangers and afraid in a world they never made'. For eight years they have waited, for eight years they have endured. Not one jot nor one tittle of justice have they received. Do you expect them to kiss our hands, to give three cheers for democracy, and to praise the policy of the United Nations?

As is well known, many of the refugees live in camps. But it is a mistake to think that they all do. In fact, only just over a third live in camps. Let me repeat that: only just over a third of the refugees—by which I mean registered refugees recognized as such by the United Nations Relief and Works Agency—live in camps maintained by that Agency. The remaining two-thirds live in caves, with relatives, or anywhere they can find to lay their heads. But camp dwellers and independents alike, they are refugees and depend on their ration cards for their livelihood.

This picture is black, and I hope that no one thinks there is any way round the problem of the guilt of the West in having created it. There is not; but there is a compensation in this thought, that if we have done nothing to solve the problem, we have done a good deal to palliate it. I refer to the United Nations Relief and Works Agency, generally known as U.N.R.W.A. To this agency the United Nations vote a large sum every year. It does not come out of the general budget, but is made up of special contributions voted for the purpose by certain nations. America pays the greatest part, between three- and four-fifths. England comes next, but with a far smaller contribution. How is this money spent?

First, on the issue of rations to all those refugees who hold cards, wherever they may be living. Secondly, on the maintenance of camps. Thirdly, on education and health. The Agency is very well run. It must be one of the best-administered organizations of its kind in the world. It has a few foreign officers, American, French, and English among them; but the great majority of its staff are Arabs, themselves refugees. It is, in fact, the limbo of that excellent administration which the Mandatory government built up over thirty years and abandoned in a night.

The health services deal with sanitation and the care of 'all women labouring of child, sick persons, and young children'—to use a phrase which, even in these days, cannot be bettered. The education department provides excellent schools, excellent buildings, that is. The Mandatory government never built anything half so fine. In or near every big camp you find them; and outside Jerusalem there is the best trade school (only, of course, it has to be called a Vocational Training Centre nowadays) that Palestine has ever known. In days gone by it was hard to induce people to send their children to a trade school because, in Palestine as in this country, no one wanted to work in a shop who could work in an office. But now things have changed. Offices pay very poorly in Jordan. Oil companies pay very well. So it is better to train as a welder, or an electronics expert, than to become a clerk. Or a teacher, either. And that has had a bad effect on the schools. The cadre of teachers trained under the Mandate were the *corps d'élite* of the Levant. But they have all been scattered now. A few do remain in Jordan, but of those not all are in education. The rest have sought and found fortune in other lands. So their place has been taken perforce by untrained tiros, little more, often, than schoolboys themselves. Not all of them have resisted the blandishments of Communism. But, let us beware of cant: is it natural that they should? What must be the attitude and the feelings of those who for eight years have had nothing to do but brood on their wrongs, men and boys alike, without work, without hope? Think of them, looking daily across the truce-line at their own lands, on which grow their own trees—the trees they planted with their own hands. Into their own houses where they were born and lived they see the stranger enter. Will these people, so used, and so circumstanced, praise the policy of the nations who drew that line? Will they not rather be inclined to favour the adversaries of those nations?

The Jordan government absolutely discourages any attempt at individual revenge. When you read of frontier incidents, and, mercifully, during the last eighteen months they have been very, very rare on the Jordan frontier, remember this. The Tel Aviv régime has repeatedly been rebuked by the Security Council—in fact, no government in the world has been censured more often—for permitting its armed forces to infringe the truce. On the other hand, such incursions as there have been from the Jordan side have been the work only of individual, dispossessed, privateers, seeking what, in their eyes, is still their own. You appreciate the difference? Remember this, too: that last year the Jordan government imprisoned more than nine hundred of its own citizens who had been arrested trying to cross the truce-line.

Yes, the bitterness is there and the causes of it. A little over a month ago I was walking near Jericho, a town in the vicinity of which there are some seventy thousand refugees living in three vast camps. Slums would be a better word. The squalid huts, the arid, listless streets, the daily round of nothing—no wonder that, despite U.N.R.W.A., they have created among a people famous, almost notorious, for its patience, a sense of despair which in the early days of 1956 showed itself in an outburst of destructive violence. (In the camps in the hills, where tents are still to be found as homes, the atmosphere of squalor, the awful contrast between school and home, are even more depressing.) As we were walking, we came up with a little lad who was conning his book. (This always had to be done in the open country, because there is no privacy in a camp, so that young wandering scholars are a common sight.) He asked me where I came from. He was reading an English primer but we talked in Arabic. As soon as I told him, he loosed off a stream of abuse of England such as, after thirty years of growing realization that we are not universally loved, took me quite aback. This boy had clearly listened to the Egyptian wireless and to nothing else, for a very long time. He had believed, or pretended to believe, all it told him. Finally, after tearing Britain to shreds, he said: 'And then that Baghdad Pact. . . .' 'Listen,' I said. 'Mohammed, how old are you?' 'Sixteen,' he said. 'Well, then,' I said, 'you come back in ten years' time and we'll have a good talk about the Baghdad Pact, because I don't talk politics with children.' He laughed and, in that irresistible Arab way, said: 'But can't we just be friends, we Arabs and you English?' That encounter ended in smiles; but I am convinced that Mohammed is only one of thousands who have been brought up to regard England as a villainous Power, and who see around them no evidence which would persuade them to the contrary.

Which means that, after eight years, the refugee problem is not only no better: it is actually a good deal worse. The refugees are fed and housed and looked after; many, but by no means all, of those squalid, tattered tents have gone, but only to be replaced by hopeless little huts. Meanwhile, the original refugees have become a grave social problem, not least for the Jordan government, whose subjects they are; and their children, who increase rapidly every year, have been born and brought up to a life of aimless, resentful idleness.

I hope that no one will ask me: 'Why have the Arab governments not solved the problem?' The answer is that they did not create the problem, we did. Every Arab, be he statesman or peasant, regards the refugees' problem as part of the Palestine problem in general. Without restitution of some kind, without either return or compensation—and by compensation I mean the payment of a just price for each piece of property alienated from its lawful owners—the problem never will be solved. That is our responsibility; so why should we try to shuffle it off on to the shoulders of the people whom we have wronged? It makes neither sense nor justice.

Now, I have said enough about the problem in general. I want to let you look at some of the facts of the case through the eyes of an artist, Mr. David Brewster, who has taken the pictures we are now going to see. Mr. Brewster is the representative on the Bishop's staff of the Cambridge Undergraduate Committee for Arab Refugees, and is at present a teacher and scoutmaster at St. George's School in Jerusalem.

(*The remainder of the lecture was illustrated with slides.*)

Given the fact that the refugees are peasants; given the second fact that their plight is a problem which can be solved only as part of a major political solution of the Palestine problem, the commanding question is: 'How can these people be helped?' It is not a question of 'Who is my neighbour?' There he is, wounded by the roadside: it is a question of 'How can I help him?'

It was in this light that the Bishop in Jerusalem, among many others, both Arabs and their friends from other lands, viewed the problem.

First of all there was education to be thought about. St. George's School is famous. It has produced many of Jordan's best sons and is now training many more. An education is the one door which may open on to a life of hope and self-respect for many a refugee, provided he can afford to obtain a good one. I have spoken of the U.N.R.W.A. schools, of their merits and drawbacks. Many parents would prefer their children to grow up in the proven atmosphere of St. George's. So the Bishop set out to raise funds for bursaries to enable deserving boys to go to St. George's. And that scheme for bursaries is still one of the most rewarding of the Bishop's contributions to the refugee problem. It is also one of the most expensive. Two-thirds of St. George's boys are now refugees.

Then, thought the Bishop, what about those who had nowhere even to live, except some dank cave? Could something be done for them, and even more for their children, so that in due time these same children might grow up healthy boys and girls, and perhaps become scholars of St. George's?

At this point the Bishop and Mrs. Stewart consulted a friend of theirs, someone with a long connection with St. George's, where his own first-born and many of his family are now at school. He is called Mahmud Abu Rish. He lives at Bethany, the village, you remember, in which the story of the Good Samaritan was originally told, the village which stands at the head of the very road in which that story is set. Mahmud is the head of a very ancient family, and he is a Muslim. So are all the refugees in the camps, every one of them. There are Christian refugees; but, as it happened—largely owing to an accident of geography—the chief centres of Christian residence and industry were untouched by the disaster, and so have been able to absorb a great number, in fact the majority, of their fellow Christians. Mahmud felt he had some responsibility towards, first of all, certain friends who arrived in his village. He soon had them looked after. Then his interest spread, and with his friends—the Bishop and the Bishop's wife, Mrs. Stewart—he decided that something might be done to make the lot of other refugees more stable and more hopeful. Mahmud is one of eight brothers. They are a typical Palestine family. One was killed in the Zionist War. One lives in Haiti, one is the representative in Beirut of a world-famous American newspaper, one works for the Jordan Government, one for U.N.R.W.A. That leaves three—Mahmud, Musa, and Daud. They live at home in Bethany and devote their time and talents to work for their fellows.

So there was the team: the Bishop, Mrs. Stewart, Mahmud, and the two brothers. They decided to help a group of villagers from the plain—who were living in such filth and overcrowded squalor that they could not, tough as they were, long survive in such conditions— to build some houses. The villagers saw no objection. After all, they said, the Bishop was a man of religion and he had nothing to do with their future, which was the business of the politicians (you see, this attitude is universal); all he was offering was the means of facing the future, whatever it might be, as healthy householders, with healthy children. Why not do it? That was how the Bishop's housing scheme originally started, and that is how it works today. The first village was built nearly four years ago, with funds raised in England in response to a letter in *The Times*. Since that small beginning, the Bishop and Mahmud Abu Rish have built five other villages.

The general idea was that the new villages should be built so as to harmonize with the existing ones. Funds for them have been contributed by individual friends, in England, America, and Canada, by Arab refugees who have made good in other lands; by the Arab statesman and business man, Mr. Emile Bustani, and by three oil companies—the Arabian-American, or ARAMCO; the Iraq Petroleum Company; and the Trans-Arabian Pipeline Company, or TAPLINE. The American Episcopal Church and the American Congregational Church jointly have given one village. The American Gulf Oil Company, which is one of the owners of the Kuwait Oil Company, has recently given the Bishop a sum of £2,000, a large proportion of which is being devoted to the afforestation of the villages with fruit trees, vines and shade and fuel trees. Altogether this project has received a sum of some £35,000, with which it has been possible to provide decent homes for some one thousand souls. This is not a big achievement; but it does show that homes can be provided—and the sort of home that seems to meet the wishes of the people; and the individual cost is not high.

First a site is bought, and surrounded with a ring-wall, to protect it from goats. Then the building begins. From the start, the new villagers help to build their own homes. Here is a Bedu, a refugee from Beersheba, and his little boy. You can see from his face how earnest and anxious he is: is it really possible that, after shivering for eight winters on these cold hills, he is to have a house to live in? Yes, if he helps to build it. So he sets to work.

The stonemason is a professional. Here he sits under his improvised sunshade, cutting with a practised instinct the stones which are to form the new house. They are soon laid in position, and the walls begin to rise—with astonishing speed. For before the eyes of the workers are the finished houses in the background: when are WE going to have houses?, they say. As soon as you finish them, is the answer.

Soon the house looks like this. It is a two-roomed block, each room about 13 feet square. Each room will house a couple, and adjacent rooms are occupied, of course, by members of the same family, who will not mind sharing the verandah and the kitchen—which, like the verandah, they will build themselves to the design of the head of the house, or more likely of his wife.

At last the top course is reached, the stones being passed up from hand to hand and shoulder to shoulder.

The mortar is made of earth and lime mixed. Cement is used to point the outside and to make it watertight. Here is a load of mortar being brought up by one of the younger generation. He will always remember the day he helped to build the house. Whatever the future may be for him, and his children, whatever other dwelling, old or new, he may acquire, this will always have an appeal for him.

The house is measured for its doors and windows. When it is finished it looks like this. The roof is corrugated iron on a wood

frame, coped with stone. The group grows until it begins to fit into
the landscape. When the ground round the houses—and there is half
an acre to each block—is cultivated, and when the hundreds of trees
which have been planted round the walls and along the streets of the
villages come up, the houses will look even more appropriate. You
notice that they are not set in straight lines, but in groups, which is
the way houses are in Palestine.

Finally comes the day when the stone of dedication is engraved
and set up. This one is an old Roman pillar which gives its name to
the village. The inscription starts, as all of them do, with a verse
from the Qur'ān. It reads: 'God is the surest protector.' Then
'Al-'Amudiya' (the name of the village, meaning 'the Village of the
Pillar.') 'It was founded by the American-Arabian Oil Company.'
And then comes the date according to the Muslim and the Christian
calendars—1374 and 1955.

And here is a mother at home in her house with her baby. It is one
of the oldest and best pictures in the world, so I will say no more
about it. Only that the rolls of mattresses in the alcove, neatly stowed
away by day, are the family's beds at night. They are, of course,
exactly the same as they were in the days when the once lame man
was told to take up his and walk.

In the older-established villages it has been possible to provide
communal amenities. This is the inscription of one of them. It reads:
'The Children's House' (between two dates, 1374 and 1955). 'It was
given to the model villages of Al-Mansur, Al-Bustan, and Al-Manara
by the employees of the Near-East Arab Broadcasting Station,
themselves children of this land.' The last phrase is a modest cloak
for the fact that although they are all refugees, they wanted to help
their less fortunate countrymen and so contributed the very considerable sum of money necessary to build this infant-welfare centre.

This is the inside. The blackboard shows the number of children
who have on that particular day come to the centre for their daily
ration of milk.

Another amenity, particularly loved by the ladies, is the communal
oven, or *furn*. In biblical times, as still in most villages, the pots had
to be made hot with thorns, the kind of thorn depicted here. It
takes hours and hours of arduous work for the women to go out on
to the hill-sides and gather enough fuel even for one week. And think
of the harm it does to the countryside by encouraging desiccation
and denudation. How much better and more convenient to have a
general oven, which can be lighted with just one bit of thorn, like
this, and then fired with *jift*—the residue left after the olives have
been crushed; such a good, oily, hot fuel. All the ladies now have
to do is to take down each her own prepared dough, made from the

flour which U.N.R.W.A. provides, and the baker does the rest of the baking. The gossip is the province of the ladies, and I assure you they do it to perfection. This bakery was the gift of two English friends whose names I should like to tell you, only I know they would not wish me to.

There stands a finished village—our second, Al-Mansur—with Bethany in the background.

Here is a group of villagers in the neighbouring Al-Bustan, three generations of them.

This is a picture of the headman of Al-Bustan.

And this is the baker's father, from down near Hebron. He has known bewildering changes in his life. Born under the Turks; seeing the coming of the English as a young man. And now, in his old age, a refugee. What do they think of, these men? What do they look forward to? I do not know all their thought. But I can tell you this: they are never vindictive. Critical of governments, yes. But you never hear them—at least I have never heard them—say one revengeful word as individuals about those who now occupy their homes and lands. They think of them not in the mass, as Zionists, but individually, as Jews; which is a wholly different thing. It is also an extremely important thing. It was Weizmann himself who said that the ultimate test of the Zionists would be their ability to get on with the Arabs. In the long run, it cannot be alien arms that can maintain a minority amid a majority of different race and religion. It can only be civility and decency and sympathy. My own belief is that if ever the Zionists come to realize that, and act towards their neighbours as man to equal man, they will find that reciprocal sympathy will not be lacking.

But what these people chiefly think about is work. How can they get a livelihood? It is remarkable how the mere fact of once more possessing a home stimulates this desire to be independent and self-respecting. Even more remarkable is their success. They travel all over the kingdom, these men, to find work, and every cultivable inch of the gardens is planted. The result is that the first village is to all intents and purposes now an independent community, as the Bishop always hoped it would be. The second has gone a long way in the same good direction. The third and fourth in a lesser but encouraging degree. There is every prospect that, in a matter of a few years, these people will be as stable as their neighbours, and that their children will grow up free—loved and happy.

Here is one of them. He is called Faris, which means knight or horseman. He is known as the Crown Prince, and is a great character. If only for his sake, and the likes of him, surely the Bishop's work is worth doing.

Somehow, in Palestine, life always renews itself. Here in Jericho, today's refugees are at work bringing to light the oldest town yet known to have been built by man, more than eight thousand years ago.

Here, in the forsaken street of Jerash, the hyssop still springs from the wall.

Here, in the Garden of Gethsemane itself, are the sweet flowers of this very spring. However hard it may be at times to hope, it is far harder to despair.

* *A Lecture delivered before the Royal Central Asiatic Society on May 16, 1956.*

THE ARAB REFUGEES: A STUDY IN FRUSTRATION

by MIZRA KHAN

FEW HUMAN TRAGEDIES in recent years have held the attention and the sympathy of the world as has that of the Palestine refugees, and rarely has the international community rallied so readily and with such generosity in an effort to rehabilitate uprooted masses, consisting mostly of innocent victims of events brought about by the follies and ambitions of a bankrupt leadership.

But just as rarely has an essentially local problem like this been allowed to bedevil international relations to such an extent and for so long a time, or human suffering been so cynically prolonged and exploited to serve a reckless political game. Seldom has history been so brazenly rewritten, and once-accepted facts so shamelessly distorted beyond recognition.

The following pages aim to recapitulate, briefly, and in the light of the record, the salient points of the problem and its origins, its treatment by the international community at large, by the parties most directly concerned, and by the United States, on whose shoulders rests the major financial burden of refugee relief and attempted rehabilitation.

I. THE PROBLEM

In the wake of the Arab War on Israel in 1948, hundreds of thousands of Palestinian Arabs fled the country and became refugees in neighbouring Arab states, in the Jordan-held Arab sector of Palestine, and in the Egyptian-occupied part of Palestine known as the Gaza Strip. Their plight immediately engaged the attention of world opinion and the energies of the international relief agencies. A small number of well-to-do Arab families emigrated at leisure at the first signs of the impending violence and transferred enough of their possessions to resume life in their accustomed manner in the countries of their refuge. But the vast majority, caught in the flux of war, saved little or nothing of their belongings, and these masses soon fitted the U.N. Relief Agency's definition of an Arab refugee as 'a person normally resident in Palestine, who has lost his home and his livelihood as a result of the hostilities and who is in need'. All became dependent on relief for their food, clothing, medical care, and the education of their children. Two-thirds of the refugees found at least shelter in existing towns and villages; camps were set up for the remainder.

The world was not slow in recognizing the dual nature of the problem which had arisen: the human aspect—an urgent case of misery to be alleviated; and the political and social aspects—the impact on its surroundings of an uprooted multitude, bewildered, unwanted, not knowing where to place the blame for its unexpected sufferings, a potential prey to agitators, 'rich and tempting soil for exploitation by those with other motives than the welfare of the refugee' (report of U.N. Relief and Works Agency, 1951). Though the Arab refugees comprise only a small fraction of those displaced by the upheavals of the last decade (some 700,000 out of 60 million, as estimated by the Foreign Policy Association), they are located in a sensitive part of the world, an area which is itself in the throes of violent social, economic, and political convulsions. It was therefore soon realized that the perpetuation of this human problem would serve to prevent peace between the Arab states and Israel, and would be used to sharpen the conflicts and the hatreds arising from the war.

Nearly $200 million has been spent on relief alone during the past eight years. An additional $200 million has been set aside for various projects designed to improve the economies of the host countries, and to assist the reintegration there of increasing numbers of refugees and thus reduce the relief-ration rolls. Year after year, the problem has been debated at the U.N. sessions. A variety of survey missions, sub-committees, and 'special ambassadors' have gone to the Middle East to assess the situation or to suggest solutions. Several U.N. agencies, each charged with working towards a solution, have followed one another, each succeeding agency with a bolder programme than its predecessor. New hopes have been held out by those agencies, with simultaneous requests for fresh funds. The international community responded unfailingly, not, however, without a note of increasing urgency in its resolutions advocating an early transition from relief to reintegration. Yet each time, failure had to be admitted. The annual reports of the Director of the U.N. Relief and Works Agency for Palestine Refugees (U.N.R.W.A.) are full of such tell-tale phrases as 'obliged with regret to report that little progress . . . ,' 'not as rapidly as the General Assembly might wish . . . ,' 'timing has gone awry . . . ,' 'failed to produce . . . ,' 'mixed record . . .' Invariably one finds the explanation of these failures: 'Programmes depend for their existence and success on the approval and support of the host governments'; '. . . depends partly on political decisions over which the Agency has no control . . .'; 'lack of co-operation . . .'.

The Sub-Committee on the Near East and Africa of the U.S. Senate Foreign Relations Committee, which held hearings on the refugee problem, reported on July 24, 1953: 'Each time the Foreign Relations Committee has considered the . . . matter since 1949, it has been encouraged to believe that substantial progress in the settlement of the matter was soon to be made, but year after year it has come up again with little change, except for increased requests for funds.'

And again:

'The Sub-Committee was extremely disappointed to find that after nearly five years of effort and expenditures . . . virtually no progress has been made in developing projects for resettlement, or reaching political agreements relative to resettlement and rehabilitation.'

Some of the worst anticipations have come true. The solution of a human tragedy has been thwarted on political grounds. The refugees have indeed provided that 'rich and tempting soil for exploitation' envisioned in the 1951 Report of U.N.R.W.A. Many brilliant careers have been built in Arab governments on the misery of the refugees and through the perpetuation of the problem as an instrument of international blackmail. The bogey of Communism among refugees—disproven by authoritative surveys—has been brought into play. Arab governments hold all the major rehabilitation projects at a standstill, all negotiations deadlocked. Unrealistic expectations of 'repatriation' are recklessly fostered and the refugees are denied the humane solution of reintegration. History is constantly being rewritten to make the United Nations, the Western Powers, and of course Israel, the whipping-boys for the whole problem.

Meanwhile, contrary to all hopes, the number of refugees receiving relief has increased and not diminished. A 'typical refugee mentality, and its passive expectation of continued benefits', has taken root (U.N.R.W.A. *Report to Ninth General Assembly*, 1954).

In many instances, the material conditions of the refugees compare favourably with those of many of their neighbours, or with their own former existence. 'It is probably true to say that the refugees are physically better off than the poorest levels of the population of the host countries, and in some cases better off . . . than they were in Palestine,' the above-cited report continues. It is also true that nutrition is maintained 'at satisfactory levels', and that social and medical services are of a high standard. 'Many refugee camps are increasingly taking on the appearance of villages and towns, with school buildings, small workshops and communal facilities such as bathhouses and recreational centres, as well as small shops. . . .'

These developments may in some instances have contributed to the aforementioned 'refugee mentality'. Yet the fact remains that these hapless people are uprooted, that their present artificial distribution, resulting from the Arab refusal to permit them free movement, 'is such that great numbers exist where economic opportunity is the least' (U.N.R.W.A. *Report to the Seventh General Assembly*, 1952); that, except in Jordan, they have not been offered citizenship, that they are on sufferance among their own kin, that they 'are people apart, lacking, for the most part, status, homes, land, proper clothing and means of livelihood' (*ibid.*).

U.N.R.W.A. itself has evaluated the relief it has administered as worse than waste in terms of the solution of the problem:

'The existence of vast numbers of able-bodied individuals who for . . . years have looked to the United Nations for the provision of all their basic needs . . . is a social and economic plight of incalculable dimensions. The presence of refugees in host countries is more than the measurable economic waste of manpower and of economic potential. The intangible waste in terms of lost pride, emotional conflict, despair, and hopelessness cannot be measured' (*ibid.*).

The task of assessing the possibilities of a solution has not been rendered easier by the apparent uncertainty about the true number of refugees. Estimates have ranged from an original 550,000 to 850,000. Many Arab propagandists have decided to simplify matters by making the figure a round 1,000,000. Ration-card holders, it is true, exceed 900,000. There is, however, a vast difference between a genuine refugee and the recipient, real or fictitious, of relief. This difficulty of determining the true number has plagued U.N. organs ever since the first refugees crossed the borders.

Wild exaggerations have been repeated so often that by sheer inertia they are to be found not only in Arab publications, but in statements of neutral statesmen, and are occasionally repeated even by Israeli representatives at the United Nations and elsewhere. The great discrepancies between the various estimates are easily explained by the registration of large sections of the surrounding resident population as refugees in order to share in the benefits of international relief. As early as May, 1949, the International Red Cross stated that 'it was becoming increasingly difficult to differentiate, as far as destitution is concerned, between the refugees and the residents'. It therefore asked for the inclusion of these 'resident refugees' among those eligible for refugee relief, ignoring the dangerous contradiction in terms.

U.N.R.W.A. itself (*Interim Report to the Fifth General Assembly*) called the 200,000 difference between two particular estimates 'the result of different approaches'. The lower one 'was obtained from mathematical calculations', while the other was 'compiled by voluntary agencies dealing with hundreds of thousands of hungry people claiming need'. Hungry people everywhere deserve care, but it would seem somewhat irresponsible to let them increase the political magnitude of a completely different problem.

In 1951, U.N.R.W.A. said: 'In Western Jordan the whole population is Palestinian and the refugee is therefore not distinguished from his neighbour by speech, appearance, or necessarily by poverty, rendering still harder the task of the investigator, himself a Palestinian, which is already complicated by . . . all the pressure that can be brought to bear.' In its 1952 report, U.N.R.W.A. said: 'To increase or to prevent decreases in their ration issue, they eagerly report births, sometimes by passing a new-born baby from family to family, and reluctantly report deaths, resorting often to surreptitious burial to avoid giving up a ration card.'

The nearest correct approximation of the number of refugees is today probably in the vicinity of 700,000. The U.N. Economic Survey Mission, which studied the problem thoroughly in 1949, put the figure of Arab refugees in need of relief at 635,000. The first director of U.N.R.W.A. referred to 'the 600,000 refugees' in November, 1950. The U.N. Conciliation Commission accepted the figure of 711,000, and an analysis of the population records of the Palestine Mandatory government shows the total Arab population of what is now Israel at less than 800,000, of whom about 180,000 are now in Israel, leaving little more than 610,000 refugees. To this number, the natural increase since 1948 should be added.

The question of the size of the refugee population has been dealt with at some length not in order to belittle the gravity of the problem. However, it is not irrelevant to realize that this matter has been allowed to degenerate to a point where the international community is made to submit to an expensive, if subtle, kind of extortion, and significant interests have grown up around the benefits from the continued distribution of vast quantities of relief goods provided for about 200,000 non-existing refugees.

II. THE ORIGINS

What were the immediate circumstances that gave rise to the tragic Arab mass flight? Attempts have been made in the United Nations and through all media of mass information to rewrite the history of this tragedy so as to put the blame everywhere but where it rightly belongs. Arab leaders have persistently tried to saddle the U.N. with the original responsibility through its decision to create Israel. The United States is constantly attacked for supporting that decision (ignoring the part played by the Soviet Union and thirty-odd other nations). Israel has been accused of evicting and expelling the refugees and of perpetrating atrocities that caused a stampede.

Only the Arab states are made to appear immaculate and virtuous, bearing no shred of guilt or responsibility. Though it would be best to concentrate on a solution instead of debating the past, the question of original responsibility is important and must be answered truthfully and comprehensively before a wise and morally tenable solution can be found. The circumstances attending the phenomenon of the Arab exodus will presently be closely examined, but first it is essential not to lose sight of the basic fact that the Arab refugee problem arose from the war that the Arab governments launched against Israel—and would not have arisen without it. The problem is a result, not of the resolution of the United Nations General Assembly on November 29, 1947, to partition Palestine, but of the Arab attempt to overthrow that resolution by force—the war launched first to prevent the emergence of Israel and then to destroy it.

As early as September, 1948, Mr. Emile Ghoury, Secretary of the Arab Higher Committee and at one time commander of Arab forces in the Jerusalem area, declared in the Beirut *Telegraph*: 'I do not want to impugn anyone but only to help the refugees. The fact that they are there is the direct consequence of the action of the Arab states in opposing partition and the Jewish state. The Arab states agreed upon this policy unanimously, and they must share in the solution of the problem.'

On May 15, the day Israel was established, the Secretary-General of the Arab League promised at a Press conference in Cairo: 'This will be a war of extermination and a momentous massacre which will be spoken of like the Mongolian massacres and the Crusades' (B.B.C. broadcast of that date). Wherever he could, he kept his word. Arab brutality during the fighting was unprecedented. No mercy was shown nor was quarter given. *One hundred and eighty thousand Arabs live in Israel today, but in all the areas which came under Arab occupation not a single Jew survives.*

The record testifies eloquently and irrefutably to the efforts made by the Jewish leadership, first to prevent the outbreak of hostilities, then to nip them before they spread and grew to war proportions, and later still, to terminate them by a formal agreement of the parties; and also to prevent the Arab exodus. On October 2, 1947, two months before the partition resolution, the Assembly of Palestine Jewry (forerunner of the Knesset), declared: 'The Jewish people extends the hand of sincere friendship and brotherhood to the Arab peoples and calls them to co-operation as free and equal allies for the sake of peace and progress, for the benefit of their respective countries.'

On November 30, the day after the U.N. General Assembly had adopted the partition resolution, in the face of Arab threats to oppose it by force, David Ben Gurion pleaded: 'If we are attacked, we shall take up the challenge, but we sincerely hope there will be no need for that. The Middle East needs peace more than anything else, and we need peace more than anything else. Let there, then, be an end to all threats of violence.'

Four days later, after the Jewish Commercial Centre in Jerusalem had been sacked, and while reports were coming from all over the country of organized Arab attacks, the Jewish Defence Organization distributed leaflets in the Arab villages pleading 'to keep the peace and remain calm.'

On May 14, 1948, with five Arab armies converging on the newly born Israel, its Proclamation of Independence appealed: 'In the midst of wanton aggression, we call upon the Arab inhabitants of the State of Israel to return to the ways of peace and play their part in the development of the state with full and equal citizenship and with due representation in all its bodies and institutions.'

And on August 6, 1948, in the midst of war, when the Arab flight was already assuming mass proportions, Moshe Sharett, Israel's Foreign Minister, appealed to the United Nations Mediator asking him to 'be kind enough to transmit to the governments of the Arab states now at war with Israel our offer that . . . representatives . . . should meet . . . for the purpose of peace negotiations.'

As the fighting grew more severe, the Arab exodus increased. The first single large-scale flight occurred in Haifa, in late April, 1948. After Iraqi troops in the Arab sector of the city had launched abortive attacks against the Jewish quarter, the Jews counter-attacked and captured the port city. Many neutral observers have described what happened. The London *Economist*, not known for Zionist sympathies, said in its account: 'The Jewish Authorities, who were now in complete control . . . urged all Arabs to remain and guaranteed them protection and security. . . . However, of the 62,000 Arabs who lived in Haifa, not more than 5,000 or 6,000 remained. Various factors influenced their decision to seek safety in flight. There is but little doubt that the most potent of these were the announcements made over the air by the Arab Higher Executive, urging all Arabs in Haifa to quit. The reason given was that upon the final withdrawal of the British (on May 15), the combined armies of the Arab states would invade Palestine and drive the Jews into the sea, and it was clearly intimated that those Arabs who remained in Haifa and accepted Jewish protection would be regarded as renegades' (October 2, 1948).

On April 26, 1948, the British police in Haifa reported to headquarters: 'Every effort is being made by the Jews to persuade the Arab population to stay and carry on with their normal lives . . . and to be assured that their lives and interests will be safe.' Two days later a further report confirmed that these efforts were still being made.

The British High Commissioner in Palestine reported to the Colonial Secretary in London that 'the Jewish attack in Haifa was a direct consequence of continuous attacks by the Arabs over the previous four days. There was no massacre'.

In a report to the Arab governments on the second anniversary of the Haifa flight, the Arab National Committee of Haifa, which had held authority during the crucial period, admitted that 'the removal . . . was voluntary and carried out at our request. The Jewish representatives expressed their deep regret and the Jewish Mayor . . . adjourned the meeting . . . with a passionate appeal to the Arabs to reconsider their decision. . . . It seems that the Jews intended to . . . prove that the Haifa Arabs could live safely and securely. . . .'

The representative of the Arab Higher Committee told the U.N. Security Council on April 23 that 'the Arabs would not submit to a truce . . . but rather preferred to leave their homes in the town'.

The present writer, who happened to be in Haifa at the time, vividly recalls the fantastic and almost unbelievable sight of tens of thousands of Arabs crowding the harbour area under orders of their leaders, waiting for launches and barges to ferry them across the bay to Acre, where the fighting had not yet reached, or a little farther north into Lebanon. This was done leisurely, in two days, while Jews were passing through the multitude trying to dissuade personal friends from leaving.

After the Haifa exodus, there was no holding the Arab population, and similar scenes soon occurred in Jaffa, Safed, and other towns. 'The Arab civilian population panicked and fled ignominiously,' wrote General Glubb, the British Commander of Jordan's Arab Legion, in the London *Daily Mail* of August 12, 1948.

Not the entire Arab population, however, acted on the orders of their leaders, and others were overtaken by the advancing Israeli army, especially during the later stages of the fighting in Galilee. Disillusioned, sceptical of their leaders' promises of a speedy victory, they stuck to their homes. It was thus due to a change of heart in some of the Arabs themselves that they were spared the sorrows of their kin who fled. Nothing refutes the accusation of mass expulsion more clearly than the continued presence of those who at the time simply decided to stay behind.

Later, when masses of Jewish refugees from Arab and other lands were filling the country, and fierce hatreds dashed hopes of an early peace, Israel no longer regretted the Arabs' exodus and found their return impracticable. But this development is irrelevant to the present inquiry and cannot alter the historical truth of the events of 1948.

What, then, made the Arabs leave as they did? Recently Nimr Al-Hawari, a well-known and gifted Arab lawyer, published a book called *The Secret Behind the Disaster*. Hawari had been the commander of the para-military Arab youth organization in Palestine. He became a refugee himself during the war. Disillusioned with the Arab leadership, he returned to Nazareth, where he is now a courageous Arab spokesman. After testifying at length to Jewish attempts to dissuade the Arabs from fleeing, he sums up: 'The Arabs' eyes were blinded and their brains clogged. They were confused by promises and deluded by their leaders.' And later: 'The Palestinian Arabs were ignorant and easily led astray. They were shortsighted and unthinking, and subjected to a gangster-leadership . . . which herded them like docile sheep. . . . Many left temporarily, they thought, to await the passing of the storm. . . . The leaders rattled their sabres, delivered fiery speeches, and wrote stirring articles. Iraq's Prime Minister had thundered: "We shall smash the country with our guns, and destroy and obliterate every place the Jews will seek shelter in. The Arabs should conduct their wives and children to safer areas till the fighting has died down." '

Msgr. George Hakim, the Arab Greek-Orthodox Archbishop of Galilee, wrote on August 16, 1948: 'The refugees had been confident that . . . they would return within a few days—within a week or two. Their leaders had promised them that the Arab armies would crush the "Zionist gang" very quickly.'

And a Lebanese paper, published in the United States, wrote in 1951: 'Brotherly advice was given to the Arabs of Palestine urging them to leave their lands, homes, and property, and go to stay temporarily in neighbouring, brotherly states, lest the guns of the invading Arab armies mow them down' (*Al Huda*, June 6).

The Arab flight under orders, as part of a deliberate policy to clear areas for the invading Arab armies and to prevent stagnation of the war by the conclusion of local truces, accounted for very large numbers of refugees. But other, equally grave factors were involved. Nearly thirty thousand persons had left before trouble started in earnest. These were the well-to-do, the merchants, landlords, professionals, men in high public office, those who could afford to ride out the storm in the comfortable safety of hotel lobbies in Cairo or Beirut or in the spacious distant homes of relatives. Their early departure undermined the structure of Arab society and economy, demoralized great numbers, and accelerated the panicky stampede of unguided masses once it became evident that the promised Arab victories would fail to materialize.

The name 'Deir Yassin' is often conjured up to show that Arabs fled out of fear of being massacred. The destruction of the village of Deir Yassin by a disowned Jewish terrorist group, the only case of Jewish atrocity during the war, no doubt contributed to the confusion. But the fear of 'Jewish atrocities' was really effective in another way. We have quoted the promise of the Arab League's Secretary-General to produce a 'Mongolian massacre'. That promise was not an idle threat. The Arab onslaught on the Jews of Palestine was conducted with a savagery not easily comprehensible to the civilized mind. Killing was indiscriminate, and neither civilians nor prisoners were spared. Bodies were stripped and mutilated, and these scenes, recorded in photographs, proudly peddled in the streets. Captured Jewish localities were razed. Little wonder, then, that many Arabs who had participated—or belonged to groups which had participated—in such exploits feared vengeance. Guilt-inspired fear often sufficed to make a whole vicinity pack up and run. A striking example is given by Kenneth W. Bilby in his book *New Star in the Near East*. During the fighting in Manshieh, a district connecting Jaffa with Tel Aviv, the Mayor of Jaffa (Dr. Yussef Haikal, later Jordanian Ambassador in Washington, and now in London) told Mr. Bilby, then the New York *Herald Tribune* correspondent, that hundreds of trapped Arabs had been slaughtered by the Jews. Mr. Bilby 'never found the slightest shred of evidence to support this contention, and I examined Manshieh carefully just after the battle. But the fact was that Haikal's story had spread like sage fire among the Arabs of Jaffa and they needed no urging to get out.' Both their leaders' threats and atrocity propaganda thus boomeranged with far-reaching consequences.

These, then, were the chief circumstances that caused masses of Arabs to stream across the borders. In their reckless folly, their leaders had played havoc with countless human lives. But, as the

London *Economist* said even on August 7, 1948, when the tragedy had not yet run its full course: 'Now they dare not tell their people what happened.'

III. THE WORLD AND THE ARAB REFUGEES

The United Nations. The world quickly understood both the human and the political aspects of the refugee problem. It addressed itself first to the relief of human suffering. The stream of refugees had begun during the fighting that preceded the termination of the British Mandate on May 15, 1948, the simultaneous proclamation of the State of Israel, and the launching of the full-scale attack by the Arab states on the same date. As the flood increased, the United Nations Mediator on Palestine appealed to all nations for assistance on humanitarian grounds. By August, the United Nations International Children's Emergency Fund (U.N.I.C.E.F.) made a substantial contribution in money, and its personnel were in the field within a few weeks. The Mediator then established a disaster relief project. Numerous voluntary agencies responded splendidly with cash and supplies, and helped in their distribution. In November, 1948, the General Assembly set up the U.N. Relief for Palestine Refugees (U.N.R.P.R.) to co-ordinate all relief activities. Some $40 million was contributed, in money and in kind, during U.N.R.P.R.'s operation.

The General Assembly also hopefully attempted to grapple with the political aspect. On December 11, 1948, it established the Palestine Conciliation Commission to 'assist the governments and authorities concerned to achieve a final settlement of all questions outstanding between them'; to 'seek arrangements . . . to facilitate the economic development of the area'; and to 'facilitate the repatriation, resettlement, and economic and social rehabilitation of the refugees and payment of compensation' (Resolution 194). The same resolution also contained the much-debated Paragraph 11, providing that 'refugees wishing to return to their homes and *live at peace with their neighbours* should be permitted to do so at the earliest *practicable date*, and that compensation should be paid for property of those choosing not to return'.

As will be shown, the sponsors of this paragraph were soon to regret its phrasing, which is at the root of much of the failure to solve the refugee problem. Originally the passage was quite clear in its intent: the refugees should be allowed to return if they wanted to, if the envisaged conditions of 'living at peace' and 'practicability' existed. But by trying to say too many things in one mouthful, it left room for wilful misinterpretations and provided the ground on which later rose the 'repatriation issue'. The phrase was not a compromise on substance. It was the result of a desire to satisfy in principle the demand for return, and yet to provide such safeguards as reality now dictated. As such, it was both a symptom and a cause of the fumbling and hesitancy, the lack of courage and firmness, which have characterized the handling of the refugee problem to this very day. Since then, responsible opinion within the U.N. and outside it has recognized the original error, and now simply pleads for resettlement of the refugees in Arab countries. But Arab intransigence exacts its annual tribute when the General Assembly considers the problem.

Shortly after its creation, the Conciliation Commission concluded that 'a settlement [of the refugee problem] on a purely political basis was not possible at present'. The deadlock could be broken 'only through an economic approach . . . mainly along the lines of the refugees' integration in their present countries of residence'. The need to find a realistic solution to the refugee problem led the Conciliation Commission to appoint, in August, 1949, an Economic Survey Mission for the Middle East to make recommendations 'for an integrated programme . . . in order to reintegrate the refugees into the economic life of the area on a self-sustaining basis within a minimum period of time'.

Under the chairmanship of Gordon R. Clapp, head of the Tennessee Valley Authority, and composed of representatives of Great Britain, France, and Turkey, the Mission worked intensively in the field for two months. It shunned 'grandiose plans' because a less ambitious programme would bring results earlier and without too heavy expenditure. But the Mission was frustrated by Arab obstruction. Having started courageously, Mr. Clapp was soon persuaded to substitute in his statement the euphemism 'refugee employment projects' for the blunt 'resettlement'. However, the Mission did not lose sight of its objective, and in its report recommended a plan for a combined relief and works programme consisting mostly of small-scale projects, under which direct relief would be gradually replaced by useful projects furnishing employment. Its purpose was 'to abate the emergency by constructive action and to reduce the refugee problem to limits within which the Near Eastern governments can reasonably be expected to assume . . . the responsibility for the maintenance of such refugees as may remain within their territories'. A new agency was to administer the programme; direct relief would be terminated at the end of 1950, while the works programme would be continued until June 30, 1951. The programme was to cost $55 million.

The Clapp report had severe shortcomings. It underestimated the cost of this work, and by limiting itself to small-scale local projects such as afforestation, terracing, road-building, and utilization of water resources, it did not seek to break up the refugee concentrations. But it had the great merit of putting the Arab governments on notice to prepare 'for the time when U.N. funds for relief and works projects shall no longer be available'. Had this been firmly stressed, we might not today be as far from a solution as we are.

The General Assembly endorsed the Clapp report and on December 8, 1949, set up the United Nations Relief and Works Agency (U.N.R.W.A.) to carry out the recommended programme 'with a view to the termination of international assistance for relief'.

In its first report the new agency had to admit failure, due largely to difficulties in interesting refugees and governments in a work programme and to lack of opportunities for considerable programmes in some of the centres of refugee distribution. A maximum of only twelve thousand refugees was employed at any one time. 'Local governments contributed no funds; the full burden of wages fell on the Agency; the cost was five times that of simple relief. The approved projects were roads and public structures, and when they were finished, the refugees returned to tents and ration lines. . . .' On December 2, 1950, the General Assembly had to admit 'that direct relief cannot be terminated'. U.N.R.W.A.'s recommendations were to continue relief for another year and to add $30 million for a Reintegration Fund 'as a first step [without commitment about the future] in a major undertaking which may ultimately entail the expenditure of several hundred million dollars over a period of years'.

The General Assembly accordingly voted the funds 'for the *permanent establishment* of the refugees and their removal from relief', though of course 'without prejudice' to the provisions of the by now famous Paragraph 11 of the December 1948 resolution.

U.N.R.W.A.'s next report to the Sixth Session of the U.N. at the end of 1951 sounded encouraging. 'There is now considerable agreement among governments', it stated, 'that the refugees cannot continue indefinitely in their present condition.' This, and the conviction that there must be a firm goal of terminating relief operation, encouraged U.N.R.W.A. to recommend the establishment of a $250 million programme for three years, starting retroactively from July 1, 1951, until June 30, 1954. Of this sum, $50 million was to be for relief, and $200 million for reintegration. Relief expenditure was to decrease annually, investment expenditures to increase. Relief administration was to be transferred to the Arab governments not later than July 1, 1952.

The basic political premise was that the refugees be 're-established', principally in Near East countries. The general objectives: to help refugees obtain adequate housing and employment; to move them from camps and temporary shelter to suburban housing projects and rural villages; to move them from ration-lines to self-supporting employment, and to make them economic assets. One hundred and fifty thousand families, that is, the entire refugee population, was thus to be re-established within the prescribed time. They were to move within the Arab countries to areas of greatest opportunity. But above all this hovered the usual 'without prejudice' to the resolution of 1948.

On January 26, 1952, the General Assembly adopted the programme and urged the governments concerned to assist in its execution.

This imaginative programme, endorsed in the Assembly even by the Arab states, was energetically pursued by U.N.R.W.A. Major projects were negotiated (but not implemented) with Syria and Egypt. But by the end of 1952 the Agency had to report that 'the pace has been slow. *Deep misunderstandings and misinterpretations* of the new programme have to be faced.' The General Assembly refused to face this fact and thus did an incalculable disservice to the programme and the objective that had prompted the contributors to make such efforts. As a result, U.N.R.W.A. had to present to the Eighth Session (end of 1953) a gloomy picture. The entire relief fund intended for three years had been consumed in two, while the rehabilitation fund remained largely untouched. The general tone of the report was one of both lassitude and impatience, though 'the outlook is not, however, entirely dark'. It recorded 'the growing reluctance of contributors to continue'. Reporting numerous instances of illegal interference with the Agency and its privileges and immunities, and its use by the Arab governments as a convenient whipping-boy, U.N.R.W.A. suggested that 'it would be more appropriate for the governments to relieve themselves of . . . the presence of U.N.R.W.A. and to assume responsibility themselves'.

Finally, U.N.R.W.A.'s Mandate and its fund were extended for another year, until June 30, 1955, and all concerned were urged 'to seek acceptable projects to enable the fund to be utilized for the purpose for which it was intended'.

When the Agency and its advisory commission reported to the Ninth Session (November, 1954) 'with regret . . . that little progress has been achieved', it was clear that the programme as a whole had failed dismally. Unable to admit failure, and reluctant to assert itself, the General Assembly, dejectedly and as a matter of routine, extended U.N.R.W.A.'s operations once more, this time until July 1, 1960. This, it was said, would make possible 'longer-term planning' and give U.N.R.W.A. 'the opportunity to organize its work more efficiently and economically'. From a dynamic, bold, spirited enterprise, the Agency was being transformed into a frustrated bureaucracy.

Under these circumstances, the 1955 report was not unexpected: 'lack of co-operation', 'obstacles', and general gloominess and dejection. There was every reason for this mood. After six years of operation, ration-lines had grown longer instead of shorter. Projects to which great hopes had been attached, such as the Sinai irrigation project and the Syrian agricultural project, had been left unimplemented, for obvious political reasons.

The action taken by the Tenth Session of the Assembly (December, 1955) on U.N.R.W.A.'s latest report has been more than usually diffident. The Agency was directed 'to pursue its efforts', but specific relief funds have not even been voted. On January 28, 1956, U.N.R.W.A.'s director was reported to have told the Press in Damascus that his Agency might cease operations for lack of funds, since the regular contributors had so far supplied only a fraction of what was needed. Such an eventuality is not likely at present, but the report is indicative of the international community's exasperated dissatisfaction with the lack of progress made towards the envisaged solution.

The Arab States. 'It is perfectly clear that the Arab nations do not want to solve the refugee problem. They want to keep it as an open sore, as an affront against the United Nations, and as a weapon against Israel. Arab leaders don't give a damn whether the refugees live or die,' said Mr. Galloway, former U.N.R.W.A. representative in Jordan, to an American study-group meeting in Amman in 1952.

'We shall be most insistent in perpetuating the Palestine problem as a life question. . . . The Palestine war continues by dint of the refugees only. Their existence leaves the problem open.' This from Abdullah Nawas, member of Jordan's Parliament, on June 6, 1952.

In *Falastin* of August 26, 1955: 'Those human beings, whom political ambitions and intrigues turned into cave-dwellers overnight —what have the Arab rulers done for them these past eight years? Is their ray of hope to be found in the politicians' haggling at our expense? Or is it in the execution of the Johnston Plan and of the Sinai project?'

'We refugees have left our homes merely to enter a world of intrigue on the part of those who are our own flesh and blood. . . .' —*Difa* of September 10, 1953.

The above representative quotations—the first by an American experienced in refugee relief work, the second by an Arab politician, and the last two by refugee journalists—tell the same tale of Arab obstruction. They go to the root of the matter. To Arab leaders, the refugee problem is exclusively a political issue. Its human aspect counts only to the extent that, by arousing sympathy for the refugee in the world, it serves as a weapon in the political and propaganda warfare against Israel, and in the game of extortion against the Powers most interested in Middle East security.

The existence of the refugee problem, said another member of the Jordan Parliament, 'is an important harassing factor *vis-à-vis* the Jews and the West. As long as it remains unsolved, Israel's political and economic existence are acutely endangered' (*Falastin*, June 3, 1952).

The refugee camps are a valuable propaganda asset, both locally and internationally. The disorganized, uprooted, embittered masses that inhabit them, kept in endless suspense, are easily aroused, and only a few among them both know who is to blame for their misery and dare say so aloud. Their bitterness can thus be quickly pushed in the desired direction.

The official Arab thesis states that the only acceptable solution to the refugee problem lies in 'repatriation'. This claim is based on the oft-cited Paragraph 11, whose intent and context we have already discussed. But authoritative Arab leaders and publications have left no doubt about the design behind the demand for repatriation. Let us consider only two of countless statements:

'In demanding the restoration of the refugees to Palestine, the Arabs intend that they return as masters . . . more explicitly: they intend to annihilate the State of Israel' (Mohammed Salah ed Din, then Egyptian Foreign Minister, in *Al-Misri*, October 11, 1949).

In 1952 another important Cairo daily wrote: 'The Arab League must constantly demand the return of the refugees and strengthen in their minds the spirit of revenge' (*Akher Sa'ah*, January 16, 1952).

As recently as January 28, 1956, the Syrian Minister of the Interior met with representatives of refugees of military age to discuss 'their training in preparation for the day of revenge'.

There has never been any attempt to conceal the intention that refugees returning *en masse* should provide a fifth column to help destroy Israel from within. Yet, by deftly exploiting political opportunities and by playing on human compassion, the Arabs have succeeded in exacting an annual tribute from the United Nations in the form of provisions, in all later resolutions calling for the reintegration and rehabilitation of the refugees in Arab countries, to the effect that such reintegration was 'without prejudice' to repatriation. These two seemingly innocuous words have been the undoing of all efforts to solve or at least to reduce the refugee problem, because Arab governments have preferred to undertake themselves the task of interpreting what would constitute 'prejudice'. In order to frustrate any development that might reduce the prospect of repatriation, they have sabotaged all major rehabilitation schemes. They have suppressed any tendency among the refugees themselves to become self-supporting in large numbers. They have deprived the refugees of political rights lest they should sink roots somewhere. They have prevented them from moving across Arab borders. They have in most cases refused to allow them to seek employment in the Arab labour market.

U.N.R.W.A.'s annual lament and its pleas for Arab co-operation have been mentioned earlier. Only in one instance did co-operation on a significant scale seem to be forthcoming. Early in 1951 the Egyptian government, after much deliberation, signified its willingness to co-operate in the reintegration of fifty thousand refugees in Sinai if conditions in that area should prove suitable. The Egyptian Press then reported that the decision sprang from the fear that international contributions for relief would cease if absolute refusal to co-operate continued. This should have been a guide to U.N.R.W.A.'s future policy in its negotiations; but the hint was not taken. Much U.N. money was spent on surveys of permanent value to Egypt, but in U.N.R.W.A.'s latest report we learn that the agreement has lapsed.

Although the Arab economies gain important and lasting benefits through relief and rehabilitation operations (road construction, afforestation, vast local purchases of supplies, transportation, etc.), their own financial contributions to the international fund by which U.N.R.W.A. lives are practically nil. 'The host governments made no cash pledges for 1954–55 and paid nothing against pledges made in previous years,' the U.N. was informed. They did provide some services and storage and warehouse facilities, valued by U.N.R.W.A. at $373,000. This sum was amply recouped by the imposition on U.N.R.W.A. of taxes and charges, despite the privileges and immunities the Agency is entitled to as an arm of the United Nations. U.N.R.W.A.'s annual reports invariably bristle with complaints of violations of immunity, 'centrally inspired' attacks, 'strong pressure from commercial interests', and other kinds of costly interference, so that at one juncture U.N.R.W.A. warned it 'will have to retire from the field'.

The refugees themselves have been the subjects of economic envy on the part of their fellow-Arabs. Thus an exhaustive article in an Egyptian military journal (*Al-Tahrir*), written by an army officer, compares the refugees' condition with that of the Egyptian peasant: 'I spent three days [in the Gaza camps] where I came to recognize as such all the lies we read about refugees, disease, cold, hunger, misery and injustice. . . . Hunger, misery, and distress are not to be found. . . . I saw people eating their fill, drinking milk and living in comfort. The men lay on their backs in the sunshine, or played dice. . . . Do our weak children drink milk? Have you ever heard of an Egyptian *fellah* wearing shoes?'

What about the refugees themselves? Their real mood is difficult to ascertain. Their leaders (many of whom do not themselves live in the camps), politically ambitious, speak for them. Many people who have talked freely to individual refugees have failed 'to find the first refugee who would say that he would go back to Israel and live under the Israeli government'. In its 1953 report, U.N.R.W.A. records that though the official attitude of the refugees has not been appreciably modified, there are signs that individual refugees, when invited to take advantage of minor projects, are ready and willing to abandon the enervating life of the camps, and there are refugees who have approached the Agency for a chance to become self-supporting.

In its latest report, U.N.R.W.A. still did not know the refugees' minds. Though recording signs of continued opposition to resettlement, it states: 'None of the large-scale projects has progressed to a point where refugees have in fact had an opportunity to decide whether or not to participate. . . . It is indeed gradually coming to be accepted by an increasing number of refugees that . . . without prejudice to their political rights, it is in their own interests to find . . . a temporary means to overcome *their enforced idleness*.'

It may be assumed, however, that were the refugee asked to state his view publicly, he would submit to pressure and echo the position taken by the politicians.

Israel. Israel's position on the refugee problem has been firm though not unbending. In 1948, when hopes for a speedy peace settlement were high, Jews sought to prevent the mass flight of the Arab population. These hopes were soon dashed. In the new reality of unrelenting Arab hostility and threats of a renewal of their war, Israel refused to aggravate further the precariousness of her security by admitting those who were hostile to her. In July, 1949, under heavy pressure to make tangible concessions in the refugee matter as an essential preliminary to any prospect for a general settlement, Israel first offered to incorporate the Gaza Strip with its 70,000 permanent Arab residents and 200,000 refugees. When this offer was rejected, Israel made the further concession of offering to place the refugee problem as the first item on the agenda of peace negotiations. Finally, in August, it offered to accept 100,000 returning refugees, as part of a general solution of the problem. Though this, too, was rejected by the Arab states, Israel kept it open for some time. In July, 1950, Israel's Foreign Minister withdrew the offer. Since then Israel has refused to consider the repatriation of the refugees as part of a solution and has pointed to the obvious impossibility of risking the admission of a large and avowed fifth column. The arming of Arab states and their continued genocidal intentions towards Israel have not been conducive to allaying Israel's fears on this score.

Grave economic and social arguments also have been brought forward to show the impracticability of repatriation. In seven years the places of Arabs have been filled by at least an equal number of Jewish refugees, including entire communities from Arab countries totalling 350,000. The pattern of life in Israel has been fundamentally transformed, and returning Arabs would be confronted with a severe problem of readjustment. Dangerous friction between returning Arabs and Jews recently driven from Arab countries would be inevitable. Israel, therefore, demands 'to be accepted as we are, with our territory [and] population' (Moshe Sharett, Israel Foreign Minister, before National Press Club, Washington, D.C., on April 10, 1953).

Israel has consistently insisted on the refugees' resettlement in Arab countries as the solution to the problem. She has pointed to the vast possibilities in sparsely populated countries like Syria and Iraq. International authorities agree that from the economic point of view the entire problem could be solved in these two countries alone, with room to spare and immediate benefit to their economies. Israel has supported the Johnston Plan for the utilization of the Jordan and Yarmuk Rivers because it would help settle over 150,000 refugees. She has pointed to the psychological, cultural, religious, and social factors which would make refugee absorption in Arab countries appear logical. She has recalled the historical fact that all refugee problems created throughout the world in this century have been solved through the exchange of populations or other forms of resettlement; none has been solved by trying to turn back the clock.

Israel's objection to repatriation applies also to what has in recent years been termed 'token' repatriation, a device to save Arab face without disrupting Israel's security or economy. This seemingly plausible device, Israel holds, would automatically stifle all progress towards resettlement, since it would either make every refugee genuinely believe that he would be among those selected, or enable political leaders artificially to stir up such belief or expectancy, thereby increasing tension.

Despite this position, and the well-substantiated contention that the problem is not of her making, Israel has not been insensitive to the human tragedy involved and has taken a series of measures to alleviate it. By 1952, Israel had absorbed and restored to self-support the nineteen thousand Palestine Arabs who were refugees within its own borders (displaced from other areas of Palestine during the fighting). This figure compares more than favourably with the total achievement of the combined Arab states to date.

On November 4, 1951, Israel's Foreign Minister announced in the Knesset that the government 'is prepared without delay, to discuss . . . the amount of compensation due' (to Arab refugees for abandoned lands). This has been reiterated since then, even within the context of political tension.

As a further measure, Israel agreed to release all the liquid assets (the so-called 'blocked accounts') left by Arab refugees in Israel banks, though it is most unusual for governments to arrange for the flow of foreign currency into countries which are doing everything possible to strangle their economy by boycott. This was done in two stages, early in 1953, and again in the fall of 1954. The total amount involved was between $11 and $12 million, not including the contents of many safe-deposit boxes. Little appreciation seems to have been expected, and still less received.

Israel has also readmitted a substantial number of returning Arabs. Some thousands of relatives of Arabs living in Israel were permitted to come in under a scheme for reuniting separated families, and tens of thousands who had infiltrated into the country have been legalized and given citizenship. These two processes are responsible for the rapid growth of Israel's Arab population from one hundred thousand in 1948 to nearly twice this number at present.

As far as can be gleaned from Israel's statements and publications, the only further readmissions Israel might be prepared to consent to would be through some extension of the family reunion scheme. Such individual cases clearly do not touch the core of the refugee problem. Israel's answer to the problem continues to be total resettlement in the Arab lands and payment of compensation.

United States. The United States has borne the major share of the financial burden imposed by the continued existence of the refugee problem, and has also shown more initiative and active interest in the search for a solution—both within and outside the framework of the United Nations—than any other Power. Its policies on the question therefore require separate consideration.

Originally, the U.S. government supported the right of repatriation as qualified by the safeguards of the December, 1948, resolution. In the months that followed, it made full use of its influence in the Palestine Conciliation Commission to press for maximum concession by Israel in this respect. It was also reported to have urged the Israel government directly to admit up to two hundred thousand refugees over a period of time, the remainder to be resettled in Arab lands. But having recognised 'the stalemate in the peace negotiations and the need to find a realistic solution' (Department of State Publication 375), it substantially reversed its early position, and fully endorsed the 'economic approach . . . mainly along the lines of the refugees' integration in their present countries of residence' (Mr. Paul Porter, U.S. member of the Conciliation Commission). The head of the Special Survey Mission set up to advise on the implementation of this new approach was an American, T.V.A.'s Chairman Gordon R. Clapp.

From then on, the U.S. has favoured and worked for resettlement as the solution, although in major statements of policy mention of the idea of some measure of limited or 'token' repatriation is rarely absent. The impression that has been gained over the years is that a verbal commitment to the idea has been thought necessary for psychological reasons, though many feel that greater frankness would ultimately prove more beneficial to all concerned.

In December, 1949, the U.S. was instrumental in the establishment of the U.N.R.W.A. In November, 1950, it was one of the sponsors of the $20 million Reintegration Fund, proposed by this agency. In January, 1952, it took one long stride further by largely underwriting the $200 million Rehabilitation Programme. It has consistently taken the view that this programme was important, not only to the refugees but also to the Arab states, 'to which it means a substantial increase in financial and human assets', and that they 'must come to consider the refugees as an important asset, not as an unwanted liability. The leaders of the Arab countries should stop clinging to a *status quo* which benefits no one.'

On June 1, 1953, after his return from a tour of the Middle East, Secretary of State John Foster Dulles said in his televised 'Report to the Nation' that most of the refugees 'could more readily be integrated into the lives of the neighbouring Arab states' (though some could be settled in Israel).

On July 24, 1953, a report of the Sub-Committee on the Near East of the U.S. Senate Foreign Relations Committee, without passing judgment on the feasibility of any repatriation, said that 'such a solution cannot handle more than a small proportion of the total number'. It went on to say that 'the Arab states should develop definite proposals for ... rehabilitation outside Israel. ... They cannot escape responsibility to their fellow Arabs', and concluded with a warning: 'American aid cannot continue indefinitely . . . unless considerably more progress is shown in the near future. . . . Congress would not be justified in continuing aid for this programme through the United Nations. . . .'

Ever since 1953, the U.S. government has been making great efforts to gain Arab support for its Johnston Plan, so far without decisive success. The position taken by most Arab states has been that they would rather forgo the immense benefit inherent in the plan than allow any—even limited—benefit to accrue to Israel too, or risk the merest suspicion of co-operation with Israel on a joint venture. The refugees continue to languish? So what?

On August 26, 1954, Secretary Dulles said in another major speech: 'These uprooted people should, through resettlement and, to such an extent as may be feasible, repatriation, be enabled to resume a life of dignity and self-respect. . . . Compensation is due from Israel. . . . There might be an international loan to enable Israel to pay. . . .' And after outlining large resettlement projects in the Arab states, he continued: 'These projects would do much more than aid in the resettlement of refugees. They would enable the people throughout the area to enjoy a better life.'

The policies of Great Britain, France, Canada, and of many other countries have moved on lines generally similar to—and sometimes expounded with greater clarity than—those of the United States.

In their joint statement of February 1, 1956, at the end of their talks in Washington, President Eisenhower and Sir Anthony Eden reiterated their governments' readiness, *inter alia*, 'to contribute to such a settlement [generally between the Arab states and Israel] by assisting financially in regard to the refugee problem'.

A significant contribution to the literature on the refugee problem is the report issued by the Special Study Mission to the Near East (the so-called Smith-Prouty report) of the House Committee on Foreign Affairs, 1954, made after investigations in the field lasting five weeks. The Mission declined to obscure its meaning by the customary qualifications. After stating hopefully that 'Arab government officials are beginning to realize that holding out against all U.N. proposals is not certain to result in the ultimate return of the refugees', the report proclaims the need for a new approach. It does not mince words: 'The status of the refugees as a special group of people who are the wards of the U.N. should be terminated as soon as possible. The objective should be for refugees to become citizens of the Arab states and, if necessary, they should be made [their] wards pending admission to citizenship. This process should not be delayed. . . . Ten years from now the transition will be much more

difficult.' And later: 'The U.S. should announce that it will contribute no further assistance *to the refugees as such* after a specified
future date. This would put the refugees and the Arab states on
notice that the *status quo* cannot be maintained indefinitely.' This
does not mean that the U.S. would be washing its hands of the
problem. 'We should give help to the host countries in developing
their resources so that a substantially larger population can make a
living.' Refugee owners of immovable property should be compensated. If necessary, Israel should be assisted in doing so.

The Mission's final recommendations are concrete: 'The U.S.
should serve notice that it will not support the return of the Arab
refugees . . .' and 'The U.S. should press for compensation by Israel
to the refugees. . . .'

There is no evidence to indicate that the above report differs in
any substantial manner from the most authoritative thinking in the
U.S. government. The Congressional mission has merely chosen to
translate thought into words without hem-ing or haw-ing.

IV. CONCLUSION

In seven years of activity on behalf of the Arab refugees, the
United Nations—as a body and through its agencies and major
powers—has striven devotedly to alleviate human distress and to
create the conditions for a constructive solution. In this it can take
just pride, and it has no cause for apology. Yet thus far it has failed.
Why? Because it has hesitated and temporized, because against its
recorded better judgment, it has allowed generous, bold plans to
degenerate into palliatives, and has compromised its true intentions
by fostering illusions. By the ceaseless, monotonous reiteration of the
repatriation idea as a kind of useless though inflammable appendix
to its main theme, it has enabled the Arab host countries to adopt an
attitude paralysing to all progressive work. Its much too gingerly
approach to psychological sensitivities has robbed its finest efforts
of the possibility of bringing results.

Today we seem perhaps no nearer to a solution than eight years
and hundreds of millions of dollars ago, and the recent appearance
of new forces on the Middle Eastern horizon makes a solution more
problematical than ever. Yet the present dangers and uncertainties
also provide a unique opportunity and an unprecedented challenge
for those Western nations who have shouldered the burden for so
long, to assert themselves decisively. The preceding pages have
shown, it is hoped, that enlightened and constructive world opinion
considers resettlement in Arab countries and compensation for
abandoned property the obvious solution. 'Resettlement' and

'repatriation' are mutually exclusive terms. The one cannot be effected without 'prejudice' to the other. Why, then, equivocate? The nations of the Middle East should not be left in doubt about the undreamt-of economic opportunities and benefits to be gained from co-operation in effecting this solution, or about the consequences of an intransigence feeding on perpetual appeasement. It would be a disservice to the interests of the free world and to the cause of Middle East peace and stability, and also a cruel disfavour to the refugees themselves, if the present Arab gamble were to continue through miscalculation of the world's mood.

1956.

DEVELOPMENT IN IRAQ

Part I

by HAL LEHRMAN

NOT LONG AGO the tomb of an obscure Moslem holy man, over-looked in the road-planners' charts, turned up across the path of wreckers and steamrollers cutting a modern boulevard through Baghdad. The awesome taboos of sainted ground paralysed further advance; it appeared the thoroughfare might have to make a detour. Then one morning the city awoke to find the sepulchre gone and the area around it transformed into a delightful park to grace the new street. Before so clear and benevolent a miracle, not even the most pious could cry desecration.

Baghdad's Mayor of the moment was the responsible magician. Covered by darkness, after secret preparations, a small army of workmen with machines and all essentials including trees and grassy turf had moved in under his intrepid command and accomplished the feat in a single, incredible, new-style Arabian night.

Such phenomenal energy rarely stirs in sun-cooked Iraq (or anywhere else, for that matter). Yet Iraq itself today is making a prodigious national effort, no less remarkable in the Arab world.

Seventy per cent of the state's revenues from oil have been flowing unswervingly into the account of a Development Board established in 1950 to build up the country. The Board has begun digging dirt for a score of massive projects, and has actually completed a few already. It has installed Western experts in key positions, has given some of them a full vote in policy-making, and has never gone counter to their major recommendations.

This is precisely the sort of 'boot-strap' self-help the United Nations and the United States have long been urging if the Arab world is ever to lift itself up out of medieval backwardness and mass destitution. President Eisenhower's special cache of $200 million for

Middle East aid would be intended to assist just such programmes—with the long-range aim of soothing Arab nationalist fevers by reducing the virus of poverty.

Yet nowhere else among the Middle East's independent Arab states can comparable progress, or even an inclination towards improvement, be detected. Like Iraq, Saudi Arabia has been enjoying a mammoth oil income—more than a quarter of a billion dollars yearly. But King Saud spends more on one extra palace than on his government's entire budget for education. After his numerous brothers and sons have drawn their annual allowances, and a legion of tribal sheikhs their stipends as a fee for non-rebellion, little is left over for public works and welfare. In Egypt, Colonel Nasser's start on economic reform has limped to a halt. In hyper-nationalist Syria, even free economic aid has been rejected as 'colonialism'.

By contrast, Iraq's seven-man Development Board Executive Committee, working with the Prime Minister and the Ministers of Development and Finance, has an average annual budget of $250 million to disburse. Its five native members—an ex-Premier and four senior statesmen, all former cabinet members—authorize nothing without the concurrence of their two full-ranking foreign colleagues, an American and a British engineer. Its irrigation and drainage section is headed by a Dutchman and an American, the bridges and highways section by an Englishman, industry and mining by a Frenchman.

In the bazaars 500 fils ($1.50) is the standard 'price' for a smuggled copy of any confidential Board document; and every foreign firm is assailed by agents offering to purchase the ear of a high official for a fee.

Immersed in this classic baksheesh climate, the Board nevertheless screens contracts and projects rigorously on merit. Perhaps the one dubious item is an air-conditioned palace for 21-year-old King Faisal, to cost $7 million. But even this can be justified as part of a public-building programme that includes a new Parliament building, a royal guardhouse, a museum, a library, a jail, and a tourist hotel to cost $6 million.

The Board's programme of major public works will literally change the face of the country. Already a set of dams at Samarra on the Tigris and at Ramadi on the Euphrates has lengthened to a cycle of five years instead of one the prospect of regular and ruinous inundation for the Mesopotamian Plain. Two more dams, one of them 450 feet high, are now being erected on Tigris tributaries.

A petrol refinery has been completed at Daura with Board funds, an asphalt refinery is going up at Qaiyara, a cement plant near Sulaimaniya, and a cotton textile plant at Mosul. Contracts

have been awarded on another cement plant, a sugar factory and
two thermo-electric power plants totalling 85,000 kilowatts. A six-
year road programme had laid down four hundred miles of first-class
highway by the beginning of 1957, and was scheduled to complete
one thousand miles by the end of that year. Of twelve new main
bridges projected for Iraq's great rivers, three were already in use at
Kirkuk, Kufa, and Hindiya, and two more to be opened at Baghdad
before the end of 1957.

The bridges symbolically point to another Iraqi eccentricity—by
Arab standards. When five iron bridges span the Tigris at Baghdad,
according to ancient prophecy, 'an invader will come down from the
north'. On modern maps this means the Soviet Russians. The two
new bridges will give Baghdad a total of five for the first time in
history—and another two are already being planned.

Not that the Iraqis are indifferent to menace from Moscow. On
the contrary, Iraq is the only Arab state sufficiently aware of it to
have entered a Western-led regional defence system, the so-called
Baghdad Pact, with Britain, Turkey, Pakistan, and Iran. Iraq's
defence forces get weapons and training from Britain and substantial
armaments, by separate treaty, from the United States. Early in
1957 Crown Prince Abdul Illah, uncle of the King, turned up in
Washington to negotiate still more arms aid.

Iraq faces squarely Westward, despite abuse from her neutralist
'allies' in the Arab League. Outwardly, she takes the same angry
stance as they against Israel—and even against Britain in the Suez
crisis. After the Franco-British attack on the Canal, two meetings
of the Baghdad Pact states were ostentatiously held without inviting
the British. But that estrangement, churned up mainly for public
Arab consumption, seems safely past. The Hashemite dynasty which
reigns in Baghdad feels much less threatened by Western 'imperialism' than by nearer dangers.

The dynasty that rules in Saudi Arabia has long been a hated rival;
and the carefully contrived Washington meeting of Saud and Abdul
Illah obviously cannot be expected to erase the old enmity. Ambitious Egypt and quarrelsome Syria, both under increasing influence
from Moscow, have been driving for Iraq's isolation in the Arab
world. King Saud, Nasser, and the Syrians are deep in intrigue
inside Jordan, which sits at Iraq's door and has a Hashemite kins-
man of Iraq's, King Faisal, on the throne. The Soviet Union, within
easy march of Iraq's oil-fields, looms larger still.

Against all these perils, and in mutually profitable oil exploitation
through the British-controlled Iraq Petroleum Company and other
outlets, Britain remains Iraq's closest ally—and the United States
her strongest friend. When the Soviets were making alarming

military gestures in the Middle East recently, it was Washington which warned Moscow that any move hostile to Iraq or her Baghdad Pact neighbours 'would be viewed by the United States with the utmost gravity'.

Iraq has much to defend. Other territories in the Middle East possess oil or water or an excess of potentially fertile land over inhabitants. But Iraq alone has all three combined.

Once, populous Sumerian and Babylonian civilizations flourished in antique Mesopotamia. On the great plains between the Twin Rivers there are desert stretches paved with remnants of classic pottery that turn up at every step. One can still see the vestigial mounds of ancient cities, some of them five miles long. As late as the ninth century A.D., Baghdad under Harun al-Rashid was the eastern capital of Islamic culture and power. But afterwards came Mongol destruction of the irrigation system, the Turkish conquest, unrestrained floods, erosion, deforestation, and other hazards. By World War I the region was the 'Siberia' of the Ottoman Empire, administered by Turkish officials temporarily banished there.

Today Iraq has a population of only 5 million. Egypt, with less than a third as much tillable soil, has 22 million people. 'Almighty God', cried Development Minister Dhia' Ja'afar in Parliament, 'has given us a wealth very seldom bestowed on countries with such a small population!' But Iraq will need large-scale immigration if the challenge of projects already in work is to be met.

From a guaranteed annual minimum of $70 million negotiated in a fifty-fifty split with four oil companies in 1952, Iraq's share swelled to better than $205 million in 1955. This represented 65 per cent of total government income. Between 1951 and 1955, Development Board allocations amounted to $470 million. For 1955–60, estimates of expenditures were calculated initially at $850 million. But within a year, with the mounting flood of oil royalties and taxes, these were revised upwards to $1,400 million.

An Iraq Petroleum Corporation pipeline from Kirkuk normally carries 75 per cent of Iraq's export oil to the Mediterranean. Last November the three pumping stations on Syrian territory were blown up by the Syrian Army. The action, ostensibly a defensive military measure provoked by the Anglo-French invasion of Egypt, has been costing Iraq around $700,000 daily. The magnitude of Iraq's resources is attested by the fact that, despite this blow, the development programme has continued until now without pause. Plans not yet put into work are being slowed pending negotiations with Syria for pipeline repair. But all projects already under way are going forward uninterruptedly, thanks to $385 million of Board reserves banked in Baghdad and London. Iraq's credit, the soundest in the Arab Middle East, is expected to obtain financing for her abroad easily if these funds give out before full income is restored.

In other oil-rich Arab countries—Saudi Arabia, for instance—the land is either parched desert or stony steppe. Iraq, however, has so much fresh water that damage from periodic river overflow in some years has cost $80 million. Hitherto, floods that ravaged the land each spring ran futilely off, leaving a water shortage in the dry autumn season. Storage and irrigation works now in progress are expected in five years to redeem four hundred thousand wasted acres and bring supplementary water to a half-million other acres. The Board aims ultimately at supplying extra water to 7 million of the 8 million acres which represent Iraq's total irrigated area today— and at reclaiming 6 million acres more.

Such stupendous expansion could multiply native farm output at least five times. But skills are notoriously lacking in Iraq. Despite the general advance already noted, it is far from certain that the basic long-range development programme will be able to move steadily forward.

In Baghdad, modern homes sometimes get completed before someone remembers that a kitchen should have a sink and that a fireplace performs better if equipped with a chimney. A $5 million railway station started under an earlier development programme was finished in 1954 near the Baghdad airport—but nowhere near the railroad.

At the start, the Board itself also committed monumental boners. In one case, close study finally revealed that a large patch of reclaimed soil could never drain properly and hence would yield malaria instead of crops—but the study which proved this was undertaken only after expensive canals had been dug and hundreds of settlers brought in.

Under discreet foreign guidance, the passion to spend huge sums quickly has faded. If anything, the Board errs now on the side of slow motion. Years of study are being put into each project. The countryside swarms with survey teams exploring potential resources.

But excessive precautions are not the main obstacle. A prime roadblock is the Ministry of Development, the Board's liaison with the government. Whenever a cabinet falls, the Board's work halts while a new Minister of Development learns his job. In four years, eight governments have fallen.

Iraq's shortage of technical personnel is an even graver problem. There is a surplus of lawyers, but a shortage of plumbers (the Government Law College was grinding out seven hundred graduates yearly until a recent decree cut new classes to one hundred). Too few vocational and advanced technical schools exist. The Board's total staff is only one thousand five hundred—including a battalion of coffee-bearers—as against ten thousand in the United States Bureau of Reclamation, which has a programme of roughly the same magnitude.

Equally serious is the bottle-neck produced by Iraq's backward civil service. Between 1933 and 1956, the cost of living rose 500 per cent, but salaries of middle and upper government employees inched up only 50 per cent. Better pay in private enterprise lured away most of the more competent personnel. Promotions for merit and discharges for incompetence being virtually unknown, the civil service suffers from a built-in apathy. Iraq has had no facilities for special training in government and, until recently, no awareness of the need for them. With a super-billion-dollar development programme to manage, the state machinery might fairly be described as a one-cylinder motor in a Rolls-Royce body.

Last summer, Parliament voted a scaled pay hike up to 75 per cent for government workers. The major immediate result was only that cigarettes and other 'white-collar' items quietly doubled in price. There is some prospect of bolder reforms, however. Prodded by the United States International Cooperation Administration—which supports a 110-man Point IV mission in Iraq—top native leaders are even contemplating the possible utility of establishing a school of public administration.

The largest question-mark in the Development Board's future is its social goal. Is the programme truly designed to help the whole Iraqi people, or merely to make the rich grow richer? Despite the lavish funds available, projects executed or planned for the direct short-range benefit of ordinary Iraqis were of paltry scope in the programme's first half-decade.

In 1954, the Development Board invited a British economist, Lord Salter, to make a critical survey. He recommended that the Board find ways to hasten the impact of its good deeds. He pointed especially at the appalling need for housing. Three-quarters of the nation still live in miserable huts, largely without fresh water or sewerage. Even in Baghdad, almost within sight and smell of government offices, over two hundred thousand occupy squalid *sarifa* of mud walls and reed roofs.

A 'crash programme' has now been launched to erect in five cities during the next two years around five thousand one-family houses with modern insulation and sanitation. The houses, ranging in cost up to $2,800, will be sold or rented on easy terms. Other government departments are being assisted with housing programmes for employees.

By 1960, the Board intends to have spent around $70 million on perhaps twenty-five thousand new dwellings. Even this scratching of the surface is impeded by the dearth of specialized labour. In addition, $45 million has been allotted for schools, clinics, and hospitals and $242 million for roads and bridges, with priority for roads that afford farmers better access to markets.

Sober foreign observers are hopeful these noble works may yet be accomplished, along with other grand plans of the Board. But all agree that first there must occur a dazzling enlightenment of Iraq's economic and political rulers.

The sweeping progress of which the Board dreams implies a revolution in Iraq's social patterns. It would wash away the pillars of mass poverty, illiteracy, and semi-feudal subjugation. It would diminish the caste which now rides high on the backs of the Iraqi people. Such drastic change could be made only with the voluntary consent of the riders—or by their violent overthrow.

Over 60 per cent of the population subsists on agriculture, but nearly 70 per cent of the land consists of large holdings which employ the bulk of the farm labour. At least four out of every five peasants in Iraq get no cash return for their toil. Their landlords pay them in kind, sometimes as little as a two-seventh share of the crop. Perpetually debt-ridden, forbidden by law to quit their places as long as they are in arrears, trapped by low productivity and high interest rates, most peasants live in virtual serfdom.

Their lords and masters constitute a corps of medieval-minded sheikhs, with some absentee urban potentates. The sheikhs are hereditary rulers. Their power rests on ingrained fealty from below and on their personal armies of tribal riflemen. In Parliament the sheikhs form the hard centre of Premier Nuri as-Said's support. A measure of their rooted strength is the fact that Iraq, despite its predominantly agricultural economy, levies no land tax or inheritance tax.

The landed caste has been persuaded thus far to go along with the Development Board. Flood control, irrigation, and other improvements obviously raise the worth of the private properties affected. Until now, the state has largely classified such improvements as in the 'common interest', absolving the owners from having to compensate the public coffers for benefits received.

On the other hand, the rural oligarchy has no zeal for civil service reform, which might build up cadres of lively officials with reformist notions about entrenched privileges. Nor are the sheikhs likely to relish the growing unrest among their landless followers as the area of reclaimed acreage available for distribution expands. (To date only fifteen thousand peasants have been affected by various agrarian reform schemes.)

Will the government give this land to those who need it, and help them survive by easy credit—or, instead, will the land go eventually, by default, to those who already have too much? Can the wealthy be allowed continually to grow fatter from the development programme's contributions to the value of their properties, or must not some apparatus for adequate repayment on these benefits be devised? How long, finally, can sound economic and social management tolerate a fiscal régime which gives immunity from taxes to the one group best able to pay?

The best that can be said is that recommendations on all these matters have been prayerfully drawn up by foreign consultants and that the Iraqi government has begun gravely to read them instead of filing them in back drawers. It is too early to predict whether the feudal class can recognize in time that its best interest demands a relative reduction of its own top-heavy wealth in exchange for the tranquillizing effects of reduced mass resentment.

Part II

from 'THE ECONOMIST'

INTO ACTION

ALL OVER Asia and Africa, under-developed countries have plans for development. All are fingering estimates and blue-prints, but only a few can display finished works that are already raising productivity. Some have drive but no capital (Egypt), others money but no scope for creating productive enterprises (Kuwait), yet others resources but, through nationalism, no mind to borrow the capital or hire the advice to develop them quickly (Syria). Only nations that have both resources and either investment capital of their own, or else enough stability to be thought a good investment risk by outsiders, have the means to execute their plans. Even these sometimes pause out of mistrust of the foreign technical advice without which, for the present, they cannot get on (Iran).

Of the thrusters, Iraq and India are the two nations that have accomplished most, and Iraq is the better placed for forging still farther ahead. For the Iraqis have capital and need not operate on credit, or worry—as India has to do—over shortages of ready cash and balance-of-payments crises. Indeed, they have far more money than they can as yet effectively spend, as Table 1 reveals.

TABLE 1—DEVELOPMENT BOARD
Million Iraqi Dinars

	1951–52	1952–53	1953–54	1954–55	1955–56*
Revenue . . .	7·5	24·0	35·3	40·7	60·6
Estimated expenditure† .	9·4	20·4	28·4	31·6	46·6
Actual expenditure . .	3·1	12·8	12·3	20·9	29·5
Surplus . . .	4·3	11·7‡	23·0	19·9	31·1

Source: *Quarterly Bulletin of the Central Bank of Iraq*, No. 20, 1956.

* Eleven months to February, 1956.

† Source: Development Laws, Nos. 25 (1951), 35 (1952), 43 (1955), and 54 (1956).

‡ ID 5 million transferred to ordinary budget.

Their direct revenue from oil, 73·7 million Iraqi dinars in its peak year (1955), was ID 68·8 million in 1956 and, but for the Suez crisis, had been expected to reach ID 80 million in that year. The Iraqi dinar is at par with sterling and the £ sign will be used henceforth. The source of this wealth—the oil-production industry—is not covered in this review, which deals only with the way the Iraqis handle the proceeds.[1]

The Iraqis enjoy several advantages other than money, some of them gifts of nature, others the result of effort or heredity. Their greatest national asset is plentiful and accessible water. The length of Iraq from its northern mountains to its featureless southern river mouth is six hundred miles—about the distance from the source to the mouth of the Rhine. At the northern end, the hardy Kurds in the highlands and the rolling plains at their foot have the benefits of snow and rain; while in the south there is compensation for the torrid summer heat of Mesopotamia in the everlasting flow of the Tigris and Euphrates; indeed, a large tract in the south of the land between the rivers is undrained marsh.

A second asset is demographic. Unlike Egypt or India, with their nightmare problem of a birth-rate that is outstripping resources, Iraq is under-populated. Its population of 2·8 million in 1930 has risen to about 5·5 million today, but results obtainable by irrigation and drainage can produce more living-space; there is room for expansion.

Among man-made, self-made advantages must be reckoned relative efficiency over the management of money. The Iraqis have kept

[1] For the impact of the oil companies see 'Oil and Social Change in the Middle East', supplement to *The Economist*, July 2, 1955.

a much more effective check on the expenditure of their oil revenue than any of their neighbours. Their accounting system is good (though their Development Board is sadly behindhand with published audits) and it is possible to trace virtually every penny they have spent from the early days of their 'Projects Section' of the Ministry of Communications and Works to their Development Board of today. At present the allocation of oil revenue is 70 per cent to the Board and 30 per cent to Ministries for ordinary budget expenditure. The Board spends some of its share through Ministries. It also uses its unspent balances as a cash reserve from which to make loans to public authorities for local developments of importance; about £40 million is lying out in this form at present. Some of this is likely to be irrecoverable, but municipal power-stations in most small towns, silos breaking the monotonous line of the Mesopotamian horizon, and—more romantically—the silver water-tanks that now flank the golden domes of pilgrimage cities, are a testimony to its usefulness. The Board's estimates are embodied in successive Development Laws sanctioned by Parliament.

Another Iraqi merit is a sense of continuity. This is Nuri Pasha's gift to his country, and his critics hold that he has furnished it at the expense of the liberty of the individual. Originally, he intended the Development Board to be a body of permanent members, plus one or two Cabinet Ministers. But after experiment he was defeated on this issue and for some years the Board has been a Ministry; in other words, its directing spirit changes with a change of cabinet. Nuri's answering expedient has been to organize a stacked Parliament and to render cabinet upsets a matter of control. When they occur, they make no difference to the economic and social pattern that is described in the following pages. So that whereas for some years the Board hesitated inordinately over what to do, and kept changing its membership and filling cupboards with unused reports submitted by expensive specialists, in the two years 1955–57 it has finished many jobs.

This sudden flowering is partly the outcome of old work coming to a head, but partly, also, that of a new state of mind that is illustrated by the invention of 'Development Week'. This gala was instituted in 1956 and, held in March, is an orgy of inaugurations that forces the pace of completion. The new attitude of mind was illustrated when an Iraqi criticized the 1957 programme: 'Next year's performance must not be padded with so much laying of foundation stones,' he said. 'Development Week is the time for cutting tapes.'

What produces this purposeful outlook? Why did Iraq opt for business as usual both at the time of Abadan, despite the emotional inducements to copy Dr. Mossadeq, and again during the Suez crisis? Some say 'Because of Nuri', and think that when he finally quits, the country will disintegrate into factions as quarrelsome as those in Syria. But there are deeper reasons—reasons of temperament—for thinking that this fate may be avoided.

The Iraqis have in their blood a more dogged strain than is usual among Arabs. It may owe something to centuries of admixture with mountain races. Some hold that it owes a little to the British Mandate; certainly, the notion among older civil servants that their calling is hard work and not a repaying sinecure dates from those years. Whatever its origin, this strain imparts a strength to the national fabric which is increased by another national characteristic: the endearing quality of humility. ('Of course Ali has written the best essay,' says the class, 'didn't you know? He has an Armenian (or a Turkish . . .) mother.') An Iraqi, unlike an Iranian, does not mind admitting that he does not know. Alone among the 'developing' Asian nations, he has appointed two foreigners to full voting membership of his Development Board. 'We shall be able to do things for ourselves in due course,' he says, 'but meanwhile we prefer to pay for the best work that is to be had.' And when they have paid for the advice, they nowadays tend to take it. Alone in Asia they have commissioned a single report to end reports and then acted upon it—as they have done with considerable parts of Lord Salter's masterly 'Plan of Action' of 1955. In it, the Iraqis own a document worth study by any country engaged on development.

Is this dependence on foreigners a weakness? Many Asian nationalists think so and brand present practices as a 'sell-out to the imperialists'. But the criterion, surely, is whether or not Iraqis are training themselves to fill all the foreigners' shoes. Their country's only two major natural resources are its oil, offering the basis of a petro-chemical industry, and its agriculture, on which many processing industries could be based. Already educated men are beginning to conquer their prejudice against dirty hands and are advising their sons to qualify in engineering. Accomplishment will not be complete until the same can be said of scientific farming.

THE DRIVE FOR VARIETY

Diagonally across a wall in the office of the Iraqis' Greek housing consultant runs a huge and unusual map of Iraq, dotted with red circles of varying sizes denoting the present distribution of communities throughout the country. In the rain-fed north, they make a 'normal' sprinkled pattern of cities, market towns, and villages. But south of Baghdad the grouping changes, and the whole of life is thickly clustered along the two rivers, with wide empty spaces in between. No wonder that the flyer from Baghdad to Basra sees nothing (except where the plane crosses the fertile ribbon of the rivers) but sand, salt, and marshy emptiness that looks like the surface of some sodden moon. This is the pattern that must be altered before there can be an adequate increase in productivity.

Irrigation and drainage will help to disperse the clusters, but cannot do it unaided. The Development Board's other main sections are each contributing to the job.

Railway, port, roads, a power grid: once these four are available the people can fan out from the rivers, though the spinal cord of all communications—Basra to Mosul—must clearly be the main line of each system. From 1958 or '59, there will be two railway lines from one end of the spine to the other, instead of one as at present; the lines will meet at Baghdad, but elsewhere will serve new centres, such as Kut, and remedy missing links such as that between Erbil and Mosul. The state railways are to get £24 million of Board money in the six years 1955–60, but cannot do the spectacular part of their construction work till some new bridges are built. Meantime, their principal loading-point, which is the Port of Basra, deserved more attention from the Board than it received until 1956.

Iraqis are not sea-minded; they get abroad by land or air. Their port and gateway at Basra is many miles up their river and—because they do not use it much for personal exits or for oil export—they forget its importance as a point of intake when they are importing six times as much as they export, excluding oil. Only in 1956 did Basra get its first belated grant of Board money (£4 million) for improvements. Happily, it had meantime helped itself. Run by a semi-independent Port Authority, it is self-supporting and well managed; indeed, in the years of pinch and scrape, it saved on its port services enough to lend money to keep Basra city going on electric light. It is up to date by port standards anywhere else in the Persian Gulf, but needs more capital for investment in port facilities if it is to do its bit in the diversification of the economy by handling the output of some export industries that are to be sited near it. It deserves more tributes, as well as more money, than it has had.

New trunk roads and main bridges are handled directly by the Board. Its bridging work has gone ahead, but the road map is a disappointing display after six years of work; only a few small sectors of main road are finished. Admittedly, there were many roads in the south on which it was not worth starting till the floods were mastered; at other points bridges had to come first. But there is no good reason why the traveller of March, 1957, should still have had to bump all the way from outside Baghdad to Mosul or Kirkuk in the classic discomfort of ruts and dust, or mud. Two years hence, he will purr along the tarmac, but he ought to be doing it now.

The trouble seems to have been an assumption that whereas it takes a foreign expert to design a dam, anyone can build a road. The programme has been disorganized by bad estimating and arguments over specifications, by contractors preferring to pay their penalty clause and pull out, and disagreements over the value of work partly done. (One of the contractors' difficulties has been the local prejudice that has obliged them to shed unskilled labour and take on new men each time a road enters new tribal territory.) Some of the snags were unforeseeable, or at any rate unforeseen, by the world's most experienced firms, one or two of whom are completing their contracts only at heavy loss. A combination of such set-backs has left the main Baghdad–Kirkuk road untouched for a year. Now, however, push is being applied to the road network. Two years hence, places that are backwaters will be on trunk lines to market and in process of transformation from a non-monetized to a cash economy.

Cheap electric power is also within sight. Two of the three main power-stations—at Dibbis in the north and at Baghdad—are under construction now, and the third, at Basra, is due to be started in 1958. Those near oil-fields will run on natural gas; both the dams now building have been equipped to generate hydro-electric power, but, for the present, gas or oil is a cheaper source of energy.

Now that these networks are on their way, the Board is beginning to make its main contribution to another Iraqi target—diversification of the economy by the establishment of industry; for its principal role in this field is to provide the services that will cause Iraqis to start industries for themselves. As elsewhere in the 'under-developed' world, they are slow starters except in light industry—soft drinks, pasteurization, matches, and the like—because they are reluctant to plough big sums into ventures that may not yield returns for some years. Furthermore, they are mistrustful of organizing mergers, except within a family, with the object of accumulating funds for an investment of magnitude. The Board has therefore itself undertaken the establishment of various major industries, but on the basis that there is as soon as possible to be some private stake in the operation, and that private management is to be encouraged to take over once the industries are on their feet. (The precise form of ultimate government participation has yet to be determined; in one or two cases construction costs have been so high that private enterprise could scarcely take over unless capital costs are largely written off.)

On the advice of its American consultants, the Board has concentrated chiefly on industries which process Iraq's two main raw materials—agricultural products and the by-products of the natural gas and oil industries. These it has spread all over the country as far as is compatible with availability of materials, and of markets both at home and abroad. Large bitumen, cement, and cotton-textile plants are already operating in the north, with sugar to follow. For oil refining, the Board has granted £6 million to an independent Government Oil Refineries Administration which has its principal plant just south of Baghdad, and allocated a further £2½ million in 1957. So far, the south feels neglected; but its turn will come in the next year or two when it will get plant for processing its marsh reeds into paper for export and its dates into date syrup and cattlecake. In the field of petroleum-chemicals, fertilizer, and rayon textiles, plants are also scheduled to start at Basra; a sulphur-processing plant at Kirkuk is out to tender.

A step that the Board has not yet taken, but plans to take, is improvement of industrial credit facilities for the private entrepreneur. In its concentration on big business, it has forgotten the little man whom it could help to start with enterprises, such as jam and canning factories in the fruit- and meat-producing valleys of the north. Till now, the small entrepreneur's only means of borrowing is from an Industrial Bank that is run on an old-boy basis over cups of coffee, and without relation to the return on the investment or to national need. The Board's idea now is to funnel loans out to would-be industrialists through an Industrial Finance Corporation which would scrutinize their plans from the angle of value to national development as well as of relationship to imported goods of the same quality.

There is much grumbling among white-collar liberals about the Board's delay in making a good display of industrial expansion; in fact, once it gets credit facilities going, it will be moving at a pace and along lines that ought to enable the private entrepreneur to get an early share of the cake. But to the Iraqi's mind it is only wheels actually humming that count as accomplishment.

The grumbler likes results he can see, and it was partly to pacify him that Lord Salter advised in 1955 that housing financed by the Board should be on a much larger scale. Another reason for pressing on with it was that providing houses is a quick way of spreading the population, reducing the drift to the towns, and making workers available where they are needed. This piece of his advice was at once taken and the allocation for housing raised from £6 million (1955–59) to £24 million (1955–60). In addition to the private building that is in full swing in all main towns, therefore, and to much oil-company building of employees' houses on a home-ownership basis in Basra and Kirkuk, Development Board housing on a community basis has started all over the country; it is well advanced just outside Baghdad and round the northern factories; a big estate is out to tender at Basra.

The idea is to build communities, not mere shelters. 'School here, market there, no road to cross to the playground, and here is the gossip square.' The enthusiasm of the Greek firm that is laying the plans is infectious. Town dwellers are at once delighted with their work and the envy of all the unhoused; so will farmers be in the districts where they have always returned to villages at night for security. But the Middle Euphrates farmer who has liked living on his farm does not yet want to be herded into the kind of community that makes overheads cheap. Only when he has seen what happens— that is, when a pilot project has played its essential role—will accessibility to drinking-water, sewage, electricity, a store, a school, and, perhaps, even a cinema make him change his conservative mind.

NEED FARMING BE IGNOBLE?

If, in talk with students in Baghdad, you mention that Iraq is an agricultural country, or deplore the lowness of the Development Board's current allocation for agriculture (£14 million for 1955–60) as opposed to industry (£67 million), you are shouted down. The much-too-glib assumption is that your idea is to keep a backward people pinned down to manual labour, and to thwart modernization. You answer that agriculture *is* an industry, and that Australian farming is just as modern as dark Satanic mills in England, but your point is not easily accepted. Many young Iraqis who work in the Farm Extension Service tell you with a sigh that they would far rather have been a doctor, or an engineer, because these careers are not only better paid but are rated 'more dignified'.

Yet, apart from oil, Iraq's main source of wealth present and future is its agriculture. To give peasants the incentive to remain farmers, and cause the educated youth to stop sighing for a desk, is the first corollary of spending £153 million on water works in the next six years. Why, then, is the Agricultural Section of the Development Board the Cinderella financially?

Is its money allocation supposed to reflect the fact that rural Iraq will be first beneficiary under other expensive heads—notably irrigation and communications? Or is agriculture low in priority because the Board reckons the job a maintenance and educational matter which is the province of Ministries? Or is the more backward and passive part of the electorate neglected to permit window-dressing in the more vociferous towns? Agriculture is underweighted for such reasons in the development budgets of other countries, notably India. Or is the reason political? Is it that major changes in the agricultural pattern of Iraq undermine the power and wealth of the landlord class that still dominates politics, and so are pursued only gingerly by a Board that is under the control of Parliament?

Whatever the reason, the Agricultural Section of the Board is confining its work to the *Miri Sirf* (pure state) lands where new smallholder settlements can be organized without a political fuss. And, indeed, to get these new areas to yield the results they are capable of yielding will absorb all its capacities for the present. Two main impressions are left on a visitor to established *Miri Sirf* experiments in the north, south, and middle of the country. One (which may well escape a visitor who is unfamiliar with traditional Iraqi farming) is that they are a tremendous advance, both statistically and to the naked eye, on any other form of peasant life. The other is that, nevertheless, they fall depressingly far below the level they could attain. They are below it for causes that it would be within the Board's capacity to prevent and cure.

One important step that the Board is beginning to take is to make a better choice of settler; families that already have a bent for farming will both produce more crops and advertise the Board better than intransigent nomads (chosen at Hawija in the north as part of the government's settlement policy) or retired government servants (chosen for certain holdings at Latifiyah near Baghdad, and apt to lease their plot to some more menial worker).

A second step as yet untaken is to see that the Ministries to which services are transferred when the projects get to the running stage— Agriculture, Health, Education—do not treat them as stepchildren, and fail to mother them, let alone act in unison. This dovetailing will not materialize unless the Board organizes one of two developments. The choice would be either to vest its Agricultural Section with the prestige and authority and cabinet support that would enable it to chivvy Ministries, or else to set up local committees of the representatives of the various Ministries in each province so that each project manager could get them to help him push for services. The farther afield one goes, the wider yawns the gap between the desk in Baghdad and the man on the project. Even at the project nearest to the city, a visit on a bitter day in January, 1957, revealed 437 families gathered to be vaccinated; as a result of a great publicity effort they had ridden, walked, and carried their babies miles through the winter mud only to find that, without even telephoning to let them know, the Ministry had neglected or forgotten to send the van.

Instruction, supervision, encouragement, attention—all are in short supply, and yet applications, many thousands in excess of the number of holdings available, pour in each time new plots are distributed. A tribute should be paid to the training staff who, by living on the job, set the example that creates this demand. They are, as yet, only a handful of Iraqis and two notable American stayers whom an Iraqi on the Board described to the writer as 'three points of Point IV'.

Perhaps the hope is that if—in the existing *Miri Sirf* settlements and the huge new one inaugurated (March, 1957) in land between the rivers just below Baghdad—these failings are set right, a precedent will be set for carrying managed crop-patterns into that Old Tom Tiddler's Ground, the large estates.

Some of these are very well farmed already by owners who are quick to see the virtue of new methods, and who would react at once to visible evidence of rising yields whether of crops or—in the north —of better fed and bred animals. A few such men already admit that if government expenditure causes less land to yield more money, it might be just to pay for the services by surrendering some acres. For other more crustacean types, particularly on the enormous estates in the Kut and Amara area, acres good or bad have an intrinsic worth that still makes them prize-worthy, even if lying idle because uselessly salty.

Seeing is believing. Successful pilot projects are one of the keys to social change. Even the following impressive figures—all available in published reports submitted to the Development Board—have made no mark on most Iraqi minds:

(a) In Iraq as a whole, 20 to 30 per cent of cultivable land has been abandoned in recent years as a result of salination due to irrigation without drainage. Where land has more than $\frac{1}{2}$ per cent salt content it grows no wheat; more than 1 per cent, no barley; more than 2 per cent, no dates.

(b) Much of this land is recoverable. During a recent experiment at Dujaila forty days of 'laundering' removed 65 metric tons of salt per meshara (0·62 acre) and reduced the salt content of a trial area of 200 mesharas from 5 to 0·1 per cent.

(c) Drainage alone would increase the average yield of grain by 72 per cent, rice by 36 per cent, and dates and citrus by 60 per cent.

(d) All Iraq uses the fallow system; only half the cultivable land is cropped each year. On land for which expensive irrigation works have been installed, the cost of these works per unit is double what it would be if the land were continuously cropped. The Board's American water consultants estimate that the introduction of crop rotation and managed summer cropping could raise the three figures given above to 190 per cent, 129 per cent, and 200 per cent respectively.

(e) By introducing pest control and improved irrigation methods, and less hidebound practices about dates of planting, it could be doubled again.

(f) It could be further increased by improvement of varieties, seed selection, and the use of fertilizers. 'There is 4 dinars profit on each dinar invested in fertilizer.'

Who on reading of such possibilities can contest that farming is a noble profession and that this ever-renewable resource deserves to be a first call on Iraqi brains as well as Iraqi hands?

FLAWS IN A GOOD PLAN

When an under-developed country is galloping to catch up with Europe and America, critics are apt to find fault with it to an extent that would be justifiable only if all 'developed' countries worked without a hitch. Before commenting on the shortcomings of Iraqi development, perspective must be sought by making comparisons only with other countries in the same boat. Thanks to more continuity of effort than anywhere except India, and more readiness to speed matters by trusting experienced foreigners than anyone else, Iraq has made more of a start than any of its neighbours towards creating productivity; admittedly, it has worked in more favourable conditions than any of them except Iran.

The Development Board's effort is on the whole so estimable that some of its weaknesses are worth mentioning if only because the cure lies well within its reach.

The first is a failure to encourage the expansion of credit for people ready to help themselves. Iraq has for years had three banks that perform this function, an Industrial Bank, a Mortgage Bank, and an Agricultural Bank. The first will do better than hitherto if it is transformed into the new Industrial Finance Corporation that has been recommended; the second (which is the most efficient of the three) lately had from the Board a £5 million loan at $\frac{1}{2}$ per cent and the benefit it is bringing to the middle-class income group wishing to build houses in city suburbs is visible. But the third, the Agricultural Bank, is Cinderella over again. How can a peasant better himself, even if he is granted land and a house, if he starts in arrears of debt and has no money to buy seed or fertilizer? Unless credit on easy terms is available to him, he either farms in the bad old way or else borrows at the old usurious rate from a money-lender or his former employer. Even a loan at low interest from a government organization will not convert him into a solvent farmer if he simply uses it to pay old debts.

Supervised co-operative credit, of the kind that the British instituted in Cyprus and Jordan, or that the Ford Foundation is beginning to promote with a pilot programme in both Iraq and Iran, is one of Iraq's main needs. 'Such associations, to be sound and successful, must have substantial support and guidance during their early years,' says a Ford Foundation report. To attain this level, Iraq's Agricultural Bank would need reformation, much money from the Development Board, and much more trained staff than it has got. Experience of well-run co-operative credit systems suggests that, given considerate terms, peasants are good payers. In Jordan, 75 to 80 per cent of the money due for repayment is wont to arrive on the dot. Why should Iraq be any worse at making a revolving fund stimulate initiative and in time turn peasants into minor capitalists?

A second sin of omission by the Board is under-estimation of the need for training. Trainees for the new Mosul textile factory were sent abroad well ahead of time, but at the opening of the factory they were only a sprinkling in great halls of French machinery. Agricultural training is given far less forethought. If peasants accustomed only to the fallow system are to use all the water that big investment is making available for intensive farming, they will need to be given at least enough instruction to realize how badly they need more of it. In a country developing as fast as Iraq, training 'on the job' is the only possible recourse for some years to come. Doubtless it will take place in industry, since machines cannot be handled by the light of nature, but there are not nearly enough arrangements for giving it on the farm. Even in the north, where the merchant landowner of Mosul or Erbil has on his own taken to tractor farming and has increased production, the way he is doing it is, from lack of knowledge, not increasing yield per acre. And, farther north still, afforestation proceeds only in patches of a size that can be wired, because no one has undertaken the kind of teaching about stopping the ravages of goats that has been such a success in Cyprus.

Next—decentralization. The depressing insistence that every decision be referred back to Baghdad blights many improvements that would take place at once if the job were entrusted to local initiative. The manager on the project could do much better with a little more authority; what he wants is a budget of his own and a right to encourage his farmers to help him manage the show and penalize or evict the failures.

A striking example of the initiative that flowers when local authorities are given incentives and responsibility is shown by the Municipalities Department of the Ministry of the Interior—the body responsible for light and water in the country towns of Iraq. There are 152 of these municipalities. They get their revenue from local

TABLE 2—ECONOMIC AND SOCIAL PROGRESS IN IRAQ

Year	1951	1952	1953	1954	1955	1956
Electricity consumption, million units	147	207	272	390	489	505
Pure water consumption, thousand cubic metres	44	51	55	64	77	..
Motor lorries licensed, thousand	6·5	7·3	7·5	8·2	9·0	..
Railway traffic, million ton-kilometres	647	726	711	855	843	..
Building licences issued, thousand	3·0	4·3	5·4	5·6	7·0	10·0
Oil exports, million long tons .	8	18	27	28	30	16*
Other exports, million dinars .	27	19	19	18	16	7*
Imports, million dinars . .	51	62	68	73	97	57*
Government budget expenditure, million dinars . . .	29	31	45	50	54	51†
Expenditure by municipalities, million dinars . . .	5·0	5·7	8·4	9·8	13·2	..
Primary school pupils, thousand	181	199	226	258	295	333
Secondary school pupils, thousand	23	24	30	35	41	45
Hospital beds, thousand . .	5·4	6·1	6·6	7·2	7·7	..

Source: Central Statistical Department, Ministry of Economics, Baghdad.
      * First six months.   † Provisional.

taxation, and the enterprising ones have had cash loans from the Development Board and much technical help from the Ministry. In 1945, 33 of them had electric light and 31 pure water. By 1956, the figures were 95 and 109 respectively, with 27 extensions to electric plant and 54 to water. A good agricultural-project manager could match their strides if he were given the same chances; as things stand, he even sows on the day designated by Baghdad, instead of on that ordained by the weather.

Within the very precincts of the Board improvements are possible that could hasten every end it is seeking. Incredibly, it has no professional publicity section. It lacks even the straight information section that would save its technicians from the importunities of journalists; it has more aptitude than it had, though is still lacking in capacity, for telling the Iraqi public what it is doing, so that few northerners have any idea what the flat and palmy south is like, and few southerners have ever seen a relief model of a hill, let alone a dam. It ran good exhibitions in Baghdad during Development Week, and these ought to travel the country for the rest of the year. The same department could with advantage keep students informed of the technical openings that lie ahead and save them from the quite needless restlessness and anxiety they feel about getting a job.

But more than either of these does the Board need to conduct a publicity function of another, subtler, kind. One of the obstacles in the way of development is conservatism; landlord as well as peasant is set in ways he does not want to change. Unless both are acquainted insistently, yet subtly, with what they are missing by failing to co-operate in new schemes, those schemes will never wholly succeed. For instance, cannot a landlord learn, through articles, pilot projects, television, and other media, that he would make more money per acre were he to cease preferring private pumps under his personal control, and instead to hook on to the main canals and drainage outfalls. Unless he is confronted with inducements to join the national water-grid, this will prove unduly costly per acre watered and drained, and the gap between large landowners and the rest of Iraq will remain as wide as ever.

Next, if the Board is to go on lending from its liquid reserve for long-term projects undertaken by other public authorities, it needs a finance officer with experience of public lending, so that it may be advised consistently about what to write off or convert to grants, or what to convert into investments by means of stock or bond issues. The falling-off in oil revenues since the Suez crisis, and the Board's consequent need to use its unspent balance for keeping going, has been a lesson to it to watch, though not necessarily to curtail, its lending policy.

Last, but not least, the Board needs to tune up the economic advice it gets from day to day. Its economic section is only a fact-finding unit. In 1955, it employed Lord Salter to sift all the propositions before it and to advise it what weight to attach to each, and in what order to deal with them. He advised; much of his advice has been taken. But what is needed is a permanent Board member of the Salter stamp. Were such a character to be added to its strength, it might pay more attention to the two topics which should from now on govern all its judgments: Does this or that piece of expenditure arrest the alarming flow of manpower away from the land and into the towns, and does it quickly create productivity? As things stand, credits are being voted without demur for high-cost public buildings that retain in Baghdad building operatives desperately needed for low-cost rural building, and peasants are being planted on to land before there is the credit system without which they cannot be brought to produce more than they consume.

PEOPLE AND PRODUCTIVITY

Is development moving fast enough to satisfy the growing demand for social change? Is it bringing people enough of what they want to give them a foretaste, if not a taste, of benefits they have so far lacked—an education, a steady job, a house, a bit of property? When a member of the Development Board remarked that he envied bridge-builders, because their work, once completed, was put to full use right away, and without discrimination between the users, he put his finger on the most sensitive nerve in the Board's frame: the relative simplicity of its technical feats by comparison with the daunting complexity of its social and political task. Every observer of Iraqi development, from Lord Salter down, has emphasized that 'the nation's economy exists for man, not man for the economy'. Once the fine flush of dam- and bridge-building is over, Iraqis will no longer be able to live in an engineer's paradise, generating great works without need to reflect on their social effects.

As yet this thought is rather a warning than a criticism, but it could with ease become the latter. So far, the Board has catered in generous measure for human welfare; its building of schools, hospitals, and dispensaries is illustrated in Table 2 on p. 275; its start with housing illustrates a concern for improving life at all levels. Has it satisfied its public, or merely increased their craving for more?

At first, it rendered everyone impatient. The years between 1952 and 1955 resounded with grumbling at its apparently interminable preoccupation with blue-prints and surveys. In 1956–57, there was a change of outlook, but one stimulated chiefly by spectacle. The public is excited at feats of engineering such as the Baghdad bridges and the Mosul textile factory. There is now a risk that this excitement will pall and will be followed by disillusionment.

Iraqi society still divides, roughly, into two classes: a rich one growing nervous at hints of a threat to privilege, a poor one awakening to chances of advancement. The precedent in Egypt is in both their minds. In between them two groups seethe and argue; one is a small, educated, urban class, but its aims and discontents are rather political than social. Its grumbling is directed at the muzzle of censorship and the way it has been elbowed out of seats in Parliament. It would do much as Nuri has done were it in power. The other is a younger, poorer group of genuine socialists who now despair of land reform except at the hands of some leader sprung from the people— a Gamal Abdul Nasser.

The social aspect of the Development Board's work, reduced to its simplest terms, is a straight issue between haves and have nots— landed gentry and landless peasants. Over the next few years, the matter that must command attention, in a country one of whose only two great natural resources is agriculture, is whether the relationship between them is to jog on in its present uneasy and uneconomic shape, or, if not, by what means it is to be changed.

The problem of easing social tensions is beyond the scope of the Development Board and in the realm only of cabinet and Parliament. Will a Parliament composed chiefly of landlords ever agree to alter the pattern, or must it be altered violently, as in Egypt? Some dispassionate outside observers think that an imposed land reform is the only way of making the irrigation programme pay its way, since to settle peasants at £300 a head on second-best land is financially as well as socially unsound. Others contend that if only existing laws were applied and landlords paid the taxes for which they have voted, all would be well. Yet others believe that owing to development works, the landlord's position is crumbling anyway, and that even if brusque land reform is shirked, change will happen, without tears, in this generation.

A growing number of factors bears out the last view. One is the increasing availability of alternative employment. Sheikhs in the Amara area were complaining early in 1957 that they had no one to row them to market, and no beaters, because 'their' peasants had gone off to work for the American builders of the Kut–Basra road. Another such factor is the very existence of new smallholdings, however expensively created; once peasants know they can put their name down for a plot and a house, their relationship to a master alters. And if, to replace them, he has to resort to machinery and pay a tractor driver 1½ dinars (30s.) per day, who will stick to sharecropping? Yet another factor that is undermining the landlords' old supremacy is the growth of communications. When peasants who were once confined to poor, disease-ridden surroundings are able to reach a town and a labour exchange by bus, landlords will need either to make rural conditions attractive or else will find themselves bereft of labour and income. The exodus from Amara to Baghdad is already proverbial; more would be disastrous.

'As a long-term policy, Iraq cannot abandon cultivation and live entirely on canned food. A country which is undertaking investment in irrigation on a large scale is indirectly investing in agriculture, and must make some provision for the future of the agricultural population. But by the time that perennial irrigation allows intensive cultivation, the cultivators may not be there.'[2]

There are faint signs that the mind of some landlords is moving towards a grasp of the need to forestall this awful contingency. In 1952, for instance, Parliament passed without demur a short-sighted law—the Amara Land Law—which, nominally, gave peasants title to claim land, but was in fact so worded and executed that sheikhs and their families grabbed most of the lands available. By 1954, the

[2] Doreen Warriner, *Land Reform and Development in the Middle East* (London, Royal Institute of International Affairs, 1957), p. 133.

lower house had passed a bill which entitled the government to recover by instalments from landlords the cost of drainage of their lands undertaken by the Development Board; but the landed gentry in the Senate threw it out. By 1956, a law passed by both houses rendered income from the rent of agricultural land liable to income tax. In 1957–58, to meet an anticipated deficit in the ordinary budget, the proposal is to tax the capital value of landed estates. If that measure is passed by both houses, if the assessment is just, and if landlords begin to surrender acres in exchange for services or in order to meet their obligations, a corner will have been turned in Iraq's social history.

Whether social change will happen gradually or after an upheaval is still an open question. By contrast, it is certain that unless some means is devised of breaking up the many estates at present doomed to perpetual inefficiency, Iraq's productivity will never be what it could be, however great and efficient its investment in irrigation and training.

A point never to be forgotten is that this fortunate nation has not merely water but good human material in which to invest. Often, Iraqis may seem to be lacking in initiative and inclined to wait for orders, but on the whole the evidence is that they warm to responsibility. Give them a co-operative and a budget, prizes for the efficient farmer and a keen instructor to teach them how to work the new apparatus, and—Arab and Kurd alike—they forge ahead. 'I joined the Iraqis for a year,' says the man from Leicester or Utah, 'and that's six years ago, and here I still am because I like them.' There is something compelling about helping with the fortunes of this eager people.

ISLAM AND THE THEORY OF
ARAB NATIONALISM

by SYLVIA G. HAIM

IT IS OFTEN argued that Islam and nationalism, being systems different in origin and inspiration, are contradictory almost by definition, and that no useful purpose can be served in discussing them in connection with each other. In this essay I will, however, try to examine Islam and Arab nationalism as systems of belief, and to discover the point of contact between them, and whether a reconciliation between the two creeds is possible or not.[1] It will be necessary to study the literature of the Arab nationalist movement, to trace any Islamic elements that it may contain, and to endeavour to relate these elements to the traditional system of Islamic belief. Such a study will involve the discussion of the changes that have come over certain terms, Islamic in origin and character, as a result of the infiltration of Western ideas into Arabic thought.

Nationalist doctrines in Europe have usually encouraged xenophobia, an exaggerated pride in race and language, and a desire to seek inspiration in a pre-Christian past; Eastern nationalisms naturally followed suit in these as in other, perhaps less aggressive, tendencies of nationalism, since it was from Europe that nationalist theories were learnt in modern times. The literature of Arab nationalism does not lack illustrations of these tendencies. To take an example, Sāmi Shawkat, a Director General of Education in Iraq in the 1930's, spoke as follows to the teachers of private and foreign schools in Baghdad in 1939:

'We have up to now neglected a most vital aspect of our glorious history; we have made it start at the prophetic message, and this is

[1] See also 'Islam and Arab Nationalism', in *Die Welt des Islams* (New Series), Vol. III, p. 201.

a period of less than fourteen centuries. In reality, however, the history of our illustrious Arab nation extends over thousands of years, and goes back to the time when the peoples of Europe lived in forests and over marshes, in caves and in the interstices of the rock; at that time our own ancestors used to set up banks, sculpt statues, and lay down canons and codes of law; they invented then the first principles of medicine, geometry, astronomy, the alphabet, and the numerals. On the stele of Hammurabi in the Louvre, we find inscribed the basic law given by one of our ancestors, Hammurabi; one of its clauses concerns the legal punishment of an eye for an eye and a tooth for a tooth; this took place before the Torah, the Gospels, or the Qur'ān. In the same way we find that everything makes us lift our heads high when we consider the histories of the Semitic empires formed in the Fertile Crescent—the Chaldean, the Assyrian, the African, the Pharaonic, or the Carthaginian; all these things must persuade us that the civilization of the world at the present time is based on foundations laid by our ancestors. These empires and their dependencies are all our property; they are of us and for us; we have the right to glory in them and to honour their exploits, just as we have the right to cherish and exalt the glories of Nabuchadnezzar, Hammurabi, Sargon, Rameses, Tutankhamen, in the same way that we glory and take pride in 'Abd ar-Rahmān ad-Dākhil, 'Abd al-Malik b. Marwān, Hārūn ar-Rashīd, and al-Ma'mūn.'[2]

Sāmi Shawkat went on to say that this pride in the Arab past had to be systematically inculcated: 'No other history', he ended his address by saying, 'is to be taught in an attractive and sympathetic manner except the history of the Arab nation (al-umma al-'arabiyya), and when I say the Arab nation, I mean the history of all the Semitic waves.'[3] A more detailed exposition of his views on the role of the

[2] Sāmi Shawkat, *Hādhihi ahdāfuna, man āmana biha fa huwa minna* (Baghdad, 1939), p. 11. See also Muhammad Jamīl Baiham, 'Al-'Arab qabl al-Islām wa ba'duhu fī Filastīn', in *Al-'Irfān* (Sidon, 1952), pp. 440–1. The author there maintains that the Arab nationality (*qaumiyya*) and language precede Islam in Syria.

[3] Shawkat, p. 14. Sāmi Shawkat is not the only one to make the Arabs the ancestors of all known civilizations in the Middle East; 'Alī Nāsir ad-Dīn, an ideologue of Arab nationalism, does the same, and affirms that what are commonly called peoples (*shu'ub*), such as the Assyrians or the Chaldeans, are Arab tribes and not nations or peoples. He considers that Islam, although important as an event because of the expansion it made possible, is but an accident in the larger and older being of Arabism. See his *Qadiyyat al-'Arab* (Beirut, 1946), pp. 30 n. 1, 55 n. 2, 57 n., 104 ff. Edmond Rabbath, a Syrian Christian, at one time Deputy in the Syrian Parliament, elaborates the same point of view with greater precision and a show of scientific method. See his *Unité Syrienne et Devenir Arabe* (Paris, 1937).

teaching of history in fostering nationalist pride occurs in another address to teachers of history:

'You see how history is made up according to the needs of the moment: this is formative history. History for history's sake, on the other hand, has no place in our present society; it is a matter for the specialist and for those who devote themselves to learning alone. The histories which are written with this aim in view are buried and nobody reads them. I believe that the Arab masses which are instinct with deep national feeling and with sentiments of pride and glory, must desecrate the tomb of Ibn' Khaldūn for his saying "The Arabs are a people who cannot unite, and a people without political capacity", and just for his blaspheming in such a manner.

'Science is called science because emotion plays no part in it; but emotion has a share in the arts such as poetry, painting, music, and acting, and he who has no strong emotions cannot sense the meaning of pictures or of acting. I believe that the teacher of history, if he has no feeling of love for his nation and of adoration for its great men, will not be able to teach history. In this respect, therefore, history is in the category of the arts.'[4]

It is clear that sentiments such as those expressed by Sāmi Shawkat owe much to the European doctrine of nationalism. The question is how and by what stages such a doctrine came to be acclimatized in the Muslim Arab East, and what elements in the indigenous political tradition facilitated its reception. The nature of the change in Muslim political theory may be grasped through a consideration of the gradual and successive attempts to invest with meaning and content the conception of an Arab 'nation'. And it is perhaps worth while to start with the case of a person like Sāti' al-Husri. Sāti' al-Husri, a native of Aleppo and an official of the Ottoman government, became a follower of Faisal and an ardent Arab nationalist. He has occupied various high educational posts in Iraq and Syria, having been at one time Director General of Education in Iraq and later Educational Adviser to the Arab League. In his book, *Safahāt min almādi al-qarīb*, he defines in Hegelian terms the concepts of freedom, of order, and of the state; this definition, he claims to be that which the West

---

[4] Shawkat, pp. 43–4. The expression used about Ibn' Khaldūn is *yanbush qabr*, no equivalent of which in English can fully convey the primitive violence of the action described by the Arabic expression. Sāti' al-Husri supplies the rational basis for Sāmi Shawkat's pedagogy. In his essay *A'al-'ilm li 'l-'ilm, am al-'ilm li 'l-watan?*, *Arā' wa ahādīth fī 'l-wataniyya wa 'l-qaumiyya* (Cairo, 1944), pp. 135–44, al-Husri argues that though knowledge is for the sake of knowledge, teaching is not for the sake of teaching. It is a means towards an end, namely education. Therefore it implies selectiveness, and selectiveness in the teaching of history should be inspired by the desire to inculcate the spirit of patriotism and nationalism.

universally understands. He recalls a scene from a play he had seen in Paris and in which the European officer tells his mistress, the Moroccan dancer, who tries to turn him away from his military duties by appealing to his sense of freedom:

' "Liberty for us Westerners", the officer is made to say, "is not as you Easterners understand and desire it. You understand by freedom that a person should put on his burnous, mount his horse, and ride straight into the desert wherever he may wish to go. . . . As for us, we do not demand this kind of freedom; every one of us carries round his neck ties and chains . . . ties and chains made of spiritual gold . . . of the gold of tradition, of history and of duty. . . . We love those chains with all our hearts, and we carry them with great joy. . . . We venerate those ties and chains and we indeed hold them sacred. . . ." The author comments: "The generation which spoke in these terms carried France to glory and to victory, but the generation which forsook the sanctity of the social ties, and adopted the notion of absolute freedom . . . the generation which set aside social solidarity and sanctified individualism . . . this generation . . . has carried France to these calamities . . ." [of 1940].

'I believe that this outcome must be a precious lesson to all Arab youth. . . .

'I wish it realized that freedom is not an end in itself but a means towards the higher life. . . . The national interests which may sometimes require a man to sacrifice his life, must perforce entail in some cases the sacrifice of his freedom. . . .

'He who does not sacrifice his personal freedom for the sake of his nation's freedom [*hurriyyat*[5] *ummatihi*]—when necessity requires, might lose his own freedom along with the freedom of his people [*qaum*] and of his country [*watan*]. . . .

'And he who refuses to lose himself in the nation to which he belongs, might—in some cases—find himself lost within an alien nation which might one day conquer his fatherland.

'This is why I say continuously and without hesitation:

'Patriotism [*wataniyya*] and nationalism [*qaumiyya*] before and above all . . . even above and before freedom. . . .'[6]

---

[5] *Hurriyyat* is not much used in older books, and then only in the sense of 'non-slavery'; see E. W. Lane, *Arabic-English Lexicon* (London, 1863–92, Vol. I, Part II, p. 540, and R. Dozy, *Supplément aux Dictionnaires Arabes* (Leiden, 1881), Vol. I, p. 262.

[6] *Safahāt min al-mādi al-qarīb* (Beirut, 1948), pp. 57–8, from an address, 'Haul inhiyār Fransa', given to *Nādi al-Muthanna* in Baghdad, in 1941. The author uses '*yufni*' *nafsahu* for what is rendered here 'loses himself'; he uses inverted commas for this expression no doubt because it is such a new expression in Arabic. For the state of the soul when it is 'lost' in a mystical trance, the mystical writers use the term *al fanā*.

The originality of these ideas in Arabic merits a detailed exposition. According to Sāti' al-Husri, then, the individual is not a solitary human being, but part of a society, and must, therefore, not give in to every whim and desire that seizes him. This would be not freedom, but anarchy. Real freedom consists in losing oneself in one's own nation or society, in fulfilling the dictates of tradition laid down by one's ancestors. But this freedom is not an end in itself; the true end is the attainment of a higher mode of being. The individual cannot attain this higher mode of being by himself, but must reach it in company with his society or nation. To appreciate how new such a departure is in Arabic thought, we may compare this doctrine with an exposition of the meaning of happiness which Muhammad 'Abduh attributes to Jamāl ad-Dīn al-Afghāni.

' "Undoubtedly", says al-Afghāni, "every man, by nature, desires happiness and tries to avoid, as much as he can, unhappiness; all his actions are designed towards this end. But the happiness of man is in the happiness of his community [milla] and of his countrymen [ahāli watanihi]. He is one of the members of his community, and there can be no doubt that the member grieves when the other members grieve and is hurt with what pains them, unless he is paralysed and devoid of feeling. The greatest happiness to be desired is surely the happiness of the umma and of the milla within which the person has grown. But the paths leading to this desired happiness are rough: the seeker might lose his way and find himself far from his goal and from what he sought; he might succumb to misery. The duty, therefore, of every man is to prepare himself, to look into all the possible ways, and to take the way most likely to lead him to his lofty goal." '[7]

It may seem at first glance that this passage is directly inspired by European sources. Does it not maintain, like the European organic theory of the state, that man is not alone, that his interests are not to be understood apart from the interests of the other members of his community, and would it not be legitimate to conclude from this passage that the interests of the individual are the same as the interests of the community? Muhammad 'Abduh explains this identity of interests by comparing the social unit to a body, the many different organs of which perform their functions in such a way as to benefit all of them.[8] If these extracts are examined in the light of some hadīths concerning the body politic of Islam, it would perhaps appear that they derive from a purely Islamic

---

[7] Muhammad Rashīd Ridā, Ta'rīkh al-ustādh al-imām (Cairo, 1931), Vol. II, pp. 46–7; from Muhammad 'Abduh's At-tuhfa al-adabiyya.

[8] Rashīd Ridā, op. cit., Vol. II, p. 112; from Muhammad 'Abduh's essay Hājat al-insān ila 'l-zawāj.

tradition. The comparison of the Muslims to a body is not a new one. The hadīths dealing with the body politic have been collated by Ibn Taimiyya to illustrate his definition of Muslim solidarity:

'Dans le *Sahīh*,' translates H. Laoust, 'on rapporte que le Prophète a dit: "Les croyants, par l'affection qu'ils se portent mutuellement, par leur pitié réciproque, par leur sympathie commune, ressemblent à un seul corps; lorsqu'un membre se plaint, les autres membres compatissent à sa peine par la fièvre et l'insomnie." Un croyant de même est, pour un autre croyant, comme une construction dont tous les éléments se renforcent les uns les autres.—Et le Prophète entremêla ses doigts [*tašbik*]. Dans le *Sahīh*, le Prophète dit encore: "Par celui qui a mon âme entre ses mains, nul parmi vous ne saurait être croyant tant qu'il ne souhaite pas pour son frère ce qu'il souhaite pour lui-même." ' [9]

There is great similarity between the temper of thought shown in these hadīths and in the quotations from al-Afghānī and Muhammad 'Abduh. They both lack the metaphysics necessary to the thought of Sāti' al-Husri. Jamāl ad-Dīn and Muhammad 'Abduh are inspired from the Qur'ān and the hadīth to stress the solidarity of the Muslim community, a solidarity which is one of the recognized duties incumbent on the Faithful. Consequently, in the hadīth and the teachings of the 'ulamā', even the Reformist among them such as Muhammad 'Abduh, the theories about *al-umma al-islāmiyya*, although they appear to be similar to Western organic theories of government, in fact insist on the benefits which the individual reaps in such a solidary community, and on the material services rendered by one individual to another; they do not know a collective being higher than the individuals who make up the society. Al-Fārābī had previously used the comparison of a human society to the human body, but he made a clear and fundamental distinction between the two:

'Cependant les organes du corps sont naturels et leurs dispositions sont des puissances naturelles. Tandis que les parties de la cité bien que naturelles, leurs dispositions et habitus par lesquels elles agissent pour la cité ne le sont point; ils sont (au contraire) volontaires. Toutefois, les parties de la cité sont douées de natures hiérarchisées qui font qu'un homme est utile à un homme en une chose à l'exclusion d'une autre. Mais elles ne sont point partie de la cité par leurs aptitudes naturelles uniquement, mais aussi par leurs habitus volontaires acquis, tels que les arts et les (activités) similaires. Aux puissances formant les organes naturels du corps

[9] H. Laoust, *Essai sur les Doctrines Sociales et Politiques de Taki-d-Dīn Ahmad b. Taimīya* (Cairo, 1939), p. 55, quoting from *Majmū'at al-rasā'īl al-kubra* (Cairo, 1905), Vol. I, p. 307.

correspondent dans les parties de la cité des habitus et des disposi-tions volontaires.'[10]

The conclusion to be drawn from al-Fārābī's argument is that there could have been no reference to abstract duty, i.e. duties of self-abnegation and self-sacrifice for the greater good not of the individuals in society but of the society as a whole superior to the sum of its components.

But a certain ambiguity about the correct translation of some of the terms is not altogether absent. Muhammad 'Abduh's sentence, translated above as 'every organ will function in such a way as to benefit all of them', reads in the original '*yaqūmu kull adū minhu bi-maslahat al-kull*'. It can be interpreted—depending on the attitude of the reader—as benefiting all the other members separately, or benefiting them as a whole. And indeed, Jamāl ad-Dīn had already introduced in the passage quoted above the idea that man's happiness is in the happiness of his *umma* or *milla*. The ambiguity, then, in the language of Muhammad 'Abduh, and in a passage from *Al-'urwa al-wuthqa* which will follow, lends itself to legitimate but opposite interpretations: the one in the direction of individualism, the other in that of totalitarianism. One difference, however, between Jamāl ad-Dīn's theory of happiness, and the organic theory of Sāti' al-Husri, is that the former makes everything emanate from God. In the opinion of the writers of *Al-'urwa al-wuthqa*, to perform one's task in life, just as an organ performs the function for which it is meant in the human body, helps to ensure the survival of the social unit to which one belongs, as well as to ensure for oneself a share of the general benefit; existence-in-society (*kaun al-ijtimā'*) is the gift of God to man—it makes him superior to the rest of the animal species with whom he shares the faculty of self-preservation. To preserve, then, the social unit to which one belongs has a higher purpose than merely to preserve the species; it is obedience to God who willed the superiority of man over the animals by endowing him with existence-in-society.

'Every individual', write the authors of *Al-'urwa al-wuthqa*, 'has his own particular existence. Divine providence has endowed him with the faculty of protecting his own existence and of preserving the species by reproduction. Man is like other animals in this respect. But the Divine Wisdom decided to make man superior to the other animal species by giving him another attribute and a higher kind of existence. This attribute is existence-in-society. All the individuals in society make up one structure subsumed under one name; they

---

[10] Al-Fārābī, *Idées des Habitants de la Cité Vertueuse*, translated by R. P. Jaussen, Youssef Karam, et J. Chlala (Cairo, 1949); for Arabic text, see F. Dieterici, *Alfārābī s Abhandlung 'Der Musterstaat'* (Leiden, 1895), p. 55.

are, in that structure, like different organs performing different functions, just as God has entrusted different functions to the organs of the body. Each performs his function to preserve the enveloping structure [al-bunya al-jāmiʿa], to strengthen it and to increase its chance of existence. . . . Each member is able to perform his function but cannot do more, just as the hand can fight and seize but does not see, . . . but they are all alive with one life. . . .

'Fortunate is the umma . . . every member of which works for the good of everybody [al-kull], aiming at nothing which contradicts their aim, neglecting nothing which pertains to the umma. Then they will be like a firm structure, shaken neither by tempests nor by earthquakes. It is from the strength of every one that the umma gathers its strength [wa bi-quwwat kull minhum yajtamiʿ li 'l-umma quwwa]. . . . This is the umma in which virtues have prevailed. . . .'[11]

The hadīths cited by Ibn Taimiyya refer to the attitude, compassionate and helpful, of the members of the group towards the individual. The corresponding obligation of the individual towards the group is not stressed. The one obligation can, of course, be logically argued from the other, but the question to ask is, why has this not been done earlier than the nineteenth century; is it that Western influence was essential before this step could be taken? In order to decide on such a question, the stages through which the reaction to Western thought went must be reviewed for us to appreciate the importance of the terminology used, such as watan, umma, and to determine the process of change by which they have come to mean what they now mean. In the passage from Sātiʿ al-Husri, I have translated umma as 'nation' without any hesitation or qualification, while I have retained the words milla and umma in the passage of al-Afghāni. This is because the views of al-Husrī are to be understood only in the light of romantic European thought which culminated in the growth of totalitarian doctrines and forms of government in Europe; but the Islamic tradition apparent in the extracts from Jamāl ad-Din and Muhammad ʿAbduh is still too strong to allow one to give ready-made European equivalents to the Arabic expressions which confront the reader. When the translation of European works and modes of thought became necessary for the intellectual life of the Middle East, the Arabic equivalents of the terms 'nation', 'people', 'patrie' were of course taken from the current Arabic vocabulary, and the words 'watan', 'qaum', 'milla', 'umma' were used to denote these European notions. But just as the European counterparts of these terms were themselves adaptations from past philosophical and juridical systems, these terms themselves in Arabic were full of connotations peculiar to Islam. Umma,

[11] Al-ʿurwa al-wuthqa (Beirut, 3rd ed., 1933), pp. 132–4.

a term used more than once in the Qur'ān, is generally understood to refer there to 'ethnical, linguistic, or religious bodies of people who were the object of the divine plan of salvation'.[12] The same with the word '*milla*', which, up to the end of Ottoman rule and in some cases even later, meant a religious community. B. Lewis, however, considering perhaps Turkish as well as Arabic usage, has found it necessary to translate it both as a 'creed or religious community' and as 'nation'.[13] The attempt to present the secular doctrines of Europe in Arabic was therefore bound to result in confusion so long as these specifically Islamic terms were used indiscriminately. Jamāl ad-Dīn, who is by no means free from foreign influences, makes no special reference in the above quotation to *al-umma al-islāmiyya*, but speaks in general of the *umma* and the *milla* in which one has grown. In this approach might be detected an attempt at a generalization about the place of the individual not only in the *umma*, which is the Muslim *umma*, but in all the *ummas* whether religious groupings or national ones in the European sense; it may well be that the distinction was not present in al-Afghāni's mind. There is nothing in this passage which an orthodox Muslim, whose mind is still untainted with Western ideas, would reject as new, unorthodox, or unacceptable. Even if al-Afghāni himself had been aware of such a distinction and wanted to introduce new notions, it will still remain true to say that the average Muslim reader would understand the traditional words which al-Afghāni used, in terms of the allusions they would conjure up for him; he would still not take the words '*umma*' and '*milla*' to mean anything else but *al-umma al-islāmiyya* and *millat Muhammad*. The mental interpretation of purely Western theories into Islamic concepts is therefore possible and easy; no '*tour de force*' is required when one is ignorant of the linguistic and doctrinal difficulties involved. The point may be further illustrated by examining how the sense of the word '*watan*' shifted slowly from being 'the place where one is born and resides' to that of '*patrie*', with all the contemporary political connotations of loyalty and duty attached to it. Writing in the late 1870's, Husain al-Marsafi, in his tract *Al-kilam al-thamān*,[14] defines *watan* as follows: 'In general,' he says, '*watan* means the land in which the *umma* lives, but specifically *watan* means a habitation: the soul is a *watan* because it is the habitation of the perceptions, the body is a *watan* because it is the habitation of the soul, clothes are a *watan* because

[12] R. Paret, article 'UMMA' in *Encyclopaedia of Islam*.
[13] B. Lewis, *A Handbook of Diplomatic Arabic* (London, 1947), p. 59.
[14] Husain al-Marsafi, *Al-kilam al-thamān* (Cairo, 1881), p. 16. In spite of its promising title and, for that period, unusual approach, the tract remains an interesting curiosity and no more.

they are the habitation of the body, the house, the street, the town, the country, the earth, the world, are all *watans* because they are habitations.' Even as late as the Reformists, the word '*watan*' had a limited, specific, well-understood meaning, and neither signified nor in any way implied a mystic 'genetic-cultural' boundary, as for instance, Charles Malik, as will be seen, would like to give it today. This is how Muhammad 'Abduh defined the concept of *watan*:

'Linguistically, *watan* means, without exception, the place where the person lives; it is synonymous with the word "*sakan*": to say "*istautana al-qaum hādhihi al-ard wa tawattanūha*" is the same as saying "they have made it their abode". The word as used by those who study politics [*ahl as-siyāsa*] means the place after which you are called, where your right is safeguarded, and the claim of which on you is known, where you are secure in yourself, your kin, and your possessions. It has been said: "There is no *watan* without freedom." La Bruyère, the French philosopher, said: "There is no *watan*, properly speaking, compatible with tyranny, but only private interests, personal glorification, and exalted places."[15] *Watan* was defined by the ancient Romans as the place where the person has rights and political duties.

'This latter Roman definition does not contradict the saying that there is no *watan* without freedom. They are indeed identical. Freedom is the right to fulfil the known duty, and if it does not exist there can be no *watan*, since there are no rights. When political duties exist, then they imply the existence of both right and duty, which are the motto of all the *watans* to which lives and possessions are sacrificed, and which are put before kin and friends; in generous souls, the love of *watan* reaches the height of adoration and of passion.

'But the abode where the dweller has no rights, and where he is secure neither in his life nor in his possessions, is, in short, the resort of the powerless, and the abode of him who can find no way to another; if it grows bigger, there is no ease, and if smaller, then life in it cannot become worse. La Bruyère, mentioned above, said: "What is it to me that my *watan* be large and great, if I am sad and lowly in it, living in humility and misery, a prisoner and afraid?"[16]

---

[15] 'Il n y a point de patrie dans le despotisme; d'autres choses y suppléent: l'intérêt, la gloire, le service du prince.' Jean de la Bruyère, *Caractères*, ed. Nelson (Paris, 1954), p. 315: 'Du Souverain ou de la République.'

[16] '. . . Que me servirait, en un mot, comme à tout le peuple, que le prince fût heureux et comblé de gloire par lui-même et par les siens, que ma patrie fût puissante et formidable si, triste et inquiet, j'y vivais dans l'oppression ou dans l'indigence; si, à couvert des courses de l'ennemi, je me trouvais exposé dans les places ou dans les rues d'une ville au fer d'un assassin, et que je craignisse moins, dans l'horreur de la nuit d'être pillé ou massacré dans d'épaisses forêts que dans ses carrefours . . .'—*ibid.*, p. 331, *loc. cit.*

But to belong to a certain *watan* means that a connection links the *watan* to the person who dwells in it, a connection based on personal honour; so that he will be jealous for it and will defend it as he defends his father after whom he is called, even if he is a bad-tempered and strict father. This is why it has been said that the relational ending "i" in *Misri, Inglīzi, Fransāwi*, is of a kind which inspires regard and jealousy in the heart of the Egyptian for Egypt, of the Frenchman for France, and of the Englishman for England. This has been denied by some people, but this was no doubt due either to misunderstanding or to unclear exposition.

'The conclusion of the matter is that there are three things in a *watan* which compel love, solicitude, and vigilance for it. They are as follows: First, *watan* is the abode where there is food, protection, kin, and children; Second, it is the place of rights and duties, which are the focal points of political life and the importance of which is obvious; Third, it is the place with which one is associated and through which man is exalted and honoured, or cast down and humbled; and this is purely spiritual.'[17]

In Muhammad 'Abduh's doctrine, then, a man's *watan* is the place where he feels his security preserved and to which, therefore, he owes certain duties. The criterion is thus clear, and in the discretion of the individual to apply. The following passages from Sāmi Shawkat are equally clear in their diametrical opposition:

'The foreigner, according to the definition of the *futuwwa* of Iraq,' he writes, 'is not he who does not possess an Iraqi nationality card; but, in our creed, the foreigner is he who does not feel as we do and does not hold sacred the dignity of Iraqi unity even though he possessed ninety such cards and even though our cemeteries be filled with the bones of his ancestors for thousands of years. The foreigner for us is he who intrigues . . . against Arab unity; and he is not only a foreigner to us in creed, spirit, and belief, but is also our sworn enemy.'[18] 'We have, like all other nations,' he goes on to say, 'enemies; the enemy of the nation [*umma*], like the enemy of the family, is of two types: the internal and the external. Usually the internal enemy is more harmful and destructive than the external one. No nation can have a real renaissance unless she first of all defeats this internal enemy, uproots him completely from the bedrock of her foundations. This internal foe consists of those persons

---

[17] 'Al-hayāt as-siyāsiyya,' in Rashīd Ridā, *Ta'rīkh* . . ., Vol. II, pp. 194–5. This definition had been previously given by Adīb Ishāq (1856–95) in his essay 'Al-hayāt as-siyāsiyya' in *Ad-durar*, edited by 'Auni Ishāq (Beirut, 1909), pp. 453–4. This does not detract from the historical value of the argument; the fact that Muhammad 'Abduh gave Adīb Ishāq's definition verbatim goes to show how much he must have been impressed with it.

[18] Shawkat, pp. 5–6.

or groups who, both at school and at home, come to feel like strangers in the midst of the being of the state, and feel that the majesty and loftiness of the state are harmful to their interests and diminish their power and position, and are humiliating to themselves. As the strength of such persons or groups is not sufficient to make them stand up against their state and declare their enmity openly, they strive in secret, stretching their hands under cover of the dark, to the external enemy, shaking hands with him and conspiring to become his agent, while their heart is full of envy, anger, and vengeance. Thus is the pact made between the external enemy and the internal one.'[19]

Great indeed is the gulf between the ruthlessness of these passages and the benevolence of Muhammad 'Abduh's attempt at a definition of the *watan*. The last two passages assume many things: the existence of a nation in the Western sense of the word, the unity of the nation and the state, and that the nation is superior to the individual. The final conclusion is that all criticism, whether voiced or otherwise, constitutes disloyalty, and that such disloyalty deserves the most systematic and scientific method of elimination. Muhammad 'Abduh, on the other hand, is, in fact, justifying the absence of loyalty for one's *watan* from the moment that the *watan* ceases to safeguard certain minimum rights. The *watan* changes from a place where one feels most secure, to an omnipotent force which must crush the individual if it suspects him of withholding any part of his personality from its control and dominion.

The dictionaries will shed further light on the evolution of the word '*watan*'. In Butrus al-Bustāni's *Muhīt al-Muhīt*, *watan* is defined as the place where a person dwells, irrespective of whether he was born in it or not. Al-Bustāni enumerates: *al-watan al-aslī*, which is, according to the law, the birthplace of a man, the place where he grew and the town where he dwells, which is also called *watan al-fitra wa 'l-qarār* or *al-ahli*; *watan al-iqāma* or *al-watan al-musta'ār* or *al-hadīth* or *watan as-safar* is the place where one decides to stay for fifteen days or more without taking it as a personal habitation.[20] Dozy, who reviewed all available material, does not list the word '*wataniyya*', although *watani* does appear as 'provincial'.[21] Ellious Bocthor, in his French-Arabic dictionary, on the other hand, has recourse to a paraphrase to express what would now be unhesitatingly termed *wataniyya*. He gives:

'Patrie: pays, État où l'on est né, *watan, ard mīlād, bilād, maulid*; l'amour de la patrie: *hubb, mu'izzat al-watan.*

[19] *ibid.*, p. 36.
[20] *Muhīt al-Muhīt* (Beirut, 1867), Vol. II, p. 2264.
[21] Dozy, Vol. II, p. 820; see the preface on material used.

'Patriote: qui aime sa patrie par-dessus tout, *kathīr al-muʿizza li-watanihi.*

'Patriotisme: caractère du patriote, *muʿizzat al-watan.*

'Nation: he defines as "habitants d'un même pays", *tāʾifa, milla.*

'National is *yakhussu at-tāʾifa*; and Garde Nationale requires a circumlocution, *ghafar ahl al-bilād li-bilādihim.*'[22]

Al-Bustāni mentions the hadīth '*Hubb al-watan min al-īmān*', but Bocthor wavers between *hubb* and *muʿizzat al-watan* when he has to translate the European notion of patriotism. The difficulty of translating it was a real one. The relation between a person and his *watan* was not always clear-cut in Arabic, and the notion of having duties towards it was a late accretion. Bichr Farès has a useful note on the question: 'Le *hima* se distingue du *watan*; celui-ci, à notre sens, désigne la patrie du point de vue sentimental, celui-là du point de vue guerrier.'[23] The word '*watan*' is used in a purely descriptive way in this passage of Rashīd Ridā: 'I have two *watans* in this world: the *watan* of origin and upbringing which is Syria . . . and the *watan* of work which is Egypt where I have lived for eleven years. . . .'[24] And here is another use of the word '*watanī*' in the sense of local or native: '. . . that the merchants send every year wool worth millions of pounds to London or Marseilles, and after this wool is woven there, it is sent back and these merchants sell it at a very high price to the local people (*al-wataniyyīn*).'[25]

The synthesis between Islam and Western political thought is possible without immediately upsetting the balance of the Muslim tradition. The foreign character of many political theories disappears through the use of words with definite Islamic connotations. One transition at least is thus smoothly made. The necessity for understanding the success of Europe with which the Muslim thinkers found themselves confronted was a real one. They were greatly concerned with the reason of their own decline, and with the obvious superiority and prosperity of Europe. In order to fathom the reasons for the success of Europe, European works had to be read and translated. They would be pored over and minutely examined in the hope that, maybe, they would be efficient in dispelling the apathy of Islam. Of course, these works had to be translated, whether mentally or literally, into the existing language, Arabic, as it had developed during many centuries of theological and philo-

[22] Ellious Bocthor, *Dictionnaire Français-Arabe, revue et augmenté par A. Caussin de Perceval*, 4th ed. (Paris, 1869), pp. 58 and 527.

[23] Bichr Farès, *L'Honneur chez les Arabes avant l'Islam* (Paris, 1932), p. 66 n. 4.

[24] *Al-Manār*, XI, 1326/Jan. 1909, p. 904.

[25] Hāfid 'Abd ar-Rahmān al-Hindi, 'Baghdād wa 'l-tijāra' in *Al-Manār*, I. 1316/Jan. 1899, p. 860.

sophical studies. This was done without difficulty, because the translators were not themselves always aware how different were the traditions of the learning which they admired and attempted to transmit
to their fellow Easterners. They tried to prove that what they found
excellent in the West did not contradict the tenets of Islam, but was
a mere extension and development of notions already known among
them. It becomes, especially after a process of translation, as will be
seen below, not too difficult to superimpose on the concept of the
umma in Islam an alien conception of nationhood, since the conception of the *umma*, as a body different from and superior to every
other form of society, already existed in Islam. Such a procedure
would not cause a revolution in the thought of the Muslim intellectuals. In the nineteenth century the nature of the *umma* was very
much discussed, especially because the Muslims were aware of their
weakness and wished to study the causes of that weakness in order
to revive the *umma* in all its strength, glory, and cohesion, and make
it such as it had always been ideally conceived in Islam. The Europe
which the East knew then was influenced both by utilitarianism and
by a kind of liberalism based on German idealist philosophy which
superseded utilitarianism little by little, and which inclined to a
Romantic belief in self-determination. It may be asked whether,
given the time and conditions under which the Arabic revival was
taking place, it could have been different from what it was. The
West was there and account had to be taken of it. It could evoke
admiration or hostility, but not the superior indifference which was
customary in Islam till then. Jamāl ad-Dīn is a prominent instance
of the preoccupation of the most confirmed anti-European with
European ideas.

The key notion in al-Husri's definition of freedom is that of
'society': the individual is not a solitary human being, he is part of
a society, a nation. This conception of man as a person unable to
exist by himself as a solitary being is not new in Islam. Al-Fārābī
and Ibn Khaldūn had already developed the Greek idea that man
is a 'political' animal. Al-Fārābī, in *al-Madīna al-fādila*, discusses
the organization of the perfect city, as first pictured by Plato; Ibn
Khaldūn's axiom '*al-insān madanī bi 'l-tab*' is at the basis of his
doctrine that social co-operation is made necessary by man's need
to live in a society. This condition of man has become the accepted
and obvious assumption for all discussion on the nature of government in Islam. Such a starting-point makes possible the acceptance
of Sāti' al-Husri's premise that a man is aware of his place in his
society or nation through his feeling of solidarity and identification
with his society and its past. 'Abd al-Rahmān al-Kawākibi, a Janus
figure in modern Arabic political thought, makes this statement as

well: 'Free man is a complete master of himself and is completely owned by his *qaum*.'[26] But there is a slight, though significant, difference between the traditional account of the relation of man to his society and that of al-Husri. Traditionally, a Muslim has to be solidary with the *umma* because the Qur'ān dictates it and Islam expects it. But Sāti' al-Husri bases his doctrine on individual feelings. It is the individual who feels the call of tradition, it is he who feels that he must answer it, it is he who does not feel fulfilment and total realization if he does not lose himself in his nation. Fichte and not the Qur'ān inspires Sāti' al-Husri. Once it is established that man must live in society, there is only one step from the enumeration of the benefits he reaps to the description of the duties he has to perform. Muhammad 'Abduh takes this step: rights and duties become the same in his definition of the term *'watan'* given above. *Watan*, the place where one feels most secure, is also the place where one has the right to perform one's duty towards it. Muhammad 'Abduh, striving in his gentle and moderate way to assemble together a workable theory of the state, borrows from the same sources which al-Husri was later exclusively to draw upon.

Another concept which would make the definition of Sāti' al-Husri acceptable to the average Muslim, is that of the *umma* in Islam as a compact body of all the Muslims, one of whose primary duties is the Holy War. The conception of the *umma* in modern Arabic has become almost inseparable from the notion of nationalism, a secular notion imported from the West. But just as the passages from the Qur'ān where the word occurs are so varied that it is difficult to define its meaning more rigidly than R. Paret has done, so are the uses of the word at the turn of the century. Even Rashīd Ridā, who spent forty years preaching the unity of the Muslim *umma*, uses the word in the sense of 'nation' or 'people', a sense devoid of all religious content: 'The Turks are a warrior nation [*umma harbiyya*] but they were not more valiant than the Arabs. . . .'[27] And the word was indeed used in the same sense in the classical period of Arabic.[28] When European books were being read and translated for the first time in Arabic, it would have been very difficult to render, without being pedantic, the secular concept of nationhood by any words other than *milla* or *umma*. *Milla*, although it did lend itself to some form of secular interpretation,

---

[26] *Tabā'i' al-istibdād wa masāri' al-isti'bād* (Cairo, Ma'arif Press ed., n.d.), p. 156. The work was first published in 1900–1. See *Oriente Moderno*, XXXIV, 321; XXXV, 132.

[27] 'At-Turk wa 'l-'Arab', in *Al-Manār*, III, 1318/May 1900, p. 172.

[28] See for instance Abu 'l-Hayyān al-Tauhīdi, *Kitāb al-imtā' wa 'l-mu'ānasa*, eds. Ahmad Amīn and Ahmad az-Zain (Cairo, 1939), Vol. I, pp. 70 ff., for a classical essay on the superiority of the Arab *umma* over the Persian *umma*.

must have been still too much connected in people's minds with the idea of a religious community within the much larger and more powerful *umma*, especially as long as the official adoption of the term by the Ottoman government in 1839, to denote the Jewish and Christian communities of the Empire, remained in force till 1908.[29] These communities did of course have some features of nationhood, for they had their own autonomy inside the Muslim community. The word '*umma*', however, denoted a much larger entity than the word '*milla*'. Its meaning fluctuated in the early period of Islam until the Muslim conquest gave it an immutable significance. Muhammad first regarded the people of Mecca as a closed *umma*, and when he emigrated to Medina, he considered the people of Medina —including the Jews—to form one *umma*; but as time went on the *umma* came to consist more and more of the believers. When he finally broke with the People of the Book, he resumed his original idea of an *umma* embracing the community of the Arabs, but of the Arabs who were Muslim. With the conquests after his death the *umma* came to include all the Muslims, whether Arab or not.[30] Al-Kawākibi defines *umma* as follows: 'An *umma* is the sum of the individuals with a common ancestry or *watan*, language, or religion, just as a building is a collection of stones. When one member of the *umma* progresses or degenerates, the totality of that *umma* will be affected, just as a flea, standing on the side of a great ship, will weigh it down and make it lean sideways, although the movement cannot be felt by the senses.'[31] The author of this definition has made more than one step to meeting Western secularism, and indeed al-Kawākibi worked out an almost racial theory of nationality, while remaining an orthodox Muslim; the result was pan-Arabism. In any case, racialism is not wholly absent from the history of Islam—the *Shu'ūbiyya* movement is proof enough. The definition of *umma* given by al-Kawākibi, therefore, permits a purely secular concept to replace the traditional one; and such a secular concept is now taken for granted by many writers:

'After all, what is this *umma*?' asks Nicola Ziyāda, 'and what is *qaumiyya*? *Qaumiyya* in essence and origin is a feeling, and the *umma* is the result of this feeling. It is the result of the feeling of the individuals and their belief that the *umma* exists. But such a feeling cannot be, except when the common characteristics obtain, those characteristics that enable the members to realize that they are different from others. These common characteristics obtain when people live in one spot of the earth, and enjoy the goods of this spot in an organized community. This goes together with a general philosophy of life, based on history, custom, experience, thought, language, and literature, distilled from the heart of their past and present life, outlining for them their future aims and indicating the plan of their lives.'[32]

It may be remarked here that the word generally used now to denote nationalism is *qaumiyya*. Sāmi Shawkat had already adopted this word in the early 1930's. 'We have to be firm in our belief,' he says, 'that our age is the age of nationalities [*al-qaumiyāt*], not the age of religions.' He again says: 'We hold sacred all the divinely inspired religions; this is our motto; we shall not allow anyone to lay sacrilegious hands on them. But of the worldly creeds, we will only adopt the national creed [*al-mabda' al-qaumi*], without which nations cannot be formed, nor the foundations of states laid.'[33] The distinction made by Bishr Farès between *hima* and *watan* may give the clue to the preference shown to the word '*qaumiyya*' over the word '*wataniyya*'. *Wataniyya*, by derivation, attaches a person to his dwelling-place, an attachment which was sentimental rather than implying duties of war and defence. *Qaumiyya*, on the other hand, is derived from the word '*qaum*', the unit—in Bedouin usage—to which one belongs and to which allegiance is owed, especially in time of war; the *qaum* usually comprised only the male members of the group. A man attached to a *qaum* owed them assistance when they were engaged on a razzia or in defending themselves.[34] *Qaumiyya*, therefore, is a word which defines the position of a man in relation to the other members of his group, rather than in relation to his place of birth or of residence.

'The belief of the members of one tribe [*qabīla*]', writes Nicola Ziyāda, 'in one common origin or ancestor tied them to each other, and they felt that they were all one *qaum* affected equally by prosperity or misery. Therefore, when a member meets with calamity or misfortune he goes to his *qaum* asking for their help, and crying out to them. And as a member of a tribe [*qabīl*] he can expect every individual in the tribe to ward off evil from him, against whoever means him ill. . . .

'This feeling which we notice in the relationship between the members among themselves on the one hand, and between the

[32] Nicola Ziyāda, *Al-'urūba fī mīzān al-qaumiyya* (Beirut, 1950), pp. 66–7. This book is a second edition of his previous book, *Al-qaumiyya wa 'l-'urūba*.

[33] Shawkat, pp. 59 and 13.

[34] *Muhīt al-Muhīt*. Vol. II, pp. 1777–8; Dozy, art. '*Qaum*', Vol. II, pp. 424–5; Bichr Farès, p. 47; A. J. Wensinck, art. 'Kaum' in *Encyclopaedia of Islam*, where the uses of the word in the Qur'ān are given. This use of word '*qaum*' has passed into French in the North African 'goum' and 'goumiers'; see A. Cour, art. 'Goum' in *Encyclopaedia of Islam*.

individual and his *qaum*, is what may be called *qaumiyya*. It is therefore clear that the idea of *qaumiyya* is as old as human society; that
this form of relationship used to be called *'asabiyya* does not detract
from its values.'[35]

From Nicola Ziyāda's analysis, it must appear that *qaumiyya* is,
on the whole, a more emphatic term than *wataniyya*. The contributors to the periodical *Al-Abhāth*, published at the American University of Beirut, use both terms equally frequently but, it seems,
with a vague difference in emphasis. For instance, in the article
entitled 'Ta'rīb al-'Arab', where the author argues that the arabization of the Arabs is far from complete, he puts forward a plan which
would result in 'an intellectual and spiritual *wataniyya*, different
from this dry *wataniyya* taking roots in us. We are *wataniyyūn* geographically not intellectually, and great is the distance between the
two kinds of *wataniyya*.'[36] But an article of a general nature on
national education, which assumes the full existence of a nation
(*umma*), has for title 'At-tarbiya al-qaumiyya'.[37] Are we to infer,
then, that *qaumiyya* is a more complete and exacting form of
wataniyya? It has to be guessed, from a general knowledge of the
subject, whether the words are being used interchangeably in a
particular context or whether the author attaches a specific meaning
to each of them. Al-Husri gives his reasons for using the word
'qaumiyya':

'One of our Egyptian brethren . . .', he writes, 'considered the
question from the purely legal and canonical standpoint, and his
concern was therefore only with the state [*ad-daula*] and not with
the nation [*umma*].

'He spoke about nationality [*jinsiyya*] and mentioned the French
word "nationalité", saying: "There is an Egyptian 'nationalité'
[*jinsiyya*], and there is an Iraqi 'nationalité' . . . but there is no Arab
'nationalité'. . . ."'

'In this connection, I wish to draw attention to an important
truth: the word "nationalité" has two different meanings in French,
the legal, which denotes that a person belongs to a certain state, and
the social, which denotes that a person belongs to a certain nation
[*umma*] even though this nation does not form a state.

'I call to witness the dictionary of philosophical terms published
by the French Philosophical Society. Look up the word "nationalité"
in this dictionary. You will find that Professor Lalande distinguished
clearly between the two meanings. He mentioned the first meaning

[35] Nicola Ziyāda, pp. 9–10.
[36] Ishāq Mūsa al-Husaini, in *Al-Abhāth*, Vol. III, No. 1, March, 1950, pp.
26–41.
[37] Habīb Kūrāni, *ibid.*, Vol. III, No. 3, June 1950, pp. 228–35.

under the heading (A) and quoted many examples of that use, and he mentioned the second one under the letter (B) and again quoted other examples of its use in this latter sense.

'Thus we have before us a word which means two different things, but the French found no objection to expressing these two meanings by one word.

'As for the Germans, they were, in this question, deeper in thought and truer in expression than the French: they express each of these meanings by a special word absolutely different from the other. They express the legal meaning that I have mentioned above by a word similar to the French word, "Nationalität", but they express the second meaning—the social one I have mentioned—by quite a different word, "Wolkstum" [sic].'

Al-Husri goes on to say that because the French belonged to one national state for many centuries, they found no objection to expressing these two senses by one word, but the Germans, who had been, until recently, divided into many states, found it necessary to distinguish between the two meanings, the legal one and the social one. Al-Husri goes on to apply this analysis to Arab conditions:

'Since the legal sense', he points out, 'is fixed by the existing laws by the word "*jinsiyya*" in Egypt, and the word "*tābiʿiyya*" or "*raʿawiyya*" in other Arab countries . . . we have to agree to use another word to express the social meaning of the word "nationalité".

'I have been in the habit—and so have many of the Arab writers and thinkers—of using the word "*qaumiyya*" to denote this latter sense.'[38]

The word '*qaumiyya*' therefore denotes the nationhood of a nation whether or not it has achieved its unity and independence. The following passage is a good illustration:

'It would follow', argues ʿAli Nāsir ad-Dīn, 'that . . . the Syrians, being Syrian in relation to the land, would not be Arab!

'This is a scientific, historical, and social mistake, and there would not be today a single nation on the face of the earth which could be correctly called a nation. Then each of the Arab countries [*kull qutr min al-aqtār al-ʿarabiyya*] would be a nation independent by itself, with a geographical "territorial" nationality particular to itself. But it would be a counterfeit nation. And there would not remain in the world an Arab nation [*umma*], nor an Arab nationality [*qaumiyya*] . . . because there is no land called *ʿArab*, so that we may be able to say " *ʿArabi*" in relation to this land.'[39]

A curious and premonitory instance of the use of the word '*qaum*'

[38] Sāti' al-Husri, *Arā' wa ahādīth fī 'l-qaumiyya al-ʿarabiyya* (Cairo, 1951), pp. 22–4.

[39] *Qadiyyat al-ʿarab* (Beirut, 1946), pp. 30–1.

is recorded by Rashīd Ridā. Some time before the First World War, the editor of a Beirut newspaper, *Al-Mufīd*, was prosecuted by the Ottoman authorities for publishing a poem in which the expression '*Yā qaum*' appeared. The editor protested that this was merely a rhetorical expression of no political significance, and that the word in Arabic meant a group of people. But the tribunal contended 'that the word *qaum* meant the Arab race ['*unsur al-'arab*], and its mention promoted disunion among the Ottoman races [*al-'anāsir al-'uthmāniyya*], and this, because the Turks use the word "*qaum*" in the sense of *jins*, or, as some people would say, '*unsur*'.[40] The word '*wataniyya*', used by the pioneers of Egyptian nationalism,[41] would not be equally suitable to use, as it might imply a regional nationalism, Egyptian or Iraqi for instance. The distinction is made even clearer by Jalāl al-Urfali, who speaks about *al-wataniyya al-'irāqiyya* and *al-qaumiyya al-'arabiyya* as complementary forces working to achieve what he calls 'the national aims' (*al-ghāyāt al-qaumiyya*) which are common to all the Arab countries, namely, the realization of the desired Arab unity.[42] *Wataniyya*, as the pan-Arabs use the word, would probably be reserved either to a sentimental attachment to one's homeland—much in the old sense of *hubb al-watan min al-īmān* [43]—or to regional nationalism,[44] or very often to mere

---

[40] *Al-Manār*, XVII, 1332/June 1914, p. 535.

[41] See Muhammad 'Atiyya al-Ibrāshi, *Abtāl ash-sharq* (Cairo, 1947), where the author gives extracts from the speeches of Muhammad Farīd and Sa'd Zaghlūl, and where the word '*wataniyya*' is the only current one; see especially pp. 70–1, 75, 78, 107, 152 ff.; for the speeches of Mustafa Kāmil, see 'Abd al-Rahmān al-Rāfi'i, *Mustafa Kāmil bā'ith al-haraka al-wataniyya* (Cairo, 1939).

[42] Jalāl al-Urfali, *Ad-dibl ūmāsiyya al-'irāqiyya wa 'l-ittihād al-'arabi* (Baghdad, 1944), Vol. I, pp. 4 and 326.

[43] Rifā'a Rāfi' at-Tahtāwi defines the notion of *hubb al-watan* as follows: '*Hubb al-watan min al-īmān*. It is the nature of the freeborn to yearn for their *watan* (birthplace); a man always loves his birthplace; his place of origin is familiar and desirable; that where you live claims the respect due to a birthplace just as your mother may claim her due for having sustained you. . . . Even though Cairo has bestowed her benefits on me and raised me above my peers in knowledge . . . and I cherish it greatly, having received its benefits and lived forty years in it, I still yearn for my particular *watan*, am always on the look-out for its happy news, and will not hold anything equal to Tahta. . . .' Quoted by 'Abd al-Latīf Hamza, *Adab al-maqāla as-sahafiyya fī Misr*, Vol. I (Cairo, 1950), pp. 140–1. This is the traditional approach in Arabic literature, as may be seen from an extract of al-Jāhiz's *Asās al-balāgha*, given in *Al-Manār*, XVII, 1333/April 1915, pp. 220–6. Al-Tahtāwi uses some of al-Jahiz's expressions.

[44] It is in this sense that Sāti' al-Husri uses it, *Arā' wa ahādīth fī 'l-qaumiyya al-'arabiyya*, pp. 65–6; see also J. Heyworth-Dunne, *Religious and Political Trends in Modern Egypt* (Washington, 1950), pp. 64–5, where the author mentions a similar distinction made by Hasan al-Banna between *wataniyya* and *qaumiyya*, and lists the different kinds of *wataniyya* and *qaumiyya* defined by al-Banna.

description as in *mashrūb watani* or *aqmisha wataniyya*. The conception of *qaumiyya*, therefore, starts from the assumption that there
exists a nation [*umma*]. Since the writers who use the term are
mainly exponents of pan-Arabism, their assumption is the existence
of an Arab nation.[45] The efforts to prove the existence of such a
nation and to define the terms 'Arab' and 'nation' are so profuse in
Arabic publications at present that it is difficult to decide what
passages to choose for the sake of illustration and which to leave
out.[46] It would perhaps be least confusing to confine the discussion
to the books dealt with so far, as they are the most interesting of
their kind.

Qaumiyya implies a predetermined scheme of things and requires
conformity. It is not within the choice of a person to be Arab in the
'social' sense that Sāti' al-Husri gives to the word.

'Some people asked me,' he writes, "You say that every person
who belongs to one of these peoples [the speakers of the *dād*] is an
Arab, but suppose he does not wish to be an Arab? suppose he does
not acknowledge himself as an Arab? that he does not care for
Arabism ['*urūba*], but despises it? how can we consider him an
Arab in such a case? Is it not better to say: 'The Arab is he who
desires to be an Arab'? or at least should we not make this desire
one of the conditions of being an Arab?"

'As for myself, before I answer these questions, I want to shift the
discussion from the question of Arab nationhood [*qaumiyya*] generally, to that of Egyptian nationality [*jinsiyya*] in particular. And
I ask myself: "When we attempt, for instance, to define this Egyptian
nationality, do we demand those conditions and ask those questions?"

'And does it occur to any of us to say: "A person is not considered
Egyptian unless he himself wants to be Egyptian, unless he acknowledges that he is such, and is attached to his Egyptian nationality"?

[45] But the sophisticated Charles Mālik sees a problem: 'The word "Arab",'
he writes, 'denotes neither a race nor a religion. For the most part its connotation
today is "Arabic-speaking". The overwhelming majority of the Arabic-speaking
peoples (or Arabs) are Moslem, just as the overwhelming majority of Moslems
are non-Arabs: so that the two terms do not coincide. Although there are vast
diversities of culture among them, the Arabs have certain general traits in common. They also have common aspirations. Whether all Arabic-speaking peoples
constitute a single nation depends first on the meaning of the term "constitute"
and second on the "Arab" adaptation of the European concept of "nation".
All this of course is independent of the question whether they should constitute
a nation.'—'The Near East: the Search for Truth', in *Foreign Affairs*, January,
1952, p. 232.
[46] Nicola Ziyāda, 'Recent Arabic Literature on Arabism', in *Middle East
Journal*, Autumn, 1952, pp. 468–73, gives some idea of the amount of literature
being written on the subject.

'You all know that the son of the Egyptian is considered Egyptian whether he likes it or not, whether he cherishes his Egyptian nationality or not. He is an Egyptian by custom and law. But if he does not know or does not acknowledge it, this may be because he is ignorant and needs educating; because he is unaware and needs to be wakened up; or because he is a traitor and deserves to be punished.

'It is the same with Arab nationhood [*qaumiyya*]. Every Arabic-speaking people is an Arab people, and every one who belongs to the Arab peoples is an Arab. But should he not know that himself . . . or should he not cherish Arabism [*al-'urūba*] . . . then we must find out the reasons that make him adopt such a stand.

'It may be due to ignorance, in which case it is our duty to teach him the truth . . . or it may be due to unawareness or credulity, and we must awaken him and direct him to the right path. And if it is due to excessive selfishness, then we must try to put a stop to his selfishness. But, in any case, whatever the reason, we may not say: "He is not an Arab, since he does not want to be an Arab, or because he is ashamed of Arabism." . . . He is an Arab whether he desires it or not, whether he recognizes the fact in the present or not. . . . He is an Arab . . . ignorant or unaware . . . ungrateful or treacherous. But he is in any case an Arab, an Arab who has lost his consciousness and his feelings, and probably has at the same time lost his conscience.'[47]

This is a view directly opposed to that expressed by Muhammad 'Abduh. A man's feeling towards his nation does not depend on the manner in which his rights are safeguarded and his security protected within the nation; this feeling is decreed, predetermined, and inevitable. Not to feel that one belongs to the 'Arab nation' is treason, which should be punished severely. Sāmi Shawkat's short way with such traitors is complete and systematic liquidation.

Another step in the transition of nationalist doctrine can be appreciated by examining the definition of the word 'Egyptian' given by Ahmad Lutfi as-Sayyid. This definition is different in tone from the writings of both Muhammad 'Abduh and Sāti' al-Husri: it assumes a secular theory of the state but does not prohibit dissent.

'One of our great thinkers was asked . . .', Lutfi as-Sayyid writes, ' "What is an Egyptian?" He answered: "The Egyptian is he who knows no other *watan* beside Egypt. But he who has two *watans*, who

---

[47] Sāti' al-Husri, *Arā' wa ahādīth fī 'l-qaumiyya al-'arabiyya*, pp. 44–5. Note how al-Husri uses here the 'legal' argument which he rejected above. The founder of *Nādi al-ittihād al-'arabi*, founded in Baghdad, in 1943, comments on a proviso in the statutes of the club, pledging the club to oppose *iqlīmiyya*, as follows: 'As Iraq is made up of many minorities, and some of these minorities are not inclined to join the Arab union which Iraq, both government and people, desire, it is our duty to combat this trend which is contrary to the general principles of Arabism.' Al-Urfali, Vol. I, p. 316 n. 1.

lives in Egypt and takes for himself another *watan* for safety, he is far from being an Egyptian in the full sense of the word."

'The *Salaf* used to say that the land of Islam is the *watan* of all the Muslims. This is an imperialistic rule ; one that is applied by every nation desiring continually to enlarge its possessions and increase its influence over neighbouring countries. It is a rule which fits in easily with the designs of a strong element which after conquering a country in the name of religion, wants to endow all the subjects of its empire with all national rights, so that the different races in the conquered countries become united ; do not forsake their allegiance or become discontented, with the higher authority, or look forward to the enjoyment of independence and self-government. But now that the Eastern countries have become the target of Western imperialism, and their own imperialist ambitions have been arrested, they are on the defensive rather than the offensive, and they seek only to preserve their identity and the existence of their national being. Independence becomes, therefore, the ambition of every Eastern nation.

'So that now, conditions being what they are, this rule is not compatible with the actual situation of the Muslim nations and their ambitions. There is no other alternative but to replace it by the one faith consonant with the ambition of every Eastern nation, that has a defined *watan*. And that faith is the faith of nationalism [*wataniyya*].

'We must therefore declare that the Egyptians are the original people of this Egyptian land, as well as every Ottoman who has lived in Egypt as a resident, and who has adopted it as his *watan* exclusive of other Ottoman *watans*. This faith is not new, it has long been the doctrine of Egyptian law.'[48]

It may be that the word for nationalism has become *qaumiyya* rather than *wataniyya* because of the change in influence which has come over the Middle East. The Egyptian nationalists who were active at the turn of the century had all come under French influence, and under the spell of the French Revolution; they had mostly received their education in France and to some extent in England where liberal and positivist creeds were the rule. But the intellectual influences to which the Middle East was being subjected gradually changed as the nineteenth century turned into the twentieth. The utilitarian and positivist philosophy which one generation of thinkers had imbibed from Europe came gradually to be replaced by a romantic creed, the chief feature of which was a belief in the sacredness of the national personality and in the necessity of its self-realization. There is perhaps more than one reason why this change

[48] Ahmad Lutfi as-Sayyid, *Ta'ammulāt* (Cairo, 1946), pp. 68–9; the piece quoted above first appeared in *Al-Jarīda* of January 16, 1913.

of attitude did not manifest itself first in Egypt, but in the countries that used to form Turkey-in-Asia. For there is no national problem in Egypt; it is a reasonably homogeneous country. The case is otherwise with the Fertile Crescent; and the very heterogeneity of the area may explain the extremes to which nationalist doctrines have run there. Another reason may perhaps lie in the disturbed political conditions of the Ottoman Empire towards the end of 'Abd al-Hamid's reign and afterwards, when the Young Turks acquired power. Clandestine associations, plots, and assassinations do not lead to moderation in political thinking.

Qaumiyya makes a deeper impression. It implies that *qaum* is bigger, better, and holier than the sum of its components. It has therefore a 'mystical' hold over the individual. The individual loses himself mystically in the *qaum*, as in the passage in al-Husri where he defines liberty, or in the following passage from Charles Mālik:

'These things dominate the Arab mind in general: independence and unity. There is a deep-seated mystical element in both these feelings. The only analogous situation I can think of is the radical sense of unity and independence which determined the history of German peoples in recent decades. Independence springs from the Arab sense that has been sharpened in recent centuries by the relative isolation of the Arabs from the rest of the world. Unity takes on many modalities: from the mild form of general community and consultation enshrined in the Arab League to the extreme form of complete unification desired by certain nationalist movements, partly in Iraq and Syria. But regardless of its modality every Arab feels an immediate mystical unity with every other Arab. The investigation of the ultimate causes and the real structure, limitation, and promise of these two creative Arab persuasions is one of the most fascinating philosophical-cultural tasks to be undertaken by the loving and understanding mind.'[49]

Such is the character of Arab nationalism, perhaps the most powerful trend in modern Muslim Arab political thought. Its derivation from Western thought has been indicated. Sāti' al-Husri and his successors, trying to come to terms with European modes of thought, have naturalized Fichte and Hegel as teachers of Arab Muslim thought. Sāti' al-Husri requires the individual to lose himself within his own community. This requirement is new in Islam, but it has one thing at least in common with the orthodox Muslim approach, and that is the demand for unlimited, implicit obedience. According to the *Sunna*, the power of the Caliph is, in principle, not absolute, since absolute power belongs only to God. All temporal power, on the other hand, restricts the liberty and independence of

[49] Charles Mālik, *loc. cit.*, p. 240.

the individual, attributes bestowed on him by God. Consequently the power of the ruler, which restricts individual freedom, must itself be restricted to the aims of tutelage and protection only. Moderation, kindness, temperateness are incumbent on the ruler. He must be just, and must follow strictly the prescriptions laid down in the Qur'ān. Only thus does his power remain valid, and his edicts command obedience. The ruler of the Faithful who follows the dictates of the *Sunna* is entitled to the obedience of the Faithful. The subjects obey because it is in their own interest to do so, and because God ordains that they should, since the commands of the ruler are merely executive prescriptions based on the Divine Law. It is thus that obedience is grounded and justified in the *Sunna*. But this justification of government may be developed in two opposite directions. On the one hand, the doctrine of obedience to the just ruler may lead to a system of checks and balances designed to test the rectitude of the ruler and to correct him when he errs. It may, on the other hand, lead to an attitude of completely passive obedience. This is what had happened in Islam. Passive obedience is in turn justified on two grounds. The criterion by which a ruler is held to rule justly or not is that of the Canon Law, which only the *'ulamā'* can authoritatively interpret and apply. In the second place, even if the *'ulamā'* decide that a ruler is unjust, it is not open to the Faithful to rebel. Al-Ghazāli has a classical essay on the religious duty of obedience to the ruler.

'The first point', he writes, 'is the explanation of the obligation to set up an *imām*. It must not be thought that the obligation to do this is derived from reason, for, . . . it is derived from revelation. What is obligatory, however, is interpreted as the action which is beneficial and the omission of which is harmful in this world; and on this interpretation, it is not denied that the setting up of the *imām* is obligatory because of the benefits in it and because it avoids what is harmful in this world (and this is in accord with the demands of reason). . . . We maintain that the right ordering of religion was certainly the purpose of the agent of revelation. This is an absolute premise on which there can be no disagreement. We will add to it another premise, to the effect that the right ordering of religion can obtain only where there is an *imām* to whom obedience is given. . . .

'If it be said, however, that the second premise is not granted, to wit, that the right ordering of religion can obtain only through an imamate to whom obedience is given, therefore prove it, then we will say: "The proof is that the right ordering of religion can obtain only where there is right ordering of the world, and the right ordering of the world can be obtained only through an *imām* to whom obedience is given." . . . And if it be asked: "Why do you say that the right ordering of religion can result only from the right ordering of the world, when, in fact, it can result only from the ruin of the world, for are not the spiritual and temporal opposites, and does not the prosperity of the one entail the ruin of the other?" Our answer is: "This is the speech of him who does not understand what we mean by the 'world' in this context. It is an ambiguous word which may, on the one hand, refer to excessive self-enjoyment and pleasure beyond need and necessity, and, on the other, it may refer to all the necessities in the life before death. In one sense it is indeed against religion, but in the other, it is the very condition of religion." . . . We say, therefore, that the right ordering of religion comes through knowledge and worship, and these can be attained only through a healthy body, the preservation of life, and the satisfaction of the exigencies of cold, hunger, exposure, and insecurity, the ultimate evil. . . . Religion cannot be rightly ordered except through the fulfilment of these essential needs; otherwise how can a man who spends all his time defending himself against the sword of the oppressors and seeking his food in the face of those who overreach him, how can such a man find time to devote himself to learning and endeavour, these being his means to a blessed after-life? . . .

'As for the second premise, i.e. that the world and security of life and possessions cannot be organized except by a ruler to whom obedience is given, it is confirmed when we observe the civil wars which break out at the death of the rulers and the *imāms*, especially when there is a lapse of time before another ruler is nominated. Disorder, violence, and scarcity rule, cattle perish, and manufactures die out. Might seizes what it can; no one devotes himself to worship or to learning, even if he remains alive, while the majority perish by the sword. This is why religion and rule have been called twins. It is said that religion is a foundation and rule a guardian; what has no foundation is destroyed, and what has no guardian is lost. On the whole, no sensible man will doubt that human beings, with all their classes and variety of desires and opinions, if they had been left to their condition, and if there had been no one opinion to command obedience and to unify them, would have perished altogether. This is a disease which has only one cure: a strong ruler to command obedience and unify the diversity of opinions. It is clear that power is necessary for the right ordering of the world, and the right ordering of the world is necessary for the right ordering of religion, and the right ordering of religion is necessary to win eternal happiness; this is indeed the aim of all the prophets. The obligation to set up an *imām* is therefore enjoined in the *shar'*, which it is out of the question to abandon.'

Al-Ghazāli goes on to discuss the qualities that a suitable *imām* must have, and then says: 'He may be deposed on condition that he is replaced by another who has all the qualifications, and on condition that his deposition does not arouse any dissension or violent commotion. If this is impossible, then obedience is due to him, and his imamate must be accepted. . . . For if we cause a revolt to break out the consequences of which we do not know, this may lead to the loss of life and possessions.'[50]

Such is al-Ghazāli's view of the exercise of power among the Faithful. It is the traditional Sunni view. It is extremely reluctant to counsel opposition to government, however tyrannical the government may be. In practice, orthodoxy had always to accommodate itself to political tyranny.[51] Sunni opinion agrees with Ibn Taimiyya that obedience is due even to the unjust and ignorant ruler, so long as his orders do not constitute a breach of an injunction laid down by God or by Muhammad. In such a case, disobedience is allowed only when the orders of the *imām* are manifestly in contradiction to a prescription which is based on a precise text of the Qur'ān or the *Sunna*, and agreed upon by the *ijmā'* of the *Salaf*.[52] More recently, Rashīd Ridā tried to answer this question in the light of modern developments. He prefers *Ahl al-hall wa 'l-'aqd* to the *imām*, saying that the Sultan must execute what they agree upon, because they are the representatives of the *umma*, and it is their prerogative to elect the *imām*; so that if the *imām* contradicts them, the *umma* must obey them and not him. In spite of this effort to interpret the power of the ruler in terms of national sovereignty, and in spite of the very categorical condemnation of blind obedience which Rashīd Ridā makes, his views do not, in practice, differ from what has been quoted above; he ends his analysis by saying that 'the resistance of the *umma* to the tyrannical ruler must be carried on with wisdom, foresight, and care not to cause civil strife, upon the principle of following the course of the lesser evil.'[53] All forms of government, then, as they are more or less powerful, can be made more or less acceptable. Whatever the reason given to justify obedience to powerful and arbitrary government, whether to maintain the unity of the Faithful, as the traditional teaching has it, or to

[50] I. Al-Ghazāli, *Al-iqtisād fī 'l-i'tiqād* (Cairo, n.d.), pp. 105–7.

[51] This has been noticed by many writers on Islam, but the relevance of this attitude to modern politics and international relations has not been widely dealt with. M. Halpern, 'Implications of Communism for Islam', *The Muslim World*, January, 1953, and B. Lewis, 'Communism and Islam', *International Affairs*, January, 1954, are to be noticed in this connection.

[52] H. Laoust, *Essai . . . sur ibn Taimīya*, pp. 313–14. Laoust discusses the different theological positions taken by the Shī'ites and some other sects. My study is, however, concerned with the orthodox developments only.

[53] *Al-Manār*, XIV, 1329/October, 1911, pp. 740–1.

attain a higher mode of being as the new nationalist doctrine claims, there is, for the ordinary subject of government, no difference in practice. Another feature of the modern doctrine which fits in with the Muslim past is the emphasis which both of them lay on communal solidarity, discipline, and co-operation. The *umma* in Islam is a solidary entity, and its foremost duty is to answer the call of the *jihād*. This brings us to the third feature which both modern and ancient systems have in common, to wit, the glorification of one's own group. The traditional attitude of the Muslims to the outside world is one of superiority, and the distinction between *Dār al-harb*, *Dār al-Islām*, and *Dār as-sulh* is an ever-present one in the mind of the Muslim jurist. It may therefore be said, in conclusion, of this modern doctrine of nationalism, that although it introduces into Islam features which may not accord with strict orthodoxy, it is the least incompatible, perhaps, of modern European doctrines with the political thought and political experience of Sunni Islam.

Part Two

COMMUNISM, THE SOVIET UNION,

AND THE MIDDLE EAST

COMMUNISM AND ISLAM

by BERNARD LEWIS

MY PURPOSE HERE is to try to see how far Islam and Communism are compatible—how far, that is, Islam predisposes those who have been brought up in it to accept or to reject the Communist teaching. I shall not attempt to examine Communist infiltration and propaganda in Islamic countries or the degree of their success or failure—that is a task calling for professional skills and sources of information other than those which are at my disposal. Rather shall I try to consider what qualities or tendencies exist in Islam, in Islamic civilization and society, which might either facilitate or impede the advance of Communism.

The obvious objection will no doubt at once be raised that Islam is after all a religion based on revelation, belief in which is clearly incompatible with Marxist ideology. That is undoubtedly true, and the same could be said with equal truth of Orthodox, Catholic, or Protestant Christianity, of Judaism, or any other religion worthy of the name. Nevertheless, that doctrinal incompatibility has not prevented many former followers of these religions from becoming Communists. No doubt, the devout and pious Muslim theologian who has studied and understands the implications of dialectical materialism will reject that creed, but such a combination of circumstances is not of common occurrence, nor likely to be of far-reaching significance. The question before us should rather be put thus: in the present competition between the Western democracies and Soviet Communism for the support of the Islamic world, what factors or qualities are there in Islamic tradition, or in the present state of Islamic society and opinion, which might prepare the intellectually and politically active groups to embrace Communist principles and methods of government, and the rest to accept them?

Before proceeding any further I feel that a writer on a subject of this nature owes his reader some definition of his own political attitude. Let me confess right away that I lack one qualification which nowadays is generally accepted as conferring both authority and respectability—I am not an ex-Communist. I can however plead as an extenuating circumstance that I grew up in a generation which was deeply affected by what was happening in Russia, and which felt, generally speaking, that, with all the brutalities and crimes of the Russian Revolution, it nevertheless represented something valuable and significant for humanity—'bliss was it in that dawn to be alive'—and I am therefore perhaps able to understand something of the attraction as well as of the repulsion of the Communist creed. Of my own political attitude let me say this, that I believe that parliamentary democracy as practised in the West, with all its manifest faults, is still the best and most just form of government yet devised by man. But at the same time I believe it to be the most difficult to operate, requiring certain qualities of mind and habit, of institution and tradition, perhaps even of climate, for its effective working. It has taken firm root only among the peoples of the northern and north-western fringes of Europe, and in the territories colonized by their descendants overseas. It has maintained, or maintains, a precarious existence in a few other regions, and is showing signs of promising but still immature growth in a few more—but otherwise it is unknown to the rest of the human race, in most of the world, and through most of recorded history.

Knowing, then, that parliamentary democracy is far from being the common experience of mankind, I am, to my regret, by no means certain that it represents the common destiny of mankind, and I shall therefore try to avoid the too frequent practice, which has the fault of being both inaccurate and inexpedient, of representing the world's dilemma as a straight choice between Communism and parliamentary democracy; of making, therefore, an appearance of parliamentary government the universal test of political and even moral virtue —in other words, of making our own present way of life the sole pattern of goodness, all deviations from which are necessarily evil, all alternatives to which are lumped together in a mass of undifferentiated wickedness. This principle, not even consistently applied, leads us to such logical and political absurdities as simultaneously courting the favours of some slave-owning and polygamous autocrat on another continent, while snubbing the government of Spain— because of their disregard of civil liberties. The unfortunate and unpalatable fact is that it is we who are the exception in both history and geography, and that authoritarian and not representative government approximates most closely to the common experience of mankind. In most of the world, autocracy, if less attractive, is more familiar and more intelligible than democracy, and even the arbitrary and capricious dictatorship of Moscow is neither as strange nor therefore as repellent to much of Asia and Africa—even much of Europe—as it is to us. We should certainly do our best to encourage the growth of free institutions wherever possible; but at the same time we would do well to recall that, for a great part of the human race, parliamentary democracy remains something remote, alien, and incomprehensible, an object sometimes of wonderment, even envy, more often alas of mistrust and hatred, which we must concede is not entirely unjustified when we recall the examples of democracy by which alone they can judge it. If the peoples of Islam are forced to make a straight choice, to abandon their own traditions in favour of either Communism or parliamentarianism, then we are at a great disadvantage.

It is, however, fortunate, both for Islam and for the Western world, that the choice is not restricted to these two simple alternatives, for the possibility still remains for the Muslim peoples of restoring, perhaps in a modified form, their own tradition; of evolving a form of government which, though authoritarian, and perhaps even autocratic, is nevertheless far removed from the cynical tyranny of European-style dictatorship. I do not wish to be misunderstood— I would much prefer to see all Islam enjoy the benefits of constitutional government, democratic liberty, and the free development of the individual, and I by no means exclude the possibility of this desirable consummation, which in a few favoured countries is already in sight—but I wish to make clear my view that in large areas of the Islamic world this consummation is not in prospect and, furthermore, that the present circumstances, and indeed the ancient traditions of Islam, do not wholly favour us but, on the contrary, contain much which might incline the Muslim individual, class, or nation, which is ready to abandon traditional values and beliefs, to accept the Communist rather than the democratic alternative.

I propose now to select and discuss a few of what seem to me to be the more important elements favouring the success of Communism in the Islamic world, and to deal with them under two headings: first, the accidentals, those that are part of the present historical situation, and then the essentials, those which are innate or inherent in the very quality of Islamic institutions and ideas.

The first and most important of the accidentals is the anti-Western motif. The Communists are against the West and for that reason can at once count on important elements of support in the Islamic world, just as the Nazis were able to do in their time—to a considerable extent the same elements of support and for the same reasons. Like the Nazis, the Communists are anti-Western in the double sense—they are against the Western Powers and they are also against the Western way of life, Western institutions and ideas. Under both headings they have a strong appeal. The present anti-Western reaction in the Islamic world is obvious and well known. After the period of admiration and imitation of the nineteenth and early twentieth centuries, there is now a general and growing revulsion. Public attention has been focused in the main on a series of specific grievances of the Islamic world against the West—Morocco and Tunisia, Suez and the Sudan, Palestine, Abadan, and the rest, of which now one, now another, has been adduced as the main cause of anti-Western feeling. There are always those in the West who will seek to grind an axe or titillate a prejudice by attributing all troubles to the misdeeds of their favourite scapegoats—the French or the Jews, the Americans or the British—and they will always find enthusiastic agreement from somebody in the Orient. Muslims tend to stress the importance of any specific issue in the measure of their own involvement in it—Westerners, of their own freedom from involvement. All of these grievances are symptoms or aspects of a fundamental and universal revulsion from all that is Western and, as we have seen of late, even the removal of one or another grievance cannot bring more than a local and temporary alleviation. This movement is made up of various strains, of which I may mention the reaction against colonialism, which grows stronger as the latter is manifestly dying; against Western privilege and arrogance, economic, social, political; against the dislocations and upheavals resulting from the impact of the West, the changes brought about by Western influence and activities, by no means all of which are—as we like to flatter ourselves—beneficial.

The liberal and constitutional movements in the Islamic countries, which were launched with such high hopes in the nineteenth century, have, with few exceptions, ended in failure, disappointment, and frustration. The local leaders have all too often relapsed into a cynicism and opportunism that has outraged the moral sense of those whom they professed to lead, or else have sought comfort in a rabid and xenophobe fanaticism, damning indiscriminately all and everything that has come out of the West. They expressed the blind protest of the masses against the alien and powerful forces that had dislocated their traditional way of life, destroyed their traditional social equilibrium, and posed new problems for which they offered no effective answer. It is no doubt unjust of Muslims to blame the West for the exuberant and destructive haste of their own reformers and for the incompetence and selfishness of their own parliamentarians. But we must admit that the record of the West in its dealings with the Islamic world and for that matter in its own internal affairs does not furnish material for any very striking rebuttal.

Communist propaganda against the West can therefore always count on a ready response, especially when striking the anti-imperialist drum. It may seem strange to us that the Soviet Empire, still audibly eructating after having bolted half of Europe, should be able to pose successfully as the champion of the rights of oppressed peoples against the imperialists—that the state which rules with no light hand over so many Muslim subject peoples, should nevertheless be able to carry off this pose among the other peoples of Islam. Yet so it is. For most Islamic peoples the notion of 'imperialist'—and I am speaking here, of course, of the popular image—is rather restricted and surprisingly precise. The imperialist is always Western—in fact, 'Western imperialist' is a natural and normal collocation of terms, like German measles or Spanish 'flu. The Arab who protests against imperialism does not think for one moment that his putative ancestors who conquered an empire from the Pyrenees to the Oxus were also imperialists, nor the Persian that the vaunted glories of Cyrus and Darius were also of an imperial quality. Even the modern Japanese, except of course among their immediate victims, are somehow regarded as different and as belonging fundamentally among the sheep rather than the goats—black sheep perhaps, but still sheep. The imperialist of the popular prototype, the stock figure of contemporary political demonology in the Orient, is Western, and is moreover always maritime and commercial. The imperialist is a man who comes across the sea in a ship, lands on the coast, buys and sells, works his way inland, and finally, by various devices, mostly dishonest, establishes his rule.

This is of course a distillation and in some measure a distortion of the experience of most of Asia and Africa of Portuguese and Dutch, French and British expansion since the sixteenth century. It is in fact the sole direct experience of most of these countries, in the last few centuries, of the phenomenon of imperialism. The other kind, overland military expansion, is not really grasped, except again by those who have experienced it directly. Turkey, for example, has for centuries fought a defensive action against the successive stages of the Russian overland advance, first to the Black Sea, then down through the Balkans and the Caucasus. Turkey, moreover, is related by language and origin to the Tatar peoples who are now under Soviet yoke. Hence the greater degree of awareness among the Turks of the nature of Soviet imperialism, and the vastly different attitude adopted by Turkey to the present world problems. In the rest of the Islamic world Soviet imperialism may perhaps, in some circles, be apprehended intellectually, but it fails to evoke any real emotional response. It is remarkable how Islamic opinion generally refuses to accord to ancient Muslim centres of culture like Bukhara and Samarkand one-hundredth of the interest and attention given to, say, Casablanca, Ismailia, and Abadan. Even those who are anti-Communist will often say—most of us must have heard it—'At least, the Russians are not imperialists'—and really believe that the Soviet régime, despite its other faults, is somehow free from that particular stigma which renders the Western Powers so odious. Here it must be stated that the Russians are greatly helped by Western racial and colour prejudice and by their own apparent freedom from it. This is an immense asset to them, both in Asia and in Africa, and one that is wantonly presented to them.

The second accidental with which I shall deal is the present discontent of the Islamic world, and more specifically the social and economic discontent. The abject poverty of the masses and the callous irresponsibility of the possessing classes are often mentioned as sources of possible danger. Quite clearly, warnings of the threat to liberty and property are unlikely to move those who possess neither; on the contrary, Communist ideas and promises will have a ready attraction for important groups in a society which, as has often been pointed out, in many ways resembles that of Russia on the eve of the Revolution.

This point is self-evident and has often been made, and there is no need for me to dwell on it. I would, however, like to mention three facts which we might bear in mind when we speak of the immemorial poverty and irresponsibility of the Orient. The first is that this poverty, at any rate in its present form, is in fact not immemorial. Obviously, the gap between rich and poor has always existed, but as far as we can ascertain, it has not in earlier times been as wide and as unbridgeable as it is now. In its present form, this gap is largely the result of the Western impact, the effect of which has been to make the rich richer, and the poor poorer than they were before. The economic effects of Westernization and of contact with the West are a complex problem; I propose here to mention only two aspects. One is the greater opportunity to amass wealth afforded by Western industrial, commercial, and financial techniques, and the consequent growth of fortunes on a scale unknown in earlier and simpler economies; the other is the rapid increase of population, made possible by Western hygiene and security, but unaccompanied by any corresponding increase in food supplies.

Moreover, the disparity between rich and poor is not only greater than before, but, what is perhaps more important, is more visible, thanks to the introduction of Western amenities and the flow of

Western consumer goods, which afford vastly greater opportunities for the public display and enjoyment of wealth. These changes are not due to the villainy of the West or even in any great measure to the direct intervention of Westerners; they are rather the consequences of the process of Western contact, Western influence, and Westernization generally. The West is now doing something to remedy them, and can do very much more.

I have said that the poverty of the Orient was not, in its present form, immemorial. Nor for that matter is the irresponsibility of the Oriental ruling classes. Before the impact of Westernization from, say, the late eighteenth century onwards, the corporative structure of traditional Islamic society, though worm-eaten, was still standing, and the complex system of social and moral duties associated with it was still functioning. Then the old order was shattered, not by the wicked imperialists, but by native reformers, men of the stamp of Mahmud II in Turkey and Muhammad Ali in Egypt, who destroyed better than they built. Nothing has come to replace the old bonds. That is the cause of the social and political formlessness which has struck so many observers of modern Islamic societies, the absence of any but purely personal and family loyalties—since the family is the only surviving social unit with any real life or meaning. So that, we might remember, what we condemn as the vice of nepotism is, for those who practise it, the virtue of family loyalty, the only intelligible form of loyalty that remains. The disappearance of the old social ethos and the breakdown of the old social cohesion have left a dangerous gap which Western social ideals and institutions have failed to fill.

My third point is that the centre of danger is not the starving peasantry so often referred to, but rather the aspiring mechanics, who are the main recruits to the Communist cause. The peasantry are still, to a large extent, integrated in their traditional social units, and sustained by the loyalty and cohesion of the family and village group. It is the semi-skilled or unskilled labourers who are uprooted from their tribal and village communities, deprived of the support of their usual system of social relationships and mutual aid, and placed in alien and unfamiliar surroundings. In the Communist cell the transplanted proletarian or mechanic may hope to find some substitute for his lost social armature, as well as encouragement in the ambitions and resentments that he acquires together with his new skills.

I turn now from the accidental to the essential factors, to those deriving from the very nature of Islamic society, tradition, and thought. The first of these is the authoritarianism, perhaps we may

even say the totalitarianism, of the Islamic political tradition. It is
by now lamentably clear that any totalitarian government, however
anti-Communist its professed creed may be, does in fact provide the
starting-point for a swift and easy transition to Communist dictatorship. The democratic Finns, isolated and abandoned to the mercies
of Russia, have nevertheless succeeded in maintaining their democratic liberties through long and difficult years. The more or less
Fascist régimes of eastern and central Europe, by a few simple
adjustments, were soon transformed into Communist states, for
which the machinery and personnel of repression, and the habit of
acquiescence in it, were ready to hand. The political experience and
traditions of Islam, though very different from those of eastern
Europe, do nevertheless contain elements which might, in certain
circumstances, prepare the way for Communism.

Many attempts have been made to show that Islam and democracy
are identical—attempts usually based on a misunderstanding of
Islam or democracy or both. This sort of argument expresses a need
of the uprooted Muslim intellectual who is no longer satisfied with
or capable of understanding traditional Islamic values, and who tries
to justify, or rather, re-state, his inherited faith in terms of the
fashionable ideology of the day. It is an example of the romantic and
apologetic presentation of Islam that is a recognized phase in the
reaction of Muslim thought to the impact of the West. There are of
course elements, even important elements, in Islam, especially in the
early period, which we might not unjustly call democratic, but on the
whole the tendency which is usually adduced in support of this thesis
is equalitarian rather than democratic; a very different thing, and
one that goes with authoritarian at least as well as with democratic
institutions. In point of fact, except for the early caliphate, when the
anarchic individualism of tribal Arabia was still effective, the political
history of Islam is one of almost unrelieved autocracy. I say autocracy, not despotism, since the sovereign was bound by and subject
to the Holy Law, and was accepted by the people as rightful ruler,
maintaining and maintained by the authority of the Holy Law. But
still, it was authoritarian, often arbitrary, sometimes tyrannical.
There are no parliaments or representative assemblies of any kind,
no councils or communes, no chambers of nobility or estates, no
municipalities in the history of Islam; nothing but the sovereign
power, to which the subject owed complete and unwavering obedience as a religious duty imposed by the Holy Law. In the great
days of classical Islam this duty was owed only to the lawfully
appointed Caliph, as God's vicegerent on earth and head of the
theocratic community, and then only for as long as he upheld the
law; but with the decline of the caliphate and the growth of military

dictatorship, Muslim jurists and theologians accommodated their teachings to the changed situation and extended the religious duty of obedience to any effective authority, however impious, however barbarous. For the last thousand years, the political thinking of Islam has been dominated by such maxims as 'tyranny is better than anarchy' and 'whose power is established, obedience to him is incumbent'. The classical formulation of Islamic political quietism may be found in an often-cited passage from the Syrian jurist Ibn Jamā'a, who became Chief Qādi of Cairo and died in 1333:

'*Forced homage.* This happens when a chief seizes power by force, in a time of civil disorders, and it becomes necessary to recognize him in order to avoid further troubles. That he may have none of the qualifications of sovereignty, that he be illiterate, unjust or vicious, that he be even a slave or a woman, is of no consequence. He is a sovereign in fact, until such time as another, stronger than he, drives him from the throne and seizes power. He will then be sovereign by the same title, and should be recognized in order not to increase strife. Whoever has effective power has the right to obedience, for a government, even the worst one, is better than anarchy, and of two evils one should choose the lesser.'

It will be clear that these are not the words of a time-server or flatterer trying to make his career at an autocratic court. They are the words of a pious and devout believer, putting bluntly and sadly an unpalatable truth as he sees it. It will be remembered that the writer is a doctor of the Holy Law and speaking in terms of the Holy Law. When he prescribes recognition and obedience, he is laying down the duty of the believer under the Holy Law—that is to say, he is formulating a rule the violation of which is, in our terminology, a sin as well as a crime, involving hell-fire as well as such anticipatory chastisement as the sovereign might see fit to impose in this world. 'Even a slave or a woman', says Ibn Jamā'a; only one thing worse can be imagined—an infidel, and that stage too was reached when, after the Norman conquest of Sicily from the Muslims, a Muslim jurist of Mazara laid down that even a Christian ruler must be accepted and obeyed, provided he accords religious toleration to the Muslims. A community brought up on such doctrines will not be shocked by Communist disregard of political liberty or human rights; it may even be attracted by a régime which offers ruthless strength and efficiency in the service of a cause—anyway in appearance—in place of the ineptitude, corruption, and cynicism which in their mind, one may even say in their experience, are inseparable from parliamentary government.

Even the Communist doctrine that the state must direct economic life is not as alien to the Muslim as might be thought—rather is he accustomed to look to the state for direction and control of certain central aspects of economic life. The classical Islamic social order was evolved in Iraq and Egypt, and conformed to the ancient pattern of river-valley society. In those lands of little rainfall there was an intensive agriculture, based on artificial irrigation from the river. This required armies of engineers and officials, employed and controlled by a central authority, whose task it was to maintain the elaborate structure of dykes, dams, canals, and other irrigation works, by which alone the economic life of the country could be maintained. For this system a strong central authority was a paramount necessity, and one does not have to look far to find examples of the ruin and impoverishment which followed the breakdown of the central authority in times of political weakness and the consequent neglect of the irrigation works. In countries blessed with rain the farmer can look to God for his water and maintain a certain independence in other respects. In the river-valley societies he must look to the central authority to maintain the system and to supply the life-giving stream, and he knows himself to be at its mercy. It is in such communities that we find the type of social order that Wittfogel has called 'the hydraulic society', where the régime and the ruling class are based on the supply of water for irrigation. Its characteristics are well known: a docile and helpless peasantry, at the mercy of a centralized and bureaucratic authority and a ruling class of officials and landowners in unchallenged, and indeed unchallengeable, control of the sources of economic life and therefore of political power. The same basic type of society exists in Egypt and Iraq, in the river valleys of India, in China, and, one may perhaps add, in the river valleys of Russia. Whether the historic Russian society is 'hydraulic' in this sense I would not pretend to say; there are, however, certain striking similarities. The traditional Islamic autocracy rests on three pillars: the bureaucracy, the army, and the religious hierarchy—and I may recall in passing the interesting suggestion made in *International Affairs* in 1953 by Mr. Albert Hourani, that we may be witnessing a return to this pattern in the recent changes in Egypt. In this pattern, only the third, the religious hierarchy, need be changed in order to prepare the way for a Communist state.

That third, however, is by no means unimportant. Quite obviously, the *'Ulama* of Islam are very different from the Communist Party. Nevertheless, on closer examination, we find certain uncomfortable resemblances. Both groups profess a totalitarian doctrine, with complete and final answers to all questions on heaven and earth; the answers are different in every respect, alike only in their finality and completeness, and in the contrast they offer with the eternal questioning of Western man. Both groups offer to their members and followers the agreeable sensation of belonging to a community of believers, who are always right, as against an outer world of unbelievers, who are always wrong. Both offer an exhilarating feeling of mission, of purpose, of being engaged in a collective adventure to accelerate the historically inevitable victory of the true faith over the infidel evil-doers. The traditional Islamic division of the world into the House of Islam and the House of War, two necessarily opposed groups, of which the first has the collective obligation of perpetual struggle against the second, also has obvious parallels in the Communist view of world affairs. There again, the content of belief is utterly different, but the aggressive fanaticism of the believer is the same. The humorist who summed up the Communist creed as 'There is no God and Karl Marx is his Prophet' was laying his finger on a real affinity. The call to a Communist *Jihad*, a Holy War for the faith—a new faith, but against the self-same Western Christian enemy—might well strike a responsive note.

I have referred to collective obligations. Here too there is a possible point of contact between Communism and Islam, the collectivist tendencies of which have struck many observers. A good deal has been written about the innumerable religio-Communistic sects and movements that have arisen all over Islam, almost since its beginning. Let me quote from an almost contemporary Arabic chronicle, describing the activities of an agent of one such sect in Iraq, in the neighbourhood of Kufa, about the middle of the ninth century. This agent, we are told, having converted the inhabitants of some villages to his doctrine, imposed on them an ever-increasing series of taxes and levies and finally:

'The duty of Ulfa . . .; this consisted of assembling all their goods in one place and enjoying them in common without any one retaining any personal property which might give him an advantage over the others. He assured them that they did not need to keep any property because all the land belonged to them and to no one else. That, he told them, is the test by which you are proved so that we may know how you will behave. He urged them to buy and prepare arms. The missionaries appointed in each village a trustworthy man to assemble all that the people of the village owned by way of cattle, sheep, jewellery, provisions, etc. He clothed the naked and met all their needs, leaving no poor man among them, nor any needy and infirm. Every man worked with diligence and emulation at his task in order to deserve high rank by the benefit he brought. The woman brought what she earned by weaving, the child brought his wages for scaring away birds. Nobody among them owned anything beyond his sword and his arms.'

This is no doubt an exaggerated description of the proceedings of these groups, but it is not untypical. And this is but one of many such movements recorded in Islam, and in Persia also long before Islam. All of them failed and were duly condemned by the orthodox as heresy, but they reveal the recurring tendency in Islam to throw up such ideas and groups, and they also help to explain the otherwise mystifying connections which are reported from time to time between certain extremist Islamic religious organizations and Communism. It was precisely in organizations of this sort, the popular, semi-secret, mystical brotherhoods, of dubious orthodoxy and mistrusted by the regular 'Ulama, that these religio-Communistic tendencies usually appeared. Nor is this collectivism limited to what one might call the 'popular sub-stratum' of Islam. It is also discernible in many aspects of orthodox Islamic life and thought, in the attitude to society and government, which I have already mentioned, even in literature. The classical Arabic book is often presented not as an individual and personal creation of the author, but as a link in the chain of tradition, the author effacing his own personality behind the prestige of authority and the ranks of previous transmitters. Many of the great works of Arabic literature are as impersonal and as collective as a medieval cathedral. This collectivism is perhaps clearest in the Muslim idea of the Perfect Man and the Perfect State as given, immutable patterns externally applied, to which all must in theory attempt to conform by imitation, instead of, as in the Western ideal, by developing their own potentialities from within.

But all this, it may be objected, could equally well be said of any other religion as of Islam, and amounts to no more than saying that Communism is itself a religion. I concede that some of the comparisons I have made, though by no means all, also apply to some other religions. I would add that had these religions retained the same formative and determinative power over their adherents as Islam still has, the observation might have some practical relevance. But I cannot accept the statement that Communism is a religion, and nothing, I would suggest, illustrates more clearly the decayed state of religion in our Western world, than that such a comparison can be made at all. Admittedly, the resemblances are at first sight striking. In Communism, as in most religions, we find ritual and hierarchy, revelation and prophecy, scripture and exegesis, orthodoxy and heresy, excommunication and persecution. Even some of the deeper spiritual strength of religious faith seems to fortify the truly convinced Communist. Despite his professed materialism, he has objectives beyond his own self-interest, and beyond his own lifetime. He is filled with an evangelic fervour and a messianic faith. It is this quality which has given Communism its special strength— the dangerous fascination which it exercises in so many Oriental countries. Fascism and Nazism, with their naked appeal to greed, hate, pride, and envy, could in the long run address themselves only to the evil instincts of man, and were correspondingly limited. Communism, while exploiting these to the full, has also perverted to its service some of the noblest aspirations of the human race—as peace, social justice, the brotherhood of man—and has used them with deadly effect. We shall fail to understand and meet the threat of Communism if we do not recognize its attraction for the best, though not the brightest, as well as for the worst spirits.

Communism thus has many features in common with religion, but those that are lacking are perhaps the most important. I would like to quote a passage from the Danish writer Vilhelm Grønbech, who says:

'The trouble is that we confuse religiosity with religion. Just because people are so devout in their personal way, they are unable to conceive a religion which is the soul of society, the obverse of the practical, a living and real religion, the practical relationship of the people to God, soul and eternity, that manifests itself in worship and works as a life-giving power in politics and economics, in crafts and commerce, in ethics as in law. In this sense the modern state has no religion.'

In this sense, one may add, Communism is not and cannot be a religion, while Islam, for the great mass of believers, still is; and that is the core of the Islamic resistance to Communist ideas. Though their belief in liberty be too weak to sustain them, their belief in God may yet be strong enough. The Islamic peoples are still profoundly religious in the simplest and deepest meaning of the word. Islam as a religion is no more anti-Communist than Christianity; in fact, as I have suggested, rather less so. But it is more potent as a force affecting the lives and thoughts of its adherents. Pious Muslims— and most Muslims are pious—will not long tolerate an atheist creed, nor one that violates their traditional religious moral principles which, because they do not tally with our own, are too often overlooked by Western observers. The present revolt of the Muslims against the immorality and opportunism of their own and of some Western leaders may temporarily favour the Communists, with their appearance of selfless devotion to an ideal, but will work against Communism when Muslims come to see the realities behind the propaganda. Let us hope that they will not take too long over it.

In any case, there is not a great deal that we can do about it. Our own public and political morality is undoubtedly better than that of the Communists, but the difference is apparently not large enough or striking enough to make any notable impression on the rest of the world. The people who represent Western democracy in its dealings with Islam are certainly estimable men, doing important and meritorious work, but as promoters of moral and religious revival they are unlikely to carry conviction. We of the West can do much to promote the material well-being and raise the material standards of the lands of Islam. We can also perhaps do something to encourage—and that means to justify—a more positive attitude towards ourselves, our ideas, and our aspirations; but in the present crisis it is from within that Islam must find the moral strength and spiritual resources to resist the great secular heresy of our time. We can do no more than refrain from offering impediments.

October, 1953

SYRIA: NATIONALISM AND COMMUNISM

by WALTER Z. LAQUEUR

I

THE SYRIAN CRISIS of August, 1957, brought into dramatic relief certain trends in that country, and made known to the general public a course of events that had started at least eighteen months previously and possibly earlier. What happened in August, 1957, was not really of world-shaking importance: the replacement of some military leaders by others and the signature of another Treaty with the Soviet Union for the supply of arms and economic aid. Syrian spokesmen were thus not entirely unjustified in deploring the Western 'hullabaloo' about the logical culmination of their policy between 1955 and 1957. But the gradual Syrio–Soviet *rapprochement* during those years seemed to have escaped Western attention, and the *dénouement* in summer, 1957, came as a shock to Western and some Middle Eastern capitals. The question generally asked was whether Syria had already become a Soviet satellite, or whether it would soon be the first Middle Eastern popular democracy. These questions baffled many observers, not perhaps because the situation itself was so complicated, but because the Syrian phenomenon was a new, and hence an unfamiliar one. As a possible standard pattern for other Arab and Asian countries, it is worth exploring in detail.

II

The rise of the radical forces in Syria has to be viewed in the wider context of Syrian domestic politics during the last twenty years, the failure of parliamentary democracy, the disintegration of the traditional parties. Torn by factional strife, the old parties had become identified with the rule of individuals and economic vested interests, with financial scandals, and with gross incompetence while in power.

Although economic crisis was more or less permanent, Syrian developments cannot really be explained on economic grounds, for this was a crisis of growth. Syrian agriculture has doubled its output during the last fifteen years, and industry has also made notable progress. But economic advance was not conducive to political stability, and certainly not to the growth of a democratic régime.[1] Between 1949 and 1954 Syria was ruled by military dictators. Public opinion, for some time at least, was not unsympathetic to the colonels who had taken over; military dictatorship, it was believed, could hardly be worse than the rule of the old discredited parties. But the government of Shishakli (who was longest in power) did not accomplish much either; he was overthrown early in 1954 and from then on Syria was, at least in name, again a parliamentary democracy. However, the old tensions and the old discontent were not eliminated; the coalition of nationalists and People's Party which first took over soon disintegrated, and the influence of various radical groups increased greatly: first in the streets of Syria's cities and among the peasants of some regions, later among the officer corps, and eventually in the government itself.

The most interesting, and at present probably the most important of these radical groups is the Arab Socialist Renaissance Party (Ba'ath). In view of its close contacts with the army command and its connections with similar groups in other Arab countries, the emergence of the Ba'ath is of more than local significance. It came into being as the result of the merger, in September, 1953, of two separate factions: the Arab Renaissance Party and the Arab (or Republican) Socialist Party. The history of both groups goes back to the early 'forties; they were orginally pro-Fascist in ideology, in organizational structure, and in their foreign political orientation. (Many of today's leaders of the Ba'ath, such as Aqram Hourani and Colonel Afif al-Bizra, took part in the abortive pro-Axis Rashid Ali revolt in Baghdad in 1941.)

The Renaissance group was originally headed by Michel Aflaq

---

[1] One of the most discouraging aspects of the Syrian situation is the fact that there seems to be no facile correlation between economic development and political progress. Rapid economic development (between 1944 and 1955), due mainly to private enterprise and an exceptionally high rate of capital investment, did not show the anticipated positive political results. Some Western observers have argued that the prospects for democracy in Asia would be bright if India (for instance) could only attain and maintain a yearly rate of investment of about 10 per cent of the gross national product. In Syria the rate of investment during the early 'fifties reached 13–14 per cent—without having the desired political effect.

(a leading member of the Syrian Communist Party up to 1943) and Salah ad-Din Bitar, at present Foreign Minister; it relied chiefly on small groups of young intellectuals in Damascus, and Deir az Zur. After the defeat of the Axis Powers it stood for neutralism in world politics and a Socialist programme at home. The demand for equality for women and for the disestablishment of Islam brought the group into sharp conflict with the authorities, and it never attained much importance; in the 1949 elections only one of its members was elected. The party executive thereupon decided to act as an educational organization for the propagation of political theories rather than as a political party. Subsequently, this faction collaborated on occasion with the 'feudal' government to which, in theory, it was unalterably opposed. Aflaq served as Minister of Education in 1949 and undertook, possibly under some pressure, to collaborate with Colonel Husni Zaïm and later with Shishakli. On the whole, however, the policy of this group was based more on principles and less on expediency than was the line taken by the other faction that joined with it to constitute the present-day Ba'ath.

Aqram Hourani, the head of the Arab Socialists (or Republicans) is a different, and even by Levantine standards a remarkable, political character. A brilliant speaker with a dynamic personality, his political career has been distinguished by the most determined efforts to gain power, whatever the means, and by a willingness to ally himself with all and any individuals or parties, rather than by consistency of idea or principle. In the late 'thirties and early 'forties he stood for an orientation towards Germany, Britain, and the United States, in that order, and his domestic alliances were similarly checkered. The most recent phase in his career began in 1949–50, when he organized a group of young intellectuals in Hama and Homs under an 'anti-feudalist' banner, and sought to gain influence in the army and in the peasant movement in Northern Syria. This group also organized small detachments of storm-troops which frequently came into collision with the members of the old parties and the feudal clans. Its programme promised everything to everybody: the party was to be 'nationalist-socialist-popular-progressive', standing for reform in all walks of life, higher living standards, destruction of feudalism, nationalization of physical resources, and a republican-parliamentary régime. All this did not, however, prevent Hourani from collaborating with Colonel Shishakli's military dictatorship in the early 'fifties, when for a time he became Minister of Defence.

After the restoration of the parliamentary régime in 1954 the united Ba'ath Party remained at first in opposition. Within the party Hourani, with his extremist nationalist slogans, gained the upper hand over Aflaq, who put the main emphasis on social reforms. Hourani, a man of great ambitions but less experience than Aflaq, who had at one time been a leading Communist, also stood for close co-operation with the Communists, while Aflaq had some misgivings on that score. While in opposition the party consolidated its influence among the urban intelligentsia, and especially among the students and army officers, who were extremely dissatisfied with the incompetence of the traditional ruling parties. It made considerable headway in the September, 1954, elections, when sixteen of its members were returned, and it won most by-elections between 1955 and 1957. Well-wishers of the party among the army command presumably had some part in this success; there is reason to believe that the election campaigns were at least partly financed from unspecified army funds. With Arab unity high on its programme, Ba'ath gradually became the most anti-Western group in Syria, outstripping temporarily even the local Communists, who were somewhat handicapped by Moscow's 'peaceful co-existence' strategy. In its Arab nationalism it tried to be second to none, even attacking Colonel Nasser for compromising with the British over Suez in 1955. Shortly after the elections the party agreed to enter a government coalition, obtained several key positions (including the Ministries of Foreign Affairs and National Economy), and gradually came to dominate Syrian politics, largely as a result of its alliance with the army command which, after a temporary withdrawal, again took a decisive part in shaping the country's destinies.

The army has intervened at times in many other countries; when other institutions have broken down or become discredited, ambitious young political soldiers have taken over with or without invitation. In Syria, as in other Arab countries, the officer corps has shown a passionate interest in politics, although until comparatively recently it has not really been united in purpose. It was only as a result of several purges (the Maliki affair in 1955, and subsequent reshuffles in 1956–57) that the group headed by the Ba'ath (members and sympathizers, including presumably some Communists) prevailed over other trends. Their political convictions were and are radical; they want changes in Syrian politics, and in the Arab world as a whole, in accordance with the lead given by Colonel Nasser, the Ba'ath, and the Communists. This radicalism is admittedly in any case of a vague character, and their foreign political orientation has less to do with Marxism–Leninism (or any other ideology) than with a general feeling that these are dynamic, purposeful movements which somehow 'get things done'. Back in the 'thirties the same officers would almost certainly have become pro-Fascist (as indeed the older ones among them did). Their anti-Westernism has similar roots. The Soviet Union seems to be surf-riding the wave of the future, whereas the decadent West stands for the *status quo* and has been allied with the old and discredited forces in Iraq, Jordan, and the other Arab countries which these officers want to overthrow.

The Syrian Communists emerged from illegality in 1954 as a small but extremely active and well-organized party, with undoubtedly the best leadership of any Communist Party in the Middle East.[2] It has put much stress on its patriotic convictions, and its leader, Khaled Bakdash, has in effect declared more than once that his party was radical-nationalist rather than Communist: 'Syria is Arab nationalist, not Communist, and will remain so,' he stated in Parliament. The party has been at great pains to drop all the more radical planks in its programme, including its agrarian demands; it has followed a national front line *par excellence* and on occasion has even censured its Ba'ath allies for their excessive intransigence towards right-wing and orthodox Muslim groups (which is perhaps unwarranted, since the Ba'ath eventually discarded its agrarian programme too). It worked mainly through front organizations such as the League of Arab writers, the Syrian Students' Union, and numerous other 'progressive' leagues of women, lawyers, etc. It has gained control of all three Syrian trade-union organizations; the third and largest fell into its hands early in 1957. On occasion the party has shown that it can draw the largest crowds at meetings, but on the whole it has been content with gaining strength rather than demonstrating it with much sound and fury (the unsuccessful policy of the Lebanese comrades during 1950–53). Confident that the tide is running in its favour, and that any 'separatist' activity could only antagonize other political forces and block Syria's road into the Soviet camp, it has been most moderate and restrained in its policy. This has not prevented it from becoming the largest and best organized Communist Party in the Middle East, and one of the leading political forces in Syria. By summer, 1957, it might perhaps have been able to make a bid for political power: but any such venture was quite obviously opposed to both Soviet and general Com-

---

[2] Some of the Western comment about Arab Communism has been slightly disingenuous. A writer in the London *Observer* (September 15, 1957) announced that a Communist *coup d'état* in Syria was unlikely, if not impossible, because Communist membership was only 0·3 per cent of the adult population. According to the same logic the Bolsheviks in Russia could never have been successful, for their number in June, 1917, was 11,500 or 0·01 per cent. It is therefore grossly misleading to talk about the 'numerical weakness' of the Communists—what other Syrian party has ten thousand cadres? But the whole discussion is beside the point; why should the Communists engage in *coups d'étât* if time was working for them anyway?

munist interests in the Middle East. It would have acted as a
deterrent to other Arab countries. It was, moreover, unnecessary,
for a 'gradualist' approach appeared much more promising; as a
guide and mentor behind the Ba'ath, the fellow travellers in the
traditional parties (such as Khaled al Azm), and especially the army
command, it already had a decisive say in shaping the course of
events.

III

All these developments go back to 1955–56, and the crisis of July,
1957, did not really inject any basic new element into the situation.
While Colonel Nasser had to a certain extent curbed Communist
influence at home, and continued his attempts to play East and West
against each other within the limited freedom of action remaining
to him, the ruling forces in Syria had moved from 'positive neutralism' towards an openly pro-Soviet orientation during 1956 and 1957.
Early in July, Khaled al Azm, Minister of Defence, left for Europe,
ostensibly for health reasons, but in fact to conclude a military and
economic Treaty with Moscow. (Azm had been a close collaborator
of the French under the Mandate and one of the country's largest
landowners; subsequently, as the result of personal feuds, he became
one of the leading fellow travellers.) According to the Damascus
daily *Al Rai al am* (August 1, 1957), the Syrian mission in Moscow
had succeeded in reducing the amount Syria was supposed to pay for
arms and other goods from Russia by 70 per cent. The reduction
amounted to $280 million, out of a total of $405 million. Such
terms had never been given by Moscow to even its most loyal satellites; clearly Syria was regarded as a safe investment. This cementing
of closer relations was followed by the discovery on August 12,
1957, of an 'American conspiracy' aimed at 'overthrowing the Syrian
government' which led to the expulsion of three American diplomats
from Damascus, and, in retaliation, to the declaration of the Syrian
Ambassador to the United States as *persona non grata*. Whether
these charges of American conspiracy were Moscow-inspired or
locally fabricated is not known; local initiative is perhaps more
likely, for Moscow was hardly interested in impairing its chances in
other Arab countries by overplaying its hand in Syria, where the
outlook was promising anyway. Another outcome of the Syrian–
Soviet agreement, which may or may not have been planned in
Moscow, was the purge of some of the leading army officers, including the chief of staff Tewfik Nazimudin, who were known not to be
pro-Soviet. He was replaced by Afif al-Bizra, who was identified as a
member of the Communist Party by the Lebanese Press (Bizra

denied this report after some hesitation). There was less far-reaching reshuffling in the civil service and the police command. The old-time politicians such as President Shukri Kuwatly and Sabri al Assali were rendered harmless, and in any case did what they were told. Indeed they were needed to give the régime that aura of continuity and respectability in the Arab world which was considered necessary. The only real danger might have come from opponents in high military position; these key posts had to be taken over by entirely trustworthy people.

All these developments were probably less sensational than their description in the Western Press suggests; there had been no dramatic change in the domestic balance of power in Syria. The real shift had taken place much earlier, and what really happened was that the hold of the Ba'ath-Communist-army bloc was somewhat strengthened by the expulsion of unreliable elements, and that the alliance with Moscow was somewhat strengthened by an additional agreement. This, however, sufficed to produce a state of alarm in the West, and of uneasiness in most Middle East capitals: it was realized that things had gone much further in Damascus than was previously assumed. This, and not the events of August, 1957, was the real cause of the shock. More important than the immediate diplomatic reaction (such as Mr. Loy Henderson's mission to some Arab countries) was the reappraisal that had become imperative. What was the character of the régime that had emerged in Syria? Was it Communist, or on the way to becoming a 'popular democracy'? Or was the West merely facing a temporary alliance between Arab nationalism and Moscow, in which Communism was not involved at all? Or, if both these hypotheses were wrong, had perhaps some new form of 'popular democracy' and voluntary satellite status emerged in the Arab East? And if so, what were its characteristics, and in what way did it differ from the more familiar political patterns of the past?

IV

The debate as to whether the Syrian régime is Communist or part-Communist, or non-Communist, bears a slight resemblance to the conversations of the people waiting for Godot. Some believe that, like Godot, Communism will never come. But in contrast to the play, somebody or something has arrived in Syria: from an unexpected direction, to be sure, wearing different clothes and talking in a strange voice; it is this somebody or something whose identity must be established.

It is largely a question of semantics: if one thinks of Communism as it was in the 'twenties, as a revolutionary, radically left-wing movement, internationalist in outlook, militantly atheist, whole-heartedly in favour of the class struggle, a party claiming to represent and lead the industrial working class, then it follows beyond any shadow of doubt that there is no Communism in Syria today. Nor is there any reason to assume that Communism in this sense will gain any influence in the Middle East in the foreseeable future, and those who contend that all talk about Communism in the Middle East is an invention of malevolent outsiders would appear to be quite right. One may go further and argue that the régime is not even left-wing (as so many Western observers seem to think); the traditional divis-ion between Left and Right made sense only in Europe, and that, moreover, only until the emergence of totalitarian movements such as Fascism and Communism. In the Middle East the label 'left wing' is either meaningless or its meaning is different. Of the traditional values of the left wing in Europe—radical democracy, humanism, pacifism, internationalism—little, if anything, will be found.

All this is quite true, and yet it is very misleading. Most people have become conscious of Communism only during the last decade or so, and they have learnt to regard it, quite wrongly, as a static ideology and movement, which of course it is not. If Syria is not Communist by the standards of the nineteen-twenties, nor is China, and some doubts arise even with regard to the Soviet Union. Com-munism is continually changing, and not only on the tactical level; the idea that only the industrial proletariat could lead the revolution was abandoned in Asian Communism long ago. Generally speaking, the class struggle has been replaced in Asian Communism by the cold war and anti-Westernism. Throughout Asia and the Middle East there is a trend towards some new form, communist Populism or populist Communism, whose distinctive features are anti-capital-ism and anti-colonialism. Even Mr. Khrushchev was called by the late Josef Stalin (as we now know) a 'Narodnik', and there may be a small grain of truth in the charge. (There are some interesting parallels between the new Communist Populism in the Middle East, and Russian and American Populism in the nineteenth century— anti-Semitism for instance—which may warrant further investiga-tion, although, like all historical comparisons, this one would pre-sumably be quite misleading if stretched too far.) A non-Communist leader, Sabri al Assali, declared that he would not remain Prime Minister if Syria were really Communist, and Ba'ath leaders like Aqram Hourani have said that the Communists are the smallest party in Syria. This is all very interesting, but it should be recalled that Khaled Bakdash, head of the Syrian Communist Party, has also stated that his party is not really Communist, and that he wants a nationalist, not a Communist Syria, which tends to show that what politicians say about themselves should not be accepted without due critical analysis. The common implication in these statements was that they disagreed with the old style of Communism, and in this context Bakdash may have been sincere in dissociating himself from it, too. But the whole point is that a new form of popular democracy has developed in Syria (and may develop subsequently in other Arab and Asian countries), and in this sense the Syrian non-Communists are thinking and acting like good 'popular democrats' without even knowing it, just as Molière's *bourgeois* had talked prose all his life without ever realizing it. The distinctive features of this new form of popular democracy are an anti-Western and pro-Soviet orientation in foreign policy, an aggressive nationalism, and the attempt to modernize and industrialize the countries in question by the methods of bureaucratic state capitalism.[3] There may be some social reform, but all *radical* change is omitted: the existing social structure in the Middle East and Asia in general has in any case been disintegrating, and the industrial *bourgeoisie* is so much weaker than in the West that it is possible to forget about the class struggle and to concentrate on modernization and industrialization.

These prolegomena towards a new theory of 'popular democracy' in the Middle East may be criticized on several counts. It could be argued that bureaucratic state capitalism can be found in the West too; how, it may be asked, does the Syrian development differ from Kemal Atatürk's collaboration with Moscow in the 'twenties? The issue of bureaucratic state capitalism is a complicated one and cannot be discussed in detail here; but it should at least be mentioned in passing that not a few observers have described the Soviet régime as state capitalism or state socialism; once there is total control by the state over the economy the differences between the two forms tend to diminish and even to disappear. There are, in addition, two important differences between Atatürk's Turkey in the 'twenties and Syria in the late 'fifties: one is the change in the world balance of power, which has made Russia now a much more formidable and unequal partner than thirty years ago. Moreover, Atatürk's alliance with Moscow was strictly limited to the field of foreign relations: far

---

[3] One ingredient of Communist ideology has strongly affected this neo-Populism, the Leninist theory of imperialism which became 'the binding link between Marxism-Leninism and Asian resentments' (as Benjamin Schwartz wrote on China in *Mao and the Rise of Chinese Communism*). 'So widespread has been the acceptance of the Leninist theory of imperialism even in circles far removed from the Communist Party, that wherever imperialism was discussed the Leninist interpretation came to be taken for granted.' These observations on the China of the nineteen-twenties also apply to the Middle East in the 'forties and 'fifties.

from opening his country to Communist influences, he actively suppressed all such activities. What distinguishes the Syrian situation is the fact that the alliance from above is complemented by Communist pressure from below.

A second argument runs roughly as follows: events in Syria (and elsewhere) are merely a manifestation of radical Arab nationalism, of its feeling of frustration and disappointment with the West; its alliance with Russia has nothing to do with Communism. This is based on the belief that Arab nationalism is a factor equal to Communism, a possible countervailing force, which is a quite unwarranted assumption. Arab nationalism and Communism move, at least in the present stage, on different levels and therefore do not clash. The central aim of Arab nationalism, some form of Arab federation or union, may be achieved in a Communist framework as well as in any other; it would surely be ludicrous to deny that Mao Tse-tung is a Chinese nationalist as well as a Communist. Arab nationalism has no social or political philosophy of its own which would necessarily bring it into opposition to the Communism of the late 'fifties.

The third criticism is the only one which may have some validity; wherever Communism has prevailed so far, it may be argued, it was brought about by a Communist Party. The Syrian landowners and merchants who, together with the Ba'ath Party, constitute the bulk of the fellow-travelling régime, may be stupid, but they are no Communists. Is it possible to envisage the advent of a 'popular democracy'—even of a new style—without the Communists playing the main role? This is a question which for the time being remains open. But experience suggests that a determined minority with a clear programme may well have a decisive influence on the course of events provided the majority consists of confused men who do not really know what they want or where they are going.

The Syrian trend towards a new form of 'popular democracy' may not be irreversible; this will depend largely on the over-all balance of power in the world two or three years hence. Full Soviet control in Damascus is unlikely for various reasons, but there should be no undue illusions; Russia's only satellite that does not border on the Soviet Union, Albania, is its most faithful and orthodox ally. There is one essential difference between Moscow's satellites in eastern Europe and countries like Syria, and to a lesser degree Egypt. Communism in eastern Europe has little if any attraction, as events in Hungary and Poland have shown. The east European countries resent Soviet domination, regard Soviet Communism as a reactionary system, are not anti-Western in outlook, but want 'to return' to Europe. There can be no doubt how they would opt if the choice were open to them. They are most reluctant satellites, whereas a country like Syria is a voluntary and most enthusiastic convert, something Moscow never found in Europe. In contrast to Poland, Hungary, and all the other east European countries, there is a strong pro-Soviet and pro-Communist sentiment, because Moscow appears to many people in the Middle East, including a majority of the political *élites*, as a carrier of the torch of progress. (It may be suggested that in the Middle East, unlike eastern Europe, Soviet Communism can promote progress, in view of the inability of the local industrial *bourgeoisie* to give a political lead to their countries. But this argument cannot be analysed here.) Be that as it may, Western statesmen have completely disregarded the specific emotional brand of anti-Westernism which is so characteristic of radical movements in the Middle East and unlike anything known in eastern Europe, or probably even in the Soviet Union. Granted this hostility it is extremely unrealistic to argue, as it has been done, that national Communism in the Middle East would be preferable to what is called 'international Communism'. This involves a completely unwarranted equation between national Communism in eastern Europe and in the Middle East. A student of Chinese affairs has said that 'we need to examine carefully and more explicitly whether a Communist China, left to its own devices, may not actually be more aggressive and a greater threat to world peace than one allied with the Soviet Union. There is a real question whether irrational xenophobic and nationalist ingredients are not much more potent in the Chinese Communist revolution than in the Soviet leadership of today. . . . It can be argued that the Soviet Union may be potentially the more responsible of the two partners, the one which might serve to curb aggressive moves.'[4] The same could be said, *mutatis mutandis*, for Soviet–Syrian relations. It is misleading to portray the innocent Syrians as the unsuspecting victims of the bad, scheming Russians. Moscow moved into the Middle East in the middle 'fifties with considerable delay, after explicit invitations had been extended by Cairo and Damascus. The angry Soviet denials of Western allegations of 'penetration' and 'invasion' are technically correct: they have come as guests, not invaders. President Eisenhower was equally mistaken when in September, 1957, he warned international Communism not to push Syria towards aggression against her neighbours: Syria does not need pushing. If there has been any pushing, it was probably in the reverse direction. Moscow's influence in Damascus is more likely to be one of moderation, if only because it is believed that too great aggressiveness on Syria's part (and too fast progress towards Communist Populism) would antagonize the other Middle Eastern

<hr>

[4] Alexander Eckstein in *Moscow–Peking Axis* (Harper, 1957).

countries and make Soviet progress throughout the area more difficult.

There are still some misconceptions in the West about the new radical movements in the Middle East. On the immediate political level the most dangerous is the disregard of their irrational, xenophobic, and nationalist ingredients which may make these movements and régimes at the present stage not more, but less tractable than the Soviet Union and 'international Communism'.

October, 1957

THE ARAB SOCIALIST MOVEMENT

by GEBRAN MAJDALANY

BEFORE GIVING any account of the Arab Socialist movement, one has to lay down a simplified definition of Socialism. I shall call that party Socialist whose programme includes the abolition of social classes, the vesting of the principal resources of the country in the community, and the struggle against capitalism—first international and then national capitalism. I shall take account only of parties that answer to this criterion, and neglect the rest. Many parties adopt the label of 'Socialist' in the hope of attracting the Arab masses, whose condition in some regions is so wretched that they are all too likely to fall for the magic of the word. I shall say nothing, therefore, of the 'Corporative Social Party' of Syria (whose leader, Faisal Assali, has no connection with the present Syrian Premier), nor of the 'Socialist Party of the Nation' in Iraq (whose leader, the late Saleh Jaber, has more than once been Prime Minister); nor of the old 'Socialist Party' of Egypt which has points in common with the Muslim Brotherhood; nor, finally, of the 'National Socialist Party' of Jordan, which in the last two years has gained in prestige by its hostility to the Baghdad Pact. These parties may, in certain cases, take up positions which are healthy from a Socialist point of view, but their record, their organization, their programmes, and their leading personalities give no guarantee of continuity or progress.

There are two main currents in the Arab Socialist movement. The first, and by far the stronger, is represented by the 'Ba'ath al-Arabi al-Ishtiraki', or party of the 'Arab Socialist Renaissance', often called simply the Ba'ath (Renaissance). This party holds that the Arab world, by its unity of culture and of aspiration, forms 'one nation' and that its present political divisions are artificial. The party is organized to bring about this union, in which all its members are required to believe. Its general secretary has authority over all the party's sections and cells in all Arab countries.

The party preserves, however, a certain degree of autonomy within each country, which has its own executive committee and secretary-general, who look after purely internal affairs. The secretary-general for each country is *ipso facto* a member of the National Executive Committee, which alone can take decisions of wider purport. In each country an annual congress meets to lay down the plan of work for the following year, strictly in accordance with the policy projected by the National Executive Committee, and by the National Congress of delegates from all the Arab countries.

The other main current of Arab Socialism is represented by certain parties which base their action upon present possibilities. This current is weaker, because such action produces none of the 'chain reactions' set up by the deeds of the Ba'ath. The 'National Democratic Party' of Iraq and the 'Progressive Socialist Party' of the Lebanon are the chief representatives of this secondary current. Acceptance of the political realities of the countries in which they work (though the party in Iraq also looks towards Arab union) imposes limitations upon their aims, which have to be adapted to their own field of action. The Lebanese party has the merit of having convened an Arab Socialist Congress some years ago, although, for lack of preparation and of precise objectives, this was not followed up; and since then they have moved further away from the Ba'ath and other Arab Socialist Parties.

Both the Lebanese Socialist and the Iraq Democratic Nationalist Parties have now a considerable popular following, but they tend to a gradual effacement of their original character. The Iraqian party has been declared illegal by Nuri Sa'id, and its last gestures were hardly distinguishable from those of the Communist Party. The Lebanese party, on the contrary, has been gradually slipping towards the Right, until now its leaders seem even to envisage the possibility of a *modus vivendi* with the U.S.A. and Great Britain. The Lebanese party has, however, the better chance of surviving as a political force; primarily because it has legal recognition, but also because of the personality of its leader, a descendant of one of the most powerful families of the Lebanon, whose name alone assures him of the loyalty of half the Druses of Lebanon. But from the standpoint of Socialist, as distinct from political, force these parties are of very limited influence. The Arab Socialist movement is in reality led by the Ba'ath.

Characteristics of the Ba'ath

This movement is very violently anti-colonialist. Colonialism in the Arab lands is not a nightmare of the past; it is a reality under all its forms, from the most subtle economic imperialism to the most primitive Protectorates of the peninsula. That is why the struggle against imperialism has, for the Arab Socialists, as much importance as the raising of wage-rates has for the American or European worker. They regard it as the acid test for any Socialism or even reformism. Hence the lack of sympathetic contact between the Ba'ath and the European Socialist Parties, especially those of France and Britain, who are accused of over-indulgence towards capital interests in the colonies.[1] Hence, also, an erroneous opinion entertained by a good many Western publicists (such as those of *Le Monde*) who see the Ba'ath as a 'more nationalizing than socializing' force; and also the more discriminating opinion which stresses its opposition to the Communists—for it is, on the whole, anti-Communist, though more for political than ideological reasons, and the Ba'ath is never obsessed by this antagonism. It did, indeed, during the last elections, refuse to make a common front with the Communists in Syria and Jordan, but this was dictated by electoral calculations. When a limited agreement promises a gain for the Left, the Ba'ath does not refuse it.

The second important point about Arab Socialism is its systematic opposition, from its beginning, to the politics of the rival blocs, and its attachment to what is called 'positive neutrality' or 'the third force'. Its success in getting Syria and Jordan out of the rut of British policy is undeniable. There has been constant Anglo-American pressure for the last four years to get the Arab countries into a Mediterranean pact of mutual defence and thus into the Baghdad Pact. All the arguments in favour of this looked attractive. The first propaganda point, cunningly put forward by the British-controlled papers, was Islam. Were not Turkey, Pakistan, Iraq, and Iran all Muslim countries? And who was the chief opponent of the pact but India, which had 'persecuted and expelled' the Pakistan Muslims? Turkey, it must be said, lent its generous aid to this campaign even at the risk of sabotaging what remained of the work of Atatürk. Another trump card played by the British advocates in Iraq and the other countries was the need for arms to deal with Israel; for if we could not get arms from the Eastern bloc (this was before the delivery of Czechoslovak arms) the West was the only

[1] Note, moreover, that the British Labour Party was reinstated in favour by its courageous denunciation of the Anglo-Franco-Israelian attack in October, 1956.

source of supply for the Arabs: it followed that, in all realism, one ought to make a few minimal concessions for the sake of guaranteeing the common cause. By a deviation from their own policy these advocates concentrated attention upon Israel as the only danger; and the third stratagem of these Baghdad Pact advocates was to urge union between Syria and Iraq, in order to create a 'strong state' against Israel and lay the basis for a future union of all Arab peoples.

To expose the methods used by Britain and her allies and satellites may seem irrelevant to the subject of Arab Socialism; but it is necessary to recall the amount of pressure and of seduction to which the Arab states were exposed, if we are to realize the influence exerted by the Arab Socialists, and what persevering effort they must have put forth, effectively to resist a temptation which was so 'rational', besides being often accompanied by the menaces, more or less veiled, of British and American ambassadors at Damascus. To anyone who knows the sentimentality of the Arabs—the trait which explains their weakness for religion and their hostility to the State of Israel—the failure of the Western arguments to break Arab neutralism is most significant. The politics of 'bloc-formation' may be said to have definitely failed.

The open support of the Ba'ath and other Socialist Parties for Nasser's régime in Egypt is principally due to his foreign policy. Socialists have every reason to believe that the encouragement of this progressive foreign policy will inevitably lead the régime to depend more and more upon the Egyptian masses, and on the progressive movements in other Arab countries, who alone will support it as a movement of emancipation.[2]

Lastly, an essential characteristic of the Ba'ath is its aspiration to Arab union. The two principal slogans of the party are 'A Single Arab Nation' and 'Unity, Liberty, and Socialism'.

For a European Socialist the Ba'ath may perhaps seem to be too nationalistic, to put too great an emphasis upon the Arabs' unity as a nation. But we must remind our European comrades that a

---

[2] This support has never implied an unreserved approval of the Egyptian régime. The Arab Socialists were the first to attack Nasser when he appeared as the spoilt child of the American and other Occidental sponsors. Today he has become the symbol of Arab emancipation: for he has not only to stand up against a Great Britain whose colonial interests are threatened, and a France wounded in its self-esteem, but also against the reactionary Arab coalition, centred in Iraq and elsewhere, which has some support throughout the Arab world. The Socialists, by giving Nasser their frank but conditional support, help to unify the anti-imperialist front, and weaken the Arab reaction, which is the most dangerous and violent enemy of Nasser's foreign—and his economic—policy.

French Socialist, for example, finds his national problem practically solved already (except perhaps for some Socialists of the Right who still think that 'Algeria is in France' and therefore insist upon a Franco-Algerian union), and so it is for a British Socialist. For the Arabs, the existing fragmentation of their territory into little, more or less 'ricketty', states—which was the work of the Ottomans and then of the French and British after the First World War—has never ceased to handicap their efforts towards a real emancipation, political and economic. On the other hand, Arab union is impossible under present conditions except upon the basis of progress. Of the traditional factors making for unity, language and culture alone remain; it is above all to the unity of aspiration and the will to a common life that the Socialists give prominence. In their view, religion is far from being a unifying element. The current confusion of thought which, even in the Arab world, identifies Islam with Arabism is vigorously, though discreetly, combated by the Socialists. It is maintained by certain heads of states and Arab leaders who appeal to religious sentiment in order to win an artificial popularity, and by the 'Muslim Brotherhood', who sincerely believe that the Qur'an can take the place of *Das Kapital* for the Arabs. The open conflict between the Socialists and the Muslim Brotherhood in Syria and in Jordan has enabled fundamental socialists to secularize their ideal more firmly, and helped the general public to distinguish the Socialist movement from the numerous semi-political and semi-religious movements.

The principal enemies of unity at the present time are the foreign Powers, the dynasties in power, and all those who benefit most from the divisions between the landed proprietors and the merchants, and whose privileges are menaced by any attempts at union. The whole struggle for union is therefore a struggle against imperialism, feudalism, and the reactionary elements.

For Socialists, unity is not conceivable without a progressive content: no project, therefore, is to be encouraged which will not gain a victory over the internal reaction or the foreign Powers and trusts. Similarly, the Ba'ath is firmly opposed to Iraq–Syrian unification, since Syria might then become another outpost of the British hegemony. By the same token the Ba'ath has led the campaign for federation between Syria and Egypt; and the party's acceptance of two ministerial posts in the present Syrian cabinet has no other explanation but the Ba'ath's desire to promote this plan. Any idea of federation with Egypt would have been unthinkable by Socialists two or three years ago: it is only since they became convinced that Egypt was sincerely seeking political and economic liberation from all foreign interference, and lending moral support to all the movements for Arab liberation, that the Socialists have accepted this idea of a federation, which the Ba'ath now regards as a basis for their unified action.

SOCIALISM IN IRAQ

The Ba'ath challenges all the traditional conceptions that are current in the Arab world: that is why it attracts at first only a minority of rebellious intellectuals. For many years it had to be content to inspire new currents of thought, until the day when the Arab defeat in Palestine shook confidence in all the traditional leaders. The masses, weary of the methods and the régimes which, in their eyes, had brought about the catastrophe, were ready for new leaders, and all the dynamic movements gained by this. One may say that, on the whole, all the parties of moderation have seen their influence diminish to the advantage of the 'extremists' both of the Left and of the Right. Because of this nervous tension the military régimes have leapt into prominence, the Muslim Brotherhood has enlarged its audiences, and the parties of the Left have made a rapid advance. The Ba'ath has at last seen its intellectuals succeed in reaching the hearts of the masses, and thus escape from the isolation which would, in the end, have turned them into utopian idealists.

Today the Ba'ath is unquestionably a party with mass support in three Arab countries—Syria, Jordan, and Iraq. In Iraq it has to work underground, for it is violently repressed. For having undertaken to distribute leaflets against the Baghdad Pact, eleven of its members have been condemned to a month's imprisonment or more; some students in the party have been arrested for transmitting the call to a general strike to leaders in the principal towns. This appeal to strike, on the opening day of the first London Conference, was ignored by the Press, and bill-posting about it was forbidden by the government.[3]

But repression is not always a real handicap: it weeds out those 'liberal moderates' who abandon all activity as soon as their ideas put them in danger of prison—which is, in fact, what happened after Sa'id's police measures in Iraq. The traditional and liberal parties left the way open to the forces of the Left.

The Ba'ath's chief rival in Iraq is still the National Democratic

[3] Such measures look mild today, when Parliament has been suspended and twenty-three leaders of the Opposition arrested whose only crime was the publishing of a message sent to King Faisal. That message contained a sharp criticism of the policy of Iraq during the last two years, and demanded the dismissal of Nuri Sa'id and the denunciation of the Baghdad Pact.

Party, which is older and better known. Its leader, Kamel Jadirgi, remains one of the most popular and highly respected figures in the country; and although he is kept under strict observation, he is very active in the Arab interest. His party, however, has been badly intimidated by Sa'id's coercive measures. Socialist though it is, the National Democratic Party has lost influence through lack of organization, and of balance in its doctrine; and under the pressure of events it has been driven into a negative position. Its militants retain a clear enough notion of the aims and activities that they object to, but are more hesitant when it is a question of supporting or formulating positive demands.

The National Democratic Party has agreed to join with the Istiqlal Party in forming a National Congress which, in its turn, has been pronounced illegal by the Iraq government. This congress is not a party but an alliance. The Istiqlal is a nationalist party which may play a progressive part during the period of liberation, but it will repudiate its partner as soon as independence is achieved: the objectives of this new front are therefore purely provisional. Its paramount aim is to co-ordinate all the efforts of the opposition towards the guaranteeing of democratic liberties, the annulment of the Baghdad Pact, and the promotion of the cause of Arab unification. The front will not survive the present régime. Further speculation about the future of Iraq would seem pretentious: but the longer Sa'id's dictatorship lasts the better it may be for the Ba'ath, as a party, and for Jadirgi as a personage and a symbol.

THE SOCIALISTS IN SYRIA

The Ba'ath is the only Socialist Party in Syria. In Parliament it takes third place in order of numerical strength; after the People's Party (33 deputies) and the National Party (23), but the Ba'ath's 16 deputies with their allies form the most homogeneous and the most formidable combination in Parliament.

During the negotiations which preceded the formation of the present 'national' government, the delegates of the People's Party, which is known for its pro-Iraq sympathies, tried to take the Ministry of Foreign Affairs away from the Socialists. They argued that, for the last two years, the Socialists had in fact dominated the foreign policy without being part of the government, and that they need not cling to a Ministry whose policies they would be directing in any case. In the end the Socialists insisted on obtaining this portfolio as well as that of National Economics; two key positions which show how much the Socialists' influence exceeds their weight in Parliament. The Western Embassies of Damascus never cease to be surprised by this paradox of a Parliament of the Right following a policy of the Left—just the opposite of what happens in France!

The influence of the Ba'ath is to be ascribed to several factors, economic as well as political. First, it was the only party that gained in number of seats at the last elections—which were said to be the first *free* elections ever held in the Arab world. After having had only three seats the Ba'ath suddenly reappeared with sixteen; a success which impressed the electorate more than the greater number of seats held by other parties. The Ba'ath has profited by this to keep the political initiative: it has never ceased to force the other two parties to take up positions upon problems that divide conservative opinion. On the whole, the two conservative parties, mostly representative of big landed proprietors and of commerce and industry, have followed suit, for fear of making trouble. The Ba'ath has regularly backed up its demands upon Parliament by pointing to the threat of strikes or popular demonstrations. The fall of the last government, which was of People's Party formation, shows how the Socialists, although a minority, were able to make the majority resign, simply by manoeuvring and keeping the initiative. The Minister of National Economy had signed an agreement with France for the delivery of a quantity of corn, and the French wanted it shipped to Algeria. It was an advantageous deal; the price was better than the Syrians could usually count upon in good seasons, and the government (mostly men of the landed interest) could not but welcome the agreement. But the Syrians are highly sensitive about the Algerian War, as they are about every Arab cause; the government therefore sought to disguise the destination of this wheat, which, however, became known to the Socialists by an indiscretion. They immediately distributed a pamphlet in every town in Syria denouncing the People's Party for conniving with the enemy to feed troops who were killing our Algerian brothers. The workers of the party at Latakia called a strike and refused to load the wheat; and presently a great crowd of demonstrators led by the Ba'ath forced their way into the Ministry of National Economy, occupied the offices, and said they would remain there till the government resigned—which it did, the following morning.

Two earlier events had shown how Socialism was advancing in Syria. The first was a trial of strength between the Left and the conservatives, occasioned by the death of a conservative deputy of Homs. The conservatives had controlled this town at the general election and gained most of the seats in the department: naturally they expected to replace the deceased conservative by another. But the Socialists and Communists combined to put up a candidate of the Left, with the result that the People's Party found itself beaten in one of its chièf strongholds. The second trial of strength took place at Aleppo, the second town of Syria and the nerve-centre of the People's Party. A Socialist there had been chosen to represent Labour in a Commission upon wage-rates, and the 'populists', irritated by this Socialist success in their midst, invoked an ancient law promulgated by Shishakli, to disqualify him. The effect of this law would have been to exclude from his employment every syndicalist who did not undertake to abstain from all political action; and the government, with its populist majority, accordingly annulled the election of the syndical populist and replaced him by an ally of the People's Party. But the day after that decision a demonstration in the town by fifteen thousand workers forced the government to go back on its decision and promise to revoke the law of Shishakli.

Impartial observers agree that the Socialists are likely to double the number of their seats at the next elections, a prospect that is disquieting for the Western Embassies and the conservative parties. Negotiations are afoot for the merging of the two main parties, and leaders of the National and the People's Parties seem to envisage this as a possibility in spite of their great personal differences. In any event, some electoral alliances are to be expected; and either alliance or a merger would doubtless reinforce the conservative bloc. On the other hand, it will simplify the political map and give the Syrian voter a clearer choice between progressives and reactionaries.

SOCIALISM IN JORDAN

Parliamentary representation has not, until now, been a reliable measure of the strength of the Left in Arab politics. This is strikingly evident in Jordan, where the elections used to be effectively organized by General Glubb. The army represented the only force capable of manipulating the administrative machine. The seven Socialist candidates had been jailed on the morning of the election and were not released until after the Glubb Parliament had held its first sitting.

Today there are four main forces in the country: the King (who has succeeded in regaining favour since the time when the refugees from Jericho demanded a republic and General Templar arrived in Jordan); the army, which since Glubb's departure has become a pliant instrument in the hands of the monarchy; the organized parties, which are Socialist and Communist; and, finally, the traditional authorities.

At the last elections the Socialists and Communists formulated three principal demands:

(1) Denunciation of the Anglo-Jordan Treaty;

(2) The 'Arabization' of the army—that is, the removal of Glubb and the British officers, and the negotiation of Arab financial aid to replace the British subvention.

(3) Action against the Baghdad Pact, and the signing of a treaty with Egypt, Syria, and Saudi Arabia, the upholders of the neutralist policy.

Glubb's faking of the previous elections, and the sanguinary consequences that ensued, now provoked an additional demand —the dissolution of Parliament.

No one can deny the value of the part played by the King in facing these demands, although the young, easily-influenced Hashemite monarch agreed to them only under popular pressure and in order not to be outbid by the forces of the Left. When General Templar came at the beginning of 1956 to impose the Baghdad Treaty upon a state almost entirely financed by Britain, the nonplussed government could signify its refusal only by the negative gesture: it resigned. The British quickly replaced it by a fresh cabinet, all pro-Iraq, under the premiership of Hezaa Majali; but now, for the first time in Jordan's history, the government had to resign under pressure from the masses, and did so five days after its formation. In the towns and even in the smallest villages the people forced the barriers and demanded the dismissal of 'the traitors'. Western observers, astonished at this unanimity, tried to explain it as the work of the 'unholy trinity' of Saudian bribery, Egyptian wireless propaganda, and the Communists. Only later, by the American periodical *Time*, was the insurrection recognized as the work of the Ba'ath Socialist Party.

The King was obliged to proclaim the opposition of Jordan to the Baghdad Pact and to dissolve Parliament—which, however, he soon had to recall to fend off an attack from the Right. To avoid further trouble he promised to dismiss Glubb, and again to dissolve the Chamber: he even took part himself in a public demonstration on the Algerian question where he delivered a resounding speech—and this at a meeting held in defiance of its prohibition by his own Prime Minister.

Rightly or wrongly, Glubb's dismissal was regarded as a triumph for the Socialists; and they, for their part, could not but see their influence increased by the turn of events, Glubb having been their most fierce and active enemy for the last eight years. Abdullah Rimawi, the secretary-general of the party, and his henchman Nawas had been imprisoned six times, and the seventh time interned in a remote desert camp, within the last four years. Stimulated by success, the party quickened its march, demanded the removal of the Glubb Parliament and a new election, which took place on October 27, 1956. This election was watched with the liveliest interest in all the

Arab lands and by the British, for it was the first to be held without police and military supervision: the Socialists and Communists, whose parties had so recently been illegal, now presented official candidates under their own party labels. The results have been interpreted as, in effect, a swing of public opinion to the Left; as undoubtedly a gesture of opposition to Britain—and, therefore, of solidarity with Egypt.

THE LEBANON

The Lebanon is, of all Arab countries, the most refractory to Socialism: the weakness of its Socialist movement is largely due to the strength of a middle class composed chiefly of traders; to the number of religious communities, none of which includes a majority of the population; and, not least, to the mistakes made by the Progressive Socialist Party, so far the only spokesman for Socialism in the Lebanon. This party was founded in 1949 by a young landowner who also enjoyed the privilege of being the temporal head of a religious community. At first it attracted a number of intellectuals and workers who, while playing up to its founder's attachments to the past, hoped they would be able to counteract the pressure exerted upon him by his personal supporters. In this they failed: between the conflicting claims of the past and the present, the leader at first took up contradictory positions, and then appealed more and more to ancestral aspirations. In the end the ideals of the past carried the day, to the detriment of Socialism in general in the Lebanon, for by discrediting his party the founder discredited the movement itself.

A recent schism led by five old and close colleagues of this 'feudal Socialist' was immediately welcomed by all the Arab Socialists who were tired of this 'progressive' party's deviations. The dissidents were known to have a decided sympathy with the Ba'ath, and they may to some extent improve that movement's foothold in the Lebanon. Here the Ba'ath's support is almost wholly limited to the Mohammedans, for most of the Christians have an instinctive fear that any appeals to union or Arab federation may lead to Mohammedan domination; but the secessionists are all Christians, a fact which may soften the 'alarming' aspect of Arab unity and help to introduce the Ba'ath's ideas into Christian circles. The progress of Socialism in the Lebanon is bound to be slow, for it goes against the economic grain of the country. Here, where the doctrines of the physiocrats are applicable even today, nothing short of an economic disaster could enable the people even to imagine such a thing as a 'planned economy'; and the present prosperity, though based largely upon unstable revenues (from *émigrés*, transport, and tourism), precludes any serious inclination towards the Left. The organization of a sound Socialist movement will, however, prepare the ground for the future: an economic crisis cannot be very far off.

THE ARABIAN PENINSULA

Political parties are absolutely forbidden throughout peninsular Arabia. Individual liberty depends, in most places, wholly upon the goodwill of the prince or the sheikh. But the expansion of the oil industry and the importation of large numbers of technicians and workers from Palestine is developing a politically conscious proletariat. Excepting Jedda and two or three other towns, one cannot speak of a *bourgeoisie* in the accepted sense of the word: every political claim or political movement has to originate in the working class and to be stamped with its approval. On the east coast, in the region of the oilfields, the workers number more than thirty thousand; and we saw from the Press how this throng of humanity arose to welcome Abdul Nasser during his latest visit to the Saudi Arabian King; but the Press did not know that these workers were all organized into cells and committees.

Farther south, in Aden, the British authorities have for some months past suspended *Ba'ath* (the local organ of the movement), which they accuse of having originated all the strikes in the principality; but the suppression of political parties has helped them perforce to improve their organization; and all their demands are disguised under economic arguments or general considerations. They also make use of cultural clubs and of formations with ambiguous titles such as the 'National Unity Front' at Qatar or the 'National Front' at Bahrein. By such means the Socialists, though only a minority, have been able to resume their activity.

But for their ultimate penetration of the backward regions of the peninsula, the strength of the Socialists will come from the universities. The growing numbers of students sent from Saudi Arabia, Kuwait, and elsewhere to the Universities of Beirut, Damascus, or Egypt are opening up a new future for Socialism. It was at the American University of Beirut, and the Syrian University of Damascus, that the present leaders of the Socialist Parties in Jordan and Iraq made their first contacts with the movement.

*   *   *   *   *

The nationalization of the Canal Company of Suez precipitated events which have upset all the data of the Middle Eastern problem.

On the side of the West, France, which had to some extent followed a neutralist line in opposing the Baghdad Pact and the entry of Iraq's troops into Jordania, has now completely gone over to the Anglo-Iraqian policy. The Franco-British have adopted the purely negative policy of anti-Nasserism: having nothing positive in view, they take the line that they think will be the most damaging to Egypt; but this has driven them to measures which alienate more and more of the Arab masses, not only of loyalists of the Egyptian régime.

The West has thus indirectly helped Nasser to consolidate his position in the Arab world. France was persuaded, for anti-Nasser reasons, to offer a quantity of arms to Israel and, moreover, a number of tanks and aeroplanes to the reactionaries. But Arabs regarded that aid to Israel as an aggression against them all and not only against Nasser, whom it therefore made them want to protect.

The aggression against Egypt after the act of nationalization (which Arabs saw as a step towards emancipation) furnished another proof that Egypt was the champion of Arab independence. The moderates who sought a compromise between nationalism and pro-Western ideas found themselves faced with a difficult choice, for it was no longer possible to keep neutral: one had to choose either Egypt and independence, or the West as represented by the members of the Baghdad Pact. The stiffening of Arab opinion had the further effect of isolating the leaders of Iraq, whose attempt to form an Arab belt out of the countries of the traditional Fertile Crescent was now doomed to defeat. Hashemite Jordan, their surest ally, had become clearly aligned with Egypt's policy; and Syria, the only other Western-Arab neighbour of Iraq, had fully endorsed the Egyptian attitude, thereby paralysing the Syrian People's Party, and even menacing Iraq's economy by blowing up her oil pipelines.

In the face of this diplomatic defeat, Iraq fell back upon a counsel of despair: she sent arms to her partisans in Syria to enable them to overthrow and supersede the government. The plot was discovered in time, and the People's Party—which until then had been the ruling party in Parliament—now fell under the grave accusation of treason. Many of its influential members are in prison, while others have fled to the Lebanon or Turkey. Thus the anti-Iraqi bloc has emerged in greater strength, and the People's Party, if it wishes to survive as a political force, will not only be obliged officially to sever connections with Iraq, but to compete in the anti-Iraq campaign. The party has already, in an official declaration, violently denounced the Baghdad Pact and Nuri Sa'id in person.

Thus the Franco-British solidarity, newly achieved in the Middle

East, has raised up against itself a new anti-Western, Arab solidarity comprising Egypt, Jordan, and Syria. The complete independence of Jordan and its development no longer depend upon the will of the British, but rather upon that of Damascus, Cairo, and Riad. The Jordan government has officially expressed its desire to abolish the Anglo-Jordan Treaty, a desire which awaits fulfilment as soon as the three other interested countries provide the funds necessary for Jordan's survival, in replacement of the British subvention for maintaining military bases in Jordan.

This whole situation is one in which the Arab Socialists should be able to realize a part of their programme, by hastening unification with a country situated outside the Fertile Crescent—namely, with Egypt—and putting an end to Nuri Sa'id's dream of creating a strong Arab bloc in opposition to Egypt. They will succeed in this if they can force their own Arab countries to pursue policies against the interests of the Western colonial Powers, and those of their natural allies in the heart of the Arab world—that is, the conservative parties who owe their survival to Western financial aid, and who now see themselves being cut off from their supplies.

The weakening of these economic and political links will have the effect of speeding-up the industrialization of the Arab countries, and the opening-up of new markets with nations who do not threaten them with a new colonialism. The industries of Germany (Eastern no less than Western), of Czechoslovakia and the other 'popular democracies' have to a great extent supplanted those of French and British firms. Exchanges with them are increasingly carried on by barter, and this encourages the development of the natural resources of the Arab lands.

But if Socialist aims are effectually to guide the course of Arab politics, it is necessary that the Socialists should continue their present collaboration with Egypt. That collaboration is not likely to be called in question so long as the tension in the Arab world persists; but when quieter times return, the Socialists will be able to pursue this policy of the outstretched hand towards Egypt only in so far as Egypt presses on with the liberalization of her régime, which has already begun. Egypt, which is completely isolated from the Arab reaction, seems prepared to fulfil that condition; and if she does so, Arab Socialism will be equally ready to inspire and direct the same development in the Arab countries during the next few years. If not, the struggle must go on without Egypt: in which case the contest may be a finer one, but will certainly be more arduous and sanguinary.

Spring, 1957

THE ISLAMIC COMMUNITY AND COMMUNISM

by DR. NABIH AMIN FARIS

IS ISLAM, because of its hostility to materialist atheistic beliefs, a guarantee against the spread of Communism among Muslims? The question has recently acquired more than academic interest and urgency. The world has been divided into two conflicting ideologies, each trying with all the means available to it to gain control over the minds of men everywhere. A large number of spokesmen, however, both in the West and among Muslims, have been reiterating that in this struggle Islam stands as a barrier against the onslaught of Communism. On the surface, this position seems assuring, but on closer investigation it loses all the talismanic charms with which its advocates endue it. In this study, the entire problem is examined in the light of traditional Muslim orthodoxy and current Islamic practice. Needless to say, the writer has no desire whatsoever to criticize either Islam or Communism. As a matter of fact, this article would never have been written had it not been specifically requested.

In reviewing a recently published book on the history of the Arabs,[1] I concluded the review with the following observation:

'Another myth which seems to be as ubiquitous as flying saucers, and as unreal, is the claim that among the factors which stand a barrier against the spread of Communism in the Arab world is Islam's "hostility to a materialist, atheitsic creed and way of life". The reviewer is inclined to believe that Islam, in spite of its hostility to materialist atheistic creeds, is no guarantee against the spread of Communism at all, but perhaps a preparation for it. The final answer

[1] Edward Atiyah, *The Arabs* (London, Penguin Books Ltd., 1955). The review appeared in the *Middle East Forum*, Beirut, December, 1955, pp. 30–32.

might come from wholly unexpected places—from Egypt, Iraq, and Indonesia, all predominantly Muslim.'

A few weeks later, I received a gracious letter from Mr. 'Abdul Majid, Editor of *The Islamic Review*, London and Woking, in which he expressed his interest in and agreement with the review, 'especially the observations in the concluding sentences'. The letter goes on to say: 'The smug comfort and sense of complacency from which leaders of the Muslim world suffer in the belief that their religion is proof against the encroachment of Communism is a theory which must be destroyed if we really wish the Middle Eastern countries to be free from the disaster that might overtake them otherwise.' Would I, therefore, he asked, though not belonging to the Muslim faith, be willing to share with readers the reasons which have led me to the conclusion that Islam, in spite of its hostility to materialist atheistic creeds, is no guarantee against the spread of Communism, but perhaps a preparation for it?

Although on purely doctrinal grounds Islam and Communism are irreconcilable, yet there are striking similarities in the two systems. It must be said at the outset, and quite emphatically, that on purely doctrinal grounds it is perhaps impossible to reconcile Islam with Communism. The central theme of Islam, and indeed its *raison d'être*, is God and belief in God as the Sovereign Ruler of the Universe. As a system, Islam measures all things in terms of its all-inclusive divine code, even to the recognition of the institution of private property, and the regulation of its possession, disposal, and inheritance.

There are, however, similarities and parallels in the two systems which make transition from Islam to Communism easy and natural the moment emphasis is shifted from the spiritual to the temporal. Since Communism recognizes nothing spiritual, the reverse process— transition from Communism to Islam—is not likely unless it is brought about by a conversion as thoroughgoing as that of Paul or al-Ghazzali.

What, then, are those similarities and parallels which expose Islam to the danger of being swallowed up by Communism?

The Authoritarian Character of Both Systems

The first is the authoritarian character of both systems. Though theoretically subject to the *shari'ah*, the Caliph, from earliest times, has been the fountain-head of all authority. Obedience to him was obedience to God; disobedience to him carried, besides the most extreme penalty the state could mete out to offenders, the penalty of hell-fire in the hereafter. A classic expression of this is to be found in the certificate of appointment issued by the Abbasid Caliph al-Nasir (1180–1225) to Muhammad Ibn Barz al-Qummi when the latter was named vizir:

'Muhammad Ibn Barz al-Qummi is our representative throughout the land and amongst (our) subjects. Therefore he who obeys him obeys us; and he who obeys us obeys God, and him will God cause to enter Paradise. On the other hand, he who disobeys our representative disobeys us; and he who disobeys us disobeys God, and God shall cause him to enter hell-fire.'[2]

It is true that the Caliphate as an institution is no more, but the *shari'ah*, in the name of which modern Muslim governments rule and the ordinances of which they enforce, remains subject to no limitation or amendment. Furthermore, piety and virtue lie in obedience and conformity (*ittiba'*), while nothing is more repugnant than change and innovation (*ibtida'*). In spite of the fact that most Muslim countries have adopted, side by side with the *shari'ah*, constitutions and codes derived from European counterparts rather than from the Qur'ān and the Sunnah exclusively, sanction for such practices is read into the Qur'ān and the Sunnah, and the prevailing atmosphere remains one of conformity.

Similarly, most of the so-called religious reform movements in Islam today, and certainly the most articulate, such as the Muslim Brotherhood in Egypt[3] and Syria, the *Hizb al-Tahrir* (the so-called *Nabhaniyyah* movement) in Jordan, the *Jama'-at-i-Islami* in India and Pakistan, and the *Fida'iyan Islam* in Persia, view any government not based on their conception of Islam as satanic, constituting *kufr*.[4]

This raises the problem of freedom itself, on both the metaphysical and the practical levels. The individual in Muslim society is twice compelled, by predestination on the metaphysical plane, and by the social and political system built upon the *shari'ah* on the practical.

The advocates of free will and of predestination have from the beginning sought and found equally convincing support for their respective positions in the Qur'ān. The position championed by al-Ash'ari attempted to reconcile the predestination dogma with the

---

[2] Ibn al-Tiqtiqa, *al-Fakhri fi 'l-Adab al-sultaniyyah* (Cairo, p. 108).

[3] Though suppressed in Egypt in 1954, this movement is still active in other Muslim lands, and its idea and ideals continue to represent the innermost aspirations of Muslims from Morocco to Indonesia.

[4] *Report of the Court of Inquiry Constituted under the Punjab Act II of 1954 to Enquire into the Punjab Disturbances of 1953* (Lahore, 1954), pp. 243–54. See also Ishaq, Musa al-Husaini, *al-Ikhwan al-Muslimun*, 2nd ed. (Beirut, 1955), pp. 75–84.

requirements of justice, by building on certain Qur'ānic texts his doctrine of *kasb*. But in the over-all picture the balance has continued to be tipped in favour of *jabr*. This is also the position of al-Ghazzali and the majority of Muslim thinkers after him. It finds its classic support in the Qur'ānic verse. 'Moreover, had they been desirous to take the field, they would have got ready for that purpose the munitions of war. But God was averse to their marching forth, and made them laggards.'[5] As to the general public, the broad limits of *qada' al-lahi wa-qadarih* rule their lives and actions.

'The basic principle of Islamic politics is that both individually and collectively human beings should waive all right of legislation and all power to give commands to others. No one should be allowed to pass orders or issue decrees in his own right and no one ought to accept the obligation to carry out such decrees and obey such orders. None is entitled to make laws on his own authority and none is obliged to abide by them. The right vests in Allah alone.'[6] According to this theory, sovereignty belongs to God alone, and no person, group, or even 'the entire population of a state as a whole can lay claim to sovereignty. . . . All legislative power, too, vests in God. The believers cannot frame any law for themselves nor can they modify any law which God has laid down, even if the desire for such change in it is unanimous. The Islamic state, at all events, must be founded upon the law laid down by God through His Prophet. The government which runs this state shall be entitled to obedience in its capacity as a political agency set up to enforce the laws of God and only in so far as it acts in that capacity.'[7]

Objection may be raised that Maudoodi does not represent Muslim thought at its best. Be that as it may, Maudoodi's position is not basically different from that of al-Ash'ari, the father of Muslim orthodoxy, who denied any right of popular rebellion against the state, even if it were evil.[8] Nor is it different from that of the *Ikhwan al-Muslimun* as stated by their founder, the late Hasan al-Banna, and by his first and latest successor Hasan Isma'il al-Hudaybi. Both have reiterated that the establishment of the Islamic state was at the head of their programme. They were not content that the constitution should stipulate, as does the Egyptian Constitution, that the religion of the state is Islam, but insisted that legislation in its entirety should be first of all Islamic, and further that practical and

---

[5] 9:46. See also al-Ghazzali, *Risalat al-Tayr*, English translation by Nabih Amin Faris in *The Moslem World*, Vol. XXXIV, No. 1, January, 1944, pp. 46–53.

[6] Sayyid Abdul A'la Maudoodi, *Political Theory of Islam* (Pathankot, n.d.), pp. 27–8. See also the Qur'ān, 12:4, 3:154, 5:43, 3:79.

[7] Maudoodi, *Political Theory of Islam*, pp. 29–30.

[8] Al-Ash'ari, *al-Ibanah 'an Usul al-Diyanah* (Cairo), p. 12.

applied legislation should also be Islamic.[9] While there is a sharp cleavage among Muslim thinkers, it would seem that the position of al-Ash'ari and of al-Maudoodi, al-Banna, and al-Hudaybi, is more representative of the majority than any of the positions of its more liberal opponents. For in the final analysis what the theologians of old sought, and the thinkers of today are seeking, is the welfare of the *jama'ah* and its solidarity rather than freedom for the individual; both the *jama'ah* and the individual are in this world for the enforcement of the Divine Law.

In view of all these, therefore, it would seem justifiable to conclude that on the metaphysical and practical planes the tendency is to negate freedom, or at least limit and restrict it to a point where it would seem non-existent. And when the metaphysical is not constantly underscored and borne in mind, predestination can, for all practical purposes, be equated with historical determinism.

The Supra-national Character of Both Systems

Another similarity is the supra-national character of both systems. Both Islam and Communism claim universality and cut clean across nationalities to bring them all within the faith. Recent Muslim writers have reiterated this idea and called for an Islamic state which transcends national boundaries and linguistic divisions to embrace all Muslims and to unite them in the Muslim Fatherland.[10]

The Conception of Evil

Still another basic belief in Islam which finds a striking parallel in Communist thinking is that of the nature of evil. 'Everyone who is born is born with a sound nature; it is his parents who make him a Jew, or a Christian, or a Magian.'[11] Islam does not believe in original sin. Man goes astray because of the effect of external factors. Modern Muslim writers have reiterated that the evils in human society are actually a matter of unbalance in certain forces in that society. 'Intransigence on the part of man is no part of his general nature but the outcome of upsetting certain balances. . . . This degradation

[9] *Al-Ikhwan al-Muslimun*, pp. 115–16.

[10] See memorandum submitted by the Ikhwan al-Muslimun to the Egyptian government and published in *al-Ahrām*, October 9, 1952. See also Sayyid Qutb, 'Mabadi al-'Alam al-Hurr,' *al-Risalah*, No. 1018, January 1, 1953; Ahmad Hasan al-Zayyat, 'al-Jami'ah al-Islamiyyah Hiya 'l-Ghayah,' *ibid.*, No. 730, June 30, 1947.

[11] Al-Bukhari, the *Sahih*, Jana'iz, 80, 93; al-Tirmidhi, the *Sahih*, Qadar, 5. See also al-Ghazzali, *al-Munqidh min al-Dalal*, Dar-al-Ma'mun (Cairo, 1936), Vol. III, p. 97.

can be checked and stopped by proper action. Every irregularity committed by human beings is the product of some external force that tends to direct consciously: this force can and must be resisted and nullified ere it subjugates the human self.'[12]

All social injustices and ills afflicting this world would be rectified and a sort of Utopia would prevail when the external factors which throw society out of balance are done away with and balance is restored by the establishment of the Muslim state. In other words, 'perfect society can be hoped for by the establishment of the external order within which, apart from human inward change, it can be actualized'.[13]

The Communists, too, believe that the proletarian Utopia is attainable once a set of external factors replaces another set, once Communism replaces capitalism. Society would ultimately become so perfect that the restraining hand of government would become superfluous. The only difference between Islam and Communism in this respect is the means by which their respective Utopias are to be brought about. Essentially they are very similar in their denial of original sin.

In these ways there exists a striking similarity between the two systems. This does not necessarily mean that they are identical. Indeed, under certain conditions, Islam need not be wary of the inroads of Communism at all, or fear that it could ever be a preparation for it. But unless Muslims place their emphasis on the spiritual mission of Islam, unless they bear in mind that the *raison d'être* of their faith is belief in and worship of God, the Sovereign Ruler of the Universe, the danger of sliding into Communism is real and imminent.

Islam, as all know and agree, does not draw a clear line between the two realms—the spiritual and the temporal. There is in Islam no such thing as 'render therefore unto Caesar the things which are Caesar's and unto God the things that are God's'. For in Islam everything is God's. The most accurate statement of this view came from the pen of the late Hasan al-Banna, when he stated:

'You are able to say, and no one will censure you, that the Muslim Brotherhood is a Salafite movement, a Sunnite way, a Sufi truth, a political organization, an athletic club, a cultural and a scientific society, an economic company, and a social doctrine.'[14]

[12] Q. Ahmed-ur-Rahman 'Alavi, 'Notes on Islamic Law', in *The Islamic Literature* (Lahore, March, 1951), pp. 139–40. See also Kenneth Cragg, 'The Intellectual Impact of Communism upon Contemporary Islam', in *The Middle East Journal* (Washington, D.C.), Vol. 8, No. 2 (Spring, 1954), pp. 127–38. I am greatly indebted to this excellent article by Mr. Cragg and believe that it deserves serious study by all interested persons.

[13] *ibid.*, p. 134.   [14] *Al-Ikhwan al-Muslimun*, p. 79.

The struggle for independence, therefore, is no less a part of Islam than is fasting, and the boycott of Israel is as much a part of the faith as is almsgiving.

Because the spiritual and the temporal in Islam are not kept distinctly separate, the common man in Islam is exposed to the danger of obliterating the spiritual when the temporal is over-emphasized. Most heresies in the history of religion have been the result of groups or individuals taking one religious truth or doctrine out of its context and placing emphasis on it to the near or total exclusion of the remaining truth or doctrines. With the realms of the spiritual and the temporal in Islam not kept distinctly separate, as they are in reformed Christianity, for example, it has become extremely difficult, especially for the common people, not to obliterate the one when they over-emphasize the other. Herein lies the danger, and this is exactly what is happening throughout the Muslim world today, as Muslim thinkers and masses face the inroads of conflicting ideologies competing for the minds of the rising generations everywhere. The newest and the most ominous of these is Communism. Its threats confront both Christianity and Islam. In the Christian West the determined emphasis on freedom by most thinkers and the equally determined insistence on belief in God by the Church have been able to stop the onslaught of Communism in its tracks. But wherever these slackened their vigilance, Communism has gained; wherever they kept the initiative, Communism either withdrew or stood still.

Unfortunately, this is not so in the case of Islam. Muslim leadership, to quote the words of 'Abdul Majid, has not begun to face this problem. Most are hardly aware of it. Instead, one finds a race between modern Muslim writers and Communists, aimed at showing which system offers more of the fruits of this temporal world, which can better bring about social justice, security, and solidarity. These writers are more concerned with solidarity than with freedom, with the welfare of the *jama'ah* than with that of the individual. By placing most of their emphasis on the temporal, modern Muslim writers[15] have in effect reduced Islam to a social programme. The result of this transformation, irrespective of all good intentions, is twofold. It first undermines the *raison d'être* of Islam itself: belief in God as the Sovereign Ruler of the Universe. Once this is done *in toto* or in part, the second result becomes inevitable. Muslims will find their social programme in a more attractive form, and buttressed with an apparently perfect and comprehensive philosophy, in Communism. They can find in Communism all the temporal

[15] Sayyid Qutb, *al-'Adalah al-Ijtima'iyyah fi al-Islam* (Cairo, 1950); English translation *Social Justice in Islam* (American Council of Learned Societies, Washington, D.C., 1953).

blessings of Islam, improved, refined, and embellished by technology and freed from all metaphysical difficulties.

It should be remembered that the stubborn resistance to Communism in the West is rooted in a specific philosophy based on an absolute belief from which all other beliefs and values emanate, namely the belief in the dignity and freedom of man. No such philosophy is discernible in the writings of modern Muslim writers yet. Furthermore, the confidence of the average Muslim in Western democracy which revolves around the individual, his worth, dignity, and freedom, has been seriously impaired as a result of Islam's unfortunate political experience with the West. It is not likely, therefore, that the average Muslim would defend democracy with the same zeal with which its Western devotees have been defending it. Nor is the average Muslim likely to resist the spread of Communism in any earnest or effective manner.

Resistance of Islam to Communism is unlikely because of the place of reason in Islam and the unfriendly relations between the West and Islam. Two other factors, one basic and the other secondary, tend to render such resistance unlikely. The first stems from the place of reason in Islam. Its function is 'to bear witness to the trustworthiness of prophecy and to confess its own inability'.[16] Furthermore, 'it does not point the way to that which is useful or (warn against) that which is harmful in words, works, ethics, and doctrines. It does not distinguish between the propitious and the baneful. . . . When it is, however, told, it comprehends and believes.'[17] This is what al-Ghazzali asserted, and what has become the accepted function of reason in Islam. It is the handmaiden of religion, and rarely has a Muslim writer in recent times made another use of it. Reason which doubts, investigates, and rejects, if need be, authority, is equally negated by Islam and Communism. Both use it to justify authority.

In making this statement, I am not oblivious of the various attempts within Islam to give reason its rightful place in human history. The very fact that such attempts were made would indicate that in the continuous struggle of 'aql with naql, of reason with authority, a final victory for reason is not impossible. However, all previous attempts have ended with defeat and have left little influence on the collective mind of Islam.

Noteworthy among these attempts are those made by the Mu'tazilits, by Averroes (d. A.D. 1199) and by Ibn Khaldun (d. A.D. 1406). The influence of the first on Islamic thought has been in giving Ash'arite theology the weapons with which to fight rationalism. The influence of the second, while enormous in the West, is less than

[16] *Al-Munqidh min al-Dalal*, p. 174.
[17] Al-Ghazzali, *al-Iqtisad fi 'l-I'tiqad* (Cairo, 1327), pp. 80–1.

negligible in Islam. The influence of the third is, to all practical purposes, non-existent.[18]

The other factor stems from the long and unfriendly history of the relations of Islam and Christianity and their respective followers. The struggle of the rising Muslim Empire with the Byzantine determined not only their temporal relations but also their attitude towards their respective faiths. This was further complicated and embittered by their struggles during the period of the Crusades, whose legacy of ill-will still rankles in the hearts of both peoples; during the period of the early Ottomans, when a resurgent Muslim Power menaced the Christian citadel of Europe; and during the century and a half of one-damn-thing-after-another in Muslim experience of the colonialism of the so-called Christian West. Rightly or wrongly, the average Muslim came to view the West as his mortal foe. Every action taken by the West was interpreted as a direct attack upon Muslims, their homeland, institutions, society, culture, and religion. Muslims, therefore, became understandably jubilant at the ills of the West, their hearts often bursting with gratification whenever the West faltered or suffered a set-back. This has softened Muslim resistance to Communism and has already made many of them, particularly among the intellectuals, what might be described as fellow travellers or spite Communists. And when these intellectuals, with the tradition of transcendentalism behind them, shift their emphasis to the temporal in response to the crying needs of their fellow Muslims who suffer from poverty, ignorance, and tyranny, the danger of Communism becomes more and more imminent.

True Islam, as stated before, cannot on doctrinal grounds be reconciled with Communism. Only when the emphasis is shifted from the spiritual to the temporal would transition from it to Communism become easy and natural. The grievances most of the Muslim world have against the West, the conditions under which Muslims live, and the legitimate urge felt by them to break the spell of Western hegemony, tempt the faithful to make league even with the devil, especially when the devil has donned a turban, has partly concealed his hammer and sickle under his newly acquired burnous, so as to make it look more like a crescent—and finally has started to quote the Qur'ān!

[18] Ibn-Khaldun's remarkable contribution to social thought has been discovered by the West and only boasted of in current Islam.

THE 'NATIONAL FRONT'

In Communist Strategy in the Middle East

by A. BENNIGSEN

SINCE THE DEATH of Stalin, a new policy of expansion has been worked out by his successors and applied to the Middle East with a success that alarms most Western observers. Some of the latter predict the imminent sovietization of that part of the world—within two years according to the most pessimistic, or ten years according to the most optimistic.

But in fact the notion of 'sovietization' has lately become transformed, and to ignore its new meaning is to misunderstand the whole political development of the U.S.S.R. In Stalin's time, sovietization could come about only through the violent seizure of power by the local proletariat, or through occupation by the Red Army. Stalin, one of the old Bolsheviks, despised and distrusted the *bourgeoisie*, and had no confidence in anything less than revolt—a civil war waged by the proletarian masses themselves and led by Communists. The sovietization of the Middle East could therefore be conceived only in three possible forms—(*a*) violent proletarian revolution, (*b*) the break-up of states with multi-national populations (such as Iraq, Persia, and others) by the action of dynamic minorities such as the Kurds or Azerians looking towards the U.S.S.R., or (*c*) a Soviet military occupation—this last solution being, however, improbable.

In reality, neither the Soviet theorists nor Stalin himself ever thought these methods likely to succeed. That is abundantly proved by their refusal to assist the separatist movements of the democratic republics of Azerbaidjan or the Kurds of Mahabâd. Such revolts could be easily throttled by police and authoritarian régimes which, as in Iraq, are on guard against internal subversion; such revolts are also repugnant to the popular feeling, the pan-Arabian or pan-Iranian mind being opposed to any Kurd or Azerian separatism. As for military intervention, there was always the risk that the Western Powers would automatically react by launching a third world war.

If such solutions were inconceivable during Stalin's lifetime, they have since become much more so; for the doctrine of 'co-existence' excludes any military solution—at least for the present. The support that Russia gives to the dictatorial and conservative Arab governments not only reinforces them, but deprives the local Communist Parties of all possibility of revolutionary action. And finally, by its recognition of pan-Arab idealism and the Oriental nationalisms, the Kremlin is at the same time abandoning the cause of their national minorities.

How, then, can the U.S.S.R. sovietize this region, where the 'objective conditions' of proletarian revolution are not yet attained, and where anarchic developments ought logically to bring the *petit bourgeoisie*, and not the proletariat, to power? If the spectres of revolutionary action and military intervention are both dispelled, the Western Powers will see only two aspects of the strategy of the U.S.S.R., the economic and the diplomatic: that is, the competition for the economic hegemony of the Middle East (which the Eastern bloc as a whole feels confident of winning in the end) and its political neutralization.

If that were the only danger, the West might take an optimistic view. Attacked by the U.S.S.R. on their own commercial grounds by purely capitalistic methods, the Western Powers could defend their interests, and the social and political structures of the Middle East might long endure. But alas, something very different is in question: the aim of Soviet policy is precisely to modify, by its new methods, the social structures of the Middle East, and thereby to bring about the 'objective conditions' required for their overthrow. Western observers are misled by not having seen that the notion of 'revolution' has itself evolved: it is no longer limited to phenomena like the Russian explosion of 1917: it now includes that of a 'painless revolution'—leading, however, to the irreversible eviction of the Western Powers. This, it may be objected, is a merely intellectual interpretation. Perhaps so, but it finds solid support in arguments recently authorized by the U.S.S.R.

WIDENING THE 'REVOLUTIONARY' FRONT

The Stalinist vision of the political universe was the narrowly manichaeistic one of which Zhdanov formulated the principles in

1947; and they remained orthodox until 1953. An imperialist and anti-imperialist dichotomy was supposed to divide the world into two camps, centred in Moscow and Washington respectively; and to this postulate was added another—that the proletariat alone was anti-imperialist. But for the Middle East, practically destitute of a proletariat and dominated by a national bourgeoisie whose class interests inevitably ally them with imperialism, what are the consequences of this doctrine? It compels these countries to go on living as clients of the West; it gives them no middle way between maintaining the 'pro-Western' bourgeoisie in power and violent seizure of power by the proletariat.

The first correction of this intransigent dualism was made at the Twentieth Congress of the Soviet Communist Party, when Khrushchev recognized the existence, between the two opposites, of a *neutral zone*, neither Socialist nor capitalist but pacifist. To this thesis was attached another and no less important modification of the Stalinist doctrine—that a neutral country, even though capitalist, could attain to national sovereignty and independence.

Before 1954, Soviet theorists held that India, as well as the countries of the Middle East, was still at the 'colonial stage' of evolution, because its national bourgeoisie had merely come to a compromise with the British imperialists, for fear of the local proletariat. They said that national liberation depended upon social emancipation, and that politically separate countries could achieve independence only after having shaken off the yoke of foreign capital.[1] These ideas are now abandoned in favour of a more elastic doctrine, already foreshadowed by Varga in 1948, which was restated in the review published by the Oriental Institute of the Academy of Sciences.[2] In the words of an editorial writer:

'Since the Second World War, owing to the radical change in the balance of international forces, the predominant position of foreign capital in some Eastern countries no longer means that imperialism necessarily overrules their political life. States such as Indonesia and Saudi Arabia, though not yet free from Western imperialism, are nevertheless enjoying political sovereignty today.'

This reference to Saudi Arabia, an absolute, theocratic monarchy dependent for its revenues upon foreign oil concessions, is especially significant.

The recognition of a 'third way' includes, moreover, the approval of a new function for the bourgeoisie. In Stalin's time, the Soviet doctrinaires always insisted that 'only the working class, led by the Communist Party and united with the international working-class

---

[1] *Doklady Akademii Nauk S.S.S.R.*, No. 3, 1950.
[2] *Sovetskoe Vostokovedenie*, January, 1956.

movement' could 'realize national independence'. The role of the bourgeoisie was reduced to very little, for 'its natural class interests compelled it to make compromises with its Western patrons, and such freedoms as it might win from them were rendered nugatory'. But now *Sovetskoe Vostokovedenie* itself, in flagrant opposition to innumerable writings of Stalin and even of Lenin, proclaims that:

'It is incontestable that, at certain stages of the struggle against imperialism, the interests of the bourgeoisie are essentially at one with the popular interest, and that the claims of the bourgeois leaders in their dealings with the colonial Powers are an objective reflection of the interests of the whole people united in the struggle for emancipation.'[3]

These astonishing—and how far from Leninist!—pronouncements might easily be attributed to Mensheviks or to deviationists of the Right: at any time between 1924 and 1939 they would certainly have cost their authors their lives. By 1956 they have become the key concepts of Soviet policy in the Orient. They are meant to make up for the absence, or the extreme weakness, of the Eastern proletariat, by saddling the national bourgeoisie with the burden of leading these countries towards Socialism. The new watchword that 'there are different paths to Socialism' means that in the Middle East the bourgeoisie can and ought to assume the leadership, and be authorized to lead the Arab countries to revolution by ways that the Russians have not known.

TACTICAL APPLICATION OF THE NEW PRINCIPLES

These doctrinal developments alone make it possible to understand the recent activities of the Communist Parties in the East. Working-class vigilance is now concentrated upon a new enemy: whereas all its mistrust used to be directed against the bourgeoisie, the 'foreign tyranny' has now taken their place and become 'public enemy No. 1'. The class struggle is now relegated to secondary importance, hard though it may be for the local Communist Parties to make such a transfer of animosity. To reduce proletarian demands to a minimum; to subordinate these to the primacy of national claims; and to reassure the bourgeoisie—these are the new marching orders.

All unconsciously, this is a return to the methodology advised as early as 1920 by the Mohammedan Communists of Russia, who wanted to dissociate national from social liberation. For the Russians, and Stalin above all, purposely confounded the two aims in order to keep indigenous Communists out of the leadership of the revolution in the Mohammedan fringe. Between 1924 and 1939

[3] *Sovetskoe Vostokovedenie*, January, 1956.

Stalin and his henchmen physically destroyed their best Muslim Communists, who had realized that national freedom should be put before the class struggle in Russia's colonial and semi-colonial regions, where the nationalist movement had to be anti-Russian. That was the reason for the 'liquidation' of the Turkmenian Communist leaders Boriev and Akmurad Orazov; Ramzi of the *Narkompros* in Uzbekistan; Khodjibaev, president of the Tadjik *Sovnarkom*; and of prominent Kazakh leaders who had been transferred to the Communist Party (Ryskulov, Sultanbekov, and others)—all of whom were condemned for complicity with 'bourgeois nationalism'.

The Kazani Sultan Galiev, who was the first theorist of the colonial revolution, had the ideas that could and should have been adapted to the whole colonial world: when he was executed in 1937 it was not just a pan-Turkish separatist who was put to death, but the author of a formidable doctrinal deviation; and now, less than twenty years after, his heresy has become the new orthodoxy.

From this time onward the local Communist Parties are no longer to regard themselves as the independent and separate vanguard, but as only one of the sections, of a very wide front formed to attain two fundamental aims—the maintenance of peace and national emancipation. As the Communist Party of the Lebanon announced in May, 1955: 'The National Front is the union of all the forces of the country, against imperialism, and for the co-operation of all Arab states concerned about their economic development'[4]; while the Syrio-Lebanese Communist Party celebrated the ninth anniversary of Syrian independence by issuing a manifesto declaring that 'the National Front ought to unite all who oppose the Pact of Baghdad'.

The design, then, is that of a front embracing every class in society —in which workers, peasants, and intellectuals will rub shoulders with members of the petty, the medium, and the big bourgeoisie, with the clergy—and even with the army, which Khaled Bakdash, first secretary of the Syrian Communist Party, now calls 'a potent and democratic instrument for peace'. Everyone is included, excepting only a few 'flunkeys of imperialism' past praying for, who, moreover, 'represent nothing'. This 'handful of individuals who ignore the national aspirations consists only of a few big financiers and shareholders of the imperialist banks, and of trade-monopolists connected with foreign capital'.[5] Also excluded are the large, so-called 'feudal', landed proprietors.

This 'national front' is not, of course, an invention of Stalin's successors; as a formula it has a fairly long history. What is, how-

[4] *Al Talia* (Damascus), May 9, 1955.
[5] 'Appeal of the Communist Party to the Lebanese people', *Al Sarqha*, February 24, 1954.

ever, new in the present conception is the function assigned to the working-class members of the front. Traditionally, the working class is its vanguard and the Communist Party has, beyond all question, to assume leadership of it. But now, according to *Sovetskoe Vostokovedenie*, this applies to colonial countries only in certain cases where capitalism is relatively well developed: one must not draw from this generalization, justifiable in itself, the conclusion that the proletariat alone can assume leadership. There are countries such as Egypt, where 'the proletariat, the vanguard of the forces of patriotism, is not yet in a position to take the lead, and sovereignty has to be fought for under the shield of the bourgeoisie'.

Another innovation in the strategy of the national front is that it is meant to *endure*.

Lenin and Stalin regarded any alliance between the bourgeoisie and the proletariat as of necessity conditional and temporary. The proletariat, after having triumphed over foreign imperialism with the aid of the bourgeois nationalists, would have to turn against them and usurp their power; the class struggle would follow immediately after the struggle against alien exploitation. This doctrine, if not officially abandoned, has been considerably watered down. Any rupture with the united front is postponed to the Greek kalends; and the idea of enduring collaboration between all classes is emphasized. *Sovetskoe Vostokovedenie* tells us that national emancipation is not a definitive conquest: it is a victory that remains ever in question. 'The colonizers cannot resign their power . . . they take steps to re-establish it over the countries that have won their freedom. They are obliged to institute new forms of colonial exploitation of the under-developed countries.' The Communist journal *Al Sarqha* writes even of the Lebanon, which is the most independent of the Arab countries: 'It is certain that the Lebanon will not free itself completely from colonial exploitation until it breaks its shackles of foreign, imperialist capital.'

In other words, the alliance between bourgeoisie and proletariat will last just so long as the integration of the region with the Eastern half of the world (eliminating all possibility of a return to colonialism) is not yet realized.

Besides being lasting, this alliance is *sincere*, resting as it does upon a real community of interests.

As lately as 1949, the social and economic policy of the ruling classes was condemned root and branch, in such statements as the following about India and Pakistan, applicable equally to the Middle East:

'Since their independence, there has been no reform to the advantage of the mass of the population. The contradictions which oppose their interests to the interests of those who exploit them are even accentuated . . . agrarian reform, the fundamental problem, cannot be achieved so long as imperialist big business still overrules the country: the situation of the peasants grows steadily worse; the level of industrial production declines. The Nehru government ignores the interests of the workers.'[6]

That thesis, too, is now repudiated, as 'lacking in objectivity and depth'. While certain shortcomings of the economic policy of the national bourgeoisie are criticized, it is now admitted that their policy may have *progressive significance*: 'Supported by the people as a whole, by all the democratic and patriotic forces of all parties and all classes at every social level, the Oriental states will be able successfully to fight their way to a higher standard of life for the masses.'[7]

One can easily see how unacceptable all this must seem to local Communists still being hunted by the police. Nevertheless, it must be admitted that the leaders in Moscow have a more dialectically valid conception of the present situation. The economic policy of Nasser's government, for instance, which is directed to a fairly rapid industrialization of Egypt, is 'progressive' even if that government is persecuting the progressives. By promoting industrialization any government, however authoritarian or reactionary it may be, increases the numbers and raises the efficiency of the working class, from which emerge those trade-union groups upon which any effective Communist Party depends.

Such, briefly stated, is the strategy of Arab Communism in the post-Stalin epoch. On the practical side, it is based upon three methods of action: first, the indefinite multiplication of groups inspired by pacific, neutralist, and cultural ideas; secondly, exchanges between Arab and Soviet intellectuals; and thirdly, the promotion of alliances with other parties into which the Communist Party merges and effaces itself, thereby gradually disarming the suspicions of the bourgeoisie. Of this last manoeuvre there are plenty of examples. Though it is a manoeuvre which in the West has commonly led to set-backs, it succeeds in the Orient, where the bourgeoisie is unstable, and is defenceless against Communist solicitation. To cite one instance among many: at the National Arab Congress convened in 1955 at Damascus, Arab intellectuals were invited by the Syrian progressives and Communists to protest 'against alliances with imperialists' (the Baghdad Pact), and every kind of political tendency was represented. There were eminent representatives from the universities, the clergy, the law, and the

---

[6] *Voprosy Ekonomiki*, 1949, 10.
[7] *Sovetskoe Vostokovedenie*, January, 1956.

Parliaments of all the Arab countries. But although these men had come together from every quarter of the political horizon, this congress degenerated—thanks to the Communists and especially to the Lebanese Georges Hanna—into a manifestation of violent hostility to the West and of pro-Soviet propaganda.

Rather sooner than later—if the Soviet theorists are right—these tactics will have effectively paved the way for a Socialist régime. However, since the Twentieth Congress of the Soviet Communist Party, it is conceded that there are several approaches to Socialism; and also that the transition may be peaceful. Civil war, though formerly reckoned indispensable, is no longer so except in countries 'where capitalism is particularly powerful; where the military and police establishment is enormous, and where savage resistance from the reactionaries is inevitable'. This is not the case in the Middle East, where 'the capitalist structures lack foundations, and a revolutionary class struggle may not be required'. Since there is also a national bourgeoisie, numerically weak and without class traditions of its own, while the administrative system is inadequate and feeble, why not admit the possibility of a peaceful and legal conquest of power by the working class? The more so since the example of China proves that one may include in 'the working class' all the 'convertible' elements of the bourgeoisie—that is, almost all of it excepting only the small minority of large landed proprietors and capitalists who are irretrievably condemned by their compromises with imperialism.

What this means is that Socialism—and this is a major innovation —can triumph in other ways than those of the Russian Revolution; therefore *without recourse to violence*.

*   *   *   *   *

The future of the Middle East is thus accorded a definite place in the dialectic process of world Communism. Will that process be halted, or even retarded, by external opposition or internal resistance? Which are the decisive factors? These are questions now being anxiously revolved in the minds of Western observers.

Can the Western Powers put a brake upon this revolutionary dynamism by their political action? Apparently not, or not as yet, while their action remains so clumsy and incoherent. The Soviets— and this is their trump card—took the right measure of the force of Arab nationalism while the Westerners still assumed it was negligible. And, in the words of one observer: 'It must not be supposed that the nationalism of the Middle East is hostile to Communism. Quite the contrary: nationalism has prepared the way for Communism, and sometimes collaborated with it.'[8] Since 1956 the tactics of the Communists have been redefined; and henceforth it is the business of Communists to identify and to merge themselves with the nationalists.

Can we look more confidently to the Western policy of economic aid, intended to raise the standard of life of the Oriental peoples? Certainly not: people forget that Communism can do nothing with the unorganizable *lumpen-proletariat*; that it appeals only to fairly advanced proletarian workers. And industrialization, promoted by Western aid, hastens the transformation of the poor and 'unawakened' masses into a proletariat upon which Communism can base its operations. The goodwill of the West is thus drawn into a vicious circle from which it can hardly escape: the choice is between anarchy, unfailingly profitable to 'the Left', and a kind of order which gives that same Left the very basis that it wants.

Since we can see so little hope for the West, can we feel more confident about the national *bourgeoisie*? Even less so: here too the Soviet politicians have shown foresight, in their cultivation of the petty bourgeoisie—'the rising class of the Middle East'—rather than of the proletariat. It has been well said that 'in the Middle East, Communism presents itself as a movement encouraging the revolt of the middle classes against the feudal rulers'.[9]

The result of the confusion of issues we have been seeking to unravel is that there is no longer, in this region, more than a feeble minority of individuals who feel genuinely anti-Communist or anti-Soviet. In Egypt, for instance, a military régime brought about by the petty and the middle bourgeoisie has been hunting down the Communists, while turning, for its own part, more and more towards the U.S.S.R. pro-Soviet but anti-Communist is a subtle political distinction; but how long will it wear? In Iraq, where the political fashion is both anti-Soviet and anti-Communist, the progressives are so clumsily persecuted that they claim the aureole of martyrdom and the exclusive right to be called pure nationalists.

Why, then—since there is no force that can effectively oppose them—have the national fronts not seized power? Because they are doubly weak, weak both in their organization and in their ideology. The cause of that weakness lies chiefly in the social origins of the revolutionary leaders, the majority of whom come from the Arab *bourgeoisie*, and from minority groups such as Orthodox Christians, Armenians, and Kurds. The Middle Eastern parties are enfeebled by their lack of authentic trade unionism, which alone would be competent to organize and maintain strong parties, ready for any hardships and capable of holding a line of doctrine without any

[8] *Middle East Journal*, 1955, No. 4.   [9] *ibid.*

deviations. Only a Communist Party that was ideologically un-shakeable could lead a national front to its appointed ends, by pro-tecting itself from 'rotting away' and from being enticed into hetero-dox ways by its bourgeois allies. The directives from Moscow have to be understood, correctly interpreted, and applied to local circum-stances. And it appears, for the present, that the Communist Parties of the Levant are not in a position to do these things.

The West has therefore a period of respite: but will Western governments have the knowledge and the ability to profit by it?

RECENT SOVIET ATTITUDES
TOWARDS ISLAM

by GEOFFREY WHEELER

THE ACTIVE INTEREST in the Middle East and South Asian Affairs which the Soviet Union has been developing during the past two years is calculated to bring it in much closer contact with the free Muslim world than ever before. In addition to extending all-Union political and commercial relations with the independent countries of the East, there are clear indications that the Soviet government intends to use the Muslim republics of the Union both as a kind of cultural bridge between Russia and the Middle East, and also as a shop window to demonstrate the effectiveness of Soviet methods in under-developed countries. The present policy is far more ambitious than previous ones and requires tact and judgment which have been lacking in former Soviet approaches to Eastern countries.

The object of the present brief study is to consider the nature of the latest Soviet tactics and how they are affecting or likely to affect the Soviet attitude to Islam and the Islamic way of life.

The classic policy of the Stalin era towards the Muslim world assumed that the ruling classes and the clergy must be fundamentally hostile to the Soviet Union and irrevocably sold to Western imperialism. A corollary to this was the conviction that only the proletariat—virtually non-existent in the Middle East—and the peasantry could safely be regarded as anti-imperialist. Another feature of Soviet policy before 1953 was the segregation of the six Muslim republics of the Union from their co-religionists in the Middle East. For a short period after the Revolution, plans existed for the fusion of the Muslims of Russia with those of the outside world. But the rapid development of internal opposition to the

Soviet régime during the early 1920's soon put an end to any such ideas. The Soviet government evidently feared that, so far from attracting their Muslim neighbours into the Soviet fold, the peoples of the eastern republics might wish to break away from the Union.

The earlier attitude of reliance on the proletariat and peasantry and hostility to the 'reactionary' *bourgeois* nationalist governments brought no dividends, and, apparently during 1955, it was decided to abandon it, at any rate temporarily. At the same time, the Soviet government seems to have made up its mind that segregation of the eastern republics is no longer a vital necessity, and that the considerable material progress which has been achieved there could be an important means of enhancing Soviet prestige in Eastern and particularly Muslim countries. The West is now witnessing Soviet endeavours to apply these two new principles in their dealings with independent Muslim countries not only in the Middle East but also in South Asia.

Before proceeding to examine how the Soviet government is handling the delicate matter of co-ordinating its attitudes towards Islam both inside and outside the Soviet Union, it is necessary to review briefly the Soviet conception of Islam as a religion and a way of life. As a religion Islam comes under the general fire directed against all supernatural beliefs and is not subjected to any special treatment, except that since Islam, like Communism, has oecumenical claims, it is regarded as potentially more dangerous than, for instance, the Orthodox Church. As a way of life, however, Communism regards Islam as infinitely more pernicious and objectionable than any branch of Christendom. It sees it as backward, as militating against material progress, and as having been promoted and perpetuated, first by feudal Eastern potentates and later by Western colonialists, for their own anti-social ends. The incompatibility of the Islamic with the Soviet way of life has been stated and restated over and over again, and early attempts by Soviet orientalists to suggest that Communism and Islam have something in common were unequivocally condemned.

Soviet antipathy to Islam on materialist grounds is a conviction which is sincerely held and is to some extent understandable. It is indeed widely accepted that whereas, through the Reformation and the Renaissance, Christendom as it were came to terms with modern life, Islam has not hitherto done so. Without examining the reasons for this phenomenon it may be observed that nationalist reformers in some independent Muslim countries have so far elected to ride roughshod over Islamic traditions and practices rather than initiate reforms in the fabric of Islam itself. But Soviet and Communist objections to Islam go much further than intolerance of an outworn way of life: the Soviet propaganda machine has constructed out of the concept of pan-Islam a formidable bogy which, with a few intervals for political reasons, has figured prominently in all propaganda directed to the Muslims of the Soviet Union. Since the war the fury generated against pan-Islam by Soviet propagandists has been to some extent synthetic—pan-Islam is nowadays represented principally as a tool in the hands of the Western imperialists—but Soviet fear of Islam as a political force had a genuine origin in the early years of the régime, when the supporters of Jadidism, a Muslim reformist movement born many years before the Revolution, showed clearly that they were more interested in some kind of nationalism associated with Islam than in the class war advocated by Soviet Communism.

Soviet opposition to Islam is fundamental and axiomatic; but this does not prevent the Soviet government from regulating and modifying its overt expression of this opposition as circumstances may require, or even from enlisting Islam in its service. Past examples of this can be found in the moderate and even benevolent attitude developed towards Islam in Central Asia when the Soviet government had become seriously alarmed at the oppression exercised by the local Russian element during the Civil War; and in the attempts made to gain the support of the Muslim clergy of Persia in the 1920's. Again, in 1941 when Germany attacked the U.S.S.R., Mufti Abdurrahman Rasulev, so-called leader of the Soviet Muslims, in company with other religious leaders was permitted to issue a manifesto to his co-religionists urging them to 'Rise in defence of the fatherland against the enemy threatening destruction and misfortune to all Muslims, children, brothers, and sisters in our religion', and to 'organize religious services in houses of prayer and mosques and consecrate them to victory of our army'. In the event, the war must have accentuated Soviet hostility to Islam, for a large number of Muslims serving in the Red Army, who were taken prisoner by the Germans, elected to fight against the Soviet Union. Some of the Muslim nationalities of the North Caucasus and the Crimea were accused of collaborating with the Germans and were deported from their homes to the number of nearly a million.

After the ignominious failure of its venture in Persian Azerbaidjan in 1945–46, the Soviet government showed no particular inclination to become involved in the affairs of Islamic countries outside the Union. Between 1947 and 1954, therefore, no significant change can be noted in the general Soviet attitude towards Islam. Inside the Union, anti-Islamic propaganda continued in the eastern republics. In metropolitan literature, however, the tendency was to ignore Islam, or at any rate to play down its importance. Thus, the articles in the second edition of the *Soviet Encyclopaedia*, which began to appear, in 1950, were far shorter than analogous articles in the first edition. They seemed designed to display cold indifference rather than active hostility.

Detailed consideration of the questions why and when the Soviet Government decided to intervene in the Middle East would be out of place here. Suffice it to say that although misgivings about the soundness of its Middle East policy probably began to assail the Soviet Ministry of Foreign Affairs after the Azerbaidjan incident of 1946, it was not until after Stalin's death that the formulation of a new policy and new methods began. The final collapse of Mossadeq's administration in Persia and signs of the formation of the Baghdad Pact confirmed the need for a new policy, while over-eagerness of the West in the matter of Middle East defence provided a favourable opportunity for a new Soviet adventure.

During 1954 there were several indications of increased Soviet interest in the Middle East and of a growing consciousness that to break down the barrier which the Soviet government had erected between the Muslim republics and the adjacent Muslim countries would soon be not only inevitable but potentially useful. Nevertheless, the government must have realized that such a fundamental change would carry with it an element of danger: the Muslim East might react unfavourably to the hostile attitude which the Communist Party had taken up towards Islam inside the Union; and the Muslim republics might see a strange contradiction in the Soviet government's making overtures to 'bourgeois nationalism' in foreign countries after it had ruthlessly uprooted it from Central Asia and the Caucasus. Any action which the Russians take in order to obviate or minimize these dangerous possibilities must clearly be conditioned by their assessment, firstly, of the strength of Muslim opinion in the non-Soviet East, and secondly, of the survival of any genuine nationalist feeling among the Muslims of the Union.

A study of Soviet publications on the Middle East and on Islam which have appeared during the past three years reveals a good deal of inconsistency, and it is not easy to extract from them any clear pattern of Soviet thinking. Nor can it be easy for the Soviet government to devise propaganda programmes for both internal and external use which do not contain dangerous contradictions: the all-party and all-class type of nationalism now favoured and supported by the Russians in the Middle East is difficult to explain to the republics of the Union, where it has been consistently stigmatized; and the theme of hostility to Islam as the main obstacle to progress—so constantly emphasized to the Muslims of the U.S.S.R.—cannot safely be extended beyond the Soviet frontier. In face of this dilemma the Soviet propaganda machine seems to have decided on a kind of compromise. In the Middle East the main enemy of progress is shown to be Western imperialism, which has cunningly exploited and debased Islam for its own ends; at the same time Soviet interest in Middle East culture and cultural contacts between the Soviet Muslim and Middle East intellectuals are to be widely extended. In the Muslim republics of the Union, on the other hand, anti-Islamic propaganda has been greatly toned down, although by no meansd iscontinued; at the same time a show is being made of 'playing down' the importance of the Russian connection and of drawing more attention to the achievements of native genius and heroism; and some of the victims of past campaigns against Islamic and nationalist movements have been posthumously rehabilitated.

A few instances of recent Soviet propaganda tactics may be given. At the end of 1956 the review *Sovetskoe Vostokovedenie* gave the keynote of Soviet propaganda to the independent countries of the East as follows: 'A characteristic of the national liberation movement of today is the participation in it of all patriotically and anti-imperialistically inclined representatives of widely varying social strata and religious and political convictions. These range from workers and peasants, who constitute the chief driving force of the movement, to the national *bourgeoisie* and to some extent even to the landowners; and all of them are united in their aim of freeing their countries from the colonial yoke.' These are the lines on which the Soviet government is thinking and on which it would like the non-Soviet Muslim world to think too. During 1955 a vast expansion of Soviet Oriental studies was planned and since the beginning of that year the volume of literature on the Muslim countries of the Middle East and South and South-East Asia has enormously increased. There has been very little mention of Islam in all this literature beyond some derogatory references to its practice in the countries of the Baghdad Pact and particularly in Pakistan.

Soviet writing on Islam in the U.S.S.R. has passed through a good many changes in the past two and a half years. Up to the decree of November, 1954, which warned against offending religious susceptibilities, the output of crude and violent anti-Islamic propaganda had been fairly regular. Smirnov's book, *An Outline of the History of Islamic Studies in the U.S.S.R.*, although strongly hostile to Islam might conceivably be called a serious and objective work. Appearing in February, 1954, it had presumably been written before Soviet plans for a new attempt to penetrate the Middle East had been formulated. Apart from a number of articles in periodicals and newspapers, the only other considerable study devoted to Islam in recent years has been L. I. Klimovich's *Islam: Its Origin and Social Character*, which appeared in February, 1956, and must have been timed to coincide with the Twentieth Party Congress. Klimovich has written extensively on Islam and always from a strictly Marxist and strongly anti-religious aspect. His latest work attacks Islam from almost every conceivable point of view, but in terms which would probably not be offensive to many Muslim intellectuals and would be largely unintelligible to simple believers. His main concern is with the history and origin of Islam, which he presents in the most derogatory light possible, and with the scientific inaccuracy of the Qur'ān. Reference to the Prophet is restricted to a few contemptuous lines suggesting that he was posthumously built up as the founder of Islam in order to serve the requirements of the 'personality cult'.

The first impression of Klimovich's book is given as 138,000, but it would not be surprising if it were not available in the Muslim republics. Anti-Islamic material appearing in the Press of these republics since 1954 is of a much milder description, but desultory shots are still fired at traditional Islamic practice. There seems to be a desire in the Soviet mind to distinguish between what it regards as the essential fallacy and harmful effect of Islamic dogma and practice and the achievements of Muslim peoples throughout the ages. Such a distinction must be, and clearly is, highly confusing to the Muslim intelligentsia inside the Soviet Union and they are frequently pulled up for apparently misinterpreting the party line. There have been two instances of this in the recent past. The author of a book on the Kazakh poet Abay, who believed he was doing the right thing in emphasizing the extent to which Abay had drawn for his inspiration on Russian literature, was strongly criticized on this very account; he was told that it was quite unnecessary to devote a whole chapter to the civilizing influence of the Russian connection and that he would have done much better to examine more closely Abay's debt to the traditional literary genius of the Kazakhs. In January, 1957, a Kazakh newspaper published a series of articles criticizing the past official attitude towards Kazakh oral literature, and even going so far as to accuse the authorities of excluding Kazakhs from higher and technical education in the Kazakh S.S.R. This excursion into the field of liberal criticism met with a sharp reproof in the official organ of the Kazakh Communist Party.

An instance of the attempt being made to flatter Muslim opinion by a reference to past achievement can be found in an article appearing in *Voprosy Istorii* of June, 1956, by O. D. Chekhovich. This flatly contradicted the doctrine hitherto insisted upon that the century before the appearance of the Russians in Central Asia had been one of internecine strife and retrogression. Chekhovich claimed to have established what Barthold had known in 1920, namely, that 'at the time of the [Russian] conquest the economic welfare of the greater part of Turkestan was much higher than it had been a century earlier, and that in the three Central Asian khanates of Bukhara, Khiva, and Kokand there had been very considerable progress'. The civilization and culture of the khanates before the coming of the Russians were, of course, almost exclusively Islamic. Finally, evidence of the Soviet desire to atone for the early repression of nationalism among Soviet Muslims can be found in the partial rehabilitation not only of victims of past purges but of traditional Muslim heroes of pre-Revolutionary times such as Shamil of the Caucasus. In this connection, the speech of the Uzbek Communist Party First Secretary Mukhitdinov at the Congress of the Intelligentsia held in Tashkent in October, 1956, is of particular interest. Mukhitdinov announced the rehabilitation of a number of Uzbek writers who had been wrongfully condemned for association with Jadidism and '*bourgeois* nationalism'. He even said that the case of Ikramov, the Party First Secretary, who was executed in 1937 in company with Fayzulla Khodjaev (Faizullah Hoja), the Prime Minister of Uzbekistan, on charges which included that of 'nationalism', was being investigated. It is perhaps significant that an Egyptian delegation was present in Tashkent at the time of the congress, and also that there has since been no further mention of Ikramov.

Certain other steps point to the Soviet desire to make the eastern republics as fit places as possible for the reception of delegations from Muslim and other Eastern countries, the frequency of whose visits to Central Asia has greatly increased during the past year. Thus, the repatriation to their homelands of the displaced Muslim communities of the North Caucasus has recently been announced, and the restoration of Muslim monuments has been speeded up and given publicity by the Tass News Agency.

Any attempt to deduce Soviet intentions by examining the propaganda machine in action or to correlate propaganda methods with declared Soviet policy is bound to encounter illogicalities and inconsistencies which sometimes defy explanation. Soviet attitudes to Islam are no exception, and the controversy which raged during 1956 over the nature of Shamil's revolt and of 'Muridism' are an excellent case in point: the officially inspired attempt to rehabilitate Shamil produced unexpected nationalist stirrings and the authorities were eventually constrained to reduce their recognition of his merits and those of his movement to an absolute minimum. The resolution passed at a discussion on the subject held in October, 1956, in Daghestan (Shamil's place of origin) found that the religious trappings of the movement were reactionary; Muridism inflamed religious fanaticism and provoked hatred towards people professing Christianity.

The discussion held in Moscow in November did not produce any precise resolution, but it was abundantly clear that the Party is now strongly against any whole-hearted rehabilitation of Shamil.

Rent by schism and weakened by nationalism and Western and Communist materialism, Islam is still a force to be reckoned with—not a united force in the practical sense, but one with great reserves of passive resistance. After a generation of Soviet regimentation, the Islamic way of life still persists in the Muslim republics of the Union to an extent which is at once surprising and mortifying to the authorities. Even a partial lifting of the barrier between the Soviet Muslims and those hitherto supposed to be in thrall to the West might bring with it disturbing consequences: Muslims both inside and outside the U.S.S.R. might realize for the first time that there is a world of difference between nationalism which is tolerated by or which can be wrested from the West and the synthetic nationalism permitted in the Soviet Union; and that no part of the so-called colonial Muslim world has been colonized by non-Muslims to the same extent as Soviet Central Asia and Kazakhstan. Even if hatred of the West and love of the Russians were but half as widespread among Muslims as the Russians so persistently maintain, the task of the Soviet propaganda machine would still be a formidable one.

SOVIET CULTURAL PROPAGANDA
IN THE NEAR AND MIDDLE EAST

by IVAR SPECTOR

THE YEAR 1956 was marked by an intensification of Soviet cultural propaganda in the Near and Middle East, with some shifts in emphasis as compared with 1955.[1] In the first place, Soviet policy makers have attempted to establish a pattern for the conditioning of Asian minds with reference to the significance for the liberation of the Orient of the Russian Revolution of 1905, the October Revolution of 1917, and the 'Soviet victory' over Nazi Germany in 1945. Secondly, it has become apparent that the U.S.S.R. no longer acts alone in the Near and Middle East, but in collaboration with the Chinese Republic and the Soviet European satellites. Finally, the Soviet government has ceased to focus its programme exclusively on the Near East or the Far East, but strives rather for the 'solidarity of Asia' as a whole, with Moscow functioning as its cultural Mecca.

I

(1) Since 1954 a whole series of Soviet monographs has linked the rise of the national movements in Turkey, Iran, India, China, Korea, and the Arab countries to the impact throughout Asia of the Russian revolutionary events of 1905. Although as early as 1922 M. Pavlovich, the editor of *Novy Vostok*, claimed that the 1905 Revolution played the same role in the lives of the peoples of Asia

---

[1] For Soviet cultural propaganda in the Near and Middle East prior to 1956, see Ivar Spector, *The Soviet Union and the Muslim World, 1917–1956* (Seattle, University of Washington Press, 1956), especially Chapter VIII.

as did the French Revolution among the peoples of Europe, little or no attempt was made to capitalize on this theme. Since the celebration in 1955 of the fiftieth anniversary of the Revolution of 1905, it has been exploited in scholarly and popular journals, as well as in the daily Press of the U.S.S.R. Brushing aside all other factors, both external and internal, that provided the impetus for the rise of the national liberation movements in Asia, Soviet historical propaganda has attempted to focus the attention of Asians on the impact of the Revolution of 1905. By so doing, the U.S.S.R. expects to condition the Asian peoples to recognize their indebtedness to the Russian revolutionary movement for the origin and development of their own national liberation movements.

(2) Since 1921, Soviet writers have neglected no opportunity to remind Turkey, Iran, and Afghanistan that they owed their national independence to the existence and support of Soviet Russia. In the autumn of 1956 the Soviet Press began to indicate that the fortieth anniversary of the October Revolution in 1957 would give rise to an avalanche of articles and literary works emphasizing Asian indebtedness to this event. Persistent Soviet emphasis on the connection between the October Revolution and the retreat of 'colonialism' in the Near East and throughout Asia has in the past had an impact on the thinking of some Asian leaders, including the Kemalists in Turkey, Mr. Nehru, and President Sukarno of Indonesia.[2]

(3) In 1956 the U.S.S.R. embarked on a new line of propaganda to mould and shape the thinking of the Arab world. The gist of it was that the Arab states, like the rest of Asia, owe their independence to the Soviet Union, as the country primarily responsible for the defeat of Hitler in World War II. Had Hitler been victorious, according to Soviet propagandists, there would have been no independent Arab or Muslim states in the Near and Middle East. Although this new line of Soviet 'cultural' propaganda has not yet been fully articulated, the Soviet Press and periodicals, and even Soviet text-books, emphasize that Soviet support not only protected the Arab states from Nazi domination, but ensured their liberation from 'Anglo-French imperialism'. Thus, in addition to 1905 and 1917, there has been added a third significant date, namely, 1945. The extent to which the Russians are prepared to push this thesis was evinced in the case of Iran. Soviet writers have been busy claiming that Soviet intervention during World War II actually saved Iran from the

[2] See, for instance, the speech of N. A. Mikhailov, Soviet Minister of Culture, 'Strengthen Soviet-Indian Friendship', *Pravda*, January 27, 1957; and President Sukarno, 'The Influence of the October Revolution on the Awakening of the Peoples of Asia', *Pravda*, October 11, 1956.

ignominy of being classed with Germany as a defeated Power, with all the consequences that that would have entailed.[3]

II

In its efforts to win over the Near and Middle East, the Soviet Union in 1956 made no pretence of relying solely on its own resources, whether political, military, economic, or cultural. The European satellites not only supplied arms and industrial equipment to the Arab states and India, but they participated in trade and cultural exhibits, furnished dancers, musicians, and scholars, in order to establish closer contacts with the peoples of Asia. In September, 1956, for instance, Yemen accepted a Czech offer to train Yemenite students *gratis* for six years in engineering and medicine at Czech universities.

Far more significant from the Asian standpoint, however, has been the collaboration in the Near and Middle East between the Soviet Union and China. On the occasion of the seventh anniversary of the Sino-Soviet Alliance of February 14, 1950, the Soviet government voiced its profound satisfaction over the strong position of the Chinese People's Republic, not only in the Far East but also in the Near and Middle East. N. A. Mikhailov, the Soviet Minister of Culture, likewise gave his blessing to Sino-Soviet collaboration: 'These are new times. China and the U.S.S.R. stand together.'[4]

The joint action of the U.S.S.R. and China, each of which boasts a large Muslim minority, has greatly improved the prospects for the spread of Communist propaganda in the Near and Middle East. Beginning in 1952, China began to make its Muslim population conscious of their co-religionists in Asia, especially of the Arabs.[5] Although the Chinese Communist régime has been manifestly unfriendly towards Christian sects, it has avoided some of the gross errors of the Soviet régime towards the Muslims of Central Asia and the Caucasus. In Sinkiang, for example, where the Muslim clergy were the principal landowners, not only have the Chinese left the lands belonging to religious foundations untouched, but in the matter of land redistribution the mullahs and imams have shared equally with the peasants.

The Eisenhower Doctrine, announced January 5, 1957, demonstrated the extent of Sino-Soviet collaboration in the Near and

[3] See K. Ivanov and A. Vasilyev, 'A Slippery and Dangerous Path', *International Affairs* (Moscow), No. 2, 1956, pp. 36–7.

[4] 'A Great Force', *Izvestia*, February 14, 1957.

[5] See *Moslems in China* (in Chinese, Arabic, and English), edited by the China Islamic Association (Peking, 1953).

Middle East. After a series of articles denouncing it in the Soviet Press,[6] the Soviet and Chinese governments on January 18 signed in Moscow a joint declaration condemning the Doctrine and announcing their readiness to support the peoples of the Near and Middle East in order to prevent 'aggression' and interference in their domestic affairs.[7] This joint declaration, as reported in the Soviet Press, met with immediate and favourable response in Cairo, Damascus, and elsewhere in the Arab world.[8]

That Egypt is fully conscious of the significance of Sino-Soviet collaboration in the Near East appeared from Colonel Nasser's determination to visit not only Moscow but also Peking during the summer of 1957. A Sudanese cultural delegation followed a similar procedure in 1956. The end of March, 1957, found a seven-man trade delegation from China engaged in an extensive tour of Egypt, Sudan, Jordan, and Lebanon. It seems significant that on the day the joint declaration was signed in Moscow, a Sino-Soviet programme for cultural collaboration in 1957 was signed in Peking.[9] Although this plan expressed no direct intent with respect to joint Sino-Soviet cultural action in the Near and Middle East, it no doubt set the pattern for future Chinese and Soviet cultural agreements with the Muslim countries of that area.

Of special significance since 1955 from the propaganda standpoint has been the fact that Soviet and Chinese political leaders travelling abroad have frequently included Muslims in their entourage. When Chou En-lai went to Bandung, he took with him a 'pious Imam of the Islamic faith', and during the course of the conference he assiduously wooed the Arab states.[10] Bulganin and Khrushchev took to India Jabar Rasulov, Zykhra Kakhimbabayeva, and Sharif Rashidov, described as representatives of the Muslim peoples of Uzbekistan and Tajikistan. Both Chinese and Soviet Muslims performed the pilgrimage to Mecca in 1955. In March, 1956, when the Stalin Peace Prize was conferred on Sheikh Muhammed al-Ashmar, Chairman of the National Committee of the Partisans of Peace in Syria, the Soviet delegation to Damascus included Ziyautdin Babakhanov, Chairman of the Spiritual Administration of the Muslims of Central Asia and Kazakhstan, who addressed the assembled guests in Arabic.

[6] See especially, *Pravda*, January 9 and 13, 1957.
[7] *Pravda*, January 19, 1957.
[8] *ibid.*, January 22, 1957.   [9] See *Pravda*, January 17 and 19, 1957.
[10] George McTurnan Kahin, *The Asian-African Conference, Bandung, Indonesia, April, 1955* (New York, Cornell University Press, 1956), pp. 16, 54.

III

The pressure within the U.S.S.R. for more person-to-person contacts between Soviet citizens and the peoples of Asia, which has been mounting ever since the Bulganin-Khrushchev visit to India, Burma, and Afghanistan demonstrated its value, has led the Soviet government to proceed, albeit with caution, to lower its barriers against Soviet travel abroad. In particular, it has become obvious that Soviet Muslims permitted to venture forth to the Near and Middle East are thoroughly indoctrinated as to their superiority over foreign Muslims, and that they are ready and willing to assume the role of missionaries to their less fortunate co-religionists.

Following the precedent set the previous year, in 1956 a large delegation of Soviet Muslims under the leadership of Kamaretdin Salikhov, Imam of the Moscow Mosque and member of the Muslim Council for the R.S.F.S.R., undertook the pilgrimage to Mecca by air.[11] This delegation, comprising mullahs and lay Muslims, peasants and workers from Uzbekistan, Tajikistan, Turkmenia, Kirghizia, Kazakhstan, Azerbaidjan, Bashkiria, Daghestan, Moscow, and the Urals, performed all the customary religious rites of the *hadj* at Mecca, visited Muslim shrines at Medina, and spent some time in Cairo. A young Uzbek doctor among them ministered to the needs of sick pilgrims unable to secure medical attention. Not only did they join with Egyptian Muslim leaders in the reading of the Qur'ān, but they assured all who would listen that there is freedom of religion in the U.S.S.R., that they are permitted to have their own *madrasahs*, to print religious literature, and that a new edition of the Qur'ān had been issued in the Soviet Union in 1956.

The role of these tourists has not been confined to the dissemination of Soviet propaganda throughout the Muslim East. They have played host to an increasing number of Islamic and non-Islamic visitors from abroad. With this purpose in mind, the Soviet régime has created what may be termed Islamic oases in such centres as Tashkent, Samarkand, Ashkhabad, Baku, etc., in Central Asia and the Caucasus. Mirzo Tursun-Zade, perhaps the most prominent literary figure in Soviet Central Asia, who has himself travelled widely in Iran, Afghanistan, India, Pakistan, and China, claims that hundreds of foreign tourists have visited Tajikistan in recent years. It was his conclusion that '... in language, music, literature, and folklore, there is close affinity between the peoples of Soviet Central

---

[11] 'Mecca 1956: Pilgrimage of Soviet Muslims', *News*, No. 19, October, 1956, pp. 22–3. This emphasis on religious propaganda did not receive the same publicity in *Pravda* and *Izvestia*.

Asia and India, Afghanistan, and other neighbouring countries'.[12] Uzbekistan is fast becoming one of the major scientific centres of the U.S.S.R., and already serves as 'Exhibit A' for Asian tourists. Indeed, according to Anvar Kutchkarov, Uzbek Minister of Culture, the hundred research institutes under the Uzbek Academy of Sciences steadily increased their contacts abroad in 1956, especially with the Academies of Sciences of China, India, Pakistan, Iran, Afghanistan, etc.[13] In January, 1957, M. Abdullaev, President of the Uzbek Academy of Sciences, attended the Indian Scientific Congress.

The Congress of the Intelligentsia of Uzbekistan, which opened in Tashkent on October 11, 1956, and was attended by twelve hundred Uzbek representatives, as well as delegates from the other republics of Central Asia and the Caucasus, was used to bring scholars from China, India, and Korea, and especially an important delegation of members of the Association of Egyptian Writers under the leadership of Dr. Muhammed Mandur, philologist and critic.[14] Invited to the U.S.S.R. by the Union of Soviet Writers, this delegation was primarily interested in the Arab settlements in Uzbekistan on which considerable research has been in progress under the direction of Professor I. Vinnikov.[15] The Egyptian delegation, which spent five days in Tashkent, and visited Samarkand and Stalinabad, included Muhammed Said al-Erian, a writer, Shawki Diaf, a professor of Arabic literature at Cairo University, Ali Bakasir, an Egyptian dramatist and poet, and Abdurrakhman ash-Sharkawi, novelist and dramatist.

IV

Following the pattern of Soviet-Chinese cultural relations since 1950, the U.S.S.R. has worked assiduously in recent years for the conclusion of cultural exchange agreements with the countries of Asia. The opening months of 1957 witnessed the renewal or establishment of a whole series of such agreements with China, Vietnam, the Mongol People's Republic, and with several of the European satellites. The high-water mark of Soviet success among the Arab states came on August 21, 1956, with the Egypt–Syria–Lebanon tour of Sergei Kaftanov,[16] First Deputy Minister of Culture of the

---

[12] See his article, 'Bright Prospects', *New Times*, No. 2, 1956.

[13] See 'Uzbekistan: Culture for All', *News*, December, 1956, p. 7.

[14] See *Literaturnaya Gazeta*, October 4, 13, 18, and 27, 1956. Articles by Dr. Mandur were published in this official organ of the Soviet writers on November 3 and December 11, 1956.

[15] *Literaturnaya Gazeta*, October 11, 1956.

[16] See 'Egypt–Syria–Lebanon', *News*, No. 20, 1956, for an interview with Sergei Kaftanov. See also *Sovetskaya Kultura*, October 25, 1956.

U.S.S.R., who in Damascus signed a broad cultural co-operation agreement covering Soviet-Syrian exchanges in the fields of science, art, general and technical education, physical training, and sports. The agreement provided for exchange visits of delegations and individuals, the pooling of cultural information, the holding of exhibitions, concerts etc., co-operation in broadcasts, the exchange of films, the establishment of university scholarships to encourage student exchange, and the staging of Soviet-Syrian sports events. Kaftanov's hopes of concluding similar agreements with Lebanon and Egypt did not advance beyond the preparatory stages. As to Syria, however, the implementation of the agreement could scarcely fail to make of the country a 'cultural satellite' of the U.S.S.R. Judging by V. Borisov's report on the Second Congress of Arab Writers in Damascus in the latter part of 1956, Soviet thinking in regard to the role of literature and the state has already had an impact on the outlook of a substantial part of the Arab intelligentsia.[17]

Until the Suez crisis, Soviet-Egyptian cultural contacts proceeded more slowly. Since 1955 VOKS (the Society for Cultural Relations with Foreign Countries) has maintained a permanent exhibit in Cairo, with the object of popularizing Soviet cultural achievements. In May, 1956, Intourist and the Misr Travel and Shipping Company concluded an agreement for tourist exchanges. About the same time, a group of Soviet archaeologists and ethnographers visited Egypt to establish contacts with Egyptian scholars, and to collaborate in preparations to safeguard Egyptian monuments located in the area due to be inundated by the construction of the projected Aswan Dam.[18]

In the spring of 1956, the first delegation of Egyptian cinema specialists arrived in Moscow, their visit timed to coincide with the showing of the first Egyptian feature films in the U.S.S.R., namely, 'Struggle in the Valley' and 'Blazing Sun'. It was admitted that Egyptian knowledge of Soviet films was still very slight, having included up to that time only *Sadko*, *Men of Daring*, *The Big Top*, and the Soviet Albanian film, *Skanderbeg*. Egyptian publication of *Film Art*, by Vsevolod Pudovkin, and of a study of *The Soviet Cinema* by two Egyptian directors, Tlemseni and A. K. Musa, was regarded as an important step towards bridging this gap.

In June, 1956, the Soviet Publishing House for Foreign Literature brought out a collection of nineteen stories, entitled *Egipetskie Novelly*, designed to acquaint Soviet readers with 'the creative family of Egyptian writers', namely the 'progressives'.[19] Included

---

[17] *Novy Mir*, No. 1, 1957, pp. 246–9.

[18] *Vestnik AN, S.S.S.R.*, No. 9, 1956, pp. 67–70.

[19] *Literaturnaya Gazeta*, June 16, 1956; *VOKS Bulletin*, No. 9 (104), September, 1956, pp. 54–5.

were several works by Mahmud Teimur, the so-called founder of the Egyptian short story. Abdurrakhman ash-Sharkawi, author of *The Land*, whose anti-American outlook won him a trip to the U.S.S.R. in 1956, was also represented, as were the young Egyptian writers, Youssef Idris, Is Ubeid, Mahmud Bagasir, Mahmud Tahir Lashin, and one Egyptian authoress, Ibnat ash-Shati. These stories emphasized such themes as the plight of the Egyptian peasant and the Egyptian woman, the revolting Muslim customs of the past, the corrupting influence of American films on Egyptian youth, etc.

In recent years, the U.S.S.R. Academy of Sciences has promoted a book-exchange programme, not only with Red China and India but with the Near and Middle East, including Turkey, Iran, Egypt, Syria, and Lebanon. In all, according to a report by A. Kh. Rafikov, ten countries of the Near and Middle East have taken part in the book exchange with the Library of the U.S.S.R. Academy of Sciences, through eighty-five institutions, including five Academies of Sciences, eleven universities, two biological, nine agricultural, and sixteen historico-philological institutes, etc. Although this programme has shown a marked increase since 1950, the visit of the Soviet historian, V. I. Shunkov, to the Cairo and Alexandria libraries in May, 1956, suggested that in Egypt, at least, the book-exchange programme was still in its infancy.[20] In spite of the lively interest in things Russian, Shunkov found 'almost no books in Russian' at the National Library in Cairo, and in the Music Library a complete absence of Soviet publications on Russian music and art.

V

The year 1957, which from the Soviet standpoint began so auspiciously in January with the opening of the first Soviet industrial exhibition in Cairo, the Soviet film festival, and the performances of the U.S.S.R. State Ensemble of the People's Dance, almost ended in disaster with the première of the Soviet film, *Mother*, on January 19. The works of Maxim Gorky, especially his novel, *Mother*, have long been popular among left-wing industrial workers and the intelligentsia of the Near East, who demand deeds instead of words. But although *Mother* is a blending of great art and revolutionary propaganda—a combination which appeals strongly to the younger generation in the Near and Middle East—the Soviet film based on this novel was shown in the wrong place at the wrong time.[21] Its em-

[20] See his article, 'In the Libraries of Cairo and Alexandria', *Vestnik AN, S.S.S.R.*, No. 11, 1956, pp. 83–5.
[21] See the *New York Times*, January 23, 1957.

phasis on the organization of an underground movement, methods of bribing the police, the printing and distribution of subversive literature, and instigation of strife in factories, was tantamount to an invitation to overthrow the Egyptian government, which itself claims to be revolutionary.

It is an established fact that Nasser has encountered opposition, not only from the extreme right wing but also from left-wing intellectuals who regard his régime as transitional, to be superseded sooner or later by an authentic Socialist government.[22] The inflammatory nature of the film, *Mother*, alarmed the Egyptian leaders, who abruptly terminated the entire Soviet festival and substituted a Hollywood 'Western'. (The fact that the elaborate and widely distributed Arab-language brochure on the U.S.S.R. advertising the Soviet industrial fair was printed backward proved to be another blow to Soviet prestige.) However, neither Cairo nor Moscow permitted this incident to affect Soviet-Egyptian relations. According to the Soviet Press, the première of *Mother* was a tremendous success, with an ovation for the Soviet film star, V. Maretskaya, and there the matter was dropped.[23] When Nasser visited the Soviet industrial fair on January 26, I. G. Bolshakov, Deputy Soviet Minister of Foreign Trade, announced that a large part of the 10,000 items on exhibit would be donated to the Egyptian government. The Soviet Dance Ensemble directed by I. A. Moiseev, which carried out a strenuous schedule of performances in Egypt and Syria, was reputed to be a huge success. The mission of the Soviet Red Cross and Red Crescent Society to Egypt, bringing food, medical supplies, and ambulances amounting to 15 million roubles in value for the 'victims of Anglo-French-Israeli invasion', was warmly received.

In view of what happened in Egypt, it is interesting to note that in the Sudan, according to L. Izzedin Ali Amer, leader of a Sudanese cultural delegation to China and the U.S.S.R. in the summer of 1956, translations of the works of Maxim Gorky enjoy high priority among Sudanese readers.[24] Perhaps the most significant event in the brief history of Soviet-Sudanese relations to date has been the presence of a large delegation from the Sudan at the International Seminar on the Equality of Women in the U.S.S.R., held in Moscow in the summer of 1956. The head of the delegation, Fat'ma Talib Ismail, herself a teacher and the first woman in the Sudan to receive a university education, was particularly interested in the status of

[22] See Georges Ketman, 'Du Papier et des Fèves—Portrait de l'intelligentsia égyptienne,' *Preuves*, January, 1957, p. 22. See infra, pp. 479–87.

[23] *Pravda*, January 21, 1957.

[24] 'Sudano-Soviet Cultural Exchange', *VOKS Bulletin*, No. 8 (103), August, 1956, pp. 43–5.

women in the Soviet Union.[25] Upon her return to the Sudan, she planned to write a book on the U.S.S.R. She and her associates hoped to create a Union of the Women of Africa, to organize a Conference of the Women of Asia and Africa, and to establish a Society for Sudano-Soviet Friendship. Already Sudanese students have begun to go to the Soviet Union to study medicine, etc. The announced intent of the Soviet Government to expand its efforts in Africa in 1957 appears to be under way in the Sudan.

VI

There has been particular emphasis in Soviet propaganda on the need for 'solidarity' among the Asian peoples as a whole. As a result of the Conference of Fifteen Asian Countries in Delhi in 1955, the U.S.S.R. established a Soviet Committee for the Solidarity of Asian Countries, with headquarters in Moscow, to promote the extension of the 'Peace Zone'. The most significant outcome to date has been the arrival in Egypt on February 9, 1957, of representatives of the Committee of Solidarity, headed by Anap Singh, a member of the Indian Parliament, and including delegates from China, Japan, and the Soviet Union.[26] The delegation arranged with Colonel Nasser for the calling of a new conference to stress the solidarity of the Asian and African peoples—a second Bandung—to be held in Cairo in October, 1957. Significantly enough, although the first Asian-African Conference was held in South-East Asia, the forthcoming session was scheduled for Eygpt; and whereas the U.S.S.R. was not formally represented at Bandung, the holding of this conference under the auspices of the Egyptian National Committee for the Solidarity of the Countries of Asia practically assures Soviet participation.

With Asian solidarity in mind, the U.S.S.R. is placing great emphasis on the development of Asian studies, in the expectation of making the Soviet Union a centre for Asian scholars of the Near, Middle, and Far East. Out of Asian solidarity the U.S.S.R. looks for the evolution of a new society, largely self-sufficient economically and culturally, to be achieved by degrees in the non-Soviet Asian orbit. From this new society, needless to say, Western influence is to be eliminated.

[25] See her article in *Literaturnaya Gazeta*, October 6, 1956.
[26] See *Pravda*, February 9, 17, 1957; *Izvestia*, February 16, 1957.

THE BACKGROUND OF SOVIET
POLICY IN THE MIDDLE EAST

by H. CARÈRRE D'ENCAUSSE

AT THE VERY moment when the Soviets' penetration of the Middle East is causing alarm in the West, the policy of the group now in power is being pursued, apparently, at the cost of a certain loosening of the world-structure of Communism. In eastern Europe the Poznan trials, the rise to power of Gomulka, and the Hungarian revolt look like so many cracks in the monolith. Even in the Soviet Union itself difficulties of similar kinds are appearing. The Azerbaidjanis, rebelling against Russification, demand the exclusive use of their own Azerian-Turkish language; while the Dagestan nationalists have to be conciliated by the official rehabilitation of their national hero the Imām Shamil, venerated for his resistance to the Russian occupation in the last century. Khrushchev's policy seems, indeed, to be provoking outbursts of national feeling which take the form of antagonism to the U.S.S.R. Is it, however, the same in the Middle East? Will the relations between that region and the U.S.S.R. be modified by the fact that there is now agitation on the Soviet's own fringe? To answer these questions we have to look into the background of Soviet policy in the Levant.

If one starts by drawing up a balance-sheet of Communist activity in the region in 1954,[1] it looks decidedly deficient. There were only 5000 Communists in the official party in Israel; in the 'unofficial' Syrian party less than 10,000; 1000 to 1500 adherents to the (particularly active) Communist Party of the Sudan, and 10,000 in the Lebanon, where the Communist Party was somnolent. Everywhere

[1] W. Z. Laqueur has done this in his article, 'The Appeal of Communism in the Middle East' (*Middle East Journal*, 1954, 4).

else the situation looked hopeless. In Iraq and Jordan (1000 to 1500), Egypt and Turkey (3000 'progressives'), the parties appeared to be paralysed by the vigilance of the authorities. These figures, it is true, must be seen in context: no political party in the Middle East can claim more than 10,000 adherents; and all, excepting the Communist Parties, are primarily the personal following of local politicians. One must add, moreover, that the Communist Parties of the region infiltrate, and are the real directors of, a number of 'parallel' organizations, such as the important 'Partisans of Peace', which reinforce or relieve them at need. But taking these factors into account, the condition of Middle Eastern Communism in 1954 was far from flourishing. What could the U.S.S.R. expect from such scattered forces? What reliance could it place upon Communist Parties that were generally crippled by repression; some of which, like the Tudeh in Persia, had more than once bungled a revolution[2]; parties which, after all, were everywhere made up of minorities of little importance in the national life[3]? Moreover, these Communist Parties were mostly groups of intellectuals from the *petit bourgeoisie* whose precarious situation made them susceptible to Marxist solicitation, but who had no working-class connections. (In the Middle East, instead of a proletariat there is only the *lumpen-proletariat*, which is hardly organizable.) All in all, these Communists aroused no great response in the minds of the faithful Muslims, whom their clergy had always kept well on guard against a purely materialist ideology. The revolutionary future of such parties in such conditions must have seemed highly problematic.

THE AWAKENING TO 'NATIONAL CONSCIOUSNESS'

Does this balance-sheet, drawn up during 1954, still give a fair idea of the situation? In his latest writings Walter Z. Laqueur[4] replies in the negative; he says that in the space of two years Middle Eastern Communism has made progress 'in depth' and achieved a strong position in the balance of political Powers. It is a question, moreover, whether this portentous development is not something much more than Communism itself—whether this is not the awakening of national consciousness.

Until quite lately, the masses of Islam were far removed from any

[2] 1945–46: the Democratic Republic of Azerbaidjan and the Kurdish Republic of Mahabad. August, 1953: Revolt against the power of the King.

[3] For instance: the outstanding personality of Middle Eastern Communism, Khaled Bakdash, Secretary of the Syrio-Lebanese Communist Party, is a Kurd: and the Israeli Communist Party consists to a great extent of Arabs. Comparable cases are common throughout the Middle East.

[4] *Communism and Nationalism in the Middle East* (New York, 1956).

political speculation, and farther still from any temptation to Marxism, the materialist teaching of which shocked their sensibility. The very structure of their societies made it hard for them to understand such preaching. On the one hand, there was the landed aristocracy, protected by its wealth; and on the other hand, impoverished masses, illiterate and backward, the *lumpen-proletariat* which Communism ignores. Between the two extremes there was a petty bourgeois intelligentsia, very responsive to Communism by its nature and its situation, but this was a small minority.

The awakening and the politicization of these masses, whose poverty, insecurity, and disordered surroundings kept them in a state of dull despair or even drove them (as in Iran) to suicide[5]— these are surely the most portentous aspects of the present ferment in the Middle East. Exposed to a skilled propaganda, from within by the Communist Party and its 'parallel' groups, and from abroad by the U.S.S.R. and its satellites, the populace is being awakened to national aspirations solely in opposition to the 'foreign imperialism' to which all its miseries can so easily be ascribed. What is this 'imperialism' by which they are 'enslaved'? For some it is Britain; for most, it is the United States, whose political and economic presence in the Middle East is 'only a new form of the old colonialism'. The tyrant is always 'the West'; it is also the world of democracy. Is it, then, surprising that these Muslim masses have in their hearts confounded *democracy* with foreign *imperialism*? The consequences of this are grave indeed. For, having lately been deprived of their traditional social structures, they are plunged into a world where democracy and Communism are presented as irreconcilable opposites without any middle way between them. How, then, are these populations of the Orient, destitute of political experience, to come to any reasonable decision? Their authoritarian governments, set up and sustained by the West, have everywhere hunted down the Communists, but also all the nationalists who opposed pro-Western policies, thereby helping to confound Communism with nationalism. The Communists, because they alone have some political organization, seem to have known how to canalize in their own direction all the forces of opposition, simply by subordinating all their own watchwords to that of nationalism. The result is that gradual growth of collusion between nationalists and Communists which

[5] Suicide for political reasons is extremely common in Persia. This is well known, and was exemplified during the fall of the Mossadeq government, when the number of voluntary deaths among the intelligentsia as well as the populace was very large. The clergy of the Shia warned the government against the dangers of 'collective despair' in the religious organ *Setarèh Eslam*, November 19, 1955.

Western observers have been alarmed to discover. A confusion of purpose so dangerous ought, no doubt, to have been resisted by Islam; but here too it seems that expert propaganda, combined with a complication of circumstances, has blinded the masses to the antinomy that it implies. To nationalism, now the ruling idea in Middle Eastern politics, Communist propaganda has linked not only hatred of 'foreign imperialism' but, above all, the necessity of one's fervid resistance to it, as a nationalist but also as a Muslim. The 'Western imperialist' is 'the foreigner', but worse still he is the *Kafir* —the 'infidel'. This *addition of nationalism to the duties of a good Muslim* makes the deepest appeal to the sensibilities of the masses, and it is this, apparently, which is awakening them to politics. Henceforth they think of themselves as Muslims and nationalists, over against the West and its imperialists.

What is the real value of such a development to Communism— what does it gain by it? May it not be to have feathered a nest (though by means of an equivocation) in the midst of the national community? One remembers Khaled Bakdash's recent declaration in the Chamber of Deputies: 'Syria is not Communist; *it is nationalist and will remain so!*'

That is the striking development of the situation since Mr. Laqueur's study of it in 1954. Communism, formerly confined within the dogmas and slogans of Communism, is breaking new ground by identifying itself with nationalism; and this arouses repercussions in Soviet policy.

THE EVOLUTION OF SOVIET POLICY SINCE THE TWENTIETH CONGRESS

Whilst the Middle East of its own initiative is awakening to national consciousness, the U.S.S.R. is revising its doctrines and devising new formulae, breaking away from the Stalinist vision of the world. Near the end of Stalin's reign, about 1949–50, the Soviet theorists, true to the most orthodox Marxism, still excluded the *bourgeoisie* from any part in the emancipation of the dependent countries, for they said that 'historical experience proves that the national *bourgeoisie* in the colonial countries, linked in innumerable ways with the feudal classes and with foreign imperialism, cannot lead a movement of national liberation to victory. The anti-imperial and anti-feudal revolution will triumph only through the alliance of the workers and peasants, directed by Communists.'[6]

That theory is now abandoned as 'sectarian'. A few months later we read in the same review that 'the national *bourgeoisie* is not

[6] *Sovetskoe Vostokovedenie*, Nos. 5 and 6, 1955.

always prone to betray the cause of national independence: on the contrary, it is the natural and almost irreconcilable enemy of imperialism'.[7]

Still more recently *Party Life*, the review published by the Central Committee, has elaborated the role that the national *bourgeoisie* may, in some cases, be induced to play in the struggle for independence. The writer of the article admits that 'liberation from the colonial yoke may be attained in different ways in different countries':

'In some cases the people first fight for and win their complete political and economic independence, and then undertake the task of bringing about not only a democratic but a Socialist transformation.'[8]

This is true for some popular democracies such as China and Korea, where 'the working class plays the leading part and directs the struggle for Socialism'. However, emancipation is a very long and complicated process and one must admit that, at the present time, many other forces participate in the struggle side by side with the proletarian class—peasants, artisans, technicians, traders, officials, intellectuals—and even, for a time, 'some feudal elements'. In that alliance the part played by the peasantry 'is small, because the peasantry does not come on the political scene with a programme of its own . . . because it is dispersed, divided against itself, and does not form a single and compact mass'. The peasantry in decline, and the proletarian class weak because as yet insufficiently organized, are thus obliged to ally themselves with the national *bourgeoisie*, 'an organized force made up of numerous sections, and with an independent political programme'. This recognition of a leading function for the *bourgeoisie* in the conflict with imperialism is reinforced by another innovation no less noteworthy—namely, that in this new orthodoxy the alliance between the proletariat and the *bourgeoisie* is to be *sincere and lasting*. Lenin, it will be remembered, allowed it only as *conditional and provisional*; he thought the national *bourgeoisie* might, in certain circumstances, support an anti-imperialist movement, but that only the proletariat could lead it.

This brings us to another aspect, no less astonishing, of the evolution of the Communist Party in Russia—its new appreciation of the notion of 'independence' in the Orient.

Theorists of the Stalinist epoch asserted that the independence achieved by the national *bourgeoisie* ('still ready to collaborate with the enemies of yesterday') was a mere myth. They appealed to the strict Marxist-Leninist teaching that 'social liberation is the condition of national liberation': the prerequisite of independence was 'first to

---

[7] *ibid*, January, 1956.

[8] M. E. Zhukov, 'The break-up of the Imperialist Colonial System', *Partiinaya Zhizn*, August, 1956.

be freed from foreign capital'.[9] Thus, they said: 'The concessions to the Dominions of India, Pakistan, and Ceylon have in no way modified their real situation.'[10]

One must, of course, admit that the independence lately gained by many Oriental peoples is highly artificial: 'Political independence is not complete independence. . . . In some sovereign states of Asia and Africa, foreign monopoly capital has retained important positions. In many cases, the old colonies and the old dependent countries which have recently acquired sovereign status, continue for a fairly long time to be burdened with unfair, even usurious obligations. . . . The banks, which hold the keys of industry, often remain under the control of foreign capital.'[11]

What, then, is the use of the sovereignty achieved by these countries? M. Zhukov gives two answers. First that 'political independence is the most important of the prior conditions for economic liberation'. Sovereignty enables the governments of African and Asian countries to pursue a policy that will 'redress their economic backwardness and lead to complete independence'. Such a policy naturally includes the nationalization of foreign companies (such as that of the Suez Canal, 'the just assertion of its natural rights by a young sovereign state'), but it requires above all the creation of state undertakings, within the frame of a planned economy, which, in spite of their non-Socialist character, are regarded as most important.

Still more important in order to guarantee the sovereignty of these young states is the development of their international relations: 'If the domination of the capitalist system were still unrivalled as it was before 1917, the political independence achieved by the colonies would be without substance. It would inevitably remain merely conventional and formal. But after the triumph of the Great Socialist Revolution of October, and still more now that the Socialist system is fully established, the character of the political independence achieved by peoples struggling against imperialism is essentially modified. The new sovereign states are no longer isolated over against the powerful capitalist world which engendered the capitalist system. The liberated colonies and semi-colonies can rely upon the Socialist states which, by their very existence, make the struggle against colonialism easier.'[12]

All this is a marked departure from the Stalinist thesis; and is the more striking in view of its having evidently made a complete change in the Oriental tactics of the U.S.S.R., not in a merely accidental and opportunist sense, but consistently with the purpose that Mr.

[9] *Doklady Akademii Nauk S.S.S.R.*, No. 3, 1950.
[10] *Voprosy Ekonomiki* ('Economic Problems'), July, 1948.
[11] *Partiinaya Zhizn*, *loc. cit.*   [12] *Partiinaya Zhizn*. *loc. cit.*

Khrushchev outlined at the Twentieth Congress and that different organs of the Press have since restated.[13] What are the precise implications of this development? Greater independence in relations with Moscow, and the recognition that there are different paths to Socialism. In Stalin's time the value of an anti-imperialist movement was reckoned in terms of its relations with Moscow and its alignment with Soviet policy. Henceforth these 'over-simplified and sectarian' criteria are rejected. Similarly, it is henceforward admitted that national liberation may take on various aspects. In some countries such as China, it is the work of the Communist Party; in others, like India or the Middle Eastern states, the *bourgeoisie* can, and ought to, be at the head of the movement for national emancipation. It is true that no reconciliation between the national *bourgeoisie* and the Communist proletariat is ideologically possible, but their practical alliance is dictated by the imperative needs of a nationality at grips with the common enemy.

It is therefore around nationalism that the Eastern policy of the U.S.S.R. must henceforth be organized. But this is an old preoccupation within Russia herself, where the appearance of the previously unpublished notes of Lenin[14] shows that there is a renewed attention to the same problem. To have published these notes about the national minorities may well be a sign of intentions that reach far beyond the frontiers of the U.S.S.R. *Pravda*,[15] for instance, has an article disclosing another of Stalin's 'impostures'. His name had been associated with the solution of the national problems in the U.S.S.R., while in reality, as Lenin shows, he was in favour of a unified and centralized Soviet state which gave little scope to the legitimate aspirations of the nationalists, and he did not scruple to use violence against them. The publication of Lenin's comments shows that the party wants to prove that the Union of Soviet peoples is based upon their equality, and that it reaffirms the simple motive expressed by Lenin and quoted in *Pravda*'s article, that 'it would be an inexcusable opportunism if we, on the eve of the re-birth of the Orient, at the dawn of its great awakening, were to ruin our prestige in their eyes by the least brutality, the slightest violence towards non-Russians'.[16]

In deeds as well as in doctrine, the U.S.S.R. now shows the desire to reconsider its relations with the Oriental countries and take their

---

[13] *ibid*. One may also usefully consult an article by the economist Varga in 1948, the gist of which is reprinted in *Sovetskoe Vostokovedenie*, January, 1956.

[14] Written in December, 1922, and January, 1923, and communicated to the Twentieth Congress during the reading of Khrushchev's secret report.

[15] Article on Lenin's part in organizing the Soviet Republics, *Pravda*, July 11, 1956.

[16] *Cf.* pp. 410, 411 of the present book: article on Sultan Galiev.

national aspirations into account. The evolution of its policy towards the Middle Eastern states, if one studies this over the last few years, shows that here especially the Soviet Union is reversing the tactical policy in vogue since the Second World War, and is playing the 'nationalist' game which is the essence of the new doctrine. Excellent relations have been established with governments that are not in the least Socialist, which indeed are pitiless persecutors of the Communists. Such is the case in Egypt, Persia, and elsewhere, including Saudi Arabia, a theocratic state living upon its revenues from Aramco, but which, we are now told, is 'a really independent state'.[17] In taking this line the U.S.S.R. is apparently betraying the Communist Parties in those countries. But can one say that this is the abandonment of Communism? Or is it not, rather, the pursuit of a realistic policy that takes account of existing conditions—i.e. of the defective Communist organizations, the absence of a proletariat, the unorganized peasantry, and, finally, of a public opinion crystallizing around the nationalist idea?

The Communist groups in the Middle East, after a period of hesitation—nay, even of bitterness and resistance to their abandonment[18]—have come into line with Soviet policy and completely changed their tactics. In Syria, Khaled Bakdash, whose doctrinal orthodoxy is beyond question, has led his party into the wilderness, as it were, of *self-effacement and submergence in the national community*. This undoubted Communist now avoids any word of Communism: he never claims that his party is *avant-garde*; he completely subordinates the claims of the class struggle, which is now kept in the background, to the exigencies of the national emancipation[19]; and, finally, he proclaims his desire to enlist his forces in a common front uniting the whole country. A striking example of the new attitude was Khaled Bakdash's declaration after the triumph of the 'progressive' candidate in the election at Homs,[20] that 'this victory is not a Communist success: it is the birth of a Front in which all patriots of all opinions stand together'.

[17] *Sovetskoe Vostokovedenie*, January, 1956.

[18] At the moment when the U.S.S.R. was extending an ostentatious friendship to Nasser's Egypt, the *National Democratic Front* put out an 'appeal to the masses' in which it denounced 'the tyrannical military dictatorship' of Nasser; and the Sudanese Communist Party followed suit. Similarly, the Tudeh in Persia redoubled its attacks on General Zahedi whilst the U.S.S.R. was negotiating with him.

[19] 'Agrarian Reform', the great battle-cry of the Syrian Communist Party, wholly disappeared from the party's latest manifestoes (*cf. Al Sarqha*, May 25, 1956).

[20] The Communist Party not being officially recognized in Syria, Communist candidates present themselves for election under the label of 'progressives', but figure as Communists in the reported proceedings of Parliament.

Similarly, in the Lebanon the Communist Party professed itself 'ready to support any government produced by the National Front', without demanding participation in the government as a condition of its support.[21] And, finally, even the Egyptians who were imprisoned rallied round their government in February, 1956, by affirming in an open letter that 'we Communists offer complete and conscious support to your government . . . for we think it is in the interest of our country to constitute a broad National Democratic Front, uniting the people with the government . . . a Front that will fight against imperialism'.[22]

Thus Communism is effacing itself behind the power of the *bourgeoisie* supported by the U.S.S.R. Which of the two will in the end be paralysed by the other—the Communists or the *bourgeois* power? The progress of Communism would certainly seem to be imperilled by such an alliance, reducing Communists as it does to the rank of government supporters: opposition is an attitude with much more popular appeal. But Communism never had very much prestige among the masses of the Middle East. The great question is whether a *bourgeois* régime, upheld by the whole of the Left in the name of national freedom, will not be drawn into the politics of leftist demagogues competing for mass support. And is there not a further danger—that the *bourgeoisie*, as their apprehensions are gradually allayed by the Communists' self-effacement, may confuse issues by unconsciously identifying the cause of nationalism and Islam with the aim of their temporary allies? For that seems to be part of the Soviet tactics. Observers of Turkish national life are already wondering, with anxiety, whether the promoters of the Islamic renaissance in that country are not mixed up with the apostles of dialectical materialism. Whether these apprehensions are justified or not, they arise from the very real and grave question about the final outcome of this kind of politics.

*　　　*　　　*　　　*　　　*

Thus the sovietization of the Middle East presents itself in quite a new form. Communism, properly so called, gives place to nationalism encouraged by the U.S.S.R. But is it not in the name of this same nationalism that the popular democracies are rebelling against the U.S.S.R.? May not nationalism, if fortified by precept and example, be a rock on which Soviet politics will split? Seductive though it may

[21] *Al-Sarqha*, February 24, 1956, 'Appeal to the Lebanese People'.
[22] This document, published in the clandestine multigraphed organ of the Cairo Communists, *News of Egypt*, is signed by Ahmed Ali Qadr, Fakri Labibi, Mohamed Mohamed Shata, and Zaki Murad.

be to entertain that idea, an important distinction must be drawn between the popular democracies and the Asian and African countries of the Bandung group. For in the Russian 'satellite' states, and even in those on the fringe of the U.S.S.R. itself, the Soviet system came in with the Red Army, by which it was imposed upon peoples in no way prepared for it by their own previous evolution: in such countries Communism is inevitably identified with Russia, and Russia has the grim visage of an occupying Power. Here, nationalism can hardly be allied with Communism, and patriotic reaction against the U.S.S.R. often takes on the aspect of antagonism to Communism. In the Afro-Asiatic world, on the other hand, alliance between the two forces is facilitated by their common enmity to the 'imperialist West'. The U.S.S.R. being absent (in theory), it does not present any of the repellent features that it does in eastern Europe. Moreover, the development of Oriental countries towards Communism, so far as it is taking place, seems to be inspired chiefly by the example of China: this is especially the case in India.

The gradual weakening of the Soviets' position in eastern Europe is also likely, in the end, to disarm the Muslim *bourgeoisie*'s deep suspicions of the U.S.S.R., and incline them to accept alliance with it. It is also worth while to recall the fact that a 'colonial' form of Communism—that is, a form suitable for non-Western societies— was outlined long ago, and that it included all the tactical ideas that we now find in the new Soviet ideology of colonialism. This was the work of Sultan Galiev, a Tatar of Kazan and a Communist theorist, who first put forward the idea of a *colonial* International. Based upon a tactical alliance between workers, peasants, *bourgeoisie*, and even the advanced elements of big industry, this International, which was to be open to all the colonial world, envisaged the subordination of the class struggle to the aims of national liberation.

The growth of 'Titoism' in the Communist world lends additional force to this idea. To the U.S.S.R., which kept the idea under condemnation as an inexpiable 'deviation' until very recently, it is certainly a formidable challenge. But is it not even more so for the West?

SULTAN GALIEV

The U.S.S.R. and the Colonial Revolution

by A. BENNIGSEN

> It is true that Marx wanted the union of the proletariat of the whole world, but he never claimed that all the Russians ought to unite at Tiflis.—TSERTSVADZE.[1]

THE IMPLANTATION of the U.S.S.R. in the Middle East marks a very grave, perhaps a crucial moment of world history. After hesitating for nearly forty years, Communist Russia appears suddenly to have decided to extend Socialism to the whole of the colonial world, in the East above all. One may doubt whether Russia is ideologically prepared to face such an evolution of Communism, the first consequence of which would be to shift its centre of gravity towards the colonial and semi-colonial countries.

One may also wonder whether Russia has either the will or the means to employ, towards this end, the human elements which might provide a bond of union between Russia's Communism and her own Mohammedans. Nearly 30 million Turks, Iranians, and Caucasians make up a weighty factor in Soviet Russia's Oriental politics; but is it one that she can integrate in her calculations?

The first theoreticians of Communism, too preoccupied by Western affairs, had no definite doctrines about the colonial revolution or about national minorities. For Marx and Engels, the national

---

[1] Tsertsvadze, a member of the Georgian Communist Party, was a victim of the Stalinist repression. The sentence above is quoted by Alexander Tsomaïa in his 'Stalin in Georgia' in a *Report on the Soviet Union* (New York, 1956).

question was of only secondary importance beside that of the working class. They favoured certain separatist claims (notably the Polish and Irish), but they looked upon the nationalism of minorities as a 'medieval' phenomenon, a hindrance to the development of proletarian class-consciousness, and one which the triumph of Communism would automatically eliminate.

Some of their disciples—notably Rosa Luxemburg—reckoned that the national problem, insoluble under a capitalist régime, would disappear of itself with the inauguration of Socialism; and meanwhile, any support given to the national minorities might, under certain circumstances, tend to strengthen *bourgeois* nationalism and therefore retard the advent of Socialism. Others, particularly the Austrian Socialists Renner and Bauer, were afraid that the progress towards Socialism, far from eliminating the national problem, might aggravate it, and they became preachers of cultural and territorial autonomy for nationalities.

Before 1917, Lenin's attitude, which was so largely to determine the future of the minorities in Russia, was changing and ambiguous. Like Marx, he saw nationalism as a medieval survival and was violently hostile to the '*bourgeois* and reactionary' notion of national culture. Thus he resolutely opposed any form of federalism or of administrative decentralization, for the simple reason that capitalism (and Socialism *a fortiori*) required for its development that states should be as large and as centralized as possible.[2] On the other hand, appreciating the nationalist movements according to their tactical value, he acknowledged that non-Russian nations had an *absolute* right to dispose of themselves, but he limited the right to that of separation, not to any special form of autonomy.[3]

As the Bundist Kossovsky wrote in 1913[4]—the formula that a nation has the right to dispose of itself throws no light on the question of how to regulate relations within a given state between nations who cannot or will not secede from that state.

With the advent of the Soviet power the national problem was bound to enter upon a new phase. Certain peoples of Russia—Poles, Balts, and Finns—took advantage of the disintegration of the Tsarist power to create new national states; others—Georgians, Armenians, and Azerbaidjanis—tried to imitate them; others again —Bashkirs, Kazakhs, and Mohammedans of Central Asia—gave themselves national *bourgeois* governments in order to obtain, if not full independence, at least some form of autonomy within a frame of federation. The whole Empire was falling apart. That is why Stalin, devoting himself to the national problem after 1918, settled

[2] V. I. Lenin, *Critical Notes on National Questions* (Paris, 1952).
[3] *ibid.*, p. 87.   [4] In *Nasha Rabochaia Gazeta*, No. 3.

the fate of the peripheral peoples not according to any doctrine, but by purely economic and military imperatives—by reconquering them.

From 1917 onwards, the Bolshevik leaders, and Stalin above all, decided to subordinate the interests of the national minorities to that of the Russian centre and, therefore, subordinated the colonial revolution to the revolution in Europe. They never quite ceased to be interested in the colonial revolution, but they saw it only from a tactical point of view as a means of weakening the capitalist world. Perhaps this was because, prior to 1917, no Russian or any other Communist theorist had really attempted to define the conditions proper to the development of Socialism in a colonial setting; the Germanic prototype was assumed to be universal. The self-interest and opportunist indifference of the Russian Bolshevist chiefs was matched by the ideological poverty of Marxists elsewhere. But for very rare exceptions, Asiatic theorists of the colonial revolution were lacking. There are many reasons for this: first that the indigenous revolutionaries seemed unable to get beyond the phase of *bourgeois* revolution and of the *national liberation* of their countries; moreover, the idea of *social revolution*, born in the West, remained the exclusive prerogative of Western Marxists, who were interested in the Orient only so far as it offered something in their own line—that is, social revolt on the 'Germanic' model in the setting of industrialized society.

One name, however, stands out in the void of Oriental thinking upon the subject—that of Mir Sayid Sultan Ali Ogly (Sultan Galiev to the Russians), a Mohammedan Tatar of Kazan. He was an authentic Marxist, and the author of a doctrine of colonial revolution which, in its time, might have extended Socialism to the whole of Asiatic society, although it would have struck a mortal blow at the Russian supremacy. In Soviet Russia his name has become synonymous with 'traitor' and 'imperialist agent' since Galiev's condemnation in 1923 and his execution in 1937; and his theories have fallen into complete oblivion. His teaching can be reduced to a few clear maxims, forged in the course of his long struggle against his Mohammedan compatriots, against revolutionary Socialists, or simply modernists, as well as against the Russian Bolsheviks, especially Stalin. His theories, confused, contradictory, and incomplete, are often hard to grasp; nevertheless they represent the only attempt to define the revolutionary process in the colonial world.

The whole of Sultan Galiev's doctrine is derived from the purely Marxist idea of the revenge of 'the oppressed' against their 'oppressors'. The colonized peoples have a better right than the proletariat of the West to the title of 'the oppressed', for they are doubly so—oppressed by their own feudal rulers and *bourgeoisie*, but also by their foreign colonizers. From this postulate Sultan Galiev drew two direct conclusions:

(1) The colonized peoples are all proletarians, even if their industrial proletariat is numerically small.

(2) Their movements for national liberation are Socialist in character and therefore progressive.

This was expressed by a disciple of Sultan Galiev, Hanafi Muzaffar, when he wrote: 'The Mohammedan (colonial) peoples are proletarian peoples, for they are the only people genuinely oppressed. They are more authentically proletarian than are the English or the French proletariat. One may therefore affirm that the national movements in the Mohammedan lands have the character of a true social revolution.'[5]

Moreover, all social classes among these peoples, having been victims of the foreign oppression, may be regarded as altogether proletarian. The term 'proletariat' thus includes all the national forces. From this last idea it follows that the class struggle in the colonial world is of only secondary importance and should be limited to the suppression of a few 'irredeemable' elements. Thus, and in other ways, Sultan Galiev subordinated the class-struggle to the imperatives of national emancipation.

But what is most original in Sultan Galiev is that, starting from the Marxian theory created in reaction to Western industrialism, he modified and adapted it to the needs of an Asiatic, and essentially agrarian, society. Well aware that Communism was endangered by its dependence upon the Germanic model alone, Sultan Galiev also denied that the interpretation of dialectical materialism could be a Russian monopoly; for he knew that as soon as Russia was industrialized, the German prototype would become the Russian one and give birth to a Greater-Russian chauvinism superposed upon Communism.

To the 'Occidental' and Russian conception of the Revolution Galiev opposed the necessity of building upon the foundations of the Asiatic or Mohammedan cultures; of working with their own 'progressive' traditions. Like Mao Tse-tung at a later date, he demanded the progressive adaptation of traditional structures to the new régime, instead of their brutal suppression.

Finally, the keystone of his system was to be a *union of colonized peoples* against the *industrial metropolitans*, for Galiev held that the Western proletariat, which inherited the *bourgeois* colonial tradition, would be as great a menace as the *bourgeoisie* had been to the colon-

[5] In *Znamya Revoliutsii*, No. 44, March 8, 1918.

ized peoples. With this aim, Sultan Galiev drew up a scheme for a *colonial International*, independent of the Comintern. He justified his distrust of the Western proletariat by citing instances of the 'colonialist' attitudes of the French and English working classes.

'To replace the dictatorship of one class of European society, the *bourgeoisie*, by that of its adversary the proletariat,' he wrote in 1922, 'will do nothing to change the situation of the oppressed part of humanity. In fact, if that change took place, it would simply mean, for the colonized peoples, the accession to power of another master.'[6]

Just as he distrusted the Western proletariat, Sultan Galiev had no confidence in the Communists of Russia; and the savage repression of the Tatar nationalist movements showed that his apprehensions were entirely justified. He accused the Russian Bolsheviks of betraying the Socialist Revolution and setting up a bureaucratic régime of *state capitalism*, which had no ideologically valid authority over the Mohammedan fringe. That was why Galiev said that the application of the class struggle to a colonial situation was limited, and recommended a union of all the national forces under the aegis of an indigenous Communist party.

'The colonial international ought to be based upon the alliance of workers and peasants with the petty *bourgeoisie*, and even upon their—purely tactical—alliance with the progressive elements in the upper bourgeoisie.'[7]

'Alliance between all the classes of a colonial people is necessary in face of the struggle for independence.' [8]

Galiev's attitude of mistrust was wholly justified by the actions of the Communist authorities during the Revolution, for the pretext of the struggle between classes in the Mohammedan fringe was abused by the Russians in order to usurp all the positions in the party and the administration. As the President Kolesov had said, at the Third Regional Congress of Soviets of Turkestan:

'One cannot let the Mohammedans into the highest organs of revolutionary authority on account of the uncertain attitude of the local population towards the power of the Soviets, and because the native population lacks a proletarian organization. We cannot therefore let them take part in the government.'[9]

Five years later a Kazakh Communist, G. Todjanov, wrote that:

---

[6] Quoted by Arsharuni and Gabidullin in *Ocherki Panislamisma i Pantiürkisma v Rossii* (Moscow, 1931), pp. 78–9.

[7] Arsharuni, 'Ideologiya Sultan Galievshchiny', in *Antireligioznik*, No. 5 of 1930, p. 26.

[8] *ibid.*, p. 28.   [9] *Nasha Gazeta* (Tashkent), November 28, 1917.

'the Kazakh steppe has become a nest of colonialists, of criminals and toughs. The Kazakh Communists lose all their illusions and desert the party. If the present conditions persist, the greater part of the Kazakh revolutionary youth will abandon us and say, "Let the Russian colonialists decide our fate".'[10]

For Sultan Galiev and his disciples the class struggle in the colonized countries led inevitably to the filling of the local positions, taken over from the *bourgeoisie*, by Russian Communists. That is why these local, orthodox Communists soon began to stand up for the classical principles of *bourgeois* reformism.

Smagul Sadvokasov, one of the leaders of the Kazakh Communist Party, declared on April 20, 1926: 'I am terrified by the talk about a social revolution in Kazakhstan. Socialism amongst us would be demagogy pure and simple.' And he launched as his own slogan: 'Social peace on Kazakh principles instead of the class-struggle.'[11]

After the N.E.P., which in Galiev's eyes was nothing but the revenge of the Russian colonialists against the Mohammedan fringe, he applied his concept of *metropolitan tyranny* to Soviet Russia, thereby endorsing Enver Pasha's views. Enver Pasha, the man of action, had at first believed, like Galiev the theoretician, in the possibility of a colonial revolution under Russian auspices: at Baku in September, 1920, he said:

'We are happy to feel that we have beside us a faithful and sure ally in the Third International. We are united against the hypocritical European politicians, against imperialism and against colonialism.'

Two years later, having been sent by the Soviets to Tashkent to mediate between the Red Army and the Basmachis, whom it was his mission to organize and lead to the conquest of India, Enver Pasha expressed his profound disillusionment: 'I now understand that, to realize my ideal, the liberation of the peoples labouring under the yoke of imperialism, we must first do away with the Russian domination.'[12]

But unlike Enver Pasha, who broke with the party, Sultan Galiev strove thenceforward to prevent the Russians from monopolizing the Revolution to their sole profit, and with this object he continually insisted upon the absolute priority of the Revolution in the East. Writing in 1919 he said that 'Communism has made a grave strategic mistake in devoting prior attention to the revolutionary movement

---

[10] *Enbekshi Kazakh*, No. 15, March, 1922.
[11] Lekerov, *Iz Istorii Partiinovo Stroitel'stva v Kazakhstane* (Alma-Ata, 1936), pp. 177–9.
[12] M.N., 'Pod Znamenem Islama', in *Novyi Vostok*, No. 4 of 1922, p. 95.

in western Europe, forgetting that the weak point of the capitalist
world is in the Orient, not the Occident. The failure of the Communist Revolution abroad is to be ascribed to the insufficient efforts
made by the Soviets upon their Oriental fringe.'[13] He therefore
drew up a plan of action for the Communist Revolution in the East,
for, as he said, 'to liberate the Orient from the grip of imperialism—
that is to deal the world-*bourgeoisie* a mortal blow.'[14]

In itself, the idea of national emancipation for the colonial peoples
was certainly not contradictory to the declarations of such Russian
Bolsheviks as Stalin or Zinoviev. But unlike them, Sultan Galiev
really meant to realize this idea everywhere, and especially in the
Soviets' domain: he looked to the Mohammedans of that domain
to mediate Communism to Asia, the more so because Islam was an
excellent preparation for Communism. As his disciple Hanafi
Muzaffar wrote elsewhere: 'Everything predisposes us to join in
with Communism, for, from the Islamic point of view, there should
be no narrow nationalism. Islam is international and recognizes only
the *Islamiyyat*, the brotherhood and unity of all peoples under the
banner of Islam.'[15]

Sultan Galiev arranged his plan in five stages: the creation of a
Mohammedan Communist state on the Middle Volga: the inclusion
in this state, first, of all the Turkish people and then of the Mohammedan peoples of Russia; the propagation of Communism in the
East by these Mohammedans; the setting-up of an Asiatic and
colonial Comintern; and finally *the establishment of a political
hegemony of the colonized and semi-colonized countries over the
industrialized metropolises*. And Sultan Galiev refused to be merely
a doctrinaire; he wanted his theories put into practice.

In April, 1917, when he was working on the left wing of the Mo-
hammedan movement in Russia (affiliated with the Revolutionary
Socialists), he became a member of the Mohammedan Socialist
Committee, Menshevik in tendency, founded by his compatriot
Mullah Nur Vahitov *to propagate Socialism throughout the Mohammedan world*. In the autumn of 1917 Galiev broke with the Mensheviks, adhered to the Bolshevik faction, and became the People's
Commissar for Education and Nationalities in the government of
Kazan. It was then that his political career began. On January 10,
1918, at the Third All-Russian Congress of Soviets, Sultan Galiev
initiated the creation of the Tatar-Bashkir Republic of Idel (Volga)-

---

[13] 'The Socialist Revolution in the Orient', in *Zhizn Natsional'nostei*, October 10
and 12 and November 2, 1919.

[14] *ibid.*, November 2, 1919.

[15] In *National and Religious Problems*. This booklet was never published, but
is quoted by Arsharuni and Gabidullin, *op. cit.*, p. 5.

Ural.[16] This was the first stage towards the creation of a Mohammedan state in Russia, and the choice of the Volga-Ural territory was a happy one, since it comprised the true cultural centres of Islam in Russia, Kazan and Ufa.

On February 5, 1918, Sultan Galiev entered the collegium of the People's Commissariat for Nationalities, presided over by Stalin, of whom he was henceforth a colleague. Two months later he—with Mullah Nur Vahitov, whom he met again at this Commissariat —laid the first foundations for a purely Mohammedan organization of Communists. Its offices (called *Musburo*) were instituted in all the Mohammedan towns of European Russia; and provincial committees (*Gubmuskom*) at Ufa, Orenburg, Kazan, and Astrakhan. These offices and committees were to propagate Communism in the Islamic lands in Russia and elsewhere. All the delegates emphasized the part that the future Mohammedan state was to play throughout Asia and the colonial world.[17] 'We consider that the Idel-Ural Republic will be the revolutionary nucleus whence the sparks of revolt will fly all over the Orient.'[18]

Sultan Galiev's dream of a pan-Islamic or even a pan-Asiatic Communism seemed ripe for realization, needing no more than the autonomous political organization that he was seeking to create. In June, 1918, Mullah Nur Vahitov convened, at Moscow, a congress of the regional sections of the Commissariat for Mohammedan Affairs which at once set up an all-Russian party of Mohammedan Bolshevik Communists, with a central committee which included Galiev. He, at the same time, presided over an all-Russian Congress of Mohammedan teachers who, meeting at Moscow, decided for their part to found a Mohammedan Communist university.

Difficulties began to arise almost immediately. On August 7, 1918, Kazan was captured by the Czech White Army, and Mullah Nur Vahitov was executed eleven days after. Sultan Galiev, who had now gone back into Russian Mohammedan territory, realized that sovietization was leading to Russification and the destruction of the local cultures. He now sought an understanding with the Mohammedan nationalist leaders such as Zaki Validi, the head of the government of Bashkiria.

In November, 1918, Kazan having been retaken, the Mohammedan Communists of Russia met again at Moscow at a congress

[16] This decision was ratified (January 23, 1918) by special decree of the *Sovnarkom*; at the end of January by the Congress of Mohammedans of European Russia at Ufa; and in February by the Congress Extra-ordinary of Mohammedans of Idel-Ural at Kazan.

[17] The conference decided to include in the future state some non-Mohammedan 'colonials'—Mariis and Chuvash.

[18] *Pravda*, May 5–18 and May 11–24, 1918.

in which Stalin and Sultan Galiev confronted one another for the first time. Stalin demanded the fusion of the Mohammedan Communist Party with the Russian Communist Party; but the Mohammedan leader opposed this with the project for an official Mohammedan Communist Party participating in the Russian Communist Party on a federal basis. The support of the Turkestani, Caucasian, and (in part) of the Volga and Crimean delegates did not suffice to save this project; it was reduced to the creation of a separate *Mohammedan section* of the Communist Party. The Mohammedan Communist Central Committee was changed into a *Central Bureau of Mohammedan Organizations* attached to the Central Committee of the Communist Party, which was put under the chairmanship of Stalin, whilst Sultan Galiev was only a plain member. Stalin, it is true, sought to soften this rebuff to his colleague and adversary by a declaration that the Mohammedan Communists are able to build the bridge between the East and the West.[19]

Thus the Central Committee of the Communist Party established its power over all the Mohammedan organizations, and subjected the *Musburo* and the *Gubmuskom* to the control of local organs. Mohammedan Communism no longer had an existence of its own. The end of the civil war in Uralsk struck a further blow at the designs of Sultan Galiev: for in February, 1919, the Soviet government signed an agreement with the nationalist government of Zaki Validi in Bashkiria and, by proclaiming the creation of an A.S.S.R. of Bashkiria, killed the project of an Idel-Ural state.

In March of the same year the *Central Office of Mohammedan Organizations* was supplanted by a *Central Office of the Communist Organizations of the People of Russia and the Orient*—which consisted of Bashkir, Tatar, Turkmenian, Azerbaidjan, and other sections: Mohammedan unity itself was prejudiced. Shortly afterwards the Commissariat for Mohammedan Affairs was replaced by a Tatar-Bashkir Commissariat with still more limited powers. Thus, from the beginning of 1919 the Soviet government went on successfully liquidating all the attempts to build up an autonomous Mohammedan organization, and imposing its own strict control over Mohammedans. Sultan Galiev's efforts were now restricted to ideological problems; and it was then that he published his three famous articles[20] on the Revolution in the East, in which he cast doubt upon the role of the proletariat in the colonial Revolution.

At the Second pan-Russian Congress of Communist Organizations of the Peoples of the Orient, convened at Moscow, Stalin

---

[19] *Zhizn Natsional'nostei*, November 24, 1918.
[20] See *Zhizn Natsional'nostei*, October 5 and 12 and November 2, 1919.

succeeded in imposing further limitations upon Oriental Communists. Sultan Galiev met with an obstinate refusal from the Congress when he pleaded for a Communist Party of the Orient in the heart of the Comintern; and again for a Republic of Idel-Ural.

However, despite these shocks from Stalin, Sultan Galiev was still, in 1920, the leading Mohammedan in the Communist hierarchy: he was editor-in-chief of the *Zhizn Natsional'nostei*, the organ of the People's Commissariat of Nationalities, and one of the three members of the small collegium of that body. In May, Galiev once more addressed himself to the Central Committee of the Communist Party to ask for the creation of the Idel-Ural Republic; and, faced with Stalin's definitive refusal, he entered into opposition. Soon afterwards the leading Mohammedans, whether Communists or 'fellow travellers'—Sultan Galiev, Zaki Validi, Toursoun Khodjaev, Baïtoursounov, and others—met again at Moscow and founded a secret organization, Ittihad ve Taraki, which had three objectives—key posts in the Soviet system for Turkish elements; a hold over the teaching institutions and—if we are to believe their enemies—clandestine collaboration with anti-soviet nationalist organizations, notably the Basmachis.[21]

But while Sultan Galiev redoubled his efforts to extend Communism to Asia, the acts of the Soviet government checked him in every direction. In May, 1920, a decree of the *Sovnarkom* set up an A.S.S.R. of Tataristan, shattering once for all the dream of a Volga–Ural Republic, and at the same time Moscow opposed the Bashkir revolt, and drowned in blood the rising of Gandja in Azerbaidjan. In September the Congress of the Peoples of the East, convened at Baku, dispelled Galiev's last hopes. It is true that this Congress launched a declaration of *jihad* (or Holy War) for a general revolt in the colonies, but the value of that appeal was neutralized by the blundering (whether intentional or not) of Zinoviev, who raised the question of the class struggle in the colonial lands and attacked the Kemalist régime, thereby antagonizing non-Communists such as Enver Pasha.

This summer marked the beginning of the suppression of indigenous nationalism. An anti-Islamic and anti-Turkish attitude became official at the Tenth Congress of the Russian Communist Party in the following spring. To Sultan Galiev, who, supported by Safarov, demanded *national cultural autonomy* for the Turks in Russia, Stalin replied that this was *a counter-revolutionary invention meant to exacerbate hatred between peoples.*[22] After this Congress the gulf

[21] *Pravda Vostoka*, December 18, 1934: article on trial of Toursoun Khodjaev.
[22] *Revoliutsiya i Natsional'nosti,* No. 11 of 1933.

between Russians and Orientals widened. Enver Pasha turned towards the Basmachis in November, 1921, and was killed a few months after. Sultan Galiev, conscious of the dangers inherent in a Greater-Russian chauvinism, raised his demand for political ascendency of the colonies over the industrial metropolises, and proposed the creation of a colonial Comintern to counterbalance Western preponderance in the counsels of Communism. He also urged that Communism should be spread abroad, and said that the Soviet republic of the Crimea *ought to become the window of Communism opening towards the East, and first of all towards Turkey*.[23] These views of his were to be decisively condemned at the time of the execution of Vali Ibrahimov, president of the *Sovnarkom* of the Crimea, in 1927.

In December, 1921, Sultan Galiev, writing in *Zhizn Natsional'nostei*, denounced the brutal policy of the Russians in Islamic country.[24] Instead of the tactics of 'cavalry raids', he called for humane and elastic methods which would foster the 'progressive' elements of Islam; and he demonstrated the soundness of his arguments in Tataristan, where his friends in the Commissariat set up a commission of *Shari'yat*.

These partial successes did not prevent the rapid fall of Sultan Galiev. In April, 1923, the Twelfth Congress of the Communist Party met at Moscow; and there Stalin and the Georgian nationalists came to a head-on collision: the final resolution condemned indigenous nationalism in the same breath with Russian chauvinism. One month later Sultan Galiev was arrested, and at the Fourth Conference of the Central Committee of the Communist Party he was condemned without appeal. The resolution of this conference on 'the case of Sultan Galiev', following upon the report by Kirov[25] merits a place in the annals of the purest police literature. It accuses Galiev of setting up a 'counter-revolutionary' organization in the bosom of the Communist Party of complicity with nationalist organizations, especially the Basmachis, and above all of extending similar organizations abroad in order to 'prevent the liberation of the colonies from the imperialist yoke'!

Thenceforth the history of Sultan Galiev is obscure. June, 1923, saw the beginning of the 'purge' of Mohammedan nationalists which continued right up to the bloody and ludicrous assizes of 1937–38. Galiev himself seems to have been released about 1927, rearrested the following year, tried in 1929, and transferred at

[23] About a third of the members of the Turkish Communist Party were Tatars of the Crimea working in Turkey.

[24] Issue of December 14, 1921.

[25] *Revoliutsiya i Natsional'nosti*, No. 11, 1923, p. 108.

some unknown date to Moscow. There he was finally executed as an
'enemy of the people' in 1937.

* * * * *

Thus, since 1923, the Soviet government had put an end to every
attempt to mediate between Communism and Islam, and thereby
suppressed the desire to export Communism to the Oriental countries.
Why did Moscow so flatly refuse to follow Sultan Galiev's initiative
in adapting the ideology of Communism to local conditions in the
colonized lands? There were various reasons—

—*ideological*, in the first place: for the first Bolsheviks were
trained in the West and took no interest in revolutionary movements that were not supported by an industrial proletariat.

—*economic* also: for it was necessary to reconquer the peripheral
lands by the force of the Red Army, exclusively Russian, and that
brutal intrusion threw all the national Communist elements into
opposition. In the eyes of the Mohammedans, the Revolution was by
its origins a Russian phenomenon, implying the *presence* of Russians.

—but there was a *political* reason above all. If Moscow had done
as Galiev proposed and mobilized the Islamic countries of Russia
as a slip-way for launching Communism into Asia, the Russians
would thereby have made their Tatars allies, and the real arbiters
of the destiny of the Comintern. One can see, therefore, why the
nationalists of the fringe adopted Communism, in expectation that
their role in Asia would give them a political importance equal to
that of the European Russians; but one can see also why the
Russians were implacably hostile to ideals which, in practice, would
have set up strains in the Comintern, after 1923, of a 'Titoist' type;
thus depriving Russia of the 'leadership' of Communism which she
continued to enjoy until the death of Stalin.

—lastly, *Stalin's intransigence*—which was also that of most of
the Bolshevik leaders except Lenin—was rooted deeply in his
bureaucratic mentality, which could not contemplate the existence,
in the outlying Mohammedan lands, of national administrations
that would be autonomous, or even imperfectly synchronized with
the Russian bureaucratic machinery.

Lenin alone had a sound judgment about the danger of a Stalinist
policy for world Communism. As he wrote in his unpublished
notes:[26]

'The evils that may follow, for our state, from the lack of unity
between the nationalist organizations and that of Russia will be

[26] Written at the end of 1922. Published in the summer of 1956 (*Pravda*,
July 7, 1956).

incomparably, infinitely less than those which it will entail not only upon us, but upon the International as a whole, upon the hundreds of millions of Asians who, following in our footsteps, will very soon appear upon the stage of history. It would be an inexcusable opportunism if we, on the eve of the re-birth of the Orient, at the dawn of its great awakening, were to ruin our prestige in their eyes by the least brutality, the slightest violence towards non-Russians.'

After 1923 Stalin had a clear choice to make, and he chose 'Socialism in one country', which meant Socialism in the Russian style, excluding any form of autonomy for the eastern peoples. Thereby, as Lenin had warned him, he was shutting the colonial revolution out of his vision; for it was scarcely possible to extend Communism into Asia while he was persecuting his own eastern minorities. And, right up to 1938, he went on deliberately hounding down every deviation that could be labelled 'nationalist' in his Islamic territories.

The indigenous Communists were obliged, after their set-back, to abandon any hope of a colonial Comintern, or of founding a Turanian state under the wing of the U.S.S.R. Henceforth they inclined towards *bourgeois* nationalism and away from orthodox Communism, taking up a purely nationalistic attitude towards the Moscow government. They opposed primarily a cultural and linguistic resistance to Russification, but also a political resistance. Following Galiev's example, the indigenous Communists rejected the class war, so much cried up by the Russians, as a mere pretext upon which the latter inserted their own countrymen into the key posts of other countries. The leaders of the Kazakh Communist Party, for instance, opposed the campaign against the *baïs* (feudal chiefs) and the *semi-baïs* (kulaks) between 1924 and 1927, because it was used to open the doors of the local Soviets and their Communist Party to Russians.[27] Colonization by Russians was also resisted in Tadjikistan, where Nasrattulah Maksum, President of the republican Supreme Soviet, demanded the expulsion of all the Russians (he was 'liquidated' in 1933); and at Kazakhstan, where Sultanbekov, Dulatov, and Sadvokasov—all members of the party —demanded 'all Kazakhstan land for the Kazakhs'. In the end, all the indigenous Communist leaders were united in support of two essential demands; greater autonomy for the republican Soviets in relation to Moscow, and priority in local administrative posts. To these demands Stalin's invariable response was that of formal refusal, followed by physical removal of the claimants in an uninterrupted succession of purges, of which the bloodiest, in the years

[27] Kuchkin, 'Liquidation of the baïs, semi-feudal Kazakhs', in *Istoricheskie Zapiski*, No. 35, 1950.

1937–38, cost the lives of nearly all the indigenous Communist leaders. Well known, of course, are certain cases like those of Ikramov and Khodjaev, protagonists in the trials of Right-wing and Trotskyist groups executed at Moscow in 1938; but what is usually forgotten is that in the same period Tataristan lost all its people's commissars and nearly all its presidents of local executive committees, and secretaries of district and urban committees. The majority of these 'bad Communists' were executed.

After the brief respite of the war years, when the Soviet government left the outlying regions more to their own political and cultural devices (which, incidentally, led to a number of deviations), the campaign against bourgeois nationalism was renewed in 1947. Politically reduced as they were, these groups had no longer much to defend but their national cultures; and after 1948 the authorities launched another campaign against their languages (enforcing the 1938 Cyrillization of alphabets and 'purging' of vocabularies). Now their history had to be reinterpreted in a sense favourable to Russia and their literary heritage expurgated; all works of a 'feudal' or 'clerical' tendency were thus condemned and ordered to be replaced by translations or imitations in the local languages of works by Russians. The drive against the national epics began in Azerbaidjan in 1951, and was extended, in the teeth of local resistance, to all of the Islamic republics.

By the time of Stalin's death the society of the Mohammedan regions was very different from what it had been in the days of Sultan Galiev. The local life is now modernized and practically de-Islamized. The instruments of power—i.e. the parties and the administration—are now dominated by Russians. Yet in spite of this transformation, a new intelligentsia—of Soviet and Communist training—self-confident and contemptuous of the past, is turning the thesis of Sultan Galiev to its own account. What the Russian Press periodically denounces as the 'pan-Islamic' or 'pan-Turkish' deviationism of certain intellectuals is in reality their dream of carrying their own experience abroad; the will to propagate Communism beyond the frontiers of the U.S.S.R.—but a Communism Orientalized and directed by Orientals. And this, it seems, is what the U.S.S.R. still cannot allow. That is why, even in 1956, Soviet propaganda to the Middle East was carried on by Russians, excepting only a few religious bodies (a pilgrimage of Soviet Mohammedans to Mecca, for instance) and hardly ever by Mohammedan Communists.

For all its demagogic declarations of support for colonial movements the U.S.S.R. cannot be said to take a genuine interest in the Orient. The position it took up towards Galiev in 1918 remained the same until 1956, and the fear of a colonial revolution getting beyond its control still determines the attitude of the Russian leaders.

*   *   *   *   *

Notwithstanding Russia's assumption of the monopoly of Communism, the colonial revolution has been made in Asia—by the Chinese. Henceforth the U.S.S.R. is no longer the centre of attraction to the Asiatic peoples avid of independence: Peking becomes more and more the geographical focus of colonial Communism. The first phase of the dream of Sultan Galiev has come true.

The death of Stalin, however, marks a new stage in the relations of Russia with the Orient. The 'return to Leninism' is not an empty phrase. In the attitude of the new directors of Soviet policy there is a possibility of their furthering the world revolution, and this for several reasons—reluctance to yield the leadership of Communism to China; desire to break out of the encirclement by capitalism which, in the East, takes the form of the Ankara–Karachi Pact; and the consciousness of a set-back to Communism in Europe.

The return to Leninism shows itself in the abandonment of the Manichaean vision of the world that was symbolized by Zhdanov; in the recognition of different paths to Socialism (which was implicit in Galiev's enlargement of the Germanic industrial pattern of revolution to embrace the colonial agrarian sphere); in a realistic resort to the politics of the 'National Front' under *bourgeois* leadership, which, in the early stages, excludes the class struggle (another resurrection of doctrines buried in 1923!); and, finally, in the tactical alliance between Communism and Islam which was also urged by Sultan Galiev. This new Russian policy has had a warm welcome in Asia, as we have seen at the Bandung Conference. But this policy implies, as an imperative condition, a liberal policy towards Mohammedans within the Soviet frontiers.

Russia's policy towards the Orient and the problem of her national minorities thus present themselves to the Soviet leaders as closely connected. One cannot study the evolution of their Oriental policy without reference to that of their internal policy; and here indications are not wanting which confirm the course of development we have been trying to trace. The appearance of Lenin's unpublished writings was accompanied by the disappearance from the scene of Mohammedan Communists who had been over-zealous partisans of Stalin's Russianizing policy: such was the case with Bagirov, first secretary of the Central Committee of the Azerbaidjan Communist Party, executed in the spring of 1956, who was a passionate and inexorable enemy of Islam and Mohammedan separatism. Yet more significant is the withdrawal of chauvinistic versions of the history of Russian and Islamic relations.[28]

One fact which illustrates the new tendencies and throws light upon the wider aspect of Russian Oriental policy, is the rehabilitation of Caucasian *Muridism* and of its leader the Imām Shamil[29]: the interpretation of this movement which had been current from 1950 to 1956 has been condemned as 'unscientific and a falsification of history'.[30] By suddenly admitting that the revolt of these mountain folk was 'a movement of national liberation in essence progressive, against a foreign imperialism', the leaders of the U.S.S.R. seem to confer a *de facto* recognition upon all national revolts against any sort of imperialism. Furthermore, in choosing to rehabilitate the Imām Shamil's rather than another movement of the Mohammedan fringe, they apparently want to conciliate the Mohammedan *bourgeoisie* and clergy, since Muridism was a purely religious movement, under a religious leader; and, yet again, his struggle against the Tsarism is characterized as a *jihad* by the Soviet historians themselves.[31] Finally, in condemning the Tsarist imperialism, do not the Soviet authorities seek to dispel the doubt whether they themselves are not the heirs of an imperial colonialism—a doubt highly prejudicial to their relations with the Oriental peoples?

The expansion of Communism in Asia is moving on the lines that Sultan Galiev foresaw, by way of nationalism and anti-imperialism. But is it not this same nationalism which the popular democracies in revolt are brandishing against the U.S.S.R.? Is it not in the name of that same nationalism that the Soviet Mohammedans have again

[28] On the problems of the interpretation of history, see *L'Afrique et l'Asie*, Nos. 2, 3, and 4 of 1952, and No. 1 of 1953.

[29] The Imām Shamil headed a resistance movement of the mountain tribes of Dagestan and Chechnia (Eastern and Central Caucasus) which opposed—often successfully—the Russian conquests between 1829 and 1859, when they surrendered. . . . From 1920 to 1950 Shamil was esteemed by Soviet historic science as a hero of national liberation, and the resistance of his followers to the Russian conquerors was a 'patriotic and progressive movement'. But in 1950 the hardening of doctrine under Zhdanov led to a denial that there was anything 'progressive' in non-Socialist national movements; and to the condemnation of all anti-Russian revolts under religious, feudal, or *bourgeois* leadership. Thus the Muridist movement of Shamil was stigmatized as 'reactionary, imperialist, and feudal', and Shamil himself as no better than a brigand in the pay of foreigners.

[30] G. A. Daniyalov, 'The Movement of the Mountain Folk led by Shamil', *Voprosy Istorii*, No. 7 of 1956, pp. 67–72.

[31] One must not forget that the *jihad* is one of the duties of a Mohammedan as obligatory as prayer, fasting, etc. This is relevant, it seems, to present developments in the Middle East, where nationalism has become included in the duties of a Mohammedan and the anti-imperialist struggle becomes, in consequence, a 'Holy War'.

been demanding, for months past, their cultural—nay, even their political—autonomy? A decree of the Supreme Soviet of Azerbaidjan has proclaimed (August 21, 1956) that the Azerian language is the *only* official language of the republic, to the exclusion of Russian.[32]

Thus we come back, in 1956, to the dilemma of 1920—whether to export Communism to the Orient, at the risk of a backlash that might jeopardize the privileged position of the Russian people as leaders of the world Revolution; or whether to sacrifice the cause of the Revolution to their interests.

Only—and this makes the choice before the Russians look more limited now than then—the revolutionary possibilities before the Oriental people are much greater, and they intend to realize them, with or without Soviet help.

[This article was already in the press when the signs of a hardening of doctrine on the part of the Soviet authorities confirmed the fear of a return to Stalinist intransigence in national policy. The review *Voprosy Istorii* has again denigrated Imām Shamil as 'a spy in the pay of Anglo-Turkish imperialism', a 'bloody tyrant', and 'a feudal reactionary'.]

[32] See *L'Afrique et l'Asie*, No. 1 of 1957, 'De-Stalinisation in Sovietic Islam', by H. Carrère d'Encausse.

THE SHAMIL PROBLEM

by PAUL B. HENZE

HISTORICAL BACKGROUND

SHAMIL, BORN in 1797 and most active in the years 1834–59, was the last and the most successful of the great Moslem resistance leaders who fought to stem the Russian advance into the Caucasus. Based in his native Dagestan, his movement spread to include more than a dozen mountain peoples, most of whom were to some degree inspired by a form of militant, fundamentalist Islam called Muridism. While Shamil and his followers would probably have welcomed Turkish or Western assistance, they received no substantial aid from abroad. Hopes which rose high during the Crimean War were shattered as 'the Allies neglected an opportunity which will never recur of placing a belt of independent tribes in a position of vast natural strength rearwards of the Russian movement in Asia'.[1] Shamil was captured by Russian forces in 1859. Several hundred thousand Caucasian mountaineers fled to various parts of the Middle East in the years that followed. Large-scale Caucasian resistance thus ended, but Shamil has remained a legendary hero among the native Moslem peoples of the Caucasus to the present day. The fact that he lived comfortably for twelve years after his capture under protective surveillance in Russia and eventually died on a pilgrimage to Mecca in 1871 is an interesting measure of the difference between the Tsarist and Soviet régimes in treatment of resistance leaders.

Few pre-Revolutionary Russian historians were entirely negative in their evaluation of Shamil. The bravery and colourfulness of the Caucasian mountaineers have always appealed to Russians. There

[1] F. H. Skrine, *The Expansion of Russia, 1815–1900* (Cambridge, 1904), p. 134.

is much similarity between the treatment of native Caucasian resistance by nineteenth-century Russian authors and the attitude displayed towards the American Indians by writers in the United States.[2]

SHAMIL AS A SOVIET HERO

During the early Soviet period Shamil was lauded as a great fighter against Tsarist colonial expansion and a progressive precursor of Communism. M. N. Pokrovsky, most prominent Marxist historian of the 1920's, praised Shamil as an opponent of feudalism and regarded Muridism as a fundamentally democratic ideology.[3] A party handbook on the national question issued in 1930[4] reminded readers that the fact that Shamil had been the leader of a religious movement in no way diminished his progressive significance, for 'even in conditions of developed capitalist society the class struggle often takes forms which conceal its content'. The same handbook described the 'state' established by Shamil as '. . . in its essence democratic . . . but in its structure a dictatorship. A mosaic of splintered tribes and peoples gave way to a centralized state with common legal norms, with a unified power apparatus, a unified military-financial organization, and to a certain degree a regular defence structure.'

The positive line on Shamil continued unchallenged until after World War II. Much scholarly effort of varying quality was devoted to the study of Shamil in the 1930's. In Dagestan, in particular, native scholars concentrated on the Shamil tradition as a means of expressing and strengthening their own national sentiment. Marx and Engels, who had written briefly but sympathetically of the struggle of the Caucasian mountaineers against the Russians, were frequently cited to support a relatively anti-Russian interpretation of modern Caucasian history.[5]

[2] See *The Mountains of Allah* (London, 1953), by the Georgian *émigré* novelist Paul Chavchavadze, for an interesting contemporary treatment of the Shamil theme in a manner which is both typical of the nineteenth-century Russian approach and highly reminiscent of the American 'Wild Western'.

[3] *Diplomatiya i voiny tsarskoi Rossii v XIX stoletii* (Moscow, GIZ, 1928).

[4] El. Drabkina; *Natsional'ny i kolonial'ny vopros v tsarskoi Rossii* (Moscow, Izd. Kommunisticheskoi Akademii, 1930).

[5] Rasul Magomedov, *Bor'ba gortsev za nezavisimost' pod rukovodstvom Shamilya* (Makhach Kala, Daggiz, 1939), is an interesting example of relatively thorough Dagestani scholarship on the Shamil question. This work was violently criticized by another Dagestani in 1947, however, because it 'idealized and modernized' Shamil, 'depicting him at times as practically a Communist'. *Cf. Voprosy Istorii*, No. 11, 1947, p. 138.

THE FIRST ATTACK IN 1947

An Armenian writer, Kh. G. Adzhemyan, launched the first public attack on Shamil in 1947. He could hardly have decided to challenge the hitherto officially supported line on the North Caucasian resistance movement entirely on his own. He may have had the support of party elements. He found no support among historians. The Institute of History of the U.S.S.R. Academy of Sciences arranged a session to debate 'The Historical Essence of Caucasian Muridism'[6] at which Adzhemyan attacked the movement as 'an ultra-reactionary current of militant Islam' and characterized the freedom for which Shamil and the mountain peoples fought as 'the freedom of the wolf, the freedom of backwardness, of downtroddenness, of darkness, of Asiaticness'. The more cultured the peoples of the Caucasus were, Adzhemyan maintained, the more strongly they had been drawn towards Russia, as the example of the Georgians and the Armenians proved. He concluded by criticizing Marx and Engels for 'exaggerating the reactionary role of Tsarist Russia' and 'idealizing Shamil under the influence of the contemporary English Press'.

The historians who commented on Adzhemyan's views included a number of distinguished Soviet Orientalists. All attacked him sharply. To judge by the *Voprosy Istorii* report, there was no one willing to support his views publicly. Adzhemyan finally retracted his characterization of the revolt of Shamil as 'a manifestation of savagery' and agreed with his critics that the movement could not be labelled 'Asiatic', but he did not capitulate. Professor N. M. Druzhinin concluded the debate by declaring that Adzhemyan's view had not found the support of the meeting: 'Our former view remains in force.'

ALL-OUT ASSAULT ON THE SHAMIL TRADITION, 1950–55

Try as they would, the defenders of Shamil could not long maintain their position against contrary currents which were rapidly gathering official support. A tendency which developed in the U.S.S.R. during the war—glorification of the Tsarist past—gained further strength in the post-war years. All previous historical theories, no matter how firmly they had been anchored in Marxist dogma, had to be accommodated to the new line. Since Soviet leaders had openly adopted most of the traditional features of imperial Russian policy, historians were assigned the task of justifying Tsarist terri-

---

[6] Reported in *Voprosy Istorii*, No. 11, 1947, pp. 134–40; the exact date of the session is not given.

torial expansion. The 'theory of the lesser evil' was developed for this purpose[7] (though it did not prove entirely adequate) and, one by one, the heroes of the non-Russian peoples were condemned as enemies both of Russia and of progress, since the two had now become synonymous.

In the Caucasian field, the first blow was struck in May, 1950, when a Stalin prize which had been awarded a short time before to an historical work by an Azerbaidjani scholar was suddenly withdrawn.[8] The book reflected what had up until then been the official line on Shamil and Muridism. This view was now condemned because 'such an evaluation of Shamil and Muridism is anti-Marxist, contradicts historical facts and fundamentally distorts the actual sense of this movement, which was reactionary, nationalistic, and in the service of English capitalism and the Turkish sultan'.[9]

No less a figure than Beria's and Stalin's favoured associate, Bagirov, Party Secretary of Azerbaidjan, fired the next salvo in the offensive, an article in the party organ, Bol'shevik.[10] Starting off with a liberal selection of Stalin quotations, Bagirov proceeded to denounce Islam as an intolerant, nationalistic creed utilized by Mohammed—'a representative of the feudal-merchant aristocracy' —to consolidate his power and prepare the Arabs for wars of conquest. The Turks and Persians, in their turn, made similar use of Islam and, in the nineteenth century, were followed by the British: 'In the arsenal of the colonizers, especially the English, who had no compunctions about using any means to attain their aims, Islam occupied a special place. They used Islam and its various currents not only to organize mass fratricidal wars among subject colonial peoples, but also in the struggle against their competitors, in the first place against Russia.'

The ill-fated Bagirov, executed in 1956, could hardly have suspected when he wrote these lines in 1950 that by substituting 'Soviets' for 'English' in the first line, and 'Britain' for 'Russia' in the last, one could have, in 1958, a not entirely inappropriate description of contemporary Soviet tactics in the Middle East. The bulk of Bagirov's long article was devoted to 'documentary proof' of British and Turkish support of the Shamil movement. He concluded with a further vicious attack on his unfortunate compatriot

[7] For a brief discussion of this theory see K. F. Shteppa: 'The "Lesser Evil" Formula', in C. E. Black (ed.), Rewriting Russian History (New York, 1956), pp. 107–20.

[8] Geidar Guseinov, Iz istorii obshchestvennoi i filosofskoi mysli v Azerbaidzhane XIX veka (Baku, 1949).

[9] Pravda, May 14, 1950.

[10] M. D. Bagirov, 'K voprosu o kharakter edvizheni ya Myuridizma i Shamilya', in Bol'shevik, No. 13, July, 1950 (approved for printing on July 14, 1950).

Guseinov and a number of other Azerbaidjanis who had supported publication of his book.

A similar denunciation of historians who had tried to present the Caucasian resistance movement 'as progressive, democratic, and directed toward national-liberation' was published by A. D. Daniyalov, Party Secretary of Dagestan, soon after Bagirov's article appeared.[11]

The anti-Shamil campaign, combined with the effects of the deportation of four entire North Caucasian nationalities at the end of World War II and their subsequent obliteration from the historical record, crippled Soviet scholarship in the Caucasian field during the entire post-war period. Works on North Caucasian history which had been published in the late 1940's had to be put on the proscribed list after 1950. From 1950 onwards few Soviet scholars dared to publish serious works on North Caucasian history, ethnography, literature, or even linguistics. Some scholars retreated into ancient history. Others remained silent. A small minority followed the Bagirov-Daniyalov line and joined the attack on Shamil in full force, participating in the preparation of 'documents' and articles condemning the resistance struggle of the mountaineers as fraudulent and reactionary.

This was the period of the Korean War and of maximum tension between the Soviet bloc and the free world. Stalin was in his final, most megalomanic years. Soviet leaders were obsessed by fears of foreign intrigue and suspicious of disloyalty and subversion at home. The temper of the times is well mirrored in the frantic denunciations of the Shamil cult, of Turkish intervention in the Caucasus, of British threats to Central Asia, and of American plots against Siberia which filled the pages of *Voprosy Istorii* in 1951 and 1952. It was not easy for party-line historians to substantiate their charge that nineteenth-century Caucasian resistance had owed its strength to British and Turkish agents, but they combed diligently through Tsarist military reports and memoirs of the period for all hear-say evidence and concentrated special efforts on reading implications of far-reaching intrigue into such nineteenth-century classics of travel and adventure as Bell's *Circassia*, Spencer's *Travels in Circassia*, and Longworth's *A Year Among the Circassians*.[12] Urquhart,[13] a fanatic champion of the North Caucasian cause who failed to get effective

[11] A. D. Daniyalov, 'Ob izvrashcheniyakh v osveshchenii Myuridizma i dvizheniya Shamilya', in *Voprosy Istorii*, No. 9, 1950, pp. 3–18.

[12] J. S. Bell, *Circassia*, 2 vols. (London, 1840); E. Spencer, *Travels in Circassia*, 2 vols. (London, 1839); J. A. Longworth, *A Year among the Circassians*, 2 vols. (London, 1840).

[13] D. Urquhart, *Progress and Present Position of Russia in the East* (London, 1838).

support from either his own or the Sultan's government, became in the eyes of Soviet writers such as A. V. Fadeev the principal architect of the whole Shamil movement. Complex sociological analyses of the various Caucasian peoples during the eighteenth and nineteenth centuries were also made, the purpose being to demonstrate that the majority of the people had always been pro-Russian while the ruling classes had favoured Persia, Turkey, and Britain. Some writers went still further, and attempted to prove that the masses had not actually been religious at all; only the feudal nobility, it was alleged, had been adherents of the reactionary cult of Islam. All this was not without its moral for modern times; A. V. Fadeev wrote in 1951:

'The history of the Muridist movement in the North-west Caucasus completely confirms the fact that, as the product of wild Muslim fanaticism, Muridism was used as a weapon of aggression and a means of enslavement of peoples and never had anything in common with the interests of the toilers. Exposure of this reactionary role of Muridism has its timely significance in our days, when Anglo-American imperialists and their Turkish understudies are trying to utilize well-worn pan-Islamic and pan-Turkish slogans with the aim of ideological preparation of war against the Soviet Union and the countries of people's democracy.'[14]

The assault upon Shamil continued unabated after Stalin's death. A collection of documents designed to prove that Shamil had been an agent of Britain and Turkey was published in Georgia in 1953.[15] N. A. Smirnov's history of the study of Islam in the U.S.S.R. appeared in 1954, as did S. K. Bushuev's study of Tsarist foreign relations at the time of the Caucasian Wars.[16] Both authors took an entirely negative view of the struggle of the Caucasian mountaineers. Smirnov's book was hostile to Islam in all its aspects and particularly venomous in its condemnation of Soviet writers who had found kindly things to say about Islamic institutions and attitudes. Fadeev's article in *Voprosy Istorii*, No. 6, 1955,[17] was a restatement of his earlier attacks on Shamil and Muridism and rounded out a full five years of attacks on the Caucasian resistance movement in that distinguished journal.

---

[14] A. V. Fadeev, 'Myuridizm kak orudie agressivnoi politiki Turtsii i Anglii na severo-zapadnom kavkaze v XIX stoletii', in *Voprosy Istorii*, No. 9, 1951, pp. 76–96.

[15] Sh. V. Tsagareishvil (ed.), *Shamil—stavlennik sul'tanskoi Turtsii i angliiskikh kolonizatorov* (Tbilisi, 1953).

[16] N. A. Smirnov, *Ocherki istorii izucheniya Islama v S.S.S.R.* (Moscow, 1954); S. K. Bushuev, *Iz istorii vneshnikh politicheskikh otnoshenii v period prisoedineniya Kavkaza s Rossiei* (Moscow, 1954).

[17] A. V. Fadeev, 'O vnutrennei sotsial'noi baze myuridistskovo dvizheniya na Kavkaze v XIX veke', *Voprosy Istorii*, No. 6, 1955, pp. 67–77.

REHABILITATION BEGUN—1956

Revision of the negative line on Shamil began at a conference of the readers of *Voprosy Istorii* in Moscow on January 25, 27, and 28, 1956.[18] This conference laid the groundwork for a broad readjustment of the official line in many fields of Soviet historiography. E. M. Burdjalov, Deputy Chief Editor of *Voprosy Istorii*, informed the conference that several comrades had proposed re-examining the evaluation of Shamil which had been 'established in our literature after the appearance of Bagirov's article', and A. M. Pikman, identified only as a 'middle school instructor' who was apparently making his debut among Soviet historians, delivered a speech in which he 'dwelt . . . on the question of shedding light in our literature on the movement of the mountaineers under the leadership of Shamil. He remarked that a crude falsification of history has been permitted . . . the beginning of which was laid by Bagirov's article. Pikman proposed that the following should serve as a criterion for evaluating the movement of Shamil as well as every other national movement: did or did not the movement aid the liberation struggle of the toilers of Russia and western Europe? For this very reason, because Shamil's movement aided the revolution both in the West and in Russia and weakened Tsarism, the movement should be regarded as progressive. In the works of Smirnov, Fadeev, Daniyalov, and others such a criterion for evaluating Shamil's movement is lacking. Confusing the interests of the Russian state of that time with the interests of the Russian toilers, they have been unfoundedly regarding the movement of the Caucasian mountaineers as reactionary and the "work of agents". In this way a direct distortion of the evaluation which Marx and Engels gave to the movement was permitted and likewise a falsification of the views of Dobrolyubov. A. M. Pikman remarked that the opponents of such an incorrect view of the movement of the Caucasian mountaineers during the course of several years did not have the opportunity of stating their case in the pages of the Press. Only at the end of 1955 was a discussion of this question carried out among the editors of *Voprosy Istorii*.'

The next issue of *Voprosy Istorii* carried an article in which Pikman set forth his views at greater length, citing Marx and Engels repeatedly and calling for recognition of Shamil as a national resistance leader comparable to Kossuth and the nineteenth-century Polish patriots who had fought against Tsarism for the independence of their countries.[19] In the light of what transpired in Hungary and

[18] Reported in *Voprosy Istorii*, No. 2, 1956, pp. 199–213.
[19] A. M. Pikman, 'O bor'be kavkazskikh gortsev s tsarskimi kolonizatorami', *Voprosy Istorii*, No. 3, 1956, pp. 75–84.

Poland a few months later, he could hardly have chosen examples less likely to please the Soviet party leaders.

Published reactions to Pikman's article were slow in coming. A short article by a Dagestani scholar repeating most of Pikman's views appeared towards the end of the summer.[20] The subject was not taken up again until the last issue of *Voprosy Istorii* for 1956 (No. 12) which, probably because of confusion caused by Polish and Hungarian events, failed to appear until February, 1957, having been approved for printing only on January 24, 1957. In this issue, S. K. Bushuev of the University of Moscow, in a poorly organized article, made a sharp attack on practically every point Pikman had raised in a manner reminiscent of the 1950–55 period.

Bushuev's article would have given the impression that the 'un-rewriting' of North Caucasian history and the rehabilitation of the Shamil movement foreseen by the January historians' conference and Pikman's article had been abandoned as a result of the neo-Stalinist reaction which set in after the Polish and Hungarian events, if it were not for the fact that the same issue of *Voprosy Istorii* also reported discussions of the Shamil problem which took place in Makhach Kala (capital of Dagestan) in October, 1956, and at the Academy of Sciences in Moscow in November, 1956.[21] On both occasions Pikman's viewpoint had been supported by the great majority of the participants.

THE 1956 CONFERENCE IN MAKHACH KALA

The October discussion at the Dagestan branch of the U.S.S.R. Academy of Sciences included representatives from other North Caucasian regions and Azerbaidjan and scholars from Moscow. Four reports were delivered. All four of the persons who delivered these reports were, to judge by their names, non-Russians: Kh. O. Khashaev, G. D. Daniyalov, Kh. Kh. Ramazanov, and V. G. Khadzhiev. The first two reports were devoted to analysis of the social bases of the Caucasian resistance movement; the third was frankly titled, 'The Colonial Policy of Tsarism in Dagestan in the First Half of the Nineteenth Century', and the last was concerned with the Shamil movement in historical literature. *Voprosy Istorii*'s account of the session indicates that all four *rapporteurs* acknowledged the 'progressive significance of the unification of Dagestan with Russia'. Khashaev attempted to prove that the Mountaineers'

---

[20] G. D. Daniyalov, 'O dvizhenii gortsev pod rukovodstvom Shamilya', in *Voprosy Istorii*, No. 7, 1956 (approved for printing on August 16, 1956), pp. 67–72.

[21] 'Obsuzhdenie voprosa o kharaktere dvizheniya gorskikh narodov Severnovo Kavkaza v 20-50-kh godakh XIX veka', *Voprosy Istorii*, No. 12, 1956, pp. 188–98.

movement was at first dominated by progressive elements but later fell under the leadership of the reactionary local aristocracy. G. D. Daniyalov saw the reasons for the uprising in the impoverished condition of the native peoples and the harsh colonial policy of the Tsars. Ramazanov maintained that Tsarist policy had encouraged the native aristocracy to exploit the common people mercilessly, and that their revolt had therefore been caused by the reactionary excesses of Tsarist policy. The last speaker attacked the historical falsifications which had begun with Bagirov, and maintained that the struggle of Shamil had not been inspired from abroad and, in spite of the presence of reactionary features, was basically anti-feudal and anti-colonial in character.

There seems to have been little conflict in the views of the four *rapporteurs*. The discussion, even in the abbreviated form in which it is given in *Voprosy Istorii*, seems to have been remarkably lively and frank. Seventeen persons took part, thirteen of whom were from Dagestan, and all but two appeared to be non-Russian. Another person, Kara-Karaev, is identified only as 'an old Bolshevik', but his Turkic name would indicate that he too was from Dagestan or elsewhere in the Caucasus. One Ossete and one Adygei participated in the debate.

Several of the speakers who took part in the discussion criticized the *rapporteurs* for not going far enough. One 'considered that aid to the movement on the part of Turkey and England was nothing more than a myth'. The same speaker declared that it was impossible to conceal the military-colonial character of the unification of the Caucasus with Russia. The 'old Bolshevik' attacked the anti-Shamil book issued by the Georgian Academy of Sciences in 1953, in which the Mountaineers 'were depicted as foreign hirelings and bandits'. This kind of distortion, the old Bolshevik said, 'could not aid the strengthening of friendship between peoples'. Another Dagestani opposed the characterization of the Mountaineers' movement as progressive while the ideology of the Mountaineers was declared to be reactionary. Muridism at that time had been necessary, he said, as a force uniting the various Caucasian nationalities in their struggle against the colonial policy of Tsarism. A speaker from Dagestan with a Russian name said he considered the Mountaineers to have been fighting against Tsarist autocracy but not against the Russian people, and suggested that analogous uprisings in other countries should be studied. Another speaker maintained that the sole unifying force in the Mountaineers' movement had been Islam, observing that Lenin himself had noted that all peoples at a certain stage in their evolution make political protests in religious form. This speaker concluded:

'Russian Tsarism was the gendarme of Europe. . . . It is impossible to affirm that Dagestan was voluntarily joined to Russia. . . . The people did not want to submit to Tsarism and conducted a war of liberation. At the same time it is untrue to deny the connection of Shamil with the Turkey of the Sultans and capitalist England. This connection existed.'

On the other hand, a certain B. O. Kashkaev accused the *rapporteurs* of neglecting a number of important factors in their reports, such as 'the reactionary essence of the ideology of Islam and Muridism and the progressive significance of the unification of the Caucasus with Russia, the aggressive policy of England and Turkey in the Caucasus'. He also 'decisively dissociated' himself from Khashaev's report. Exercising the same kind of inverse double thinking so characteristic of Hungarian Communists after the 1956 revolt, Kashkaev 'expressed doubt whether the colonial policy of Russian Tsarism provoked the opposition of the Mountaineers', for 'most of the Tsarist troops were in the lowland regions, but there were no attacks against them there'. Kashkaev was the only participant who appeared to speak from a completely unreformed point of view.

A. V. Fadeev, representing the U.S.S.R. Academy of Sciences and sole Moscow participant in the discussion, performed self-criticism by observing that Soviet historians now condemn the anti-scientific views which were imposed upon them in 1950–52. 'Now there are no arguments that the popular masses took part in the movement under the flag of Muridism.' His self-criticism on the question of foreign intervention was a little less decisive: 'It is necessary to abandon the opinion that the Mountaineers' movement was the result of the existence of external forces, but it is impossible not to take into consideration the fact that this movement was encouraged by foreign Powers who were interested in causing Russia harm in the Caucasus.'

Fadeev's position was generally confirmed in the anonymous summary of the discussion with which the *Voprosy Istorii* report of the Makhach Kala conference concluded:

'Thus the participants of the Dagestan session came out for the necessity of discarding the viewpoint which had been confirmed after 1950 to the effect that the Caucasian Mountaineers' movement was reactionary, contrary to the interests of the people and that its leaders were agents of Turkey and England. The unification of Dagestan with Russia had objectively a progressive historical significance. However, the autocracy carried out in the Caucasus, as in other regions, a harsh colonial policy and maintained the oppression of the local feudal lords, which provoked the opposition of the popular masses.'

The Caucasian Mountaineers' movement tried to utilize Powers hostile to Russia, but it arose on the socio-economic soil of the North-eastern Caucasus. The Mountaineers' movement under the leadership of Shamil was directed most sharply against the colonial policy of Tsarism and was a struggle for national independence. The religious trappings of this movement were, however, reactionary; Muridism inflamed religious fanaticism and provoked hatred towards peoples professing Christianity.'

VIGOROUS DEBATE IN MOSCOW

The conference which assembled in Moscow to debate the Shamil question appears to have been one of the largest semi-public debates held in the Soviet Union in many years. More than five hundred persons attended. The conference was sponsored by the Historical Institute of the U.S.S.R. Academy of Sciences. Historians from all the autonomous republics and regions of the North Caucasus, as well as from Georgia, Armenia, and Azerbaidjan, 'took an active part'. The meeting was chaired by A. L. Sidorov, Director of the Historical Institute, who began by remarking that the distortions in evaluating Shamil and the history of the Caucasus which had occurred after 'the appearance of the anti-scientific and harmful article of Bagirov' had now been overcome, but that a number of questions still remained debatable.[22]

The Moscow conference heard three of the reports which had already been delivered in Makhach Kala: those of Khashaev, G. D. Daniyalov, and Ramazanov. Three new reports were also presented: M. V. Pokrovsky discussed the social struggle among the Adygei tribes in the late eighteenth and early nineteenth centuries.[23] A report by N. A. Smirnov was devoted to denouncing Muridism as the root of all the evil and reactionary tendencies in the movement of Shamil and the Mountaineers. A. V. Fadeev delivered the final report on 'The Caucasus in the System of International Relations from the 20's to the 50's of the Nineteenth Century'.

[22] The equally 'anti-scientific and harmful' views of A. D. Daniyalov were, incidentally, never mentioned at either the Makhach Kala or Moscow conferences. Blame for the distorted line was conveniently placed entirely on the liquidated Bagirov; though as late as mid-1955 Daniyalov had written that 'the continued wars of the Murids and Shamil against Russia resulted only in further ruination of the peoples of Dagestan, in their complete impoverishment', in his introduction to the symposium *Narody Dagestana* (Moscow, Akademia Nauk S.S.S.R., 1955). A. D. Daniyalov is still Party Secretary of Dagestan.

[23] Pokrovsky's report was published as an article in *Voprosy Istorii*, No. 2, 1957, pp. 62–74. His argumentation and social analysis were extremely complex, but were generally aimed to prove that the rank and file of the Western Caucasian peoples had leaned towards Russia, while the aristocracy favoured Turkey.

Admitting that the Caucasus 'always played a noteworthy role in the plans of conquest of Russian Tsarism', Fadeev also maintained that the 'English *bourgeoisie* was striving to tear the Caucasus away from Russia'. The fact that the view of the Mountaineers' movement which had prevailed from 1950 to 1953 had been abandoned did not mean that 'Turkey and England did not try to utilize Muridism as their own weapon', Fadeev continued. He concluded by trying to demonstrate that the 'masses' of the North Caucasian peoples had been opposed to the pro-Turkish and pro-British policy of their leaders.

The reports of Smirnov and Fadeev complemented each other. It is the views of these men, both Russians, which come closest to the line which the party leadership probably wished to have confirmed as the 'result' of the discussions as a whole. Their position involves a general rejection of the Bagirov viewpoint tempered by continued adherence to a totally negative position in respect to Muridism. Muridism is made out to be a much more extensive, systematic, and independent religious philosophy than it ever was in fact, because it has now become inexpedient to attack Islam as a whole. Too direct an attack on Islam would not only antagonize sensitive Caucasian feelings; it would likewise be out of keeping with Soviet efforts to woo Middle Eastern peoples. Fadeev and Smirnov attempted to salvage other aspects of the Bagirov line, particularly the allegation of British and Turkish support for the Caucasian peoples. They conceded as little as possible on the question of the 'reactionary nature' of Shamil and his immediate supporters, and tried to picture them as unprincipled, self-seeking, and fundamentally anti-democratic, particularly during the later stages of the Mountaineers' struggle.

The views of these 'neo-Bagirovites' found remarkably little support among the participants in the lively discussion that followed the lectures of the six *rapporteurs*. Thirty people took part in this debate. The remarks of twenty-five of them were given at some length by *Voprosy Istorii*. By far the most noteworthy thing about the debate is the frankness with which the overwhelming majority of the participants spoke. The exponents of the Bagirov line, several of them present at the session, were vigorously attacked. Smirnov and Fadeev were subjected to scathing criticism by the majority of the speakers. If the dryly written and no doubt carefully edited report in *Voprosy Istorii* gives such a vivid impression of free discussion, it can well be imagined how stormy and hectic the actual session must have been!

A. M. Pikman, who was the first to speak, defended himself vigorously and dared to differ radically from N. A. Smirnov's views by declaring that 'no special religious sect called Muridism existed at that period either in the Caucasus or in Turkey. One can talk about Islam as a religion but not about a special Muridist ideology. In appearing to criticize *non-existent Muridism*[24] the general dogmas of Mohammedanism which are allegedly several times worse than the Christian ones are being criticized.' Pikman then attacked Smirnov directly for characterizing Shamil and the Mountaineers' movement as reactionary in his book on Islam, and accused him of distorting quotations from Marx and Engels in the book.

Pikman's attack on Smirnov was followed by another by R. Aliev, of the Oriental Institute of the U.S.S.R. Academy of Sciences. Aliev, apparently of Moslem origin, implied that Smirnov had failed to understand the nature of Sufism, the powerful tradition of Islamic mysticism of which Muridism was an offshoot; declared that Smirnov failed to distinguish between earlier and later Islam; and observed that 'all movements in the East in the feudal period had such religious trappings'. Like many other participants in both the Moscow and the Makhach Kala meetings, Aliev displayed considerable skill in manoeuvring within the framework of Marxism and official Soviet terminology while still making universally valid and respectable historical and sociological observations. Many of the participants in the debate on Shamil and related problems of Caucasian history appear to be clear thinkers and capable researchers cleverly taking advantage of the limited freedom allowed them, cloaking their ideas in Marxist trappings and Soviet historical jargon in order to be able to defend themselves, but under few illusions as to the real relevance of the jargon to the problems at hand. They can speak knowingly of the 'religious trappings' (*religioznaya obolochka*) of movements which were in reality much broader in scope because they have become skilled in covering their own search for truth with a carefully pieced-together cloak of 'pseudo-religious' Marxist-Leninist phraseology.

Of the twenty-five participants in the Moscow debate whose remarks were reported by *Voprosy Istorii*, only two attempted to defend their former views and took a position completely contrary to the general trend of the discussion. Two others, both Georgians, expressed partially negative views.

Adzhemyan, unrepentant and as blatantly outspoken as he had been in 1947, boasted that as early as 1944 he had proved the Shamil movement reactionary. He still maintained that Shamil had been an irresponsible adventurer and that Russian classical literature had

---

[24] Dissociating themselves from the use of this challenging phrase, the editors of *Voprosy Istorii* placed it in quotation marks to make clear that it originated with Pikman.

'correctly portrayed Shamil as the same kind of dark despot as Nicholas I'. It was entirely wrong, he said, to consider the struggle of the Mountaineers a national liberation movement.

Adzhemyan's remarks were too much even for B. O. Kashkaev, the only Dagestani who had taken a neo-Stalinist line at the Makhach Kala meeting. He reminded the Armenian that the conference in Dagestan had taken place 'on a high scientific level' and had contributed to the strengthening of friendship among peoples, and concluded: 'We want to prove the popular-liberation character of the struggle of the Caucasian Mountaineers and at the same time uncover the reactionary features of Muridism.' Most of Kashkaev's compatriots, of course, both at Makhach Kala and in Moscow, displayed little interest in 'uncovering the reactionary features of Muridism' and were apparently not convinced that such elements existed.

S. K. Bushuev, whose neo-Bagirovist article appeared in the same issue of *Voprosy Istorii* as the report of the debates, attacked Pikman strongly, maintained that Shamil had hindered the spread of democracy among the Caucasian peoples, and accused Pikman of inaccurately quoting Marx and Engels.

Z. V. Anchabadze of the Abkhaz Institute of Language, History, and Literature, affirmed the 'moral right' of the Mountaineers to fight for their independence, but maintained that the struggle had been pointless because it had had no chance of succeeding. The Russian rebellions led by Pugachev, Razin, and Bolotnikov had likewise had no chance of success, he said, but they were at least progressive, while the struggle of the Mountaineers was not. Criticizing the introductory article to the collection of documents published in Tbilisi in 1953, Anchabadze maintained that the collection nevertheless contained much valuable material. A. P. Ioseliani, of the Georgian Institute of History, said that he felt that the unification of Georgia with Russia had encouraged the spread of progressive influences to the other peoples of the Caucasus. Shamil led the masses in their fight against feudal oppression and Tsarism, but he also carried out raids into neighbouring countries, particularly into Georgia, and tried to link up with the Turkish Sultan. This threatened Georgia's separate position (*samostoyatel'nost'*).

The refusal of the Armenian, Adzhemyan, to abandon his anti-Shamil position, and the reluctance of the two Georgian participants in the discussion to concede a positive view of the Caucasian Mountaineers, reveal a remarkable persistence of historical patterns. Forty years of stress on the community of interests of all Soviet peoples have not altered traditional nationalist attitudes. The Christian peoples of the Caucasus, the Georgians and the Armenians, have always found it difficult to sympathize completely with the anti-Russian attitude of Caucasian Muslims or to judge them with a full sense of detachment.

Two of the participants in the discussion gave the impression of being bureaucrats concerned primarily with preserving their positions, eager to avoid taking a firm stand in respect to any of the major issues involved. These people consequently stressed the complexity of the problem and devoted themselves to discussion of questions of terminology and procedure. A Russian from a North Caucasian teachers' training school thought that to speak of 'Mountaineers' was incorrect, because people from the plains had also taken part in the resistance movement. A gentleman from the Historical Institute of the Academy of Sciences in Moscow said that the only way a national movement could be judged was whether it served the class struggle of the proletariat or not. The authors of histories and papers on the movement of the Mountaineers, he felt, had failed to apply this criterion.

Thus the persons who opposed or seemed doubtful about revision of the line on Shamil—two unreformed Bagirovites, two partly negative Georgians, and two bureaucrats—totalled six. The *nineteen other* participants in the debate all supported the essentials of the Pikman position vigorously. A few seemed somewhat confused, but most of them were remarkably clear in their thoughts and courageous in expressing them. *Voprosy Istorii* does not report who was applauded and who was not, nor is there any indication of calls from the floor. With more than five hundred people assembled to listen to the kind of vigorous, spontaneous oratory in which many of these people indulged, there must have been moments of great excitement and perhaps even outbreaks of what the text of the Khruschchev secret speech parenthetically referred to as 'commotion in the hall'.

M. N. Osmanov, of the Oriental Institute of the U.S.S.R. Academy of Sciences, was critical of Fadeev's report. He said that researchers tended to base their conclusions too much on the reports of nineteenth-century Russian military commanders, and made far too little use of local sources. Another non-Russian speaker, M. A. Mamakaev, attacked the views of Adzhemyan and Bushuev, and concluded with a vigorous declaration: 'The Mountaineers were not fighting out of love for Shamil nor from sympathy for Turkey; they desired neither the knout of Nicholas I nor the noose of the Janissaries; the Mountaineers were seeking their own freedom and independence!'

A Dagestani from the Makhach Kala Teachers' Training Institute, R. M. Magomedov (who had also participated in the discussion in Makhach Kala) declared that the freedom-loving Mountaineers had inspired 'Pushkin, Lermontov, Tolstoy, Chernyshevsky, Dobrolyu-bov, and other glorious sons of the Russian people'; it was therefore impossible to consider them a passive mass following the will of religious fanatics. A colleague of Magomedov's (apparently from the same teachers' training institute), A. A. Abilov, pointed out that the struggle of the Mountaineers had not only inspired the best repre-sentatives of Russian cultural traditions, but had also been positively recognized by prominent Soviet Communist leaders: 'During the Civil War M. V. Frunze, G. K. Ordjonikidze, S. M. Kirov, and A. I. Mikoyan appealed to the Mountaineers to struggle against Denikin by recalling the glorious traditions of the struggle under the leadership of Shamil.'

It is interesting to note that several of the participants in these discussions were from the staffs of teachers' training institutes. Three persons from the Makhach Kala institute participated in both the debates there and in Moscow. A woman from the Woman Teachers' Training Institute in Makhach Kala also participated in the debate there. Two other participants in the Moscow discussion were from a North Caucasian and a Moscow teachers' training institute, respectively, and A. M. Pikman, the spokesman for revision of the anti-Shamil line, is a teacher at a middle school in Moscow. If these people—teachers and teachers of teachers—are inculcating upon the younger generation the ideas they expressed during the Makhach Kala and Moscow debates, and the general tendency towards independent liberal thinking which they display, then many young Soviet citizens are not learning in school the things the party would like to have them learn. Local nationalism would seem to be a strong force in Dagestani teachers' training institutes. The Caucasian participants in the debates who were not involved in pedagogical activities seemed for the most part to come from local 'scientific' institutes—local branches of the U.S.S.R. Academy of Sciences, local Institutes of History, Language, and Literature, of which practically every Caucasian autonomous republic and region has at least one. The local intelligentsia who dominate these institutes, in spite of the fact that they owe their positions to the Soviet system, appear also to be strongly influenced by local nationalism and display independence in their approach to historical and political problems. Education and cultural progress are two-edged swords. A historical pattern is again repeating itself. British schools in India produced Indian nationalists just as French schools in Algeria turn out Algerian nationalists and Austro-Hungarian schools used to equip Czech, Slovak, and Croat patriots with training and ideas which they used against their imperial masters. The older intelligentsia of the Soviet minorities was slaughtered off during the Great Purges, but a newer generation, apparently just as nationalistic as the previous one, has emerged.

L. I. Lavrov, a Russian ethnographer from Leningrad, declared that many mistakes were made in judging the movement of the Mountaineers by 'comrades who approach history like politics slapped on to the past; we need science which reveals the objective truth. In the struggle of the Mountaineers the main thing is their struggle for freedom.'

V. G. Gadjiev, of the Dagestani branch of the U.S.S.R. Academy of Sciences, in one of the strongest speeches of the discussion, accused Fadeev, Bushuev, and Smirnov of trying to divert criticism from themselves for their earlier mistakes by criticizing Pikman. Bushuev, he said, was one of those who had originally shown some understanding for the Mountaineers' movement,[25] but after 1950 he had merely repeated the harmful distorted propositions of Bagirov's article. He concluded: 'Pikman's article has its shortcomings but in general it poses the question correctly, and furthermore it raised the question at a time when our leading Caucasian specialists were simply sitting, waiting the problem out.'

I. Kh. Kalmykov, from the Circassian Scientific Research Institute, pointed out that Shamil had exercised no religious influence on the peoples of the western Caucasus, . . . but, all the same, these peoples 'considered themselves independent and did not want to permit any outside interference in their affairs. The dissatisfaction of the Mountaineers and their lack of desire for unification with Russia were utilized by the Turkish feudal lords and the English *bourgeoisie*. . . . The harsh measures of the Tsarist authorities alienated the Circassians from Russia.'

A Kabardin declared that it was a mistake to forget that peoples like the Kabardins, Ossetians, and Balkars carried on the anti-colonial and anti-feudal struggle without ties to the Muridist movement. Muridism, he implied, could not be blamed for the uprising of the Mountaineers or cited as an adequate reason for it.

Perhaps most significant of all the remarks made during the discussion are those of E. Yu. Bogush, representative of the Institute of Marxism-Leninism in Moscow. He offered little consolation to the neo-Bagirovites. It was incorrect to maintain, he said, that Marx and Engels had written their articles on the Caucasian question with the aid of the Englishman Urquhart. Marx and Engels knew that Urquhart was a Turcophil who was working for maintenance of the

---

[25] Bushuev had published a pro-Shamil book before the war, *Bor'ba gortsev za nezavisimost' pod rukovodstvom Shamilya* (Moscow, 1939); this book as well as that of R. M. Magomedov were both strongly attacked by Smirnov in his *Ocherki istorii izuchenii Islama v S.S.S.R.*, p. 250.

Ottoman Empire. But 'Bushuev, Adzhemyan, and others propose to consign the articles of Marx and Engels on the Eastern question to oblivion. In actual fact it is necessary to study them more deeply. In Marx's and Engels' articles . . . there are inaccuracies and mistakes, but in respect to principles their line . . . is completely correct. Marx and Engels came out in support of the liberation struggle of the mountain peoples of the Caucasus as well as all other national liberation struggles of that time. They maintained a position of proletarian internationalism and represented the viewpoint of European democracy, of the European workers' movement.'[26]

The next speaker, A. F. Miller, let another great draught of fresh air into the discussion. This member of the Historical Institute of the U.S.S.R. Academy of Sciences pointed out that nineteenth-century Russian policy in respect to Turkey and Islam had by no means been consistent:

'It is impossible to present Turkish policy of that time as pan-Islamist or even pan-Turkist. The Tsarist government, on the basis of its own interest, at one time supported the notion that the Turkish Sultan was the Caliph of all the faithful and sometimes appealed to his authority. . . . Turkey had fallen at that time into the position of a semi-colony and could not have given much help to the Mountaineers even if she had wanted to. . . . Tsarism was at that time carrying out an arch-reactionary policy inside the country and in the international arena, and the struggle of Tsarism against Mountaineers was envisaged as a struggle against revolution. The religious trappings of the Mountaineers' movement are completely natural. An ideology reactionary in form has often concealed a progressive movement.'

Burdjalov, deputy chief editor of *Voprosy Istorii*, referred to Marx, Engels, Lenin, and Pokrovsky as the first who had approached the problem of the struggle of the Mountaineers from the viewpoint of proletarian internationalism. In the 1930's, he said, a generally correct view of the problem had been developed. Bagirov's article set everything on the wrong path.

'. . . The Mountaineers were fighting for their freedom and independence. In demonstrating the progressiveness of the unification of peoples with Russia it is impossible to remain silent about the colonial policy of Tsarism. It must also be noted that in many places what took place was not unification but conquest. It is untrue to maintain that the struggle of the Mountaineers under Shamil was absolutely without hope of success. It is impossible to forget that

---

[26] Bogush's remarks could be applied to Poland or Hungary as well as to the Caucasus. For a representative of the Institute of Marxism-Leninism he spoke in a remarkably direct and unqualified manner. Note his use of the phrase 'European democracy', without any qualifying term.

this was the time of the development of the revolutionary movement in the West and the ripening of the revolutionary situation in Russia.'

The Moscow discussion was summed up by L. M. Ivanov, of the Historical Institute of the U.S.S.R. Academy of Sciences. He said that a series of serious monographic works 'which would give a correct, Marxist-Leninist elucidation' of various aspects of nineteenth-century Caucasian history should now be prepared, and noted that 'the overwhelming majority of the participants in the discussion recognized that the anti-colonial movement of the Mountaineers led by Shamil had been provoked by the aggressive and colonial policy of Tsarism and the sharpening of the class struggle inside Mountaineer society'.

Ivanov placed more emphasis on the internal class struggle among the Caucasian peoples than was given it by most of the participants in the discussion, particularly those from Dagestan and other North Caucasian regions. His concluding remarks likewise seem to be more a revelation of what certain directing elements *wanted* the discussion to conclude, and a reflection of the only partially reformed viewpoints of the neo-Bagirovites, rather than an accurate summary of the predominant opinions expressed during the discussion:

'In examining the course of this movement it is impossible not to consider the influences of external forces, the efforts of the ruling circles of England, Turkey, and other Powers to utilize the movement of the Caucasian Mountaineers in their own interests. In exposing the harsh colonial policy of Tsarism, Soviet historians must demonstrate from every point of view the objectively progressive consequences of the unification of the Caucasus with Russia.'

Burdjalov's remarks, much more than Ivanov's, summarized the views most frequently expressed during the discussion. The Moscow conference revealed even more forcefully than the one in Makhach Kala the strength of the national spirit and sense of history of the North Caucasian peoples. The vicious attack on their national traditions which began with the Bagirov-Daniyalov articles in 1950, and continued unabated for five years, appears to have strengthened rather than weakened their national consciousness.

To any thinking person, repeated frantic assertion that England and Turkey were scheming to take the Caucasus away from Russia must seem patently absurd. As the nineteenth century opened, Russia possessed *none* of the Caucasus. Seventy years later *the entire* region had been incorporated into the Russian Empire. It was Russia who took the Caucasus away from others during the nineteenth century—from the independent peoples who wished to be tributary to none of their neighbours and from the Turks and the Persians who *legally* held title to substantial Caucasian possessions. Something can in all fairness be said for Tsarist rule in the Caucasus, in contrast to that of the less efficient and far more decrepit Turkish and Persian Empires, but how, in the last analysis, can one blame any state worthy of the name for opposing encroachments on its territory? The Turkish Sultans, in their ineffectual way, tried to stem the Russian advance, which at times seriously threatened the eastern marches of Anatolia itself, but this hardly constitutes the kind of 'intriguing' against innocent Russia which the Bagirovs and neo-Bagirovites have made it out to be. To accuse the British of plotting to steal the Caucasus from Russia is to attribute a degree of long-range planning to British nineteenth-century Caucasian policy which was never there, not to mention a capability for interfering actively in the Caucasus which the British never possessed. British Caucasian policy was a very subsidiary aspect of British Near Eastern policy in the nineteenth century. In general, Britain favoured bolstering the Ottoman Empire sufficiently to keep it from collapsing and falling entirely to Russia. In principle, therefore, Britain generally opposed Russian gains at Turkish expense, but only during the Crimean War did the British undertake military operations to further this aim. The Caucasus did not figure in these operations, however; if Britain had been as determined to pry the Caucasus away from Russia as some Soviet historians have pretended, it is curious that her military effort at this time was concentrated in the Crimea.[27]

The Moscow meeting concluded with agreement by the participants (1) to continue discussion of the Mountaineers' movement in *Voprosy Istorii*, (2) to issue a collection of documents and other materials, and (3) to publish each year a scientific symposium on questions of the history of the peoples of the Caucasus.

The four deported North Caucasian peoples had not been rehabilitated at the time of the discussion in Moscow, and it was apparently not yet common knowledge that they would be, for there was practically no mention of them: the Balkars were mentioned once in passing by one Caucasian speaker, and there were a few references to Chechnia and one to Ingushetia, but none to these peoples themselves, in spite of the fact that they played a major role in the Shamil movement. The Chechens were from the very beginning of the nineteenth century among the bitterest opponents of Tsarist expansion into the Caucasus. The rehabilitation of these peoples[28]

---

[27] For a more balanced view of Russia's nineteenth-century Caucasian policy and the relation of Britain thereto, see W. E. D. Allen and P. Muratoff, *Caucasian Battlefields* (Cambridge, 1953), pp. 46–53 and 66–80.

[28] The Chechens, Ingush, Karachai, Balkars, and Kalmyks were rehabilitated and their former territories were partially restored by a decree of the U.S.S.R. Supreme Soviet dated January 9, 1957 which was publicly announced on February 11, 1957.

makes it possible for the first time, since World War II, to write on North Caucasian history without circumventing the role and practically denying the existence of the deported nationalities.

DEVELOPMENTS IN DAGESTAN

The Dagestanis lost no time in taking advantage of the meetings in Makhach Kala and Moscow to reverse the measures which had been imposed upon them in 1950. No less eminent a body than the Bureau of the Dagestan Regional Committee of the Communist Party of the Soviet Union met, apparently some time in December or January,[29] and formally revoked the resolution which it had passed in August, 1950, implementing the Bagirov-Daniyalov line. The Dagestani party bureau drew somewhat more positive and far-reaching conclusions from the debates than L. M. Ivanov, who had summarized the Moscow discussion. There are interesting differences in terminology: the resolution refers twice to Dagestan *and Chechnia* as the base of the resistance movement of the Mountaineers. Instead of speaking of the *unification* (*prisoedinenie*) of Dagestan with Russia, the resolution refers to the 'incorporation of Dagestan into Russia' (*vkhozhdenie Dagestana v sostav Rossii*). Instead of restricting the re-examination of Caucasian history to the period from the 1820's to the 1850's, as the final paragraph of the report on the Moscow meeting implies the participants decided to do, the Dagestani party resolution sets a wider variety of tasks, including 'the character of the uprising of 1877' and 'the history of the struggle of the peoples of Dagestan for the establishment of Soviet power and Socialist construction in the republic'. Finally, the Dagestani party bureau took the positive step of instructing the Dagestani Ministry of Culture to restore materials on the history of the Shamil movement to the local museum, while the Propaganda and Agitation Department was ordered to prepare within a month a proposal for transmitting literature on Shamil and the Mountaineers' movement to libraries 'for public use'. The name of Shamil is mentioned eight times in the brief report of the Dagestani resolution, which occupies less than a page.[30]

Dagestan was not directly affected by the wave of deportations at the end of World War II. Its local society remained intact. It was the scene of repressive measures against the local culture during the final years of the Stalin era, but in spite of the anti-Shamil campaign

---

[29] The report carried by *Voprosy Istorii*, No. 1, 1957, pp. 195–6, gives no dates.

[30] The Dagestani Communist Party resolution on Shamil was reported only by *Voprosy Istorii*. It was not mentioned by any other journal, by the central Press, nor, as far as is known, by the provincial Press or radio.

and a certain degree of forced Russification, it fared less badly than many other parts of the North Caucasus. It is natural, therefore, that once the bonds were loosened, evidence of local nationalism should come to the surface there more rapidly than in many other regions.

It is not surprising that national pride should still be strong—and perhaps be growing—in Dagestan. Dagestan means literally 'mountain country'. It is inhabited by some of the fiercest and sturdiest of Caucasian Moslem peoples. There are four major and more than a dozen minor national groups among them, some of whom speak entirely unrelated languages. Until long after the Revolution, Arabic continued to be the common language of Dagestan. Strenuous, and among the younger generation largely successful, efforts have been made by the Communists to supplant Arabic with Russian.

The republican paper, *Dagestanskaya Pravda*, has always been published in Russian, but local papers in native languages had also been encouraged until 1950. On January 1, 1951, all these papers were converted to native-language translations of *Dagestanskaya Pravda* because 'of the need to eliminate some local limitations and peculiarities which had been cropping up in the newspapers and because of the fact that at that time there were not enough qualified newspaper cadres capable of publishing regional papers independently'. In early 1957 this measure was reversed. It was claimed that six years had seen much progress and national cadres of intelligentsia had grown. Among the disadvantages of the translated versions of *Dagestanskaya Pravda* the fact was cited that this arrangement 'limited possibilities for the development of native languages . . . the language of the translations of the materials from the Russian text into the languages of the local nationalities was at times difficult for readers to understand'.

Dagestanskaya Pravda reported on January 26, 1957, that 'in accordance with the decision of the Bureau of the Central Committee of the C.P.S.U. of the R.S.F.S.R. and the Bureau of the Dagestani Regional Party Committee', four independent papers in different local languages would start publication shortly. They began to appear on February 5, and were called upon by *Dagestanskaya Pravda* to help, among other things, 'in mobilizing the masses for the successful implementation of the historic decisions of the Twentieth Party Congress'. They were also expected 'to better satisfy the growing spiritual requirements' of the working masses, 'to liquidate patriarchal feudal survivals and to wage a decisive struggle against *bourgeois* ideology and morals'.

COUNTER-OFFENSIVE OF THE ANTI-SHAMIL FORCES

The anti-Shamil elements had been completely outnumbered at the Moscow meeting in November, but they were not to be easily silenced. Bushuev's article in *Voprosy Istorii* No. 12, which has already been mentioned, was the first counterblow against the freer course which the pro-Shamil historians had charted out for themselves. The tone of this poorly organized article, which is internally contradictory and shows signs of having been hastily written, was in keeping with the frightened bombast characteristic of most Soviet official pronouncements in the period following the Hungarian Revolution: 'The aggressive intrigues of the Turkey of the Sultans and capitalist England were aimed at hindering the voluntary unification of the peoples of the North Caucasus with Russia and at sowing hatred among them.'

Bushuev accused Pikman of idealizing the Shamil movement 'without citing a single new document' as evidence for such a view. With peculiar illogic he implied that Pikman wished to ignore the fact that Tsarism was also the most evil enemy of the Russian people themselves. He accused him of misusing the word 'colony' and of being un-Leninist in doing so. To counter Pikman's minimization of the threat of Anglo-Turkish aggression against the Caucasus in the nineteenth century, Bushuev boasted that he had studied the military-historical archives from the 1780's to the 1870's and that these materials confirmed the aggressive character of English and Turkish policy. But he then committed the same error of which he accused Pikman, for he cited practically none of these materials and fell back on the standard items used during the Bagirov period to support his case.

When he took up the problem of Muridism, Bushuev's style degenerated to the 'howling jackal' level of the Stalin era, with vitriolic adjectives heaped one upon another: 'An Oriental-theocratic, feudal-monarchistic despotic system of military-religious Muridist administration was created by Shamil and other leaders. . . . The Mountaineer-murids knew nothing but war. . . . The misanthropic character of Muridism was given expression in legalization of a continual state of war [*gazavat*] between Muslim and non-Muslim peoples. Muridism was directed against all friendship among peoples, against all democracy, against all humanism.'

And later in the same article: 'The imāms of Chechnia and Dagestan were creating a theocratic, despotic structure, wound in a web of tribal, patriarchal institutions. Shamil, in contrast to his predecessors, established an hereditary monarchy. He himself, like his predecessors, was nothing more than a chief of tribes. In conditions of semi-patriarchal, semi-feudal life, there were not only no nations, there were not even any nationalities. The Soviet historian cannot be allowed to depict imāms as leaders of a national movement.'

Bushuev drew far-reaching and quite unjustified conclusions from a twelve-word citation from Lenin's *Development of Capitalism in Russia*, which he took out of context[31]: 'The peoples of the Caucasus, and especially the Mountaineers, according to V. I. Lenin, "stood on the periphery of the world economy and even on the periphery of history". In connection with this it is incomprehensible why A. M. Pikman equates the Caucasian Mountaineers with the Poles and Hungarians, who were at a much higher stage of development.'

His indignation at the fact that Pikman dared to draw parallels between nineteenth-century East European liberation struggles and those of the Caucasian peoples probably reflected the after-effects of Polish and Hungarian events in the autumn of 1956.

Bushuev's second-rate article exhibited the same combination of belligerent bad taste and dubious scholarship characteristic of Stalinist times. Bushuev had not been selected to deliver a report at either the Makhach Kala or the Moscow meetings. His still largely unreformed viewpoint had been denounced by several of the participants in the discussions. Nevertheless he was given seven pages to air his views in *Voprosy Istorii*, while they were not. Probably the editors of *Voprosy Istorii*, among whom there is at least one person as unreformed in his views on Caucasian problems as Bushuev, namely N. A. Smirnov, had reason to anticipate the coming party attack on their journal, and wished to demonstrate that they also gave space to views contrary to those of Pikman.

An unsigned article entitled 'Observe Strictly the Leninist Principle of *Partiinost'* in Historical Science' appeared in issue No. 4 of *Kommunist* for 1957 (approved for printing on March 15, 1957) and took *Voprosy Istorii* to task for shortcomings in many fields, particularly party history. E. N. Burdjalov, who had publicly associated himself with Pikman's views on Caucasian history on at least two occasions, was singled out as having committed 'serious mistakes' which were 'the result of direct withdrawal from Marxist-Leninist dialectical methods of research, from the principle of *partiinost'* in historical research'. Striking out at Burdjalov again, the *Kommunist* article continued: 'Selection of factual material and its evaluation and treatment in the articles of Burdjalov contradict the requirements of science.'

[31] The passage in Lenin's work from which Bushuev extracted his quotation is concerned with proving the *colonial status* of the Caucasus after it had been incorporated into Imperial Russia. See Lenin, *The Development of Capitalism in Russia* (Moscow, Foreign Languages Publishing House, 1956), pp. 650–4.

Burdjalov was not directly attacked for Pikman's 'unsound article which introduces nothing but confusion into the basic problems under discussion', but *Voprosy Istorii*'s editors as a group were accused of irresponsibility in publishing such an article. Pikman himself was denounced in phrases which implied that he was immature and foolish, but it was also implied that he might be deliberately propagating an anti-Soviet and perhaps anti-Russian viewpoint. In dogmatically bureaucratic phrases which leave the impression that the author of the *Kommunist* attack never actually read Pikman's article, he termed it 'shrill in tone and weak in argumentation', and self-satisfiedly asserted that Pikman's 'unscientific' article was unnecessary because: 'Long before the publication of the article the well-founded opinion had been formed in our scientific collectives that the attempt to portray the movement led by Shamil as inspired by enemy agents was unscientific, just as the denial of its anti-colonial character was incorrect. However, no one among serious Soviet scholars casts doubt on the progressive nature of the unification of the peoples of the North Caucasus with Russia.'

The most surprising thing about the *Kommunist* article is the next passage, which claimed that the debates on the Shamil question held in Dagestan and Moscow had 'confirmed most convincingly' the viewpoint which *Kommunist* expressed. The party bureaucrats who compiled the attack on *Voprosy Istorii* must have been judging these meetings on the basis of carefully doctored official reports of them, for the meetings, if they proved anything, certainly proved that Pikman had the majority of speakers behind him and that the smug views of the party *apparatchiki* which *Kommunist* championed had only two Bagirovite *rapporteurs* and a mere handful of other participants to support them.

The purge of the staff of *Voprosy Istorii* had not yet occurred when the *Kommunist* attack appeared. The next issue of the journal (No. 2, 1957) came out in April (approved for printing on March 26, 1957) and listed an unchanged editorial board. Two months elapsed before the next issue (No. 3, 1957) appeared, however; meanwhile the troublesome journal had been brought under strict party discipline. This issue (approved for printing on May 21, 1957) revealed that seven members of the former eleven-member editorial board had been dropped and replaced by eleven new members. Burdjalov, protector of Pikman, had fallen; Smirnov, neo-Bagirovite, had remained. The first sixteen pages of the issue were devoted to an editorial entitled 'For Leninist *Partiinost*' in Historical Science', in which the journal took itself to task for its past errors in the same scathing fashion employed by *Kommunist* in its earlier attack.

Burdjalov was accused of displaying excessive zeal in attacking Stalin,[32] and the previous editorial staff was berated, article by article, for a considerable portion of the contents of the journal during the preceding year. Pikman's article was termed 'a negation in camouflaged form of the progressiveness of the unification of the Caucasus with Russia'. The Moscow conference on the Shamil question was not mentioned.

Subsequent issues of *Voprosy Istorii* during 1957 avoided Caucasian problems entirely. According to the 'purge' editorial in *Voprosy Istorii* No. 3, 1957, the journal is henceforth to concentrate on 'the most important problems' in the field of history, 'freeing itself from the elucidation of narrow specialist questions'. The Shamil problem no doubt comes under the heading of 'narrow specialist questions'. Actually the way had been cleared for complete elimination of *Voprosy Istorii*, should the journal continue to be troublesome. Three new historical journals dealing respectively with party history, U.S.S.R. history, and world history began publication in the U.S.S.R. in 1957.

The Shamil debate has not been reflected in other Soviet publications, but the literary journal *Novy Mir* (which originally serialized Dudintsev's controversial *Not By Bread Alone*) began in its second issue for 1957 to publish a posthumous historical novel by Piotr Pavlenko, entitled *A Caucasian Story*, which deals sympathetically with the Shamil movement.[33] The editors of *Novy Mir* prefaced the first instalment with a note stating that the work was being published for the first time. Having been started in 1933 and finished in 1938, 'the manuscript was preserved in the author's files'. Pavlenko, who died in 1951, had gained pre-war fame with his novel *In the East* (1937) and a post-war Stalin Prize for *Happiness* (1947).

CONCLUSIONS

The campaign for the re-writing of nineteenth-century Caucasian history and re-evaluation of the role of Shamil was fought on a semi-public plane for more than a year. *Voprosy Istorii* was the sole journalistic instrument which the forces behind the campaign were able to use. A. M. Pikman, the principal spokesman of the campaign, was obviously a frontman for a more substantial group of Russian and Caucasian academicians who did not care to expose themselves by being the first to revive a highly controversial issue.

[32] In two articles in *Voprosy Istorii*, Nos. 4 and 8, 1956, neither of which touched upon Caucasian questions.

[33] P. Pavlenko, 'Kavkazskaya Povest', in *Novy Mir*, No. 2, 1957, pp. 60–119; No. 3, 1957, pp. 58–134; and No. 4, 1957, pp. 80–115.

After a vigorous beginning in the period immediately preceding the Twentieth Congress, the campaign was no longer publicly evident after the appearance of Pikman's article in *Voprosy Istorii* in March, 1956, until a similar article by G. D. Daniyalov was published in August. Heated debates may have occurred within the editorial board of *Voprosy Istorii* during the summer of 1956; both there and in Dagestan the pro-Shamil forces appear to have gained greatly in strength and courage during this time. The Makhach Kala and Moscow conferences marked the public triumph of the views of Pikman and his supporters and revealed the intellectual weakness of those who were trying to retain substantial features of the old line. The Dagestani Communist Party resolution, reversing the measures implementing the Bagirov line taken in 1950, marked the high point in the campaign to restore Shamil to his former position of honour.

At the Moscow meeting in November, however, a counter-trend was manifested in the selection of neo-Bagirovites such as Fadeev and Smirnov to deliver reports, and in Ivanov's summary of the discussion which involved only a minimal recognition of the strength and breadth of ideas of the pro-Shamil forces. Bushuev's viciously polemic article in *Voprosy Istorii*, No. 12, proved to be a forewarning of the attack on Pikman by *Kommunist* and the purge of *Voprosy Istorii* which followed it.

The partisans of Shamil were unfortunate in bringing their campaign to a head at the very time when the most severe period of neo-Stalinist reaction since the death of the old dictator had set in. Events in Poland and Hungary in October and November, 1956, had demonstrated to Soviet Party leaders how the force of ideas generated by intellectuals, fused with mass discontent, could shake the structure of Communist power to its foundations. Consequently, their enthusiasm for reform lessened appreciably and the 'unrewriting' of history was slowed almost to a standstill. It is not surprising that in this kind of atmosphere the 'neo-Bagirovites' found it easier to gain official backing for their only partially reformed views. The far more numerous pro-Shamil historians found themselves without support from above. But whether there had been a period of neo-Stalinist reaction or not, the party would most likely have had to step into the Shamil debate sooner or later and call a halt, for the campaign, which had generated considerable dynamism of its own, clearly threatened to develop far beyond what the Communist Party regards as a permissible degree of revision of the line on the incorporation of non-Russian peoples into Russia. Ever since the mid-1940's the Soviet Communist Party has been trying to find a formula to justify Tsarist conquests as progressive. It has never succeeded, and Soviet historians continue to be beset by 'the Shamil complex'.[34] Though conformity with varying official lines has repeatedly been imposed from above, controversy and potentially 'antagonistic' contradictions continue to seethe beneath the surface. If the pro-Shamil forces had been allowed to carry their demands through, their success would not have gone unnoticed by Uzbek, Kazakh, and Tatar historians and intellectuals, perhaps even by Ukrainians. The party leadership cannot risk this, for such a process, once begun, might not be easily checked.

Recent Soviet political ventures in the Middle East have added a new ingredient to the problem of justifying past Russian (and present Soviet) colonialism, but they have not changed the fundamental issue. It is remarkable, in fact, how little effect Soviet courting of Muslim peoples in Asia and Africa has had in changing Soviet policies towards the Muslim peoples of the U.S.S.R. and their traditions. There has been some softening of official attitudes, but the line on Islam for internal consumption is still essentially negative. It will be extremely difficult for Soviet Communists, however, to continue their active pro-Arab 'anti-colonial' policy for several years without running the risk of provoking unrest among their own Caucasian and Central Asian peoples. The Shamil debate shows that an alert, proud, nationalistically-inclined intelligentsia has again developed among these peoples. They are likely to draw their own conclusions from the Communist line as propagated to the Egyptians, the Indonesians, the Sudanese, and the Cypriots, and they will not be conclusions the party wishes them to come to. The Soviet Union is not immune from Algerian situations of its own, though the day when issues which are still in an incipient stage might reach such proportions is still far off.

To return again to the Shamil debate. The *Kommunist* and post-purge *Voprosy Istorii* editorials clearly state the line the party would like to have followed: the party is willing to admit that errors were made in 1950, but prefers to have no more talk about them now than is necessary. The party desires that several important aspects of the Bagirov line on Shamil and the Caucasian resistance movement be preserved in less odious form. Therefore the reactionary nature of Muridism continues to be stressed and the element of foreign intrigue is still allotted an important role in explaining the scope and intensity of the Mountaineers' struggle. The myth that the struggles were anti-Tsarist and in no way anti-Russian must continue to be propagated vigorously and is to be supported by pseudo-sociological

---

[34] *Cf.* Moshe Perlmann, 'The Study of the Islamic Middle East in the Soviet Union, 1940–56' in *Report on Current Research on the Middle East*, Spring 1957 (Washington, D.C., Middle East Institute), pp. 23–4.

analyses proving that, while the Caucasian native aristocracy opposed everything Russian, the 'masses' always had great love for the Russian people. A good case could be made that in actuality the situation was often quite the opposite, but the maintenance of the Soviet imperial system, as a continuation and extension of the Tsarist Empire, requires that many facts continue to be overlooked or obscured in a mass of dialectical, Marxist-Leninist verbiage, while the writings of Marx and Engels on the Caucasian problem are, so far as possible, to be ignored.

Such is the line the party would like to have followed. It even pretends that this line was supported by the Makhach Kala and Moscow conferences. It is in all its essentials the same kind of line the party is trying to enforce in all fields of Soviet intellectual activity—in respect to other aspects of history, literature, art, music, most fields of science, in the interpretation of the role of Stalin himself. But to get Soviet academicians, scientists, and writers to conform to the party line *in general*, the party must now make concessions to them on *particulars*. This gives them far more leeway than they ever enjoyed in the Stalinist period, and in one way and another many of them will use it.

The campaign for revision of the anti-Shamil line has had positive results. Views which were for many years suppressed were publicly aired and are no doubt now held all the more vigorously by those who uttered them. None of the participants in the Shamil debate, even those most strongly denounced such as Burdjalov and Pikman, was called upon to make, or has made, self-criticism. There must still be considerable private discussion of these questions. Though historians in Moscow may for the time being be restrained from further ventures in all-out revision of Caucasian history, those in Dagestan will probably move ahead more freely. The way ahead will not necessarily be easy for any of them and there may be new set-backs, but there is no reason to assume that further progress will not eventually be made.

September, 1957.

NATIONALISM AND COMMUNISM IN THE ARAB WORLD: A RE-APPRAISAL

by A. V. SHERMAN

THE SURPRISE which the political developments of recent years in Egypt and Syria have occasioned is as good a hint as any that our ideas not only on Arab nationalism, but also on Communism, are due for critical revision, and that, so long as this apparently painful task is put off, we shall be due for further cycles of the illusion and disillusionment which have characterized the attitude of allegedly 'informed circles' on Middle Eastern affairs during the past decade.

In this essay I should like to suggest that the assimilation and 'Arabization' of Communist techniques and ideas by Arab nationalist movements was not accidental, a product of the whims or personal idiosyncrasies of one or two leaders, nor was it the fruit of a mistake made by the West at some point or other in 'antagonizing the Arabs', or failing to 'win them over' by some stratagem or other. On the contrary, it resulted from the inherently authoritarian tendencies of the Arab nationalist movements themselves.

I shall further suggest that Communism, as it reaches the Arab nationalists, is not a creed of social revolution aiming at justice for the underdog and based mainly on the aspirations of peasants and workers; it is the ideology and technique of ruling classes (or aspirants to power); of soldiers and bureaucrats. These ideas and techniques, far from leading towards the establishment of a new and more advanced form of society in the Middle East, serve to provide the military-bureaucratic classes with instruments and rationalizations for re-establishing the traditional Middle Eastern despotism, where exploitation of the inhabitants is effected through control of the levers of political power, based on armed force.

Such a society constitutes, in effect, the resurgence of the old Ottoman social structure, which was generally believed to have collapsed under the impact of the West. It proved more resilient, apparently because its social basis had remained unchanged, and reasserted itself in this new form, having digested what had been considered the disrupting developments in the military, economic, ideological, propaganda, and mass-communications fields, and indeed pressed them into service.

*　　*　　*　　*　　*

Anyone who takes the trouble to look through what was written on the Middle East in specialized journals and those which deal with foreign affairs during the decade 1946–55 will be struck with how little was written at all on the subject of Communist penetration in the Middle East, and how optimistic the experts were on this score. Most writers took it for granted that Communism and Arab nationalism are two antithetic and mutually exclusive forces, of which Arab nationalism—backed by Islam—was bound to prove overwhelmingly the stronger. These assurances emanated both from Arab nationalists, their sympathizers, and those influenced by them to a greater or lesser extent, and from Socialists or leftish circles which have traditionally taken it for granted that nationalism is an obstacle to the spread of Communism or Socialism, and that Arab army officers are not sufficiently 'politically educated' to take seriously to Communism.

True enough, those who gave the assurances made certain reservations: sympathizers of the Arab nationalist movements would warn that an unfavourable Western attitude to the Palestine question could open the door to pro-Soviet and even Communist sympathies out of sheer despair, while Socialists warned that inequality and poverty would prove 'fertile breeding-grounds for Communism'. But in neither case was actual evidence of Communist penetration adduced, and it was left to be tacitly assumed that the warnings were not intended to be taken literally but were meant rather as an admonition to accept the writer's remedies: to show a more favourable attitude to the Arab struggle against Israel, or to implement the writer's pet social theories, as the case may be.

It was taken for granted that serious Communist penetration would have to be through the medium of an organized Communist Party. As a rule, commentators attempted to gauge the attitude of

Arab nationalists to Communism and allied political problems not by empirical study of their actions and internal propaganda—where many disquieting signs could be observed by 1951—but by speculation as to what attitudes Arab nationalism would logically involve towards such problems as the cold war. This usually boiled down to guessing what the commentator in question would think if he were an Arab nationalist—hence the optimism.

Instead of trying to divine either the mental processes of individuals or the inherent logic of the nationalist idea, we had better study the character and dynamics of the Arab nationalist movements themselves, as organizations, groups, or social strata which either hold power or aspire to gain it, and whose aims and policies are not confined to specifically Arab affairs but run the whole gamut of political, economic, and social life over which governments or parties can aspire to rule.

Indeed, the vagueness and lack of consensus shown by Arab nationalist ideologists with regard to the tenets of Arab nationalism contrast strikingly with their emphatic insistence on extensive government control or power of intervention in social and economic life.

For example, when Nusseibeh[1] writes on the meaning of nationalism, we are hardly wiser at the end than at the beginning. 'What is needed most of all is a synthesis of current ideas into a coherent whole—a total conception of ideology conformable to the fundamental unity of human existence. . . .'; 'Nationalism is the principal instrument through which the Arab peoples are seeking to reconstruct the foundations of their life. . . .'; '. . . to bring out and inculcate what are thought to be unique national concepts. . . .' So writes the best-known exponent of Arab nationalism, but he admits that what is specific in the idea has yet to be worked out. Musa Alami, who has won wide respect for his practical social reform and rehabilitation activities in Jordan, writes that the 'Arab people are in great need of a myth . . .', but what the myth is and how it is to be made he does not add.

The new Egyptian Constitution, which is more a statement of Nasserist ideology than a practical framework for running a state, is as vague on the nature of Arab nationalism as it is insistent on whole-hearted devotion to its service.

But where the importance of massive state control over economic

---

[1] *The Ideas of Arab Nationalism*, by Hazem Zaki Nusseibeh, 1957. Nusseibeh's book is not only the most recent but the most coherent and, by Western standards, the best-written work on the subject. Nusseibeh has held important government and ministerial posts in the Jordan government, and is as near to being authoritative as one can be on such a subject.

life is concerned, Nusseibeh and the other sources are outspoken and exigent. 'Arab political thought is now irrevocably committed to positivism as the proper conception of the state. The increasing complexity of social organization has rendered wholly obsolete the earlier conception of the state as a limited agency. . . . This is particularly true in under-developed areas where governments represent the largest constellation of talents, skills, and resources [*sic*] and find themselves compelled to undertake responsibilities which in more developed countries depend upon private initiative. . . .'

To undertake these responsibilities he proposes the 'nationalization of life' as a corollary of nationalism, where 'social, political, and economic policies are keyed to the requisites of popular welfare as distinct from class privilege'. Remember that this was written and published in 1956, not by an opposition theorist but by a Minister in the Jordanian government, which was still in receipt of British subsidies.

The other sources of Arab nationalist ideology, like the Egyptian Constitution, Musa Alami, the Syrian-Lebanese Socialist-Renaissance Party (now ideologist for the colonels), are equally emphatic. All lay the same stress on 'positive social policies' and nationalization.[2]

*   *   *   *   *

Now, the possibility that a growing measure of state control over economic and social life, together with an increasing degree of actual state ownership, when combined with a one-party dictatorship and leader-cult, might produce a *communizing* régime, and that this communizing régime should look to the strongest and senior Communist Power for ideas, techniques, and aid, ought to have surprised almost no one: yet it amazed almost everybody. Because Communism in the Soviet Union had began with the seizure of power by a group which had developed a Communist (i.e. modified Marxist) ideology of sorts prior to its organized drive for power, it was somehow taken for granted that this was the only sequence in which Communism could arise, unless it were imposed directly by the Soviet army. The idea that a ruling class, or section of a ruling class, in any country might take over important elements from

[2] The Egyptian Constitution proclaims: '. . . having wrested our rights to a life of freedom after an uninterrupted struggle against enemy forces without and the forces of exploitation within . . . building a welfare society . . . the extinction of feudalism . . . the eradication of monopoly and the control of capitalistic influence over the system of government . . . the establishment of social justice . . .'

'mature' Soviet Communism where this suited its purpose was simply not mooted. This blind spot may well show that thinkers are still so dazzled by Communism's revolutionary past, its use of class-struggle symbols, of humanistic and internationalist slogans borrowed from the Western liberal tradition, that they continue to think of Communism in terms of the distortion of these ideals rather than as an actual society which has to be studied empirically through its institutions and behaviour like any other. In short, a clearer understanding of Communism, as well as of Arab nationalism, is needed to explain the impact of the one on the other.

The touching faith which Western observers placed in the Arab officer corps, and their certainty that army officers and bureaucrats would behave more or less like their European counterparts in playing a stabilizing role, sprang from the implicit assumption that the political and social orientation of these groups must be fundamentally similar to that of their Western counterparts. But owing to the completely different social structure of the Arab-Muslim world, the officers and intellectuals stood in quite a different relationship to society, and their basic political reactions were correspondingly different.

In Western society, army officers, higher civil servants, and bureaucrats form an integral part of a larger *élite*, or upper and upper-middle class, which includes property owners, industrial and commercial entrepreneurs, the higher clergy and higher intelligentsia, newspaper proprietors and editors, and many political figures. These groups are linked not merely by common interests, but first and foremost by ties of family and marriage, common education, background, and social life, which produce a common outlook and loyalties.

Muslim-Arab society, however, did not develop a single social *élite* unifying the wielders of political power and armed force, active figures in economic life, and intellectual activity into one social class. Social stratification was mainly along ethnic lines. Political power and the means of coercion were the prerogative of Muslims, and were the traditional and accepted source of economic and social privilege.

A large part of the economic activities and intellectual functions (apart from those with direct religious, legal, or political significance) were marginal to Muslim society proper, and were concentrated in the hands of religious minorities, i.e. various Christian denominations and Christian-ethnic groups, and Jews. These groups did not intermarry with Muslims, and shared no common educational background, values, or common loyalties with them, or, in fact, with other minority groups.

The officer class, police, bureaucrats, and 'lower intelligentsia',[3] on the other hand, were recruited from the Muslim population, the sons of officers and civil servants, of small landowners, tradesmen, and peasants. Islamic society has always provided avenues of social mobility through its educational institutions, which lead to government, military, and religious careers. Lacking the cultural inheritance and sense of responsibility inculcated by either feudal or patrician family background, this class of soldiers and white-collar workers (or job-seekers) is narrow-minded, under-educated, and uncultured (most of them come from semi-literate or illiterate homes, and in most cases their mothers and wives were completely illiterate), emotionally unstable and jealous, but quite ambitious. Their jealousy of the wealth and privilege of the Muslim upper classes was traditionally expressed as Muslim puritanism, while their jealousy of the commercial and industrial middle classes and higher intelligentsia found expression in the form of Muslim xenophobia. (Later, this resentment was to find modern totalitarian expressions.)

With the introduction of modern educational systems, this group grew numerically far more rapidly than the country's need for it or ability to support it. (In Egypt, the number of civil servants increased by about 25 per cent per year, thanks to the rapid and continuous expansion of the school system, eked out by falling standards, whereas industrial and agricultural production managed a few per cent per year increase at the best.)

Its rapidly growing numbers, both absolutely and relatively to other groups in the population, its access to the means of power (army, police, and political agitation), its ability to sway the urban masses by the use of their common symbol Muslim-nationalist xenophobia, all increased its political significance. At the same time, the vast increase in numbers of the civil service and army were obtained in part at the expense of a considerable deterioration in pay-scales and declining prestige. This combined with white-collar or intellectual under-employment to produce a feeling among graduates and students alike of having been deceived after making sacrifices in order to receive an education with the sole purpose of entering govern-

---

[3] I use the term 'lower intelligentsia', for want of a better one, to describe the large numbers of sons of poor and uncultured families, who received a secondary education and possibly took or attempted a university degree, with all the pretensions that this brings in a country where a large proportion of the population is illiterate, but without the training and discipline which would permit them either to appreciate their limitations or to think problems through logically. Very few of them know a foreign language well enough for serious reading, while there is very little in Arabic—either translations or originals—to provide the basis of a serious education, even for those who might be inclined to seek it.

ment service. (A study made in Egypt just after the Revolution showed that some 33 per cent of all those with primary education, 50 per cent of those with secondary education, and over 75 per cent of university graduates worked for the government. For Muslims alone the proportion would be higher still. In the other Arab states, the proportion is believed to be higher; one studies in order to get a government job.)

There could be no parallel in these societies to the political influence of the 'solid' middle classes in the Western sense of the word, the commercial, industrial, and learned classes, since the non-Muslims who formed the majority of these had no tradition of power-sharing, military service, or political life (excepting inside their own community). They had no special prestige or standing in the eyes of the masses, or the 'small men' whose prejudices are still first and foremost Islamic. They had no internal solidarity, nor that civic courage that the Christian burgher class in Europe had developed from late feudalism onwards. They lacked even a municipal tradition, and being without that tradition of political struggle which played so important a part in the genesis of European liberalism, their substitute for the class struggle was bribery, or the protection of a foreign Power.

The class above them, the superficial copy of a Western ruling class built around a monarchy, or republican institutions which had been built or renovated under British and French influence, lacked most of the essential qualities of its model. The European ruling classes were descended from feudal ruling classes (culturally, at least, if not always biologically), possessed ample courage, self-confidence, and capacity for leadership, and had proved capable of adjusting themselves to new social conditions and of absorbing and digesting rising economic, intellectual, and political *élites*. The ruling classes in most Arab countries, on the other hand, were prevented by religious and social factors from any symbiosis with their propertied and higher intellectual classes, while the lack of inculcated sense of duty and responsibility, which is needed to keep a ruling class on top in the long run, caused them to play a smaller part than they should have done in army and administration, which they left in the main to the 'lower intelligentsia'.

Moreover, in a world where fashionable ideas coming in from the West were all in favour of democracy, social change, and welfare, this upper class was hindered in developing the ideology—or *mystique*—of rule which is so essential to any class struggling to keep in the saddle.

The growing potential power of the officers and lower intelligentsia, therefore, combined with their increasing dissatisfaction at their lot, produced a revolutionary situation which had ample opportunity to express itself through the perpetual crises in foreign affairs and internal policies in which the upper classes found themselves, and which helped to sap their self-confidence. The social-nationalist movement was, in effect, the political expression of this revolution: it appears that every revolution needs its ideology.

As the officers and intelligentsia had no native political philosophy to fall back upon, apart from Muslim xenophobia, they had to pick out ideas to suit their needs from among the foreign ideas available, by a process of trial and error. Just as the Middle East takes its technological developments, economic and military organization, educational system, constitutions, and police systems from Europe, it also picks out its ideologies. But in shaping the ideas its own needs and context, this new revolutionary class altered them to such an extent that they finished up by meaning something quite different from, or even diametrically opposite to, what they had signified in their original habitat.

Nationalism, though originally a European importation, had been naturalized in one form or another in the Middle East for generations, so was ready to hand. The officers and lower intelligentsia subjected it to further transformation till it became the opposite of what it had signified when it first appeared in the Levant around the turn of the century. Then it had signified the antithesis of Ottoman-Islamic cosmopolitanism, a liberal trend based on language and culture as against conservative religiosity, aspiring to a secular liberal society on the western European model. The lower intelligentsia finally turned it into an extension of Muslim xenophobia, anti-liberal and anti-Western.

This nationalism, which took a couple of decades to reach its full development, brought them several practical advantages. Muslim xenophobia allowed them to harness the anti-Christian and anti-Jewish sentiments of the masses. 'Modern' anti-Westernism also provided an outlet for feelings of inferiority and insufficiency, which arose for a number of reasons, but not least among those who had been educated to emulate—or imitate—the West (which can hardly help being the world's yard-stick), and whose awareness of their own failure needed a scape-goat. Yet at the same time, the use of romantic nationalist slogans which recall the Greek and Italian national movements served to gain them the sympathy of many well-meaning intellectuals, politicians, and public in the West, who take it for granted that slogans always retain the same content, whatever the circumstances.

The fact that nationalism was a gambit in the internal struggle for power explains the apparent paradox that as Western presence or influence in the Arab countries became slighter or was eliminated entirely, anti-Western nationalism became stronger and more extremist. But being 'against' often non-existent foreigners was only half a programme, and the need for an ideology was widely felt. During the 'thirties and early 'forties Nazi and Fascist ideology made the greatest appeal; they had the advantage of being aggressive, simple, anti-British, anti-French, anti-Semitic, and of promising endless power opportunities and glory to young officers and radical intellectuals without being too precise about the uses to which power would be put. The influence of these ideological currents on the mental climate was far greater than would appear merely from the organization strength of Fascist movements built up on the Axis model, like Ahmed Hussein's Greenshirts and the People's Party of Syria.

*   *   *   *   *

Communism made no great impression at the time, mainly because of its insistence on retaining in its propaganda those elements which were distasteful to the radical intelligentsia and officers, like internationalism, denunciation of anti-Semitism, emphasis on the welfare and rights of workers and peasants, and anti-militarism—in short, all the trappings it had taken over from Western liberalism and whose use was still *de rigueur* in Europe. So long as Communism was presented in this guise it attracted only young intellectuals and semi-intellectuals from the religious-ethnic minorities, who discovered it as a rule via France or England, and accepted it as a variant of Westernism. The adoption of Communism by members of the Levantine communities, many of whom knew little or no Arabic, but used 'local French', Greek, or Armenian as their languages, helped, if anything, to repel Muslims.

It has lately become fashionable for commentators to attribute Soviet wooing of Arab nationalism to changes which took place after Stalin's death,[4] but in fact there is ample evidence to show that many of the major decisions had been taken by the end of the 'forties. After the stalemate in Europe and their victory in China the Soviet government was able to make the Middle East a major object of policy. ('Now that China is ours, we can turn to the Middle East,' was the way the new line was given at a Soviet embassy conference

---

[4] Two examples to hand at the time of writing are an article by Geoffrey Wheeler, *Political Quarterly*, special number on the Middle East, April–June, 1957, and a series of articles on the Middle East in the *New Statesman* of July, 1956, by the assistant editor Paul Johnson.

in 1949, according to a high-ranking defector who 'crossed over' early in 1951.)

Stalin did not prevent the drawing of conclusions from earlier set-backs in the Middle East; indeed, he purged several of the executives concerned. The Tudeh had failed to win over the masses in Persia with slogans of social reform when it had a free hand between 1941 and 1946; Communism had become unpopular in the Arab world because of Soviet support for Israel, without winning any compensating advantages among Israelis. It was decided, therefore, to place the main emphasis on working through anti-Western nationalist movements, whatever their ideology, rather than through the mostly negligible Communist Parties, a thesis which could be given respectability by references to Comintern proclamations on Asian affairs of the early 'twenties.

Soviet financial support was given to the Mullah Kashani (leader of a fanatically anti-Western Islamic movement which used assassination as one of its main arguments) and to other nationalist politicians in Persia, through the intermediary of merchants with whom the Soviet authorities traded. The Tudeh was diverted to supporting Mossadeq rather than to planning the social revolution—for the time being, at least.

When the Mossadeq affair had proved the method's efficacy it was decided to extend the new policy to the whole of the Middle East and Pakistan.[5] References to Arab nationalists in the Soviet Press and in local Communist publications swung from one extreme to the other. From 'fascists', 'reactionaries', 'exploiters', etc., they became 'patriots', 'national and progressive forces', or 'anti-imperialist and freedom-loving sections of the *bourgeoisie*'. The Soviet government began to invite delegations to 'peace campaign' meetings and other functions, and show them a 'world fit for bureaucrats to live in', and to send delegations of tame Muslim dignitaries and other specialists to Arab capitals. Soviet propaganda directed to Arab countries began to concentrate on anti-Westernism, praise of Arab nationalism and Arabs in general, and agitation against Israel; it was backed up by the anti-Semitic and anti-Israeli campaign in Russia and the satellites which culminated in the Prague trial and the Doctors' plot in 1952.

The Communist Parties inside the Arab countries were gradually brought into line, and one of the results was a marked change in

---

[5] The Communist plot in Pakistan involving high army officers and officials was nipped in the bud. But the lessons to be drawn from this development, from events in Persia, from the defector's explicit information, and from the re-orientation of Soviet and Communist policies towards the Middle East, were unable to make any serious impact on Western thinking.

their ethnic-religious composition, from Christians and Jews and members of minorities to Muslim Arabs.

* * * * *

After the *coup* in Egypt, the officers and their advisers among the radical intelligentsia were forced to seek methods of consolidating their power and finding allies at home and abroad. The idea of nationalizing property, first Jewish and foreign, later Egyptian limited companies', was especially attractive, since it provided funds for supporting an enlarged political apparatus and also placed an increased number of well-paid administrative posts at the disposal of the junta. As the resistance of the Wafd and the Brotherhood grew, and differences of opinion appeared among the junta themselves, the idea of a one-party dictatorship became more attractive.

Whereas acceptance of Communism—or elements of Communist policy—demands a sharp re-orientation of outlook on the part of Western officers or intellectuals, the Arab officers and radical intelligentsia, as we saw, had no such inhibitions, since neither the rights of property nor the rights of man were part of their own political traditions, but belonged to the baggage of ideas imported from the West.

They began to discover that the Soviet Union offered them techniques for bureaucratic anti-capitalism and new justification for confiscating property, procedures for economic control and organization; it offered methods of building up a party-state apparatus and manipulating the masses, of organizing propaganda at home and abroad.

Soviet-style anti-Westernism, with its more sophisticated arguments (compared with those of Arab xenophobes, that is to say), proved a valuable supplement to nationalist-Muslim anti-Westernism for use among both non-Muslims in Asia and those progressive circles in the West which are traditionally averse to violent nationalism but approve of blaming the ills of the world on to the West.

(There has been some discussion recently on the relationship of Islam to Communism. The older and comforting belief that Islam was automatically antagonistic to Communism was challenged, among others, by Professor B. Lewis, who claimed, on the contrary, that Islam had many elements in common with Communism, a viewpoint challenged in its turn by spokesmen of Arab nationalism and its sympathizers, with counter-quotations from Islamic theologian-jurisprudents and references to communizing tendencies in various Christian *milieux*—after all the first successful Communist revolution took place in a Christian country.)

The whole argument limps, on both sides, for two main reasons. In the first place, our social and historical sciences have not yet developed far enough in this field for us to know really what the essential characteristics of Islamic society are, or what are the specific contributions of Islam to the shaping of the Middle East. Secondly, even if we were to accept Professor Lewis's thesis, or that of his opponents, it would still not help us to understand why Communist influence is stronger in Egypt and Syria than in Turkey and Iraq, or what we should do about it.

In the foregoing analysis I have tried to demonstrate that Arab-Muslim society as it exists today is prone to Communist influence. The extent to which this susceptibility is caused by specifically Islamic traits or, alternatively, by social and historical factors, is of secondary importance.

*   *   *   *   *

As early as 1953, Albert Hourani pointed out that the new régimes in Syria and Egypt appeared to presage something of a return to the old Ottoman system of absolute rule by the military assisted by the bureaucracy and served by the ideologists (in the former case Islamic quietists, in the latter social-nationalists). In the old Ottoman Empire, however, where political power was the main source of social and economic privilege, the ruling class was satisfied to hold the levers of power (including, of course, taxation): It afforded a measure of toleration to diversity, non-conformism, or initiative, so long as they contained no challenge to its power; and left economic life very much to its own devices.

But the material conditions which permitted Ottoman indifference to economic organization and social life are being destroyed by the economic impact of the West. Large numbers of individual peasants, small craftsmen, traders and manufacturers, merchants and financiers dependent largely on the authorities for their business do not represent such social power as is wielded by the big firm, the large banking house, the cartel, or manufacturers' association. The films, newspapers, and radio, too, introduce quite a new element of power into political life.

The 'neo-Ottoman' ruling classes (or aspirants to rule), who wish to achieve the same measure of absolutist power under new conditions as the Ottoman enjoyed under the old, are committed, therefore, to seeking control over a much wider range of human activities. They are consequently intolerant of all independent concentrations of economic power or communications-media, and dare not permit the existence of independent foci of loyalty or intellectual activity. Not only opposition, but also non-conformism and non-participation by any segment of society turn out to be incompatible with their 'positivism'.

At the same time, disposal of a large and growing proportion of the national income is essential if they are to satisfy the economic demands of the intellectual proletariat. Every extra salaried post brought under the disposal of the state, or every function converted into a salaried post, increases their power over loyalties, as well as their control over activities.

In this way, Arab social-nationalism developed its totalitarian elements, which predispose it to Communist influence. True enough, totalitarianism does not *eo ipso* signify Communism; there have been other autochthonous varieties of totalitarianism which have remained free of Communist influence: besides German Nazism and Italian Fascism, there are examples like Chiang's Kuomintang régime, and Syngman Rhee's, which for one reason or another were precluded from comparison with European totalitarian movements.

But the Arab social-nationalist movements and régimes developed under the shadow of a powerful and technically advanced totalitarian empire in their vicinity, with a developed propaganda apparatus, economic resources which permit them to promise aid, and the facilities which allow them to send advisers and delegations and invite visits and, in general, to exert the influence that larger, stronger, and more developed states can exert on smaller, poorer ones.

Moreover, the feeling that they had a basic social outlook in common with the Soviet Union and the Communist world was comforting to the nationalists, since it offered the assurance that Soviet support, and indeed the support of Communists and fellow-travellers the world over, would turn out to be permanent and not a mere passing phase of Soviet foreign policy. Acceptance of certain Communist theses, including the essential goodness of the Soviet Union and its community of interest with the anti-imperialist nations, seemed to offer membership in a powerful club which gave arms and political support and demanded little in return—for the time being, at least.

Soviet propaganda has not only been given freedom to circulate inside Egypt and Syria, but is propagated extensively by the social-nationalist movements themselves. In Egypt, and in Syria, where the colonels and their advisers soon learned not only to imitate but to surpass their big brother, Nasser, and also in the Lebanon, Jordan, and Iraq (till its virtual suppression) the nationalist Press began to read like something out of the people's democracies with articles praising Soviet and Communist achievements. The West and its institutions, capitalism, Israel, Jews are pilloried as something essentially wicked and responsible for all the ills of the Arab world, and yet somehow stagnant, degenerate, and weak, while Communism and the U.S.S.R. are presented as something essentially dynamic, constructive, benevolent, and powerful.

A movement in search of a programme found itself drawn step by step into the Soviet-Communist orbit, therefore, not so much because of any special skills on the part of Soviet propagandists and diplomats, but largely by the interplay between its own inner logic and a world situation where Russia has the initiative while the West is on the defensive and lacks faith in its own remedies.

This fact makes nonsense of the strident assertions that Soviet influence in the area is the punishment for the West's sins over the Palestine issue from 1947 onwards, as pro-Arabs claim, of having failed to 'win over progressive elements among the Arabs', having 'leaned on reactionary and feudal elements', or of having 'failed to recognize the new forces of social progress and aspirations for higher living-standards and democracy at work in the area', as the Left still fondly believes.[6]

During the years 1947–49, which were decisive for the Palestine question, Britain was the most strongly and actively pro-Arab of the Powers, Russia the most actively pro-Zionist, while the U.S.A., as usual, vacillated between a number of policies. Yet Britain became the main target of Arab nationalist hatred. By now, the social-nationalists are, if anything, more anti-American than anti-French or British, in spite of Nasser's having been saved by U.S. intervention during the Suez affair.

As for strengthening 'progressive elements' in the Arab world: Arab-Muslim social structure and political traditions being what they are at their present stage of development, any strengthening of the state, politically or economically, *vis-à-vis* the individual citizen serves only to strengthen totalitarian tendencies and increase receptivity to Communist ideas. And economic aid to such governments, by strengthening them *vis-à-vis* their citizens, also brings Communism nearer. Far from having appeared as a sign of despair at Western repression, communizing tendencies have been strongest where the social-nationalists have gained most power—and even most Western support.

Those who claim that neglect of the masses, low living standards,

[6] The identity of these 'progressive elements' on whom the West should lean is seldom divulged; until recently the few Socialist critics who actually visited the area, or at least troubled to sort out names and parties, gave the junta and the Syrian Ba'ath Party as their 'progressive elements', though they would not be so certain today.

and lack of civic rights for the peasantry and urban poor bring out communizing tendencies have yet to demonstrate how and where. In none of the Arab countries has the Muslim peasantry played a political role (as distinct from Kurdish and Arab tribesmen or Allawi and Druse peasantry). The only group which seriously endeavoured to organize the peasantry instead of merely talking about it was the Egyptian Muslim Brotherhood, but this brought it no political benefits. The urban masses have been brought on to the scene for brief demonstrations or riots—rarely on social or economic questions—but so long as the rulers feel confidence in themselves, a battalion of troops can dispose of any mob in half an hour at the outside.

Furthermore, wherever the social-nationalists have achieved power, the standards of living of the masses and balanced economic development have been sacrificed to military adventures and to showy schemes like the Aswan steel plant and 'liberation province', which may be impressive to photograph and convincing to gullible foreign visitors (techniques of deception pioneered in the Soviet Union) but which place a heavy strain on the national economy and give very little in return, least of all employment.

Soviet experience has shown that excuses can always be found to postpone improvements in the standard of living of the masses and developments towards political freedom. If the Russian postponements can still find pleas of justification among non-Communists after forty years of Soviet power, how long will they not justify continued poverty and repression in the far more backward Arab countries?

The tendency in the West to include Arab nationalists in the ranks of the 'forces of the future with whom we must come to an understanding' and their opponents as 'reactionaries' and 'feudalists doomed to be swept away', has led to over-estimates of the nationalists' strength which are tantamount to sheer defeatism. When King Hussain of Jordan brought in loyal regiments and deposed the social-nationalist government, lib-labs and right-wing supporters of Arab nationalism united in prophesying his immediate downfall: that the 'masses' and educated elements would not stand for it was proclaimed by the *Observer* and the *New Statesman* alike. Much the same abuse and prophecies were directed against the Iraqi government, for its temerity in joining the Baghdad Pact, and against the Lebanese government for accepting the Eisenhower doctrine, yet these three governments proved to be quite stable once they made up their minds to fight back; will-power was perhaps more important than any other form of aid.

The social-nationalists are still confident that they can take over elements from all ideologies which suit their purpose and flirt with Communist Russia without losing their virginity, but their optimism may prove to be unjustified. The centralization of political and economic power, the 'organized spontaneity', organized hate-campaigns, grandiose economic plans which make the country more and more dependent on foreign economic aid, the enlarged bureaucracy, army, police, and political apparatus, which have a vested interest in increased nationalization and still wider powers, will all make it increasingly difficult to dismount from the back of the tiger. The social-nationalists have been actively indoctrinating their younger generation with a belief in the righteousness of the Soviet Union and the wickedness of the West; it would not be so easy to reverse these beliefs at a time of crisis.

In view of the fact that many elements of the situation in the Arab world can be found in other Asiatic and African countries, the possibilities of the Levantine 'short-cut' to Communism are most disturbing, and the question naturally arises how it is possible to turn the tide. The experience of Turkey, Persia, and Iraq, each in its own way, encourages guarded optimism that, given the right conditions, Islamic society can develop its own anti-bodies to social-nationalism and its communizing implications.

It has become fashionable to compare Nasser, the series of military dictators in Syria, and their emulators elsewhere in the Arab world, with Kemal Atatürk. From the point of view of historical parallel it would be far more profitable to compare the Nasser, Shishakli, or Serraj régimes with the short-lived 'young Turk' governments set up by Western-influenced officer-intellectual groups in revolt against the Hamidian régime. Unlike Atatürk, who established his political régime as a victorious general and who had real control over his brother officers as well as over the country as a whole, the Young Turks were goaded into action by a series of defeats which Turkey had suffered; they aimed, like Nasser, at restoring former glories, and they finally dragged Turkey into even worse disasters than Abdul-Hamid had done. Kemal's revolt was directed as much against them and their ideology as against the Sultan, though of course he had begun as one of them and shared many of their assumptions.

Though Kemal's dictatorship of the soldier-bureaucrat class led to the establishment of one-man party rule and strong *étatist* tendencies in economic life, it brought no proneness to Communist influence, if only for the good reason that Turks of all classes traditionally viewed Russian expansion southwards as the greatest danger to their existence, not only politically but even biologically, and this predisposed them against accepting Russia's ideology.

Following the drastic scaling down of non-Muslim participation in Turkish economic life after the First World War and the stepping-up of state enterprise, a new Turkish industrial and commercial class began to grow up. As far as its social background was concerned it was an offshoot of the Turkish Muslim military-bureaucratic class. This sub-class, with its roots in the power-wielding *élite*, has been able to play a political role, which the minorities could never aspire to. It played an important part in producing the mental climate which assured the victory of the Democratic Party, though, as the Menderes-Bayar government's adventures prove, they are far from having things all their own way.

These developments, together with massive American aid encouraged by Turkey's genuine opposition to Soviet expansionism, have all helped to produce attitudes and social structure which are leading away from social-nationalism.

(In light of the present fashion of preaching land reform—meaning land distribution—as a catalyst to social progress, it is worth noting that in Turkey the predominance of peasant ownership and the rarity of large-scale capitalist farming or of a resident rural upper class has been one of the main causes for the disappointing slowness of social, economic, and educational progress in the countryside—in spite of huge government expenditures devoted to this aim—which still endangers the whole of Turkey's social reform.)

In Persia, the first country where Russia tried out its system of aiding the 'right-wing nationalists' (as they were called earlier), the royal family, supported by the army and upper-class intellectuals, proved capable of defeating the social-nationalist-Communist coalition, which turned out to be far weaker than we had been led to believe. In Persia, too, the danger of Russian imperialism has always been of real concern.

In Iraq, though fear of Russian invasion is limited to smaller circles, Arab social-nationalism is tainted by its use as a Trojan horse by the Egyptian-Syrian governments. The social-nationalist movement has been weakened partly by the determined repressive measures undertaken by Nuri Sa'id, and partly by the impetus given to middle-class employment by oil-financed development plans and the mass exodus of the Jews.

* * * * *

Any study of the Western impact on the Middle East must be ready to turn a critical eye on the West itself. Though Russia is the beneficiary of Arab social-nationalism and its absorption of Communist thought and methods, the ideas often arrived from, or via, the West in the first place. Significant and vocal groups of the

Western intelligentsia, though not necessarily Communists or even fellow travellers, have at one time or another taken for granted that the Soviet Union is of a generally progressive character and a model for rapid progress in backward countries. Ideas regarding the out-modedness of capitalism and the generally sinful or impure character of private property, and the unquestioned superiority of state ownership, have had long periods of currency in the West.

It would be interesting to know to what extent the guilt complex of sections of the Western intelligentsia creates the need for objects of identification outside their own class or society—in particular for a proletariat or a 'young nation' in revolt. But there can be no doubt that these circles have encouraged Arab nationalists to find rationalizations for blaming everything which is short of perfection in their countries on to the West. And far from 'liberating them from inhibitions', as these sympathizers believed, this merely aggra-vates one of the Arab intellectual's worst shortcomings—his tendency to blame everything on to factors beyond his control and to shirk self-criticism (traits whose causes have to be sought in Arab family structure and education).

When Western intellectuals compensated for their own degree of 'alienation' by teaching the social-nationalists that they were the 'rising young forces', and that they should impress their power upon society in the form of expanded government control, they did not stop to ask whether, in fact, government was not already over-powerful in the Middle East; to what extent it was capable of implementing new social and economic policies; and whether, indeed, it was so 'scientific and rational' to accept as axiomatic that solutions, whose applicability even to their native West was by no means proven, should automatically be a cure for the ills of other regions. But the more the tide turned against their ideas in the advanced countries (the defeat of Labour in Britain, Australia, and New Zealand; the swing to the right in the U.S.A., etc.), the more eagerly they turned to backward countries to see their ideas vindicated. This is one aspect of the 'impact of the West' which urgently needs attention.

As we see, the result is to intensify some of the worst features of Middle Eastern political life. Indeed, this sublime assurance that they could lay down the law on the Middle East, on the basis of a few hurried conversations and the mastery of 'progressive' catch-phrases, without any knowledge of the history, social structure, and problems of the area, is a reminder that brashness is not a monopoly of the Arab radical intelligentsia. The difference is that Western societies as a rule are strongly enough built to withstand such foibles by fringes of one kind or another, whereas in the Middle East it is the different ratio between fringe and centre which is so disturbing.

THE FUTURE OF CULTURE IN ARAB SOCIETY

by DR. MUHAMMAD KAMEL AYYAD

EVEN A CURSORY comparison between the present standards of culture in the Arab countries and those of half a century ago would show that very great progress has been achieved in this sphere of our life. This is apparent in the far greater number of literate people and of educational institutions, as well as in the greater volume of writing, translation, and publication; above all in the ever-growing variety of research methods, ways of thinking, and means of expression.

As is generally the case, however, with historical developments, this progress has not been absolute and all-embracing. It would not be difficult to cite examples of retrogression in some departments of our cultural life. For instance, we used to take more interest in our own religious and literary heritage fifty years ago than we do now. In the fields of religious reform and the study of Arab and Islamic history, we have nothing to match the movement of Imām Muhammed Abduh or the treatises of El-Alusi and Jurji Zeidan. In our poetic output, again, we do not find anything comparable in fertility and power to the works of Hafiz Ibrahim,[1] Ahmed Shawqi,[2] Ma'aruf Al Rusafi,[3]

[1] Hafiz Ibrahim, 1871–1932. Born in Cairo of poor parents and studied in the Military Academy. He is considered one of the two best modern poets of Egypt, the other being Shawqi.

[2] Ahmed Shawqi, 1868–1932. Born in Cairo and raised in the Court of Khedive Abbas II. He was called the Poet of Princes because most of his poetry was composed in praise of the royal family. Joined the nationalist movement and was regarded as the greatest of the period's poets.

[3] Ma'aruf Al Rusafi, 1875–1945. Born in Baghdad, was known in Iraq, Istanbul, and Jerusalem. Famous for his political poetry, especially in criticism of the Hashemite court.

or Jamil Sudqi Al Zahawi.[4] And perhaps the sphere in which our cultural life has most noticeably lagged behind is that of scientific journalism, which should, on the contrary, have made the biggest advances to keep pace with our increasing needs. No one with a concern for our culture can help deploring the degree to which the standard of our scientific and literary publications has fallen off—publications which, in the past, were well-known for their scholarship and their dissemination of true learning.

There is, however, no doubt that the cultural evolution of the Arab countries, which began over a century ago and has been accelerated in the last four decades, has been in many ways a genuine progress and has had salutary effects. Knowledge has spread, the horizons of thought have widened, specialization has been fostered, scientific studies have matured; while literature and the arts, freer from convention and imitation, have become more imaginative and creative. Progress is evident first and foremost in the language: the Arabic spoken by the masses has improved and developed, while the written language has become easier, lighter, and more flexible, better adapted to the capacity of the masses. The complaint of certain conservatives that our contemporary writers deviate from 'the ways of the Arabs' is quite unjustified. The ways of the Arabs, despite their age-old tendency to imitation, have changed with the times, and we cannot deny living authors their right to adopt a style of their own. For all its recent progress, Arabic is a language in need of reform and innovation, in order to keep up with the general cultural advance and adapt itself to the requirements of an age of technology, invention, and new ways of thinking.

* * * * *

No one denies the fact that the recent cultural progress of the Arab world has been the result of its encounter with the nations of the West. For four centuries after the raids of the Crusaders, Moguls, and Tatars had been succeeded by the Turkish conquest, the Arabs were living in a state of cultural obscurity and stagnation. They began to awaken early in the nineteenth century, when the Ottoman Empire was beginning to disintegrate; when the European Powers were raiding its borders, trying to interfere in its domestic affairs and aspiring to annex its territories. The Arab regions of that Empire were of the highest importance to British and French imperialism, owing to their geographical situation on the world's trade routes;

[4] Jamil Sudqi Al Zahawi, d. 1936. A pioneer of poetic innovation in Iraq. Wrote on many topics, and was reputed for his pessimism, scepticism, and feminism.

Napoleon's conquest of Egypt was primarily a manifestation of the competition between these two great imperial Powers. But the presence of the French in Egypt left a deep impression on the minds of the population; it was their first meeting with the superior strength of the civilization of the West; and it awakened them to their need of Western learning, science, arts, and crafts.

Although the early attempt of Sultan Selim III to organize the Turkish army upon modern principles had been abortive, Egypt succeeded in adopting many European ideas in building up its army and navy and in founding scientific and industrial institutions. Egypt also sought the aid of foreign experts and dispatched study missions to the West. There were similar movements of modernization within the Ottoman Empire, extending also to the Arab countries; but these efforts encountered many difficulties and were not very fruitful. Meanwhile, Western interest in the Arab domain was growing: Western nations set up consulates and commercial agencies in several countries; Western goods and manufactures found their way into Arab markets. But the most effective imperialist infiltration was that of the missionaries: the schools and hospitals that they founded were ubiquitous sources of unrest and discord among the various communities. Missionary schools provided the youth with a superficial and limited education which could only produce confusion of thought and disagreements. These schools did much, however, to spread the knowledge of foreign languages, and to facilitate those contacts between the East and the West which gradually familiarized the Arabs with Western culture.

Moreover, the French invasions of Algeria, Tunisia, and Morocco; the British occupation of Egypt; the conquest of Libya by the Italians, and the policy of Turkization pursued by the Society of Union and Progress in all the Arab countries—all these things aroused the Arabs to the necessity of a political struggle for independence. It was natural that, at the same time, our attention was directed to the revival of our own cultural heritage and to the memories of our historic glories as the greatest incentive to the re-creation of national consciousness. We could point to the examples of several nations— to the Greeks, Serbs, Bulgars, the Italians, and the Germans—in whose steps we should follow. All these factors—the memories of past glories, the impact of Western culture, the intensification of Turkish oppression, and a realization of the menace of Western imperialism—played their part in the outbreak of Arab revolts during the First World War and the subsequent rise of liberation movements in every Arab country.

Although we have no doubt whatever that the Arabs will at last be liberated from the last vestiges of imperialism and foreign control, and will advance together to a glorious future, they will have to study their situation and circumstances very closely if they are to overcome all the difficulties, avoid the obstacles, and make rapid progress. Germany and Italy were able to attain their position in the last century, and they have recovered their position in the world after military collapse in the last world war, because they were not behind other European countries in their economic, social, and cultural development, but perhaps even in advance of them in some respects. Not so the Arab countries. The German and Italian attitude to their cultural inheritance from the past also differs essentially from that of the Arabs.

Since the beginning of the present century the Arabs, well aware of the material strength of Western civilization, have realized that they will never be able to resist Western imperialism until they adopt its methods. Thus the practice of borrowing from Western culture continued uninterruptedly since about the middle of that century, but did so without definite plans or aims. One need only examine the list of works translated into Arabic during this long period to see what chaos has reigned in our cultural life. Not only is the number of works translated small; but they have been chosen simply according to the translators' personal preferences, or because they were easiest to translate or were expected to have a good market. The Arabs consequently remained unaware of the greatest and most representative works of Western literature and of its essential and fundamental tendencies. For example—as the German Orientalist Professor Carl Becker remarked in one of his classes—of all the works of Schopenhauer, the only one translated into Arabic was his polemic against women; a piece of work which, though it may represent the philosopher's personal opinion, certainly does not reflect a cultural attitude prevalent in the West.

This cultural chaos is still more strikingly illustrated in the studies relating to our own cultural heritage where, strange to say, our encounter with the West has been the most important factor. For the Orientalists of the West were ahead of us in collecting the earliest Arabic manuscripts, editing the works of our ancestors with infinite care and scholarship, scrutinizing them with depth and discrimination, and in appreciating their merits; whereas our own efforts were, until very recently, limited to publishing the more trivial of them, plagiarizing the work of the Orientalists and republishing it, mostly in distorted versions. And although this state of affairs has changed for the better in recent years, we still lag behind Western scholars in the study of these works, in showing their significance in the advance of world civilization, and in using them to illuminate our own history and civilization.

While we do not deny that some of the Orientalists have been motivated by purely objective scientific aims and have had no political axes to grind, we are at the same time aware that most of them were, and still are, engaged in promoting imperialist designs. They often distort our history and misrepresent our culture; and we, on our side, often fall into the trap, repeat their opinions, and take them for our guides.

I do not intend here to go into the distortions and misrepresentations of these Orientalists in any detail, but there is one general aspect I must deal with, because it is of importance for the orientation of our culture, although this is a point upon which many hold different opinions. I refer to the contention that the nature and destiny of the East is fundamentally different from that of the West in respect of culture and civilization.

Following the rise of racial theories towards the end of the nineteenth century, some European writers—particularly in Germany—rejected the idea of the unity of world civilization and culture: they introduced distinctions between various cultures, each of which, they said, had a unique 'temperament' of its own. Oswald Spengler, the most famous of these writers, enumerated eight basic civilizations in history, and claimed that they differed completely in their respective cultures, their ways of looking at life and the universe, in their beliefs, traditions, and habits, their sciences and arts—and even in their conceptions of mathematics and the natural sciences. Among these eight civilizations Spengler includes 'Arab civilization' together with the Babylonian, Assyrian, Phoenician, Aramaic, Judaic, and Christian, as all of a type which he distinguishes as 'Magian'—as a culture radically different from that of the West today.

A distinction of the same kind is assumed by most writers who contend that the Eastern cultures are more 'spiritual' than the Western. Their definitions of this alleged spirituality are diverse: some identify it with religious faith and all that this implies for the purification of the soul and moral behaviour; others associate it with mystical beliefs in self-revelation and emancipation from the senses. They agree, however, in regarding spirituality as dependent upon intuition and emotion in opposition to rational thinking based upon sensory observation, experiment, and the objective attitude. The intention is clear—to emphasize the difference between Western and other peoples, encourage the latter to cling to their own traditions, habits, and ways of thought; and to dissuade them from adopting modern culture and thereby liberating themselves from Western domination.

That is why we find Orientalists at work in the Foreign Ministries of Western governments, assiduously editing and publishing the works of Muslim and Hindu mystics; and fostering the opinion that there is no hope of saving world civilization from decline and disaster except in a return to the 'spirituality' of the East. A year ago, a representative of the Rockefeller Institute came to the Syrian University to explain the aims of that institution and its interest in promoting cultural projects among all peoples. But when some of the teachers urged the need of the university for laboratories and technical equipment, this American visitor immediately made excuses, pointing out a number of difficulties in the way of acquiring such things. As soon as the discussion turned towards the subject of Islamic mysticism, on the other hand, he pledged assistance to any institution set up for studies of such immense importance.

To understand this Western interest in the 'spiritual' culture of the Orient, we should do well to study the opinions published by certain Western scholars and statesmen after the First World War. These gentlemen—notably the well-known Dutch Orientalist Snouck Hurgronje—explained the unrest and revolt which had then broken out in the colonies as consequences of the assimilation of Western ideas among Eastern peoples. He pointed out that the leaders of the revolutionary movement in Indonesia had studied at the University of Leiden in Holland, and advised his government to send no more Indonesian youths to study in the West, but to set up a university in Indonesia, devoted especially to Oriental culture.

The English were ahead of the others in following this practice. France, on the other hand, pursued a policy of cultural extermination in Algeria and Tunisia, countries situated not too far from France for the French to expand into them and take the lands of the original settlers, or for some of the latter to be absorbed into France. Thus the French have sought to extend their language and some aspects of their culture to North Africa. With the expansion of France's colonies and spheres of influence, however, French statesmen began to advocate adoption of the British and Dutch policy. We had an intimation of this trend when the College of Ancient Literatures was created in Damascus in 1933. A famous French Orientalist came from Paris to help compose its curricula. He emphasized the importance of concentrating upon Arabic rhetoric and figures of speech, and upon the study of the various schools of Arabic grammar; but he opposed the teaching of comparative literature, or of modern criticism, or of the art of the novel.

*   *   *   *   *

The scope of this paper does not permit me to delve into the question of 'spiritual' versus 'material' culture, or of the alleged difference between the Orient and the Occident. But what do we mean by Orient and Occident, and where is the dividing-line between them? Are there not obvious differences between Anglo-Saxon culture and Latin culture? Are the Spaniards and the Italians nearer, in temperament, sentiments, and ways of thinking, to the Scandinavians and the English than they are to the Egyptians, the Lebanese, or the Syrians? Was Japan prevented by her Oriental nature and situation from adopting Western culture and civilization? Lastly, did not the civilization of, e.g., ancient Egypt when it was in full flower spread over most of the world, followed by Greek civilization, and then by Arabic Muslim culture? And did they not benefit all nations by promoting the progress of the human race?

Why, then, this desire that modern civilization should be reserved to the Western nations and that other peoples should cling to their ancient cultures? Did not Western culture, in its day, borrow most of its elements from the Greeks, the Chinese, and the Arabs?

From these and similar questions we arrive at the inevitable conclusion—that our traditions do not forbid our borrowing from contemporary Western culture. Indeed, apart from a group of conservatives in certain Arab countries—which has fortunately dwindled to a small minority—no one among us disputes the necessity of such borrowing. There is a group, who call themselves moderates, who urge that our borrowing should be limited to what is good in Western civilization, to the adoption of those elements which can be harmonized with our traits, traditions, and customs. The weakness of this argument, however, lies in the difficulty of defining the characteristics that we must preserve, or clearly distinguishing the bad from the good in Western culture. In any case, it is advisable, when we talk of our culture, traditions, and customs, that we should trace them to their roots in history, consider the circumstances in which they were first formed, and then modified and remoulded. Above all, we must ask ourselves whether we ought to preserve everything that we have from the past; whether the persistence of a custom for one, or ten, generations entitles it to preservation, even though circumstances have changed—even if, in fact, it was originally the product of a period of decline or of foreign domination.

We are all—conservatives, moderates, and modernists—proud of our Arabic culture in its days of splendour, of its ability to adapt itself, to widen its horizons and keep abreast of world progress. Indeed, our ancestors were prompt borrowers from all nations, and that on a very large scale. They borrowed the methods of government, administration, and finance, as well as the arts of architecture, music, and decoration, from the Persians and Byzantines; irrigation and agriculture from the Nabateans; mathematics from the Hindus, and the manufacture of paper and ceramics from the Chinese. They also went to the Greeks for medicine, mathematics, physics, and philosophy; nor did they fear to study other creeds and religions, such as Judaism, Christianity, Mazdaism, and mysticism, all of which they discussed and by some of which they were influenced.

Moreover, the successive phases of this borrowing from other cultures reflect the advances of society and the multiplication of its needs. We find, for instance, that it begins with vital, practical requirements, such as administration and postal services; then it turns to medicine, arithmetic and geometry, the arts and crafts, and last to science and philosophy. This is the natural course of the evolution of a culture, in reaction to man's direct needs and his environment. With the progress of societies, however, and their mutual encounters, we find that ideas acquire an existence of their own; they become independent of the people who arrived at them through experience; they begin, in their turn, to influence life and even to create a life of their own. But to be effectual, they must still fulfil the real needs of a society; otherwise they will lose their driving force, or may even become causes of confusion, stagnation, or decline.

Arab culture has played an important part in the creation of modern civilization. The Renaissance in Europe was a direct result of its impact upon Europeans when the Arabs were in Spain and Sicily, and during the Crusades. Europeans derived much of their mathematical science, algebra, physics, medicine, and astronomy from Arabic works. Those of Abu Bakr el-Razi, Avicenna, Ibn Rushd, Ibn el-Haitham, and Abu el-Qasim el-Zahrawi continued to be studied in European universities until the sixteenth and seventeenth centuries. The influence of Arabic literature was not confined to the rise of lyric poetry in the south of France and to Dante, Boccaccio, and Cervantes. It is still evident in the works of Goethe and Rueckert early in the nineteenth century.

*   *   *   *   *

But let us return to the present position of Arabic culture in its relation to the world. First, consider the difference between that position and what it was in the periods when the Arabs did borrow and assimilate foreign cultures. We are now weak, with most of our homelands under foreign occupation or influence, in sharp contrast to the situation of our ancestors who were conquerors and rulers. Such a contrast has deep psychological consequences. The dangers of it naturally incline us to cling to our own customs and traditions and fight shy of Western culture. . . . Unlike our ancestors, we face the world with a glorious past, and with a rich cultural heritage which, however, is old. This may be an incentive to awakening and progress, but it can also be a heavy burden, hindering us from free, confident movement into the future.

There is another difference. The cultures from which our ancestors borrowed were dead or moribund—the Greek, for instance—and the social set-up in which they had sprung and flourished was no more; whereas the modern culture which we seek to emulate is still in a state of growth and development, striding on from strength to strength within an energetic, dynamic society. Every day it is growing in extent and complexity.

This age is unprecedented in the predominance of mechanized industry, the multiplication of inventions and of the means of communication. Distances have shrunk until man's world has become one indivisible whole: the destinies of all nations are now interconnected and no nation can remain aloof from the others. And in such a world, pervaded by competition and strife, only the strong can survive—which means those who are equipped with the latest means for carrying on the struggle in science, industry, propaganda, and organization. It is a world of ever-quickening movement where there is no salvation for any nation that lags behind.

The most important conclusion to which this compels us is that we cannot choose our ways of living and fighting, to our own liking: they have to fit into a pattern quite literally imposed upon us. During the past fifty years, while we were discussing what our attitude to modern culture ought to be, Western civilization was already flooding us with its industrial products, with its own laws and ideologies. During that period our public life developed in ways we had never imagined would be possible for generations to come.

The transformation of our life is manifest, not only in our adoption of new industrial techniques and inventions, but also in architecture, in the expansion of cities and the planning of them; in administration and government, commerce, education; and in the changes taking place in the status of the family, the position of women, and in social relations generally. Many of these phenomena have penetrated far into the country, where they are revolutionizing ways of life that are thousands of years old. In all Arab countries there is a movement of the villagers into the cities and industrial centres, where they mingle with the new working class whose consciousness, solidarity, and organization are steadily developing. Most significant of all, however, are the collapse of feudalism in most of these countries and the demands of the rising masses for their rights, for higher standards of living and a general amelioration of their condition. And these countries now occupy a prominent position in international affairs, and in the struggle between the

Great Powers, owing to their strategic situation and their oil resources.

It is not for us to decide whether all this is good or bad, whether we approve or disapprove of it. Our problem is—what ought we to do in order to hold our own under these conditions; how can we succeed on this battlefield of modern life?

The first task imposed upon us is, undoubtedly, to increase production and develop our national wealth in order to keep pace with the growth of population, meet the demands of the new civilization, and guarantee the necessary implements of strength. This requires a concentration upon the exploitation of our agricultural resources. We have to build up industries that rely upon agricultural products, as well as light industries whose raw materials can be easily obtained. Nor can the Arab world do without armament industries of various kinds.

All this implies scientific knowledge and technical expertise: it calls for the training of skilled workers and good managers. Its success also depends upon the planning of our economic, social, and cultural life, for such planning has become indispensable to modern society. And by this we mean the large-scale planning which only governments can carry out and which embraces every aspect of public activity.

Modern economic and social problems cannot be dealt with except by organization and planning, i.e. by the drawing-up of long-range programmes to define aims, to fix an order of priority for the various projects, to decide upon the stages of their execution and provide the means necessary for their implementation. Planning necessarily includes the educational and cultural development which has so much influence upon economic as well as social life. Modern governments have for some time past been extending their control over educational policy, and also allocating funds to cultural institutions such as scientific and artistic bodies, museums, exhibitions, theatres, radio, and the cinema. Most governments still spend too little in these directions, however, and although they exercise a certain amount of direction and supervision over cultural institutions, they do so in a poor and irregular manner, with little reference to their social and economic planning. Since we are here concerned with the future of culture in Arab society, we must try to elucidate its connection with planning, enlarging a little upon the content of culture and its effects upon public life and national renaissance.

*　　*　　*　　*　　*

Culture (*thaqafa*) is a new word in Arabic, which we use as the equivalent of the Latin word '*cultura*' meaning originally the tilling and tending of the land. The word has acquired its present meaning in French and most European languages only in recent times. In German, the word '*Kultur*' signifies the spiritual aspect of a civilization, as distinct from the material and organizational aspects covered by the term '*Zivilisation*'. For what we mean by culture the Germans use another word, '*Bildung*', which means the giving of a shape or form to things; and that is nearer to the meaning of the Arabic word '*Tathqeef*'—literally, the tending of leaves and hence figuratively the tending and improvement of the mind.

In its widest connotation culture embraces science, literature, the arts, educational systems, ways of entertainment—indeed, everything that determines the behaviour and regulates the relations of individuals in a society, and enables them to express their needs, desires, dreams, and opinions. Culture in this sense cannot be understood apart from its time and place, since it expresses a certain phase in the evolution of a human society, its style of life in a given environment. The dominant factor in a culture, therefore, is determined by its historical and social circumstances. Thus, at one time science may be dominant, and at other times literature, art, religion, or materialism.

Culture is transmitted from generation to generation through tradition, teaching, imitation, and suggestion, but its content changes and develops at varying rates according as it is or is not enriched by discoveries, inventions, and by borrowing from cultural developments elsewhere. As the common legacy from the past, which is also the foundation for future endeavours, culture is that which enables the members of a society to live purposefully together, in harmony with their inner selves and with their environment. Its progress is the condition of cohesion and solidarity in any growing society.

At the same time, changes in the social structure change, in their turn, the pattern of culture. The higher cultural activities cannot arise before the formation of an educated class and an *élite*, and this again is the product of prior social conditions. Thus the cultural attainments of individuals are related to, and limited by, the state of progress attained by their society. We cannot expect the appearance of a brilliant architect, physicist, or geographer in a primitive agricultural community.

There may be a scarcity or even absence of the creative impulse at a certain period in the history of a nation. Such a phenomenon does not mean that a sudden change has occurred in their human capacity, and it is no explanation to say that talent and genius are inexplicable phenomena; we have to look for the cause in the social environment. There we shall find evidence that the flowering or the decline of a culture depends upon the presence or absence of a group within the society who can devote themselves to study, meditation, and contemplation—a group usually called the *élite*, or the select few. The function of such a group is to mobilize the surplus spiritual energy which society does not use up in its day-to-day struggle for existence; to provide the means by which this energy can be sublimated and the primitive urges of the masses can be directed towards knowledge, the appreciation of beauty, and towards self-expression. In the nature of things such a group attains to a privileged status in society. But if it presumes upon this and monopolizes culture, it inevitably stagnates and then disintegrates, as did the priestly castes in ancient societies. On the other hand, such a group will increase in vitality and productivity if it is open to the talented of all classes— provided it remains select enough to maintain its distinctive characteristics, and assumes the guidance and leadership of society.

If the *élite* is subjected to infiltration by waves of other elements, if it splits into antagonistic groups, or if its membership exceeds a certain limit, then it loses the quality of leadership and fails to make a deep imprint upon society. In such a case the masses will have no one to direct and sublimate their desires and drives, which therefore degenerate into raw ambitions and base urges, into psychological complexes and confusion. And this finally sets up a craving for new sensations, one after another in rapid succession, excitements which are of no permanence or value. Modern metropolises have become full of such masses, clamouring for the entertainments, intoxications, and illusions which the traffickers in culture are all too ready to supply: and, although here and there we find men sincerely devoted to real culture, who try to disseminate knowledge and good taste, their efforts are nullified by the absence of a public with constancy enough to follow their lead and example.

We begin to detect similar developments imperilling the future of culture in the Arab world, and they can be forestalled only by combined cultural and social planning.

* * * * *

Now that public opinion is everywhere preoccupied with politics and international relations, because of their direct bearing upon everyday life and security, too little attention is paid to cultural affairs. Though it is generally realized that culture is the mainstay of civilization, it is commonly regarded as an independent function, quite separate from economic and social life. It is surprising to find this view still current even among scientists and men of culture— even more prevalent among them, one may say, than among the populace. The increasing division of labour, the rise of institutions specializing in cultural departments, and the fact that the *élites*, in times of peace, devote themselves to intellectual pursuits that are not always free from subjectivity—these things obscure the intimate relationship between culture and society. A highly developed intellectuality is capable of creating an imaginary world which it can elaborate in isolation from its real surroundings. For instance, towards the end of the eighteenth century, when the German middle classes failed to transform their political and social condition, they turned inwards to seek solace in dead historical reminiscence and illusory idealist theories; transferring their cultural life into an imaginary sphere where they could be alone with themselves and their dreams.

One consequence of the distortions of the idea of culture by the various factors we have mentioned above is that, having accepted its separation from everyday life, many people tend to regard culture as a luxury or an ornament. This is a source of many erroneous theories and sterile developments in science, literature, education, and the arts. A theory of 'art for art's sake', for instance, is still widely held in spite of critical exposures of its futility. History shows that art has always been an effective weapon in the service of gods, kings, and governments, but also in the hands of revolutionaries defending the rights of peasants, workers, and the populace. If poets think their art is superior to the life and preoccupations of the people, that is only a sign of the poets' sterility. They too are products of their age and their community; nay, they ought to be nearer than others to the people and more responsive to the challenge of the times. This does not mean that they should go into politics; the poet should avoid involvement in politics in the narrower sense, in order to keep a comprehensive vision of life. The poet who cannot see far enough to warn his people of what is to come is an anomaly; he lacks contact with life or has defective vision; and in either case he should leave poetry and enter the struggle of life with the others.

It is a sign of promise for the Arab literary renaissance that many Arab writers have lately been discussing the role of the man of letters in society, and even 'the mobilization of literature' for the service and liberation of the people. We must, however, distinguish the genuine man of letters from the writer who turns into an official, merely executing orders or disseminating propaganda. The mission of the man of letters today is to teach people how to appreciate nature, how to understand events and to see the connection between them, as well as to initiate them into the mysteries of the human heart and enable them better to understand one another. He should heighten their imaginative understanding of both the past and the future, and appeal to their spirit of courage and adventure, their love of work and struggle.

Another theory tending to distort the conception of culture is that of science for science's sake. It is true that the scientist does not arrive at true knowledge except through abstract theoretical research. Yet if his mission were confined to the contemplation of the universe for the sake of that contemplation alone, science as we now know it could not have existed. Science was born and grew up because it provided the necessities of material existence. It enables man to master nature, to combat disease, to increase production and provide himself with the means to comfort. And science also frees men from darkness, delusion, and fear. The real value of science is that it can promote and illuminate human life—the life which, as Nietzsche said, 'comes before knowledge. Knowledge that neglects life destroys life, and itself as well.'

The most remarkable consequence of the growth of science to its dominant position in modern culture is the change it has wrought in man's thinking. Scientific method has made us believe in reason, and take cognizance only of tangible realities verified by experiment. Emancipating us from magical and psychic beliefs, prejudices, and illusions, science trains us in objective, accurate observation, emotional detachment, and impartiality. Moreover, the disciplines of science, the co-operation between research workers, and the co-ordination of techniques can effectually promote solidarity and mutual aid between nations.

There is no need to enumerate the impressive achievements of the scientific method; for modern civilization in all its manifestations—its discoveries, inventions, political and social organization, and its military might—is first and foremost the product of scientific thinking. There are admittedly many problems which science has not solved; it is true that modern civilization has produced new evils and led us into dangers which threaten the world with catastrophe. But can we pretend that the old, unscientific way of thinking was less harmful or that it proved better able to solve the problems of mankind? Could we not more easily explain the continued existence of inherited evils and the recurrence of new crises, by our adherence to obsolete ideas and by our failure to indoctrinate all classes with the principles of scientific thinking? While the enemies of scientific thinking ascribe our social corruptions to 'the evil nature of man', thus confessing their inability to deal with them, the advocates of the new thinking explain how these things are caused by wrong conditions and erroneous ideas, which they endeavour to remove by reforming the social system and by disseminating knowledge.

In any case, no nation today can save itself without keeping abreast of the civilization which now pervades the world. No nation can survive without adopting, first and foremost, the mechanized industry upon which that whole civilization is based. But we cannot mechanize industry, increase our productivity, and thus acquire the means of survival unless we go in for scientific culture on the largest possible scale. For it is not enough that an *élite* should acquire that culture: it is imperative that the toiling masses should receive their full share of scientific and technical education. The peasant cannot be equipped with modern agricultural machinery until he has learned how to use and maintain it. The industrial worker cannot acquire the skill to use modern techniques to the best advantage unless he has learnt to think mechanically: he must also have the presence of mind, the diligence and attentiveness that the machine requires. Moreover, since industrial equipment grows steadily more costly and complicated, and in the future we shall need workers who can not only use machinery but produce it, we shall have to provide training in the higher technical knowledge that is acquired only through mathematics, physics, chemistry, and abstract scientific thinking.

Again, it is futile to make a worker the master of a machine with the strength and ability of two hundred and forty slaves, if that worker remains stupid, lazy, and incapable of criticism or independent thought; or if he is unable to discriminate between true and false news, easily led astray by suggestion and deception, and unable to control primitive instincts and inclinations. Mass education also is necessary, to produce citizens who know something about the makings of a state, the rights and duties of the individual—citizens who realize the meaning of responsibility, solidarity, and co-operation.

Above all, the *élite* cannot develop its higher culture unless it remains continuously in touch with the community around it, drawing from it renewed strength and vitality, by reciprocal influence. The popular culture is the ground from which the culture of the *élite* must grow, in separation from which all higher culture is cut off from its roots and rendered lifeless. And the more widely the popular culture is spread, the higher the demands it makes upon the leadership of the *élite*.

* * * * *

A great and majestic role awaits the *élite* of intellectuals and the educated classes of Arab society. They have, firstly, to revive the cultural heritage upon which our future culture must be built. Secondly, they will have to bear the heaviest burden of the new culture that we have to assimilate if we are to fulfil the requirements of the age; especially of the modern scientific thinking which must become the predominant characteristic of our own culture. They will also have to study the main intellectual trends of the times and the forces which govern the development of modern societies.

Thirdly, the *élite* will have to achieve that unity between the mind, the sentiments, and the will which does not, however, rule out a variety of forms and a plurality of forms of expression. For variety is indispensable for the vitality, growth, and efflorescence of a culture —up to that limit beyond which variety becomes an impediment to harmony.

Fourthly, the *élite* must fully discharge its responsibilities to the public, maintain continuous contact with it, and take upon itself the enlightenment, guidance, and orientation of the public mind. For men cannot grapple with the problems of their common life unless they are sustained by a comprehensive conception of the universe, a vision of the ends of life which is in keeping with their knowledge and in harmony with their sentiments and predispositions. In every age and every nation this has been, and will be, the supreme function of the cultured *élite* and the intellectuals—the dissemination of a universal, guiding point of view.

THE EGYPTIAN INTELLIGENTSIA

by GEORGES KETMAN

IF A FOREIGN intellectual passing through Cairo a few months ago had asked to meet representatives of the Cairene intelligentsia, he would have been introduced to persons who have now been divested of all importance by the Suez-Sinai campaign. He would have met Copts, Jews, or Lebanese from stocks rooted in Egypt for at least a century, or persons of mixed ancestry disparagingly called *bazramites* in Arabic slang. Olive-skinned, swarthy, or having that ivory pallor one finds only in the Orient, they spoke, for the most part, a perfect French learned from the Jesuit fathers of Faggalah, or an Oxford English acquired from British governesses.

They were always up to date on what was going on in the world, read *Foreign Affairs* and the polylingual Roman review *Botteghe Oscure*, had digested authors as dissimilar as Marx, Heidegger, and Stirner, and—what is more unusual than one would suspect—they had also read Hallaj and Djabarti. Some went abroad every year to renew their contacts with such illustrious Western figures as Jaspers, Abellio, or Papini. George Henein, Munir Hafez, Magdi Wahba, Lutfallah Soliman, and Ali el-Shalakani are writers of the kind we are referring to.

The talents of these latter-day St. Petersburghers were not limited to imitation. During the first years of the war, for instance, Georges Henein, a friend of André Breton, founded an Arabic journal, *Al Tattawur*, which combined Communism with surrealism. About the same time a movement no less surrealistic brought together all the best writers and artists to be found in Egypt, in a little paradise for intellectual refugees. It is true that, excepting Cossery and those named above, none of the talents that bloomed in this hothouse (of which the most exalted wrote incendiary poems and went to prison with equal gusto) survived the break-up of the coterie. All that remains of this effort is a glowing memory, three or four good drawings by Ramsès Younan, and a few fine tracts and pamphlets not without sparks of true fire. But it was a momentary blaze soon put out by business troubles, the public danger, and everyday cares.

'THE SANDS' SHARE'

Later on, an occasional publication appropriately called *The Sands' Share* tried to provide a platform for the survivors and certain Western expatriates such as Jean Grenier or Jean Wahl, Henri Michaus and Ponge. One issue apiece was devoted to anniversary celebrations of Nietzsche, Kafka, and Kierkegaard. In the light of subsequent political developments the artificiality of the enterprise became all the more evident. Published by a very restricted group, and intended for a *happy few* readers, the magazine fulfilled no real need, was not addressed to any specific public, and pretended, not without a certain presumption, to teach the West about its own thinkers. An exceptionally high quality might have justified the publication of these essays, but this was by no means the case.

Such writings could be justly considered untimely and out of place, published as they were in a foreign—almost an enemy—language, by scions of feudalism or pseudo-Europeans who hardly concealed their nostalgia for the days of the capitulations or their anxiety about the nationalist movement looming up on the horizon.

These publisher-intellectuals were unaware of the situation of their class and that it was in its death throes. In the face of an ascendancy of Socialist thought, and in the midst of the agrarian reform, they went on collecting paintings of the Paris School and the old rugs and gewgaws of Fabergé. Indifferent to the great social and political metamorphosis taking place under their noses—which heralded, if not their extermination, then at least their moral and economic decline—they thought they were the heirs, at a distance of twenty centuries, of the ancient Alexandrian *élites*.

They claimed as their own the contemporary Alexandrian poets Constantine Kavafy (who wrote in Greek) and Giuseppe Ungaretti (in Italian), as well as that exceptional offshoot, the novelist Albert Cossery. But they had forgotten that if the composite sixth-century population spoke Greek in Alexandria it was because that was the most widespread language in use in the eastern Mediterranean, and that cosmopolitanism flourishes only in an atmosphere of tolerance and under the aegis of a strong empire, while Islam is essentially xenophobic. Nor did they seem to grasp that their preoccupation with metaphysics, dandyism, Julian the Apostate, and the *Sephirot*—

in a nation 80 per cent illiterate—was not only paradoxical, but scandalous.

Then came the great break. The direction of Egypt's revolutionary politics hardly left any choice: they had to opt for the West or for Egypt. More precisely, for an Egypt whose language most of them spoke rather badly, and which was throwing up social classes hostile to the world they represented. Some left for Europe: others, however, remained, and before the Suez crisis found themselves exceptionally placed in the confrontation between the East and the West, morally as well as geographically. That part of the Western conscience which feels guilty about colonialism, which applauds the withdrawal of the French in Indo-China and hopes to see them leave North Africa, offered these Westernized Egyptians a line to follow, fortified by the line taken up in France by Louis Massignon, François Mauriac, Jean-Paul Sartre, and others. The declarations of the independent French left wing reminded them of their youthful Communist enthusiasm, when they had learned the words of the *Internationale* and had sold the family rugs and jewels to buy books. They declared themselves left-wingers while the Nasser Republic actually prohibited them from indulging in political activity, threatened them with further nationalization of their property and sold at auctions the valuables of the royal family, whose drawing-rooms they had once frequented. It must be said, however, that by no means all of them took this line; and those intellectuals who did are now dwindling like the ten little nigger boys; only two or three survive who speak Arabic fluently and whose Communist preaching has played into the hands of Egyptian politicians, as it may do again.

If we use the word 'survive' it is because the measures promulgated by Nasser regarding all French and English cultural activity have reduced all the others to silence, or to mute conformity. It has been compromising in recent months to speak French or to maintain relations with France. We should deplore this in the name of cultural freedom, but not in the name of French culture. The legend of French cultural influence in Egypt is one of the most extraordinary deceptions to which this culture has fallen victim. The balance-sheet of French cultural losses in Egypt has little more to show than several dozen poems written in the manner of Anna de Noailles or Gustave Kahn, a score of lectures, and a number of film-shows.

Well, then, you are bound to ask, hasn't anyone taken over, is Egypt a country without a head or brain? It would not be entirely fair to answer with an outright 'no'. There are several persons in Cairo who bear some resemblance to those whom one is accustomed to call intellectuals, and who are not cosmopolitans without a future. They already came forward about five or six years ago, and one would have to be quite naïve not to know what formed and directed them. One would have to be even blinder than Taha Hussain to explain his anti-French measures only by base personal reasons for long, before the Revolution, as Minister of Education, he closed down the French archaeological sites in Upper Egypt and the French Law School in Cairo—even though his wife was French and his son spent many years studying in France. These measures already showed the significance of the nationalist movement, which was at work agitating during the last years of the former régime, and which was producing the new intelligentsia at students' meetings and street demonstrations.

Unlike their predecessors, the new intelligentsia are very rarely polylingual. They have read very little, mostly bad translations of Dostoyevsky and Sartre. They are badly dressed, they don't wear glasses, and they have been hungry. Almost all of them write for the newspapers and some write film scripts for the movies.

NO LEISURE OR MONEY

The absence of culture seems to me to be the outstanding characteristic of these new intellectuals. To read a lot, you have to have leisure and money, because foreign books cost two or three times as much in Cairo as in their countries of origin. They have very little leisure and almost no money. Furthermore, there are few Arabic translations of the masterpieces of world literature, and many of them are very poorly done. To read Dostoyevsky in a French translation, or Stendhal in the original, calls for a knowledge of French—or of English, if it is Toynbee or Joyce—which hardly any of them possess.

Finally—and perhaps above all—culture is the province of the rich and exhausted classes, it is the property of those 'who do not belong'. There is small cause for wonder, then, that these intellectuals know Gide, Huxley, Moravia or Faulkner only by name.

Almost all of them come from the villages of Egypt. They have been hungry because they are the sons of peasants or of impoverished petty officials, and this explains their attitude to the people who would go to Europe to overload their stomachs, and who were the exploiters of their fathers. Even today, under a régime which appeals for their services, they have hardly more money than can buy a watery stew for lunch, and a plate of beans and salad for dinner. Their lack of money is almost a metaphysical state; as Cossery put it, they are 'eternal beggars in the best of all possible worlds'. They tolerate American cars and 400,000-franc pink refrigerators, with which the U.S. floods the Egyptian market, but believe that those who acquire them do so dishonestly. Their unique authority does not come from their position as intellectuals—white-collar workers are not very highly thought of in the Orient, where only poets and journalists enjoy a certain amount of prestige—but from the fact that they are in the same social position as most of the nest-feathering officers of the new régime.

Here it would be worthwhile to clarify our terms. In the West, the word 'intellectual' describes a certain type of thought capable of dealing with general problems and of approaching them from a new point of view. This does not apply to the new Cairo intelligentsia. For them, the essay is a difficult, unrewarding, and foreign form. Newspaper articles about the influence of Western culture on Egyptian students—one of the most difficult subjects a 'nationalized' journalist could undertake, because both of his own limited knowledge and the level of his six hundred thousand readers—are tiresome complications of commonplaces and anecdotes stuck together any old way. One of the rare theoreticians of the new régime, the only one perhaps who has thought of the problems of a modern Egypt with a certain breadth, is Gamal Abdul Nasser!

EGYPTIAN WRITERS' DEAD END

The officers surrounding Nasser can hardly spare any time for culture from the exercise of power. The two 'intellectuals' among them, Salah Salem and Khaled Mohiedin, are the editors of dailies supported by invisible funds, *Al Sha'ab* (*The People*), and *Al Massa* (*The Evening*). Only Khaled Mohiedin, who, it may be recalled, initiated an ineffective Communist-inspired *coup d'état*, displays a certain amount of curiosity. This characteristic could perhaps be explained by the influence on him of a French journalist who was a great admirer of T. E. Lawrence, and who acted as a sort of professor of revolution in Egypt. Mohiedin's paper is the only one which maintains a certain level.

What then, are the 'intellectuals' who are neither thinkers nor journalists, like Mohammed Hassanein Heykal or Ibrahim Amer? They are writers of fiction, and we can add the names of Yussef Idris, Ihsan Abdul Kuddous (editor of *Rose el Yussef*), Lutfi al Kholy, Naguib Mahfuz, and Yussef Amin Ghorab. Their stories usually describe lower-middle-class and peasan life and their literary level is not very high. Naguib Mahfuz in his *Zukak el Medak*, could be considered a disciple of Eugène Sue and the Victor Hugo of *Les Miserables*, Lutfi al Kholy and Yussef Amin Ghorab remind one of the second-rate popular novelists inspired by the spirit of 1848. The stories of Ihsan Abdul Kuddous are suffused with a desolate insipidity. Only Yussef Idris, a son-in-law of the Mexican painter [Diego Rivera, has shown—in *Arkhas Layali* (*Fourpenny Nights*)—a talent worthy of his seniors, especially the two 'grand old men' of Egyptian literature, Tewfik el Hakim and Taha Hussain. (Eleven months of imprisonment without trial for having attended a Communist youth congress three years ago in Syria will doubtless make him toe the line.) These writers are not, therefore, thinkers.

This serious lack, which could at the very least be called unfortunate for an intelligentsia worthy of the name, also holds for the problems which face modern Egypt. The main difficulty is the absence of any Arab literature in the real sense of the word, except for religious and scientific writing (if one can call the da Vincian notes of Ibn Sina literature). The *Arabian Nights* is an exception, and an inadequate one. The Islamic poets are no more than lyrical sensualists, and neither the Sufic texts nor the Qur'ān, the chief literary work of Islam, provide any foundation for an intrinsically oriental evaluation of the problems of the modern world.

This frightful gulf separating the birth of Islam from the rebirth of contemporary Egypt dooms to destruction or to anguish any sign of specifically Arab thought. The average educated Westerner knows that the man who envisioned the prototype of the electronic brain was a tortured religious thinker called Pascal, and that the automobile and air conditioning were foreseen by Leonardo da Vinci. Between the camel and a Cadillac there is nothing but a void for the Egyptian, which his ignorance can hardly bridge. Islam's most serious failure in the modern world is its inability to master the language of technology. When one is aware of the links which bind philosophy and sociology to technology, one understands why the small Egyptian *élite* remains in vassalage to the West. Is there any reason for wonder, then, that the Muslim Brotherhood considered elevators and automobiles to be the devil's own devices, and rejected banking as sacrilege?

INFLEXIBILITY OF ARABIC

Another reason for the poverty of Egyptian thought is the inflexibility of the Arabic language. While its grammar is relatively simple, it is difficult to read, because it is practically impossible to take in the drift of a page of Arabic at a glance, as it is with languages printed in the Latin alphabet. It is a language almost exclusively destined to serve as an instrument for the understanding of, meditation on, and recitation of the Qur'ān. That is why Egyptian intellectuals can devote so little time to reading, and can absorb so little printed matter, compared to English or French.

This poverty of a language which is inexact anyway, like all languages forged by poets and preachers, turns into paralysis as a result of the intransigence of Al Azhar University (a religious institution and a sort of Sorbonne for all Islam) in regard to all projects of reform. By declaring in his Constitution that Egypt is a Muslim state—thus ignoring some three million Copts who consider themselves to be natives of the land—Nasser has allied himself with Al Azhar. One can therefore easily understand the lack of influence of intellectuals who aspire to nothing so much as to change, to a complete secularization of the state, and even to the adoption of the Latin alphabet, as the Turks have done.

The only chance remaining to the Egyptian intelligentsia is vested in its total atheism, which alone is capable of breaking the archaic social structure, a vestige of Ottoman domination and a feudal society, and one which was scandalously plutocratic, until very recently at least. This atheism is quite widespread among the university students and petty officials, who for better or for worse—rather worse—have acquired a political consciousness as a result of the revolutionary régime.

The new intellectuals who are recruited from these two groups—students and petty officials—are essentially concerned with getting a foothold in some faction of the party in power and in attaining a position one rung above the one they hold. Their leisure is divided between mornings in a café, taking hashish, and the cinema. *Rose el Yussef*, the crypto-Communist weekly which gathers round it the new left wing, chiefly devotes itself to society gossip.

The chief income of these proletarians, who are almost as short of culture as of money, is the translation and compilation of reading matter for city-dwellers and provincials eaten by social anguish. 'Compilation' is a mild word for what they do; it would be more correct to say 'plagiarization'. Take, for example, Ahmed Auda's *Al Sin al Sha'abia* (*People's China*). The author has never been to China and his book is made up of borrowings from various reports. But one had to take advantage of the fashionable interest in Communist China when Nasser was beginning to flirt with the East, and to express opinions which not so long ago would have landed the author in prison.

There is one man above all who maintains a rigorous atheism among the intellectuals and keeps track of them, and who has considerable influence, since he is both a publisher and a bookseller. His name is Lutfallah Soliman. He is a former anarchist of the *Al Tattawur* group, and looks like the most haggard intellectual type you could meet at Saint-Germain-des-Près or in Bloomsbury. He is tall and so emaciated that his faded clothes look as if they were hung up on a clothes-hanger. His perfectly concave face—surmounted by a mad tangle of black hair—is devoured by a passionate expression which cannot fail to fascinate. A sabre-shaped mouth speaks perfect French or Arabic, according to the interlocutor. One can—or rather could—meet in his bookshop Allal el Fassi and Ben Bella, as well as Cyril Connolly, Audiberti, Roger Stéphane or André Pieyre de Mandiargue, not to mention the correspondents of *Le Monde* and *The Times*, and most of the special correspondents who had no preconceived ideas about what was going on.

It will be observed that this is a world of the left, and in actual fact, Marx, Lenin, and Engels, plus a number of Communist dialecticians, make up the substance and criteria of the reading and discussions of these emancipated intellectuals.

We must admit that these left-wing Stalinist convictions are very often quite superficial, and of an idealism which sometimes finds it difficult to follow the ups and downs of Soviet foreign policy. It was doubtless in order to avoid confusing the Communist-inspired masses and upsetting the new *élite* which supports him almost unreservedly in his anti-Western policy that Nasser had his censor forbid any mention of the Hungarian uprising in the Egyptian Press.

COMMUNIST INTELLECTUALS

The Communist convictions of the intellectuals stem from the feeling of the absolute necessity for social reform in Egypt. If, on the one hand, one can only share this feeling when one has seen the immense misery of the Egyptian people, one can only be amazed, on the other hand, that certain Egyptians who have some pretensions to intelligence should have espoused a policy so diametrically opposed to social reform. They know well enough that it is not in selling their baubles at auctions, in spending millions in secret propaganda funds in Jordan and Saudia, and above all in swallowing up the meagre reserves of the country in arms purchases, that the standard of living of the fellahin and the urban proletariat will be raised. It is true that a good many Egyptian intellectuals consider the Nasser régime to be only a transitional one, and that in the near or distant future a really Socialist government will succeed it, but for the moment they seem to be confusing demagogy and Socialism.

This mistake betrays them twice over: it reveals their lack of perception, and the basically emotional nature of their thinking. The same applies to the students, whose level of studies is quite low, and who were 'quietened' by a purge two years ago; the same could be said for the 'thinking' officers. For all of them the revolutionary adventure was an opportunity for revenge—for the Muslim petty-

bourgeois intellectuals, revenge against a West which did not understand much about their problems and overwhelmed them with condescension; for the Levantine intellectuals, revenge against a West to which they had never really succeeded in assimilating themselves; for the officers, as everyone knows, revenge against Great Britain and France, their former overlords, and against Israel, which had defeated them in 1949.

One can affirm that the Communism of these intellectuals, which has no influence whatsoever on the rulers and acts on public opinion only in the direction determined by Nasser, is a transparent mask—worn only because it frightens the West which disappointed them. The Levantine intellectual—and this label also applies to the Egyptian intellectual—is not so very different from the Oriental as such: always smiling at the man holding the sword. Many Egyptians were Nazis at the height of the last war, and have remained so. Rommel is a real hero in Cairo and, as for the rest, the Oriental lives in his dream-world. He still has not freed himself from his ancient position of being an official scribe.

GRAND OLD MEN

What about Taha Hussain? Tewfik el Hakim? Abbas al Aqqad? They belong neither to the banned cosmopolitans nor to the young revolutionaries. Though they write for the government papers, their advanced age has freed them from wild passions. Educated in a khedival, and then monarchical Egypt which pretended to be democratic, they nevertheless acquired a taste for liberty and pure knowledge. Their literary output remains the most valuable point of departure for the intellectuals of contemporary Egypt. Though mentioned too often, works like *The Book of Days* and *The Call of the Karawan* by Taha Hussain, and *The Journal of a Country Judge* by Tewfik el Hakim, have not been equalled by the younger generation. They represent neither the medieval and poetic Egypt of a Louis Massignon, nor a spartan one, but an Egypt still in existence, patient and shrewd, with its sense of humour—an Egypt which will have to be rediscovered when the present Egyptian intellectuals start looking for hardier fare than Nasser's *Philosophy of the Revolution*.

TWO SOVIET VIEWS ON THE MIDDLE EAST*

I

The Growth of National Consciousness among the Arab Peoples (1945-55)

by L. N. VATOLINA

THE PEOPLES of the Arab countries,[1] having lived for four hundred years under the heavy yoke of the Ottoman Empire, then became the object of most cruel exploitation by the colonial Powers, who divided the Arab countries between themselves and turned them into markets for the sale of their goods, sources of raw materials, and areas of capital investment. This predatory exploitation by foreign monopolies of the natural wealth of the Arab countries, semi-feudal and capitalist exploitation, made for a one-sided development of the economy of the Arab countries, hampered the growth of their productive forces, and led to the impoverishment of the labouring masses.

In all Arab countries large-scale landownership prevails. In Iraq, for example, half of all the cultivable land is concentrated in the hands of the landlords. In almost all Arab countries labour rents and share-cropping are widespread. The landlords, representing an

---

* Note.—Professor Vatolina's article was published in *Sovetskoe Vostoko-vedenie*, No. 5, 1955. Professor Lutskii's essay *ibid.*, No. 2, 1957. Cuts are indicated by '. . .'.

[1] The area covered by the twenty Arab states and seven principalities is roughly 11·1 million square kilometres, with a total population of more than 76 million.

insignificant proportion of the population, exploit millions of small-holding and landless fellahin, leaseholders, and labourers, taking advantage of the enormous cheap labour market created as a result of the growing impoverishment of the peasantry and the slow development of industry. The domination of foreign capital—robbing the people by means of its banks, capitalist undertakings, export firms which buy agricultural raw materials for a trifle and ruin the peasantry—adds capitalist servitude to the servitude on the land.

As the general crisis of capitalism grows deeper, the oppressed peasant masses are still further impoverished. This is creating an anti-feudal agrarian movement in the Arab countries. Not infrequently the landless and smallholding fellahin seize the landowner's land, divide it up among themselves, and resist the measures taken by the police and gendarmerie.

The Arab countries, most of which became independent after the Second World War, are economically under the yoke of foreign monopolies. Dependence on the powerful capitalist states is most marked in the case of those Arab countries with large oil resources. The Western Powers seized the local oil-fields and other natural wealth.

The colonial Powers concluded treaties and agreements with some of the Arab countries, legalizing their occupation by foreign troops. After the Second World War the American monopolies became more active in the Arab countries. United States investment in some Arab countries increased more than tenfold.[2] Pushing their English and French competitors out of the Arab markets, the American monopolies are striving to establish their control over the economy of the Arab countries and subdue it to their rule. With this object in view, and using the pretext of so-called technical and financial 'aid' under Point Four of the Truman programme, the American monopolies have imposed enslaving agreements on Saudi Arabia, Iraq, Jordan, and other Eastern countries. By means of these agreements the American monopolists are trying to secure a privileged position for their capital in Arab countries and to draw them into military and political alliances. One of the principal objects of the struggle of the English and American monopolies in the Arab countries is oil; the reserves there represent more than half of the total reserves of the capitalist world: output in the five chief producing areas (Saudi Arabia, Kuwait, Iraq, Qatar, Egypt) rose from 16 million tons in 1946 to 132 million tons in 1954. These immensely rich resources, the use of which by the Arab peoples could raise their standard of living and help to develop the pro-

[2] *A Survey of American Interests in the Middle East* (Washington, 1953), p. 12.

ductive forces in these countries, were seized by the five largest American monopolies and two English ones.[3]

As a consequence of the atrocious exploitation of cheap labour power and the use at times of semi-serf labour, the profits of the oil companies in the Arab countries in the post-war years amounted to several milliard dollars. In Saudi Arabia the American monopolies get 700 per cent interest, but the workers in the oil-fields are paid the lowest wages in the world.[4]

The rivalry of the foreign monopolies in the Arab countries for sources of raw materials, for markets, and for fields of capital investment, is acquiring a more and more embittered character. Up to the Second World War the English monopolies controlled 80·9 per cent of Middle Eastern oil and the American 12·8 per cent. After the war the situation changed sharply. In 1952 the American share in Middle Eastern oil output amounted to 66 per cent of the total, having increased almost entirely at the expense of the English. But fear of the growing national liberation movement compels the colonial Powers, despite the contradictions between them, to act together. By their attempts to get these countries to take part in every kind of enslaving alliance, treaty, pact, and bloc, they hope not only to crush the struggle for national liberation, but also to use the territory and the human resources of the Arab countries for their own ends. This explains the great numbers of projects to create military-political blocs and pacts for the Near East, and the innumerable official and unofficial visits of diplomats and service chiefs of the Western Powers to the Arab countries.

These attempts to knock together alignments and alliances of Arab countries also reflect the anxiety of some monopolists to reinforce their own position in the Near East at the expense of others. Thus, certain English circles expended much fruitless effort in organizing a 'Greater Syria' bloc, which was to have included Syria, Lebanon, Jordan, and Palestine, and the 'Fertile Crescent' bloc, covering the same countries plus Iraq. England also tried to use the Arab League, the participants in which are bound together by a collective security pact.[5] On their side, certain circles in the United States are using every means to split the League and to create a bloc of Arab countries under their own aegis, ostensibly for the 'defence' of the Middle East. An obvious manifestation of this

[3] Standard Oil of New Jersey, Socony Vacuum, Standard Oil of California, Texas Oil, Gulf Oil Corporation, Anglo-Iranian, and Royal Dutch-Shell.

[4] *Cahiers internationaux*, 1953, No. 49, p. 48.

[5] The Arab League was set up in 1945 by the following Arab countries: Egypt, Syria, Lebanon, Iraq, Saudi Arabia, Yemen, Transjordan, and (after 1953) Libya. All these countries have ratified the Arab Collective Security Pact signed in 1951.

policy was the attempt to organize the so-called 'Middle East Command' (with the participation of the United States, England, France, and Turkey). The intention was to compel the Arab countries to make their territory, armed forces, and military bases available to the United States Army Command in the Middle East.

The peoples of the Arab countries are opposed to these plans. Egypt, Syria, and other Arab states rejected the proposal for a Middle East Command. Legitimate fears were also aroused in the Arab countries by the part which the Western Powers assign to Turkey in the creation of military blocs in the Near and Middle East. The report of the Treaty signed between Turkey and Pakistan on April 2, 1954, provoked protest demonstrations in many Arab countries. The political committee of the Arab League announced the refusal of the Arab countries to adhere to the Turkey-Pakistan Pact. In December, 1954, the Council of the Arab League endorsed this declaration.

All this compelled the said circles in the United States and England to resort to new tactics in organizing military blocs in the East—not to impose them officially from without, but to act in such a way that the initiative in creating the blocs appeared on the surface to come from the Eastern countries themselves. To this end the Prime Ministers of Iraq and Turkey early in 1955 made a tour of the Arab countries. As a result of prolonged efforts the Western circles were successful in getting a military treaty concluded (February 25, 1955) between Iraq and Turkey. The latter, as noted above, is bound by a military agreement with Pakistan and is a member of the North Atlantic bloc.

The conclusion of the Turkish-Iraq Agreement was facilitated by the presence at the head of the Iraq government of Nuri Sa'id who, as the Egyptian newspaper *Al Gumhuria* wrote on January 15, 1955, is well known in the Arab world for his irreconcilable hostility to the national-liberation movement. The news of the Treaty aroused immense indignation in the Arab countries. Arab public opinion considered that Nuri Sa'id had 'stabbed the Arab people in the back'.

In many countries, and particularly in Syria and Lebanon, and even in Iraq itself, mass demonstrations were held to protest against the Turkish-Iraq Agreement. The demonstrators, carrying anti-imperialist slogans, demanded that the shameful pact be annulled and called for the defence of the unity of the Arab countries, for ensuring peace and security.

These demonstrations bore witness to the fact that hostile propaganda had failed to deceive the Arab peoples into believing the stupid inventions about 'the Soviet threat'. The peoples of the Arab countries have learnt more than once from their own experience that

the Soviet Union has always decisively condemned, and still condemns, the policy of imperialist annexations and colonial oppression,
and that at the foundation of the Soviet Union's foreign policy lies
the struggle for ensuring peace and the security of the peoples, for a
relaxation of international tension.

Iraq's independent action, which violated the statutes of the Arab
League, compelled the governments of Egypt, Syria, and Saudi
Arabia to conclude a provisional agreement among themselves on
military and economic assistance, to be used as a basis either for the
rebuilding of the League without Iraq, or for the creation of a new
association of Arab states. This agreement, negotiated in the first
half of 1955, made it obligatory on the contracting parties not to
adhere to the Turkish-Iraq Pact or to any similar pact. The said
circles in the United States, Turkey, and Iraq demanded adherence
to the Pact from the Syrian government, offering in compensation
economic 'aid'. But Syria did not fall into the trap.

On October 20, 1955, a defence pact was signed between Syria and
Egypt in Damascus, and later a similar pact was signed between
Egypt and Saudi Arabia.

* * * * *

The unceasing struggle of millions of Arabs for peace and national
independence is undermining the foundations of the colonial Powers.
In 1946, England and France were forced to withdraw their troops
from Syria and the Lebanon. These formerly Mandated countries
achieved the status of independent republics; in 1948, English troops
were withdrawn from Palestine, formerly also under Mandate; in
1951, the enslaving Anglo-Egyptian Treaty was denounced; in 1953,
Libya was proclaimed an independent kingdom.

The desire for national independence and the hatred of colonial
oppression unites the broad masses of the workers, peasants, artisans,
intelligentsia, national *bourgeoisie*, suffering from the stranglehold
of foreign monopolies. In opposing colonialism, the peoples of the
Arab countries are fighting against the expansion of foreign capital,
against the occupation of their territory by foreign troops. They are
voicing their demand for democratic freedom, for land, for the
right to work, for independence. The national-liberation struggle in
the Arab countries is at the present stage closely interwoven with the
labour and agrarian movement.

The liberation movement in the Arab countries is developing
unevenly. It varies in the degree of intensity, in the level of organization, and in its forms, being conditioned by the varying levels of
political and economic development in the different countries. The

national-liberation movement is broadest in scope in Egypt. In 1951, the Egyptian people rose for the fight against the enslaving Anglo-Egyptian Treaty and denounced it. The English authorities tried to suppress this movement by armed force.

Having begun hostilities in Egypt, the English authorities encountered the powerful organized resistance of the Egyptian people. In the liberation struggle all the forces of the Egyptian people were united—workers, peasants, a considerable part of the national *bourgeoisie*, the middle-class urban strata. The preparatory committee for the creation of a trade-union federation, representing a hundred and four unions, came out in favour of denunciation. About seventy-five thousand workers ceased work in the English undertakings in the Canal zone. The entire population boycotted English goods. The peasants in the neighbourhood of the Canal refused to supply the English troops with food. In this area a partisan movement arose, organized by workers, students, and the peasant youth of Egypt. Relying on the King and his court, the English colonial authorities augmented the terror in the country.

In this situation a group of army officers, representing the interests of the Egyptian *bourgeoisie*, led by Nasser at the head of the revolutionary council, took advantage of the prevailing dissatisfaction with the orgy of reaction and the arbitrariness of the King and removed King Farouk from the throne in July, 1952. In 1953, Egypt was proclaimed a republic. The banishment of the King and his intimates as the personification of despotism and subjection to imperialism, hated by the entire people, the imposition of some restrictions on landownership, the abolition of the rank of pasha, and other reforms, were objectively progressive actions.

The positive element in the foreign policy of Nasser's government is that it opposes military blocs and is moving closer towards the Chinese People's Republic, India, and Indonesia, a process which was forwarded by the meeting of Egyptian representatives with the representatives of these countries at Bandung in April, 1955. On May 14, 1955, the Egyptian government proposed to the Arab League the recognition of the Chinese People's Republic. In May, 1955, an Egyptian government delegation visited People's China, followed by an Egyptian trade mission in August. . . .

*   *   *   *   *

Mass progressive organizations are taking an active part in the liberation struggle in the Arab East; often they have to carry on their work in semi-legal conditions (the national committees of the *Partisans of Peace*, various democratic leagues of youth and women, societies, committees, and other organizations). The proletariat of the Arab countries invariably links its economic and social demands with the movement for national emancipation. The proletariat and its parties act as a militant and organizing force, fighting to draw the broad masses of the labouring people into the liberation struggle.

The substantial successes of the trade-union movement testify to the growth of political consciousness among the working class of the Arab countries. The trade-union federations in the majority of Arab countries are organizationally linked with the World Federation of Trade Unions. Among them we may mention the Moroccan General Confederation of Labour, the Association of Workers' Unions in Tunis, the Trade Union Federation in the Sudan, and a number of other organizations.

The peasant masses, who form the majority of the Arab population, represent the chief ally of the working class in the struggle for national liberation. An indication of the growth of political consciousness among the peasants is given by events in Egypt, Syria, and Saudi Arabia. Soldiers—peasants only yesterday—whom the colonial authorities sent to suppress anti-imperialist demonstrations, not seldom refused to turn their weapons against the demonstrators. Thus, for example, Moroccan soldiers, sent to suppress the liberation movement in Tunis in the summer of 1954, refused to fire on the Tunisians. The struggle of the North African peoples meets with sympathy from the French workers; for example, in September, 1955, four hundred French reservists refused to take military service in Africa and demonstrated under the slogan of 'Morocco for the Moroccans'.

The policy of colonial circles is becoming an ever greater threat not only to the broad masses of the population, but to the interests of the national *bourgeoisie* as well. Their own experience brings them into conflict with the foreign monopolies, who restrict the scope for the investment of national capital, and so the *bourgeoisie*, chiefly the small and middle *bourgeoisie*, are joining more and more actively in the national-liberation movement.

In his writings, J. V. Stalin showed that it is necessary to distinguish between the revolutionary movement in capitalist and colonial countries; in the latter the oppression of imperialism is bound to hit the national *bourgeoisie* as well, and there, 'at a certain stage and for a certain time, they may support the revolutionary movement in their countries against imperialism'.

In the national-liberation struggle of the peoples of the Arab countries, the creation of a united national front acquires topical significance. The general secretary of the Communist Party of Syria and Lebanon, Khaled Bakdash, in bringing fraternal greetings to the

Nineteenth Congress of the Communist Party of the Soviet Union, described the tasks confronting the Arab countries: 'For us, Arabs, there is only one road—the road marked out by Lenin and Stalin, the road of the broad national front which must unite workers, the peasant masses, the middle strata of the urban population, and large sections of the national *bourgeoisie*. The progressive forces of the Arab countries are concentrating their activity on achieving this task.'

The process of creating a united national front is not occurring at an equal pace everywhere. It is being accomplished most successfully in those Arab countries where there is an organized and united working-class vanguard (Syria, Lebanon). A resolution of the Central Committee of the Communist Party of Syria and Lebanon states that 'the creation of a national front in Syria has now become a national necessity'. In analysing the Syrian situation, the resolution points out that the country is now going through the stage of national-democratic liberation, and this makes the struggle against imperialism and its military plans, the struggle for democratic, political, and economic reforms, a struggle in the general interest. The resolution underlines the need to assemble all forces, in the first place against imperialism and its principal ally, reactionary feudalism, democracy's worst enemy.[6]

The creation of a united front in the Arab countries is encountering considerable difficulties because of the splitting policy of certain *bourgeois* parties and because, in spite of their formal adherence, the wavering part of the *bourgeoisie* is retreating from its declarations.

In some Arab countries after the Second World War the national *bourgeoisie* tried at times to put themselves at the head of the national-liberation movement. But, wavering and inclined to compromise with imperialism, they showed themselves incapable of fighting consistently for the national liberation of their countries. The scope of this struggle usually frightened the *bourgeoisie*, and not seldom they turned to collaboration with the imperialists, as happened, for example, in Iraq.

But the conciliatory attitude of some *bourgeois* parties does not mean that there are no contradictions between the national *bourgeoisie* and the imperialists, or that the struggle of the *bourgeoisie* against the foreign robbers has ceased. When characterizing the Chinese Revolution, Mao Tse-tung noted that the national *bourgeoisie* comes, on the one hand, into conflict with imperialism and the leading feudalists, and its fight against them has a revolutionary character; while on the other hand, because of its economic and political weakness, and the existence of economic bonds connecting

[6] *As-Sarqha*, September 5, 1954.

it with imperialism and feudalism, which it has not broken, it lacks sufficient courage to wage the struggle against them to the end.[7]

This characterization applies in full to the national *bourgeoisie* of the Arab countries, relatively weak and slowly developing in conditions where foreign capital is the master.

Only the proletariat can lead the national-liberation movement, the only consistently revolutionary class which, supported by the broad masses of the peasantry, occupies the front ranks in the struggle for peace, freedom, and national independence.

An active part in the national-liberation movement is being taken by the Arab youth, the progressive students of Damascus, Beirut, Cairo, Alexandria, Baghdad, Fez, and Tunis.

Wider and wider circles of working women in the Arab countries are being drawn into the national-liberation struggle. Fettered for centuries by reactionary traditions and religious usages, Arab working women are breaking away from these survivals and entering the ranks of the fighters for peace and independence. In Morocco, in 1951–53, many women took part in the demonstrations and collisions with the troops. In the towns of Jubaila and Ras Tanura, in Saudi Arabia, in October, 1953, the first demonstrations of women were held. The women of Jordan, Syria, and Lebanon are taking an active part in the *Partisans of Peace* movement.

One of the most characteristic features of the national-liberation movement today is that it is interwoven with the movement to defend peace which has captured broad masses of the population in the Arab countries. A substantial part of the Arab intelligentsia is taking part in the *Partisans of Peace* movement, journalists, writers, artists, lawyers. In all Arab countries national committees of the *Partisans of Peace* movement have been set up, with district branches. They are doing a great deal of work among the population, mobilizing the people for the fight for peace. The appeal of the World Council of Peace to the peoples against the preparations for atomic war found a wide echo among the Arab peoples. The *Partisans of Peace* committees launched a broad campaign to collect signatures for this appeal. . . .[8]

* * * * *

The situation in the Arab countries after the Second World War testifies to the considerable growth of national consciousness among

---

[7] *Cf.* Mao Tse-tung, *Selected Works*, Vol. 3, p. 162.

[8] According to figures issued by the World Peace Council, the Vienna appeal for the prohibition of atomic warfare in August, 1955, carried 609,000 signatures from Syria alone, that is, one-sixth of the Syrian population.

the Arab peoples. This is expressed in the rise of the national-liberation movement, which has assumed wide proportions and developed to a higher stage.

The distinctive features of this movement are that it is directed against colonialism and reaction, against the involvement of Arab countries in plans and military blocs alien to their interests. This movement is occurring at a time when millions of people in the colonial world are breaking the chains of slavery, when the liberation struggle of the Arab countries fuses with the struggle of the whole of progressive humanity for peace, independence, and democracy.

II

The Revolution of July, 1952, in Egypt

by V. B. LUTSKII

A BRIEF REVIEW of the July events enables us to single out the peculiarities of the Egyptian Revolution. What inevitably had to happen in Egypt was the completion of the anti-imperialist and anti-feudal revolution. The 1952 revolution started on the fulfilment of these tasks and made considerable progress. Necessarily—not of course in all, but in a number of Asiatic and African countries—this revolution was conducted under the leadership of the national *bourgeoisie*.

But the peculiarity of the 1952 revolution in Egypt consisted in this, that it was led by the military intelligentsia, by officers. It was not a *bourgeois* nationalist party of the usual type that led the revolution, but a secret officers' society. The broad circles of the national *bourgeoisie* and the *bourgeois* intelligentsia joined the revolution not at the moment when it broke out, but afterwards—some early, some later, but the leading role remained with the military. In the revolution itself only one of the old politicians of the Hizb al-Watani collaborated with the revolutionary officers—Hafiz Suleiman; it was he who drafted the manifesto on Farouk's abdication; it was he who negotiated with the King and gave him the manifesto to sign. Watanists and representatives of the Muslim Brotherhood took part in the post-revolutionary governments. The Wafd leader Nahhas greeted Naguib as the 'saviour of the country'; but when the 'free officers' refused to hand over power to the Wafd, and promulgated agrarian reforms, Nahhas went into opposition to the new régime. But many patriotic elements, leaving the Wafd, began sooner or later to co-operate with the Revolutionary Council.

This feature of the Egyptian Revolution is obviously explained by the fact that the July *coup* occurred shortly after the savage destruction of organizations of the national-liberation movement by the forces of reaction in January, 1952. Between January 26 and July 23, 1952, only six months elapsed, and in that short time these organizations had not managed to recover from the blow dealt them. The havoc caused in January had demoralized a large part of the national *bourgeoisie*, discredited and eliminated the biggest political party, the Wafd. The 'free officers', however, had maintained their organization intact. It was still an underground organization that had not come out into the open, and it was in control of the army. This new force suddenly dealt a crushing blow against the forces of internal reaction and imperialism at a moment when it was least expected.

At the moment of the *coup* it still had no connections with the popular masses, and this circumstance explains another peculiarity of the Egyptian Revolution. Apart from the soldiery, the popular masses did not take a direct part in the July *coup*, the tasks and aims of which corresponded with their interests. Not only was the revolution led by officers; it was actually carried out by the army.[9]

But on July 26 itself the popular masses of Egypt greeted with demonstrations of wild enthusiasm the overthrow of King Farouk. On September 9, 1952, when the agrarian reform was promulgated, the people supported it. The popular masses also welcomed the proclamation of the Republic. In the struggle between Naguib and Nasser, which developed in 1954, the Egyptian working class was firmly on the side of Nasser, who stood for the further development of the anti-feudal, anti-imperialist revolution, and this decided the struggle in his favour. With the support of the popular masses the national government of Egypt is continuing to feel its way forward into the further stages of the Egyptian Revolution. The people supports the policy of fighting for Egypt's economic independence, and approves the government's foreign policy, which is to keep Egypt out of aggressive military alliances and blocs, to practise the five principles of peaceful co-existence, to establish a close alliance

[9] Gamal Abdul-Nasser, *Egypt's Liberation: The Philosophy of the Revolution* (Washington, 1955).

with Arab countries, to strengthen co-operation with the Bandung countries, with the Soviet Union, and with the people's democracies. The people supported the greatest revolutionary act of the Egyptian government, the nationalization of the Suez Canal Company, and came to the defence of the new Egypt against the predatory attack of the Anglo-French-Israeli aggressors. The development of the Egyptian Revolution is proceeding with the active and decisive participation of the popular masses.

It was precisely their support and participation which in the final analysis ensured the triumph of the revolution, although the actual *coup* of July, 1952, was accomplished without their active and direct participation. The reason for this was partly that indicated earlier: that the people's organizations—trade unions, Communist groups, the parties of the national-liberation movement—were broken up in January, 1952; partly that the Society of Free Officers had not established contact with the masses; and, most important, that the society itself was unknown to the masses; it had not revealed to the masses its programme of anti-feudal and anti-imperialist reformation. At the moment of the *coup* this programme did not, in fact, exist; it was worked out only in the course of the further development of the revolution, under the impact of the concrete relation of class forces which had taken shape in the country and the relation of international forces beyond Egypt's frontiers. The unparalleled surge forward of the liberation movement of the peoples of Asia and Africa, their growing solidarity, the broad extension of the principles of peaceful co-existence, the strengthening of the forces of peace and progress throughout the world, were bound to encourage the rapid maturing of revolutionary processes in Egypt and strengthen its revolutionary forces. But in July, 1952, the popular masses took up a waiting attitude. Their caution was due to the absence of a clear revolutionary programme among the organizers of the *coup*. Nasser himself writes: 'I confess, however, that the full picture did not become clear in my mind until after a long period of trial after July 23. It was the details of this experience which filled in the details of the picture.'[10]

The complete picture was still unclear at that time to the popular masses of Egypt too, and to outside observers, whatever their opinions, the more so that the picture was dark. The Egyptian people did not yet know who the 'free officers' were, but they knew very well that a man such as Ali Mahir, whom the leaders of the *coup* placed in power as Prime Minister, was bound to arouse serious doubts. In the nature of things, this choice was quite haphazard. It can be explained only by the political inexperience of the leaders of

[10] *ibid*, p. 32.

the *coup* and the absence of contacts with civilian circles. That the choice fell on Ali Mahir was due in part to the skilful game played by this experienced politician of the royal clique; he immediately established contact with the victors in order, by sacrificing the King, to save the old régime. The popular masses, naturally, had no confidence in Mahir's government, and the misunderstanding was very quickly cleared up. On September 7, 1952, Mahir, who opposed agrarian reform, was dismissed. His political career was ended. Naguib's government, formed on the same day, began to arrest the reactionaries, and on September 9 decreed the agrarian reform demanded by the peasants. Shortly afterwards Rashad Mohannah, a member of the Regency Council who also opposed agrarian reform, was thrown overboard.[11]

Naguib himself was also an indecisive figure. In the appeals put out by radio on July 23 he stated that the army had decided to cleanse its ranks and the entire country of traitors; at the same time he assured 'our brothers, the foreigners who live among us, that their interests will be respected. The army will be fully responsible for their lives and property',[12] and he threatened with severe punishment those who created disturbances. That was all that the people learned at that time of the aims and objects of the *coup*. But this programme differed little from the programmes of the various reactionary governments which ruled Egypt between January and July, 1952. They too had promised to cleanse the country of traitors and punish severely those who disturbed the peace, meaning by this phrase the democratic elements. Mistrust was deepened by the guarantee of the property of foreign capitalists, which disappointed the anti-imperialist expectations of the popular masses. Finally, certain steps taken by Ali Mahir and Naguib in the first weeks after the *coup* caught the attention of the masses. The law of July 31 on joint-stock companies granted the imperialist monopolies those privileges which they had sought in vain from the Wafd government. In August, Naguib appealed to the peasants to pay rent to the landlords, threatening severe reprisals should they refuse, and inflicted a bloody punishment on the striking workers of Kafr-ad-Davar. Furthermore, Naguib elaborated a programme for the large-scale penetration of foreign capital into the country and in fact directed his efforts to reinforcing Egypt's unequal relations with the imperialist West. In the end this 'fellow traveller' was cast off by history. In 1954 he was removed from the posts he occupied and placed in retirement. In the struggle against these haphazard elements the programme of the anti-imperialist, anti-feudal revolution crystallized

[11] Naguib, *Egypt's Destiny* (London, 1955), pp. 103–4.
[12] *ibid.*, p. 120; R. El-Barrawi, *The Military* Coup *in Egypt* (Cairo, 1952), p. 7.

500 V. B. LUTSKII

out, and as it did so the role of the popular masses in the revolutionary development of the country became greater.

One further peculiar feature of the Egyptian Revolution should be mentioned. When the *coup* occurred it was not only the popular masses, but the imperialists as well, who had no clear idea of its essential nature. They did not take the July revolution for what it really was in virtue of its objective aims and tasks.

In preparing the *coup*, its leaders were convinced that the balance of forces within the country ensured their success. They knew that the people would either take an active part in it, or would in any case welcome the overthrow of the monarchy; that the Egyptian army, which in the past had served the monarchy and the feudal class, was now unanimously hostile to the forces of reaction, and that consequently the reaction was without any support whatever in the country. However, as all the sources show, they seriously feared English intervention. The English army was stationed in the Suez Canal zone, and Farouk's monarchy, doomed to perish, might be saved by English tanks and guns. The leaders of the *coup* remembered very well how English intervention had crushed the national-liberation movement in 1882 and in 1919. Still fresh in their memory was the brutality of the English aggressors who had suppressed the national-liberation movement of the Egyptian people at the end of 1951 and beginning of 1952, the imperialist plot of January 26, 1952. The threat of imperialist intervention aroused doubts of the success of the *coup*. They therefore took measures to forestall the danger.

On the day after the *coup* the Arab and foreign Press carried a report of a United Press correspondent that General Naguib had immediately established contact with the representative of the American military attaché in Egypt and had asked him to bring to the notice of the English command that any intervention by English armed forces in Egyptian affairs would be resisted by the Egyptian army.[13]

In his *Memoirs*, Naguib gives the following details of this incident. The United States and English embassies, as well as the Egyptian government, were at the time in their summer quarters in Alexandria. In Cairo there remained the assistant American military attaché, with whom one of the members of the Society of Free Officers, Ali Sabri, chief of aviation research (now head of the President's Chancellery) was acquainted. On the instructions of the executive committee of the Society, Sabri called on the night of July 23 at the American embassy and asked this officer to telephone Alexandria and transmit to the American ambassador, and through him to the English representative, that the *coup* was a purely domestic affair

[13] *Al-Ahram*, July 24, 1952.

concerning Egyptians only, that the life and property of foreigners would be respected, that if the English refrained from intervention they would be treated as all other foreigners, but if not they would be responsible for the bloodshed that would inevitably follow.[14]

Meanwhile King Farouk, who was in Alexandria, cabled both the English government in London, and English headquarters in the Suez Canal zone, asking for immediate intervention, for the occupation of Cairo by English troops, for the bombardment of Alexandria by the English Navy. The United States, however, informed England that 'in the given circumstances they were decisively opposed to foreign intervention', and Farouk was deprived of external support.

There is no doubt that if the imperialists could have foreseen the consequences of the *coup* they would have tried to drown the beginnings of the revolution in blood, as they did in January, 1952. But the 'free officers' were an unknown quantity to them, and they calculated on using them in their own interests. What contributed to their mistake was not only the guarantee of foreigners' property given by Naguib, but also the fact that Ali Mahir was put at the head of the new government, and he was trusted by the Americans. With the *coup* the American imperialists linked the hope of including Egypt in the 'Middle East Defence Organization', which they had been unable to achieve previously, and also of consolidating the American economic positions and American political influence in the country. Later, when the situation became clear, when the mistake was cleared up, and the aims of the Egyptian Revolution, its anti-imperialist and anti-feudal direction, became obvious to everybody, the imperialists displayed bitter enmity to the new Egypt. But by that time the revolutionary government had already consolidated its position in the country and had received international recognition, so that nothing remained for the imperialists, in their impotent malevolence, but resort to their favourite weapons, calumny and thievish aggression. But nowadays these methods invite only defeat, and that is what they received.

The great historical importance of the Egyptian Revolution of 1952 is indisputable. The further the peculiar concrete conditions in which it occurred recede into the distance, the more clearly do its true features, its real substance, emerge. The revolution was not ended on July 26, the day Farouk was overthrown; it opened a new epoch in the life of an ancient country—the epoch of independent development. . . .

The new Egypt's foreign policy calls for the approval of all freedom-loving peoples. Egypt took an active part in the Bandung Conference; it is pursuing a policy of peaceful co-existence; it is

[14] Naguib, *op. cit.*, p. 118.

part of that great zone of peace which now includes the overwhelming majority of mankind. The occupation of Egypt was liquidated as a result of the revolution, which also made it possible to settle the Sudan question on the basis of Sudan's independence and self-determination.

The Egyptian Revolution added immeasurable strength to the national-liberation movement in the Arab countries. The Egyptian Constitution declares that the Egyptian people are part of the Arab nation. Today all the advanced progressive forces of that great nation are marching alongside the new Egypt.

In realizing the age-old hopes of the Egyptian people, the Egyptian national government returned to that people its legitimate property, the Suez Canal. The nationalization of the Suez Canal Company was made possible only by the victory of the Egyptian Revolution, as a result of which the Egyptian people found within itself sufficient strength to resist the forces of imperialism which had organized a predatory attack on their homeland in the attempt to restore the régime of colonial slavery that has disappeared for ever into the past.

[*Editor's note*: The article concludes with a résumé in English, which is reproduced below.]

RÉSUMÉ

'The revolution of July 1952 in Egypt was intended to do away with the colonial rule and with the survivals of feudalism which impeded economic, political and cultural progress in that country. Beginning with 1946, the struggle for the withdrawal of the British troops from Egypt entered its decisive stage; one of the favourable factors behind this development was the international situation obtaining after the second world war. The Egyptian army joined in this struggle in July, 1952. Characterizing the officers and soldiers of the Egyptian army, the author dwells on the formation and work of the "Free Officers" society. The intellectuals of the army who were in the leadership had no contacts at the beginning of the revolution with the mass of the people; nor could they offer a clear programme of revolutionary reforms. However, the relationship between class forces inside the country, as well as the relationship between the international forces outside, determined the subsequent course of the Egyptian Revolution; its anti-imperialist, anti-feudal programme had taken concrete shape as the revolution got under way. It is as yet too early to sum up the results of the Egyptian Revolution, which is continuing, but it is evident that great progress has been made in Egypt's independent economic, political and cultural development in the last years.'

INDEX

NOTE.—In the alphabetical arrangement of entries, the Arabic article, however transliterated (al-, el-, as-, etc.) has been neglected. Thus, e.g., al-Misri is indexed under M.